This volume provides a comprehensive account of the natural history of the organisms which inhabit the deep-sea environment. The diverse fauna is described and the methods used to collect and study it is reviewed. By examining processes of feeding, respiration, reproduction, growth and dispersal, the authors illustrate how the ecology of these organisms is related to the inhospitable nature of the environment in which they live. Finally, the nascent but potentially important impact of Man on this, the Earth's largest ecosystem, is discussed.

This book will be of interest to senior undergraduate and graduate students as well as researchers in the fields of oceanography and marine biology.

D1227431

DEEP-SEA BIOLOGY:
A natural history of organisms at the deep-sea floor

DEEP-SEA BIOLOGY:
A natural history of organisms at the deep-sea floor

John D. Gage
Scottish Marine Biological Association
Dunstaffnage Marine Laboratory
Oban, UK

Paul A. Tyler
Department of Oceanography
University of Southampton
Southampton, UK

CAMBRIDGE
UNIVERSITY PRESS

Published by the Press Syndicate of the University of Cambridge
The Pitt Building, Trumpington Street, Cambridge CB2 1RP
40 West 20th Street, New York, NY 10011–4211 USA
10 Stamford Road, Oakleigh, Victoria 3166, Australia

First published 1991
First paperback edition 1992

Printed in Great Britain at the University Press, Cambridge

British Library cataloguing in publication data
Gage, John D.
  Deep-sea biology.
  1. Deep sea organisms
  I. Title   II. Tyler, Paul A.
  574.92

Library of Congress cataloguing in publication data available

ISBN 0 521 33431 4 hardback
ISBN 0 521 33665 1 paperback

PN

To our parents,
Kathleen and Jim Gage
and Phyllis and Tommy Tyler,
to whom we owe so much

Contents

Preface

Ninety per cent of the two-thirds of the surface of the Earth covered by the sea lies beyond the shallow margins of the continents; and most lies under 2 km or more of water. We may therefore, with some justification, speak of the deep-sea bottom as constituting the most typical environment, and its inhabitants as the typical lifeforms, of the solid face of our planet. Yet, because of the remoteness of this habitat and the difficulties in observing and sampling these organisms, they are known to only few scientists; and as living rather than pickled specimens, to less than a handful. Yet the possibility of life existing at these great depths, and a curiosity about the nature of these life forms in what appears to be one of the most 'difficult' of environments has fascinated Man since the early days of oceanic exploration.

This book is intended as an introduction to our present knowledge of the biology of this environment. This is the realm of the mostly sediment-covered deep ocean floor and the immediately overlying water layer, termed the Benthic Boundary Layer (BBL). Animal life has been found burrowing within, and moving on the surface of, this sedimentary ooze, and occasionally carried along by deep currents. We now know that animals survive, sometimes in spectacular numbers, at the greatest depths of the deepest ocean trench, apparently unaffected by an ambient pressure of more than 1000 atm, by the complete absence of solar radiation and a temperature of one or two degrees above freezing. How do these forms of life survive in what seems to us perhaps the most hostile of environments? What forms of life are they – is the deep sea a refuge for archaic forms of life, long since vanished elsewhere? How can populations survive where the input of food is so low judged from the sparseness of surface plankton in the clear waters of the open ocean?

These forms of life, and the sum of their activity over the vast areas of the deep oceans, are now realized to have more than just academic importance. Both the ever-rising human population and increasing industrialization has led to massive increases in waste products released into the environment. This has resulted in a realization that Man is influencing his environment on a global scale: possibly precarious equilibria in the ocean/atmosphere systems that ultimately maintain life as we know it on the planet may be upset by such changes. It is recognized that we must gain new insights into the large-scale biogeochemical processes that control the chemical balance of the oceans and the atmosphere. This has led to a new realization of the importance of the biological processes of the ocean, and ultimately its floor, as a vast sink for CO_2 and other elements – some highly toxic. Photosynthesis taking place in the surface layers over the vast areas of the ocean fixes enormous quantities of carbon from the atmosphere. This, in the form of organic biomass or inorganic skeletal structures, eventually sinks to the ocean bed, where it is either fixed by formation of pelagic sediment or is recycled back into the water column. The effectiveness of this oceanic 'sink' may vary over space and time. Only by improving our understanding of such biogeochemical cycling and its interaction with the processes of the global atmosphere will Man be able to predict the effect of his summed activities on this planet, such as the increasing levels of atmospheric carbon dioxide.

These and similar questions are only just beginning to be considered, let alone answered, and many major discoveries undoubtedly remain to be made. Who would have conceived the existence of 'oases' of exotic fauna recently discovered associated with hydrothermal vents, colonies that represent concentrations of biomass probably higher than exist anywhere else underwater. Or even more remarkable, that these 'parallel' ecosystems could be fuelled by an energetic system, not ultimately dependent on the sun, but on chemical exchanges by bacteria!

The deep sea has excited the curiosity of some of the most fertile minds in science, and in the past two decades has helped stimulate novel ideas in theoretical ecology. In deep-sea biology, because data are sparse, opinions sometimes may be maintained and cherished longer than justified. But just as many of yesterday's ideas and assumptions are now beginning to look less useful, others come along to take their place. However, it is still arguable whether we have yet amassed sufficient basic information on the animals, their lifestyles and interactions with their environment, and their biogeochemical activity, to be able to make the crudest ecological generalizations, particularly when so little of the vast area of the oceans has been studied.

We hope this book expresses our own excitement in understanding biological processes on the floor of the deep sea, but we have tried in its writing to avoid sweeping generalizations. Rather we have aimed at including as much 'hard' information as theories in order that the reader may decide between opposing arguments. However, our rapidly changing perception of the deep sea, and of the nature of its populations, during the short period that we have been privileged to study it, has underscored both the inadequacy of our present database and the need to avoid dogma.

In its organization, we have deliberately given importance to describing the animals of the deep-sea floor, and by summarizing natural history information on them. This information has mostly been obtained from

trawled specimens or seabed photographs, or occasionally from observations from deep-diving submersibles. Such methods are summarized
in an early chapter. Later chapters deal with the structure and distribution
of whole communities of species, and with attempts to understand the
processes related to their activities. The latter topics may require highly
specialized apparatus which is able to operate and make measurements
on the seabed autonomously, without being tethered to the ship above.
The reader will find such specialized equipment described within the
relevant chapters.

As a text we have aimed this book at the final-year senior undergraduate or to the postgraduate interested in ecological processes. We hope
also that it may prove to be of interest to the enthusiastic layman who
wants to learn more of the forms of life of the largest ecosystem on Earth.
To this end it has not been possible to be exhaustive in our coverage of the
biology of the floor of the deep sea. Where possible, we guide the reader
to review articles by biologists and others more expert than ourselves in
their specific fields.

We hope this book will prove not only a useful introductory guide for
all those interested in the deep sea, but will encourage them to inquire for
themselves from the ever-increasing literature related to the biology of
this environment.

Acknowledgements

Although we accept the blame for its early genesis, the development of this book would not have been possible without the encouragement and input of many friends and colleagues too numerous to list completely. We would, however, like to thank particularly the following, many of whom have been kind enough to read particular chapters or parts of them (relevant chapter is given in parentheses; but we remain entirely responsible for any errors remaining): Dr J. A. Allen, University Marine Station, Millport, Scotland (Chapter 5); Dr M. V. Angel, Deacon Laboratory of the Institute of Oceanographic Sciences, Wormley, UK (IOS) for reading the entire text in draft form and for pointing out many errors and inconsistencies and providing numerous constructive suggestions; Dr D. S. M. Billett (IOS) (Chapter 4); Dr O. Bergstad, University of Bergen, Norway (Chapters 4 and 16); Dr A. J. Gooday (IOS) (Chapter 5); Dr J. D. M. Gordon, Dunstaffnage Marine Laboratory, Oban, Scotland (DML) (Chapters 4 and 16); Dr J. F. Grassle, Woods Hole Oceanographic Institution, Massachusetts (Chapter 8); Dr K. Harrison, Natural History Museum, London (Chapter 5); Mr R. Harvey (DML), for valuable help with an awkward but necessary transfer of wordprocessor files from one system to another, and for correcting numerous errors in spelling and expression; Dr Barbara Hecker, Lamont–Doherty Geological Observatory of the University of Columbia, New York (Chapter 9); Dr D. M. Holdich, University of Nottingham, England (Chapter 5); Dr P. A. Jumars, University of Washington, Seattle (Chapter 11); Dr R. S. Lampitt (IOS) (Chapters 4 and 11); Mme Violaine Martin, Institut Français de Recherche pour l'Exploitation de la Mer (IFREMER), Centre de Brest, France for kindly providing us with artwork providing most of the figures in Chapter 15; Professor J. B. L. Matthews and Dr J. Mauchline (both DML) for constructively commenting on the book at the outline stage and for their support and encouragement; Mr P. S. Meadows, University of Glasgow (Chapter 14); Dr A. L. Rice (IOS) for influencing our choice of title and for constructive discussions on various aspects, and for his cooperation in making available most of the seabed photographs showing deep-sea organisms that illustrate this book; Dr K. J. Richards, University of Southampton, for enthusiastic guidance in the Benthic Boundary Layer section in Chapter 2; Dr G. Robinson, NERC Unit for Thematic Information Systems, University of Reading (Chapter 2); Dr M. Segonzac (IFREMER, Brest) for sending us a copy of unpublished photographic keys to hydrothermal vent organisms; Miss Lucinda Vickers, a summer student at DML, for her patience in typing numerous and frequently barely legible pencilled corrections and for general help in wordprocessing; Dr C. Young, Harbor Branch Oceanographic Institution Inc., Florida (Chapter 2); Dr Cindy-Lee Van Dover, Woods Hole Oceanographic Institution, Massachusetts (Chapter 15); and finally Dr T. Wolff, University Museum, University of Copenhagen, for valuable help with Chapter 15 and for kindly providing originals of figures reproduced from various Galathea Reports. Lastly, we thank the Captains and Crews of the NERC and other research vessels that we have worked from over the years whose skill and patience has provided us and other colleagues, particularly at the Institute of Oceanographic Sciences' Deacon Laboratory, with the opportunities for sampling the deep-sea bed and for taking the photographs of its fauna used in this volume.

Figs 8.10, 15.13: Copyright 1978, 1984 American Association for the Advancement of Science; Fig. 15.13: Reproduced by permission from *Nature*, Copyright 1981 Macmillan Magazines; Figs 5.2, 16.1: Courtesy of *Oceanus* magazine, Copyright Woods Hole Oceanographic Institution. Figs 9.7, 9.8, 13.4, 13.5: Reproduced by permission of the Royal Society of Edinburgh; Fig. 12.1: Reproduced with permission from the Annual Review of Microbiology, Copyright 1984 by Annual Reviews Inc.; Figs 4.44, 4.47, 5.5: Published by permission of Cassell Publishers Ltd.; Figs 7.3, 8.9, 9.1, 9.14, 9.15, 12.2: Reprinted by permission of John Wiley & Sons Inc. All rights reserved; Figs 2.2, 2.6, 2.7, 4.10, 4.19, 5.14, 12.5, 13.20, 14.11: Reprinted by permission of Prentice-Hall, Englewood Cliffs, New Jersey; Fig. 5.8: Reproduced by permission of the Smithsonian Institution Press, Smithsonian Institution, Washington D.C.; Fig. 2.11: Reproduced by permission of the Lamont Doherty Geological Observatory.

Part I *The development of deep-sea biology, the physical environment and methods of study*

In the short history of the subject, the rapidly expanding knowledge of the physical nature and processes of the deep oceans has very much determined the approach and methodology adopted in the biological study of this, the most remote and seemingly 'difficult' of environments for life on Earth. At the time of the pioneering voyage of the 'Challenger', knowledge of deep-ocean bathymetry barely existed, vast areas of ocean basins had never been sounded, and a certain sameness in the catch of larger animals trawled from the depths, as the ship worked wide-spaced stations across the ocean basins, encouraged a view of an almost endless, though impoverished, uniformity in the animal life existing on the deep-sea ooze. Such a view encouraged workers to think that it is perfectly feasible to make generalizations of deep-sea biology from single and widely spaced hauls made with the relatively crude technical gear available. As graphically illustrated by Spärck (1956a), the idea of assessing the ocean's fauna by means of a few trawl and dredge hauls is absurd in relation to its vast area and volume: fishing up a postman and a policeman from a net cast randomly from a balloon floating above land might similarly lead to a distorted picture of a human population below made up entirely of postmen and policemen!

This concept of uniformity remains valid today only in a restricted way. Our ever-increasing power of resolution of the complex physical structure of the deep oceans has shown the need for biological studies at ever-decreasing spatial, and temporal, scales in order to understand the biological pattern and, sometimes transient, phenomena associated with the deep-sea floor.

1
Historical aspects

The history of the study of the populations inhabiting the interface of the floor of the deep ocean with the overlying water spans a short period of little more than the maximum lifespan of a blue whale (approx. 120 yr). We associate this with the remoteness of the deep sea and the resulting difficulties in studying this environment: our methods of study are inhibited by the need for our instrumentation and observation chambers to be encapsulated in the atmosphere of the surface, and strengthened against the crushing pressure of a water column several kilometres in height.

EARLY EXPLORATION OF THE FAUNA OF THE DEEP-SEA FLOOR

In the middle years of the nineteenth century, in his investigations by dredging for life on the bottom of the deep fjords of the west coast of his country, the Norwegian pastor/naturalist, Michael Sars, together with his son, G. O. Sars, had listed nearly 100 species of invertebrate living at depths greater than 600 m. Even earlier, in 1818, the British explorer John Ross made a fortuitous discovery of a many-armed basket star (Fig. 1.1) from a sounding line cast in a depth of more than 1.6 km during his search for the North West Passage. Later, James Clark Ross and J. Hooker on the exploratory voyages of the 'Erebus' and 'Terror' to the southern ocean in 1839–43 had obtained animals from the mud on the sounding lead in a depth of 1.8 km and described a 'teeming animal life' on the Antarctic continental slope. Such discoveries fuelled curious and adventurous minds in nineteenth-century Britain to speculate that life existed at the greatest depths being revealed by the sounding lead in surveying the oceans in order to route the new trans-oceanic submarine cables. Unfortunately for Victorian science, the collections were never adequately described and the prevailing opinion perceived the continuous darkness, lack of plant life, and water pressure of several hundreds of atmospheres as precluding the existence of living forms.

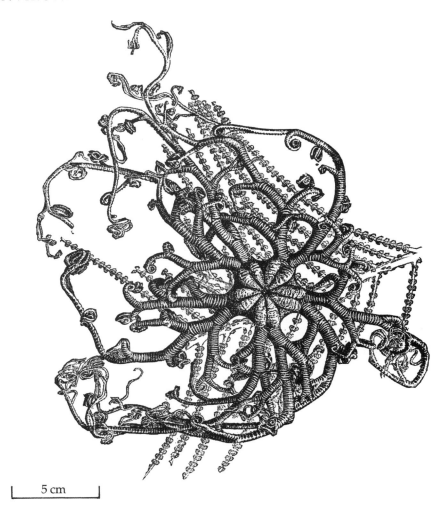

Fig. 1.1. Basket star *Astrophyton* entwined in its 'perch' on a gorgonian branch. In life, the finely branched arms are spread in a net to ensnare organisms carried by the current. (From Agassiz, 1888.)

5 cm

CONCEPT OF 'ZERO' OF ANIMAL LIFE

Although his work served to reinforce the view that life would be absent at great depths, it was a young professor at Edinburgh University, Edward Forbes, above all others, who deserves credit for stimulating the early exploration of the deep sea. His concept of an 'azoic zone' below 0.6 km depth was derived from his dredging work in the Aegean (where later work has shown that deep-sea life is particularly sparse). His idea of a threshold for life was quickly challenged by others in the lively intellectual climate prevailing in Edinburgh at this time of publication of Darwin's work on the origin of species. Attempts to sample the greatest depths available offered the chance of perhaps finding there, still living, some of the archaic forms of life then being abundantly revealed to science as fossilized remains from sedimentary rocks. Charles Wyville Thomson, a later incumbent of Forbes' professorial chair at Edinburgh,

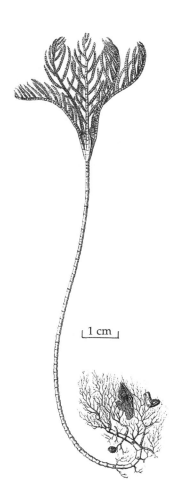

Fig. 1.2. The sea lily *Rhizocrinus lofotensis*. (From Thomson, 1874.)

visited Michael Sars in Norway in order to examine, at first hand, his collection of marine animals that he had collected from the deep Lofoten Fjord. These included specimens of the stalked sea lily, *Rhizocrinus lofotensis* (Fig. 1.2) which, as a member of a group of echinoderms hitherto only known from fossil remains, excited Wyville Thomson and led to a hope, long nurtured afterwards, that the deep sea has provided a refuge for all manner of forms of life thought to be extinct.

THE 'CHALLENGER' EXPEDITION AND THE ERA OF NATIONAL EXPEDITIONS

On his return, Wyville Thomson, together with an eminent friend, W. B. Carpenter, persuaded the Royal Society of London to get the British Royal Navy to help him organize a cruise in order to undertake the exploration of deep water. The cruises, first of H.M.S. 'Lightning' in the summer of 1868 and later of H.M.S. 'Porcupine' in the summers of 1869 and 1870, took place in the waters lying to the north and west of Britain and the

Iberian peninsula. These pioneering expeditions recovered new forms of life that were washed from the cold, clay-like ooze dredged from depths down to 4.289 km. Surprisingly, the muddy ooze was found to be almost entirely made up of the skeletal remains of innumerable tiny single-celled organisms falling from the planktonic populations at the surface.

On the basis of these cruises, Wyville Thomson was satisfied that life would be found on the bottom in the greatest depths. Their intriguing observations on discontinuities in the temperature of the deep-sea water mass opened up controversies on ocean circulation. These considerations, together with the interest of the Royal Navy in surveying routes for submarine telegraph cables, helped in the organization necessary for the subsequent circumnavigating voyage of H.M.S. 'Challenger' from 1872 to 1876. This pioneering voyage was largely organized, and later led, by Wyville Thomson. The results of this cruise without doubt laid the foundation, not only for our present knowledge of the life of the deep-sea floor, but also provided a quantum leap for the infant science of oceanography. Animal life was found from dredgings to 5.5 km below the surface, but no 'living fossils' were discovered. Instead, what appeared to be a rather cosmopolitan fauna was found which showed signs of being highly diverse (although a proper appreciation of this extraordinary diversity in animal life was delayed right up to the 1960s when fine-meshed dredges and sieves came into general use). The biological results of the subsequent studies of the samples obtained fill 34 large volumes which, together with the results of other national expeditions from other European countries and from the U.S.A. that followed, remain an indispensable source of descriptive information to this day. The names of these expeditions commemorate the ships that bore them: the 'Travailleur' and the 'Talisman' from France under the direction of the great Alphonse Milne-Edwards and the 'Hirondelle' and 'Princess Alice I' and 'II' under the personal direction of, and financed by, Prince Albert I of Monaco; the 'Ingolf' from Denmark, and the 'Michael Sars' from Norway; the 'Valdivia' from Germany, and the 'Blake' and 'Albatross' from the U.S.A. This era was effectively closed by the voyages of the Swedish 'Albatross' in 1947–48 in the Atlantic and the Danish round-the-world voyage of the 'Galathea' in 1950–52. It was on the latter expedition that the last frontiers in the quest, started in the mid-1800s, for life at the greatest depths were successfully overcome; the 'Galathea' recovering animals from the depths of the Philippines Trench (10.19 km).

MODERN QUANTITATIVE STUDIES GENERATE NEW ECOLOGICAL CONCEPTS

In the 1950s, a great expansion in deep-sea investigation was undertaken by Russian biologists, who also successfully sampled the varied benthic fauna of the deepest trenches and, following on from beginnings made by the 'Galathea', engaged in a programme of quantitative sampling of the sediments of the Pacific and other oceans with modified forms of the grabs used in coastal surveys. Their results established general 'laws' on the geographical and bathymetric distribution of benthic biomass in the deep sea.

In the 1960s and 1970s, ecological research into the life forms of the deep-sea bottom have been dominated by American work, particularly by lines of research initiated by Howard L. Sanders and Robert R. Hessler at the Woods Hole Oceanographic Institution and the latter later at the Scripps Institution of Oceanography. Their findings of unexpectedly high species diversity in the previously virtually unsampled small fauna, retained using fine-meshed screens, stimulated much theorizing by population ecologists on how high diversification could be maintained in such a food-poor and seemingly hostile environment. The advent of box-core samplers, derived from devices used by geologists, have provided, for the first time, unbiased samples of the sediment community comparable in quality to those from inshore sediments, whilst observations from deep-diving submersibles have provided not only intrepid (though cramped) observers with a wealth of data on the lifestyles of the larger fauna previously known only from the trawl or from seabed photographs, but a means to set up ecological experiments directly on the ocean bed.

MULTIDISCIPLINARY PROGRAMMES

The 1970s and 1980s have seen an international proliferation in research programmes; many having a multidisciplinary make-up and a regional focus. Oceanographers have, for the first time, monitored the organic flux from the surface, and measurements and samples have been taken at fixed stations over periods of several years. Discovery of unexpected seasonality in reproduction and respiration have challenged earlier assumptions of extreme constancy in the tempo of life on the deep-sea floor. Discovery of rich 'oases' of life depending not on sun-driven production at the surface of the ocean, but on sulphur oxidizing and methanotrophic bacterial production in emissions from hydrothermal vents and hydrocarbon seeps, and of populations of giant-sized amphipods and other scavenging animals attracted to baited traps, have shown that our understanding of the nature of life in the depths remains far from complete.

2

The physical environment of the deep sea

THE SHAPE OF THE SEA FLOOR

The topography of the floor of the deep ocean (Fig. 2.1) is a balance between the parameters of seafloor spreading and sedimentation of inorganic and organic particles. Around the periphery of the ocean basins lies a *continental shelf* of varying width ending at the shelf break, usually at a depth of *c*. 200 m, below which plant life is supposed to be absent. In the Antarctic, owing to the weight of the ice cap, the shelf edge is at *c*. 500 m. If we accept topographic criteria, the deep sea may be said to begin at the *shelf break.* This is a safer distinction than one based on photosynthetic depth since attached seaweeds have been found as deep as 268 m off the Bahamas (Littler *et al.,* 1985).

Seaward of the shelf edge there is a marked increase in the downward gradient of the seabed indicating the *continental slope* (Fig. 2.2). The slope may be a simple structure where the isobaths are parallel to each other and evenly spaced or it may contain a series of irregularities to give a very uneven gradient. The slope marks the underlying boundary between oceanic and continental crust. The theory of plate tectonics tells us that these areas of crust consist of a dynamic system of plates where crust is both being formed at mid-ocean ridge spreading centres and consumed by subduction at 'active', or seismic margins typical in the Pacific (Fig. 2.3). 'Passive', or aseismic margins are typical of the Atlantic (Leeder, 1985). The gradient of the slope may be interrupted by *terraces* and *submarine canyons.* The latter appear as irregular, fissure-like channels cut down the continental slope which may act as conduits for transport to the deep ocean basin beyond, but probably were most active as such during glacial periods when sea levels were lower, and downslope processes far more intense than today. However, bottom currents, intense enough to resuspend the sediment, may occur from internal tides focussed along the canyon axis (Gardner, 1989). Their V-shaped profiles are probably the result of erosion by turbidity currents (see p. 24). Many can be traced on to the adjacent continental shelf, often at the mouths of major rivers.

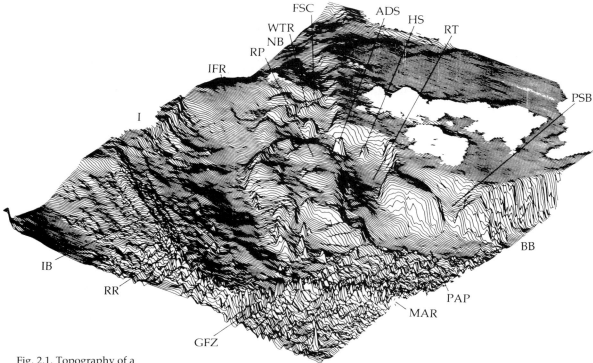

Fig. 2.1. Topography of a section of the northern N.E. Atlantic lying to the west of the British Isles showing some of the chief physiographic features of the deep ocean. The view looks northeast and shows the rugged topography of the Reykjanes Ridge (RR) extending southwards from Iceland (I), and the E.–W. trending Charlie–Gibbs Fracture Zone (GFZ) that separates it from the northern section of the Mid-Atlantic Ridge (MAR). The westward flank of the Reykjanes Ridge extends into the part of the Labrador Basin lying east of southern Greenland; while the eastward flank of the Ridge merges into the gentler topography of the Iceland Basin (IB). This basin is bounded to the E. by a chunk of almost completely submerged continental crust, the Rockall Plateau (RP) and its associated northern Banks.

continued

At the base of the slope of passive margins there is typically a thick wedge of slope-derived sediment termed the *continental rise* (Fig. 2.2) or, if the base of the slope is offshore from a large river, there may be a much larger formation of alluvial sediment called a *submarine fan*. The topography of the rise is usually much smoother than the slope, but may be cut by channels extending from canyoned slopes. By a depth of *c.* 4 km the seabed has levelled off to give a wide expanse of relatively flat *abyssal plain* which extends gently from 4 km to 6 km depth. These are often undulating or quite featureless, or they may be interrupted by numerous flat-topped *guyots* or *seamounts* (Fig. 2.1), which are inactive ocean-floor volcanoes that do not rise above sea level, and sometimes occur in chains (Epp & Smoot, 1989), Seamounts can rise several kilometres above the ocean floor and their profiles show declivities as great as 25°, much steeper than any major seafloor feature elsewhere in the ocean. The abyssal plains do not extend across the oceans but are separated by the *mid-ocean ridge* (Figs 2.1, 2.3, 15.2). The ridge is the site of formation of new ocean crust and is a more or less continuous system occupying about 33% of the area of ocean floor. The generally symmetrical process of extrusion of new crust along both sides of the mid-ocean ridge results in the separation of the flanking lithospheric plates. The solid geometry of the Earth necessitates the formation of a series of cracks, called transform faults, which appear as great slashes at right angles to the main axis (Fig.

This 'microcontinent' is separated from the continental crust of northern Europe by the Rockall Trough (RT). Shallow sills, including the Iceland–Faeroe Rise (IFR) and the Wyville Thomson Ridge (WTR) that separate the Norwegian Basin (NB) from the more southerly Atlantic basins allow overflow of cold Arctic-cooled water from the Norwegian Sea into the Iceland Basin and Rockall Trough to contribute to the deep-sea water mass via the Faroe Shetland Channel (FSC) (see p. 15). Two seamounts, the flat-topped Anton Dohrn Seamount (ADS) and Hebridean Seamount (HS) lie on the continental rise of the eastern Rockall Trough. The latter basin opens into the deeper Porcupine Abyssal Plain (PAP). The steep continental margin lying southwest of Ireland is broken by a large bight-like terrace, the Porcupine Seabight (PSB) and further S. by numerous canyons on the continental slope of the Bay of Biscay (BB). (Computer-generated chart courtesy Dr G. Robinson, NERC Unit for Thematic Information Systems, Reading University.)

2.3). Mid-ocean ridges are usually about 2.5 km below sea level, but, with increasing distance from the ridge, depth increases to about 5 to 6 km with the depression of the thin ocean crust by an ever-increasing accumulation of pelagic sediment blanketing the uneven topography of the oceanic crust. Here lie the featureless expanses of the abyssal plains with gradients typically in the region of 1 : 1000. *Trenches* occur if the abyssal plain is bordered by an active margin, when the oceanic crust (the lithosphere) buckles and deepens as it is eventually destroyed by subduction beneath an adjacent continent (Fig. 2.3). Trenches are best developed in the Pacific Ocean where 'active' continental margins are dominated by subduction zones. As a result, the Pacific, in contrast to the Atlantic, is shrinking in size despite the relatively high seafloor spreading rates found there. Trenches are seismically active areas that are best developed when associated with island arc systems where one plate is subducted under an adjacent oceanic plate (Fig. 2.3). Trenches are greater than 6 km deep and can extend to depths greater than 11 km in the case of the Challenger Deep in the Mariana Trench. The relative proportions of the Earth's surface at any given level may be shown by a hypsographic curve (Fig. 2.4(*b*)) which should not be confused with its superficial resemblance to the profile of a passive continental margin (Fig. 2.2).

The terms applied so far are physiographical whilst the ecological depth zones associated with them are labelled:

(i)   *sublittoral*, or subtidal – Low water mark to 0.2 km
(ii) *bathyal*, or archibenthal – 0.2 to 2 km
(iii) *abyssal* – 2 to 6 km
(iv) *hadal*, or ultra-abyssal – >6 km.

This terminology will be used throughout this book for the general description of depth zones. However, as we shall see, this depth zone

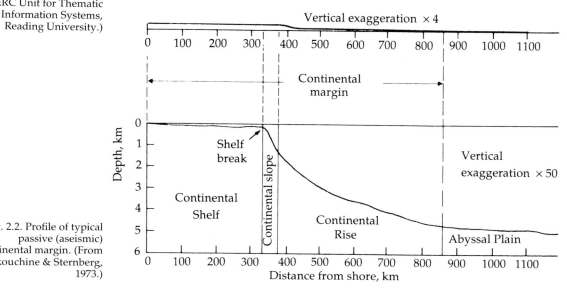

Fig. 2.2. Profile of typical passive (aseismic) continental margin. (From Anikouchine & Sternberg, 1973.)

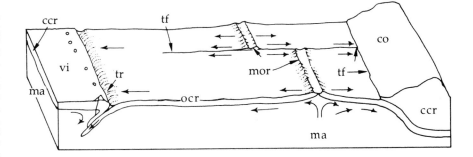

Fig. 2.3. Tectonic structure of ocean basin showing movement (arrows) of oceanic crust (ocr) overlying the mantle (ma), that is in turn overlain by the rafted continental crust (ccr) of the continent (co) along the passive margin shown on the right. The linear pattern of the spreading centre at the mid-ocean ridge (mor) may be offset by transform faults (tf). The zone of crust subduction found at the trench (tr) along the active margin on the left is shown bordered by the volcanoes and volcanic islands (vi) typical of the western Pacific.

terminology cannot be rigidly applied, and vertical zonation of fauna, which in the deep sea seems determined much more by a complex of sometimes interacting ecological factors than by simple physical variables associated with the depth gradient, needs to be described in the deep sea by multivariate quantitative methods (see Chapter 9).

DEEP WATER MASSES AND THEIR FORMATION

In terms of topography, the deep sea starts at the edge of the continental shelf but in terms of hydrography it is usually considered to be that region below the permanent thermocline (Fig. 2.5). This latter is the transition layer in the water column in which temperature falls rapidly with increasing depth until values below 4 °C are reached and the downward temperature gradients become small. In most of the world ocean this more stable temperature regime is entered at 0.8 to 1.3 km depth, except in the N. Atlantic where the injection of Mediterranean outflow at intermediate depths depresses the 4 °C isotherm to about 4 km. As

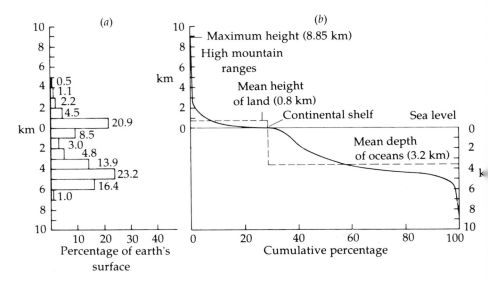

Fig. 2.4. Distribution of Earth's surface lying at different levels: (a) frequency distribution, (b) cumulative-frequency curve based on (a) termed the Hypsographic Curve. This should not be confused with the superficially similar profile of the continental margin shown in Fig. 2.2.

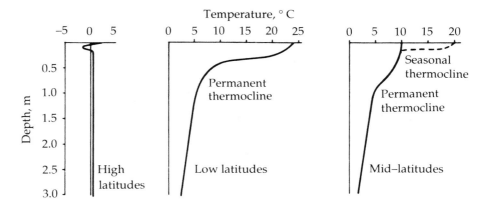

Fig. 2.5. Vertical temperature profiles for different latitudinal zones.

the upper waters are heated by solar radiation (in mid-latitudes with a seasonal cycle to form a more superficial seasonal thermocline), freshened by coastal runoff, and mixed by wind, the permanent thermocline isolates the deep ocean from the direct effect of surface parameters. Because of the much greater depth of the mixed layer as a result of wind stress (particularly evident in the N.E. Atlantic), the deep water mass below the permanent thermocline deepens at mid-latitudes, with a concomitant depression in isotherms away from the Equator. They shoal again at higher latitudes towards the areas of deep water formation nearer the poles (Fig. 2.6). This has had a marked bearing on interpreting the depth-related distributions of deep-sea animals in terms of temperature (see Chapter 9).

However, the water below the permanent thermocline is not of constant temperature and salinity. Most of the floor of the world's major oceans is bathed in water masses which originally formed in either the Antarctic or in the Greenland/Norwegian Seas of the Arctic Ocean (Fig. 2.7). For surface water to become dense enough for it to sink to the bottom of the ocean, it must become either more saline by evaporation and ice formation or colder by heat loss. The water then sinks to its new density

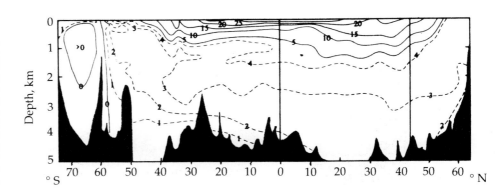

Fig. 2.6. North–South section of western Atlantic showing distribution of temperature (°C). This illustrates the sharp gradient in temperature near the Equator with a trend to submergence of isotherms towards the poles where the water mass becomes increasingly isothermal. (From Svedrup *et al.*, 1942.)

level where it spreads out. To form the very deepest waters in the ocean, the surface layers must become very cold. It eventually returns to the surface by gradual upwelling until, in time, it all returns to the surface as return flows from low to high latitudes.

The deepest waters found in the ocean are formed in the cold surface layers close to the coast of Antarctica especially in the Weddell Sea where winter-cooled surface water is exceptionally cold ($-1.9\,°C$). This water (Fig. 2.8) mixes with the upper part of the saline warm deep water (Circumpolar Water) to give a modified deep water that flows along the western shelf edge of the Weddell Sea along the Palmer Peninsula, mixing with Western Shelf Water. This proceeds to sink downslope as Weddell Sea Bottom Water. This water then mixes with deeper saline waters of the Circumpolar Water to form Antarctic Bottom Water (AABW) (Mantyla & Reid, 1983).

Antarctic Bottom Water is generally accepted as a generic term for water masses of very similar characteristics ($-0.4\,°C$; 34.66‰) which are formed in the Ross Sea and off the Adelie Coast and contribute to this bottom water. AABW sinks to form a circumpolar bottom water with branches penetrating all the main oceans (Fig. 2.7). In the Atlantic this water flows up the west side at depths >5 km but is prevented from doing so on the east side by the Walvis Ridge. Some of this water will penetrate the N.E. Atlantic by passing through the major fracture zones in the Mid-Atlantic Ridge. Branches of AABW extend into the Indian and Pacific Oceans basins unless its spread is impeded by ridges such as the East Pacific Rise.

Fig. 2.7. Main movements of water masses in a North–South section of the Atlantic Ocean, showing the origin of dense, cold Antarctic Bottom Water (AABW) from the Weddell Sea (left), which can be traced as far as 40° N, and the overlying cold, less dense Antarctic Intermediate Water (AAIW). North Atlantic Deep Water (NADW) originates in the Norwegian Sea (right) near Greenland from sinking of a mixture of dense surface water from the Gulf Stream with cold Arctic water. Warm, dense Mediterranean Water (M) intrudes from the E. from the Straits of Gibraltar. A similar northward-flowing pattern exists in the Pacific, but deep flow from the N. is only poorly developed. (From Turekian, 1976.)

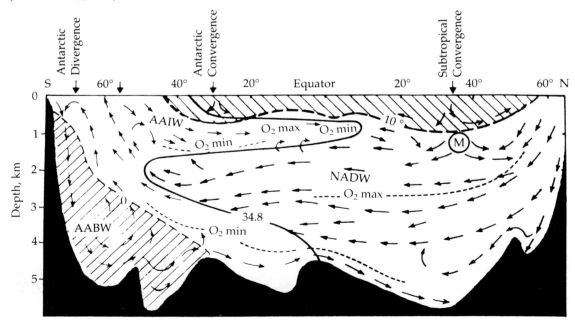

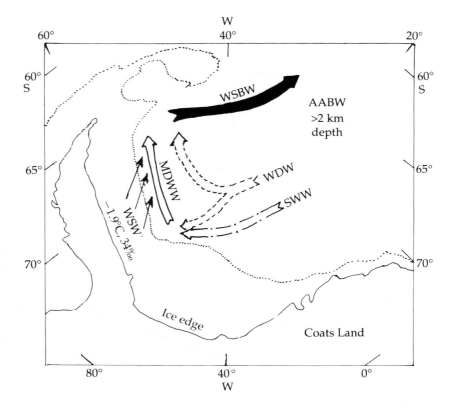

Fig. 2.8. Formation of Antarctic Bottom Water (AABW) in the Weddell Sea. WSW, Western Shelf Water; WDW, warm deep water; SWW, surface winter water; WSBW, Weddell Sea Bottom Water; MDWW, modified deep winter water. Dotted line indicates shelf edge. See text for further details. (Modified from Warren, 1981.)

Overlying the AABW and covering most of the abyssal plains of the world ocean is slightly less dense water, ultimately derived from the sinking of surface water in the Norwegian Sea, and termed North Atlantic Deep Water (NADW). Relatively warm (9–12 °C) and saline (35.3 to 35.5‰) water flows into the Norwegian Sea via the North Atlantic Current. This water is cooled: (i) by lateral mixing with polar waters and (ii) by heat loss to the very cold atmosphere in winter, weakening the density gradient between the surface and bottom, destabilizing the water column. Vertical, convective cells develop and these generate deep and bottom water in the Norwegian and Greenland Seas. The water produced has a density (σ_t) of 28.1 resulting in a virtually homogeneous water column below 0.6 km. Some of this Norwegian Sea Deep Water flows north into the central Polar Basin via the Lema Trough. The rest spills over the Greenland–Iceland–Scotland Ridge (Worthington, 1970; Warren, 1981) into the North Atlantic. In the North Atlantic most enters via either the 0.8 km deep Faroe Bank Channel or the 0.45 km crest of the Faroe–Iceland Ridge. Cold water also spills over the Wyville Thomson Ridge from the Faroe Bank Channel into the northern Rockall Trough, as shown in Fig. 2.16. The route into the N.W. Atlantic basin is by way of the 0.6 km deep sill formed by the Greenland–Iceland Rise in the Denmark Strait (Fig. 2.9; see Fig. 2.1 for details of topography). Norwegian Sea Deep

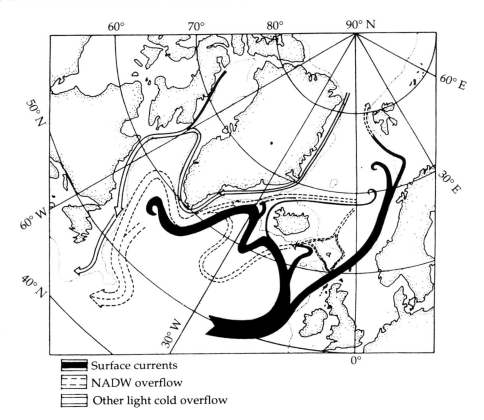

Fig. 2.9. Formation and track of dense, cold deep water (NADW) in the Norwegian Sea and subpolar N. Atlantic from cooling and sinking (denoted by curled ends) of warm (>4 °C) surface currents. Other, lighter, cold overflows are also shown. (From McCartney & Talley, 1984.) © American Meteorological Society, 1984.

Water from the first two sources entrains overlying Atlantic water to form Northeast Atlantic Deep Water. The core gradually descends the contours of the continental slope south of Iceland and then those of the eastern flank of the Reykjanes Ridge, eventually escaping westwards and northwestwards into the N.W. Atlantic basin at 1.5 to 3 km depth through the Charlie Gibbs Fracture Zone at 53° N (Fig. 2.1). There it joins the Northwest Atlantic Bottom Water formed from the Denmark Strait overflow, to produce the North Atlantic Deep Water (NADW), which flows south along the eastern continental slope of N. America at 1 to 5 km depth (Rowe & Menzies, 1968) in the Western Boundary Undercurrent. Although the NADW is more saline than AABW owing to the entrained upper waters, it remains less dense because it is warmer. Consequently wherever both water masses penetrate, NADW overlies the AABW. NADW spreads throughout the S. Atlantic and eastwards round S. Africa, and its high-salinity core may be traced into the northern Indian and Pacific Oceans (Reid & Lynn, 1971).

Although these water masses (AABW and NADW) cover a significant part of the floor of the deep ocean there are other deep waters that bathe restricted parts of the ocean floor. For example, the European Basin of the N.E. Atlantic receives only a little NADW through the Gibbs Fracture

Zone, where the deep flow is predominantly westwards. Direct evidence of AABW presence in the deepest parts of the basin is restricted to anomalously high silicate content (Mann, Coote & Garner, 1973). Northeast Atlantic Deep Water, derived from the easternmost Scotland–Greenland Ridge overflows, occurs where bottom depths are 2 to 3.5 km (Ellett & Martin, 1973; Ellett & Roberts, 1973; Ellett et al., 1986) and in the shallower northern areas Labrador Sea Water (LSW) of lesser density covers much of the seabed in the depth range 1.5 to 2 km (Lonsdale & Hollister, 1979). LSW is formed by deep winter mixing south and west of Greenland, and spreads eastwards at intermediate depths, where its density is somewhat greater than the much more saline but warmer Gibraltar, or less precisely 'Mediterranean' water (Cooper, 1952). Gibraltar Outflow Water is formed by the subsurface Mediterranean outflow plunging into the Atlantic from the Gibraltar Sill. It spreads northwards and westwards and blankets much of the continental slope west of Europe. It reaches to depths of 2.45 km in the south (Meincke et al., 1975), but to the west of the British Isles has a more restricted depth range of 0.8 to 1.2 km.

There are no major sources of deep water in the northern Pacific. This is because the surface waters in the N. Pacific are of such low salinity that even intense wintertime cooling does not increase their density enough for them to sink (Warren, 1981).

In the Mediterranean, the opposite situation creates conditions for deep water formation. The surface water flowing into the Mediterranean through the Straits of Gibraltar is relatively saline, it flows eastwards along the North African coast with branches travelling northwards. Within the enclosed basin, evaporation is high so salinities increase. In winter, in the northern Aegean, Adriatic and Ligurian Seas, cold offshore winds cool the high salinity surface water, causing massive overturning and the formation of very dense deep and bottom water. However, this is not the water mentioned above as providing a mid-water high salinity core in the Atlantic; this is the Levantine Intermediate Water (Wüst, 1961) formed with lesser density off the Turkish south coast in winter, and which flows west to the Gibraltar Sill at 0.2 to 0.6 km depth.

The main ecological significance of these deep water masses lies not in their salinity/temperature characteristics but in that they are well oxygenated. All these water masses form at the surface so that their oxygen content is in equilibrium with the atmosphere. After they sink, although the oxygen is slowly used up by metabolic processes, with the exception of limited areas such as the oxygen minimum zone and anoxic basins, e.g. the Black Sea, the supply of oxygen in the deep waters is sufficient to maintain the surficial sediments of the world's oceans in an oxidized state. In the open ocean, oxygen concentration near the seabed decreases northward in the Indian and Pacific Oceans as these areas are the most remote from the supply of oxygenated water at the main site of deep water formation in the North Atlantic (Mantyla & Reid, 1983). Beneath regions of high production (e.g. eastern tropical Pacific and in the Arabian Sea) oxygen minima form which can lead to anoxic conditions in bathyal sediments. In some regions, such as the Mediterranean, black layers in the sediments called sapropels are considered to have been derived during similar anoxic conditions during previous eras.

PHYSICAL PROPERTIES OF THE WATERS COVERING THE DEEP OCEAN FLOOR

The main feature of the physical properties in the deep sea is that, with the exception of hydrostatic pressure and current energy, these parameters show a very narrow range at any specific site below the permanent thermocline. Unlike coastal waters, solar radiation has no direct ecological significance, as all light (except bioluminescence), has disappeared by 1 km depth. It does, however, have an indirect effect by being the energy source for surface phytoplankton production, some of which enters the deep sea ecosystem via the food chain (see Chapter 11).

TEMPERATURE AND SALINITY

The *temperature* of the waters of the deep sea varies from $4\,°C$ to $-1\,°C$ (Svedrup *et al.*, 1942). Exceptions are the Mediterranean which is *c.* $13\,°C$ between 0.6 and 4 km, the Red Sea where the bottom temperature can be $21.5\,°C$ at 2 km depth, and the very high temperatures in the immediate vicinity of hydrothermal plumes (see Chapter 15). The lowest temperatures found are $-1.9\,°C$ in the deep waters of the Antarctic.

The *salinity* is also relatively constant and below 2 km is close to $34.8‰ \pm 0.3‰$, declining to $34.65‰$ at the very deepest levels (Svedrup *et al.*, 1942; Menzies, 1965).

OXGYEN CONCENTRATION

The oxygen values are near saturation except where the oxygen minimum layer, found at 0.5–0.6 km depth in the open ocean (Fig. 2.7), impinges on the upper continental slope, and in enclosed basins such as the Black Sea which, below 250 m, is anoxic and azoic. However, as the deep water masses progress further from their site of origin, oxygen will be consumed by metabolic processes, and water in the deep N. Pacific has a relatively low oxygen concentration of 3.6 ml l^{-1} (Mantyla & Reid, 1983). There is some evidence (Bruun, 1957) that, immediately above the deep-sea bed, there is a slight reduction (0.15 ml l^{-1}) in oxygen concentration.

HYDROSTATIC PRESSURE

The most predictable physical variable is hydrostatic pressure. This increases by 1 atmosphere (1 bar or 10^5 pascals) per 10 m increase in depth. This increase in pressure, particularly in relation to the low temperature, affects the rates of enzymatic catalysis in deep-sea organisms (Somero *et al.*, 1983).

SEDIMENT TYPE

Exposed hard rock is relatively uncommon in the deep sea, being found on the steep continental slopes, seamounts and along the mid-oceanic ridge. Other solid substrates are formed by inorganic precipitation from seawater such as phosphate deposits or the formation of metallic oxide and sulphide deposits around hydrothermal springs. On a smaller scale, manganese nodules form a hard substrate and have their own distinctive fauna. Coarse sediments of terriginous origin are found on the continental slopes and rises, transported there by turbidity currents and sediment slumps. Rafted sediments from melting icebergs also contribute to the coarse sediment fraction. However, the vast areas of the flanks at mid-ocean ridges and the abyssal plains are covered with either biogenic oozes or by clays, depending on the productivity of the overlying water (Fig. 2.10). Biogenic pelagic sediments are defined as sediments containing > 30% biogenic skeletal material. Siliceous oozes are derived characteristically from diatoms and are found at all depths beneath productive waters especially at high latitudes; radiolarian oozes are also siliceous but occur under productive regions in the tropics. Formaminiferan oozes composed of calcium carbonate are found beneath productive areas where the seabed is above the calcium carbonate compensation depth (CCD), the depth at which $CaCO_3$ goes into solution. Pteropod oozes contain a high proportion of the aragonite shells of pteropod molluscs and are also rich in carbonate but are less extensive because the aragonite dissolved more readily than the calcite of Foraminifera shells. These biogenic oozes may accumulate at a high rate, sometimes as much as several centimetres per thousand years. Under the centres of the oligotrophic oceanic gyres are found red clays including volcanic ash and wind-

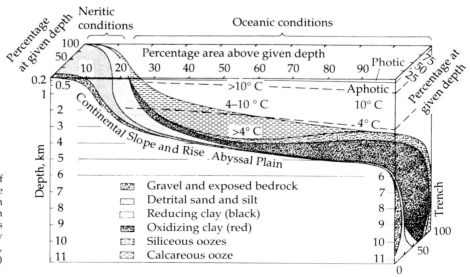

Fig. 2.10. Depth zones of the oceans showing the percentage of the ocean floor covered by ocean water and the various sediment types at any depth. (From Wright (ed.), 1977.)

transported atmospheric dust particularly from desert regions. This material accumulates at a rate of only 0.1 to 1.0 mm kyr^{-1}.

These sediments, which overlie the oceanic crust formed along the mid-oceanic ridge spreading centres, vary in thickness depending on the age of the underlying crust and the sedimentation rates. Near the mid-oceanic ridge they occur only as a thin veneer but, near the continental margin where the crust is ancient, sediments may be thousands of metres thick particularly under the abyssal plains adjacent to passive margins (Fig. 2.11). This sedimentary blanket gives the deep-sea bed its monoto-

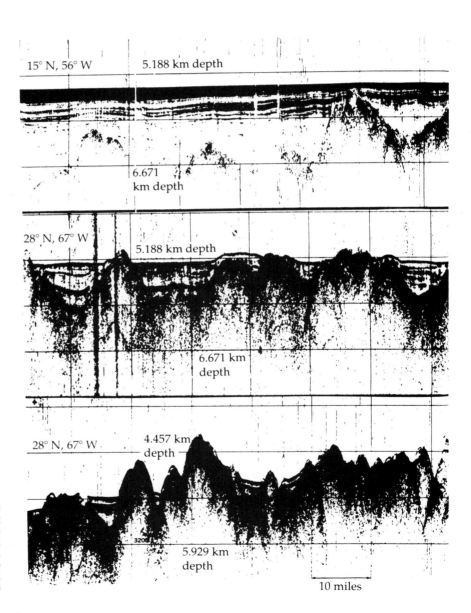

Fig. 2.11. Seismic profiles showing increasing sediment thickness overlying the crust with increasing distance from the mid-ocean ridge in the N. Atlantic. (From Heezen & Hollister, 1971.)

nous flatness broken only by undulating abyssal hills, plateaux and seamounts.

Although the sediments are predominantly inorganic, they do contain some organic matter depending on the productivity of the overlying waters. Under productive areas the organic content may exceed 0.5% whereas beneath unproductive areas this value may be < 0.1%. Most trenches are close to continental margins so not only are their sediments supplemented by terrigenous material, but they act as a trap for terrigenous material reducing the supply to abyssal plain further offshore. Trenches are seismically active, so their sides contain rock outcrops, and slumps of poorly sorted sediments are common.

BOTTOM CURRENTS

The last physical parameter of importance to be described here, bottom current energy, is the one which, up to now, has been least considered and for which data are most sparse. Most photographs of the deep-sea bed show a smooth bed with a relief broken only by deep-sea animals and their effects on the sediment (Fig. 2.12) which we will discuss in Chapter 14. The deep ocean sediments may be re-distributed on a long time-scale as a result of the deep thermohaline circulation of the oceans which is concentrated as deep boundary currents against the topographic restraints formed by the base of the continental margin. Such current activity may ripple the bottom (Fig. 2.13(*a*)) or re-suspend clouds of sediment (Fig. 2.13(*b*)). However, records from near-bottom moored current-meters show that such flow of cold, dense water is not of constant

Fig. 2.12. Seabed photograph taken by 'Deep Tow' (see Chapter 3) covering about 20 m² of muddy sediment bottom at 1.7–1.8 km depth on the continental slope off Ireland, showing the abundant biogenic mounds and craters, and evidence of only slight smoothing by bottom current activity. (Courtesy Dr P. Lonsdale, Scripps Institution of Oceanography.)

(a)

(b)

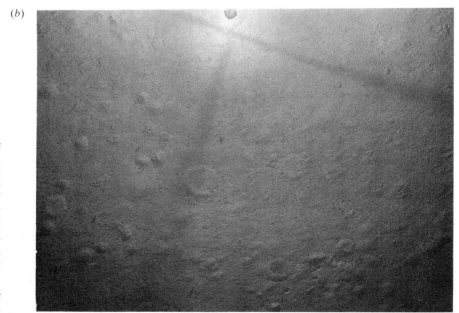

Fig. 2.13. Photographs of deep-sea bottoms affected by current activity, take on same photo-transect as in Fig. 2.12: (a) strongly rippled sediment at 1.1 km depth on the upper Irish slope; (b) current smoothed seafloor and slightly cloudy bottom water from suspended sediment at about 2.95 km depth. (Courtesy Dr P. Lonsdale, Scripps Institution of Oceanography.)

velocity, but may be enhanced by a regime of semidiurnal tidal variation in currents which, on the continental slope of the Bay of Biscay, run upslope on the flood and downslope on the ebb; furthermore, such internal tides have been measured far out into the ocean (Gould & McKee, 1973; Cavanie & Hyacinthe, 1976). Although such tides appear to have their main effect in a semidiurnal period, there are indications that they may determine a longer-period cycle in bottom-current energy by the spring-neap oscillation, with maximum effect at the equinoxes.

In areas of persistent current activity along the route of transport of deep, cold water from the poles, especially along the continental rise, sediment waves and furrow-like bedforms are commonly found. Such deep currents seem to be associated with Benthic Nepheloid Layers (BNLs), detectable when light is poorly transmitted because of the presence of transported material in suspension that has been eroded from the bottom (e.g. Eittreim, Thorndike & Sullivan, 1976; Lonsdale & Hollister, 1979).

These southward or northward (depending on whether the northern or southern hemispheres respectively are being considered) currents seem to be subject to periodic reversal as a result of the downwards transmission of the kinetic energy, and such vorticity is now thought to contribute to the overwhelming source of energy for water movement in the deep ocean. Mesoscale eddies with scales of 50–200 km are thought to contain up to 100 times the energy of the background flow. Mesoscale eddies are typically thrown off strong surface flows such as the Gulf Stream (Fig. 2.14) or formed by wind stress in stormy areas. They are analogous to the cyclones and anticyclones which give 'weather' in the atmosphere but can be much more persistent; individual eddies have been tracked for over two years (Richardson, 1985). The energy in such sources of vorticity is transmitted to the deep sea giving rise to 'benthic storms' lasting periods of a few days to weeks when reversals in cold currents flowing towards the Equator at depth have intermittently strong currents, greater than daily-averaged velocities of > 15 cm s^{-1}, and with between-storm intervals of 5–100 days (Hollister & McCave, 1984; Hollister et al., 1984;

Fig. 2.14. Diagram of supposed interaction of mesoscale eddy, shed from the Gulf Stream, with southward-flowing abyssal boundary current to give rise to a benthic storm on the continental rise off New England. The abyssal eddy is thought to take the form of an ellipse about 30×5 km long and unknown height; its coupling with the bottom current scours the bottom, entraining mud that is swept downstream and subsequently redeposited in sediment drifts. (Redrawn from Hollister, Nowell & Jumars, 1984.)

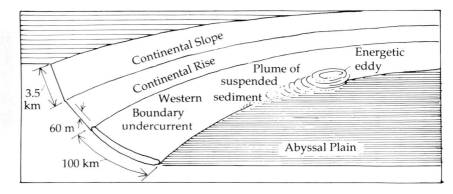

Weatherly & Kelley, 1985; Gross, Williams & Nowell, 1988). Such periods are also characterized by peaks in suspended sediment (Fig. 2.15) when vast quantities of sediment may be transported and re-deposited in a layer many centimetres thick during quiescent periods. The global pattern in eddy kinetic energy shown in Fig. 2.16 is discussed by Wyrtki, Magaard & Hager (1976) and Dickson (1983). High activity, leading to disturbance and graded bedding of the benthic sediments, can be expected in conjunction with strong bottom boundary flows, mesoscale eddies are suspected to be of common occurrence even far out on the abyssal plain as a result of wind stress (Dickson & Hughes, 1981; Klein, 1988). Such deep-sea storms are unpredictable and highly erosive; at the height of one storm in the N.W. Atlantic suspended sediment concentration was measured to be 12 g m^{-2}. Periodic benthic storms result in an erosion-deposition regime comparable to that of an estuary, and recognizable in the global distribution of sediments in beds of graded particle size. Benthic storms are geologically significant in transporting high suspended sediment loads, perhaps along with fauna not normally adapted to water-borne dispersion across the deep ocean basins. Biologically their importance is as a source of repeated, major perturbation within the lifetimes of benthic fauna (J. Y. Aller, 1989), thus affecting the structure of the benthic community (see Chapter 8).

Other sedimentary perturbations occur through internal deformation of the sediment as it moves downslope. Depending on the degree of deformation, these are described as sediment slides, slumps, debris flows and turbidity currents (reviewed by Nardin *et al.*, 1979), the last of these being the agent scouring out the rugged topography of submarine canyons (Shepard & Dill, 1966). Slides and slumps may occur on slopes as gentle as 2° and move swathes of sediment hundreds of metres thick and thousands of metres long. They involve relatively little deformation of the sediment structure, but leave a scar on the upper slope and develop a hummocky topography at the base caused by seismic activity. Debris flows are sluggish movements of sediment downslope over slopes with an angle less than 0.5°. Turbidity currents are high velocity density currents carrying a mixture of sediment and water which travel down-

Fig. 2.15. Sediment concentration in near-bed water measured over 10 weeks at HEBBLE site in the N.W. Atlantic. Peaks coincided with severe benthic storms in late July and early September. (From Hollister, Nowell & Jumars, 1984.)

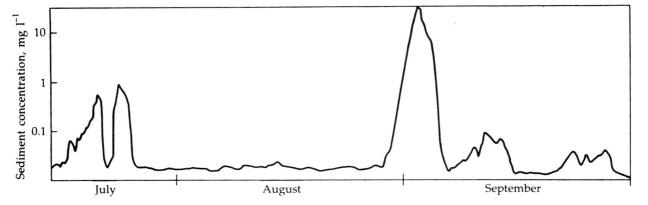

Fig. 2.16. Global pattern in deep-ocean water movement (arrows) and eddy kinetic energy (hatching) from near-surface eddies. Cold, dense water is transported away from the poles into the three great ocean basins, the currents being guided by the topography of the ocean floor and deflected westward by Coriolis force as a result of the Earth's eastward spin. The variations in kinetic energy are represented by the intensity of hatching from values (expressed in units showing the fluctuation around a mean) of 4–10 cm^2 s^{-1} (horizontal hatching), 10–20 cm^2 s^{-1} (cross hatching), to >20 cm^2 s^{-1} (black). The vorticity is transmitted to the seafloor where it interacts with deep currents to erode and redistribute the sediment to form areas where the sediment may lie in beds of graded particle size. (Modified from Hollister, Nowell & Jumars, 1984.)

slope and deposit sediment on to the continental rise and abyssal plain. Off the Grand Banks, Newfoundland, in 1929, a turbidity current transported mud and silt a distance of 640 km, initially at speeds of 55 kt; finally depositing a layer of sediment 1 m thick over the abyssal plain (Leeder, 1985). Turbidity currents and debris flows are unpredictable events, often triggered by an earthquake. Although of no significance within the probable lifetime of individual organisms, their infrequent occurrence (at frequencies within the range of 10^2–10^4 yr^{-1}) must have a marked effect on the benthic fauna, even leading to large-scale extinction. Recently it has been shown (Mayer *et al.*, 1988) that gravel waves deposited at 3.85 km depth by this event have been colonized by communities related to those of hydrothermal vents and cold seeps (see Chapter 15).

To understand how deep-sea bottom dwelling animals respond to their environment it is necessary to understand the physical properties and processes of the water column immediately adjacent to the seabed.

The friction of the seabed on the flow over it generates a vertically homogeneous, although horizontally inhomogeneous, layer of varying thickness capped by a region of strong density gradient (see review by Richards, 1990). This layer, known as the *benthic boundary layer* (BBL), extends a few tens of metres into the water column. Its thickness is limited by the attenuation of turbulent mixing, which extracts energy from the flow and the effects of the Earth's rotation. It upper boundary occurs at a height proportional to the velocity of the overlying current and inversely

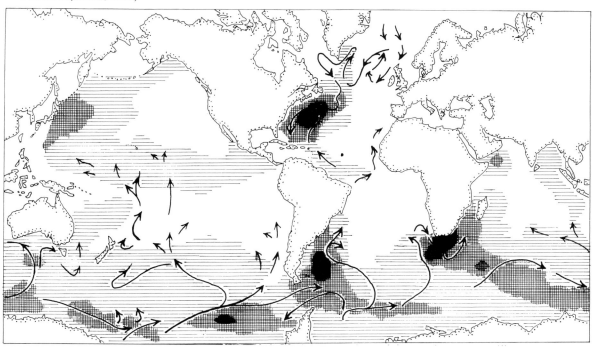

proportional to the Coriolis parameter, where the pressure gradient is balanced by the Coriolis force and the shear is no longer sufficient to enhance turbulent mixing above background levels.

There have been few studies of the ecological implications of the BBL although motion of the BBL affects numerous parameters including recruitment of larvae to the benthos, fluxes of nutrients to, and wastes from, the seabed, the survival of filter feeders and the ability of benthic animals to track scent or detect vibrations (Nowell & Jumars, 1984). Smith & Hinga (1983) define the BBL *biologically* as '. . . the sediment community and assemblage of organisms in the overlying water column associated with the bottom (within 100 m of the seabed)'. There is a migration of primarily benthic animals into the water column to feed, breed or escape predation whereas primarily pelagic animals such as fish feed at the benthic boundary layer. This concept is applied mainly to soft bottoms but even on rock surfaces a 'tiered' community of organisms may be found above the rock surface (*sensu* Messing, 1985).

Although this biological definition is adequate in determining species movements, a more rigorous description of the BBL is given by a mathematical approach. The concept of the BBL was derived from analyses of profiles of physical properties near the seabed which indicated a well-mixed region over the deep-sea bed (Wimbush & Munk, 1970; Armi & Millard, 1976). Richards (1984) has shown that the thickness of the BBL may vary between 0 and 100 m and has a horizontal scale of a few tens of kilometres. Mathematical treatments of the BBL are given by Wimbush (1976), Richards (1982, 1984), Grant *et al.* (1985), Nowell & Jumars (1984). Nowell & Jumars also consider the ecological implications in various types of flow, and a review of the physics of the BBL in the deep sea in relation to biological processes is given in Maciolek *et al.* (1987*a*).

We have based this treatment of the BBL on the work of Wimbush (1976) and Richards (1982). The BBL consists of a number of layers (Fig. 2.17) dependent on the type of flow.

The maximum thickness of the BBL (h_0) for a steady current U_0 is determined by:

$$h_0 = \frac{0.1\,U_0(f/N)^{1/2}}{f} \tag{1}$$

(Richards, 1990)

where f is the Coriolis parameter and N is the density stratification characterized by the buoyancy frequency (a measure of the stability of the water column)

$$N = \left[-g\frac{\delta\rho}{\delta_z}\frac{1}{\rho}\right]^{1/2} \tag{2}$$

where g is the acceleration due to gravity and ρ is the density of the fluid; z is the height above the seabed.

The boundary layer above the flow is referred to as 'potential' or 'frictionless'; there is no horizontal shear stress so velocity at a particular altitude remains constant as one moves away from the boundary.

Fig. 2.17. (*a*) Two-dimensional structure of the benthic boundary layer. Because of the effect of the Earth's rotation in three dimensions, there will be a turning of the structure with height above the bed. (*b*) Physical properties, such as salinity, temperature and suspended solids, are actively mixed in the turbulent logarithmic layer, where mean velocity increases linearly (on a logarithmic scale) with increasing height above bottom; above this zone properties grade into the flow speed of the overlying outer flow. In relatively slow flows a thin layer will move over the bottom in a viscous, or laminar, flow; but when the flow is more rapid, or the bottom rough, the logarithmic layer will extend all the way from 1 mm to about 10 m above the floor of the ocean. (From Hollister, Nowell & Jumars, 1984.)

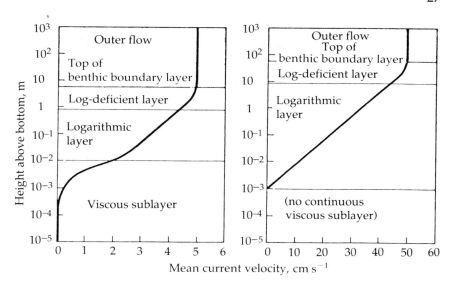

However, within the boundary layer, the flow is progressively retarded towards the seafloor until the extreme condition of no-slip is encountered immediately adjacent to the boundary where the flow becomes viscous and $U = 0$ (Maciolek *et al.*, 1987*a*).

The profile of the *logarithmic layer* lying above the viscous sublayer is given by:

$$U_{(z)} = \frac{u_*}{\varkappa} \ln \frac{Z}{Z_0} \qquad [3]$$

where $\varkappa$ = von Karmans constant (0.4); U_z = velocity at height z above the bed; u_* = boundary shear velocity ($\equiv \sqrt{\tau/\rho}$ where τ is the shear stress and ρ the density). Typically $u_* = U_0/30$, where U_0 is the flow above the benthic boundary layer; Z_0 = roughness element as a result of sediment grains or surface texture.

In hydrodynamically rough conditions:

$$Z_0 = \frac{\varkappa_s}{30} \qquad [4]$$

where $\varkappa_s$ is the roughness element or grain diameter.

In hydrodynamically smooth conditions:

$$Z_0 = \frac{9\nu}{u_*} \qquad [5]$$

where ν is the kinematic molecular viscosity ($= 1 \times 10^{-6}$ m^2 s^{-1}) for water.

Thus in smooth turbulent flow the velocity profile is determined by ν and u_*. In rough turbulent flow it is determined by u_* and the bed grain size. As u_* increases, the roughness element can increase causing the viscous sublayer (see below) to disappear and the flow to become dominated by wakes *behind* elements of the roughness component.

The 'dividing line' between hydrodynamically smooth and rough flows is determined by the balance between the inertial and viscous forces and is represented by the Reynolds number based on roughness element size:

$$R_e = \frac{\varkappa_s u_*}{\nu} \qquad [6]$$

Values < 3 are considered hydrodynamically smooth whilst those > 70 are considered hydrodynamically rough.

Clearly, there will be a straight line relationship between the velocity of flow and the logarithm of distance from the seabed (Fig. 2.17). It should be noted that as a result of the Earth's rotation there will be a turning effect with height above the bed.

The layer between the outer limit of the logarithmic layer and the outer flow beyond the BBL is referred to as the *log-deficient layer*.

The layer of viscous flow adjacent to smooth bottoms is termed the *viscous sublayer* with its thickness (Z_v) determined by:

$$Z_v = \frac{12\nu}{u_*} \qquad [7]$$

(Wimbush, 1976)

The velocity varies according to:

$$\frac{U}{u_*} = u_* Z_v \qquad [8]$$

This sublayer is very thin. In a flow, $U_0 = 3$ cm s^{-1} ($u_* = 0.1$ cm s^{-1}) then $Z_v = 1$ cm and will decrease for an increased flow speed (Wimbush, 1976).

Nevertheless, this layer will be significant to those animals whose activities are restricted close to the seabed.

If any structure such as grain size, shell or animal exceeds one third the thickness of the sublayer, the viscous flow is disrupted and the flow becomes turbulent. Turbulence will penetrate to within 0.1 mm of the seabed.

Thus the BBL must have a profound effect on movements of those animals living permanently at the seabed and those that migrate between it and the water column. Close to the seabed, the BBL is modified by seabed roughness, the mounds and pits which animals excavate and even the presence of animals themselves. The rougher the seabed the greater is the shear stress exerted on the overlying water which creates turbulence and generates a thicker BBL. There are also considerable implications for apparatus placed at the seabed such as colonization experiments (see Chapters 8 and 13) that may create their own turbulence and thus modify any natural effects.

There may also be constraints at the outer limit of the BBL. At this height above the seabed a strong density discontinuity (Richards, 1990) may occur which may act as a barrier to upward vertical movement of animals or particles. Physical processes leading to escapes from the BBL occur as a result of frontal processes, where sloping boundaries intersect isopycnal surfaces and from synoptic scale eddies. Downwards transmission of surface eddy kinetic energy may also deform the BBL (Klein, 1988).

From these studies we can conclude that the BBL forms an important physical structure over the seabed and is modified by the topography of the seabed and in turn affects the distribution of animals and particles near the seabed.

CONTINUITY AND SEASONALITY IN THE DEEP SEA

The large-scale homogeneity in salinity, temperature and oxygen throughout the vast area of the deep sea led in the past to a mistaken concept of great constancy in deep ocean ecosystems. This brief look at the physical environment shows that the main variables are pressure, which increases proportionately with depth, and the deep ocean water movements in the form of the flow regime at the BBL or the occasional turbidity current. This concept of continuity over the whole range of time/space-scales is being challenged from a variety of sources. In the physical environment, diurnal variations in bottom currents caused by deep-sea tides and the major hydrodynamic disturbances caused by benthic storms resulting from vorticity transmitted to the bottom, and which may be of widespread occurrence, suggest a hydrodynamic regime far more energetic and subject to much more episodic variation than was previously conceived. Evidence predicting seasonality in the deep sea is available from the study of the vertical flux of organic matter from surface production (reviewed by Tyler, 1988). This aspect is covered in our study of food and feeding in the deep sea (Chapter 11) where we also note seasonal variation in physiological processes in deep-sea organisms and in the sediment community. Longer-term variability, such as changes in surface productivity caused by climate variation such as an El Niño event may alter recruitment and standing crop of the deep-sea populations such as scavenging amphipods (Ingram & Hessler, 1987), whilst meso-scale eddies may be responsible for the sporadic year-to-year recruitment success of deep-sea urchins by means of their planktonic larvae (Gage & Tyler, 1985). Thus this, the largest of the world's ecosystems, is not the constant and unchanging environment it was originally believed to be. Rather, it shows physical variability, particularly in bottom-current energy along with transport of bottom particles, and a predictable seasonality in some of its ecological processes. This is one of the paradoxes to which we shall return in the course of this book.

3

Methods of study of the organisms of the deep-sea floor

To study the organisms of the deep-sea benthic boundary (which of course is well beyond the present range of deep-sea divers), the biologist requires a platform from which to deploy the special sampling gear or experimental apparatus needed to examine, observe or experiment with the biota. This platform can take two forms: a specialized oceanographic research vessel, or a research submersible, usually operated from a research vessel doubling as 'mother' ship.

Usually such vessels are engaged in voyages, or 'cruises', lasting from a few days to several months. Preparations for a deep-sea cruise have to be very thorough as the sites to be sampled are often remote from land. Although the logistics of such an undertaking are complex, involving all aspects of ship management, the scientist in charge of the cruise is responsible for identifying the equipment necessary for sampling as well as the equipment required for onboard laboratory analysis. The different categories of bottom-dwelling deep-ocean fauna (summarized at the beginning of Part II) naturally present differing problems when trying to collect samples, or in deploying other apparatus, for studying them. Furthermore, it will be necessary to accurately estimate bottom depth and positional coordinates of the ship, and for any overside gear in relation to it; while data on the nature of the bottom and the structure and dynamics of the overlying water column will also assist a successful programme. The chief scientist will also be required to programme the activities of the research cruise, and this has to be conducted with the same rigour required for experimental design in the laboratory. Sampling design has become a discipline in its own right, and the reader is referred to Barnett (1974), Elliott (1971) and Green (1979) for simple accounts. However, this has to be tempered by the realities and uncertainties of work at sea, such as bad weather, which puts any gear placed in the sea at severe risk. Hence, gear losses, along with the high cost of operating at sea, have to be accepted as a fact of life.

In this chapter we outline the main features of a deep-sea oceano-graphic research vessel. We then describe some of the supporting equipment and sampling gear necessary for collecting and observing the organisms of the benthic boundary. Some of the more specialized equipment for monitoring *in situ* the activities associated with these organisms on the seabed are described in relevant later chapters.

OCEANOGRAPHIC RESEARCH VESSELS

There is a wide variety of research vessels and a review of the different types is beyond the scope of this text; but all share some basic characteristics. Their propulsion is specialized not for speed but to hold position when on station. Although such vessels are often equipped for a variety of non-biological functions, they require specific basic equipment for biological sampling of the deep sea. A seagull's eye view of the working deck area of a typical composite monohull research vessel is shown in Fig. 3.1.

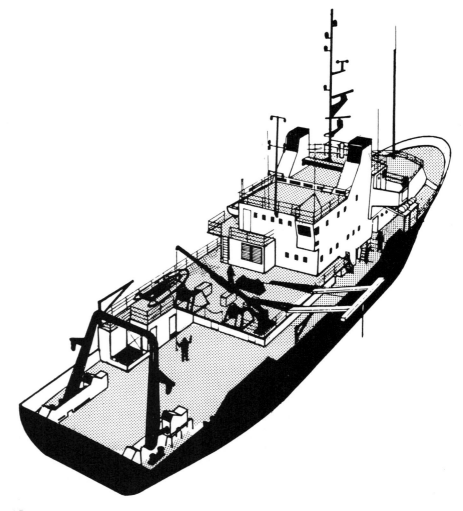

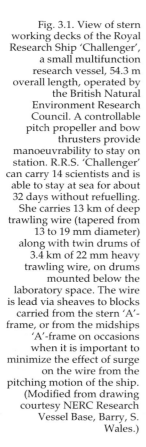

Fig. 3.1. View of stern working decks of the Royal Research Ship 'Challenger', a small multifunction research vessel, 54.3 m overall length, operated by the British Natural Environment Research Council. A controllable pitch propeller and bow thrusters provide manoeuvrability to stay on station. R.R.S. 'Challenger' can carry 14 scientists and is able to stay at sea for about 32 days without refuelling. She carries 13 km of deep trawling wire (tapered from 13 to 19 mm diameter) along with twin drums of 3.4 km of 22 mm heavy trawling wire, on drums mounted below the laboratory space. The wire is lead via sheaves to blocks carried from the stern 'A'-frame, or from the midships 'A'-frame on occasions when it is important to minimize the effect of surge on the wire from the pitching motion of the ship. (Modified from drawing courtesy NERC Research Vessel Base, Barry, S. Wales.)

FRAMES AND CRANES

To deploy sampling gear over the side, it is necessary to use a frame or crane to allow deck clearance on deployment and retrieval. The most common type is the stern – or midships mounted gantry or 'A-frame' fitted with running blocks. For the vertical deployment of sampling apparatus, cranes are also often used. The A-frame is used especially when equipment is being towed but may also be used for the vertical deployment of sampling gear, or for towing trawls or dredges. If the A-frame is mounted at the stern of the ship, it will experience maximum vertical movement during pitching. As a result, a subsidiary A-frame and cranes for deploying gear vertically, such as box-corers (see p. 48) are often placed near the nodal point of the ship (as on R.R.S. 'Challenger', Fig. 3.1) to minimize sample-damaging surge effects resulting from this vertical movement.

Tension meters, usually consisting of load-cells fitted to a sheave or in the blocks on the A-frame, measure the strain on the wire during pay-out and tell you when the sampling gear is on the bottom. The tension reading is critical in the deployment of box-corers (see below) and will also indicate when a towed trawl or dredge has come fast on the bottom.

WINCHES AND WIRES

The main wire of a research vessel can be of differing types. The wire's diameter is often 'tapered' by splicing together lengths of decreasing diameter in order to reduce the total load on the wire resulting from its weight and drag in deep deployments. These wires typically consist of 16 strands of galvanized high-tensile steel wire with a rope core and, although very strong, may 'catspaw' or kink if wrongly deployed. To remedy this difficulty, new cables have been developed which consist of three major strands that do not kink when tension is removed from the wire. In addition, wires with an electrically conducting core are available to power on-gear lights or sensors, but the length of these generally limits them to midwater.

To sample the deepest oceans, at least 11 km of wire (cable or warp) would be required to lower sampling apparatus vertically. If sampling equipment is to be towed, the amount of wire necessary to ensure the gear reaches the bottom depends on its weight and drag, the towing speed (drag on cable) and depth. The great weight of the wire payed out to great depths means that the weight and drag of the wire itself becomes evermore important in the equation, resulting in an ever-decreasing ratio of pay-out to depth (Fig. 3.2). A towed length of wire with nothing on its end will be straight, its angle dependent on its drag per unit length, pay-out and towing speed. Because of the time required to pay-out from the winch, it is important to use only sufficient wire to put the gear on the bottom and ensure it stays there. By adding a heavy weight with little drag, the wire begins to curve downwards, the angle between the outboard end and the sea surface increasing; whilst a terminal load with high drag, such as a trawl, will result in an upwards curvature with a decrease in this angle (Fig. 3.3(a)). Hence, artificially weighting a trawl by

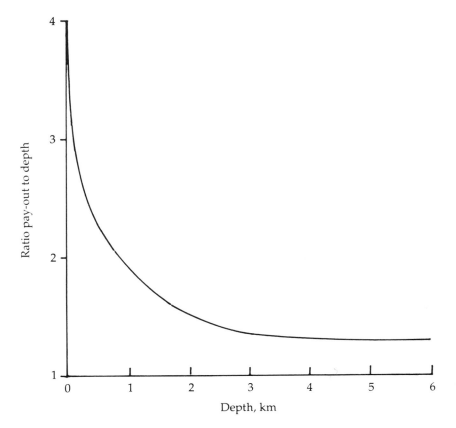

Fig. 3.2. Ratio of wire pay-out to depth (scope ratio) necessary, with the ship steaming at about 1 knot over the ground, to ensure the gear (an anchor dredge) bottoms. Because of the relatively low drag from the gear and the great weight in large pay-outs of wire, the amount of wire need be more than twice the depth only for depths less than 1 km. (Data from Carey & Hancock, 1965.)

attaching weights to the wire can allow a considerable reduction in the pay-out necessary to reach bottom (Rowe & Menzies, 1967; Laubier, Martinais & Reyss, 1972). Where weights are not used, and where the gear is light with little drag, it is reasonable for the purpose of predicting pay-out to assume a straight wire. Here the minimum pay-out at a given speed will then depend on the weight of the wire payed out. The velocity-dependent drag of the gear on the curvature of the wire, and hence the pay-out necessary over a straight wire, becomes important only with larger gear with high drag (Fig. 3.3(b),(c)), such as fish trawls. The current velocity profile of the water column can also much affect these calculations, but is rarely known. For this reason alone precision is best achieved by use of an acoustic beacon or 'pinger' (see below). A fuller treatment of the mechanics of deep wire deployment is given by Kullenberg (1951) and Laubier et al. (1972).

SWIVELS AND WEAK LINKS

When a piece of equipment is towed at the end of 10 km of wire (as trawls and sleds often are) a tremendous twisting torque develops on the towing wire as it is unwound from the drum. Ball-bearing swivels (see Fig. 3.12(a)) are inserted near the towed gear to allow the wire to turn without going into tangles which can easily weaken or even break the wire. The

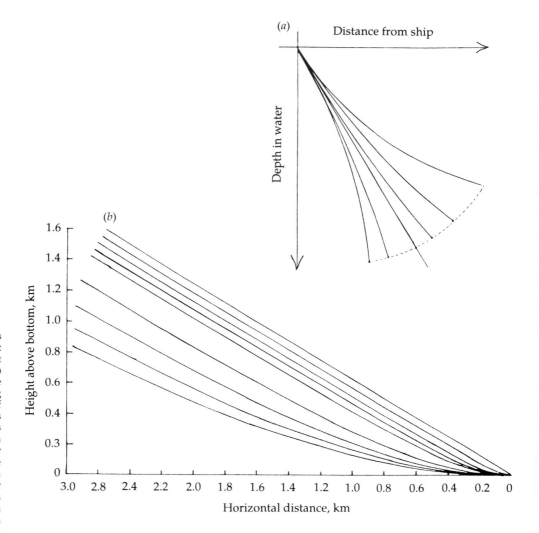

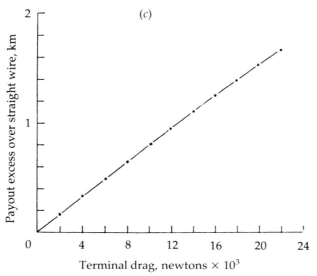

Fig. 3.3. Wire profiles assumed under different conditions at constant speed through water: (*a*) Varying shape of curve expected with increasing drag (left to right) of terminal load relative to its mass: left-hand curves show profile expected when terminal weight is greater than its drag through the water (such as for an epibenthic sled or anchor dredge); right-hand curves when this weight becomes increasingly less than its drag (such as for a fish trawl). Note a straight wire will also be assumed with wire on its own. These curves indicate the advantage gained from weighting a trawl by attaching heavy weights to the wire in order to reduce payout necessary to bottom the gear. (*b*) Family of curves showing profile assumed with increasing drag, such as would be caused by increasing the mouth opening of the sampling gear. (*c*) Calculated excess of wire required as a function of bottom drag on an epibenthic sled. (*b*) and (*c*) calculated using a numerical procedure. (From Booth & Gage, 1980.)

weak link (see Fig. 3.12(*a*)), which consists of either turns of fine gauge wire or a shear pin rated to break at a specified load (which must be less than the 'yield' point of the wire where it becomes permanently stretched prior to breaking), is used in case the towed gear becomes snagged on the seabed. If this occurs, the safety line (Fig. 3.12(*a*)), fitted from the rear of the gear to the ship-side of the weak link, pulls the sampling gear around the obstruction. This prevents the loss of the sample, sampling gear and many metres of wire.

PRECISION PINGERS

These are acoustic beacons which have a variety of uses in monitoring the depth of deployed equipment when attached to, or clamped to the wire near, the gear. They were originally used as an aid in trawling and grab sampling in order to tell when the gear was on the bottom (Bakus, 1966; Bandy, 1965). The pinger signal is often received using the same transponder as used for the Precision Depth Recorder (PDR) (see below), but for gear towed some distance behind a ship, backwards-looking or directional hydrophones are often necessary. When the direct and bottom-reflected signals converge, the gear is known to have reached bottom. It is also possible by evaluating the time delay of the two sonar

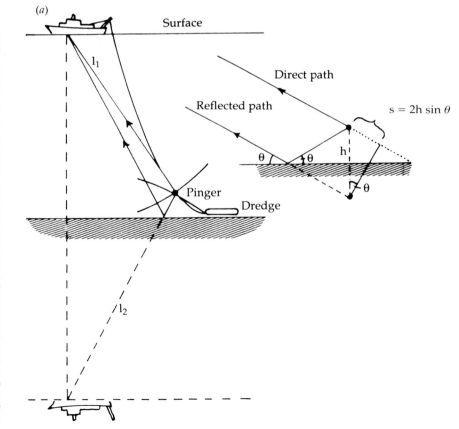

Fig. 3.4. Use of acoustic pinger to evaluate track of sampling gear on bottom. (*a*) The difference, δ, of the sonar paths between the pinger fixed to the wire near the bottom sled shown in (*a*) and the ship, and between the pinger and the ship after reflection of the 'ping' from the bottom, is equal to $2h \sin \theta$, h being the distance of the pinger from the bottom (angle θ is defined in the inset drawing). Knowledge of the two lengths of these sonar paths permits determination of the exact position of the pinger in relation to the ship in the vertical plane. The pinger is found at the intersection of two circles, one centred on the ship and the other on the 'reflected image' of the ship in relation to the bottom, whose respective radii are l_1 (direct path) and l_2 (reflected path). These circles intersect at two points, both symmetrical in relation to the vertical plane of the ship.

paths, one received directly from the pinger and the other reflected from the bottom, to determine the exact position of the pinger in relation to the ship in the vertical plane (Fig. 3.4(*a*)). The bottom track of the gear may be calculated by continuously monitoring the operation (Fig. 3.4(*b*)). Hessler & Jumars (1974) describe the use of the pinger in box-coring where it is used in determining the distance of the corer above the seabed. Relatively massive gear such as box-corers can give a pinger reflection which allows direct monitoring of the position of the gear relative to the seabed.

NAVIGATION

All modern deep-sea research vessels will be equipped with Satellite Navigation systems utilizing Transit satellites and Decca Navigator or Loran C utilizing shore-based medium-frequency radio direction-finding transmitters. The Global Positioning System (GPS) currently coming into service, and to be fully implemented in the mid-1990s, promises to provide ultra-precise, satellite-derived positional fixes from a 'constellation' of up to 24 satellites, so that at least four will be within range of the ship, i.e. more than 5 degrees above the horizon.

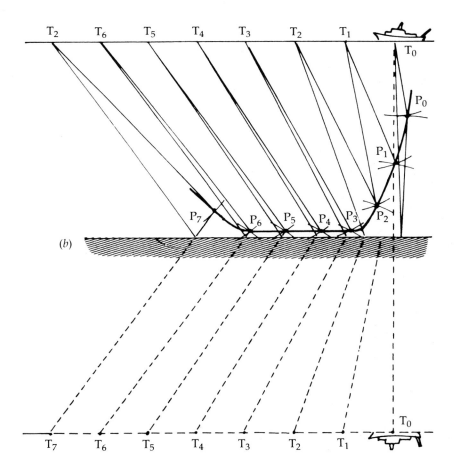

(*b*) Shows the successive positions of the ship (T_0, T_1, ...) and a pinger-monitored beam trawl (P_0, P_1, ...) plotted by means of this model. (Redrawn from Laubier, Martinais & Reyss, 1972.)

Under the constraints of each system, all can provide continuous readouts of the ship's position during sampling. Using these data, it is possible to plot the position of sampling gear on the bottom which may be 5 km or more behind the ship. A review of position fixing of ship and gear in benthic ecological studies is given by Holme & Willerton (1984). In several recent scientific expeditions to the deep sea involving intensive studies on one station, acoustic transponders (usually three or four) are deployed on the bottom (Fig. 3.5) and the position of sampling equipment is determined relative to these and to absolute position determined by Transit or GPS satellites (Rowe & Sibuet, 1983). Such transponders can be left moored on the bottom for extended periods when they are particularly valuable if the site is to be revisited in the future as part of a long-term experiment.

PRECISION DEPTH RECORDERS

The precise depth of sampling is obtained by the use of precision echosounding using PDRs, which display depth either on a paper record or digitally. These data are then corrected for the differing speed of sound through water of differing physical properties either manually, or by

Fig. 3.5. Array of four acoustic transponders as used by the French research vessel 'Jean Charcot' on the Demerby cruise in 1980 for plotting the locations and bottom tracks of the various biological deployments indicated in the diagram; tr, transponder moorings on the bottom; fi, towed 'fish' containing listening transducer; at, Agassiz trawl; bc, box core; bca, baited camera; st, sediment trap. On the right, cm is a multiple current meter mooring. (Modified from Guennegan & Martin, 1985.)

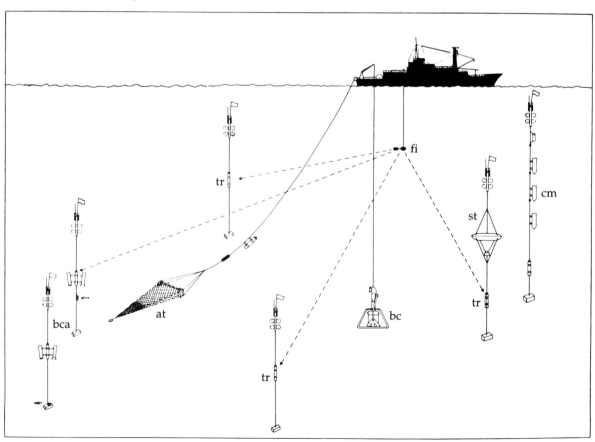

computer program, using empirical tables for geographical areas of the ocean. The PDR may be used for a rough survey of an area before sampling gear is deployed. For a more detailed topographic chart of deep-sea area, swath-mapping sonar, such as 'SEABEAM', consisting of a multibeam echosounder interfaced with a computer and high-speed plotter, will give immediate visualization of seabed topography (Renard & Allenou, 1979; Rowe & Sibuet, 1983).

RESEARCH SUBMERSIBLES

Although surface ships have been used for deep-sea biological studies for over a century, it is in the last 20 years that rapid advances have been made in the use of manned and unmanned research submersibles for ecological observations and for *in situ* experimentation (Geyer, 1977).

MANNED SUBMERSIBLES (DEEP-SEA RESEARCH VEHICLES, OR DSRVs)

These may be used for sampling as well as for observational studies, especially in areas inaccessible to sampling gear operated from surface vessels and unmanned submersibles, such as steep rocky slopes and canyons. Heirtzler & Grassle (1976) note that, compared to remote sensing, an observer from a submersible has a much clearer visualization of the interrelationships of environmental components. However, the main benefit of the manned submersible lies in its potential for manipulative experimentation at the deep-sea bed, and for detailed observation within circumscribed areas such as hydrothermal vent fields. More specifically, Grassle (1980) suggests that submersibles are the only way: (a) to sample small-scale features; (b) to sample repeatedly at a specific site over a number of years; (c) to push sampling devices into the seabed without sediment disturbance; (d) to navigate around obstacles in areas of complex topography, and (e) to sample specific layers in the water column. There are very few manned research submersibles with a depth capability greater than 1 km (Heirtzler & Grassle, 1977). Of those capable of 1 km depth, the most sophisticated is the 'Johnson Sealink' which utilizes a plexiglass rather than a steel sphere (Fig. 3.6). Of the deeper diving submersibles which require a steel or titanium sphere with portholes, the best known are the American 'Alvin' (Fig. 3.7), commissioned in 1964, and the French 'Cyana' and 'Nautile'. Of these, 'Alvin' and 'Cyana' have a depth capability of 4 km and 3 km respectively whilst only the 'Nautile' (see Fig. 15.3), the U.S. Navy's 'Sea Cliff', the Russian 'Mir I' and 'Mir II', and the Japanese 'Shinkai 6500' are capable of descending to 6 km and thus penetrate to all the deep oceans except the trenches. All experimentation must be designed within the manipulative capability of the mechanical arm fitted to the submersible and its maximum lifting capacity. Rowe & Sibuet (1983) summarize the various devices that can be operated by 'Alvin' including devices for sampling the deep-sea bed and for manipulative experimentation. The use of DSRV 'Alvin' in deep-sea experimentation is described in Chapters 6, 8, 11, 12, 14 and 15 of this

Fig. 3.6. 'Johnson Sea-Link' manned submersible shown on aft deck of mother ship under the A-frame used to lift it into and out of the water. The submersible has a 10-cm thick transparent, acrylic sphere that accommodates the pilot and one observer, and provides panoramic visibility. (Courtesy Harbor Branch Oceanographic Institution Inc.)

Fig. 3.7. The manned deep-diving submersible DSRV 'Alvin' shown with its pilot and two scientists within the titanium pressure hull (black), and equipped with rotating sample basket (sb) below the manipulator arm (ma) for collecting specimens and transporting experimentation. Other labelling: ca, camera: st, strobe; vc, video camera; so, sonar; li, floodlight; cm, current meter; mb, main ballast; vb, variable ballast; ai, air; mt, mercury trim; ba, batteries; fp, main propeller; lp, rotatable lift propeller; sr, sphere release. Hatched areas, syntactic foam buoyancy. (Modified from Ballard, 1982.)

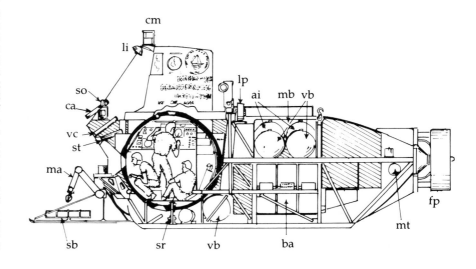

book. However, the main problem of submersible studies in the deep ocean is their expense, their weather limitation for launch and recovery, and the possible risk to the investigators (Rowe & Sibuet, 1983).

UNMANNED RESEARCH SUBMERSIBLES (REMOTE OPERATED VEHICLES, OR ROVs)

These include a range of towed, tethered or free-moving vehicles that are usually controlled from the surface. Towed ROVs have been developed from deep-towed instrument packages; they include the American Acoustically Navigated Geologic Underseas Survey (ANGUS), and the newer 'Argo', both of which are towed sleds equipped with a variety of sensors. Although possessing no independent propulsion, 'Argo' is capable of operating to 6 km depth, at altitudes above bottom of 20–40 m, towed by a coaxial cable by which it can be manoeuvred very precisely. This tether also carries power to the vehicle and data from the vehicle's various sensors. These include a wide-area TV imaging system that is integrated with sideways-looking sonar in order to provide a picture of a broad swath of seabed. The small, unmanned 'Jason Jr' vehicle (Fig. 3.8) demonstrates a successful marriage between a ROV and a larger submersible; having been used in umbilical connection to both 'Alvin' and 'Argo'.

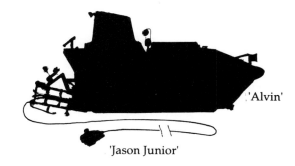

'Alvin'

'Jason Junior'

Fig. 3.8. 'Alvin' (above) with the small Remote Operated Vehicle, or ROV, 'Jason Jr' (enlarged in inset below) attached to it by a 61-m long umbilical. ca, camera; fl, flash; th, thrusters; vi, video camera; li, lights; ho, vehicle housing. ((a) Modified from Ballard (1975). (b) Modified from drawing copyright National Geographic Society.)

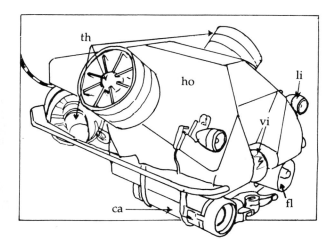

The Remote Underwater Manipulator, RUM (Busby, 1977; Jumars, 1978) belongs to a generation of remotely controlled tracked vehicles designed to crawl over the bottom. RUM is controlled and powered from an Oceanographic Research Buoy (ORB), a floating research platform (Jumars, 1978). During expedition 'Quagmire' (Thiel & Hessler, 1974), in addition to its camera and TV capability, RUM was successfully modified to take four square cores 10×10 cm each at precisely located stations at a 1.22 km depth site in the San Diego Trough (Jumars, 1978; Jumars & Eckman, 1983). Smith (1974) and Smith & Hessler (1974) have also used RUM for studies of respiration of deep-sea fish and to determine sediment oxygen demand in the San Diego Trough. Untethered ROVs that operate under their own power include the French 'Epaulard', and the Japanese 'Dolphin-3K'. These types of vehicle are under active development in many countries and promise to provide a low-cost, portable vehicle for use in a variety of applications. These will be primarily observational studies using photography and videos, but also manipulations such as coring and the emplacement and retrieval of seabed experiments (Hanson & Earle, 1987). They are also of use in broad surveys of the seabed. Photography as a tool of the deep-sea biologist is discussed below.

The role of submersibles is now firmly established in deep-sea research and offers some of the most exciting prospects for the future.

SAMPLING EQUIPMENT

The equipment used for sampling in the early voyages (see Chapter 1) consisted of coarse mesh trawls and dredges hauled up on hemp ropes often by muscle power (Mills, 1983; Rice, 1986). These apparatuses are still in use today although they have been updated and supplemented by much more sophisticated sampling devices.

Within the limitations of the research vessel, the type of sampling gear deployed depends on the sort of sample required: is it to be 'quantitative' in the sense of being representative of a known bottom area, or is it sufficient to just catch a representative or selective part of the fauna present in the area? It also depends on the size of the organism or the community of interest (apparatus needed to sample sediment bacteria will be different from that required to catch large swimming animals). The seasonal timing of the sample may also be important. As we shall see later, certain deep-sea processes are driven by seasonally pulsed production so that a seasonal sampling programme may be required. The deployment of the sampling gear also varies – some are towed, some are lowered vertically, and some are deployed untethered as 'free-fall' samplers. Thus we see that the choice of sampler and its deployment depends on a variety of factors. In this section we look at the more common types that have been developed for sampling the organisms of the deep-sea benthic boundary, and outline their purpose.

QUALITATIVE/SEMI-QUANTITATIVE SAMPLERS: TRAWLS

One of the mainstays of deep-sea biological research since the last century has been the Agassiz trawl (Fig. 3.9(*a*)), also called the Sigsbee or Blake trawl (named, respectively, after the Captain and the ship used by the American pioneering naturalist Alexander Agassiz). This is a double-sided beam trawl adapted from gear once commonly used by coastal fishermen. It has a main net of 20 mm mesh and the cod-end is lined with shrimp netting with a mesh of 10 mm. The Agassiz trawl is used principally for collecting large numbers of benthic megafauna and elements of the benthopelagic fauna (see Chapter 4). The large beam trawl shown in Fig. 5.9(*b*), which similarly has an origin from coastal fisheries, can also be used for catching megafauna.

A variety of trawls have been used to collect benthopelagic fish in the deep sea. Each obtains a different catch, reflecting variations in behaviour and lifestyle of the fish species present, so comparisons between surveys are often difficult unless similar gear is used, fished in a standardized

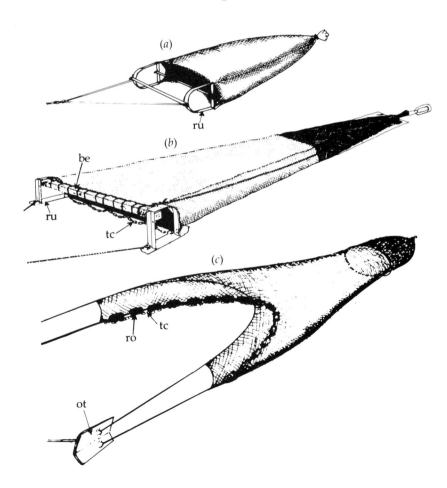

Fig. 3.9. Different bottom trawls drawn roughly to scale. (*a*) 3-m wide Agassiz trawl with: (*b*) large 6-m wide beam trawl operated in recent French studies; (*c*) semiballoon otter trawl (OTSB). ru, metal runner; be, timber beam; tc, tickler chain; ro, rubber rollers on trawl foot rope; ot, steel V-sectioned otter board. ((*a*) and (*b*) modified from drawings in Guennegan & Martin, 1985.)

manner. A large commercial-type twin warp otter trawl has been successful fished down to about 1.25 km (Gordon & Duncan, 1985), but most sampling of benthopelagic fish has been undertaken with the small Marinovitch semiballoon otter trawl (OTSB) (Merrett & Marshall, 1981; Gordon, 1986). The OTSB trawl (Fig. 3.9(c)) has a headline of 14.7 m and has been fished down to depths greater than 5 km. The progress of the OTSB during a tow can be monitored by a pinger mounted midway between the door and the wing end of the trawl. The OTSB can be fished either using a single or paired warps. The catches vary with the method used but usually the former method gives a greater catch of both large invertebrates and fish. The OTSB has been widely used throughout the North Atlantic and its catch data have been used to produce a standardized atlas of the distribution of demersal deep-sea fish (Haedrich & Merrett, 1989).

Special cod-end devices have been developed which insulate and protect the catch from thermal shock as the net is being retrieved. Many species in the net are less stressed during capture and more suitable for physiological studies or attempts to culture them. Most deep-sea animals are far less tolerant of increases in temperature than decreases in hydrostatic pressure – the obvious exceptions are those fishes which have swim-bladders.

There is increased sophistication in fishing techniques with the use of electronic instrumentation to determine bottom time of the nets as well as ambient hydrographic information. This is described in more detail for the epibenthic sleds (see below).

EPIBENTHIC SLEDS

The original epibenthic sled, developed at the Woods Hole Oceanograhic Institution during the 1960s (Hessler & Sanders, 1967), and its subsequent evolution (Aldred *et al.*, 1976; Rice *et al.*, 1982), is designed to catch the smaller animals of the deep-sea floor. The Woods Hole epibenthic sled (Fig. 3.10(a)) consists of a flattened mesh bag, resembling a plankton net, mounted in a metal frame attached to wide runners to prevent sinking into the sediment, and is designed to work either way up. The collecting net has a mouth of 81 × 30 cm. The mouth of the frame is formed by a pair of cutting plates whose edges may be raised or lowered. The main net consists of monofilament nylon with a mesh aperture of 1.0 mm. It is protected in the frame by a steel mesh cage. In order to minimize washing of the sample during its recovery to the surface, a conical cod-end extension net about 1.3 m long protrudes from the rear of the sled and is protected from abrasion by the seabed by canvas aprons. Originally the mouth edge was angled so that it would strip off the top-most layer of sediment, but in practice this resulted in the entrance of the sled rapidly clogging with sediment. An apparently minor adjustment to the hinged blade so that its cutting edge is level with, or slightly above, the runners (Fig. 3.10(b)), produced startlingly better samples of the small-sized fauna associated with the sediment–water interface (Gage, 1975).

In the absence of electronic indicators of whether the sampler is on the

Fig. 3.10. (*a*) Woods Hole pattern epibenthic sled with towing arms (ta) equipped with extension bag (ex) protected by canvas aprons (ap). ru, runners; sc, metal screen protecting the main bag; bi, biting plates shown in typical sampling angle; ga, hinged mouth closing gate shown in open position; closure is effected by release of the spring-loaded arm (ar) by means of timer-controlled release (not visible). (*b*) Probable mode of operation of epibenthic sled when used in the deep sea: the slightly upward inclining surface of the biting edge and metal plate over the front of net disturbs sediment bringing it into suspension, along with contained fauna, so that it is drawn into the mouth opening.

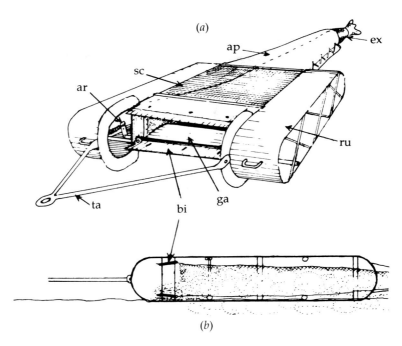

seabed or not, it is often necessary to have a portion of the towing wire on the seabed to be sure the gear stays on the bottom during a tow. The wire disturbs the sediment in front of the net, increasing the catch of small fauna, but scaring away more active species. The nylon mesh bag is designed to filter and retain sediment and fauna > 1 mm diameter; although, in practice, the catch consists of a muddy mixture of fauna and fine particles which requires careful washing (see p. 52). A timer-released metal gate closes the mouth after sufficient time has elapsed for about an hour's haul on the bottom. This both protects the samples from contamination by planktonic organisms during winching back through the water column (the weight of the gear with relatively small mouth opening prevents fishing during lowering to the bottom), and the winnowing, and consequent loss of small, light fauna, of the muddy catch through the mouth during recovery.

   Although this epibenthic sled ushered in a new era of deep-sea biology, it has operational limitations, such as a tendency towards variability between hauls taken at different speeds over the bottom (Gage *et al.*, 1980; Harrison, 1988). The need to determine the distance actually travelled on the seabed, and to record photographically the bottom before being sampled, has been addressed by workers at the Institute of Oceanographic Sciences' Deacon Laboratory in Britain with their Acoustically Monitored Epibenthic Sled. This consists of a steel frame fitted with broad, weighted skids. The mouth measures 2.29 m by 0.61 m and is equipped with an opening/closing mechanism. The main net consists of 4.5 mm terylene mesh with a 1.5 m cod-end of 1.0 mm mesh. Mounted on the top of the sled are pressure housings containing a camera and

Fig. 3.11. (*a*) Lateral view from below and (*b*) from above of the epibenthic sledge developed by the Deacon Laboratory of the Institute of Oceanographic Sciences in England; tb, towing bridles; ca, camera; ru, metal runner; od, odometer wheel; tc, tickler chain; sn, suprabenthic net; cn, coarse-meshed outer nets; fn, fine-meshed inner net. Closure of the mouth of the nets during descent and ascent from the bottom is effected by a hinged blind (bl) that is forced into the horizontal open position by quadrant levers (ql) linked to a quadrant arm (qa) by contact with the bottom. Other labelling: nm, net monitor, fl, flash. (From Rice *et al.*, 1982.)

electronic flash looking obliquely downwards and forwards over the bottom ahead of the mouth. A precision pinger mounted on the frame gives a single pulse every second when the gear is head-up as it is when being lowered to the bottom, while a second pulse is emitted when horizontal on the seabed. A third pulse from a mercury tilt switch attached to one of the opening levers indicates that the mesh covering the mouth has been lowered. If the net leaves the seabed during fishing, or at the end of the haul, the appropriate pulses are lost (Aldred *et al.*, 1976).

A modification to this design replaces the single net with three separate nets (Fig. 3.11), the outer ones having a mesh of 4.5 mm and the central net a 1.0 mm mesh. Above the central net is a suprabenthic net, of 0.33 mm mesh, for the collection of near-bottom plankton. The camera height above the seabed can be varied to give a better photographic resolution of the epibenthic fauna. An odometer wheel, coupled to a potentiometer, measures the distance travelled over the seabed which can be determined during the haul and acoustically transmits the information back to the ship (Rice *et al.*, 1982). Comparison of the bottom area photographed ahead of the mouth with the final catch shows that the gear often misses quite large epifaunal organisms which are clearly visible

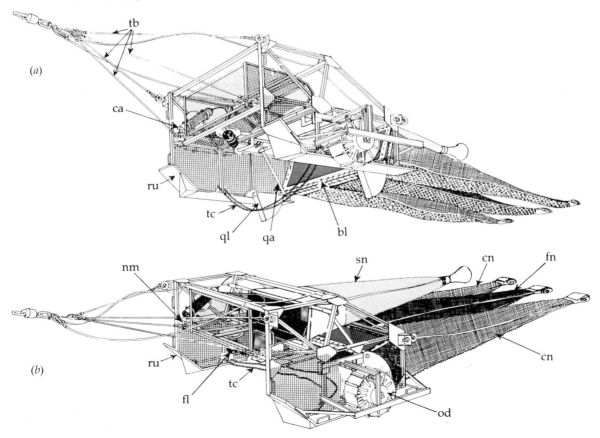

in the photographs, and the performance varies from haul to haul (Rice *et al.*, 1979; Rice, 1987). Hence, even using this level of sophistication, the results remain biased and only provide, at best, semi-quantitative estimates of the benthic community's structure and standing crop.

The sampling gear described above, along with all other towed sampling gear used on the deep-sea bed up to the 1960s, is essentially non-quantitative. This was not a major problem to that date as expeditions were mainly addressing zoogeographic problems. However, in the early 1960s, the emphasis changed from questions of zoogeography to more quantitative studies, particularly as the relative importance (both numerically and in terms of standing crop) of small-sized biota was identified. Owing to the high cost of ship time, it was impractical to use shallow water benthic samplers which sampled only a very small area.

ANCHOR DREDGES

The Anchor Dredge (Fig. 3.12(*a*)) was devised as a semi-quantitative sampler with a known depth of penetration into the sediment (Fig. 3.12(*b*)). Estimates of area sampled are made by dividing the volume of obtained sediment by the biting depth (Sanders, Hessler & Hampson, 1965). It has a collecting bag made of canvas cloth supported by a 2.5 cm nylon mesh. In the Anchor Box Dredge (Fig. 3.12(*c*)) of Carey & Hancock (1965) the mesh bag was replaced by a steel box, 57 cm wide, with cutting edges equipped with hardened steel teeth. A hinged throat valve, installed at the entrance to the dredge, is designed to prevent contamination by pelagic fauna during deployment and recovery.

Fig. 3.12. Semi-quantitative dredges: (*a*) Woods Hole deep-sea anchor dredge of Sanders, Hessler & Hampson (1965) showing planing surface (pl), mouth (mo), upper and lower cutting blades (bl), and collecting bag (cb); (*b*) mode of operation, upper shows dredge stripping off *c.* 10 cm thick top layer of sediment until entry of further material (lower) clogs mouth, rejecting further sediment. Large arrow indicates towing direction. (*c*) Anchor box-dredge of Carey & Hancock (1965) which samples similarly. The latter dredge has a similar planing surface (pl); hardened steel teeth (ht) are fitted to the cutting edge, and a V-shaped steel hinged throat valve (tv) swings up during sampling but protects the sample from washing during recovery. The sampled sediment is removed by opening the hinged end door (ed) as shown. Other labelling: sc, safety cable; wl, weak link; sw, swivel. ((*a*) and (*b*) from Sanders, Hessler & Hampson, 1965.)

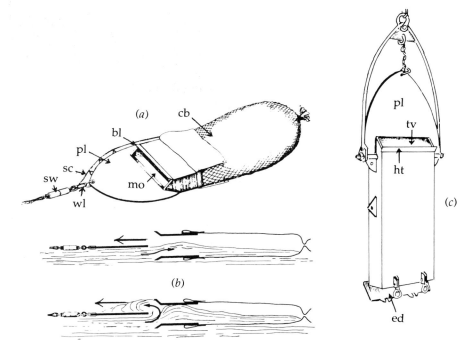

In both the Anchor Dredge and Anchor Box Dredge, a planing surface in front of the mouth prevents the dredge dipping too deeply into the sediment. This makes it capable of stripping off the top 10 cm of sediment from an area of up to 1.3 m². Diver observation of the Anchor Box Dredge in shallow water shows that probably only half this area is taken before the friction of sediment entering the box clogs its entrance (Fig. 3.12(*b*)), causing further material to be rejected (Gage, 1975). This study also showed anchor box dredge samples to be deficient in small-bodied animals capable of swimming compared to samples from van Veen grabs and from careful hand coring by divers. The anchor dredge samples contain relatively unbiased samples of the burrowed animals but, because they live at the sediment surface, they are sampled inefficiently (Hessler & Sanders, 1967; Gage, 1975).

QUANTITATIVE SAMPLERS: GRABS TO BOX-CORERS

Quantitative investigation of deep-sea bottom-dwelling animals began on the 'Galathea' (Spärck, 1951) and with the world-wide Soviet programmes from 1949 (Mills, 1983). Up to the early 1970s the main quantitative samplers were the Okean, Campbell or Petersen grabs (Spärck, 1956*b*; Eleftheriou & Holme, 1984). These grabs, which generally represent enlarged versions of gear in use in shallow water, have their own limitations; either taking too small a sample or, more importantly, having a variable penetration into the sediment depending on the shape of the jaws of the grab. Furthermore, they generate a bow-wave which 'blows' aside the surficial sediment particles along with the important light-bodied animals inhabiting the sediment interface, so once again the samples are unacceptably biased for quantitative studies. Of early samplers, the Reineck box-corer (Reineck, 1963), from which improved designs for geological coring were developed (see Bouma, 1969) was closest to the perfect design but sampled a small surface area only.

Hessler & Jumars (1974) developed the USNEL box-corer at the Scripps Institution of Oceanography in conjunction with the United States Naval Electronic Laboratory (USNEL) at San Diego. This has become the standard gear for deep-sea quantitative sampling of the smaller fauna, and penetrates a precise area of deep-sea sediments to its full depth. It retrieves relatively undisturbed samples covering an area of 0.25 m² (50 × 50 cm) which is usually a large enough area to provide meaningful number of organisms even at the low population densities existing in the deep sea. The early design has been subsequently improved at Scripps in conjunction with the Sandia Laboratories, New Mexico, and it is the later design that is shown in Fig. 3.13(*a*). The USNEL box-corer consists of a detachable, square, open-ended steel core box, attached to a weighted column. The core box sinks into the sediment guided by its passage through the gimbal mounting on the support frame. The spade, which on deployment was held in the horizontal position by a spring-loaded bolt at the top of the corer, closes the bottom of the core box. The top of the box is closed by flaps which are held open during lowering by levers to allow a through-flow of water during descent and hence minimize the bow-wave as the box-core reaches the seabed. The box-corer is lowered vertically

Fig. 3.13. Hessler/Sandia USNEL box-corer showing (*a*) view of gear cocked ready for deployment hanging from ships' wire (inset shows the sequence, I–IV, of operation of the gear before, on, and after leaving the seabed). On deck the pins (pi) are inserted in the holes (ho) at the bottom of the lead-ballasted column to prevent it from descending through the gimbals (gi) of the supporting frame (fr). A spring-loaded bolt, which is locked by means of a sliding bar, locates in a locking plate (lp), that prevents the wire being pulled through the pulley system to draw the arm (ar) of the spade (sp) to the closed position below the removable core box (bo). On bottoming (II) the heavy corer slides through the gimbals into the sediment, turning the cam (ca) that pulls the sliding bar down to release the locking bolt from the locking plate (lp) previously preventing the wire from being drawn through. A fine wire link preventing spring-loaded closure of the paired vent valves (va) over each side of the box is broken sealing the top of the box from washing during its ascent to the surface. Winching in the slack wire above the bottomed corer (III) first swings the arm down so that the spade cuts into the sediment and the spade is pulled up tight against the lower edge of the box by means of slots (sl) cut in its hinged attachment to the column. This seals the box, and the whole gear is then broken out of the seabed with its sample (IV). (*b*) The box with contained sample is removed along with the spade, which is released from the arm by undoing its attachment (sr), onto the dolley cart (dc) that is placed in position underneath. The sample is then wheeled away from the gear for processing after removing part of the lower frame (re).

from the ship with a pinger attached to the wire about 25 m above. The height above the seabed and subsequent contact is monitored by the pinger whilst the onboard tension meter provides an immediate indication of the gear bottoming.

The box-corer is quickly lowered at *c*. 60 m min^{-1} until it is close to the bottom. Its rate of descent is then reduced to 15–25 m min^{-1}. When the gear reaches the seabed, the frame rests on the bottom allowing the heavily ballasted core box to sink into the sediment (shown in inset to Fig. 3.13). This allows a spring-loaded bolt to withdraw, releasing the length of cable needed for the closure of the spade. This occurs as hauling starts, the spade arm cutting down into the sediment until it closes the bottom of the box. A lead or rubber sheet on its upper surface seals the base of the core as the gear is pulled out. As the core is pulled out, there is a marked increase in tension in the warp which suddenly decreases as the core breaks free of the seabed. The gear is retrieved at 50 m min^{-1}. A success-

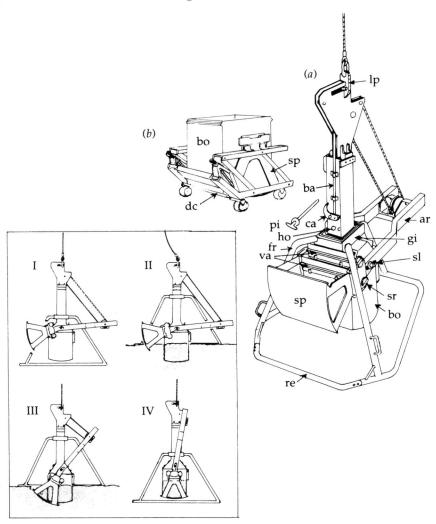

ful box-core sample will retain the clear overlying water (characterized by its low temperature) with an undisturbed sediment surface. Once on deck, the box-core can be removed from the corer (Fig. 3.14) for sieving or subsampling. The 'vegematic' modification is fitted with a liner made up of a grid of 25 10 × 10 cm square subcore tubes (Jumars, 1975*a*). This has proved valuable in understanding small scale spatial variability in the deep sea (see Chapter 6).

Carefully obtained box-core samples can provide excellent quantitative samples of the smaller animals of the sediment-dwelling community that are markedly superior to those obtained by grabs (Smith & Howard, 1972). However, they are not completely without bias. Jumars (1975*b*) showed that the outermost 'vegematic' subcores have significantly lower numbers of fauna than the inner nine subcores, indicating that there is still some 'bow-wave' on the superficial sediment where most fauna live (see Chapter 6). As a consequence, many investigations utilize only the nine inner cores for quantitative analysis. Small-diameter core tubes, pushed into the centre of the box, may be used to study the smallest animals and for microbial studies. The USNEL box-corer has become the standard quantitative sampler in deep-sea investigations, and has been used world-wide.

Fig. 3.14. Photograph of USNEL box corer on stern deck of 'Thomas Washington' showing dolley cart for supporting and positioning the sample box being wheeled into position (foreground). (Courtesy Prof. R. R. Hessler, Scripps Institution of Oceanography.)

SMBA MULTIPLE CORER

This device (Fig. 3.15), developed at the Scottish Marine Biological Association (SMBA), provides an alternative method of obtaining small-diameter cores virtually free of bow-wave-derived bias (Barnett *et al.*, 1984). The multiple corer is based on the Craib Corer (Craib, 1965) and consists of an outer framework supporting a weighted assembly of plastic core tubes of 56.5 mm internal diameter (25.1 cm^2 area) hanging from a water-filled dashpot. When lowered, the frame rests on the seabed (see inset in Fig. 3.15), the wire slackens, and the dashpot dampens the descent of the coring assembly so that the core tubes enter the seabed as slowly as possible. A ball-valve mechanism seals the top and bottom of the tube to prevent loss or disturbance of the core during recovery. The efficiency of this gear in sampling even the smallest and lightest of particles without bow-wave disturbance is testified by its success in sampling the easily resuspended phytodetrital floc lying on the seabed (Gooday, 1988). In addition to faunal and microbial sampling, this apparatus has been successfully modified for determination of *in situ* microbial metabolism (Patching *et al.*, 1986).

OTHER SAMPLERS

All these samplers are designed for use on a wire from the ship. However, Rowe & Clifford (1973) describe modifications to the Birge–Ekman box-corer (a small quantitative sampler developed in the early years of this century) for use by 'Alvin', or by scuba divers in shallow water. This

Fig. 3.15. SMBA multiple corer. A sliding framework supported by a hydraulic damper (hd) carries an assembly of core tubes (ct) within a supporting outer framework (fr). The inset shows the sequence of operation on the seabed: after contact with the bottom (I), the wire slackens as the weight of the corer is taken by the outer framework and allowing the assembly of core tubes (only two are shown in the inset drawings) to slowly descend into the sediment, damped by the hydraulic damper, with the upper core valves (uv) open. When the wire is winched in to lift the gear a special mechanism first closes the valve on top of each core tube (III) and then releases the bottom core catchers (bcc) which swing down until they rest on the seabed. Continued heaving then pulls the core tubes out of the bottom, the sediment cores being retained by the seal of each top valve. As the core tubes break out of the bottom, the bottom core catchers swing into place and help retain the cores on their ascent to the surface. (Modified from Barnett, Watson & Hardy, 1984.)

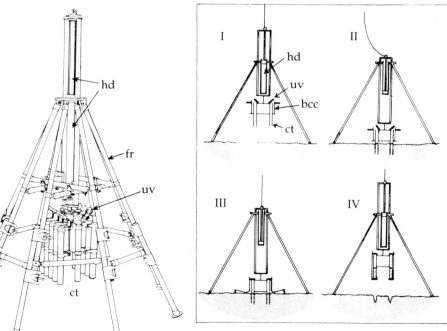

small, lightweight corer consists of an open-ended box measuring 15 × 15 cm. It is pushed into the bottom using the submersible's manipulator arm and is closed by means of spring-powered, hinged, biting jaws at the bottom.

A large multiple box-corer that can obtain nine separate box-cores, each measuring 12 × 20 cm in area, and incorporating a video camera monitor has also been built for shelf work in the Antarctic (Gerdes, 1990) and, with modification, should work well in the deep sea.

SAMPLE WASHING

Samples of the larger deep-sea animals collected in coarse-meshed trawls usually come up well washed, and the specimens can be sorted on deck into the major taxa. However, most fine-meshed trawl samples, along with box-core samples, bring up large quantities of fine sediment from which the delicate-bodied small fauna must be gently separated. Those methods used when sampling shallow water benthos tend to be too vigorous and cause unacceptable damage to the more delicate deep-sea specimens. One of the best methods of gently separating the smaller animals from the sediment has proved to be the elutriation technique of Sanders *et al.* (1965). Aliquots of the muddy sample are placed in a dustbin modified with a spout (Fig. 3.16). A suspension is created using a large-volume flow of filtered seawater. The mixture overflows through the spout on to a fine-meshed sieve that retains the fauna but allows through all the sediment particles less than the sieve aperture (with a mesh size depending on the category of fauna to be retained – see Chapter 7 for discussion of mesh sizes and the size categories of smaller fauna). The residue can then be fixed generally using 5% formalin in seawater, prior to long-term preservation in 80% ethanol. The preservative can have a small quantity of propylene glycol (1% by volume) added to prevent fauna from completely drying out during the long process of sorting the sample into the different taxa using a binocular low-power microscope.

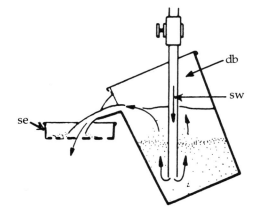

Fig. 3.16. Elutriation apparatus for washing deep-sea benthic samples. db, dustbin; sw, incoming flow of filtered seawater; se, fine-meshed sieve to screen off fauna from overflowing water. (From Sanders *et al.*, 1965.)

PHOTOGRAPHY AND TELEVISION

Much has been written about the use of photography in the deep sea (Hersey, 1967; Heezen & Hollister, 1971; Menzies *et al.*, 1973; Rowe & Sibuet, 1983). Photographs give us a permanent visual representation of the deep-sea bed better than can be obtained by any other technique, although direct observation from submersibles recorded on video is better for some purposes. In modern studies, the camera is often used mounted on a sled (sometimes in conjunction with epibenthic sleds – see above), or on submersibles, or above baited traps (see below). Analysis of oblique photographs of the bed can resolve surface structures and small organisms more clearly than those taken straight downwards. This can be aided by superimposition of a perspective grid that permits accurate quantitative measurements (Barham *et al.*, 1967; Grassle *et al.*, 1975; Wakefield & Genin, 1987). The main types of camera used in deep-sea studies include:

(i)   The downwards-looking stereo camera lowered on a vertical wire which can be used to take plan pictures of the seabed (Fig. 3.17(*a*)). The device is repeatedly 'pogo-sticked' along the bottom with an electronic flash being fired when a weight makes contact with the bottom and the film wound on. (In many deep-sea cameras a shutter is superfluous owing to the lack of light in the deep ocean.)

(ii) The obliquely mounted camera on a sled that is towed behind the ship and photographs are taken at preset time intervals (Fig. 3.17(*b*)).

(iii) Cameras are incorporated into multi-instrumented towed arrays such as 'Deep Tow' (Busby, 1977), or 'Raie' (Fig. 3.17(*c*)) which is similar to the 'Argo' vehicle described previously under ROVs. Such packages typically include sub-bottom profiling, sidescan sonar and a proton magnetometer. They are lowered to 15 to 200 m above the seabed and towed at about 1.5 kt. The large-scale photographic coverage has limitations in resolution of deep-sea organisms for identification, but is useful for broad-scale surveys of the nature of the deep-sea bed.

(iv) Free-vehicle camera system, e.g. 'Bathysnap' (Lampitt & Burnham, 1983) (Fig. 3.17(*d*)). This can be deployed at the seabed for long time periods independent of a ship and recovered later. Once deployed, the camera will take photographs at set time intervals over a long period, together with current speed and direction recordings on the moored current meter. At the end of the deployment, the camera is released from its mooring by an acoustic or timed release and floats to the surface to be retrieved by a surface vessel. 'Bathysnap' has been successfully deployed in determining seasonal changes at the seabed over a period of 6 months (Fig. 11.3).

Fig. 3.17. Gear for photography of the deep-sea bed. Common labelling: ca, camera(s); fl, flash; el, electronics. (*a*) Stereo camera system for seabed photography developed by A. J. Southward at the Marine Biological Association (MBA) at Plymouth, UK; the twin downward-looking cameras (ca) and flash (fl) within the framework are triggered by bottom contact of the small suspended trigger weight (tr). The electronics are in another pressure housing. (*b*) Camera sled used by A. J. Southward at MBA, Plymouth; the automatically firing camera and flash are protected by a metal framework mounted on runners (ru) allowing it to be towed over the seabed. (*c*) Deeply towed camera fish, 'Raie' (a similar gear is called 'Angus' in the United States). (A similar, though more sophisticated system, 'Deep Tow,' was used to take the photographs in Figs 2.12 and 2.13.) The 3-m long framework is weighted with a heavy roller (ro) that just makes contact with the bottom: at an altitude of 3 m the field of view of the camera inclined at 10° from the vertical is 7 m². There are dual flashes, batteries (ba), and the whole system is monitored with an acoustic pinger (pi) and an acoustic beacon (ab) mounted on the wire. (*d*) 'Bathysnap,' a free vehicle time-lapse camera system developed by the U.K. Institute of Oceanographic Sciences; the oblique field of view of the camera provides good resolution of relief and material such as phytodetrital 'fluff' (see Fig. 11.5) that may be difficult to see in 'straight down' photographs. The gear is also equipped with a recording current meter (cm) and compass (co).
continued

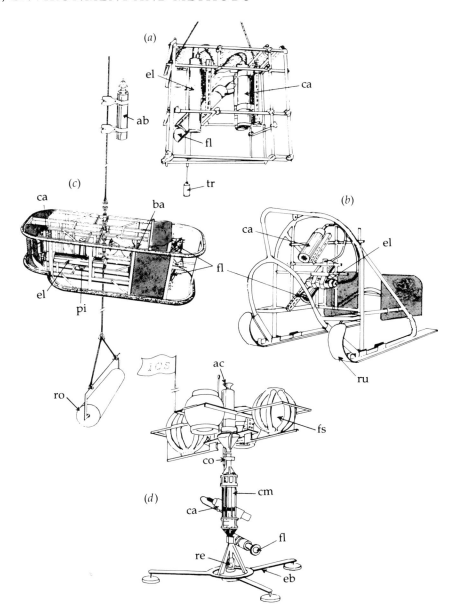

(v) Underwater television has yet to have wide application in the deep sea as there is a heavy power drain on the conducting cables from the camera to the surface vessels. However, this is being improved by the use of signal transmission using fibre optics. High-resolution video cameras and recorders attached to either submersibles or free vehicles have proved to be an excellent means of recording behaviour of deep-sea organisms (e.g. Laver *et al.*, 1985). High-resolution cameras can now yield single frames almost as good as those from still photography.

Although sent to the bottom with overall negative buoyancy the flotation spheres (fs) provide sufficient positive buoyancy to bring the free vehicle to the surface on the acoustic command system (ac) receiving a sonic signal from the ship that activates release (re) of the expendable base (eb). ((*a*) and (*b*) from photographs and drawings in Southward *et al.*, 1976; (*c*) from Guennegan & Martin, 1985; (*d*) from Lampitt & Burnham, 1983.)

Rowe & Sibuet (1983) suggest that the future of underwater television lies in the control of remote manipulators and vehicles. Future development involving electronic cameras will further help to resolve the problems associated with transmitting the information long distances through water.

(vi) Acoustic tracking. This new approach employs an array of high-resolution, narrow-beam sonar in an autonomous package that is moored on the deep-sea bed as a free vehicle. The instrument is capable of detecting and tracking individual pelagic animals by measuring their target strength, and promises to provide data on the movements of the larger swimming animals in relation to the flux of organic matter to and from the BBL (Smith, Alexandrou & Edelman, 1989).

BAITED TRAPS

These were first used at the turn of the century during the cruises of Prince Albert I of Monaco in the 'Hirondelle'. Various recent designs of baited traps mostly utilizing slow-dissolving releases to drop ballast after a period of time, in order to bring them back under positive buoyancy of glass flotation spheres, are shown in Fig. 3.18(*a*)–(*d*). It was only in the mid-1970s that Isaacs & Schwartzlose (1975) first described a baited trap and camera combination for deep-sea studies. (A similar French gear is shown in Fig. 5.18(*c*).) The apparatus is allowed to free fall to the seabed. The time-lapse camera takes photographs of the bait at predetermined intervals. At the end of the period of deployment, the camera is released on command from the surface by means of an acoustic release and it floats to the surface. Baited traps have proved particularly successful in catching, and observing, animals that are motile and well dispersed on the seabed, such as giant amphipods and large fish, that may be able to avoid trawled sampling gear (Dayton & Hessler, 1973; Dahl *et al.*, 1976; Hessler *et al.*, 1978; Thurston, 1979; Ingram & Hessler, 1987). The fate of large food falls into the deep sea may also be examined by this method (Rowe & Staresnic, 1979; Rowe & Sibuet, 1983).

IN SITU MEASUREMENTS OF BIOLOGICAL PROCESSES ON THE SEABED

All the methods discussed so far are for the collection or observation of deep-sea invertebrates or fish. Some biological processes, such as growth and reproduction, can be measured from a time series of these samples. However, there are some ecological processes than can be measured *in situ* at both the individual and population levels. Sediment recolonization has been measured in long deployments of trays of defaunated, natural sediment which are eventually recovered to the surface (Grassle, 1977; Maciolek *et al.*, 1987a,b; Grassle & Morse-Porteous, 1987; Desbruyères, Bevas & Khripounoff, 1980), while similar experiments have studied the special faunas which colonize wood by setting out 'wood islands' on the deep-ocean floor (Turner, 1973; Maddocks & Steineck, 1987). *In situ*

Fig. 3.18. Various types of deep-sea bottom traps. Common labelling: nr, nylon rope; re, magnesium release mechanism; ew, expendable ballast weight; bs, buoyancy spheres; ba, bait; en, entrance. (*a*) and (*b*) are relatively small traps of roughly 0.8 m² volume with a plastic pipe frame and equipped with a release mechanism that drops the circular expendable ballast allowing the trap to ascend with its catch by means of glass buoyancy spheres (not shown) attached further up the nylon rope. Trap (*a*) allows large predators, attracted by the suspended bait, to enter. Curtain-like sides are pulled down by springs (sp) to trap the animals when the ballast is released. Trap (*b*) is smaller and has a simple conical entrance. (*c*) is a larger trap used by IFREMER, Brest, that also operates as a free vehicle with the buoyancy (40 spheres) attached directly to the top of the cuboid cage of 8 m² volume. This trap is equipped with a time-lapse camera (ca) and flash (fl), and has an acoustic release (ar) that operates on command from the ship. The flashing light beacon (fb), flag and radio beacon (rb) aid in location and recovery of the trap at the surface. (*d*) Free-orientating trap array designed at the Scripps Institution of Oceanography for collecting scavenging amphipods. The traps are free orientating by means of a vanes (va), counterweight (lw) and jointed clamp (jc) on to the nylon rope. A release system with expendable ballast weight, similar to (*a*) and (*b*) allows recovery of the traps after a set time. The conical mesh entrance of each small, acrylic trap chamber (tr) always lies downstream to the current (arrow), the animals being attracted by the odour plume from the bait inside. (From Guennegan & Martin, 1985.)

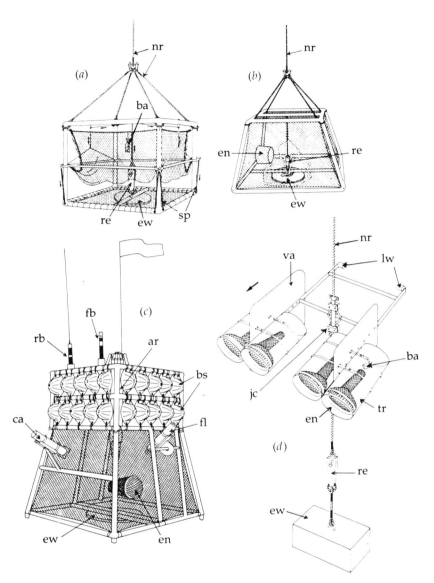

methods for measurement of metabolic processes have been developed because deep-sea organisms can not normally be retrieved alive without employing special collectors which maintain bottom temperature and pressure.

The two parameters that have been measured to determine metabolic rates in the deep sea are: rate of oxygen consumption and nutrient exchange in sealed enclosures (Smith & Hinga, 1983). These authors have described *in situ* apparatus for determining these parameters in large invertebrates, fish and in the whole sediment community. Further details of both sorts of *in situ* apparatus are provided in Chapters 8 and 11, respectively.

Part II   *Organisms of the deep-sea benthic boundary*

In this book we focus on the sorts of animal life inhabiting the benthic boundary. Deep-sea sampling world-wide has demonstrated that the evolutionary radiation of life has penetrated to all parts of the world ocean. Animal life has been recovered from the depths of the Arctic Ocean under the polar ice cap to the greatest depths of the deepest ocean trench. Only in anoxic basins where sulphide bacteria flourish are animals virtually excluded.

CATEGORIES OF FAUNA

The fauna of the benthic boundary is comprised of those animals living either on the ocean floor, the *benthos,* or those associated with the immediately overlying water, the *benthopelagic* fauna, which comprises swimming or drifting forms, some of which may spend varying amounts of time on, or even buried in, the seabed.

This is not to deny the importance of the other major categories of life which impinge on the seafloor, but normally spend their entire lives swimming (the *nekton*) or drifting (the *plankton*) in the overlying water. Biomass of these pelagic communities is highest near the surface, and decreases exponentially with increasing depth until at 4 km depth it is about 1% of that at the surface (Angel & Baker, 1982). However, Wishner (1980*a*) found, from a net attached to the deeply towed instrument package 'Deep Tow' (see Chapter 3), that abundance starts to increase 100 m above the bottom and doubles at 10 m above. She found a diverse and largely novel benthopelagic plankton community associated with the benthic boundary, dominated by small copepod crustaceans and occasionally by larger gelatinous organisms such as pelagic sea cucumbers (see p. 69) and medusae (Barnes *et al.*, 1976; Childress *et al.*, 1989). It includes some truly pelagic elements but is dominated by specialist bottom-associated species (Wishner, 1980*b*). Apart from seeming to be generalist detritivores (Gowing & Wishner, 1986), the taxomomic composition and ecology of this fauna remains little known. We shall not consider it further as a separate entity except in the context of the dispersal of larval or juvenile stages of benthic species (see Chapters 13 and 15).

Phytoplankton, the single-celled plants which photosynthetically fix the energy from the Sun, are restricted to the euphotic zone, the upper 100 m or so of the water column. Despite the surprising discovery of a specialized deep-sea fauna dependent on the chemosynthetic activity of microorganisms living in hot vents, it is believed that the vast majority of life in the deep ocean is ultimately dependent on the plant production at the surface. Consideration of the abundance of animal life in the deep sea (Chapter 7) cannot escape this fact.

In the shallow coastal seas (the *neritic*, as opposed to the *oceanic*, zone) the separation between the community of the pelagic zone and the benthic and benthopelagic community is much less well developed than in the deep sea. In shallow depths, the greater movement and mixing of the overlying water mass permits greater interaction between the two. For example, a majority of species have larval forms which feed and disperse in the plankton; while the adults of others may migrate into midwater to feed, such as certain cumacean crustaceans, or to breed, as in some polynoid worms (see below for descriptions of these taxonomic divisions). In the deep ocean, the great depths curtail such coupling between the euphotic and benthopelagic realms although, as shown in Chapter 11, it is not unknown. The early development of the vast majority of benthic animals is usually confined to the benthic boundary layer; we can infer that their larval forms are free-swimming, but they do not feed, so the length of this free-swimming phase is limited by the amount of stored food reserves that are provided in the egg on release.

The benthos can be subdivided into those usually active, crawling, or attached organisms living on the surface of the ocean bed, the epifauna, and those living buried within the sediment, the infauna. In shallow water, the epifauna comprises about four-fifths of the species of all large benthic animals (Thorson, 1955); much of this radiation is associated with the microhabitat complexity of the varied sediments and physical conditions of the inshore area, as provided, for example, by biogenic structures such as coral reefs. In the deep sea, these subcategories are less useful than ones based on size, where peaks on size spectra (see Chapter 7) seem to reflect differences in lifestyle. The largest component – the *megafauna*, comprises animals, usually living on the seabed, which are large enough to be seen in bottom photographs and caught by the trawl. Taxonomically there are some surprises *and* some difficulties. There are some large, burrowing forms, such as echiuroid and enteropneust worms, about which we know little and which are thought to be responsible for some of the larger burrows and faecal casts that are commonly seen on the deep-ocean bed (Figs 4.15(*b*), 14.2, 14.5–14.8). Most would also qualify on the basis of size to be part of the megafauna. Equally, xenophyophores which are a strange group of giant-sized fragile protozoans (single-celled animals), belonging to a testate rhizopod group, would qualify from their dimensions and conspicuousness in bottom photographs to be part of the megafauna as well! Yet protozoans are normally thought to comprise the smallest size categories amongst benthic animals. Furthermore, although most of the epifauna that live attached to the bottom extracting their food from the overlying water are large enough to be seen in bottom photographs, some of these groups of animals, such as the Bryozoa, include some very tiny forms that would certainly be invisible without a microscope.

Hence in reviewing, in the next two chapters, the groups of animals making up this diversity of animals associated with the deep-sea Benthic Boundary, we shall take a relaxed view with such anomalies and consider them, along with their cousins, at the most appropriate point in the text. The form and lifestyle of these taxa will be only briefly described with an emphasis on the creature's relation to feeding, and its special problems in the deep sea. Further details of the general form and bodily organization of the vast majority of the invertebrate taxa that we review, along with an excellent summary of invertebrate classification that we have tried to follow in the present text, can be found in the semipopular, but encyclopaedic, text on invertebrate marine life by J. D. George & J. J. George (1979), or in any good student text on the Invertebrata.

We shall start with the (mostly) larger animals in Chapter 4 followed by the, mostly, smaller forms in Chapter 5. However, in reality this sequence is less natural than it might seem in terms of the ecological processes of the deep sea as it is the vast numbers of small forms of life in this environment that (as elsewhere) lie at the base of the major exchanges with their physical environment, such as the cycling of carbon in the oceans.

4
The megafauna

THE ERRANT MEGAFAUNA

The large, active forms may be termed *errant* megafauna as opposed to attached forms which make up the *sessile* megafauna. The errant megafauna include those forms that have been most easily caught in deep-sea trawls and dredges since the earliest exploratory work in the deep sea. Hence, these species, dominated by the phylum (a major division of the animal kingdom) Echinodermata (usually spiny-skinned animals that include sea urchins and starfish) and, to a lesser extent, decapod crustaceans of the phylum Arthropoda (which includes insects, spiders and crabs) and various bottom-living fishes, are the best known, and their taxonomy the best developed of the benthos and benthopelagic fauna of the deep sea. However, discovery of a scavenging community composed of previously virtually unknown, giant-sized crustaceans called amphipods, elsewhere of generally fly-like dimensions, has shown that it is unsafe to assume that most of this errant megafauna will be caught in bottom trawls.

ECHINODERMS: BRITTLE STARS AND BASKET STARS

Of the five large classes of modern echinoderms, the Ophiuroidea (brittle stars and basket stars), Asteroidea (sea stars), Echinoidea (sea urchins) and Holothurioidea (sea cucumbers), make up by far the most important of the errant epifauna. In a relatively well-known area of the deep sea such as the Rockall Trough, the brittle stars make up 27% of the echinoderm species collected, but numerically they far outnumber (63%) the remaining megafaunal catch. Although the body form of this eminently successful deep-sea group is conservative, brittle stars may live, as in shallow water, in enormous concentrations on the seabed. They include both active, bottom-crawling species that 'row' over the sediment surface using their flexible arms scavenging for food (family Ophiuridae), to longer and spiny-armed species (family Ophiacanthidae) that utilize the branches of sessile epifauna (see below) as 'perches' in order to entrap or filter particles from currents. This trend is especially well developed in the suborder Euryalina which cling by entwining their long arms around the stems of sea pens and gorgonians. Study of trawled specimens and bottom photographs indicate that one species, *Asteronyx loveni*, catches a variety of living and non-living particulate material with one or two outstretched arms from a perch around 20–35 cm above the seafloor (Fujita & Ohta, 1988). This altitude is within the logarithmic layer of the BBL where re-suspended bottom material is actively mixed (Jumars & Nowell, 1984) (Fig. 2.17). But most deep-sea ophiuroids seem to be trophic generalists lacking in dietary specialization, with motile epifaunal species being opportunistic omnivores, since they show the greatest variety in dietary items (Tyler, 1980; Pearson & Gage, 1984). The large, bone-white brittle star *Ophiomusium lymani* (Fig. 4.1) is perhaps the best known, and, although a bottom crawler, is less mobile than smaller species. It is abundant on the continental rise and lower slope of all ocean basins except the Arctic. Even denser populations of the species *Ophiophthalmus normani* (visible in Fig. 8.8) exist in the bathyal basins of the Californian Continental Borderland where C. R. Smith (1985*a*) has observed them congregating in aggregations of 700 m^{-2} around a baited free-vehicle time-lapse camera system. Other species (families Amphiuridae and

Fig. 4.1. The large cosmopolitan brittle star *Ophiomusium lymani* photographed by 'Bathysnap' at 2 km depth in the Porcupine Seabight (N.E. Atlantic). The disc of this specimen is about 27 mm in diameter; faintly crenulated grooves in the sediment near the arms were made by its movements over the bottom. (Courtesy Dr A. L. Rice, Institute of Oceanographic Sciences.)

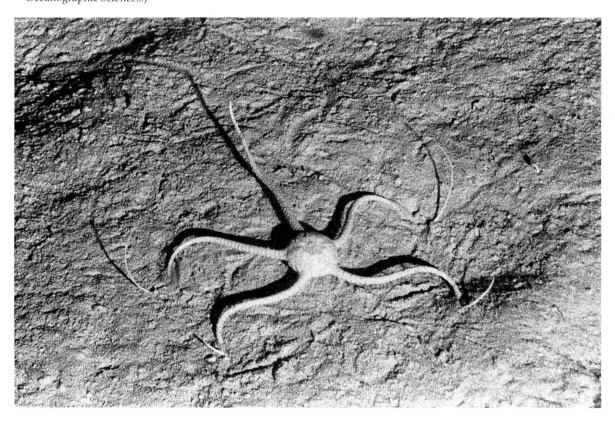

Amphilipidina) live semiburied with only the ends of their long arms exposed to explore the sediment surface for detrital food.

Ophiuroids have rather broad depth distributions compared to other macrofauna (Cherbonnier & Sibuet, 1972; Grassle, Sanders & W. Smith 1979; Tyler, 1980; Gage, 1986). However, although a number of other brittle stars besides *Ophiomusium lymani* have cosmopolitan distributions in the deep sea, in the best-known area, the N. Atlantic, endemic fauna may be further divided into an eastern and western Atlantic component (Mortensen, 1933).

SEA STARS

Fig. 4.2. Outstretched arms of the large brisingid asteroid *Freyella elegans* photographed with its 11 arms outstretched at 4 km depth at the mouth of the Porcupine Seabight, possibly swimming just above the seabed. This, and other brisingids, are thought to feed on particles suspended by near-bottom currents. (Courtesy Dr A. L. Rice, Institute of Oceanographic Sciences.)

These differ little in body form and habit from shallow-water species. The largest in size belong to a typically deep-sea family, the Brisingidae, and deep-sea photographs (Fig. 4.2) and observations from deep-diving submersibles show that they live with long, spinous arms upstretched into the current from which they probably extract food by filter-feeding. The genus *Hymenaster* includes a number of species that are thought to bury themselves in the sediment, with only the opening to a curious, muscular, nidamental chamber, exposed to ventilate the body of the animal; but in recent years they have often been photographed on the sediment surface. In the deep sea, sea stars are probably slow-moving 'croppers' (animals defined by Dayton & Hessler, 1972, as ingestors of

living particles, either exclusively or in combination with dead or inorganic particles). Off Oregon in the Pacific, from examination of stomach contents, Carey (1972) showed marked changes in the feeding types of the species of sea stars occurring along a transect with predominance by carnivores in the subtidal to omnivores at 4.25 km depth. Deep-sea asteroids are generally facultative feeders, obtaining food from both the sediment with its contained small organisms, as well as from larger prey or animal remains. The relatively large species *Plutonaster bifrons* (Fig. 4.3) has been photographed by 'Bathysnap' either ploughing through the surface sediment (Fig. 14.3), or buried at a depth of several centimetres with only the tips of its arms showing, where it may remain for several days perhaps feeding on a large buried prey item or carrion (Lampitt, 1985b). Species of the entirely deep-sea family Porcellanasteridae which have a wide distribution in the deep-sea (Madsen, 1961a), have sediment-stuffed stomachs which indicate that they feed on bulk sediment. However, analysis of the gut contents of the genera *Styracaster* and *Thoracaster* indicate some limited selectivity of larger particles (Briggs, 1985). Perhaps the commonest porcellanasterid is *Porcellanaster ceruleus* which has a cosmopolitan distribution in the world ocean. Like other porcellanasterids, this small species spends most of its time lying in a temporary shallow burrow maintaining a connection with the overlying water (Fig. 4.4), only

Fig. 4.3. Sea star *Plutonaster bifrons* photographed at 2 km depth in the Porcupine Seabight (N.E. Atlantic). Tube feet can be seen extended from the tips of the slightly upturned arms as the animal burrows into the superficial sediment. Darker patches on the heavily bioturbated sediment surface are patches of recently settled phytodetritus. (Courtesy Dr A. L. Rice, Institute of Oceanographic Sciences.)

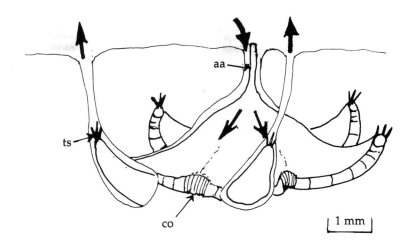

emerging periodically to ingest surface sediment or to change position (Madsen, 1961*b*; Shick, Edwards & Dearborn, 1981).

Those sea stars which are essentially abyssal in their ranges in common with other deep-sea fauna, are the most widely distributed; for example, the abyssal Porcellanasteridae are cosmopolitan (but see Chapter 10), whereas those species whose distributions are centred on bathyal depths seem more restricted (Alton, 1966; Sibuet, 1979; Gage *et al.*, 1983). Like ophiuroids, deep-sea stars do not show sharp depth-related distributions (Cherbonnier & Sibuet, 1972; Gage *et al.*, 1985).

SEA URCHINS

In the deep sea, sea urchins exhibit a wide variety of body-form based on the basic spiny design. In the Rockall Trough they provide 14% of species and 11% of individuals of megafauna. The 'regular' sea urchins retain radial symmetry, either with a rigid globular shape (Fig. 4.5) or the soft, cushion-shaped form of the family Echinothuriidae (Fig. 4.6). The latter include some large species up to about 280 mm in diameter and have a 'test' made up of imbricating plates whose shape is maintained by actively pumping water into the body cavity. After retrieval of a deep-sea haul on deck, the often brightly coloured echinothuriids can be watched slowly collapsing to a flattened, flexible disc. Most of them are probably omnivorous. One of the common N. Atlantic species *Phormosoma placenta* which feeds on the superficial deposit was described by Grassle *et al.* (1975), from submersible observations off New England, moving over the seabed in dense aggregations, 40–50 m in diameter, like 'great herds of buffalo'. Many of the rigid-test species, such as *Echinus affinis*, too, were observed to be aggregated; and elsewhere have been photographed by Bathysnap attracted to patches of phytodetritus and the faecal cast of a holothurian which was consumed within one hour (Billett *et al.*, 1983; Lampitt, 1985*a*). Irregular sea urchins are infaunal, burrowing into the sediment from which they feed on the deposit by means of highly

Fig. 4.5. Seabed photograph showing a deposit-eating regular sea urchin *Echinus* sp. (probably *E. norvegicus*) on the sediment. The urchin's test measures about 5 cm in diameter. It may be feeding on the lighter coloured sediment that appears to have been recently excavated from the two large burrow openings. 0.98 km depth in the Porcupine Seabight, N.E. Atlantic. (Courtesy Dr A. L. Rice, Institute of Oceanographic Sciences.)

Fig. 4.6. Soft-bodied echinothuriid sea urchin *Phormosoma placenta* (diameter about 10 cm) shown foraging over the sediment surface. The curious white bulb-shaped projections from the dorsal test are not evident in trawled specimens and are of unknown function. *c.* 1.4 km depth in the Porcupine Seabight, N.E. Atlantic. (Courtesy Dr A. L. Rice, Institute of Oceanographic Sciences.)

Fig. 4.7. The curious bottle-
shaped deep-sea irregular
sea urchin *Echinosigra phiale*
is shown within its
probable natural burrowing
position. This urchin most
probably feeds on
superficial sediment carried
downwards into an oral
invagination (oi) terminated
by the mouth below the
anterior burrow (ab)
maintained by the apical
spine tuft at the 'head' end.
A posterior projection
below the anus at the 'tail'
end bears a richly ciliated
band of spines, the subanal
fasciole (sf), that probably
pumps a backward flow of
water out of the burrow to
the surface. (Modified from
Mironov, 1975.)

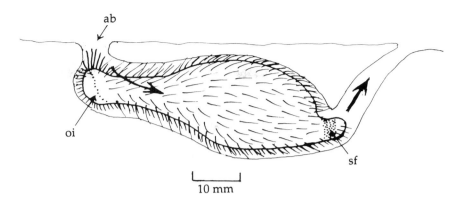

modified spines and tube feet. We can infer by analogy with shallow-water species that their burrow is irrigated by means of a funnel-like connection with the surface. The exclusively deep-sea family Pourtalesiidae, which is common on more eutrophic deep-sea bottoms (Mironov, 1975), reaches an extraordinary degree of modification to become elongated and bottle shaped (Fig. 4.7) and probably burrow superficially within the ooze. Their thin and fragile tests are but rarely recovered undamaged in deep-sea hauls.

In their horizontal range in the northern Atlantic where their distribution is best known, most echinoids occur over the whole area with only essentially shallow bathyal species showing a more restricted range (Mortensen, 1907; Gage *et al.*, 1985).

SEA CUCUMBERS

Holothurians dominate the invertebrate epibenthic fauna in many areas of the deep sea, and recent work on this group is well reviewed by Billett (in press).

Because of the large size and sediment-swallowing bioturbation (see Chapter 14) of the sediment by one entirely deep-sea group of sea cucumbers of the order Elasipodida, they are often regarded as the dominant animals of the deep-sea benthic community. However, all five orders of holothurians have deep-sea representatives, most being somewhat sausage-shaped in body form, with the orders Molpadiida and Apodida being smaller in size and infaunal. Deposit-feeding Apodida belonging to the family Myriotrochidae (Fig. 4.8) are ubiquitous and can dominate the benthic community in some Pacific trenches (Hansen, 1956; Belyaev, 1970, 1989), while the burrowing activities of molpadiids, such as the ubiquitous *Molpadia blakei*, may be responsible for many of the smaller volcano-like mounds visible in deep seabed photographs (Figs. 14.6(*a*), 14.9(*a*)). Species of the orders Aspidochirotida and Elasipodida are usually much larger, with gelatinous bodies very close to neutral buoyancy, and a ventral displacement of the mouth and anus, and a ring of oral tentacles wipe sediment into the ventral-facing mouth. These forms have been likened to 'vacuum cleaners' since they appear to take

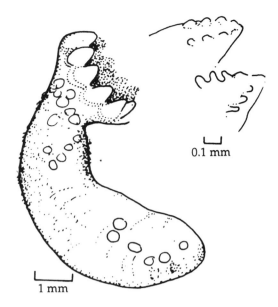

0.1 mm

1 mm

Fig. 4.8. Small apodan deep-sea holothurian *Myriotrochus bathybius*. Like other myriotrochids this small form probably feeds on superficial sediment whilst buried, with the tentacle crown uppermost, in the sediment. Inset shows tentacles drawn from preserved, contracted specimen; in life they would be extended with finger-like digits. What look like myriotrochids have been photographed on the sediment surface in the abyssal Pacific (see Heezen & Hollister, 1971). (From Gage & Billett, 1986.)

only the most superficial, and presumably most nutritious, sediment particles; although the degree to which the different tentacle morphologies reflect differing particle selectivity remains unclear (Billett, Llewellyn & Watson, 1988).

Undulations of a fused lateral 'brim' formed of fused podia in the aspidochirotids *Scotothuria herringi* and *Paelopatides grisea* (Fig. 4.9) are thought to allow a mode of swimming similar to that of cuttlefish (Hansen & Madsen, 1956; Billett, Hansen & Huggett, 1985) and observers from 'Alvin' were startled to see *Paelopatides* swimming with a 'flip-flop' motion

Fig. 4.9. The large deposit-eating aspidochirote holothurian *Paelopatides grisea* shown gently moving with undulating movements of the crenulate margin over the surface of the sediment at 2 km depth in the Porcupine Seabight (N.E. Atlantic). (Photograph courtesy Dr A. L. Rice, Institute of Oceanographic Sciences.)

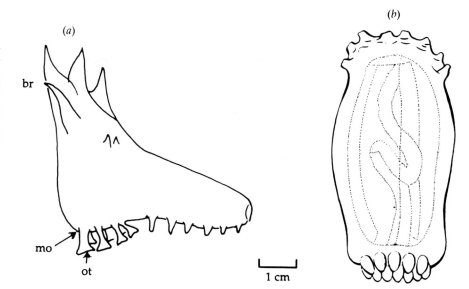

Fig. 4.10. Body form in species of the elasipodid holothurian *Peniagone*. (*a*) *P. wyvilli* showing 'brim' (br) or 'veil' of fused dorsal podia above the mouth (mo), which is surrounded by oral tentacles (ot) used for feeding on sediment particles. (*b*) *P. diaphana* in swimming-feeding mode showing 'big bag' construction typical of swimming holothurians; the oral tentacles surrounding the mouth are at the lower end and the sail-like brim uppermost. ((*a*) Redrawn from Mortensen, 1927; (*b*) from Lipps & Hickman, 1982.)

(Grassle *et al.*, 1975). The curious, long tail of species of the elasipodid *Psychropotes* may be an aid to buoyancy. The species *P. longicauda*, which can grow up to half a metre long, has been caught, along with *P. depressa*, *Benthodytes lingua* and *B. typica*, as juveniles in midwater trawls far off the bottom (Billett *et al.*, 1985), while *P. longicauda* is a swimming species from the N. Central Pacific (Pawson, 1985). In others there is a development of a sail-like brim of fused podia on the dorsal surface above the mouth (Fig. 4.10(*a*)). Species of *Peniagone*, *Scotothuria* and *Enypniastes* may be found in nets trawled thousands of metres off the bottom; *P. diaphana* (Fig. 4.10(*b*)) even at the ocean surface (Billett *et al.*, 1985). They swim with the anterior end and 'sail' upwards, but seabed photographs of the almost medusa-like species *Enypniastes eximia* on the continental slope off eastern Japan show that it does spend at least part of its time on the bottom, probably feeding selectively on the surface deposit (Ohta, 1985), so that its lifestyle might be regarded as benthopelagic (Fig. 4.11). An apparently purely benthopelagic species, *Scotoanassa* sp., has been observed and sampled from the submersible 'Alvin' to form a major part of a dense gelatinous fauna that swims in the BBL within the bathyal basins off southern California (Barnes *et al.*, 1976; Childress *et al.*, 1989).

Ohta (1983) noticed from bottom photographs that *Peniagone japonica*, along with several other holothurians with a thick gelatinous body wall or anteriorly placed velum fan of papillae, is always orientated swimming downstream (Fig. 4.12); such animals providing, in the absence of other indications, a sensitive indication of the direction of flow. The downstream movement is thought to be related to the structure of the velum, as other closely related species, such as *Scotoplanes* (see below), orientate upstream, but lack a velum.

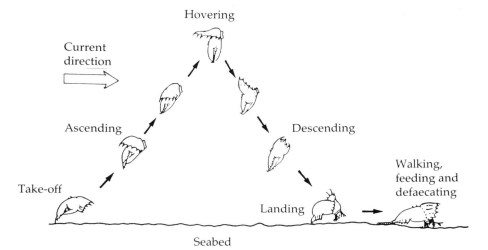

Fig. 4.11. Swimming behaviour of elasipodid holothurian *Enypniastes eximia* in the benthic boundary layer deduced from photographs taken on the continental slope off E. Japan. (Modified from Ohta, 1985.)

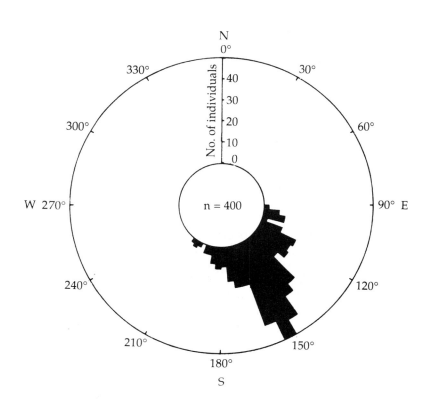

Fig. 4.12. Orientation of the elasipodid holothurian *Peniagone japonica*, recorded from time-lapse photographs taken for about 1 h at 1.7 km depth off western Japan, showing its pronounced negative rheotaxis against a weak bottom current that flowed from NNW (approx. 335°). (From Ohta, 1983.)

From submersible observations, Pawson (1976) concluded that about half the known elasipodid species are capable of swimming, and later (Pawson, 1982) suggested that swimming is a common means of transportation from one area to another. Miller & Pawson (1990) conclude that swimming is used in predator avoidance, transport – especially for locating food, and for reproductive dispersal of juveniles and adults. Elasipodids may form very dense populations in some eutrophic trenches, *Elpidia longicirrata* comprising as much as 80% of the total weight of the catch in the Kurile–Kamchatka Trench, in the N. Pacific, where the sediment is rich in detrital food. Similar, rich feeding conditions may account for the 'herds' of the related *Scotoplanes* (Fig. 8.8) that can 'walk' over the sediment using their leg-like lateral podia (Hansen, 1972). On the floor of the San Diego Trough, Barham, Ayer & Boyce (1967) observed one such herd of these deep-sea vacuum cleaners from the deep-diving submersible 'Trieste' moving, loosely orientated, upstream, in the weak bottom current and suggested they may be attracted to the more richly organic sediments. The small elasipodid *Kolga hyalina* has been photographed in dense aggregations of individuals of similar size on the seabed in the Porcupine Seabight (see Fig. 6.2), and a 'herd' of them was photograhed by 'Bathysnap' passing through the field of view within 16 hours, leaving in their wake a bottom strewn with faecal casts (Lampitt & Billett, 1984). The incorporation into the sediment of patches of phytodetritus photographed by 'Bathysnap' lying on the seabed was

Fig. 4.13. Large elasipodid holothurian *Benthogone rosea* 'walking' with its double row of ventral tube feet over the sediment on which it browses using the rosette of feeding tentacles surrounding the mouth at lower right. 1.5 km depth in the Porcupine Seabight, N.E. Atlantic. (Photograph courtesy Dr A. L. Rice, Institute of Oceanographic Sciences.)

suggested as a possible cause of such aggregations (Billett *et al.,* 1983). The occurrence of *Enypniastes* has been similarly associated with unstable conditions on the slope where frequent turbidity currents and/or slumping causes depauperation of non-motile benthic organisms, but where large concentrations of terrestrial plant debris accumulate (Ohta, 1983). Similarly, rich, but unstable conditions in deep ocean trenches probably account for the dense holothurian populations often found there. Furthermore, such an opportunist lifestyle may explain why catches of some species can be so patchy, replicate trawlings on the same station sometimes containing either hundreds or else few or none.

The holothurians, above all echinoderms, are very widely distributed in the deep ocean, with many species occurring in more than one ocean basin. A few are thought to have a world-wide, or cosmopolitan, distribution, such as *Oneirophanta mutabilis* and *Psychropotes longicauda.* Hansen (1975) persuasively argues that the, frequently wide, distribution of some bathyal and a few abyssal species is related to ocean currents transporting them either as adults or a pelagic phase in their early development.

Bathyal species such as *Benthogone rosea* (Fig. 4.13) or *Benthothuria funebris* have narrow vertical zones while species occurring deeper than about 2.6 km depth generally have a wide bathymetric range in the abyssal zone (Hansen, 1975).

MEGABENTHIC BRISTLE WORMS

There are few worms or worm-like creatures that are both epibenthic and sufficiently large to be considered part of the megafauna. Like many other of the more motile megabenthos, these are usually predators or scavengers. Of the class Polychaeta (bristle worms), which comprises the largest section of the phylum of segmented worms, the Annelida, most large deep-sea species belong to the family Polynoidae. *Macellicephala hadalis* (Fig. 4.14), for example, is widely distributed, occurring in the deepest Pacific trenches and has been photographed swimming over the bottom (Lemche *et al.,* 1976). Another species, *Eunoe hubrechti,* is common in trawlings from around 2 km depth in the N.E. Atlantic and has a, presumably swimming, juvenile stage that occurs throughout the water column. The quill worm, *Hyalinoecia tubicola* which belongs to another family, the Eunicidae, may also have a cosmopolitan distribution (but see Chapter 10) and is one of the commonest epifaunal invertebrates on the upper part of the continental slope in some parts of the N. Atlantic.

EPIBENTHIC HEMICHORDATES

At great depths, the phylum Hemichordata includes some little-known, epifaunal forms termed lophenteropneusts, whose characteristic loop-and-coil faecal casts (Fig. 4.15(*b*)) are common in the photographs of the abyssal seabed (and also in the fossil record). The animal itself (Fig. 4.15(*a*)), although occasionally photographed (e.g. Thorndike *et al.,* 1982), is very fragile and rarely collected (Bourne & Heezen, 1965; Heezen & Hollister, 1971). These animals seem to feed on superficial particles trapped in a mucous strand secreted by its proboscis. From bottom

Fig. 4.14. The large
polynoid polychaete worm
Macellicephala hadalis first
discovered by the
'Galathea' expedition from
the Pacific trenches. (From
Kirkegaard, 1956.)

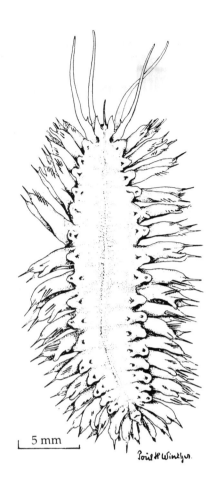

5 mm

Fig. 4.15. (*a*) Large deposit-
eating lophenteropneust,
reconstructed from seabed
photographs, showing it
feeding on the sediment
using its proboscis (pr) and
branched sensory tentacles
(te) extending from the
head end, and ejecting a
faecal 'rope' (fe) from the
other end in the foraged
area (fa) as it moves over
the sea floor. (*b*)
Characteristic coil-and-loop
faecal trace made by a
lophenteropneust on an
area of the seabed about
1 m wide. These epifaunal
hemichordate worms of the
deep sea are thought to
grow nearly a metre long.
((*a*) Modified from Lemche,
1976 and bottom
photograph in Thiel, 1979*a*;
(*b*) drawn from bottom
photograph in the New
Hebrides Trench in Heezen
& Hollister, 1971.)

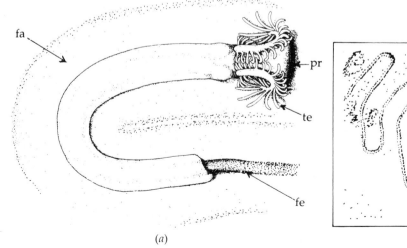

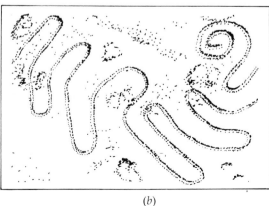

(*a*)   (*b*)

photographs Lemche *et al.* (1976) suggest the head with sensory tentacles is moved from side to side to avoid going over previously foraged areas as it feeds, as tracked by the continuous faecal trace ejected from the tail end in its efficient, non-overlapping coverage of the sediment surface. The absence of burrow openings at the abrupt beginning and end of the faecal trace strongly suggests that they swim to new feeding stations. That more normal, burrowing, hemichordates are abundant in the deep sea has been confirmed from box-cores in which acorn worms (enteropneusts) have been recovered within their branched burrow system (Mauviel, Juniper & Sibuet, 1987; Romero-Wetzel, 1989). The pattern of burrows often surrounding a large mound (Fig. 14.9(*d*)), thought to be excavated by burrowed enteropneusts, is commonly observed in deep-sea photographs taken world-wide.

MEGABENTHIC BURROWING WORMS

The Echiura are burrowing worms (Fig. 4.16), some certainly large enough to be considered part of the buried megafauna, which are often

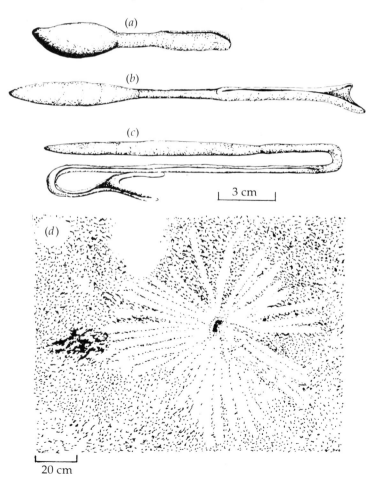

Fig. 4.16. (a)–(c) Bonelliid echiuran worm showing varying stages in body elongation and proboscis extension (see also Fig. 14.10 showing these stages in relation to proboscis feeding activity from within the burrow). (*d*) Shows the spoke-like feeding traces on the sediment surface made by foraging movements of the proboscis of a large burrowed echiuran. The area of disturbed sediment to the left of the rosette probably resulted from tension fractures caused by the movement of the body of the worm in its burrow below. ((*a*)–(*c*) from Vaugelas, 1989; (*d*) from photograph, taken in the Bay of Bengal at 4.01 km depth, in Ohta, 1984.)

3 cm

20 cm

numerous in deep-sea sediments. They may occur in dense aggregations in sediments rich in organic material at both bathyal and hadal depths, including the deepest Pacific trenches (Barnard & Hartman, 1959; Wolff, 1970; George & Higgins, 1979), and also occur in less organically rich areas of the abyssal. Most belong to the family Bonelliidae, possessing a long, tongue-like flattened, food-gathering proboscis (Fig. 4.16(a)–(c)) that is extended, ventral side up, over the sediment in different directions from the short, fat body that lies completely buried within a 'U'- or 'L'-shaped burrow in the soft sediment (see Fig. 14.10). Their grazing on the sediment surface leaves 'lick' marks around one opening on the surface which show in seabed photographs as rosette-shaped patterns on the deep-sea floor (Fig. 4.16(d)), called 'spoke' traces by Heezen & Hollister (1971). The detrital film on the sediment surface adheres to secreted mucus and is transferred to the upper surface and transported as a mucous string along the furrow to the mouth at its base. Ohta (1984) found that there was a linear correlation (Fig. 4.17(a)) between the aspect ratios and the total number of spokes making up the star-shaped pattern from the central burrow opening in seabed photographs taken in the Bay of Bengal, and he developed a simple model (Fig. 4.17(b)), optimizing the maximum spoke number for a given aspect of the spokes for most efficient foraging with least expenditure in energy, that agreed well with the star traces photographed.

The blindly ending horizontal limb of the typically 'L'-shaped burrows of abyssal echiurans may be marked by a 'gashed' mound in the sediment (see Figs 4.16(d), 14.8(c)). This overlies the burrowed body of the worm (Vaugelas, 1989); showing the gashes probably are formed as a result of the pressure of body distension when the proboscis is withdrawn (see Fig. 14.10).

'Bathysnap' deployments in the N.E. Atlantic have photographed the large, 1 cm diameter tongue-like proboscis (at least 50 cm long) emerging from conspicuous burrows to forage for food (Fig. 4.18). This is almost certainly the feeding proboscis of a very large echiuran; the animal itself

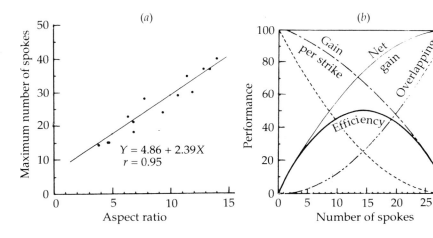

Fig. 4.17. (a) Relation between aspect ratio (length divided by width of spoke) and maximum number of spokes observed in 'saturated' spoke patterns around the feeding hole. (b) Geometrical model of foraging behaviour of bonellid echiuran, the 'strikes' by extending its proboscis producing 'spoked' feeding traces within a circle of constant radius; 'efficiency' is defined as net gain minus overlapped area with increasing number of spokes. (From Ohta, 1984.)

(a)

Maximum number of spokes

$Y = 4.86 + 2.39X$
$r = 0.95$

Aspect ratio

(b)

Performance

Gain per strike

Net gain

Overlapping

Efficiency

Number of spokes

Fig. 4.18. Time-lapse frames (part only) of a 'Bathysnap' photographic record taken at 4 km depth in the Porcupine Seabight showing the extension of the elongated, tongue-like feeding proboscis of a large burrowed echiuran worm. Since the extended proboscis measures more than 50 cm in length, the total extended length of the worm is probably about 1 m (see also Fig. 14.10). (Courtesy Dr R. S. Lampitt, Institute of Oceanographic Sciences.)

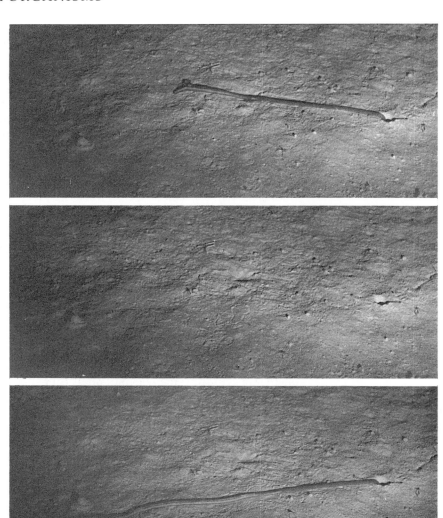

being too large or deep-burrowing to have been brought to the surface by the dredge or trawl (Lampitt, 1985a). Certainly, spoke traces more than 1 m in diameter, likely to be those of echiurans, have been photographed on the Madeira Abyssal Plain (Huggett, 1987). Furthermore, the large volcano-shaped mounds made by accumulated faecal pellets and sediment which is forcibly ejected from the typically 'U'-shaped burrows of bathyal and shallow-water echiurans, are prominent and frequent features on the bottom of the bathyal Santa Catalina Basin off California (C. R. Smith, Jumars & DeMaster, 1986). Such volcano mounds, usually associated with a feeding pit, are characteristic of shallow-water species, such as *Echiurus echiurus*, that build 'U'-shaped burrows deep in anoxic sediments. Here, accumulation of faeces and waste in the blind end of an 'L' burrow cannot be tolerated – as it evidently is in the relatively well-oxygenated sediment at abyssal depths.

The males of bonelliids are dwarfed and adopt a parasitic mode of life on the females. This may be an adaptation to the reduced opportunities of interspecific encounters by sedentary forms existing at resource-limited low densities in the deep sea. Fertilized eggs develop into trochophores that have been known to rise to the ocean surface (Gould-Somero, 1975). There are more than 20 species known from the N. Atlantic, some of which are also know from the Pacific and Indian Oceans, indicating world-wide distributions (Dattagupta, 1981; Zenkevitch, 1966).

SEA SPIDERS

Amongst the phylum Arthropoda, species of long-legged sea spiders, or Pycnogonida, are chelicerates (the group including spiders, scorpions and mites). Pycnogonids are generally large enough to be visible in seabed photographs and hence to be considered part of the megafauna. They are particularly abundant in the Arctic and Antarctic where species known elsewhere only in the deep sea are distributed into shallow water. Including only those species occurring below 2 km depth, Arnaud & Bamber (1987) list 96 known deep-sea species. The pycnogonid fauna of the deep sea is best known in the Atlantic where, of the 125 species known occurring deeper than 250 m, 51 are exclusively bathyal, 25 exclusively abyssal (> 2 km) and nine both, whilst the remainder extend from the shelf to varying depths, including seven that range to > 2 km. In the Pacific, species of the genus *Nymphon* have been found to 7.37 km depth (Arnaud & Bamber, 1987). The large-sized species of the family Colossendeidae are the most familiar deep-sea pycnogonids, the largest, *Colossendeis colossea* (Fig. 4.19), measuring up to half a metre in leg-span. The long, spindly legs, borne from a slender body, were thought to be used as 'stilts' to aid walking over the soft ooze (Wolff, 1961). However, Grassle *et al.* (1975) recorded *Colossendeis* swimming up off the bottom by opening and closing its legs like an umbrella, and then sinking down again as it moved over the bottom.

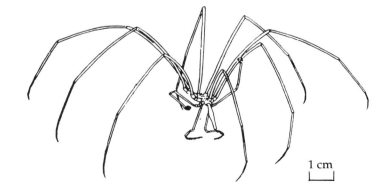

Fig. 4.19. Deep-sea sea spider *Colossendeis colossea* shown in natural position walking over the sediment. (From drawing by J. W. Hedgpeth from deep-sea photograph of living specimen in Lipps & Hickman, 1982.)

1 cm

Although the pycnogonid fauna of the deep sea is still not well known, studies show that most genera have a world-wide distribution, with several species being found in more than one, or all, ocean basins; while others show a more localized distribution within one major ocean basin (Stock, 1978). As with shallow species, the conspicuous muscular proboscis of deep-sea spiders may be used to suck out living substances from sessile, colonial invertebrates, primarily hydroids, but also antipatharian corals, sea pens and sea-anemones, with which, in the deep sea, Murray & Hjort (1912) noted that they are frequently trawled.

GIANT SCAVENGING AMPHIPODS

The usually tiny-bodied, peracarid crustaceans (see Chapter 5) are not commonly imagined as constituting part of the megafauna. However, development of baited time-lapse cameras and traps (Isaacs, 1969; Hessler, 1974; Dayton & Hessler, 1972; Hessler, Isaacs & Mills, 1972; Paul, 1973) has revealed the existence at great depths of a highly motile fauna of giant-sized peracarids, belonging to the amphipod family Lysianassidae. This, hitherto unsuspected, fauna has stimulated a significant amount of the total research effort in deep-sea biology over the past decade or so.

The best-known species is the giant-sized *Eurythenes gryllus* (Fig. 4.20) which grows to a length of 140 mm. However, the little-known 'super-giant' species *Alicella gigantea* is known to grow to 188 mm length, both species having a world-wide distribution (Barnard & Ingram, 1986; DeBroyer & Thurston, 1987). *Eurythenes,* along with other genera, are attracted in enormous numbers to traps set under both the oligotrophic central N. Pacific and more eutrophic areas in the deep N. Atlantic (Schulenberger & Hessler, 1974; Schulenberger & Barnard, 1976; Thurston, 1979; Hargrave, 1985). Although little is known of their ecology, these amphipods, along with other forms, which may include decapods belonging to the swimming section Natantia, ophiuroids, polychaetes, octopods, holothurians and many sorts of benthopelagic fishes, constitute a highly motile, scavenging fauna that is quickly attracted to, and rapidly consumes, large food falls on to the ocean floor. Scavenging amphipods possess mouthparts adapted to slicing, biting and chewing, but, since the guts of some contain sediment, scavenging might not be an exclusive way of life.

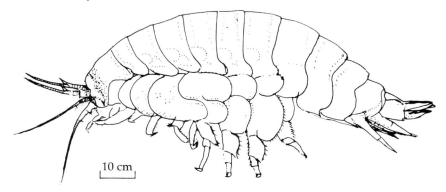

Fig. 4.20. Giant scavenging amphipod *Eurythenes gryllus* drawn from photograph of freshly caught specimen swimming in a tank.

10 cm

Baited traps set in deep trenches tend to confirm that the hadal environment is the exclusive preserve of crustacean scavengers, mainly amphipods, whereas the full range of natatory forms may be caught at adjacent abyssal depths. However, lysianassids remain the commonest scavenging crustaceans on the abyssal plain and rise while decapod crustaceans dominate on the slope (Hessler *et al.*, 1978; Desbruyères *et al.*, 1985). The rapidity with which bait attracts scavenging amphipods suggests that these animals are much more common than their rarity or absence from seabed trawl catches suggest. Thurston (1979) observes that their well-developed swimming ability would make avoiding the trawl an easy matter, and suggested that amphipods approach baited traps at 0.5 m or more off the bottom. This agrees with Wolff (1971) who observed large numbers of rapidly swimming amphipods and isopods within 1 to 2 m of the bottom from the early French deep-diving bathyscaphe 'Archimede' at 4.16 km depth off Madeira. Mean swimming rates of *Eurythenes gryllus* of about 7 cm s^{-1} were measured from video recordings of amphipods attracted to a baited free vehicle (Laver *et al.*, 1985).

Clearly, in order to achieve the high, local densities observed, they must possess highly developed sensory abilities despite total darkness. Several observations suggest that current direction is important for amphipods and other scavengers in locating food: amphipods photographed approaching a baited camera do so from the down-current direction, the response being maximized during periods of peak tidal current (Thurston, 1979; Desbruyères *et al.*, 1985), this confirming suggestions made previously (Isaacs & Schwartzlose, 1975; Guennegan & Rannou, 1979; Lampitt, Merrett & Thurston, 1983). It remains unknown where scavenging amphipods species spend most of their time between meals. Since they are large animals, it might seem possible they lie quiescent, concealed within the sediment waiting to detect prey. But, on the basis of optimal foraging theory, Jumars & Gallagher (1982) define two supposedly more effective foraging pathways for scavengers in searching for food at a distance. The first may be most appropriate for benthic animals, such as ophiuroids, incapable of swimming from the viscous sublayer (within which the 'smell' of the carrion will be carried much more slowly than in the current further up). Here, on the sediment surface, the animal should move randomly, or better, at right angles to the current until the odour is detected. It then moves upstream and, by making unilaterial or bilateral intensity comparisons, can eventually locate the source. The second strategy involves hovering above the viscous layer where turbulent mixing will widen, both horizontally and vertically, the extent of the chemical plume of the odour downstream of its source. When it is detected, the amphipod should move down- and upstream as before. Like hovering buzzards or mosquitoes, the optimal forager should use this more effective strategy if the rewards can offset the extra energetic costs of swimming/hovering. Jumars & Gallagher suggest such costs can be minimized by use of buoyancy mechanisms, and it is interesting that, at least in *Eurythenes*, the body is said to be oily with contained fat deposits.

These ideas have been tested by means of a trapping programme in the abyssal central N. Pacific (Ingram & Hessler, 1983; K. L. Smith & Baldwin, 1984a) designed to assess the distributional and feeding behaviour of scavenging amphipods: the results show that both a near-bottom (demersal) and a more pelagic, off-bottom guild exist. The near-bottom guild is composed of species of *Paralicella* and *Orchomene* which are less than 2 cm in length and which occur within 1 m of the sediment. These species can probably detect and exploit both large and small food-falls, or bottom-derived organic carrion, because of their closeness to the sediment. Since currents will be slowest at this level, their range of sensitivity to odour signals will be less than they would be higher up the water column. The much larger *Eurythenes* belongs to the off-bottom guild (that probably also includes the little-known 'supergiant' species *Alicella gigantea*) and has its greatest abundance 10–20 m from the bottom where it can provide itself with a wide chemosensory 'overview', and use the faster background currents above the Ekman (turbulent) layer in its search for food (Ingram & Hessler, 1983; Charmasson & Calmet, 1987).

At least for grenadier fish, R. R. Wilson & K. L. Smith (1984) maintain that both the local densities and the response times suggest a 'wait' strategy rather than the 'search' strategy suggested by Jumars & Gallagher (1982). Wilson & Smith argued that the detection of carrion by a scavenger hovering well above the bottom might preclude its arrival in time to optimally benefit from a food-fall before near-bottom rivals arrive from downstream. However, a 'wait' strategy might require a relatively high probability of a nearby food-fall, although the temporal and spatial frequencies of such large food packages remain unknown. In the case of *Eurythenes*, small individuals are confined to lower altitudes (< 20 m) where food supplies are more abundant and shelter from predation is provided by the sediment. Large specimens are caught at all altitudes up to a recorded maximum of 1.8 km in a depth of 5.8 km in the central N. Pacific. The large size of adults probably allows them to forage over a larger area from a higher altitude with less risk of predation. Evidence from the relatively low genetic variability of *Eurythenes gryllus* in samples from different basin areas of the central N. Pacific, indicate high dispersal capabilities and/or uniform selective pressures over a wide area, although some differentiation is shown in seamount populations, perhaps as a result of isolation or different selective pressures (Bucklin, Wilson & Smith, 1987). In the N.W. Atlantic, bait moored 20 m off the bottom is completely consumed by *E. gryllus* within 38 h, individuals residing on average only 30 min at the bait but ingesting 30–68% of their body equivalent weight during this period (Hargrave, 1985). Although females are thought to have multiple broods, brooding females have never been captured, presumably because they are not actively foraging for food at this time and hence not attracted to bait.

HIGHER CRUSTACEANS

Although abundant in shallow water, the depacod crustaceans (including crabs, shrimps and prawns) and stomatopods (ghost shrimp) are rather

poorly represented in the deep sea compared to the peracarid crustaceans. Of 300 known stomatopods there are only 14 species known
below 300 m depth, and none below 1.3 km (Manning & Struhsaker,
1976; Hessler & G. D. F. Wilson, 1983). A similar precipitous decline has
been documented for the class Decapoda (Zarenkov, 1969; Pequegnat *et
al.*, 1971; Wenner & Boesch, 1979), but, because of possible difficulties in
catching the more active forms, presently known depth maxima may not
reflect their true downward range (Hessler & Wilson, 1983). Natantian
decapod crustaceans, diverse in tropical shallow waters, are quite common in the deep ocean (Crosnier & Forest, 1973; Roberts & Pequegnat,
1970; Pequegnat, 1970*a*); glyphocrangonid shrimps (family Crangonidae)
being sometimes particularly abundant in deep-sea trawlings. Their
spiny bodies and heavy calcification may well protect them from predation as they lie with the flattened rostrum embedded in the seabed and
the body flexed (Rice, 1981). However, bottom photographs suggest that
they may also passively drift, with their legs just touching the bottom,
orientated at right angles to the current; Lampitt & Burham (1983)
interpreting this active strategy as incorporating advantages of the 'sit
and wait' or ambush predator as both efficient in energy consumption
and minimizing vulnerability to predation by fish able to sense swimming
vibrations. Their diet is macrofauna such as small bivalves that they may
dig out of the bottom. The shrimp *Bythocaris* belongs to another family
common in shallow water, the Hippolytidae. This, and large caridean
prawns such as *Acanthephyra* and a penaeid, probably *Plesiopenaeus*, swim
near the bottom as opportunistic scavengers, having been photographed
attracted to baited traps set in the Arctic and N. Atlantic (Bowman &
Manning, 1972; Desbruyères *et al.*, 1985; Rowe, Sibuet & Vangriesheim,
1986).

Amongst the Reptantia, the peculiarly flattened species of the family
Polychelidae (superfamily Eryonidae) are now confined to, and often
abundant in, the deep sea (Firth & Pequegnat, 1971; Wenner, 1978), with
Willemoesia being found only below 3 km (I. Gordon, 1955), but fossils of
this group date back to the shallow waters in the Triassic and Jurassic, and
the discovery of modern representatives of this group by the 'Challenger'
expedition was taken as confirmation of the old idea (see Chapter 10) of
the deep sea as a repository of 'living fossils' (Wolff, 1961). Seabed
photographs have shown *Willemoesia indica* occupying furrows in the
sediment; the stomach contents of trawled specimens indicating a
scavenging/predatory lifestyle (Young *et al.*, 1985). Another reptant
group, the family Nephropsidae which includes the lobsters, although
extending to the deeper continental shelf, has its centre of diversity in the
bathyal (Holthius, 1974).

The various anomuran families which include squat lobsters and
hermit crabs are the most diverse of decapods in the deep sea. One of the
most impressive is the formidably spined, pink-coloured stone crab,
Neolithodes (Figs 4.21, 4.27). This, and other members of the spider-like
family, Lithodidae, are found in shallow water only at high latitudes. Of
other anomurans the most varied are the squat lobsters (family Galathei-

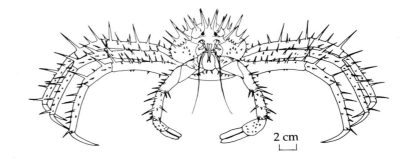

Fig. 4.21. Deep-sea stone crab *Neolithodes grimaldi* from the Rockall Trough (N.E. Atlantic) viewed from the front showing the efficient arrangement of defensive spines. These increase the envelope of body volume by about 300%. (Drawing courtesy of Dr J. Mauchline, Scottish Marine Biological Association.)

dae) (Tirmizi, 1966; Pequegnat & Pequegnat, 1970; Ambler, 1980), with over 100 species in the essentially bathyal genus *Munidopsis* (Fig. 4.22), but with less than 20 species being found deeper than 3 km (Gordon, 1955; Wolff, 1961; Birstein & Zarenkov, 1970). Large densities of *Munidopsis sarsi*, up to 360 individuals ha^{-2}, occur above 800 m depth in the Porcupine Seabight, and dense concentrations of *M. subsquamosa* are found clustered around hydrothermal vents in the Pacific (Figs 15.9(*c*), 15.10(*b*)). Next most diverse are hermit crabs (family Paguridae), but again this family is mostly confined to the upper continental slope, although

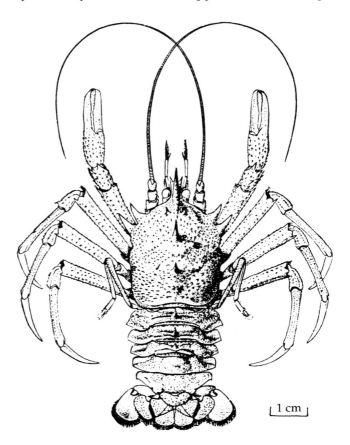

Fig. 4.22. Deep-sea squat lobster *Munidopsis rostrata* (N. Atlantic). (From Agassiz, 1888.)

one or two genera such as *Parapagurus* and *Tylaspis* range to depths beyond 3 km (Wolff, 1961; Menzies, George & Rowe, 1973). However, the greatest diversity of both groups is shown in the shallow Tropics.

The true crabs (Brachyura) have shown impressive radiation to about 3500, often highly specialized, species, but with only 125 or so rather taxonomically isolated species being found in the deep sea (Wolff, 1961; Pequegnat, 1970*b*; Griffin & Brown, 1975; Griffin & Tranter, 1986). Perhaps their more selective carnivorous/scavenging mode of life offers fewer opportunities here than the primarily deposit-sifting feeding method of hermit crabs and squat lobsters. The largest and best-known deep-sea brachyurans are species of *Geryon* and *Chaceon,* such as the red crab *G. trispinosus* (Fig. 4.23) which is most common on the upper continental slope in the N.E. Atlantic; at greater depths, on the slope, it is replaced by either *Chaceon inglei* or *C. gordonae* depending on latitude. Along the Atlantic continental slope off America, *Chaceon quinquidens* inhabits tunnels and arches that it excavates to a depth of 0.75 m in the mud, and which are dominant features of the surface of the seabed (Malahoff, Embley & Fornari, 1982), and which may contribute significantly over time to downslope sediment transport (Hecker, 1982). From differing size distributions of samples of *G. trispinosus* trawled W. of Ireland, it seems that individuals must undertake an extensive depth-related migration during their early life history from the deeper settlement areas to shallower water on the slope where they breed (Hepper, 1971). Recent tagging experiments have confirmed the migratory abilities of *Geryon* and *Chaceon* (Melville-Smith, 1987), demonstrating a maximum daily movement of up to 2 km for *C. maritae* off S.W. Africa. *Geryon* and

Fig. 4.23. Atlantic red crab *Geryon trispinosus,* photographed at 0.5 km depth in the Porcupine Seabight (N.E. Atlantic). The crab is assuming its typical threatening posture on being disturbed by the camera sled. (Photograph courtesy Dr A. L. Rice, Institute of Oceanographic Sciences.)

Chaceon are probably the only deep-sea invertebrates to be currently exploited commercially, the main fishery using baited pots being off Namibia (S.W. Africa) and off the North American east coast (see also Chapter 16).

The few species of deep-sea crabs that range to abyssal depths, such as *Ethusina*, are smaller and much less robust than *Geryon* and *Chaceon*.

CEPHALOPODS

A similar morphological strategy appears to apply to deep-sea cephalopods which include the squids, cuttlefish and octopuses. Few species have been recorded from the benthic boundary, but this may reflect sampling difficulties. However, most deep records are of occasional wanderers or because downward migration has carried them there (Roger, 1969; Roper & Young, 1975; Lu & Roper, 1979). Small species of cuttlefish belonging to the family Sepiolidae, common in coastal soft sediments, occur on the upper slope; but possibly only the deep-sea cirrate octopods (family Cirroteuthidae) with their inactive, low energy lifestyle of neutral buoyancy and sluggish jellyfish-like movements are truly adapted to deep-sea benthopelagic life (Fig. 4.24). They are rarely caught in trawls but are occasionally sighted from deep-diving submersibles and seabed photographs (see Roper & Brundage, 1972).

Although the arm-spread of a species of *Cirroteuthis* caught by Russian scientists off Cap Blanc measured about 250 cm, most are relatively small. *Opisthoteuthis* is remarkably flattened, but nevertheless rarely exceeds 20 cm in widest dimension. Their diet appears not to be the natant crustaceans of oceanic squids but rather benthic polychaetes and peracarid crustaceans. Cirrate octopods may also be scavengers, having been photographed attracted to baited time-lapse cameras laid on the bottom at great depths. *Vampyroteuthis infernalis* is a cosmopolitan species that

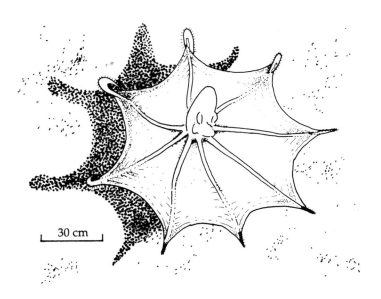

Fig. 4.24. Cirrate octopus hovering over the deep-sea bed off the Virgin Islands. Fine bristle-like cirri on the upcurled ends of the arms probably serve a sensory function in finding prey. (Drawn from a photograph in Roper & Brundage, 1972.)

30 cm

swims using its webbed arms as a pulsating bell or umbrella. Although similar in appearance to the cirrate octopods, it is actually a 'living fossil', representing a distinct group only distantly related to modern octopods, and otherwise known only from the Jurassic (Bandel & Leich, 1986).

BOTTOM-DWELLING FISH

These include a relatively small collection of species, such as skates and rays, that are clearly adapted to a *benthic* lifestyle on the sediment surface, along with a diversity of swimming forms whose range is more or less restricted to the benthic boundary. The latter, along with cirrate octopods and scavenging amphipods, comprise probably the most important part of the *benthopelagic* fauna (reviewed by Marshall & Merrett, 1977). There are close on a thousand species of bottom-dwelling fishes that are known from trawlings on the deep-sea bottom. The most representative families are illustrated in Fig. 4.25.

Benthic species include the jawless eel-like hagfishes (family Myxinidae), skates (family Rajidae) and species of several families of the most advanced, teleost or bony fish, such as the flatfish (order Pleuronecti-

Fig. 4.25. Examples of major families of fish associated with the deep-sea benthic boundary: (*a*) family Myxinidae (hagfish) *Myxine*, upper bathyal, benthic; (*b*) fam. Squalidae, *Somniosus*, upper bathyal, benthic; (*c*) fam. Rajidae, *Raja*, bathyal, benthic; (*d*) fam. Chimaeridae, *Hydrolagus*, upper bathyal, benthopelagic; (*e*) fam. Alepocephalidae, left, *Narcetes*, benthopelagic; right, (*f*) fam. Chlorophthalmidae, *Bathypterois*, bathyal–abyssal, benthic; (*g*) fam. Ateleopopidae, *Ijimaia*, bathyal, benthic; (*h*) fam. Synaphobranchidae, *Synaphobranchus*, bathyal–abyssal, benthopelagic; (*i*) fam. Halosauridae, *Halosaurus*, bathyal, benthic; (*j*) fam. Notacanthidae, *Notacanthus*, bathyal benthopelagic; (*k*) fam. Macrouridae, upper, *Trachyrhynchus*, bathyal/abyssal, benthopelagic; lower, *Coryphaenoides*, bathyal, benthopelagic; (*l*) fam. Liparidae, *Paraliparis*, bathyal, benthopelagic; (*m*) fam. Ophidiidae, *Benthocometes*, upper bathyal, benthopelagic; (*n*) fam. Moridae, *Antimora*, bathyal, benthopelagic; (*o*) fam. Bythitidae, *Oligopus*, bathyal/abyssal, benthopelagic; (*p*) fam. Trichiuridae, *Aphanopus*, upper bathyal, benthopelagic; (*q*) fam. Scorpaenidae, *Scorpaena*, upper bathyal, benthic; (*r*) fam. Zoarcidae, *Lycodes*, bathyal, benthic; (*s*) fam. Aphyonidae, *Sciadonus*, bathyal/abyssal, benthopelagic; (*t*) fam. Liparidae, *Rhodichthys*, bathyal, benthopelagic; (*u*) fam. Aphyonidae, *Aphyonus*, bathyal–abyssal, benthopelagic.

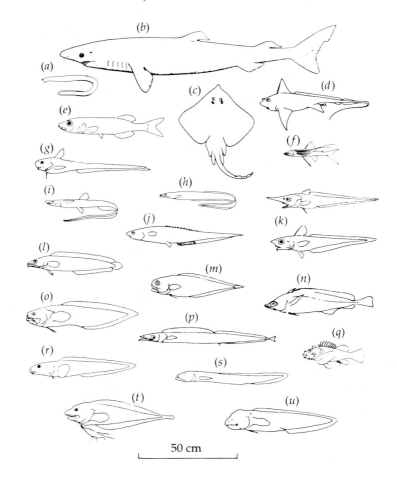

50 cm

formes) and angler fish (order Lophiiformes), which range from shallow water into slope depths. The hagfish are found only to bathyal depths where they are prominent scavengers on large nektonic foodfalls. They sequester the food by cocooning the carcase in a copious, slimy secretion that deters other fish. As in shallow water, the deep-sea rays are active predators that have often been photographed cruising over the bottom in search of small prey. These include fish and crustaceans, as well as buried molluscs which they probably 'smell' with their well-developed olfactory organs. The characteristic 'sit-and-wait' predators of higher latitude shallow waters, such as the scorpion fishes (family Scorpaenidae), eel-pouts (Zoarcidae) and sea snails (Liparidae), possess the broad, massively constructed heads on a relatively small body and extend on the deep-sea slopes. Liparids are particularly diverse in the Pacific; one species, *Careproctus amblystomopsis* taken at 7.23 km depth in the Kurile–Kamchatka Trench is one of the deepest recorded fish. In the southern hemisphere, the equivalent nototheniiform fishes also include a few species that have extended into the deep sea. However, the most extensive and typical fauna of deep-sea benthic fishes are found at lower latitudes.

These include the tripod fish (family Chlorophthalmidae) such as *Bathypterois* and their relatives. They are now well known from photographs and submersible observations to 'perch' on the ooze using much elongated fin rays in their tails and two pelvic fins in order to stand, facing upstream, into the current in ambush, with the pectorals turned forward so that the outthrust projecting fin rays resemble multiple antennae (Fig. 4.26). With their well-developed lateral line system, they are probably

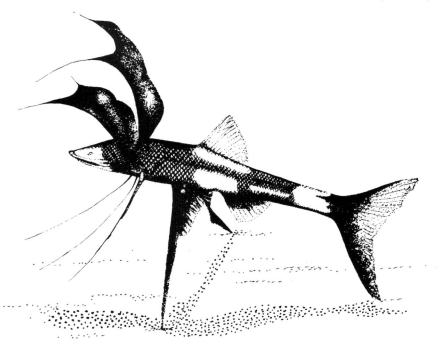

Fig. 4.26. Tripod fish (family Chlorophthalmidae) *Bathypterois bigelowi* in characteristic sit-and-wait foraging strategy on the sea bed in the Gulf of Mexico. Tripod fish can grow to more than 30 cm in length. (Drawn from photograph in Heezen & Hollister, 1971.)

extremely sensitive to vibrations from their swimming prey. Tripod fishes, along with other benthic forms such as scorpaenids are negatively buoyant, lacking a swimbladder or other means of buoyancy.

Of the benthopelagic fish fauna, only a minority lack a swimbladder. These are nearly all cartilaginous-boned sharks, chimaeras and alepo-cephalids; species of the first two groups, like the rays, possessing a large oily liver that render the fish almost neutrally buoyant (Corner, Denton & Forster, 1969); whilst alepocephalids possess a body with a poorly ossified skeleton and watery flesh that also must be close to neutral buoyancy. That there has been powerful selection pressure for neutral buoyancy in the low-energy, predatory/scavenging lifestyle of deep-sea fishes is testified by the presence of enlarged, oily livers and soft watery flesh even in the deep-sea rays (Bone & Roberts, 1969). The sharks of the deep sea are typically dark skinned and are active predators, often growing to a large size. The largest, which sometimes appear in pictures taken by baited seabed cameras, are the cold-water sleeper sharks (family Squalidae), *Somniosus* (Fig. 4.25); the Greenland shark, *S. microcephalus* growing up to more than 6 m long and ranging from the surface down to a maximum of about 1.2 km depth.

Amongst the teleost benthopelagic fish, there has been a marked evolutionary convergence towards an elongated body-form, very often with long-based dorsal and anal fins sustained by many fin rays. The rat-tailed macrourids, such as species of the grenadier fish *Coryphaenoides* (Figs 4.25, 4.27, 4.28), are best known and overwhelmingly dominate this assemblage of fishes that swim freely and habitually near the deep ocean floor, both in terms of abundance and taxonomic diversity (about 300 known species). Their distributions are centred on the continental slope in tropical to temperate areas, and in species richness and biomass rank amongst the most successful family of fishes of the benthic boundary layer. They include species for which important fisheries have developed since the 1950s (see Chapter 16).

Like most benthopelagic fish, they possess large, well-developed swim bladders, although, at least in *C. (Nematonurus) armatus*, the enlarged liver, constituting up to 13% of body weight, also serves as a buoyancy mechanism (Stein & Pearcy, 1982). They are versatile enough to feed on a mixed diet, both motile, sometimes swimming prey, including smaller fish, and carrion lying on the bottom (Sedberry & Musick, 1978). Rattails are conspicuously attracted to baited cameras and traps set on the deep-sea bed (Fig. 4.27, see also Isaacs & Schwartlose, 1975; R. R. Wilson & K. L. Smith, 1984; Desbruyères *et al.*, 1985). Some species seem better adapted to take small swimming prey which are held by the widened, small-toothed mouth and closely set, long gill rakers to screen off small crustaceans, whilst others have been photographed swimming with a slow undulation of the tail (Fig. 4.28), sometimes orientated nose-down and tail-up as they forage for food moving on or just over the sediment surface (Marshall & Bourne, 1967). They typically possess few and stumpy gill rakers, restricted first gill slits and protrusible jaws set behind the heavily built, often armoured, snouts (especially well developed in

Trachyrhynchus, see Fig. 4.25). Films taken by the baited 'monster camera' off California support earlier conjecture that this morphology allows them to root about in the ooze, sucking in the top layer of sediment with the protrusible inferior jaws and straining off small invertebrates by forcing them through the gill slits (Marshall, 1973; Isaacs & Schwartzlose, 1975).

Baited time-lapse camera records have shown a response to tidal currents, more fish being present when the current is strongest (Fig. 4.29). Baited seabed video-cameras also show they tend to head upstream into the current which, as we have seen for scavenging amphipods, seems to be part of a foraging strategy for long-range homing to food-falls following a water-borne scent trail (R. R. Wilson & K. L. Smith, 1984); whilst experiments allowing fish to ingest telemetering acoustic transmitters show *Coryphaenoides* to be nomadic, active foragers just over the seabed, with no evidence for a sit-and-wait foraging strategy; the experiments showing fish moving away and returning several times to the bait (Priede & K. L. Smith, 1986; Priede, K. L. Smith & Armstrong, 1990). Certainly, the olfactory organs seem to be quite well enough developed to enable them to detect the odour plume from a food-fall. Estimates of macrourid standing crop have been made by modelling the attraction plume of

Fig. 4.27. Deep-sea scavengers. Macrourid fish *Coryphaenoides* (*Nematonurus*) *armatus* and the large spiny stone crab *Neolithodes grimaldi* attracted to fish bait (wrapped in cloth) placed on the seabed with 'Bathysnap' at 2.456 km depth in the Porcupine Seabight (N.E. Atlantic). At a frame interval of 4 min, fish like that photographed were recorded at the bait within 15 min. (Courtesy Dr A. L. Rice, Institute of Oceanographic Sciences.)

Fig. 4.28. Macrourid *Coryphaenoides* sp. swimming by means of undulations along the long tail. The wider lower fin provides the necessary lift for a head-down posture when the fish is foraging over the sediment at about 1.4 km depth in the Porcupine Seabight. (Courtesy Dr A. L. Rice, Institute of Oceanographic Sciences.)

baited free-vehicle traps (Desbruyères *et al.*, 1985). Also macrourids possess a lateral line sensory system that is particularly well developed on the head and whose baseline is extended by the long, tapering tail. This elaborate system is thought to aid in detecting and homing on to low-frequency vibrations from prey (Marshall, 1979). Like most benthopelagic fish, the macrourids are most diverse and numerous on the continental slope, particularly in middle to low latitudes. Macrourids occurring deeper than 2 km include the cosmopolitan species *Coryphaenoides (Nematonurus) armatus* and *C. (N.) yaquinae* in the Pacific. Food partitioning

Fig. 4.29. The number of macrourids, principally *Coryphaenoides (Nematonurus) armatus*, observed in an area of 35 m^2 around a baited camera deployment in 4.7 km depth in the Bay of Biscay, showing the relationship to the tidal cycle (recorded, nondimensionally, as the indicated intensity of current. (From Desbruyères *et al.*, 1985.)

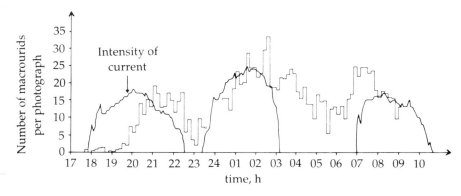

amongst the many species of grenadiers seems to be reflected in their differing bathymetric range, the pelagic feeders being most common on the slope where the vertical migration of their swimming prey may impinge on the bottom. Some species must range upwards to feed on midwater prey, *Coryphaenoides rupestris* having been caught 1.44 km from the seabed (Haedrich, 1974). However, the acoustic tracking work of Priede *et al.* (1990) showed *C. (Nematonurus) armatus* and *C. (N.) yaquinae* remained near the seafloor for 99.8% of the time they were monitored.

The brotulidiform fishes, which include the families Ophidiidae and Bythitidae, also occur in shallow, warm waters and are next most prominent (about 150 known species) and resemble grenadiers in body-form. Little is known of their diet, but, like grenadiers, the males possess a drumming mechanism associated with the swim-bladder which may be used in sound signalling in sexual encounters with other individuals. The alepocephalids are also numerous, and, with the macrourids and ophidiids, comprise the dominant three families in the N. Atlantic (Haedrich & Merrett, 1988). The alepocephalids, or slickheads, have somewhat elongated bodies with large jaws and seem to depend on quite sizeable pelagic prey, such as euphausiid crustaceans, taken near the bottom. The halosaurs and notocanths also have an elongated body-form, halosaurs possessing a wide, forward-projecting, shovel-shaped snout which they use in foraging for epibenthic crustaceans. Observers from 'Alvin' observed the halosaur *Halosauropsis macrochir* generally poised close to the bottom facing into the current, and once to swim down and pick off a sea urchin (*Echinus affinis*) from the bottom (Grassle *et al.*, 1975). The more eel-like Notocanthidae with their small terminal mouths browse on pieces of sessile epifauna such as sea pens and anemones.

The deep-sea cods (Moridae) are less elongated but quite numerous with 50-odd species known. Together with the macrourids, they often possess an elaborate light-producing organ near the anus containing symbiotic luminous bacteria. With their wide, terminal mouth, fine teeth and numerous gill rakers morids are well adapted to feed on a wide variety of motile fauna (J. D. M. Gordon & Duncan, 1985), and some may probe the bottom sediment with sensitive fin rays for food (Fig. 4.30). Morids uniquely possess 'ear pads' in the anterior chamber of the swim-bladder abutting the auditory capsules that probably function as a hydrophone. The largest species, *Antimora rostrata*, is cosmopolitan at 0.4–3 km depth.

The best known of the benthopelagic eels are the synaphobranchids, whose bathymetric range extends to more than 3 km depth. These, together with the slickheads (family Alepocephalidae), seem to take quite sizeable pelagic prey near the bottom. Deep-sea eels may live buried in the sediment for most of the time (Grassle *et al.*, 1975).

Overall, intensive studies of the trophic ecology of benthopelagic fish show that the majority have a generalized diet, usually eating pelagic or the more motile epibenthic organisms as food, and that there is minimal exploitation of the benthic infauna (McLellan, 1977; Sedberry & Musick, 1978; Mauchline & J. D. M. Gordon, 1985, 1986). Abundance and diversity

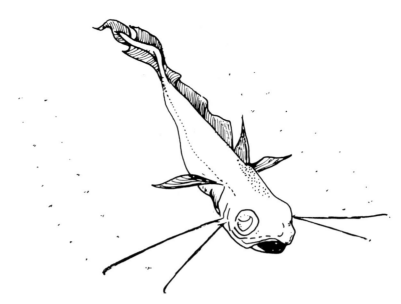

Fig. 4.30. Deep-sea morid fish probing the ooze for food with its long, sensitive pelvic fin rays. (Redrawn from Heezen & Hollister, 1971.)

of benthopelagic fishes seem to be highest in the bathyal (Haedrich, Rowe & Polloni, 1980; Pearcy, Stein & Carney, 1982; Merrett & Domanski, 1985; J. D. M. Gordon & Duncan, 1985; J. D. M. Gordon, 1986; Snelgrove & Haedrich, 1987), and there is some evidence that, overall, this may be related to impingement of bathy- and abyssopelagic organisms with the slope (Hargreaves, 1984) on which animals they feed extensively (see, e.g., Pearcy & Ambler, 1974; Marshall & Merrett, 1977).

THE SESSILE MEGAFAUNA

These animals are usually found attached to exposed rock outcrops on the continental slope, on the rugged topography of seamounts or on the basaltic rock at the oceanic spreading centres; on ferromanganese nodules and to stones that have dropped from the bottom of icebergs, or to the sediment itself. Also included are the spectacular sessile forms living associated with hydrothermal springs and sulphide-rich cold seeps on the continental margin (see Chapter 15).

Although the availability of suitable attaching substratum may limit the occurrence of sessile fauna, it is their mode of feeding on suspended particles that most clearly determines their morphology.

SPONGES

Of the multicelled animals, the sponges (Porifera) are perhaps the least complex, but nevertheless they comprise a varied and successful group. Their biology is poorly understood, especially in the deep sea. The orders Demospongiae and Calcarea, which are numerous and diverse in temperature and tropical shallow water, are nearly, but not completely, displaced in the deep sea by the Hexactinellidae, or glass sponges, which are also abundant in the cold waters of shallow, polar seas, especially the

Antarctic. Of these, the delicately beautiful, long silaceous needles comprising the spicular skeleton of the Venus's Flower Basket, *Euplectella* is best known. This, and a range of other forms of sponge, drawn from specimens trawled from the deep sea, is shown in Fig. 4.31(*b*). The encrusting habit of shallow-water demospongid sponges is much reduced in deep water, most species having an erect, roughly radially symmetrical body, often attenuated towards their bottom attachment as a slender stalk. This trend is accentuated with the vase-shaped body form of *Holascus* and *Hyalonema* (Fig. 4.31(*a*), (*c*)). The body wall of hexactinellids is particularly porous so that water for nutrition and respiration and removal of waste can enter passively in currents in addition to the active pumping by flagellated internal collar cells, or choanocytes. Clearly, the

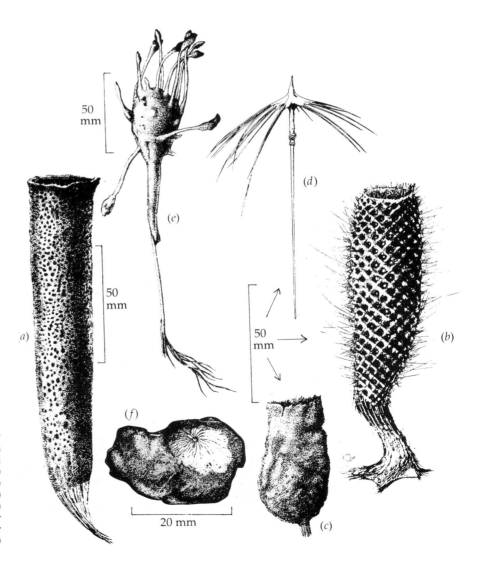

Fig. 4.31. Range of body form in deep-sea hexactinellid and demospongid sponges: (*a*) *Holascus*; (*b*) *Euplectella*; (*c*) *Hyalonema*; (*d*) *Cladorhiza*; (*e*) *Asbestopluma*; (*f*) *Sphaerotylus*. ((*b*) After Thomson, 1877; remainder from Koltun, 1970.)

microphagous feeding method of sponges requires a supply of current-borne organic particles, and they might be expected to be most abundant on the more moderately energetic bottoms where they seem to attain their greatest densities; whilst specimens on deep, oligotrophic bottoms seem to be small or very lightly built. The vase-shape of such sponges may take advantage of the current velocity gradient within the viscous layer, the relatively stronger current over the top of the sponge (the excurrent opening) creating a pressure differential so that water is drawn into the incurrent openings of the outside of the vase lower down (Levinton, 1982). Hexactinellids are sometimes found at very high densities in the deep sea, particularly on the slope. The Institute of Oceanographic Sciences in Britain has mapped the distribution of the bird's nest sponge *Pheronema grayi* (shown in Fig. 4.32) in the Porcupine Seabight area off S.W. Ireland where it can have very abrupt upper and lower bathymetric limits. Here it can reach densities up to 5 m^{-2}, and lives with a suite of other organisms largely restricted to the sponge community which is believed to be sustained by hydrographic conditions resulting in quantities of suspended matter close to the seafloor.

Those demospongids that are found in the deep sea, such as *Cladorhiza* and *Asbestopluma* (Fig. 4.31(d),(e)), have a curious, stalked form and have been found within wide depth limits from a few hundred metres to more

Fig. 4.32. Bird's nest sponge *Pheronema grayi* photographed at 1.2 km depth in the Porcupine Seabight/Porcupine Bank area (N.E. Atlantic) where it occurs in a dense band between 1–1.3 km depth. The sponges provide a 'perch' for a number of associated organisms, including ascidians and the small squat lobster *Munida* visible on the left. (Courtesy Dr A. L. Rice, Institute of Oceanographic Sciences.)

Fig. 4.33. Deep-sea
demospongid sponge
Cladorhiza concrescens: (*a*) as
trawled specimen; (*b*)
natural position in life with
outstretched appendages.
(Left, from Agassiz, 1888;
right, redrawn from
photograph in Heezen &
Hollister, 1971.)

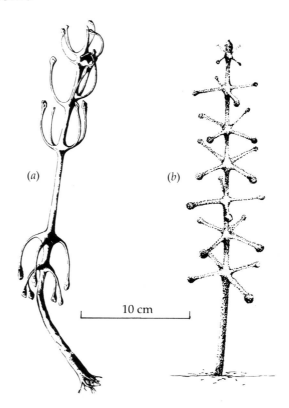

than 8 km depth in the Kurile–Kamchatka Trench (Koltun, 1970) and also on the most food-poor (*oligotrophic*) mid-basin areas under low surface productivity such as the central N. Pacific (Levi, 1964; Pawson, 1986). Somehow their strange morphology must be well adapted to tolerate life in conditions of resource depletion. However, the body-form shown by trawled specimens may not be typical of the posture adopted living on the bottom (Fig. 4.33). More 'normal', encrusting demospongids (Fig. 4.31(*f*)) are, however, found at bathyal depths.

HYDROIDS AND BENTHIC JELLYFISH

The phylum Coelenterata is characterized by 'polyps' possessing stinging cells (nematocysts) on tentacles on a body surrounding the mouth but lacking an anus. It includes the hydroids (sea firs), pennatulids (sea pens), gorgonians (sea fans), corals and sea anemones. All have representatives that are adaptable and successful forms of life in the deep sea.

The hydroids belong to the class Hydrozoa. These form distinctive shrub-like colonies where the 'polyps' are borne on the outstretched branches, and are the most diverse coelenterate group. Usually they are best developed in the more current-swept bottoms of the continental slope. But the species *Halisiphonia galatheae* was trawled from 8.21–8.3 km depth in the Kermadec Trench (Kramp, 1956), while *Aglaophenia tenuissima*, also taken in this trench, is also known at depths of less than 600 m!

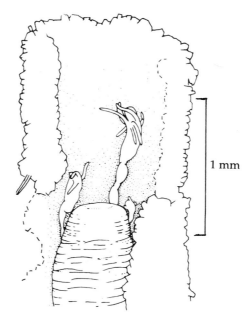

1 mm

Fig. 4.34. Epizoic athecate hydroids, resembling *Perigonimus*, attached to head end of sipunculid worm *Phascolion* sp. which, in turn, is inhabiting a tube of the foraminiferan *Hyperammina elongata*; from about 2 km depth off Spanish Sahara. (From Gooday, 1984.)

Furthermore, another species found to be common at great depths in the Bay of Biscay is known from shallow water in the Arctic and Atlantic coasts. The well-studied fauna of this area is concluded to include a mixture of true deep-sea and eurybathic species (Verwoort, 1985). *Branchiocerianthus imperator* reaches nearly 2 m in height in the Indo-Pacific deep sea (Lemche *et al.*, 1976) where it is thought to feed by sweeping the seafloor with its multitentaculate crown (Foell & Pawson, 1986). Four other congeners are known from the subtidal to hadal depths, but most deep-sea hydroids are much smaller. Hydroids reproduce by means of an often abbreviated medusoid stage resembling a small jellyfish. Some small athecate (lacking a hard covering around the polyps) forms have been found attached to xenophyophores (see Chapter 5) and even to mobile epifauna such as protobranch bivalves and sipunculids (Fig. 4.34).

The family Actinoscyphiidae include forms where the benthic, or scyphistoma, stage of species of the class Scyphozoa (true jellyfish) normally common in the pelagic zone, are widely distributed on the deep-sea bottom, but have only a very reduced jellyfish stage in their life history. The animal consists of the polypoid stage (often reduced or absent in other true jellyfish), that resembles Venus's fly trap (Fig. 4.35) living in a long chitinous tube (Fig. 4.36), and may exist in high densities (Aldred *et al.*, 1982).

SEA PENS, SEA FANS AND DEEP-SEA CORALS

It is the subphylum Anthozoa that, as in shallow water, dominates amongst Coelenterata in the deep sea. Here the medusoid phase is completely eliminated. This group includes the orders Alcyonacea (soft corals), Antipatharia (black corals), Gorgonacea (horny corals), Actiniaria

Fig. 4.35. Benthic scyphozoan *Actinoscyphia aurelia* photographed at about 2 km depth off Cap Blanc, N.W. Africa. The animal is normally orientated with the trap facing upstream in weak bottom currents; but analysis of the gut contents shows the animal probably feeds on suspended detritus. (From Aldred *et al.*, 1979.)

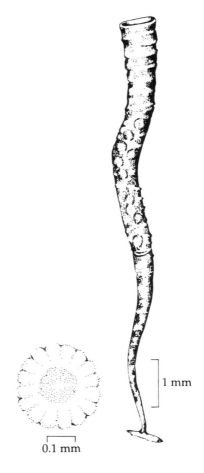

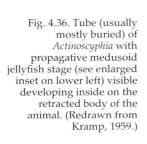

Fig. 4.36. Tube (usually mostly buried) of *Actinoscyphia* with propagative medusoid jellyfish stage (see enlarged inset on lower left) visible developing inside on the retracted body of the animal. (Redrawn from Kramp, 1959.)

1 mm

0.1 mm

(sea anemones), Zoanthiniaria (zoanthids) and the Pennatulacea (sea pens), the latter possessing a fleshy, muscular lower part of the stem anchored within the sediment, with the feeding polyps borne on the exposed upper part. These, along with the order Ceriantharia, which are sea anemones with elongated muscular bodies buried vertically within a sediment-encrusted mucus tube in soft sediments, are the only ones not requiring to be anchored to a hard substratum. Except perhaps for pennatulids, the often large and varied forms of anthozoans remain the best known from photographs. They can also be common under the more productive and energetic marginal areas, where they can reach a large size attached to small stones, shells and boulders; other deep-sea actinians, such as *Galatheanthemum profundale* (Fig. 4.37) are found at the greatest depths. Cerianthid anemones are ubiquitous in deep-sea sediments including the oligotrophic mid-basin areas, where they have been photographed with long tentacles streaming out in the current (Fig. 4.38). The outstretched tentacles touching the sediment of these and other kinds have been interpreted as indicating deposit feeding (Lemche *et al.*, 1976). However, the stomach contents of the large species *Sicyonis tuberculata*, which appears to be of widespread occurrence in the abyssal, suggests it is an opportunistic omnivore, taking small detrital particles to relatively large, motile prey (Lampitt & Paterson, 1988); 'Bathysnap' photographs show how the orientation of the oral disc actively responds to changes in bottom currents (Fig. 4.39). Furthermore, large actiniarian

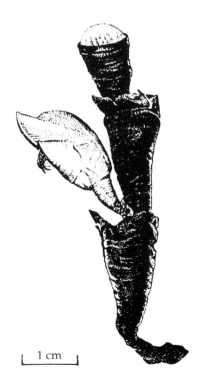

Fig. 4.37. Deep-sea actinian *Galatheanthemum profundale* (family Galatheanthidae), which has a chitinous tube into which the upper part of the body and tentacles is shown withdrawn, with an attached scalpellid barnacle. (From Carlgren, 1956.)

1 cm

Fig. 4.38. Bed of burrowing sea anemones *Cerianthus multiplicatus* at 0.4 km depth in the Porcupine Seabight, N.E. Atlantic. (Courtesy Dr A. L. Rice, Institute of Oceanographic Sciences.)

Fig. 4.39. Upper, record of orientation of tentacles surrounding oral disc and mouth in the abyssal sea anemone *Sicyonis tuberculata* from sequence of photographs by 'Bathysnap' at 4.1 km depth in the Porcupine Seabight. Black bars indicate periods when the anemone was completely contracted, and other breaks in the record indicate periods when the disk appeared horizontal. Two periods when its orientation seemed constant are labelled 1a and 2a. Lower, current direction *continued*

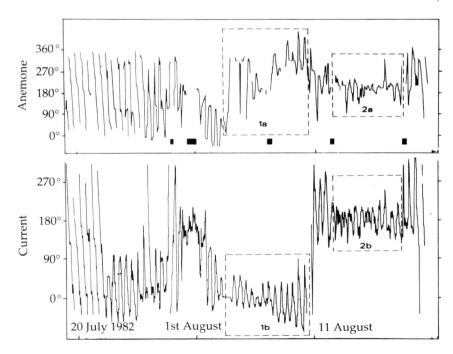

as recorded by the current meter on Bathysnap; the periods corresponding to those identified on the upper record are labelled 1b and 2b. (From Lampitt & Paterson, 1987.)

sea anemones have been photographed drifting or rolling slowly over a nodule-strewn seafloor in the oligotrophic equatorial N.E. Pacific (Foell & Pawson, 1986); such a habit perhaps increasing their chances of intercepting prey.

The Zoanthiniaria are usually colonial, anemone-like forms that frequently are epizoic – growing on other animals, species of the genus *Epizoanthus* and related genera attaching themselves to other sessile anthozoans, sponges, worm tubes and to shells inhabited by hermit crabs.

Beds of pennatulids and gorgonians are also characteristic of more eutrophic conditions and sometimes have a patchy distribution. They may also be good indicators of moderately high-energy bottoms in the deep sea; from their uniform orientation when photographed on the seabed (Figs 4.40, 4.41), it is likely that pennatulids are also able to actively orientate to the changing direction of bottom currents, and thus provide sensitive indications of current direction in bottom photographs (Ohta, 1983). The well-known, lily-like enlarged single polyp of the deep-sea pennatulid *Umbellula* (Fig. 4.42) closely resembles stalked crinoids. This genus is most common at greater depths on the more oligotrophic bottoms and may be macrophagous, perhaps being carnivorous on

Fig. 4.40. Pennatulids at about 1 km depth in the Porcupine Seabight (N.E. Atlantic). Left, *Pennatula aculeata*; right, *Kophobelemnon stelliferum*. (Photograph courtesy Dr A. L. Rice, Institute of Oceanographic Sciences.)

Fig. 4.41. Dense bed of gorgonians, mostly *Callogorgia verticillata* photographed with the sea urchin *Echinus melo* at about 0.1 km depth on the current-swept top of the Josephine Seamount, N.E. Atlantic. (Courtesy Dr A. L. Rice, Institute of Oceanographic Sciences.)

Fig. 4.42. Long-stalked, large-polyped deep sea pen *Umbellula* at 5 km depth on the Sierra Leone abyssal plain (scale approximate only). (Drawn from photograph in Heezen & Hollister, 1971.)

1 cm

swimming organisms. Such a trend towards increasing size, associated with macrophagy, in the feeding polyp has already been discerned amongst other coelenterate groups and is most noticeable amongst species of oligotrophic basins where macrophagy, or carnivory, becomes, as with benthic tunicates (see below), in energetic terms a better strategy than microphagous suspension feeding.

The bushy, colonial growths of the gorgonian *Acanella arbuscula* (Fig. 4.43(*a*)) are common at around 2 km depth on the moderately energetic continental rise areas of the N. Atlantic, while the flexible branches of others such as *Primnoa* (Fig. 4.43(*b*)), found world-wide at greater depths, branch, fern-like, in one plane which one might assume is held at right angles to the current to strain off tiny floating animals. However, this

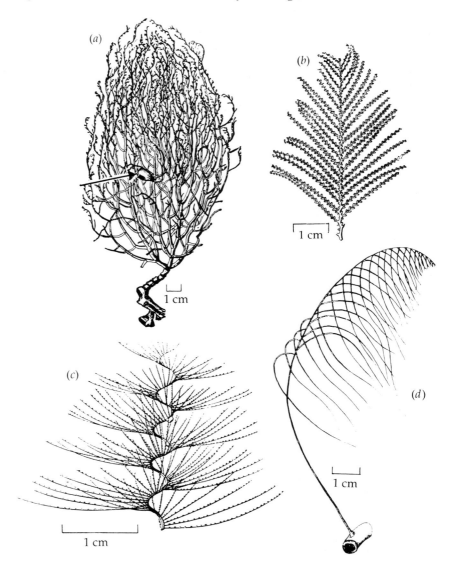

Fig. 4.43. Deep-sea soft corals. (*a*) Colony of gorgonian *Acanella arbuscula* with one small epizooic sea anemone, *Actinauge* (arrowed) attached to one of the branches with its disc wrapped around the stem; (*b*) abyssal gorgonian *Primnoa*; (*c*) *Iridogorgia* (gorgonian); (*d*) abyssal black coral (antipatharian), *Bathypathes*. (From Agassiz, 1888.)

gorgonian may well be one of the 'circle scribers', depicted in Fig. 14.8(*g*), that somehow benefits from contact with the sediment in this fashion. In the peculiarly beautiful form *Iridogorgia* (Fig. 4.43(*c*)), the branches extend from the iridescent main stem in a spiral. The black corals form slender, branched colonies with a horny axial skeleton (Fig. 4.43(*d*)) resembling gorgonians. They are known from the greatest depths in trenches (Pasternak, 1977), and may form luxuriant growths up to 2 m high on current-swept seamounts and on the sides of well-ventilated canyons.

DEEP-SEA STONY CORALS

Relatives of the true or stony, reef-building corals (order Scleractinia) of the Tropics are also well represented in the deep sea. In view of their abundance, they must have some importance in the organic flux and benthic standing crop as well as in the formation of calcite and aragonite at great depths. Colonies of *Lophelia*, *Madrepora* and *Desmophyllum* are found world-wide, including the subantarctic, at bathyal depths (Zibrowius, 1980; Cairns, 1982). These corals may form mound-like reefs up to 18 m high (J. B. S. Wilson, 1979*a*), and the rather isolated occurrences of reefs on the present-day upper continental slopes of the Atlantic may represent remnants of world-wide features that have become obliterated by slumping and erosion (Menzies, 1973). The coral patches provide an attaching substratum and refuge for a variety of other fauna (Le Danois, 1948; Zibrowius, Southward & Day, 1975; J. B. S. Wilson, 1979*b*). Deep-sea solitary corals are characteristic of the sediment at greater depths along the continental margins. They are relatively large usually with conical cup-like, skeletons (Fig. 4.44) sometimes found attached to a pteropod shell. Some of the largest species (diameter up to about 3.5 cm) are found at the greatest depths, and it seems probable that these corals are passive carnivores, catching small, swimming animals with their long, nematocyst-loaded tentacles.

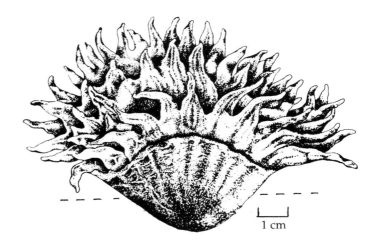

Fig. 4.44. Deep-sea solitary coral *Flabellum goodei*. The broken line indicates the approximate depth the calcitic skeleton is normally buried in the sediment. (From Menzies *et al.*, 1973 and Marshall, 1979.)

1 cm

SEA LILIES AND FEATHER STARS

These together comprise the class Crinoidea, the most primitive of the five living classes of echinoderms. The stemmed (pedunculate) forms flourished in the Palaeozoic, but they have long since declined in importance having been superseded by the more advanced feather stars, or comatulids. These become secondarily free during their early life history, attaching to the bottom by means of tendril-like ventral cirri. The 550-odd species of comatulids are most abundant in tropical shallow water, whilst the 80 known species of stalked crinoids are found at greater depths, being sometimes abundant in the more eutrophic areas of the deep sea where bottom currents are suitable for their passive filter-feeding lifestyle. The ecology, biogeography and phylogeny of stalked crinoids has been well reviewed by Roux (1987).

The central upwards-facing mouth is surrounded by the five arms (which may be branched right at their base) and bearing tube feet for transfer of particles trapped in mucus strings to the mouth. This feeding mechanism relies on currents to carry suspended food particles to the extended tube feet on the arms which act as efficient filters of the smaller size fractions of the plankton and suspended matter.

Particle selectivity is thought to be limited by the width of the ambulacral groove channelling particles along the arms to the mouth, and by the ability of the tube feet to capture active organisms. Crinoids in shallow water are capable of a complex range of feeding postures (see review by Meyer, 1982). Although little is known of the feeding behaviour of species of the family Bathycrinidae which are found on the sediment in the deep ocean basins, the few data available indicate that the arms and pinnules are splayed back into the current forming a planar filtration fan that filters predominantly horizontal water motions (Macurda & Meyer, 1976). The crinoids in the N.E. Atlantic are perhaps the best known, 12 species of nine genera of four families being known (Roux, 1985). Because of the difficulty in capturing pedunculate crinoids by bottom dredges from hard bottoms, they are best known from deep-sea photographs (Figs 4.45, 4.46). Densities of the species *Diplocrinus wyvillethomsoni* and *Porphyrocrinus thalassae* are frequently 5–7 m^{-2} and exceptionally 10 m^{-2} on the continental slope in the N.E. Atlantic; the animals being orientated with the arms recurved against the current, forming a parabolic filtration fan (Fig. 4.46). When disturbed by the submersible's arm, the arms slowly close together (Conan, Roux & Sibuet, 1981). The particle interception rate of the extended crinoid fan seems to show a clear relation to current speed (Leonard, Strickles & Holland, 1988).

In the N.E. Atlantic, stalked crinoids are present from 330 m to the greatest depths, with species richness being maximal between 1.5 and 3 km. But in the tropical W. Atlantic and W. Pacific the peak is shallower at between 0.2 and 0.6 km depth, so that an explanation for the survival of such an archaic group as refugees at great depths seems unlikely. Rather, their occurrence seems to reflect high primary production and downward

Fig. 4.45. Small ten-armed bathycrinid sea lily *Bathycrinus gracilis* photographed anchored by terminal rootlets (see Fig. 1.2) in the sediment at about 4 km depth at the mouth of the Porcupine Seabight, N.E. Atlantic. The stalk is only about 10 cm long. (Courtesy Dr A. L. Rice, Institute of Oceanographic Sciences.)

flux, perhaps with seasonal upwelling, on the continental margin (Roux, 1982; 1985). The stalked species *Metacrinus rotundus,* which occurs at upper bathyal depths off western Japan, is believed to feed on resuspended bottom material; specimens are thought to actively seek out locations of strong current where resuspended material is available, probably by autotomizing their stalks and by crawling using cirri ranged along the basal part of the stalks. Such motility may well occur in other

Fig. 4.46. Long-stalked isocrinid sea lily photographed on sediment surface from the submersible 'Johnson-Sea Link' at about 0.6 km depth off the Bahamas, N.W. Atlantic. It shows a typical, tilted parabolic filtration fan and stem that is bent downstream in the weak current. This, and similar species, are probably able to 'crawl' over the sediment using the cirri on the stem. (Courtesy Dr C. M. Young, Harbor Branch Oceanographic Institution Inc.)

species, such as that shown in Fig. 4.46, to give the rather aggregated microdistributions sometimes observed in seabed photographs. These seem to be related to local near-bottom variations in current velocity such as occur on boulders and on irregular hard bottoms (Fujita, Ohta & Oji, 1987).

ADAPTATIONS FOR PASSIVE SUSPENSION FEEDING

In the deep sea, the shapes of these passive suspension feeding invertebrates seem to be highly adapted in order to maximize capture of particles. In shallow water, flat, fan-like catching surfaces, held at right-angles to the current, occur amongst passive suspension feeders in oscillating or tidal currents, whilst more radial or bushy arrangements occur in more turbulent conditions. In persistent, unidirectional, currents, dish-shaped fans are found with the concave side facing upstream; these being more efficient than a flat surface in catching particles (Griggs, 1972; Warner, 1977). Paradoxically, the food-catching surface may be located on the *lee*ward side of a supporting structure; where microturbulence and reduced velocity may aid in particle interception and capture by the feeding mechanism, just as particles tend to accumulate on the leeward side rather than the scoured exposed face of a pebble or boulder lying on the ooze. In the deep sea, although bottom current energy may be high, current-meter records show that water movements off the bottom often show an oscillating pattern in a variety of directions superimposed on a background unidirectional movement. On moderately high-energy bottoms, sessile forms that are incapable of re-orientation, often have a stalked, but low-growing bushy habit, such as in the gorgonian *Acanella arbuscula* (Fig. 4.43(*a*)). Here the polyps may exploit currents from all directions, reflecting the more turbulent conditions within the Ekman layer or a regime where current direction is somewhat variable. Other forms capable of either active or passive re-orientation, such as hydroids, pennatulids, some gorgonians such as *Primnoa* (Fig. 4.43(*b*)), antipatharians and crinoids, adopt a filter with a dish-shaped, or less efficiently, a shallow V-shaped section, where the arrangement and tentacle disposition of individual polyps or tube-feet are also arranged to benefit from this strategy. These forms may grow tall enough to place the feeding polyps in faster currents less slowed by bottom friction. On seamounts, the abundance and reorientation of suspension-feeding epifauna appear to be related to bottom topography and their effects on local bottom-current regimes on seamounts. Photographs of the sessile, passive, suspension-feeding epifauna on the Pacific seamounts show that the nature and distribution of the fauna provide good indicators of the local topographic acceleration in prevailing current regime. A zonation in the distribution of the fauna reflects the intensity of current, with 'forests' of the spiral, black coral *Stichopathes* on the most exposed slopes, overlapping a rich sponge zone and with gorgonians and branched antipatharians occurring at less-exposed levels below (Genin *et al.*, 1986; Moskalev & Galkin, 1986).

ACTIVE SUSPENSION FEEDERS: DEEP-SEA BARNACLES

Nearly all the 50-odd deep-sea thoracican (common, non-parasitic, free-living) barnacles belong in the primitive stalked family Scalpellidae (suborder Lepadomorpha) some such as *Arcoscalpellum regium* reaching the impressive size of 6 cm less the stalk. They attach to a variety of substrata including rock outcrops and nodules, and even other sessile fauna. Scalpellids are widely distributed over depth and area in the deep sea. Of the more specialized lepadomorphs, the species *Poecilasma kaempferi* is found epizoic on decapod crustaceans, including the deep-sea stone crab *Neolithodes grimaldi* (Williams & Moyse, 1988). Of the even more specialized, stalkless, balanomorph barnacles that are familiar and abundant on wave-lashed rocky shores, there are a few, usually fairly large-sized, species found at upper slope depths. For example, the balanid *Bathylasma hirsutum* is so common on hard substrata on some energetic bottoms around 0.6 km depth on the Wyville Thomson Ridge off Scotland that the remains of its plates can make up a coarse shell gravel deposit downstream in deep holes where the current slackens.

As in intertidal species, deep-sea barnacles possess six pairs of thoracic legs ending in filamentous cirri that are typically used for straining the water of small particles. It is not clear whether the large size and solitary nature of most deep-sea species reflect a more macrophagous diet, perhaps on small living prey. They seem to be absent from the most oligotrophic basins, although scalpellids have been collected from more than 7 km depth in the Kermadec Trench.

One member of the odd group of acrothoracican barnacles, which are tiny forms that bore into calcareous material in shallow water at low latitudes, is known from the deep sea; specimens were found burrowing in foraminiferal chalk at about 1 km depth off Bermuda (Newman, 1971).

BRYOZOA

The phylum Bryozoa (moss animals) are sessile, active, suspension-feeding forms that tend to form hydroid-like branched colonies in the deep sea, rather than the encrusting colonies common on hard surfaces in shallow water. As with sponges, such encrusting forms are characteristic of the highly turbulent intertidal and shallow subtidal zones where, although the fronds of seaweeds provide additional settling surfaces, the body-form of suspension feeders may have to withstand the force of breaking waves. Each of the individual tiny animals, which live almost enclosed in a protective box-like exoskeleton, can generate a current of water that is strained of food particles by means of a ciliated feeding organ known as a lophophore. It is claimed that some, such as the large, stalked deep-sea form *Kinetoskias* (Fig. 4.47), are also able to feed on superficial sediment, since they have been photographed bent over with the zooid-bearing branches touching the bottom (Menzies *et al.*, 1973). Another erect form *Levinsella magma* from the abyssal N. Atlantic grows to 18 cm in height.

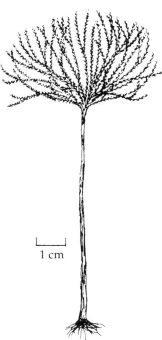

Fig. 4.47. The large deep-sea bryozoan *Kinetoskias cyathus*, first described from the Norwegian Sea, is a relatively large, erect abyssal form that is 'rooted' into the sediment by rhizoids at the base of the long, flexible stem of fused kenozoids. (From Marshall, 1979.)

1 cm

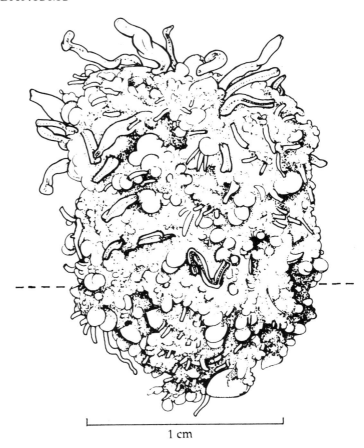

Fig. 4.48. Ctenostome bryozoan *Nolella* protruding from the 'mudball' komokiacean *Lana* trawled from 3.8 km depth in the Porcupine Seabight. The tubule mass of the komokiacean incorporates scattered *Globigerina* shells. Broken line indicates natural position within the sediment. (From Gooday & Cook, 1984.)

1 cm

A great diversity of bryozoan families and genera has been discovered in the deep sea in recent years. Although there are some relatively large forms, most are small, fragile and rarely collected intact. But they occur down to the greatest depths, sometimes in great numbers; for example, 140 specimens of the small branched form *Euginoma vermiformis* were collected from one epibenthic sled haul in the Rockall Trough (Hayward, 1978, 1981, 1985).

In addition to these forms with hard body covering, specimens of very small ctenostomatous bryozoa (lacking calcified body wall) have been discovered living in association with komokiacean Foraminifera (described in Chapter 5) and other organisms (Fig. 4.48). These forms illustrate how sessile organisms normally attached to hard substrata can adapt to living on the soft ooze of the deep sea (Gooday & Cook, 1984).

BRACHIOPODS

The phylum Brachiopoda (lamp shells), well known to palaeontologists, is another ancient group of active suspension feeders possessing a lophophore, that is moderately well represented in the deep sea. The animal is enclosed in a calcified shell that is either attached directly or by

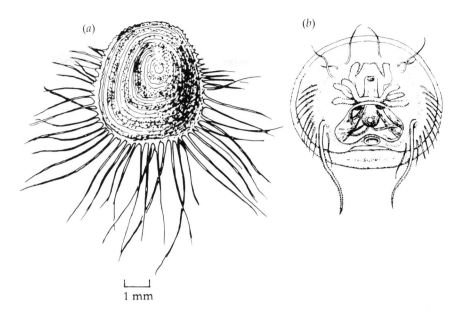

Fig. 4.49. Abyssal inarticulate brachiopod *Pelagodiscus atlanticus*: (*a*) adult, anchored by tendril-like filaments to a hard surface; (*b*) planktonic larva of *Pelagodiscus* which is modified for a prolonged pelagic existence. ((*a*) Modified from Odhner, 1960; (*b*) from Marshall, 1979.)

1 mm

means of a short stalk, or pedicle, to hard surfaces. Some species such as *Macandrevia crania* and *Terebratulina retusa* range from just below tide-mark to nearly 4 km in the more energetic parts of the deep sea. At least in the Mediterranean, *Gryphus vitreus* occurs only along the current-swept edge of the continental shelf (Emig, 1975, 1987). The few species with distributions confined to the deep sea are small in size and poorly known. Two, probably cosmopolitan, species occur regularly but in low numbers in samples from the N. Atlantic and Arctic and western Pacific, and have eurybathic distributions extending from the upper slope to the abyss (Zezina, 1975, 1981). The inarticulate (non-hinged shelled) species, *Pelagodiscus atlanticus*, has a limpet-like form (Fig. 4.49(*a*)) that attaches to hard substrata. It occurs world-wide over a wide bathymetric range, and has a *Pelagodiscus* larva (Fig. 4.49(*b*)) that is found in oceanic surface plankton. The other, *Cryptopora gnomon*, is an articulate species, where the shell is bivalved, and also smooth and transparently thin-walled. *Cryptopora gnomon* is thought to lie on the sediment surface, tethered upstream of the current by its fine stalk-like pedicle that is attached to a large sediment particle (Curry, 1983).

BENTHIC TUNICATES: MICROPHAGY TO MACROPHAGY

Sea squirts (class Ascidiacea) are benthic tunicates that are a flourishing group of active suspension feeders in shallow seas where they typically pump water through a large branchial sac to strain off suspended organic particles. In the deep sea they have achieved a high diversity on soft bottoms on which they are largely absent in shallow water. Their, probably polyphyletic, radiation to all parts of the deep sea has been reviewed by Millar (1965) and C. Monniot & F. Monniot (1975, 1978); it has

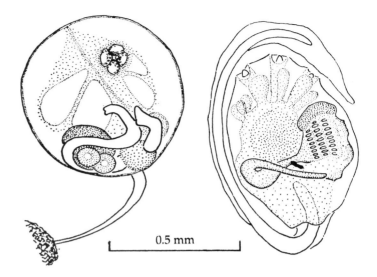

Fig. 4.50. The smallest known ascidian, the deep-sea species *Minipera pedunculata* (Family Molgulida) compared to an ascidian 'tadpole' larva of the shallow-water sea squirt *Tridemnum*. (From C. Monniot & F. Monniot, 1978.)

involved remarkable evolutionary convergence in morphology and modification of their feeding mechanism in order to cope with the scarcity of water-borne particles in the deep sea. Like many other suspension-feeding groups in the deep sea, the colonial, encrusting habit of shallow-water forms is largely absent, and individuals are nearly always solitary. However, although essentially active suspension feeders, deep-sea benthic tunicates have adopted some of the low-energy strategies of passive suspension feeders by casting mucus nets across the current, and by orientating themselves with wide-open filtering aperture facing upstream so that the current augments their own pumping mechanism. As well as species with 'normal' ciliated branchial sacs, there are, in order of degree of modification, dwarfed species with regressed but still ciliated branchial sacs (Fig. 4.50); stalked microphagous forms with unciliated branchial sacs; trap-laying species, belonging to the family Octacnemidae, which are both microphagous and macrophagous, possessing small, unciliated sacs and wide, oral siphons (Fig. 4.51); and finally relatively large-sized carnivorous forms, now placed in a separate class of tunicates, the Sorberacea, which completely lack branchial sacs. With the latter, prey are snapped up by means of muscular, finger-like lobes derived from the oral siphons, as in *Gasterascidia sandersi* (Fig. 4.52). The enlarged stomachs have been found to be stuffed full of a variety of prey items including foraminifera, nematodes, polychaetes and small crustaceans. The octacnemids are also large with reduced branchial sacs suggesting only weak filtration of fine particles; they are characterized by greatly developed oral siphons which open to form two wide-open hoods, as in *Megalodicopia* (Fig. 4.51(*b*)) in order to entrap small animals by closure of the large oral lips. In *Octacnemus* (Fig. 4.51(*a*)) there are eight large, oral lobes, but it remains unclear how the rather delicate, usually transparent, bodies of these ascidians catch the varied prey items found in their guts. Other deep-water ascidians are probably of polyphyletic origin and are

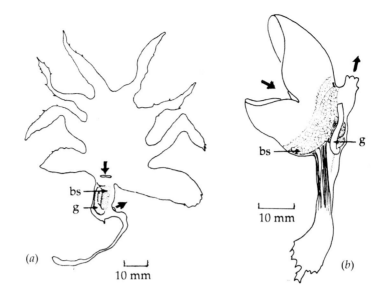

Fig. 4.51. Deep-sea octacnemid sea squirts showing the large lobed 'traps' and the relatively small gut (g) and branchial sac (bs). (a) *Octacnemus ingolfi*; (b) *Megalodicopia hians*. Arrows indicate currents into and out of the branchial sac. (From C. Monniot & F. Monniot, 1978.)

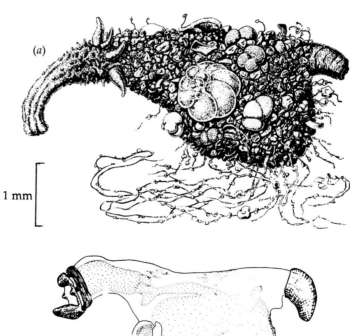

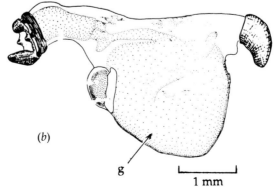

Fig. 4.52. Sorberacean tunicate *Gasterascidia sandersi*: (a) exterior view showing tunic covered with sediment particles; (b) tunic removed showing swollen gut (g). (From C. Monniot & F. Monniot, 1968.)

classified amongst ten genera from six families and three orders; some have a spectacularly large size (Fig. 4.53) borne on a stalk-like peduncle, but all have simplified branchial sacs lacking in the ciliated gill-bars (stigmata) of shallow-water species. This convergent modification is ubiquitous in the deep sea and totally lacking in shallow water, hence it must be of high adaptional significance. However, although it is known that their guts contain fine organic particles, the mechanism is not understood. Although a rhythmic muscular pumping action has been speculated, a more likely explanation on energetic grounds in the food-poor deep sea would be that the ascidian orientates itself so that bottom currents pass straight through the sac, and particles are caught on a

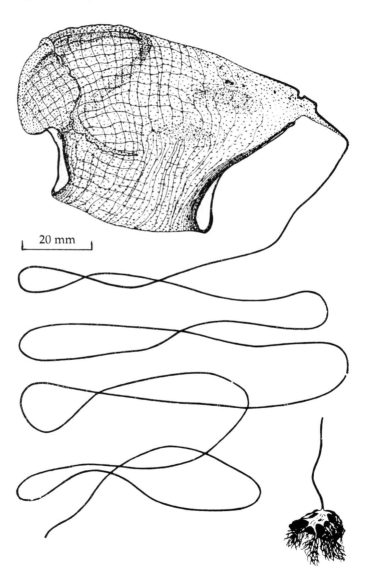

20 mm

Fig. 4.53. Giant stalked ascidian *Culeolus longipedunculatus* (family Pyuridae) from the Kuril-Kamchatka trench. The much enlarged branchial sac is lined only by a network of blood vessels, but is still much larger than the body that contains a gut containing only fine particles. In life the stalk is held erect with the siphons wide open and directed into the current. (From N. G. Vinogradova, 1970.)

mucus sheet secreted by the enlarged endostyle – as in pelagic salps. A large number of species from various families are present, all of small size and with simplified, though still ciliated, branchial sacs. They frequently have ball-like forms, half-hidden in the ooze with root-like anchoring extensions to agglomerate sediment particles over the tunic. These forms show regression of morphological structure suggestive of neoteny (attainment of sexual maturity at an early stage in development), again perhaps as a result of food scarcity. Of the 'normal' ascidians, none are abundant at great depths and those that are present belong to the family Molgulidae.

The maximum number of deep-sea tunicate species seems to peak at 70 at around 4 km depth, which is much deeper than for other invertebrate groups in the deep sea (Vinogradova, 1962a; and see Chapter 9). The much reduced number beyond 5 km probably reflects reduced sampling effort at these greater depths (C. Monniot & F. Monniot, 1978).

The relative rarity of sedimenting and resuspended particles in the deep sea seems to be responsible for the specialization towards those rarer, but more nutritious, living, particles represented by benthopelagic plankton (F. Monniot, 1979). This, conversely, has led both to an increase in size and to stalked elevation above the seabed, from where there is but a small evolutionary step to predation on small swimming fauna.

5
Smaller animals

These animals are usually subdivided into size-based categories (that are also reflected by peaks in size-class spectra (see Chapter 7); the *meio*benthos, being defined as those animals that are retained by the finest screens down to a mesh opening of 62 microns or smaller, and the *macro*benthos as that part retained by sieves with meshes of about 1 mm (Mare, 1942; McIntyre, 1969). Those mostly single-celled organisms, such as Prokaryotes (lacking the outer cell membranes of Eukaryotic unicells), yeast-like cells, certain sorts of Protozoans (single-celled animals, some with a quite complex organization such as ciliates) and some early stages of meiobenthic Metazoans (multicelled animals) in the size range from about 40 to 2 microns, make up an additional category, the *nano*benthos (Thiel, 1983) which falls between meiofauna and bacteria.

However, the division of the benthos above nanobenthos level into size-based groupings has little ecological and even less taxonomic justification in the deep sea. This is because of a trend towards miniaturization (see Chapter 7) which has occurred to the extent that the deep sea has been termed a 'small-organism habitat' (Thiel, 1975). Clearly, this trend has not affected the megafauna described earlier where in some groups, such as scavenging amphipods, a reverse trend towards gigantism has occurred. However, the trend to miniaturization is well marked amongst the macrofauna (Sanders, Hessler & Hampson, 1965; Rowe & Menzel, 1971; Rowe, 1971*a*). Furthermore, Hessler (1974) found that he had to use a 0.3 mm screen to catch the sparse macrofauna in box-cores from the central N. Pacific, noting that individuals here are so small as to be of meiofaunal size. A 1 mm sieve would, in fact, collect virtually no animals from box-cores taken from this very oligotrophic nutrient-poor area, and very few individuals from most deep-sea localities, including the more eutrophic nutrient-rich areas. Hessler & Jumars (1974) suggested the terms 'meiofaunal taxa' and 'macrofauna taxa' be used to permit these now traditional categories to be carried into the deep sea; Jumars & Gallagher (1982) commenting that is is 'more reasonable to compare oranges of different size than apples with oranges'. Another difference lies in body frailty; unless the samples are handled with great care, few of the delicate-bodied animals will be caught intact. This is because there is less need for the thick skins, heavy exoskeletons or robustly constructed shells of their shallow-water cousins in energetic shallow sediments. Hence, excessive agitation during the recovery and sieving of the sample will leave little that is identifiable.

The *macrofauna* comprise small though extremely varied forms that are virtually invisible in seabed photographs but abundant in the sediment. Together with the meiofauna, the macrofauna makes up by far the most numerous and diverse component of the deep-sea benthos. Most are small-bodied and used to be lost through the meshes of the trawls, or through the sieves used to wash samples of bottom ooze from the megafaunal catch up to the 1960s. However, the work of H. J. Hansen on the Danish 'Ingolf' expedition (1895–6) in the northern waters of the Atlantic deserves mention as an exception: by employing a fine-meshed silk screen he managed in the course of the voyage to collect 70 species of small tanaid crustaceans, 49 of them being new. A total of 106 species were previously known. The fine-meshed sampling undertaken in the 1960s by the Woods Hole Oceanographic Institution showed that the range of deep-sea animals then collected from the deep sea, still for the most part known only from pickled specimens held in museums, is only the tip of the iceberg in the diversity of life associated with the deep-sea

Fig. 5.1. Sorter's view down a microscope of washed material retained by a 0.42 mm sieve after elutriation of an epibenthic sled sample from 2.2 km depth in the Rockall Trough. A variety of macrofauna are visible amongst fragments of various calcareous and agglutinated foraminifers, including a cumacean (midbottom right) along with the scattered shells of bivalves, including protobranchs and *Vesicomya atlantica* (rounded, translucent shells), and postlarval brittle stars.

floor (Sanders & Hessler, 1969): when the muddy catch of the trawl or dredge was washed through sieves with meshes of half a millimetre or less, it was found to contain a wealth of previously unknown or poorly known species (Fig. 5.1).

Even if these smaller-sized animals, which, at least in terms of numbers, comprise the overwhelming bulk of the fauna, remain much less familiar, the forms of animal life present would easily be recognizable to anyone acquainted with the benthic fauna of coastal sediments. Not surprisingly, there is discrepancy at species, genus and, less often, at family level. However, the groupings of animals are generally familiar from studies of sheltered soft muds in shallow water. Furthermore, the taxonomic similarity of the deep sea with the shallow fauna of soft sediments seems to increase at higher latitudes, where the temperature regime is more similar to that prevailing at great depths.

THE MACROFAUNA

COMPOSITION

The macrofauna of the deep sea is much less well known than the megafauna. Yet, this group of small-sized animals has provided much excitement to students of community ecology in recent years. This has resulted from a discovery of a richness in species that was quite unexpected for such a 'difficult' habitat with low nutrient input. The various explanations that have been put forward to account for such high diversity are discussed in Chapter 8.

Despite this taxonomic diversity, the composition of this community has been shown from quantitative sampling to vary little in the deep-sea sediments world-wide; factors such as bathymetry and food input seem to have had remarkably little effect on the overall phylogenetic balance (Table 5.1). The fauna is dominated by the Polychaeta (bristle worms) which make up half to three-quarters of the total, just as they do in coastal marine sediments. Next in order of abundance are various small-bodied peracarid crustacean orders such as Cumacea, Tanaidacea, Amphipoda and Isopoda, followed by nearly all the Mollusca, including the Gastropoda (snails), Bivalvia (including mussels and clams) and Scaphopoda (tusk shells), but excluding the mostly larger and more active Cephalopoda. The other macrofaunal taxa include a rich assortment of worm-like phyla, including groups ranging from the Nemertea (ribbon worms), Sipuncula, the odd group of gutless worms – the Pogonophora, Priapulida, the Echiura (gutter worms) and the Enteropneusta, or acorn worms; the two last being large enough to have been already discussed as megafaunal burrowing worms in Chapter 4. The macrobenthic infauna would normally also include various smaller-sized representatives: groups of animals already considered under the errant and sessile epifauna, most, but not all of which, being considered as part of the 'megafauna'. These representatives include various sponges, smaller

Table 5.1. *Taxonomic composition of fauna from 21 square metres of sediment at 2.1 km depth off New England (Grassle, Maciolek & Blake, 1990)*

	Number of species		Number of families	
Coelenterata	19		10	
Hydrozoa		(6)		(3)
Anthozoa		(12)		(6)
Scyphozoa		(1)		(1)
Nemertea	22		1	
Priapulida	2		1	
Annelida	385		49	
Polychaeta		(367)		(47)
Oligochaeta		(18)		(2)
Echiura	4		2	
Sipuncula	15		3	
Pogonophora	13		5	
Mollusca	106		43	
Bivalvia		(45)		(18)
Gastropoda		(28)		(18)
Scaphopoda		(9)		(4)
Aplacophora		(24)		(3)
Arthropoda	185		40	
Cumacea		(25)		(4)
Tanaidacea		(45)		(8)
Isopoda		(59)		(11)
Amphipoda		(55)		(16)
Pycnogonida		(1)		(1)
Bryozoa	1		1	
Brachiopoda	2		1	
Echinodermata	39		13	
Echinoidea		(9)		(2)
Ophiuroidea		(16)		(6)
Asteroidea		(3)		(3)
Holothurioidea		(11)		(2)
Hemichordata	4		1	
Chordata	1		1	
Total	798		171	

pycnogonids, brachipods, small epifaunal entoprocts, brittle stars, porcellanasterid sea stars, apodous sea cucumbers, such as the small worm-like, burrowing families, Synaptidae and Myriotrochidae, and small, spherical molgulid sea squirts, which often have stalked attachments to sediment particles. A diagrammatic representation of these macrofaunal animals contained in one box-core from the central N. Pacific is shown in Fig. 5.2.

POLYCHAETE WORMS

The class Polychaeta dominates by far the marine representation of the phylum Annelida. The polychaetes typically make up around half of the total numbers of individuals, and around a third to nearly a half the numbers of species, of the macrobenthos. Together with the peracarid crustacea and bivalved molluscs, polychaetes may be regarded as the core organisms of the macrofauna. Polychaetes are taxonomically a very diverse class of segmented worms encompassing a bewildering range of morphology associated with their varied lifestyle and feeding strategies. Of the 5700 or so known species of the some 82 known families, few were known from the deep sea until the studies by Olga Hartman and Kristian Fauchald at the Allan Hancock Foundation in Los Angeles. These set a landmark by describing 374 species, more than 100 of them new, from more than 58 000 specimens examined from benthic samples taken along the Gay Head–Bermuda transect by the Woods Hole Oceanographic Institution in the early 1960s (Hartman, 1965; Hartman & Fauchald, 1971). These, and subsequent studies, have characterized deep-sea polychaetes as small-bodied, often with a reduced number of body segments compared to shallow-water species (Fig. 5.3). On the continental slope off the eastern seaboard of the U.S.A., the polychaetes have now been particularly well studied; around 400 polychaete species have been identified from extensive box-coring on the continental slope and rise, these comprising about 45% of the total numbers of macrofauna. Here, of the 47 families represented, the Ampharetidae, Paraonidae and Spionidae have most species, with up to 35 species present in each (Blake *et al.*, 1987; Maciolek *et al.*, 1987*a,b*).

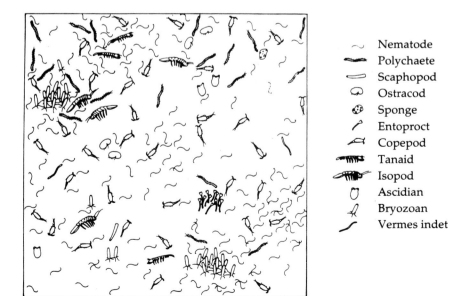

Fig. 5.2. Fauna found in 0.25 m² of bottom in the central N. Pacific (28° 26′ N, 155° 30′ W). All of the animals are much smaller than shown; but one would see nothing if they were drawn in true proportion to the area shown. (From Hessler & Jumars, 1977.)

~	Nematode
◡	Polychaete
⌣	Scaphopod
◠	Ostracod
⊕	Sponge
⁄	Entoproct
◁	Copepod
⊸	Tanaid
⊶	Isopod
⊓	Ascidian
⅃	Bryozoan
⌇	Vermes indet

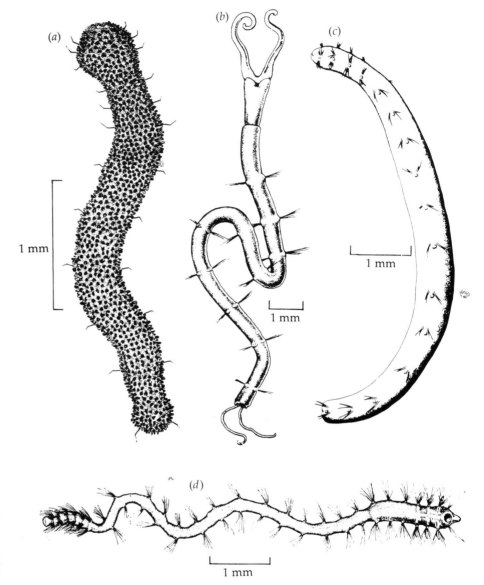

Fig. 5.3. Deep-sea deposit feeding polychaetes from the Gay Head–Bermuda transect: (*a*) flabelligerid *Flabelligella papillata* (body length 3.8 mm); (*b*) oweniid *Myriowenia gosnoldi* (length 20 mm); (*c*) flabelligerid *Fauveliopsis brevis* (length 7 mm); (*d*) paraonid *Aparaonis abyssalis* (length 7 mm). (*a*)–(*c*) anterior is at top; in (*d*) to right. ((*a*), (*b*), (*d*) from Hartman, 1965, reproduced with permission of the Allan Hancock Foundation; (*c*) from Hartman & Fauchald, 1971, reproduced with permission of the Allan Hancock Foundation.)

Polychaete species show only a limited tendency towards cosmopolitan distributions, most being restricted to single ocean basins, although these may be distributed over wide bathymetric limits. As with other deep-sea fauna there is a trend for abyssal species to have wider distributions than those on the continental slope. In the N. Atlantic, for example, 78% of the abyssal species are found in both the E. and W. Atlantic against 58% of the bathyal species. However, at least as many bathyal as abyssal species appear to have a world-wide distribution, with a eurybathic vertical range (but see Chapter 10 for discussion of possible 'sibling' species amongst these apparently widespread species), and there seems to be a bathyal polychaete fauna common to the Atlantic and N. Pacific (Kirkegaard, 1980, 1983).

Although one or two species are large and active enough to have been considered with the megafauna (see Chapter 4), most are small burrowing forms with a rather sessile lifestyle. These extend feeding palps or tentacles from the head end to explore the surrounding sediment surface for food, such as in the Spionidae (see Fig. 11.5) and Ampharetidae (Fig. 5.4(*a*)), while other surface deposit feeders, such as Flabelligeridae (Figs 5.3(*a*),(*c*); 5.4(*b*)), Opheliidae and Scalibregmidae seem to swallow sediment less selectively. Many other deposit feeders seem to have a more

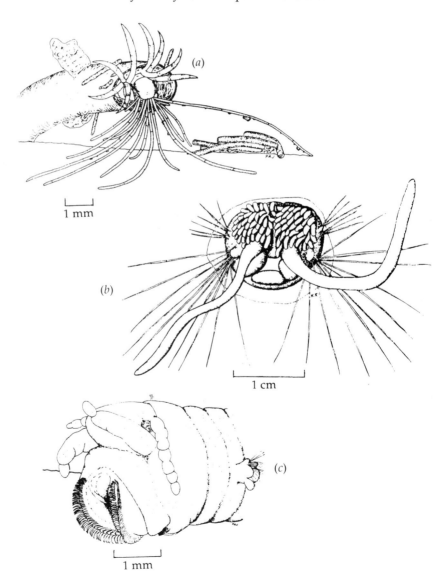

Fig. 5.4. Polychaete feeding mechanisms (drawn from observations on shallow-water species): (*a*) ampharetid *Amphicteis* shown transporting detrital particles along its feeding tentacles; particle selection may be effected by 'winnowing' during transport along ciliated tentacle; (*b*) flabelligerid *Pherusa* showing anterior feeding appendages everted (not visible in Fig. 5.3); the two large palps are used to pick up particles with the aid of the rake-like setae; (*c*) dorvilleid *Schistomeringos* with everted jaws; this form probably taking in a wide variety of food items. ((*a*) Drawn by P. A. Jumars; (*b*) and (*c*) by K. Fauchald.) (From Fauchald & Jumars, 1979.)

actively burrowing lifestyle, including species of the families Paraonidae (Fig. 5.3(*d*)), Cirratulidae, Cossuridae and possibly also the Lumbriconereidae. Some of the latter may also be carnivores, having toothed jaws and a muscular pharynx that can sometimes be everted to swallow prey, as in the carnivorous families Nephtyidae, Glyeridae and Phyllodocidae. Many, such as species of Oweniidae (Fig. 5.3(*b*)), build a protective tube from body secretions and sediment particles. Species of the small-bodied families Hesionidae, Dorvilleidae (Fig. 5.4(*c*)) and Pilargidae include carnivores. Suspension feeding is rare; the suspension-feeding family Sabellidae which in shallow water possess large, complex feeding 'crowns' being represented mostly by tiny, motile forms (subfamily Fabriciinae) with reduced tentacular crowns that seem to reflect a secondary adoption of selective deposit feeding (see Fauchald & Jumars, 1979, who provide a comprehensive review of polychaete feeding guilds and other functional types).

Polychaetes belonging to genera such as *Capitella* (family Capitellidae), *Ophryotrocha* (family Dorvilleidae), or families such as Spionidae have been found as early, and very dense, colonists in sediment tray recolonization experiments, especially where these contained high amounts of organic aggregates, decomposing *Sargassum* fragments or phytodetrital floc (see Chapter 8). Dense populations of *Ophryotrocha* have been found in petroleum-saturated sediment at a soft-sediment hydrothermal site in the deep sea in the Gulf of California (Grassle *et al.*, 1985). Clearly, populations of such forms can respond rapidly to open or unexploited habitat patches, but are soon out-competed by superiors. Hence they may be as good indicators of disturbed conditions in the deep sea as in shallow water.

OLIGOCHAETES

Discovery of deep-sea species of the annelid class Oligochaeta in the 1960s (Cook, 1970) showed that this little-known group of almost meiofaunal-sized, thread-like, deposit-feeding worms exists in deep-sea as well as shallow marine sediments where they are sometimes important constituents of the benthos (see review by Giere & Pfannkuche, 1982). Like their earthworm relatives, marine oligochaetes feed by ingesting organic particles in the sediment. One species, *Tubificoides aculeatus*, ranked fifth in abundance (making up more than 3% of the macrobenthic individuals) in extensive box-coring on the U.S. Mid-Atlantic slope, and up to 18 species were recorded from these and similar samples from the eastern seaboard of the U.S.A. (Blake *et al.*, 1987; Maciolek *et al.*, 1987a,b). Although never appearing to be very common, around 26 species alone have been identified from box-coring on the American eastern seaboard mentioned above; with more than 25 species now known from depths greater than 1 km, it is likely that many more await discovery. Most (> 90%) belong to the family Tubificidae, the deeper species appearing to have a wider distribution than bathyal species (Erseus, 1985).

SIPUNCULIDS

The phylum Sipuncula is another group of vermiform, deposit-feeding animals (Fig. 5.5(*a*)) that have been found to be relatively abundant in the deep sea. Most, such as *Golfingia* and *Sipuncula* burrow into the sediment, but several, e.g. *Aspidosiphon* and *Phascolion*, move over the sediment sheltering their body in suitable 'shelters' such as old gastropod or scaphopod shells. They are remarkable in that, in invading the deep sea, they seem to have shown only modest radiation of new species; many species, such as *Phascolion strombi*, apparently ranging from the shallow subtidal right down to abyssal depths. For example, in the N.E. Atlantic, of 31 deep-water species, only 12 are restricted to depths greater than 1 km, while 6 are both markedly eurybathic and widely distributed (E. B. Cutler & N. J. Cutler, 1987). One reason for this may be their mode of early development by means of a Pelagosphaera larva (Fig. 5.5(*b*)) which is often found in the oceanic plankton. The largest species belong to the family Sipunculidae, *Sipunculus norvegicus* often being more than 10 cm long, and hence technically part of the burrowed megafauna. Species of *Golfingia* (family Golfingiidae) have been found at high densities of nearly 400 m^{-2} in the Norwegian Sea (Romero-Wetzel, 1987) and up to 320 m^{-2} in highly organic sediment in the San Nicolas Basin off California

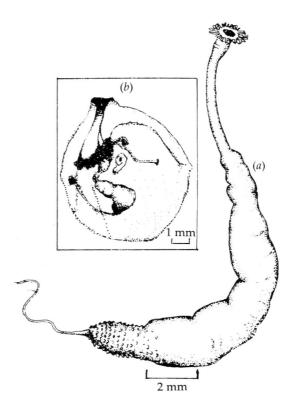

Fig. 5.5. Deep-sea sipunculid worm *Golfingia flagrifera*: (*a*) showing feeding introvert partially extended tipped by a rosette of sensitive tentacles; (*b*) planktonic *Pelagosphaera* larva, probably of the genus *Sipunculus*. ((*a*) From Marshall, 1979; (*b*) from Åkesson, 1961.)

(Thompson, 1980); whilst the sipunculid *Aspidosiphon zinni*, occurring at up to 355 m^{-2}, was the dominant species from box-cores at 1.2 km depth off New England making up about 6 or 7% of macrofaunal individuals (Maciolek *et al.*, 1987*a,b*). In the more oligotrophic Porcupine Abyssal Plain, sipunculid mean densities of 13 m^{-2} occur, yet still dominating macrofaunal biomass (Rutgers van der Loeff & Lavaleye, 1986).

The reversible pharynx of sipunculids is classically considered to reflect a non-selective deposit-feeding lifestyle (Murina, 1984). However, the gut contents of *Golfingia nicolasi* have been shown to have considerably elevated levels of organic material compared to ambient sediment (Thompson, 1980), suggesting selection of particles occurs.

POGONOPHORA

The Pogonophora are known predominantly from the deep sea. There are two main groups: the large red-plumed vestimentiferan or obturate Pogonophora which are attached to hard substrata and whose distribution is restricted to hydrothermal vents and cold seeps (see Chapter 15); and the much smaller tube-dwelling perviate Pogonophora (Fig. 5.6) which are found mainly in reducing sediments. The long, fine tubes of protein and chitin of the latter group were ignored as stray pieces of trawl twine by earlier collectors until large specimens were dredged in the 1950s from the deep trenches in the Pacific by Russian biologists. They are a morphologically compact group which, although possessing one or more long anterior tentacles, lack a mouth and gut as adults. In their natural position, extending deep into the sediment (Fig. 5.7), they are dependent for nutrition on internal symbiotic chemosynthetic bacteria capable of oxidizing dissolved reduced compounds present within sediments with high organic content (E. C. Southward, 1986, 1987; Southward *et al.*, 1986). Their phylogenetic affinities remain problematic, but they are

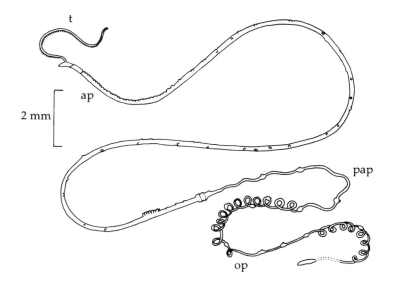

Fig. 5.6. Deep-sea pogonophoran *Siboglinum atlanticum* shown removed from its tube, showing tentacle (t), anterior part (ap) of body. The postannular part (pap) terminates in the bulb-like, digging organ, the opisthosoma (op) that normally projects beyond the lower end of the worm's tube. (From Southward *et al.*, 1986.)

Fig. 5.7. Diagrammatic representation of a pogonophoran within its tube penetrating deep into the reduced layer (rs) of the sediment that lies below a relatively superficial oxidised layer (os) in highly organic slope sediments. The bacteria-containing tissues in the postannular part of the body are shown black. Although the organic tube (tu) is shown closed over the highly vascularized tentacle (te), it is permeable to water so that the tentacle may act as a gill. Other labelling as in Fig. 5.6. (Modified from Southward *et al.*, 1986.)

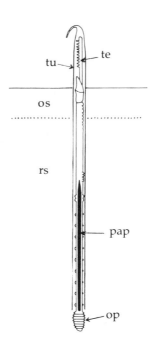

sometimes very abundant within the more organic sediments of canyons in the continental slope and in oceanic trenches, from where one of the largest known species, *Zenkevitchiana longissima* was discovered from depths of 8–9 km (Ivanov, 1963). The perviate Pogonophora are fairly rich in species, some of which appear to have restricted geographic and bathymetric distributions (Southward, 1979). The species *Siboglinum atlanticum* is a dominant element of the organic-rich sediments on the steep sides of canyons in the N.E. Atlantic; in the Santander Canyon in the Bay of Biscay, its peak abundance lying in a band only just over 100 m wide (Southward & Dando, 1988). On the well-studied continental slope and rise off the eastern seaboard of the U.S.A., pogonophorans typically make up about 1.6–1.75% of the total numbers with more than 12 species present in the macrofauna (Blake *et al.*, 1987; Maciolek *et al.*, 1987a,b).

OTHER WORMS

Of other vermiform groups, the Turbellaria (flatworms) and Nemertea (ribbon worms) are known to occur on the deep-sea floor, but little is known of their taxonomy and biology. Another relatively obscure vermiform phylum, the Priapulida, has been recorded from the deep sea only relatively recently (Menzies, 1959). Subsequently, species of *Priapulus* have been recorded from the deep sea of all oceans. They are short-bodied, deposit-eating forms. In the deep sea, specimens are small (often still postlarvae), hence lacking in adult characters and are usually never common, although reaching densities averaging 226 m^{-2} at the Woods Hole Oceanographic Institution's DOS 1 station at 1.8 km depth on the slope off New England where they make up almost 5% of the total number of macrofaunal individuals (Grassle & Morse-Porteous, 1987).

One view is that many deep-sea forms may belong to a single species, *P. abyssorum*, that is closely related to *Priapulus* in the shallow polar oceans (van der Land, 1985).

DEEP-SEA ARTHROPODS

MITES

The chelicerates (primitive arthropods which include the land spiders, scorpions and pycnogonids – see Chapter 4) have marine representatives in the order Acari, the mites and ticks. Although the vast majority are ectoparasites of land animals, including Man, a few species (family Halacaridae) are found free-living, probably as predators, in the sea. Although poorly known, deep-sea species have been found with bathymetric distributions down to 6.85 km. Some possess striking morphological characteristics, such as long legs, long protruberances and cuticular filaments which parallel those of some peracarid crustaceans living on soft sediments (Bartsch, 1988).

CRUSTACEANS

With the absence of insects, the crustaceans are by far the dominant arthropods of the deep sea, and are now thought to constitute a separate phylum. The most numerous group are the Peracarida which include the orders Cumacea, Tanaidacea, Isopoda and Amphipoda. These are mostly tiny, fairly active detritus-eating forms where the eggs develop to an advanced stage in a brood pouch (marsupium) formed along the ventral body of the female. Peracarids are numerous in both individuals and species in fine-mesh screened deep-sea samples, comprising from 32 to 51% of all macrobenthic species (Hessler & G. D. F. Wilson, 1983). Most seem to have a free-living epibenthic lifestyle, although Gooday (1984) describes various small isopods and tanaids living within the open-ended tubes of ammodiscacean foraminiferans. The other major order of peracarid, the Mysidacea, although predominantly bathypelagic, has evolved a group of benthic species distributed mainly in the upper bathyal which seem to have originated from the continental margin (Lagardère, 1985). All the remaining four classes are large and systematically complex groups the taxonomy of which is currently being developed by deep-sea workers. These studies show each group to be particularly rich in species and genera found only in the deep sea. At family level the distributional pattern varies with class.

AMPHIPODS

Although common in macrofaunal samples on the continental slope and rise, where there may be about as many species represented as isopods and tanaidaceans (Gage, 1979; Blake *et al.*, 1987; Maciolek *et al.*, 1987*a,b*), they seem to be quite rare at hadal depths and oligotrophic basins in the

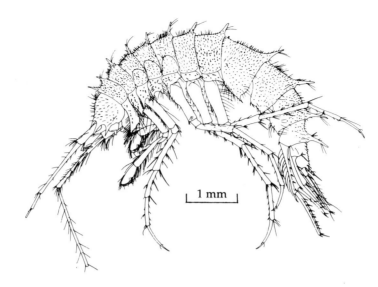

Fig. 5.8. Deep-sea, eyeless deposit-feeding amphipod *Lepechinella cura* from the E. Pacific. (From Barnard, 1973.)

1 mm

Pacific (Hessler & Jumars, 1974; Jumars & Hessler, 1976; Hecker & Paul, 1979; G. D. F. Wilson & Hessler, 1987a; Grassle & Maciolek, 1990). Most abyssal amphipods belong to predominantly shallow-water genera, and differ little from the latter species except perhaps with respect to absence of eyes (Fig. 5.8). There are, as yet, no amphipod families known with certainty as unique to the deep sea. Although 31 out of the 48 known families are represented, only six of these have over a quarter, and only two over half, of their genera confined to the deep sea (Barnard, 1969, 1971, 1973). (Of these, the family Synopiidae has four genera in warm shallow water, the remainder being primarily confined to the deep sea.) Such a broad representation, but lacking in any special development (Barnard, 1961, 1962), is thought to be indicative of a group that has invaded the deep sea many times (Hessler & G. D. F. Wilson, 1983). Nearly all deep-sea amphipods belong to the suborder Gammaridea which have arched, laterally compressed bodies (Fig. 5.8). Few measure more than a few millimetres in length, except for the giant scavenging lysianassids discussed earlier. They live in temporary burrows in the sediment, and seem to have a mostly detritus-eating, epibenthic lifestyle and can feed selectively on discrete particles, although careful examination of foraminiferan tubes has revealed one small lysianassid occupying a very specialized microhabitat (Fig. 5.9). Barnard (1961, 1962) has shown that most deep-water amphipods are stenobathic with the restricted geographical distributions typical of regional endemism; however, some eurybathic species are known. The widely differing species composition at pairs of geographically close and bathymetrically comparable stations in the N.W. Pacific are related to differences in the sedimentary regime and food availability (Dickinson & Carey, 1978; Dickinson, 1978). Many deep-sea genera belong to families whose shallow-water genera possess eyes and live at high latitudes. Although these facts suggest recent or current immigration into deep water, it might also reflect a pattern of

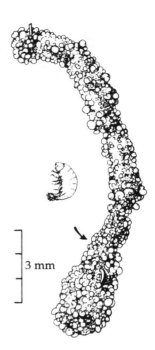

Fig. 5.9. This small lysianassid amphipod *Aristias* sp. is often found within living tubes of what has been described as an agglutinated foraminiferan *Hyperammina palmiformis* (but which may be an undescribed species of coelenterate) from the N.E. Atlantic. (Other lysianassids such as *Orchomene* and *Onesimoides* probably scavenge for woody vegetable matter that has dropped to the bottom, while the largest species of this family, such as *Eurythenes gryllus*, are well known as opportunist scavengers and are discussed along with the megafauna in Chapter 4.) (From Gooday, 1984.)

3 mm

increasing inability to cope with conditions at greater depths, such as is thought to apply with crabs (Hessler & G. D. F. Wilson, 1983). However, at least in the northern hemisphere, some species have shallow arctic–boreal distributions which extend into, and are abundant in, the deep sea (Barnard, 1971); thus supporting the idea of ongoing immigration into this realm.

CUMACEANS

The Cumacea are thought to lie within temporary burrows in the ooze (Fig. 5.10). They seem to show a similar distributional pattern to the

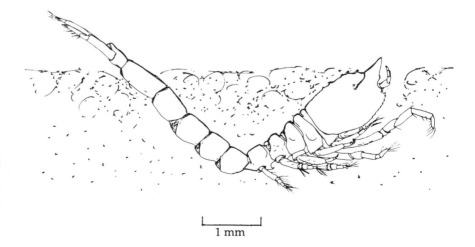

Fig. 5.10. Deep-sea leuconid cumacean *Epileucon craterus* from the abyssal N.E. Atlantic, shown in its probable feeding position in superficial sediment. (Modified from Bishop, 1981.)

1 mm

amphipods, with only one, the Ceratocumidae, of the eight known families being found exclusively in the deep sea, and the families Leuconidae and Nannastacidae are strongly represented along the Gay Head–Bermuda Transect in the N.W. Atlantic (N. S. Jones, 1969; N. S. Jones & Sanders, 1972). They are diverse, with 83 species being known from almost 8000 specimens examined from 14 hauls from this Transect (Sanders, 1977). In another well-investigated area, the Bay of Biscay, around 183 species are known to occur below depths of 200 m. Although most numerous at depths of 1–2 km, species richness seems highest between 3–4 km depth (N. S. Jones, 1985). However, cumaceans appear to be sparse or absent in oligotrophic basins and at hadal depths in the Pacific (N. S. Jones, 1969; Hessler & Jumars, 1974; Jumars & Hessler, 1976; Hecker & Paul, 1979; G. D. F. Wilson & Hessler, 1987*b*); and the oligotrophic Mediterranean deep sea has a particularly reduced cumacean fauna (Reyss, 1973). In the Pacific locations, densities are typically less than 1 m^{-2}, contrasting with more than 5 m^{-2} in the Rockall Trough (Gage, 1977).

The major ocean basins seem to show progressively fewer species in common the farther apart they are (N. S. Jones, 1985, 1986); of the 707 then known species, 92% being found in one ocean only (N. S. Jones, 1969). Analysis of cumacean distributions along depth transects in the Atlantic show that they are quite sharply zones with respect to depth (Grassle, Sanders & Smith, 1979). Although able to swim off the bottom, cumaceans usually inhabit shallow burrows in the ooze (Fig. 5.10) and usually remain close to the bottom when not buried. They sort through surface material for organic matter, without any indication of dietary specialization. As with other Peracarida, perhaps the rich diversification of this group reflects isolation of populations resulting from brooding instead of dispersing their young, rather than from resource partitioning in their environment.

TANAIDS

Species of the order Tanaidacea are generally even smaller than cumaceans. The larger epifaunal species are somewhat similar to many isopods (see below), with which they used to be taxonomically united; but are principally characterized by their markedly chelate (crab-like) second thoracic appendages and lack of a fan-like tail (Fig. 5.11(*a*)). Tanaidaceans are sometimes considered as part of the meiofauna. However, they are common in fine-screened epibenthic sledge hauls and box-cores. They comprised about 10% of the total number of macrobenthic animals in a series of box-cores taken on one position in the Rockall Trough (although many of the smaller, long-bodied individuals might have been lost through the 0.42 mm meshes of the sieve used to wash the samples, Gage, 1979) and about 19% in the abyssal N.W. Atlantic and central N. Pacific where a 0.3 mm sieve was used (Hessler & Jumars, 1974). Although their taxonomy and biogeography is still poorly developed, studies have shown that, compared to shallow water (Holdich & J. A. Jones, 1983), tanaidaceans are extremely diverse in the deep sea; in the

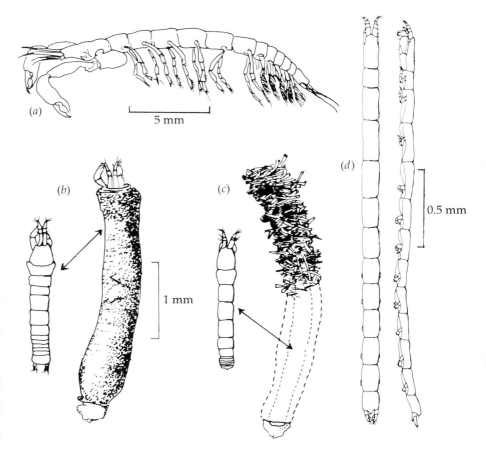

Fig. 5.11. Deep-sea tanaids: (a) neotanaid *Neotanais serratispinosus hadalis* from 8.2 km depth in the Kermadec Trench; (b) and (c) tube-dwelling infaunal typhlotanaids from the N.E. Atlantic; the tube of (b) (undescribed *Typhlotanais* sp.) is made up of fine silt with a mucous lining that projects posteriorly and sometimes also anteriorly to seal the tube when brooding young. The tube of (c) (another undescribed *Typhlotanais* sp.) is composed of sponge spicules, bryozoans and foraminiferans concentrated at the anterior end; (d) shows the leptognathiid *Nematotanais mirabilis* (N.E. Atlantic) which lives in a thin-walled, thread-like mucilaginous tube. ((a) From Wolff, 1956b; (b) and (c) modified from Hassack & Holdich, 1987; (d) from Bird & Holdich, 1985.)

best investigated deep-sea area, from the Bay of Biscay to the Rockall Trough, there are thought to be 262 species, 58% of which appear to be new (D. M. Holdich, personal communication, 1986). Similarly, in the well-sampled manganese nodule province in the north-eastern equatorial Pacific, tanaidacean diversity is also particularly high; the 77 (mostly undescribed) species from 556 individuals being about twice the number of known species listed in Sieg (1986) for the 4–5 km depth range (G. D. F. Wilson, 1987, unpublished data).

This radiation appears to be most marked in the suborder Tanaidomorpha, particularly in the genus *Leptognathia*, this genus, for example, making up 40% of the total collected by the French BIOGAS programme in the Bay of Biscay (Bird & Holdich, 1985). The latter authors also found tanaid diversity highest between 2 and 3 km depth in this relatively well-studied area. The suborders Apseudomorpha and Neotanaidomorpha (Fig. 5.11(a)), which comprise generally larger and mostly epifaunal species, are more rarely represented in the deep sea (Gardiner, 1975; Băcescu, 1985; Sieg, 1988), but can attain impressively large dimensions at hadal depths (Wolff, 1956b). In the manganese nodule province sites in the Pacific, tanaidacean densities are low, ranging from 15 to 48.3 m^{-2};

this comparing with a maximum of 491 m^{-2} at the HEBBLE site in the N.W. Atlantic. Here they are more abundant than at any other deep-sea site yet investigated, the fauna being dominated by small, elongated species possessing short, stout legs (Thistle et al., 1985). On morphological grounds these were thought to construct tubes or burrows within the sediment in which they might shelter during periods of sediment erosion and resuspension (Reidenauer & Thistle, 1985). In fact, a wide variety of tube structures occur, usually with a covering of sediment particles attached to a mucus lining (Fig. 5.11(b),(c)). Some are extremely fine and up to 30 mm in length, the animal being very elongated (Fig. 5.11(d)) as in Nematotanais (Bird & Holdich, 1985). The tube may serve as both protection for the adult, a mating chamber and a brood nursery for post-marsupial stages. Their differing construction perhaps reflects a high degree of resource partitioning in this highly diversified grouping (Hassack & Holdich, 1987).

Tanaids typically show a high sexual dimorphism (Holdich & J. A. Jones, 1983). The females are of the usual form whilst the males are more motile; indeed, tanaidaceans occurring in sediment recolonization experiments (see Chapter 8) carried out in the Bay of Biscay at 2 km depth were almost exclusively 'swimming males' of a species, not previously collected by conventional bottom sampling, that may be specialist colonizer of disturbed habitats (Bird & Holdich, 1989). Furthermore, since males possess reduced mouthparts, they are probably transient forms (G. D. F. Wilson & Hessler, 1987b; Bird & Holdich, 1989). The success of tanaids in the deep sea has mainly been the result of becoming smaller in order to escape from competition with other peracarids, along with a larger reproductive effort and improved brood care. Moreover, reconstruction of evolutionary lineages suggests that tanaids have invaded the deep sea many times, the Gigantapseudidae and Neotanaidae most probably being survivors of an ancient mesozoic fauna (Sieg, 1988).

ISOPODS

The order Isopoda are an adaptable and varied group that have species in many terrestrial as well as aquatic environments. However, it is in the deep sea that they seem to show their most impressive radiation, where they are found at all depths down to the deepest trench. They are now the best-known of Peracarida from great depths, with more species described than any other crustacean group in this environment. However, of the nine suborders, seven have species in both shallow and deep water and of these the suborder Asellota dominate by far. Eighteen families of primarily deep-sea isopods have been erected to encompass the great variety of species that have been discovered by means of using fine screens to wash samples from fine-meshed epibenthic sledges – from which more than 100 species may be collected in one haul (Hessler, G. D. F. Wilson & Thistle, 1979). Isopods have developed a particularly high diversity amongst the sparse macrofauna of oligotrophic basins; 130 species being identified from 493 individuals occurring in 0.25 m^2 box-cores from two sites in the manganese nodule province in the equatorial eastern Pacific from which densities ranged from 5.8 to 40.8 individuals m^{-2} (Hecker & Paul, 1979; G. D. F. Wilson & Hessler, 1987b; G. D. F. Wilson, unpublished data, 1987).

The detritus-eating habit of asellotes is thought to well suit them to life on the deep-sea bottom, allowing an extravagant and spectacular range in morphologies, including some very bizarre body-forms (Fig. 5.12). Some (family Ischnomesidae) have extremely elongate body segments, while others have very spinose bodies (e.g. families Dendrotionidae, Mesosignidae, and some Eurycopidae such as the splendidly large *Storthyngura* found in trenches). Yet others have slender (Thambematidae, Nannoniscidae) or fat (other Eurycopidae) bodies. The Ilyarachnidae have enlarged

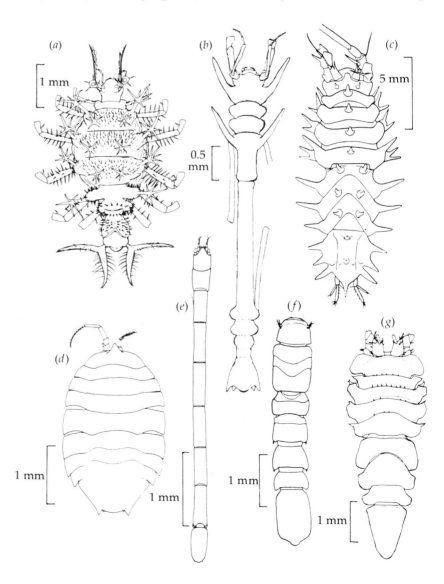

Fig. 5.12. Body form in deep-sea asellote isopods: (a) *Dendromunna compsa* (Dendrotionidae); (b) *Haplomesus gorbuvnovi* (Ischnomesidae); (c) *Storthyngura benti* (Eurycopidae); (d) *Haploniscus* (Haploniscidae); (e) *Thambema tanum* (Thambematidae); (f) *Macrostylis hadalis* (Macrostylidae); (g) *Ilyarachna affinis* (Ilyarachnidae). ((a) From Lincoln & Boxshall, 1983; (b) from Svavarsson, 1984; (c) and (f) from Wolff, 1956a; (d) from Lincoln, 1985; (e) from Harrison, 1987; (g) from Thistle, 1980.)

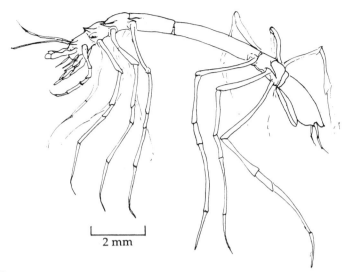

Fig. 5.13. Ischnomesid *Ischnomesus bruuni*, female specimen from the Kermadec Trench. (Modified from Wolff, 1956a.)

2 mm

heads to accommodate crushing jaws, while in others the thoracic segments have become condensed together, or even lost entirely, as in the woodlouse-like body-form of the Haploniscidae. The generally somewhat elongated bodies of species of a number of families, including the Desmosomatidae, Macrostylidae, Nannoniscidae, and Thambematidae are thought to reflect a burrowing lifestyle. Furthermore, although the long, stilt-like legs and elongated bodies of the Ischnomesidae (Fig. 5.13) give them the appearance, and suggest the habit, of stick insects, Thistle & G. D. F. Wilson (1987), considering the available evidence, suggest that this family also is predominantly infaunal, and possibly tube builders. Aquarium observations of *Ischnomesus bispinosus*, a species of this virtually exclusively deep-sea family found emerging into cold, shallow waters off western Sweden, showed it can walk rapidly over a variety of surfaces (Hessler & Stromberg, 1989). The munnopsids have attained large size by means of greatly elongated walking legs and antennae, but are able to swim (Fig. 5.14). The body plan of the Eurycopidae and Ilyarachnidae is also modified for walking and swimming; the similarly long-legged ilyarachnids in particular have greatly enlarged paddle-like posterior thoracic limbs for swimming. A backwards-swimming ability of these last three families was also confirmed in aquarium observations of cold shallow water representatives by Hessler and Stromberg (1989). Thistle & G. D. F. Wilson (1987) summarize other observations on the lifestyle and probable behaviour in the major families in the deep sea, many of these inductions being supported by the aquarium observations of Hessler & Stromberg. Finally, the family Nicothoidae include small, swollen-bodied species that are parasitic on deep-sea isopods and amphipods. In samples from the central N. Pacific, the dominant families are the Desmosomatidae, Nannoniscidae, Haploniscidae, Ischnomesidae and Munnopsidae.

In the more energetic Rockall Trough, isopod diversity (79 species identified from 5318 specimens) appears less than in the central N.

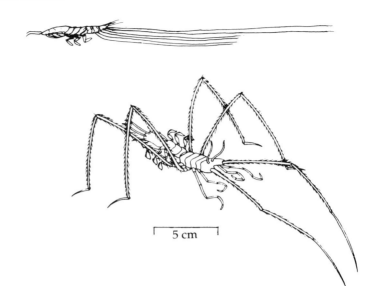

Fig. 5.14. The long-legged, large bodied munnopsid *Munnopsis longiremis* shown (lower) walking over the ooze with its anterior pereiopods, and (above) rapidly swimming backwards using its well-developed natatory, posterior pereiopods. Pacific trenches. (Modified from Wolff, 1961*a* and Lipps & Hickman, 1982.)

Pacific; epibenthic sled samples from the 2.9 km deep Permanent Station being dominated by Ilyarachnidae, Haploniscidae, Ischnomesidae and Eurycopidae (Harrison, 1988). At the very energetic HEBBLE site in the N.W. Atlantic the total isopod abundance is very high, although large epifaunal species (like apseudid tanaidaceans) are, not surprisingly, rare. These high densities may result from enhanced microbial production in sediment that is frequently disturbed or resuspended. Only six of 18 deep-sea isopod families belonging to the most advanced of the four asellote superfamilies, the Janiroidea, of Hessler & G. D. F. Wilson (1983) are represented from HEBBLE. The dominating families Nannoniscidae and Ischnomesidae are composed of elongated, thin species, suggestive of a burrowing lifestyle, rather than the broader body characteristic of other species of these families, paralleling the situation with tanaidaceans (Thistle *et al.*, 1985; Thistle & G. D. F. Wilson, 1987). Harrison (1989) argues that, for such small-sized animals as nannoniscids (Fig. 5.15), the distinc-

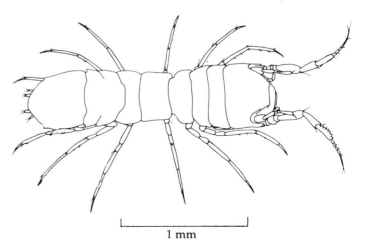

Fig. 5.15. Tiny adult body size of haploniscid *Hebefustis alleni* N.E. Atlantic. (From Siebenaller & Hessler, 1977.) Reproduced by permission of the San Diego Natural History Society.

tion between in- and epifaunal has little meaning, since in the usually highly microstructured sediment surface shown in close-up seabed photographs (Fig. 14.4(*a*),(*b*)) a distinct sediment interface is absent, and the small isopods may more accurately be said to live *amongst* the surface layer. Although isopods might be expected to show well-developed depth-related distributions, there are only limited supporting data available in the literature (Hessler, 1970; Chardy, 1979). The question of the origin of this remarkable array of species, whether they result from migration from shallow water or whether they evolved within the deep sea, is discussed (along with the evolutionary origin of other deep-sea animals) in Chapter 10.

MOLLUSCS

The phylum Mollusca, or shellfish, includes a wide variety of soft-bodied forms. In the deep sea they are the third most dominant group of animals of the macrofauna. All five classes are represented there making up about 10–15% by numbers of the total macrofauna on all slopes and basins investigated, and they occur at all depths to the deepest trench. We have already dealt with the cephalopod molluscs – the squids and octopuses – in Chapter 4.

Like that of the polychaetes and peracarid crustaceans, the diversity of the remaining deep-sea molluscs is astonishing. More molluscan species have been recorded from the relatively well-known Gay Head–Bermuda Transect in the N.W. Atlantic than are known from the entire shelf seas and intertidal of Europe (Allen, 1983). However, compared to shallow water, the composition is very different. Most deep-sea molluscs are representative of ancient groups in the fossil record which may now have only vestigial representation in shallow seas. The most striking difference is seen in terms of functional groups; the hosts of burrowing filter-feeders, mostly eulamellibranch bivalves such as the familiar clams and cockles, are almost entirely absent, the fauna being dominated by deposit feeders, with carnivores and ectoparasites running a poor second.

BIVALVES

The class Bivalvia is by far the most numerous group of molluscs in the macrofauna of sediments in the deep sea. Indications from anchor dredge and epibenthic sled hauls are that bivalves are only moderately diverse compared to gastropods and peracarids (Sanders, Hessler & Hampson, 1965). However, more recent sampling using the box-corer (which samples the burrowed fauna far more effectively than sled samplers) shows that bivalves may also be the most diverse of molluscan groups on the slope and in oligotrophic basin areas (Gage, 1979; Blake *et al.*, 1987; Maciolek *et al.*, 1987*a,b*; G. D. F. Wilson & Hessler, 1987*b*). The biology of deep-sea bivalves has been reviewed by Allen (1979, 1983) and Knudsen (1970, 1979).

In shallow and intertidal areas, the eulamellibranch bivalves are suc-

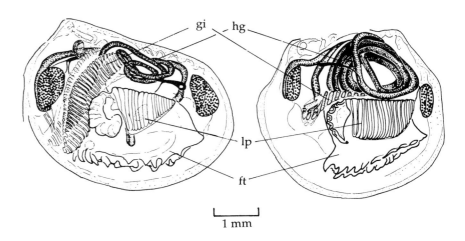

Fig. 5.16. Morphology of soft parts (shell removed) of *Nucula proxima* (left) from shallow water compared to *N. cancellata* (right) from the deep N. Atlantic, showing decreased size of gills (gi) and increased length and diameter of hindgut (hg) in the latter. Other labelling: ft, foot; lp, labial palp. (From Allen, 1978.)

cessfully specialized for suspension feeding by filtering microorganisms and organic particles from water pumped into the mantle cavity in the shell by the powerful tracts of cilia lining the greatly enlarged, sieve-like gills; the food being passed along the edges of the gills to labial palps that sort the particles before passing them to the mouth. Studies cited by the above reviews show that, in contrast, the deep-sea bivalve fauna is dominated by representatives of the much more ancient group, the Protobranchia (Allen, 1985). These possess simple, plate-like gills, often much reduced in size compared with shallow-water species, and with, at most, a subsidiary food-collecting function (Fig. 5.16). Most are surface, or sub-surface, deposit feeders, collecting food particles by means of greatly enlarged, often proboscis-like, appendages of the labial palps from a buried or possibly half-buried position in the sediment (Fig. 5.17). The protobranchs are themselves dominated by the superfamily Nuculanacea amongst which there has been great evolutionary radiation in morphology which in many ways parallels that seen in the eulamellibranchs. For instance, some have developed siphonate feeding mechanisms paralleling those amongst eulamellibranchs (Fig. 5.17), but, unlike many of the latter, the foot of protobranchs is well developed so that they are capable of active movements through the sediment.

Allen (1979) considers the most important reason for the success of protobranchs in the deep sea lies in differences in digestive physiology fitting them to cope with the low levels and often refractory nature of proteinaceous organic matter present in the sediment: protobranchs possess both intracellular digestion and extracellular proteases. The problem of having to digest such refractory organic matter quickly has led to the hind gut becoming much more elongated and coiled (Fig. 5.16) to allow a longer retention time; the coils often packing every conceivable space in the reduced body volume of the deepest living species. Where there is a range in species, then the relative length of the hind gut has been found to increase with increasing depth (Allen, 1979). The coiling pattern visible through the usually thin and semi-transparent shell of deep-sea protobranchs provides a valuable taxonomic feature for the

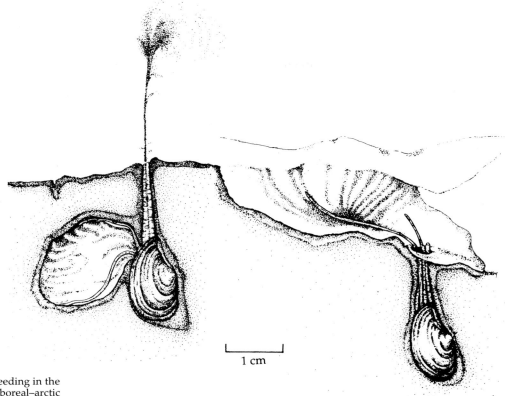

1 cm

Fig. 5.17. Feeding in the shallow-water boreal–arctic protobranch *Yoldia limatula*. Left, the bivalve is sub-surface deposit feeding using the long palp appendage to gather particles for sorting on the palps within the shell, and rejecting faeces and pseudofaeces as clouds of loose sediment and faecal pellets by periodic expulsions through the exhalent siphon. Right, surface deposit feeding using palp appendage to scrape off surface sediment, forming radial grooves in a feeding pit. (From Bender & Davis, 1984.)

separation of species whose shell form generally lacks ornamentation and amongst whom species are otherwise separable only by subtle changes in shape. It is interesting that the deep-sea eulamellibranchs *Abra longicallis* and *A. profundorum* (superfamily Tellinacea) also have a much lengthened gut compared to shallow-water congeners. But, unlike deep-sea proto-branchs (which lack any development of a symbiotic bacterial flora in their guts), it is thought that these deep-sea *Abra* may crop bacterial 'gardens' (see Chapter 11) which are cultured from pelletized pseudo-faeces (rejected particles) and faeces, whilst the pelletized material within their enlarged hind gut is thought to provide a culture medium for internal bacterial degradation of refractory scleroproteins (Allen & Sanders, 1966; Wikander, 1980).

An alternative explanation for the consequentially high gut:body volume ratios in these deep-sea bivalves (and in other deep-sea deposit feeders) is that the longer retention times allow greater conversion and absorption of the labile organic fraction of sediments as it gets scarcer with increasing depth (Jumars *et al.*, 1990).

Another feature which protobranchs share with all deep-sea bivalves is that, with the exception of the labial feeding palps, all ciliary food-sorting areas are simplified. Allen (1979) related this with the need to utilize all sizes of available food collected; Sanders & Allen (1973) judging that only in one family (Siliculidae) is particle selection possible on morphological grounds. However, deep-sea protobranchs are also distinguished from shallow-water relatives by their small size. The smallest is *Microgloma* (family Pristiglomidae) in which cell size and fecundity have been so reduced as to produce mature adults less than 1 mm long that are able to produce only one egg (Sanders & Allen, 1973). Jumars *et al.* (1990) suggest that the adaptive advantage of such small size in these, and other 'macrofaunal' species of meiofaunal size, results from intense, natural selection towards an ability for particle selection, rather than bulk ingestion of sediment, that small size permits. It is supported by the observation of Allen & Sanders (1973) of at least one case of protobranch gut contents consisting primarily of diatom remains.

The protobranch superfamilies Nuculacea and Nuculanacea have shown impressive radiation in species and morphology (Allen, 1978). At one regularly sampled station at approximately 2.9 km depth in the Rockall Trough, bivalves make up roughly 10% of the total number of benthic animals. From a total of 39 bivalve species, 17 are protobranchs, with the Nuculanacea alone contributing 12 species and protobranchs making up almost 80% of the total numbers of bivalve individuals. Although the range in morphology must reflect considerable variety in mode of life, protobranchs in the deep sea have not achieved the widest exploitation of available habitats, leaving the hard substrata, suspension feeding and carnivory to the lamellibranchs (Allen, 1983). As with peracarids, it is difficult to accept that habitat partitioning is important in maintaining such diversity (see Chapter 8 for discussion on this and other theories of diversification in the deep sea) when all are deposit feeders with no discernible differences in their stomach contents. Possibly their range of morphological adaptations, variations in locomotion, and burrowing depth, result in a degree of ecological partitioning despite an apparent uniformity in diet. In addition, since most species are small and rare at any one station, and relatively few at their optimal density, competition is reduced, allowing more species to co-exist.

Bivalve carnivores are strikingly successful in the deep sea. They fall in the lamellibranch group Septibranchia that comprises the families Verticordiidae, Poromyidae and Cuspidariidae. While species of the latter are uncommon on the shelf, the former two families are found only in the deep sea. A series with progressive gill modification can be traced from the extreme condition of a single septum in septibranchs to the typical eulamellibranch condition in the distantly related lyonsiid anomalodesmacean bivalves. Cuspidariids sense and locate their mostly copepod and ostracod prey by means of specialized cilia on the edge of the inhalant aperture, and explosively suck them into the mantle cavity (Fig. 5.18) (Reid & Reid, 1974; Allen & Morgan, 1981) while verticordiids, some of which can grow to an impressive size, extend sticky tentacles from the inhalant aperture and wipe off organisms that stick to them with a valve across the aperture (Allen & Turner, 1974). Poromyids catch small peracarid crustaceans with a hood-like structure which scoops prey into

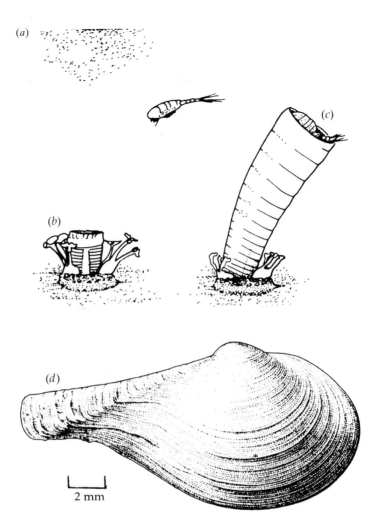

Fig. 5.18. Feeding behaviour of bathyal cuspidariid *Cuspidaria rostrata* observed from a Norwegian fjord: (*a*) siphonal apparatus withdrawn into sediment; (*b*) emerging on being alerted to presence of swimming copepod prey; (*c*) food-capturing response; (*d*) shell of cuspidariid showing elongated part housing siphonal apparatus. (From R. G. B. Reid & A. M. Reid, 1974.)

2 mm

the mantle cavity. These forms are ubiquitous but much less common in the deep sea than protobranchs. The presence of wood borers belonging to the deep-sea subfamily Xylophagainae (family Pholadidae, which include shallow-water wood borers such as *Teredo*) represent a significant extension to the range of a specialized group adapted to digestion of wood particles by means of a bacterial flora in the gut. Originally discovered in the nineteenth century, from plant-fibre covering submarine cables, they seem to be both diverse and widely distributed in terrestrial plant debris in deep water (Knudsen, 1961). Early in the 1970s it was discovered that species of Xylophagainae had colonized experimental wood blocks placed on the deep ocean bed. The wood was riddled with their tubes which gave evidence of two separate colonizations, with densities of up to 150 m^{-2} being present after 104 days (Turner, 1973; Culliney & Turner, 1976).

Of the other groups common or exclusive to the deep ocean, the Thyasiridae and Vesicomyidae, are prominent. The latter include the giant-sized species of the newly discovered genus *Calyptogena* (Fig. 15.4) which, probably along with the large-sized species *Vesicomya cordata*, harbour symbiotic chemosynthetic bacteria within their gills. These forms are conspicuously associated with hydrothermal vents and cold seeps (see Chapter 15). However, the small, round-shelled species *Vesicomya atlantica* (visible in Fig. 5.1) is common in the sediment in the Rockall Trough, but nothing is known of its feeding biology or mode of life. The little-known Thyasiridae are most common close to the continents (Allen, 1979) where they are particularly rich in species: amongst 50 species from box-cores taken from the continental slope and rise off the eastern seaboard of the U.S.A., 13 belong to the single genus *Thyasira* (Blake *et al.*, 1987; Maciolek *et al.*, 1987*a,b*). The Thyasiridae are highly specialized, feeding with their long inhalant tube formed from the highly modified, almost vermiform foot. The distribution of deep-sea forms is entirely confined to the slope and continental rise (Allen, 1983). The gut is simple and it is thought that they are non-selective suspension feeders, but both shallow-water and slope-dwelling species are known to harbour sulphur-oxidizing symbiotic bacteria in their gills, capable of fixing carbon dioxide using the same enzyme ribulose biphosphate carboxylase found in gill-symbionts of hydrothermal vent bivalves (E. C. Southward, 1986). However, the energy-providing substrate for thyasirids remains unknown in the deep sea where quantities of free sulphide are normally barely detectable.

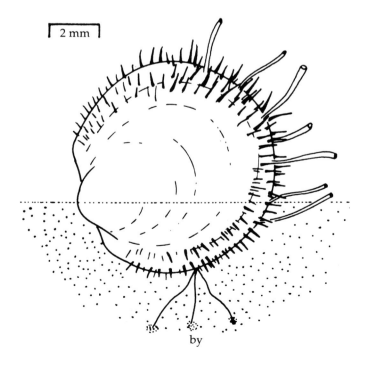

Fig. 5.19. *Limopsis cristata*, a limopsid bivalve from the bathyal N.E. Atlantic, shown in probable living position, anchored by means of byssal strands (by) secreted from the foot to clumps of sediment particles. (From Oliver & Allen, 1980*a*.)

Also present are the exclusively deep-sea Limopsidae (Fig. 5.19), along with deep-sea species of the mytilid genus *Dacrydium* (Fig. 10.2) and species of the families Pectinidae and Arcidae. All are epifaunal, probably suspension-feeding forms. One curious feature of deep-sea suspension feeders seems to be that, although the soft parts may be much reduced, the shell is proportionately much less reduced in size (Fig. 5.20), possibly to enhance protection from predation at minimal metabolic cost. As a result they include some of the largest known, non-vent bivalves of the abyss (Knudsen, 1979).

The superfamily Galeommatacea in shallow water are known to include many small bivalves that live commensally with a variety of larger infaunal invertebrates, particularly with echinoderms. At least two unrelated species of this small-bodied group are known from the deep sea: *Montacuta (Axinodon) symmetros* lives with a byssal attachment to the spines of the echinoid *Pourtalesia* (Bouchet & Warén, 1979a) while *Galatheavalve holothuriae*, collected from cavities in the skin of the elasipod holothurian *Psychropotes*, has a completely internal shell (Knudsen, 1970).

There are few bivalves in the deep sea with truly world-wide distributions; most are restricted to one or more adjacent basins with morphological differences in the populations suggesting a degree of ongoing speciation through isolation, whilst, even in the cosmopolitan species *Malletia cuneata* (Fig. 5.21), subtle changes in shell shape can be discerned (Sanders & Allen, 1985). Although vertically segregated populations can be recognized amongst the bivalves, overall, the degree of restriction in vertical range, like the vertical range of prochaetodermatid Aplacophora

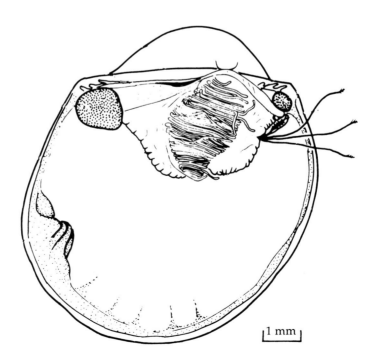

Fig. 5.20. *Bathyarca corpulenta*, an arcacean bivalve from the abyssal Pacific, after removal of right shell valve showing much reduced volume of soft parts. (From Oliver & Allen, 1980b.)

1 mm

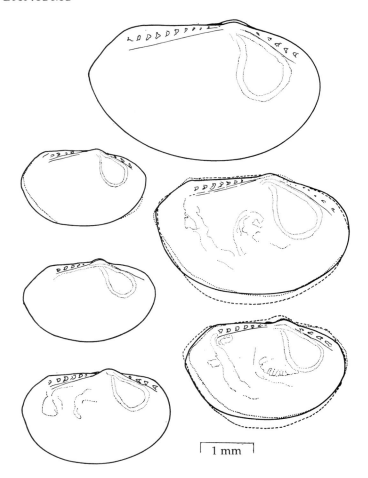

Fig. 5.21. Lateral views of shells of *Malletia cuneata* showing variation in shape from different localities in the Atlantic Ocean. (From Allen, 1978.)

1 mm

(see below), seems to be positively correlated to the horizontal range displayed by species (Scheltema, 1985).

GASTROPODA

The class Gastropoda encompasses a much greater variety in form and habit than bivalves. Most snail-like species with coiled shells are thought to be motile carnivores, probably feeding on polychaete worms and bivalves, or are ectoparasites, often on echinoderms (Fig. 5.22). However, the limpet-like shape also occurs mainly as opportunistic scavengers. As in shallow water, gastropods are probably at least as diverse as any other molluscan group.

From the Gay Head–Bermuda Transect, Rex (1976) identified 93 species of shelled marine snails (subclass Prosobranchia) and 30 species of the more slug-like subclass Opisthobranchia which have a reduced shell, or lack it completely as in sea slugs (order Nudibranchia); all with a wide range in feeding type. Deposit feeders included 20 species amongst the more primitive prosobranch families in the order Archaeogastropoda, 15 species of more primitive families of the very diverse order Mesogastro-

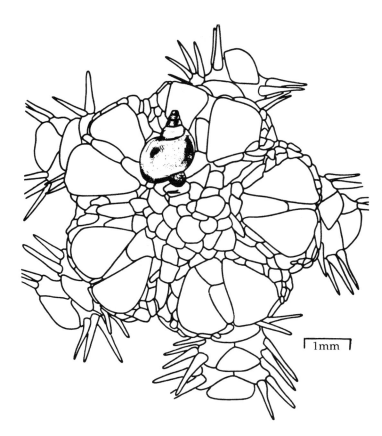

Fig. 5.22. Eulimid gastropod *Ophieulima minima* on its host, the brittle star *Ophiactis abyssicola*. Two egg capsules have been removed to show shell more clearly; a third is still attached at the base of the shell. N. Atlantic, Bay of Biscay slope. (From Warén & Sibuet, 1981.)

1mm

poda (which show particularly impressive radiation in the tropics) and five species of the more primitive order of opisthobranchs, the Cephalaspidea which retain a reduced thin shell and move semi-burrowed through the sediment. At least one species, the deposit-feeding archaeogastropod *Bathybembix aeola* is known to be selective in terms of particle size, suggesting adoption of an energetically more efficient strategy of selection of finer particles with a relatively greater microbe-coated surface area (Hickman, 1981). Bivalve and polychaete predators include one whelk-like mesogastropod; 46 neogastropods, including a variety of small poison-secreting cone shells and larger whelk-like scavenger/predators with a typical roving tentaculate nostril; 17 cephalaspids belonging to the more primitive families Acteonidae (which eat polychaetes), Ringiculidae and Retusidae (both of which seem to eat only foraminifers) and three nudibranchs which, at least in shallow water, may be highly specific in diet on colonial coelenterates. Ectoparasites of echinoderms and anthozoans include 11 and 8 mesogastropod species in the families Eulimidae and Epitonidae, respectively, the former of which have lost the jaws and radula and pump out the body fluids of their sedentary invertebrate hosts through a proboscis inserted into the body cavity (Fig. 5.22), while the latter rasp off tissue fragments with their radula; and five pyramidellids which, although with normal-looking small, spired shells, possess elaborate mouthparts that are modified for piercing and sucking, with a diet of liquid protein that is pumped out of their living mollusc or polychaete prey. Although these two groups are conspicuous, no one group can be said to predominate as amongst bivalves.

The neogastropod family, Turridae, are toxoglossan (poison-toothed) cone shells that have emerged as the single most diverse group of carnivorous gastropods in the deep sea, with a species richness, peaking in the bathyal, rivalling that of the cone shells of tropical sand flats (Bouchet & Warén, 1980). Turrids are highly specialized predators on polychaetes, killing their prey with poison from salivary glands that is injected through modified radular teeth. They are thought to have developed complex patterns of resource partitioning amongst co-occurring species (Hickman, 1984). Eulimids are one of the most diverse families of deep-sea gastropods, possibly even richer in species than the Turridae (Warén, 1984; Bouchet & Warén, 1986). It seems very likely that the high degree of dietary specialization or host specificity amongst the Turridae and Eulimidae has led to the spectacular radiation of these families in the deep sea. Other neogastropods in the deep sea include an assemblage of mostly large-sized species, some of which have a widespread distribution (Bouchet & Warén, 1985).

Although most of the different functional types amongst gastropods seem to correspond to taxonomic groupings, the cocculiniform limpets appear to have converged from at least 15 families (Hickman, 1983). These are epifaunal scavengers on rather unusual substrates such as wood, squid beaks (which can form highly localized and dense accumulations, see Belyaev, 1966), empty *Hyalinoecia* tubes, shark or skate egg cases, and fish and whale bones. Most of these have been recorded from eutrophic trenches where woody plant detritus is common (George & Higgins, 1979; Wolff, 1979). Although only some of these species, mostly belonging to the family Cocculinidae, are believed to ingest wood, the remainder graze the cover of microbes. Other cocculinid limpets have been found on waterlogged wood from oligotrophic abyssal bottoms far from land where their opportunistic, wood-ingesting lifestyle parallels that of the deep-sea xylophaginous bivalves (Wolff, 1979).

Although diverse in the abyss, gastropod diversity seems to peak at mid-slope depths (Rex, 1973, 1976; Bouchet & Warén, 1980). The distribution of gastropods also appear to be much more sharply zoned with depth than amongst bivalves (Grassle, Sanders & W. Smith, 1979), with a particularly marked compression in vertical range amongst predatory species compared to deposit-feeding species on the slope (Rex, 1977). Despite this, certain species, such as the unusually open-coiled epitonid *Eccliseogyra nitida* (Fig. 5.23), are known to be widespread, with distributions throughout the Atlantic (Rex & Boss, 1973).

Although it is becoming apparent that many deep-sea gastropods have an early development in the plankton (see Chapter 13), many of them, certainly most of those living at bathyal depths, lay egg capsules of characteristic form attached to hard substrata (Fig. 5.24) from which the young hatch directly.

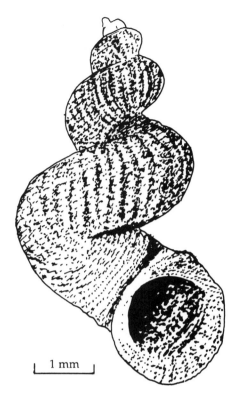

Fig. 5.23. Open-coiled
epitonid gastropod
Eccliseogyra nitida found in
the bathyal and abyssal
Atlantic. (Drawn from
photograph in Bouchet &
Warén, 1986.)

Fig. 5.24. Egg capsules of
deep-sea turrid gastropods
from the abyssal Bay of
Biscay: (*a*) capsule with
developing embryos; (*b*)
empty egg capsules after
hatching. (From Bouchet &
Warén, 1980, by permission
of the Malacological Society
of London.)

1 mm

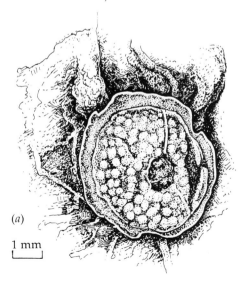

(*a*)

1 mm

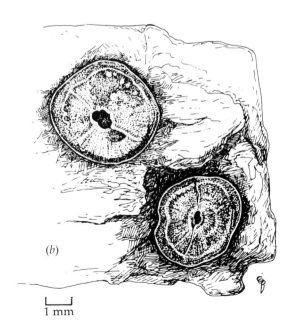

(*b*)

1 mm

SCAPHOPODS

The other major group of molluscs in the deep sea, the Scaphopoda, are far less well known. This might be because they constitute less than 1% of the mollusc fauna in shallow water. But in the deep sea this proportion is much increased (Clarke, 1962), and, although species richness may be less than that of other molluscan groups, they achieve population densities next only to those of bivalves. Modern species of this group have an ancient lineage going back at least to the Devonian. They live in cylindrical, often tapering, tube-like shells (Fig. 5.25(a)) and in shallow water are known to be expert burrowers in soft sediments using an elongated plug-like foot with a complex musculature. This is thrust down into the sediment, while the body and shell are pulled down to it by muscular contraction in a manner analogous to the burrowing movement, using the foot, of protobranch bivalves. The head bears curious bunches of ciliated tentacles terminating in a secretory bulb, the captaculum, which reach out to collect particles such as foraminifers, to which they show highly developed selectivity (see Davies, 1987, for references). These prey are crushed using a radula structure similar to that of gastropods. They are best known from species large enough to be collected by trawls: *Dentalium megathyrus* being known from 0.45–4.1 km depth in the E. Pacific measures up to 70 mm in length (Wolff, 1961). This, with other mainly larger species, is put into the order Dentalioida. These large species, at least, may be active burrowers in the deep sea leaving a conspicuous track as they move through the superficial sediment (Fig. 5.25(b)). The other subdivision, the order Siphonodentalioida may contain the majority of, mainly small-sized, species. On the basis of shell and radula morphology and the anatomy of soft parts, Scarabino (1979) has separated 59 mostly small-sized species from epibenthic sled samples taken from 0.3–6 km depth all over the Atlantic.

Fig. 5.25. Scaphopod *Fissidentalium candidum*, a relatively large species from the N. Atlantic: (a) lateral view of shell; (b) drawing from frame of 'Bathysnap' photographic record from 2.025 km depth in the Porcupine Seabight (N.E. Atlantic) showing this species moving along just under the sediment surface, leaving a conspicuous 'U'-shaped grooved track. (From Davies, 1987.)

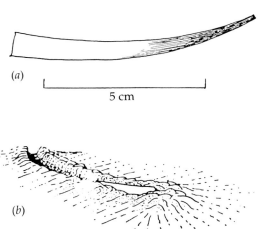

(a)

5 cm

(b)

APLACOPHORA

Although still poorly known, the worm-like Aplacophora are ubiquitous in the deep sea, occurring down to hadal depths. They include two divisions, the Neomeniomorpha and Chaetodermomorpha. Like the Scaphopoda, these forms are relatively abundant in the deep-sea macrofauna, yet are still very poorly known. Species of the chaetodermomorph family Prochaetodermatidae are found world-wide in the deep sea, with six species described from the best-known area, the N. Atlantic (Scheltema, 1985*a*). They are often numerous in deep-sea samples, being one of the numerically dominant macrofaunal animals in quantitative samples in the N.W. Atlantic slope and the Aleutian Trench (Jumars & Hessler, 1976; Scheltema, 1981; Maciolek *et al.*, 1987*a,b*), a density of 247 m^{-2} for the species *Prochaetoderma yongei* (Fig. 5.26) being recorded at 3.64 km depth off New England (Grassle & Morse-Porteous, 1987). Both divisions have a skin covered with protective calcareous spicules and possess simplified guts and a radula in the buccal cavity. The Chaetodermomorpha probably make shallow burrows in the sediment with the posterior end bearing the gills at the sediment surface (Fig. 5.26). The Neomeniomorpha have the simplest gut, and most species feed suctorially on the tissues of gorgonians and hydroids; while most species of Chaetodermomorpha feed on small organisms such as foraminifers and small macrofauna. Scheltema (1981) argued that large population densities of *Prochaetoderma* may be attributable in part to their gastropod-like rasping mouthparts allowing a wide range of particle sizes to be available to them.

CHITONS AND MONOPLACOPHORANS

Of the Polyplacophora, or chitons (coat-of-mail shells), only a few species have been collected from the deep sea, these being restricted to manganese nodules and pieces of wood, and belong to the primitive genus *Lepiodopleurus* (Paul, 1976; Wolff, 1979).

Discovery of living examples from 3.57 km depth in the Pacific of an archaic molluscan group the Monoplacophora, which are related to

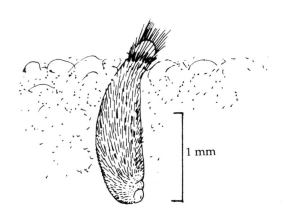

Fig. 5.26. *Prochaetoderma yongei* in probable natural feeding position in the sediment. The mouth is at the lower end and the pallial cavity containing the gills lies exposed to the water in the posterior end projecting from the sediment. (Redrawn from Scheltema, 1985*b*.)

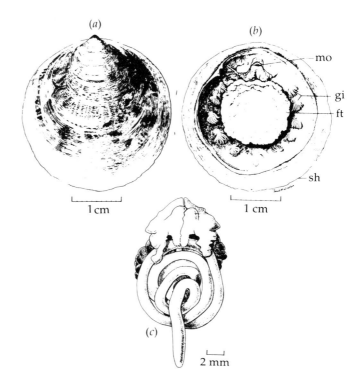

Fig. 5.27. *Neopilina galatheae*, a 'living fossil' monoplacophoran mollusc: (*a*) upper view of limpet-like shell; (*b*) view of lower side showing anterior mouth (mo), serial, paired gills (gi), broad foot (ft), lower edge of shell (sh); (*c*) dissection showing elongated gut. (From Lemche & Wingstrand, 1959.)

Cambrian and Silurian fossils and retain partial segmentation of body organs (Fig. 5.27(*a*),(*b*)), was one of the great discoveries of the 'Galathea' expedition (Lemche, 1957; Lemche & Wingstrand, 1959). However, a related species dredged in 1869 has only recently been recognized (Warén, 1988). Although having a limpet-like form, *Neopilina* has been photographed ploughing through soft sediments, the elongated gut (Fig. 5.27(*c*)) suggesting that it subsists on the sparse and refractory organic matter. Fragments of the xenophyophore *Stannophylum* (see Fig. 5.37) have been found amongst the gut contents. This, together with radula scraping marks on living specimens of the xenophyophores, from the same locality, suggests that *N. galatheae* preys on these giant protozoans (Tendal, 1985*b*). Six genera of recent monoplacophorans have now been described, the shell of the smallest, *Micropilina* from about 0.9 km depth S. and W. of Iceland being only about 1 mm in diameter (Warén, 1989). The taxonomy, morphology and relationships of the group as a whole have been recently treated by Wingstrand (1985).

MEIOFAUNAL TAXA

This category is much less well known than macrofauna. It consists of both multicelled (metazoan) animals traditionally regarded as 'meiofaunal' and larger single-celled protozoans, such as Foraminifera.

THE MULTICELLED TAXA: NEMATODA

Although little is known of the taxonomic composition or mode of life of the traditionally meiofaunal group, the Nematoda (thread worms), they are probably by far the most numerous metazoans in all marine soft bottoms. There are few data from the deep sea; but there can be little doubt that this group is as important and numerous in deep-ocean sediments as they are in shallow water (see review by Heip, Vincx & Vranken, 1985). In the Rockall Trough, we routinely see many large nematodes in box-core and epibenthic sled samples down to 2.9 km bottom depth measuring up to around 1 cm in length. However, since the modal body length, 200–350 μm, of the total nematode community from the deep N.E. Atlantic (Rutgers van der Loeff & Lavaleye, 1986) is less than the size of the meshes (420 μm) of the sieve used for washing the Rockall samples, only a tiny fraction of the streamlined body-form (diameter considerably less than body length) of these worms would have been retained by this mesh size in any case. Yet these exceptionally large specimens still number about half the total number of macrofaunal taxa (Gage, 1979). Similarly, in the abyssal Pacific, there are typically more than twice the number of nematodes retained by a 297 μm sieve than the total metazoan fauna (see Fig. 5.2) (Hessler & Jumars, 1974; Hecker & Paul, 1979).

Nematodes probably constitute the major numerical component of the meiofauna on the continental slope, but even in the abyss where, at least in terms of biomass, they may be replaced by agglutinating foraminifers as the dominating group, nematodes comprise between 85 and 96% of the remaining (metazoan) meiofaunal groups (Coull et al., 1977; Dinet, 1979; Thiel, 1979a; Shirayama, 1984a; Snider, Burnett & Hessler, 1984; Woods & Tietjen, 1985; Rutgers van der Loeff & Lavaleye, 1986; Schroder et al., 1988).

Because of the poorly developed state of deep-sea nematode taxo-nomy, species are usually separated on morphological grounds that probably underestimate the true diversity of the nematode community. However, the data available point to a high species richness, significantly greater than in equivalent sediments in shallow water (Tietjen, 1976, 1984; Vivier, 1978; Dinet & Vivier, 1979; Rutgers van der Loeff & Lavaleye, 1986). In the equatorial E. Pacific, careful examination has shown the fauna to possess an astonishing diversity with 148 species present amongst 216 individuals (G. D. F. Wilson & Hessler, 1987). A greater diversity in abyssal than in bathyal sediments may reflect the greater physical stability of the abyss. Bathymetric changes in composition of the nematode fauna are described by Tietjen (1971, 1976) from a transect off N. Carolina.

Along with other meiofauna, most deep-sea nematodes live in the topmost centimetre of sediment, abundance decreasing markedly deeper down (Thiel, 1972b, 1983; Snider et al., 1984). Some specimens have been found as deep as 20 cm in the sediment, but there is as yet little evidence of any microhabitat segregation amongst species although some seem to be found deeper than others (Jensen, 1988). There seems to be a trend towards increasing body length of nematodes deeper down in the sediment of the deep sea which may be related to a greater motility of large nematodes enabling them to penetrate the more compact deeper layers (Vivier, 1978; Soetaert & Heip, 1989). At the HEBBLE area, there is evidence that differences in sediment type resulting from frequent resuspension are reflected in the microdistribution of nematodes which seem to prefer areas where fine-grained surficial sediment has been re-deposited (Carman, Sherman & Thistle, 1987). At least in the Pacific, nematode densities seem closely correlated to calcium carbonate content of pelagic skeletal particles (perhaps increasing interstitial space) as well as sediment organic carbon, reflecting surface productivity and food availability on the bottom (Shirayama, 1984a). Nematodes can be separated into various systems of feeding types based on buccal (mouth) morphology (Wieser, 1953, 1960; Jensen, 1987). Applying Jensen's (1987) modification of Wieser's scheme to deep-sea nematodes, most seem to be microbial grazers that feed directly on bacteria and nanobiota as either deposit or epistrate feeders; the former sucking in small particles whole into the buccal cavity, the latter possessing a tooth with which they rasp material off the surface of larger particles, puncturing cell membranes to release juices that are ingested. It is thought that the considerable motility, burrows and mucus secretion indirectly help to maintain the heavily grazed microbial populations at an exponential stage of growth (Jensen, 1987). Tietjen (1984, 1989) detected a greater representation of deposit feeders in fine silt-clay deposits while epistrate feeders capable of rasping food off large particles were more abundant in the coarser deposit sands. Omnivorous predatory species decline and deposit-eating species increase in number compared to shallow water (Tietjen 1984; Rutgers van der Loeff & Lavaleye, 1986). Jensen (1988) considers that the absence, or very low numbers, of scavenging species in deep-sea samples may be related to the sparseness of freshly dead corpses on the seabed where nematodes may be outcompeted by more motile epibenthic or swimming scavengers (see Chapter 4).

The presence of species in shallow water lacking mouth and gut suggests an ability to assimilate dissolved organic matter (see review of nematode feeding by Jensen, 1987), but it is not known whether such forms exist in the deep sea. An alternative set of functional groupings for deep-sea species is based on the morphology of the posterior end (Thistle & Sherman, 1985); in the HEBBLE area in the N.W. Atlantic, individuals of one group may use their long, retractable tail to escape into the sediment in order to avoid resuspension during 'benthic storms'.

The nematode fauna has been found to be similar at family and genera level from widely separated areas in the Atlantic and Mediterranean (Dinet & Vivier, 1979; Tietjen, 1984; Thistle & Sherman, 1985), with 23–25 families and the genera *Theristus* and *Halalaimus* being two of the three genera in all three areas, but species seem to have quite narrow distributions, suggesting that current radiation is probably at species level (Tietjen, 1989).

In one locality in the abyssal N.E. Atlantic, the nematode meiofauna is dominated by the family Desmoscolecidae, which are characterized by an annulated body cuticle and which are known to be relatively abundant and particularly rich in species in the deep sea (Rutgers van der Loeff & Lavaleye, 1986). Nematodes are overwhelmingly abundant at this very carefully sampled abyssal area in about 4–4.8 km depth, comprising 87% of the total meiofauna, with up to almost a million individuals per m^2.

HARPACTICOIDS

This group of copepods is the next most numerous metazoan 'meiofaunal' group, typically comprising about 2–3% of the meiofauna in the abyssal zone (Rutgers van der Loeff & Lavaleye, 1986). Values range from about 1 to 36% at other sites in the N. Atlantic and Mediterranean, with densities from 1 to tens per 10 cm^{-2}. Like nematodes, they have been little studied. Most are thought to subsist on sedimented organic aggregates (see review on harpacticoids by Hicks & Coull, 1983, and Schriver, 1986, for recent ecological literature). There are indications of global similarity in the deep-sea harpacticoid fauna at family and/or generic level (Por, 1965), typically with genera of the families Cerviniidae, Cletodidae and Ancorabolidae occurring along with five more families; although several smaller, typically interstitial shallow-water families have also recently been found in the deep sea. Thistle (1982) recognized three functional groupings from bathyal sediments: one group, typified by the Cerviniidae, have enlarged and robust mole-like appendages bearing setae modified for burrowing (Fig. 5.28(a)). Another consists of vermiform species with an interstitial lifestyle. A third group comprises species from at least three families having well-developed dorsal spines (Fig. 5.28(b),(c)), some possessing massive dorsal processes used to anchor mucus-stabilized sediment as camouflage for life on the sediment surface.

In the deep sea, harpacticoids are thought to mainly feed on sedimented organic aggregates. Their species diversity has been shown to increase substantially along sample transects from the continental shelf out to the deep sea off Bermuda (Coull, 1972). Amongst 3935 adult individuals from 1.22 km depth in the San Diego Trough, Thistle (1978)

Fig. 5.28. Body form in deep-sea harpacticoid copepods from the San Diego Trough: (a) cerviniid showing typical broadened thorax and modified second antennae for burrowing; (b) and (c) show typical modifications of surface-living species with sediment-bound 'camouflage' associated with either comb-like rows of dorsal setae in Ameiridae (b) and Cletodidae, or horn-like dorsal projections in the Ancorabolidae (c). (Thoracic appendages omitted in (b) and (c).) (From Thistle, 1983a.)

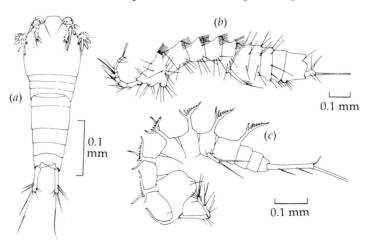

recognized 140 species, two of them numerically dominating the community.

BENTHIC OSTRACODS

The other major 'meiofaunal' group is the peculiar crustacean class, the Ostracoda. The body is enclosed in a laterally compressed, bivalved carapace, so that they superficially resemble bivalved molluscs. Although there are two pairs of thoracic limbs, it is the long antennae that are used for locomotion. The Ostracoda are apparently rich in species but very poorly known from deep-sea sediments. There appear to be considerable differences between the deep-sea forms and the relatively well-known ostracod fauna of shallow seas. These differences include large size (body length commonly greater than 1 mm) and an exaggerated ornamentation, lack of eyes and long and delicate appendages. Some segregation of distribution is evident with respect to depth, with one group of species occurring between 0.4 and 1.35 km and another group from 2.2–3.57 km and an unclear pattern between. Although species may be restricted to ocean basins, the fauna at higher levels seems to be cosmopolitan (Peypouquet, 1980; Peypouquet & Benson, 1980; Neale, 1985).

OTHER METAZOAN MEIOFAUNA

Other minor groups, traditionally regarded as 'meiofaunal' in shallow water, such as the obscure invertebrate phyla, the Kinorhyncha and Tardigrada are also found, but are never common, in the deep sea. Specimens of the newly discovered, meiofaunal phylum Loricifera discovered from coarse subtidal sand, have been found in the N.E. Atlantic deep sea (Rutgers van de Loeff & Lavaleye, 1986). They have recently also been discovered by Japanese deep-sea biologists in sediment from the Izu–Ogasawara Trench. These, and the other minor meiofaunal phyla, are thought to be ubiquitous in marine sediments.

Other constituents of the meiofauna include the young stages of 'macrofaunal taxa', such as young polychaete worms and bivalve molluscs which hence make up a 'temporary' meiofauna.

SINGLE-CELLED ORGANISMS: FORAMINIFERA

The benthic Foraminifera, or forams, of soft sediments live at or near the sediment interface, although some are infaunal (Gooday, 1986b). In shallow water, most fall within the size range of the meiofauna. There are 6000-odd recent species known, with a large proportion (including both described and undescribed species) coming from the deep sea where a wide variety in form is present encompassing the entire size ranges of other meiofaunal and macrofaunal organisms. Benthic forms can be distinguished from sedimented calcareous tests of planktonic foraminifers since the latter are without exception restricted to one taxon, the suborder Globigeriina. The latter are morphologically distinct from benthic suborders with calcareous tests such as the Rotaliina, Lageniina and Milliolina (Loeblich & Tappan, 1984; Gooday, 1986b). We must presume that the lower limit of these benthic species is related to the calcium carbonate compensation depth (see Chapter 2). Most work on living benthic foraminifers has been carried out by geologists who use them as markers in stratigraphy and palaeoecology. These studies have focussed on their relationships to bottom water masses and on the oxygen and carbon isotope content of tests which are of use in reconstructing palaeo-oceanographic environments (Douglas & Woodruff, 1981; Berger *et al.*, 1979, 1981; Murray, 1988).

However, species of some of the genera illustrated in Fig. 5.29, with tests of agglutinated sediment grains and other foreign particles

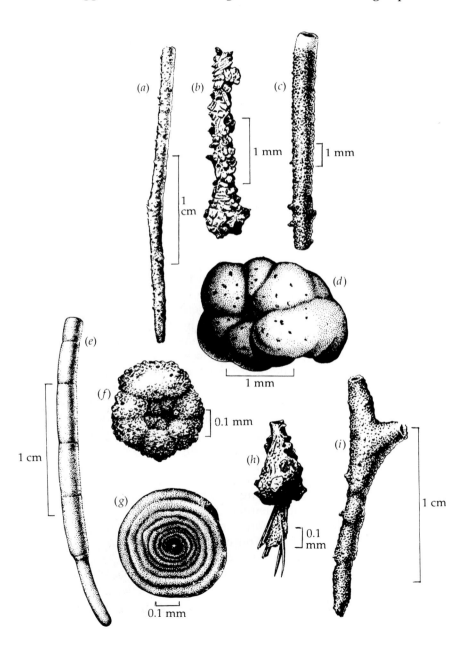

Fig. 5.29. Genera of benthic calcareous and sediment-agglutinated deep-sea foraminifers showing variation in size and form: (*a*) *Rhabdammina*; (*b*) *Hyperammina*; (*c*) another form of *Rhabdammina*; (*d*) *Cribrostomellus*; (*e*) *Bathysiphon*; (*f*) *Recurvoidatus*; (*g*) *Ammodiscus*; (*h*) *Reophax*; (*i*) *Astrorhiza*. All except (*d*) and (*g*) are sediment agglutinating forms; (*d*) and (*g*) have calcareous tests. (Modified from Saidova, 1970.)

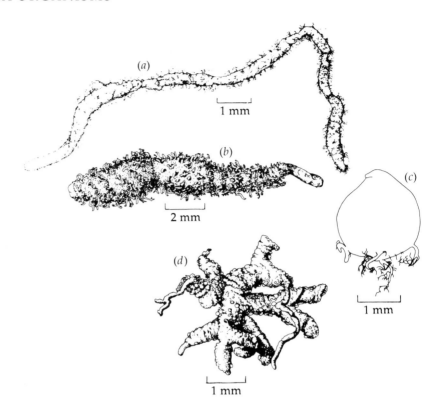

Fig. 5.30. Foraminifers with soft-walled tests. (*a*)–(*c*) are species of the genus *Pelosina* which have a thick-walled muddy test with a thin basal organic layer. Other forms of *Pelosina* are known forming tree-like arborescent growths anchored to the bottom. Forms like (*a*) and (*b*) are easily confused with a polychaete tube; while the test of (*c*) is turnip-shaped. They are eurybathic and of widespread occurrence and often abundant, comprising up to a fifth of all benthic invertebrates in some deep-sea samples. (*d*) Mudwalled astrorhizid; other astrorhizids form mudballs that superficially resemble komokiaceans. (From Gooday, 1983.)

(suborder Textulariina) have been known to make up an important part of the deep-sea macrobenthos since the early voyages of the 'Lightning' and 'Porcupine' (Carpenter, Jeffreys & Thomson, 1870). Most agglutinated forms are placed in the 'dustbin' superfamily Astrorhizacea. Careful study of samples has quite recently revealed a much wider diversity in body forms. Some have soft, tubular or flask-shaped bodies (Fig. 5.30), while others form delicate branched chains (Fig. 5.31). Many have, no doubt, been ignored in previous benthic sampling; yet these and the more familiar agglutinated foraminifers seem, overall, to be widely distributed in the world ocean. In terms of biomass, they may dominate the meiofaunal community at abyssal depths (Snider *et al.*, 1984; Schroder *et al.*, 1988). Members of the suborder Allogromiina (Fig. 5.32) have a thin, transparently proteinaceous test sometimes several millimetres long which resembles a crustacean faecal pellet, and can be enormously abundant – accounting for 41% of the meiofaunal animals in a single box-core from the Aleutian Trench (Jumars & Hessler, 1976) and 4.9–14.4% of all foraminifers at a bathyal station in the Porcupine Seabight (Gooday, 1986*b*). These forms, along with previously unrecognized foraminiferans occupying empty planktonic *Globigerina* and *Orbulina* shells (Fig. 5.33(*a*),(*b*)) will have almost certainly been overlooked in most sample sorting, and hence are little known and probably much underrated in importance (Gooday, 1986*a*,*b*). Also difficult to detect are those small

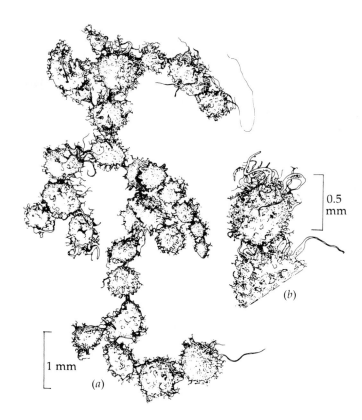

Fig. 5.31. (*a*) Foraminifer having a long, flexible chain of separate chambers; (*b*) detail of chamber. This and similar tectinous foraminifers are of uncertain affinity. (From Gooday, 1983.)

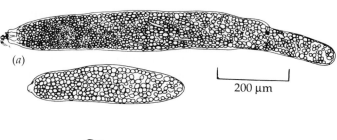

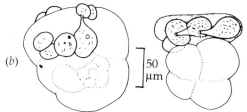

Fig. 5.32. Allogromiid foraminifers: (*a*) faecal pellet-like forms, filled with stercomata, from the upper sediment layer; (*b*) *Placopsilinella* attached to empty *Globigerina* test. N.E. Atlantic. (From Gooday 1986*a*.)

Fig. 5.33. Foraminifers inhabiting other foraminiferan tests: (*a*) and (*b*) are of forms of uncertain affinity. (*a*) Obligate inhabitants of *Globigerina* tests appear as small, but commonly occurring, conical lumps on the surface; (*b*) rarer form arising as branched structure from the dead test of *Orbulina* (another pelagic foramiferan); (*c*) *Telammina fragilis* encrusting the inside of tubes of the large agglutinated foraminiferan *Bathysiphon*, and which forms part of the small encrusting epifauna best known from ferromanganese nodules. ((*a*) and (*b*) from Gooday, 1986*b*; (*c*) from Gooday & Haynes, 1983.)

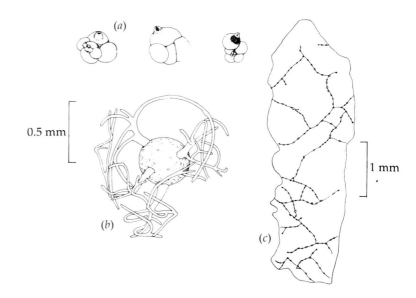

foraminifers encrusting the insides of larger agglutinated species such as *Bathysiphon* (Fig. 5.33(*c*)), and which form part of the world-wide small-bodied epifauna (see below).

Even more curious are the small, dendritically joined or anastomosing tubule clusters, with agglutinated sediment particles (Fig. 5.34), that are called komoki (from Russian, *vitvistii kamochki* – little branching clusters). Although reminiscent of xenophyophores (see below), they are much smaller, although many reach macrofaunal dimensions. They have been shown to constitute a new superfamily of Textulariina, and named the Komokiacea (Tendal & Hessler, 1977). They are widely distributed and very abundant, like xenophyophores, in both oligotrophic and more eutrophic abyssal areas, and in deep trenches. In common with other proteinaceous and agglutinating foraminifers, much of their size is made up by their test, and the volume of living *protoplasm* is much smaller, often not filling all the chambers or tubules of the test. One species (originally described as an astrorhizacean), *Rhizammina algaeformis* has been described in detail from material collected from the N.E. Atlantic at 4.5 km depth (Cartwright, Gooday & A. R. Jones, 1990). It forms a tangled system of branched tubes of almost megafaunal dimensions several centimetres across, lying on the sediment surface. The tubes are composed of a thin, inner organic layer overlain by agglutinated particles, and the lumen is filled with waste pellets, or stercomes, and an unbranched strand of protoplasm. The protoplasm is multinucleate and invaded by extracellular spaces originating as invaginations of the outer surface. These spaces may be involved in the digestion of food particles.

Problems in discriminating living tests from dead tests containing no living protoplasm, together with the fragility of agglutinating species, make it difficult to estimate the numbers of Foraminifera from deep-sea samples. But doubtless they are very abundant; at about 1.3 km depth in

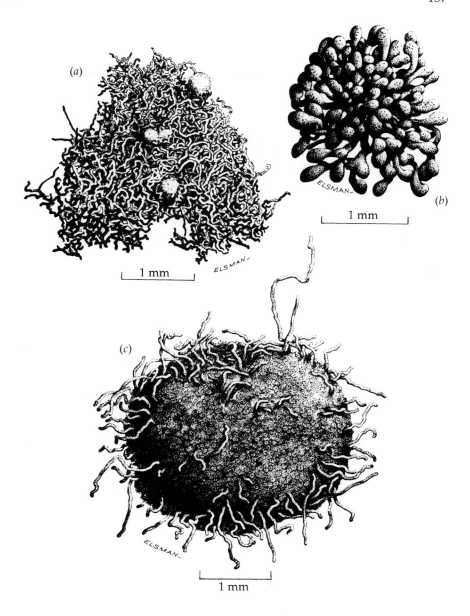

Fig. 5.34. Komokiaceans from the abyssal central N. Pacific. (a) *Lana neglecta*; (b) *Normanina saidovae*; (c) *Edgertonia tolerans*. (From Tendal & Hessler, 1977.)

the Porcupine Seabight, foraminiferans make up about half the total numbers of meiofauna (Gooday, 1986b). In the central N. Pacific, the numbers of at least one allogromiid species far exceed those of any metazoan (multicelled) species retained by a 296 μm sieve (Hessler & Jumars, 1974). Careful processing of samples shows they are also extremely diverse, with about 94–124 species occurring in each subcore (3.46 cm^2 surface area) from an undisturbed box-core sample from the Porcupine Seabight, about half of these being represented by single individuals. Careful sectioning of these cores shows that most individuals occur in the top centimetre or so of sediment; but with a distinct vertical segregation of different species at different depths (see Chapter 6, Fig. 6.6(*b*)), possibly as a result of biotic interactions (Gooday, 1986*b*).

In shallow water, foraminifers have a catholic diet, including bacteria, diatoms and other unicellular algae (Lee, 1980) and they even take up dissolved organic matter (Delaca, Karl & Lipps, 1981). Feeding methods and other biotic interactions are reviewed by Lipps (1983), and include suspension feeding by means of pseudopodial webs and other methods (Cedhagen, 1988; Tendal & Thomsen, 1988). Of deep-sea forms, little is known. The differing morphology and test contents of agglutinated species are thought to reflect different modes of nutrition; those with voluminous protoplasm often filling the test cavity but no stercomata, e.g. *Bathysiphon* and *Rhabdammina* probably stand upright feeding on suspended matter, whilst those with masses of stercomes and protoplasm either not easily visible or in the form of fine strands, e.g. komokiaceans, allogromids and some species of *Rhizammina* are probably basically deposit feeders (Gooday, 1983). One theory is that the stercomata may function as bacterial incubation chambers in providing for the nutrition of the organism (Tendal, 1979).

Along with the nanobenthos (see below), many authors have underscored the importance of protozoans in deep-sea communities (see Tendal, 1979; Thiel, 1983; Snider *et al.*, 1984; Gooday, 1986*b*). Certain benthic foraminifers with calcareous tests are believed to consume microflora associated with freshly sedimented phytodetritus. Hence, they may be an important early link in benthic metazoan food chains (Gooday, 1988).

XENOPHYOPHORES: GIANT PROTOZOANS

This strange group of large single-celled organisms is classified in the rhizopod complex of protozoans. This is because of the presence of pseudopodia, assumed from star-shaped traces visible in seabed photographs around certain forms such as *Psammetta* (Fig. 14.8(*f*)) (Tendal, 1972; Lemche *et al.*, 1976). However, xenophyophores are single-celled organisms that are larger than most macrofaunal metazoans! Although more conveniently treated with other unicells in the meiofauna, the Xenophyophorea clearly qualify on size and visibility in seabed photographs (Fig. 5.35) as part of the megafauna! The body has a wide range in size and form. It consists of a multinucleate plasmodium enclosed in a system of branched organic tubes (granellare) which ramifies through the agglutinated test. The pseudopodia are assumed to emerge from the end of the organic tubes. A distinctive feature of xenophyophores is the presence in many species of intracellular barite crystals (granellae).

The body may be a rigid disc, spherical, hemispherical, oval, star-shaped or irregular shape, or a rigid or flexible-bodied, tree-shaped form, most of whose body in life lies buried within the sediment (Fig. 5.36). The largest, *Stannophyllum* is a leaf-shaped form up to 25 cm in diameter, but only 1 mm thick (Fig. 5.37). Although first described from the early sampling off the W. of Scotland (as a foraminifer) and by the 'Challenger'

Fig. 5.35. Xenophyophore *Reticulammina labyrinthica* from 3.9 km off Mauretania (W. Africa) where it exists in densities up to about 2000 per 100 m². The density in this photograph is about 1250 per 100 m², the specimen on the lower margin is about 2.5 cm across. (Courtesy Dr A. L. Rice, Institute of Oceanographic Sciences.)

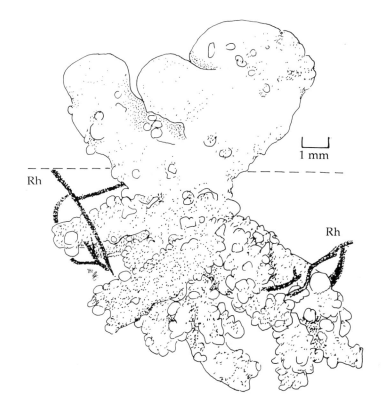

Fig. 5.36. Specimen of the xenophyophore *Reticulammina* sp. shown *in situ* from a box-core from 4.5 km depth in the N.E. Atlantic. The position of the sediment surface is indicated by the pecked line. Tubes of the komokiacean *Rhizammina* (Rh) are intertwined with the root-like lower part of the animal. (From sketch courtesy Dr A. J. Gooday, Institute of Oceanographic Sciences.)

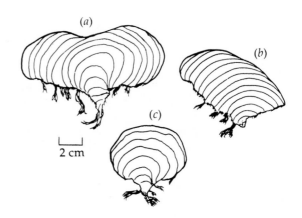

Fig. 5.37. Xenophyophore *Stannophyllum zonarium* showing different growth forms of this large species. The leaf-like body of the organism lies recumbent on the sediment, the stalk seems to be the youngest part; 'excresences' from the surface of the test of some specimens are thought to be a form of vegetative budding. The specimen on upper left is thought to represent the oldest growth form, and that below the youngest; that on upper right may result from separation of the oldest growth form. (From Tendal, 1972.)

expedition (as sponges), until the benchmark monograph on the xenophyophores of the 'Galathea' expedition by the Danish zoologist O. S. Tendal (1972), they were largely unknown by deep-sea biologists, having come to be regarded as rare benthic forms of dubious taxonomic position related to sponges. Their delicate bodies were often fragmented and unrecognizable in trawlings from great depths; and it has only been with the advent of new collecting techniques along with seabed photography and submersible observations in the 1960s and 1970s that their true abundance could be recognized in the deep sea, although their phylogenetic affinities and taxonomic rank still remain somewhat obscure. Xenophyophores have now been described from nearly all areas of the deep ocean basins, some species such as *Aschemonella ramuliformis* having very widespread distributions that extend into the Arctic (Tendal, 1985a). They generally occur at depths greater than 1 km, sometimes in very high densities that can easily be seen in seabed photographs. Up to thousands per 100 m^2 of the species *Reticulammina labyrinthica* (shown in Fig. 5.35) were estimated from the 1–6 km depth range off N.W. Africa (Tendal & Gooday, 1981), while xenophyophores may comprise up to 97% of total benthic biomass in the S. Pacific (Vinogradova, Levenstein & Turpaeva, 1978a). In some Pacific trenches, Lemche *et al.* (1976) estimated that 30–50% of the bottom was constantly covered by the slimy pseudopodia of *Psammetta*, presumably collecting particulate food (see Fig. 14.8(*f*)) or perhaps even small living animals. Xenophyophores are also abundant on the current-swept mud and sand sediments on deep (1–3.3 km) seamounts in the E. Pacific (Levin *et al.*, 1987; Kaufmann, Wakefield & Genin, 1989). Bottom photographs and body morphology suggest that such species may feed on suspended particles.

Much of the large body of xenophyophores is composed of dark-coloured excretory bodies resembling faecal pellets termed stercomes. Tendal (1979) suggests that these are colonized by commensal bacteria which break down the material to a form that can be reabsorbed by the plasma. It has been known since the early descriptions of these forms that they are also commonly the site of attachment of many small branching hydroid-like animals (Haeckel, 1889).

We now know that xenophyophores are not confined to the sediment surface: *Occultammina profunda* consists of branching tubes buried 1–6 cm deep in the sediment in the Izu–Ogasawara Trench in the W. Pacific where it is a dominating element of the fauna, possibly (as suggested by Swinbanks & Shirayama, 1986*a*) feeding on particles collected within the upper layers of the sediment (Tendal, Swinbanks & Shirayama, 1982). The existence of other infaunal xenophyophores, which seem to be characterized by smaller size, is suspected, but owing to their fragility will require special techniques, such as X-ray radiographs of sediment slices, to detect.

NANOBENTHOS

The diversity and abundance of this category of deep-sea organisms, smaller than the lower limit of meiofauna, have been revealed by pioneering work of B. R. Burnett at the Scripps Institution of Oceanography. Their separation from the deep-sea sediment is time-consuming and technically demanding, involving microscopic preparations (Burnett, 1973; Thiel, 1983). They comprise flagellates, sporozoans, ciliates and amoebae along with yeast-like cells. Their biomass is concentrated in the most superficial layer of sediment and numerically they overwhelmingly dominate the benthic fauna in the abyssal central N. Pacific and bathyal San Diego Trough (Burnett, 1977, 1979, 1981; Snider *et al.*, 1984). Although studies in the western Coral Sea indicate marked changes in composition of the nanobiota community from 0.298 to 1.604 km depth (Alongi, 1987), we remain largely ignorant of the composition and importance of these organisms in the world ocean. Yet recent work with a microflagellate isolated from phytodetritus and cultured under simulated deep-sea conditions suggests that by eating bacteria these organisms may be important in microbial decomposition pathways (Turley, Lochte & Patterson, 1988).

SMALL EPIFAUNA

Little is known of the smallest organisms living on hard substrata in the deep sea. Although larger animals have been known to attach to the surfaces of manganese nodules since the 'Challenger' Expedition (Murray & Renard, 1981), a diverse and abundant assemblage of, until recently, virtually unknown, small organisms, many fragile and easily brushed off, have been found to live on the surfaces of nodules and crusts (manganese and iron oxide coatings on rocky outcrops), which occur on roughly 70% of the deep-sea floor (Mullineaux, 1987, 1988). Eukaryotic organisms, dominated by Foraminifera, mostly odd-shaped mat- or tunnel-forming taxa, and rhizopod foraminifers were found to cover about 10% of the upper surface of nodules. Similar foraminifers occur abundantly encrusting the empty or sediment-filled tubes of the large agglutinated foraminifer *Bathysiphon rusticus* in the Porcupine Seabight (Gooday & Haynes, 1983). The taxa encrusting nodules include various small filter-feeding metazoans such as small hydroids, molluscs, bryozoans and ascidians. Bacterial cells and colonies have been described from nodule surfaces (Burnett & Nealson, 1981) and recent theories on the biological origin, or *biogenesis,* of manganese nodules have implicated bacteria isolated from nodules that are capable of precipitating manganese (Nealson, 1978; Schutt & Ottow, 1978; Ghiorse & Hirsch, 1982). However, Riemann (1983), noting that the stercomes (waste pellets) of agglutinated foraminifers contain manganese, suggested that they accumulate oxidized manganese and deposit it on the nodule; but it is possible that foraminifers accumulate particulate manganese from the nodule surface and hence do not contribute to nodule growth (Mullineaux, 1987).

Like the better-known megafaunal metazoans of hard substrata, about 40% of these tiny forms on nodules and seamount crusts are suspected on morphological grounds to be filter feeders (Mullineaux, 1987). This contrasts with the much lower proportion of filter feeders in the adjacent soft bottom infaunal community (Hessler & Jumars, 1974). Furthermore, experiments with manganese nodules in the deep sea indicate that the pattern of settlement by larvae of these small animals and the vertical distributions of the epifaunal community that develops, whether dominated by suspension or deposit feeders, is strongly affected by the flow regime (Mullineaux, 1988, 1989).

Part III *Patterns in space*

In the past, our information on the biology of the deep sea was traditionally gained from sampling designs worked on research ship cruises or expeditions having the aim of describing the composition of the fauna over vast areas of the ocean basins. The patterns revealed have necessarily been large in scale, and have addressed problems of the global and regional distributional of the fauna. Our ever-improving resolution of the physical structure of the deep sea, along with technical advances such as improvements in sampling gear and surface navigation, have permitted biologists to address a finer grain of variation, often along bathymetric transects. Such studies have involved quantitative sampling methods and bottom phototransects, allowing investigation of pattern in distribution of populations and communities associated with environmental gradients; the most important constituting one of the major environmental gradients on this planet, that relating to depth on the sloping parts of the seabed. We also consider in this section the effect on the distributional pattern of animals caused by other variation, principally that related to the amount and nature of organic material entering the deep sea, but also that related to local topographic and hydrodynamic conditions, such as canyons, seamounts and deep boundary currents.

In discussing these various sorts and scales of pattern we shall progress from the smallest to the largest scale with a discussion, in Chapter 6, of investigation of pattern at the scale of individual animals. Such study has only been made possible by means of observations and sampling from deep-diving manned and remote-controlled submersibles, and from small-scale, precisely positioned sample replication, made possible by modern navigation aids. This is followed, in Chapters 7, 8 and 9, by the changing pattern of biomass, diversity and community composition, mainly along the depth gradient. Chapter 10 concludes with a discussion of the global pattern in distribution of this great richness of fauna, following up discussion in Chapter 8 of modes of formation and antiquity of the enormous diversity of species found in the deep sea.

6

Small-scale spatial patterns

We now address the level of spatial structure existing *within* a community of deep-sea animals. We therefore concern ourselves with pattern at scales from perhaps hundreds of metres down to a few millimetres. Such pattern is, of course three-dimensional, and can be measured on both horizontal and vertical planes. Assumptions of randomness in the spatial patterns of shallow-water benthos have been shown to be grossly misleading. Frequently, what appears as 'randomness' is the resulting balance of a multitude of spatial variables affecting the pattern of individual organisms in the sediment fabric.

At a practical level, information on the intensity and scale of these patterns is vital in assessing the validity of estimates of standing crop obtained in quantitative samples from the deep sea. Beyond this, the description of the spatial structure displayed in the locations of individuals provides us with a powerful, if indirect, indicator of interaction between organisms on the deep-sea floor. We shall see later that such information is relevant in understanding the processes maintaining the unexpectedly high species diversity found amongst the smaller organisms of the deep-sea floor. Furthermore, a knowledge of the spatial patterns in locations of deep-sea benthic organisms becomes of increasing importance in modelling biogeochemical and stratigraphic processes: the accuracy and precision of such models, embodying parameters of the effect of benthic organisms on their environment, might be severely limited by unwarranted assumption of a random pattern in the distribution of biota.

TERMINOLOGY AND DETECTION OF SPATIAL PATTERN

Usually this is measured in terms of its deviation from the expectation of randomness in the disposition of points on a plane, where any point has an equal probability of occurring at any position; deviation from randomness in spatial point pattern occurring in the direction of either *aggregation* or *regularity* (Rogers, 1974; Diggle, 1983). With animals, which include both sessile and motile forms, spatial pattern usually is detected from 'snapshots', where their locations are frozen in time. These 'snapshots', may be quantitative samples preserving their spatial positions on and within the bottom, or seabed photographs or submersible observations of visible epifauna. Clearly, this 'snapshot' will be more informative for sessile or sedentary fauna in understanding underlying pattern-producing processes than for fast-moving organisms (which will be difficult to sample in 'quadrat'-type samples in any case). It is rarely possible to track the locations of motile marine organisms in time and space; this presenting great practical difficulties in shallow water let alone the deep sea. Yet such an approach undoubtedly would be of great value in understanding the underlying *causes*, or spatial point processes (Diggle, 1983), of spatial patterns appearing in our snapshots; we should, conservatively, assume that what can be detected is only the tip of an iceberg. Certainly, the more ephemeral natural patterns shown by motile organisms – such as those resulting from sexual encounters or from attraction to rare and transient phenomena such as large food-falls – will only be chanced on by luck (although we may hope to simulate and record such pattern by means of baited time-lapse camera systems moored on the seabed).

There are other difficulties inherent in detecting pattern from samples of the sediment with its contained fauna. Bias affecting the efficiency of the corer in collecting a representative sample (see Chapter 3) will affect the quality of data on the locations of fauna on and within the sediment sample. The disturbance associated with initial penetration of the corer and subsequently with the prolonged period necessary to retrieve cores from the deep-sea bed will particularly affect the validity of data on vertical pattern: while motile crustaceans can hardly be preserved in their natural positions after this initial disturbance and the necessarily long, drawn-out process of retrieving the sample to the ship. Infaunal animals such as polychaetes and sipunculids will withdraw deeper into the sediment; species with surface deposit and suspension feeding lifestyles having been found, implausibly, well below the sediment surface even in the most carefully monitored core-sampling programmes (Jumars, 1978; Jumars & Eckman, 1983). Some, mainly larger, deep-burrowing forms will probably withdraw to beyond range of the depth-penetration of the corer (see Chapter 5).

CLASSIFICATION IN TERMS OF CAUSATION OF PATTERN

Let us restrict ourselves to pattern shown by single animal species. This has been classified (Hutchinson, 1953) as deriving from several spatial point processes:

Vectorial patterns in the abundance of organisms are caused by variables in the physico-chemical environment of the organism. These may occur at several orders of scale, ranging from larger-scale phenomena such as hydrothermal vents and brine or hydrocarbon seeps, to those associated with individual faecal pellets on the sediment surface. In between, there will exist a relief, and at smaller scales a microrelief, of predominately biogenic origin (Figs. 14.2, 14.9(*a*),(*b*)), which on higher-energy bottoms will also be smoothed and moulded by currents (Fig. 2.13(*a*),(*b*)). We might wonder whether the landscape of, often tightly-packed, ferromanganese nodules likewise will have a predominating effect on the dispersion patterns of organisms at smaller scales. Within the sediment, steep vertical gradients in physico-chemical conditions occur, such as in utilization of electron acceptors in organic degradation (Berner, 1976). The reaction geometries of these may be drastically modified by irrigatory burrowing organisms, leading to fine-scale pattern in smaller organisms (Reise, 1981). Another source of spatial pattern might result from hydrodynamic effects on passively deposited larvae by microtopography of the bed flow (see Butman, 1987, for recent review of factors affecting larval settlement of soft-bottom invertebrates).

Reproductive spatial patterns result from the sexual encounters and limited dispersal of young. Such pattern has not as yet been documented in the deep sea, although aggregation amongst motile, seasonally repro-ducing species existing at low densities might be predicted. Although clutch size may be smaller and ripe eggs and larvae relatively large (see Chapter 13), the predominatingly lecithotrophic mode of larval disper-sion might be expected to sufficiently disperse siblings to prevent measurable aggregation around the parent.

Social patterns might result in either aggregation such as by schooling or herding (e.g. echinothuriids, see Chapter 4), or increase spacing between individuals (as might be envisaged to occur between the bur-rows of tentaculate surface-deposit feeding polychaetes in order to prevent their foraging from overlapping (see Fig. 11.5)).

Coactive patterns result from interactions between different species, such as might be caused by predator/prey or commensal relationships. Such interaction has been thought to be a major force in determining deep-sea community structure. Predation by larger megafaunal 'grazers' has been hypothesized to cause local lacunae giving rise to a mosaic of successional stages in recovery of the community (Chapter 8). Jumars & Eckman (1983) point out that no agreement has been reached on resulting dispersion patterns. While such processes might be expected at least to result in locally enhanced abundances, effects of interspecific compe-tition for space and resources might also be expected to lead to more even spacing of individuals.

Stochastic processes (such as a random walk) should lead to a random pattern in homogeneous conditions; but, in nature, environmental heterogeneity will lead rapidly to local aggregations, while stochastic movements that are read from feeding traces can lead to widely differing spatial patterns (Papentin, 1973). Similarly, for sessile animals it can be shown by computer simulation for randomly 'seeded' starting points that constant growth until reaching a fixed size or impingement with another can result in either aggregated, random or regular pattern (Pielou, 1960).

STATISTICAL MEASUREMENT OF PATTERN

A variety of statistics have been used in an attempt to summarize the horizontal pattern shown by benthic and other organisms (see Taylor, 1961; Elliott, 1977; Green, 1979; Andrew & Mapstone, 1987, for reviews of methodology). Usually these employ data on abundance derived from a rather narrow range in spatial dimension determined by the size of samplers or photographed area, representing the square-sided 'quadrat' of terrestrial investigations. The statistics test the observed data against the null hypothesis of randomness as exemplified by the Poisson distribution; the most commonly used statistic being the variance-to-mean ratio of the 'quadrat', or sample-unit, counts which, if they follow the Poisson, would equal one. (However, it should be remembered that sample-unit counts other than those randomly dispersed can result in a Poisson distribution.)

These methods have been addressed to abundances of single species; the multispecies pattern that is more subtle than that resulting from intimate interspecific associations such as symbioses and commensalism is far more difficult to measure; such patterns, such as aggregation of scavenging fauna around a large parcel of carrion may be so ephemeral as to be almost impossible to detect in nature.

Some deep-sea workers have attempted to provide an indication of pattern from quantitative sample replicates in terms of the summed abundances of whole taxa or size groupings (Khripounoff, Desbruyères & Chardy, 1980; Sibuet *et al.*, 1984; Dinet, Desbruyères & Khripounoff, 1985). These data are difficult to interpret in terms of pattern shown by individual species; the degree of non-random pattern expressed being dependent on interspecific concordance in pattern, i.e. whether different species 'agree' on where to be abundant or not (Jumars & Eckman, 1983).

MEGAFAUNAL SPATIAL PATTERNS

Our meagre knowledge of spatial pattern amongst deep-sea animals is best developed amongst the megafauna. This is because, although poorly sampled by quantitative grabs and corers, they are recognizable (if not always easily taxonomically identifiable) in seabed photographs or from the viewing ports of a submersible. However, any ability to bury themselves, even superficially, in the sediment may lead to imprecision in data collected by this means (Jumars & Eckman, 1983).

Transects of bottom photographs taken from the submersible 'Alvin' have allowed analysis of the *scale* (from a fraction of a metre to hundreds of metres) of pattern. Adjacent photographic 'quadrat' counts are combined into progressively larger blocks. The *intensity* of spatial patterns of the common megafauna are measured from counts in 'quadrats' compared to the random expectation by, for example, calculating a variance: mean ratio. This was first accomplished by Grassle *et al.* (1975) on the continental slope at 0.5 – 1.8 km depth off New England (Fig. 6.1). Similar data have come from 1.3 km depth in the Santa Catalina Basin in the Californian Continental Borderland (C. R. Smith & Hamilton, 1983). Not surprisingly, echinoderms dominate the taxa analysed. Although providing useful information on the natural history basis for causation of pattern, the results of these studies show the degree of complexity of pattern existing amongst even modestly motile animals. In the Santa Catalina Basin, the dense (16.5 m^{-2}) populations of the scavenging brittle star *Ophiophthalmus normani* showed tendencies towards regular pattern at the smallest scale (0.5 m) but also formed randomly located patches 1 to 4 m in diameter. On the New England slope the, probably omnivorous, large brittle star *Ophiomusium lymani* showed a tendency towards a regular distribution at high abundance (2.5 m^{-2}) at 1.8 km depth (where they could be seen to avoid touching arms) but towards an aggregated dispersion at 1.3 km depth where the population was sparser. Amongst the motile deposit feeders a tendency towards aggregation was detected in both studies. Loosely associated clumps ranged from 25 to 96 m in diameter in *Bathybembix bairdii* (Gastropoda) and *Scotoplanes globosa* (Holothurioidea). The loose aggregations of *B. bairdii* might have resulted from either vectorial or reproductive processes, with attraction to macroalgae falls seeming a likely cause; however, a regular spacing both within and outside patches possibly indicates some behavioural spacing. But the two latter species showed no significant between-species correlation in patch location (C. R. Smith & Hamilton, 1983). Off New England, the sea urchin *Echinus affinis* formed denser aggregations around short-lived patches of macroalgae lying on the bottom, and similar aggregations have been observed to phytodetritus in the Porcupine Seabight (Billett *et al.*, 1983), while less clear aggregated pattern was just detected at certain scales for the scavenging quill worm *Hyalinoecia* and a cerianthid anemone (Grassle *et al.*, 1975). These authors also observed that the patches detected in the deposit feeder *Phormosoma placenta* (see Fig. 6.1) appeared to move with a herd-like common orientation (Chapter 4), possibly determined by social interaction. Similar dense 'herds' of the holothurian *S. globosa* (Fig. 8.8) were observed by Barham *et al.* (1967) along with frequent strays; however, some of the most spectacular aggregations of holothurians have been observed in the Porcupine Seabight involving the small holothurian *Kolga hyalina* (Fig. 6.2), where reproductive processes or optimal foraging behaviour in utilization of phytodetrital aggregations may be important in such herd formation and maintenance (Billett & Hansen, 1982).

MACROFAUNAL SPATIAL PATTERN

Photographic studies are not possible for the macrofauna since individuals are too small to be resolved on photographs, and in any case are probably buried out of sight. We are therefore left with the 'quadrat' approach of quantitative benthic samplers. Given, on the one hand, the generally low faunal densities and, on the other, constraints on the

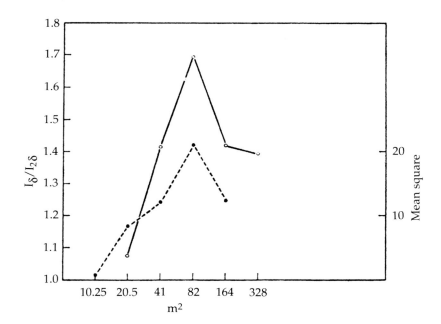

Fig. 6.1. Scale of aggregation in the echinothuriid *Phormosoma placenta* measured from counts of individuals visible in photographs taken along a contiguous band of bottom from the submersible 'Alvin'. Each photograph was overlain by a 20 × 20 grid covering 4 m² so that pattern could be measured at different scales. Two different statistics (*y*-axes) sensitive to the intensity in clumping, as deviation from a Poisson expectation in counts, are plotted at increasing scales along the *x*-axis, by combining areas into progressively bigger units from 0.25 m² up to a maximum area of 128 m² achieved by combining photographs. $I_\delta/I_{2\delta}$, solid line; mean square, broken line. The concordant peaks indicate the patches of *Phormosoma* to be roughly 40–50 m in diameter. (From Grassle *et al.*, 1975.)

maximum size of the randomly located sample that can be handled by the ship and sample-sorting manpower, the choice of 'quadrat' size has become severely restricted. In practice, the maximum size has become the 0.25 m² determined by the USNEL box corer. However, the quality of data obtained by this means is heavily dependent on whether the location of the organisms is affected or disturbed by the sampling process (see Jumars & Eckman, 1983, for a fuller discussion).

Plots of the means and variances of the abundances of taxa identified to species level in box-core replicates taken at the same time from the same deep-sea area show most values fall within the range expected for Poisson variates; with one or two occurring above but none below 95% confidence limits (Fig. 6.3). Similar results have now been obtained from studies in the Pacific and Atlantic on soft deep-sea sediments, including both bathyal and abyssal, and relatively eutrophic and oligotrophic, areas (Hessler & Jumars, 1974; Jumars, 1975a,b, 1976; Gage, 1977). But it would be unjustified to conclude that macrofauna show a random pattern on the deep-sea floor. Not only do the statistical tests applied merely fail to detect non-randomness but, given the low power of such tests as the variance : mean ratio at the very low densities existing in the samples, this is hardly surprising in any case. Furthermore, Monte Carlo methods (simulations, usually using computer-generated random variates) show that a wide variety of dispersion patterns produce identical variance : mean ratios (Jumars & Eckman, 1983; Khripounoff *et al.*, 1980). Indeed, total (unsorted) abundances of major taxa and whole size categories of both macrofauna and meiofauna in sets of box-core replicates from various locations in the Atlantic indicate aggregations of individuals to be highly probable (Khripounoff *et al.*, 1980; Sibuet *et al.*, 1984; Dinet *et al.*, 1985).

Analysis of abundances of species in adjacent subcores of subdivided USNEL box-cores permits a different approach to be applied in detecting fine-scale pattern using more powerful *distance* methods (Jumars, Thistle & Jones, 1977). Here, information is recorded in the form of distances to neighbouring points: if the presence of a point makes its presence in a neighbouring area more, or less, likely, then the pattern exhibits *spatial autocorrelation* (Cliff & Ord, 1973; Sokal & Ogden, 1978*a,b*). Pooled abundances of polychaetes within subcores from the San Diego Trough showed less autocorrelation in abundances in adjacent than in non-adjacent cores; but a similar trend was not observed amongst polychaetes in the nearby Santa Catalina Basin or amongst non-polychaete fauna, so that generalizations of even spacing of individuals at these small scales would be unjustified (Jumars *et al.*, 1977).

At a larger scale, spatial pattern has been analysed amongst macro-fauna from accurate, transponder-located positions of 124 closely spaced core samples in the San Diego Trough. These were taken using the Remotely Operated Underwater Manipulator 'RUM' in Expedition Quag-mire (Thiel & Hessler, 1974). This study shows how pattern detected by

Fig. 6.2. Dense aggregation of the small elasipodid holothurian *Kolga hyalina* gathered around a sedimentary ring structure at about 3.8 km depth in the Porcupine Seabight. (Courtesy Dr A. L. Rice, Institute of Oceanographic Sciences.)

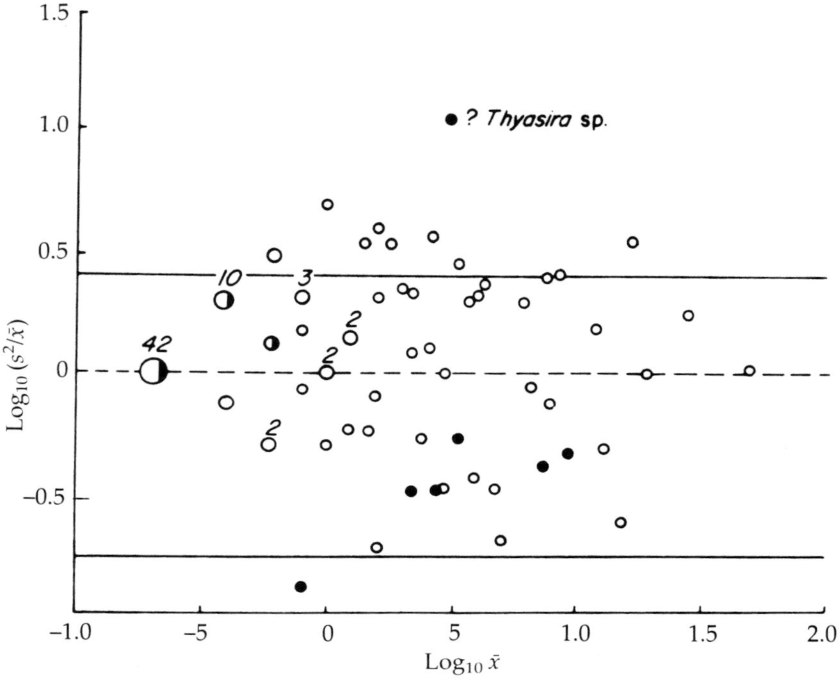

Fig. 6.3. Log/log plot of variance : mean ratio plotted against the mean abundances of 18 bivalve (filled circles) and 105 polychaete species (open circles) occurring in a series of 6 USNEL box cores from 2.875 km depth in the Rockall Trough (numerals and larger circles indicate more than one species with the same value). Continuous lines; 95% confidence limits of the Poisson expectation (pecked line). (From Gage, 1977.)

spatial autocorrelation that is sensitive to the *scale* of pattern, might remain undetected by the variance : mean ratio which addresses only its *intensity*. However, significant departures from random patterns were detected in only 2 out of 13 species; the spatial autocorrelograms for a nereid and an opheliid polychaete (Fig. 6.4), nevertheless, indicating that replicate sampling, not taking sample spatial coordinates into account, would fail to detect pattern which is evident in density isopleths interpolated over the scale of sampling (Fig. 6.5). However, Monte Carlo simulations show that the numbers of samples in relation to the densities of the remaining species probably was too low to detect any non-random patterns present in the RUM study (Jumars & Eckman, 1983).

SPATIAL PATTERN IN MEIOFAUNA AND MICROBIOTA

There are indications of aggregated pattern from analysis both of pooled meiofaunal taxa in subcores from one box-core and from a series of box-core replicates (Khripounoff *et al.,* 1980; Sibuet *et al.,* 1984; Dinet *et al.,* 1985). However, there are few data on single-species pattern owing to taxonomic difficulties in separating species. Furthermore, data from cores will be prone to all the bias previously detailed for macrofauna, and it is particularly important to minimize disturbance of natural pattern by the subsampling process (Jumars & Eckman, 1983). Analysis of results from 'vegematic' box-cores could not disprove the random expectation amongst 124 individual harpacticoid copepods from the San Diego Trough, but showed significant terms from the more powerful chi^2

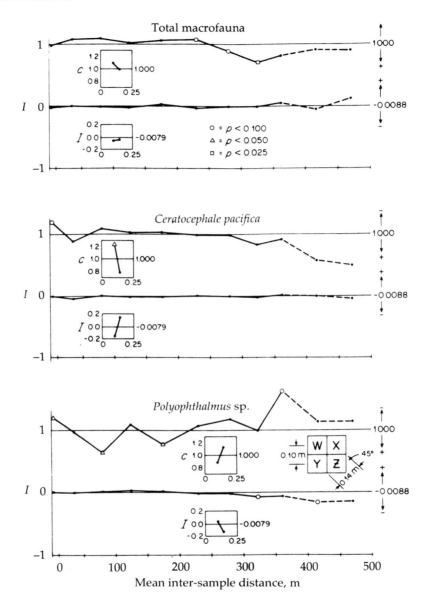

Fig. 6.4. 'Correlograms' of the autocorrelation statistics Moran's I and Geary's c (see Cliff & Ord, 1973) with a weighting of distance squared plotted at increasing inter-sample distance amongst counts of summed and two individual polychaete species in 125 subcores from the transponder-located box-cores (shown in Fig. 6.5). These statistics test the null hypothesis of no spatial autocorrelation, defined as random permutations of the variate values amongst the sample locations, against the alternatives that similarity either decreases or increases as the square of the distance between samples (for further details, see Jumars, 1978). The intervals used in calculating I and c are shown by tick marks along the y-axis. Horizontal lines; expected values. Deviations showing positive or negative autocorrelation are given at right. Pecked lines are based on sparse data and the magnitudes shown are unreliable. Inset shows the arrangement of subcores within each core and the result of within-core scale. (From Jumars, 1978.)

analysis where all species are considered together as replicates (Thistle, 1978). Positive relationships were detected amongst abundances of the species examined to various small-scale biogenic structures, such as 'mudballs' created by the tubicolous cirratulid polychaete *Tharyx luticastellus* (see Jumars, 1975b), and also to polychaete feeding types, suggesting that the high heterogeneity chi^2 values obtained derived from divergent responses to these factors (Thistle, 1978, 1979b). A similar positive correlation for both harpacticoids and nematodes has been shown to pebbles in the sediment from the HEBBLE area (Thistle, 1983b; Thistle & Sherman, 1985), suggesting that meiofauna somehow benefit

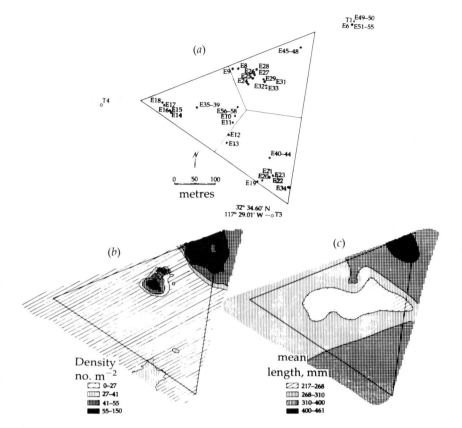

Fig. 6.5. (a) Chart of study area and positions of Ekman box-cores (numerals prefixed 'E') and the three transponders (prefixed 'T') in the RUM study area in the San Diego Trough. (b) Chart of estimated density of the opheliid polychaete *Polyophthalmus* sp. (c) Chart of individual size of *Polyophthalmus* sp. (From Jumars, 1978.)

from closeness to large non-living objects. However, one harpacticoid species (*Heteropsyllus* sp.) responds only to *Tharyx* mudballs that still contain worms, suggesting a more complex relationship, in the San Diego Trough (Thistle & Eckman, 1988). Later, Thistle and Eckman (1990) showed that the occurrence of 40 harpacticoid copepod species in cores from this area showed a response to the mudballs, four being more abundant around the structure only when the worm was in residence. Furthermore, as bacteria were more abundant around occupied mudballs their attractiveness may arise from provision of food. Three other species responded to unoccupied mudballs; experiments using mudball 'mimics' placed on the bottom and cored several months later indicating that two of the species use the mudball as a habitat, the third as a refuge from infaunal predators. However, with ferro-manganese nodules, no correlation of metazoan meiofauna to nodules or, indeed, any characteristic scale of pattern, could be detected for either meiofauna or nanobiota within or between replicate box-cores in the central N. Pacific (Snider, Burnett & Hessler, 1984).

For the microbiota, analysis of variance of biomass and community structure (assessed, respectively, by total lipid phosphate and molar percentages of fatty acids) showed the greatest variation occurs at the

Fig. 6.6. (*a*) Depth-frequencies of macrofauna within the sediment from horizontally sliced 'RUM' cores. 'Uncorrected', observed data; 'corrected' modifies observed data to take account of their probable place within functional group classification of Fauchald & Jumars (1979), i.e. probable surface-deposit and suspension feeders are placed at the sediment surface where they feed. The large discrepancy between the two distributions indicates that such data are compromised, probably by withdrawal of the worms deeper into the sediment on capture. (*b*) Vertical segregation in distribution of three species of the foraminifer *Rhizammina* that would possess ability to move within the sediment. The frequencies are expressed in terms of the total lengths of fragments occurring in each layer of the sediment in multiple corer samples from the N.E. Atlantic. ((*a*) From Jumars & Eckman, 1983; (*b*) from Gooday, 1986*b*.)

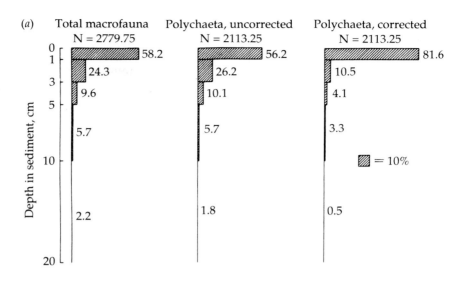

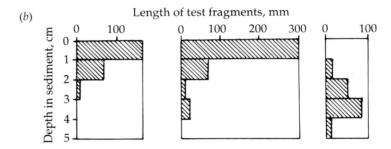

scale of subcores within, rather than between boxcores within the HEB-BLE area (Baird *et al.*, 1985).

VERTICAL PATTERN

We have discussed above how the disturbance and withdrawal of macrofauna into the sediment is likely to bias data on vertical pattern from deep-sea box-cores. The best data still available probably comes from box-cores taken by RUM (see above) in the San Diego Trough (Jumars, 1978; Jumars & Eckman, 1983). Horizontal slices of these very carefully taken samples indicated that polychaete species occur at depths in the sediment that correspond to their presumed feeding type; but such supposed vertical segregation is by no means shown unequivocally, surface deposit and suspension feeding polychaetes being sometimes found *below* the sediment surface (Fig. 6.6(*a*)).

Meiofauna might be thought to be less affected by disturbance in the sampling process because their smaller size will limit possible withdrawal deeper into the bottom. Gooday (1986*b*) analysed the positions within multiple corer samples for single species of Foraminifera, these data indicating considerable between-species segregation (Fig. 6.6(*b*)). The pattern shown by several workers shows an overwhelming concentration of individuals in the top centimetre or so of sediment, with a pattern of rapid decrease below, although single individuals of nematodes and rhizopod protozoans have been detected in the deepest (25–30 cm) layer of sectioned box-cores (Dinet & Vivier, 1977; Coull *et al.*, 1977; Shirayama, 1984*b*; Snider *et al.*, 1984; Thistle & Sherman, 1985).

MULTISPECIES PATTERN

We might expect that multispecies, or coactive, patterns would be even more diverse than those shown by individual species. One approach to the analysis of these patterns amongst the low densities typically found in deep-sea samples is by testing the concordance in abundance amongst more than two species in order to test the hypothesis that deep-sea species are independently Poisson distributed amongst samples. Hessler & Jumars (1974) found the most abundant species from the central N. Pacific 'agreed' well in which box-core replicate they were either most rare or common. By separating pattern into that *between* box-core replicates and that *within* 0.01 m^2 subcores of each, the scale of such pattern can be addressed. Since individual chi^2 distributions are additive, the *total* chi^2 determines whether species on average depart from the Poisson in core abundances; a *pooled* term determining whether core abundances of individual species when summed by core produces a Poisson distribution as would be expected if abundances are independent and individually Poisson distributed, whilst a *heterogeneity* term determines whether species tend to be concordant (homogeneous) or discordant (heterogeneous) in separate core abundances (Jumars, 1975*b*, 1976). In other words, the method tests for any unexpectedly large concordance or discordance in the local abundances of species in relation to the expected stochastic variability if their local abundances are independent; the heterogeneity chi-square component approximating its degrees of freedom if this assumption were true.

At the between-core level, the results from the San Diego Trough and Santa Catalina Basin indicated *discordance* among species within major taxa, rather than the concordance indicated from the central N. Pacific: where one species was common, others within the same taxon were rare. But further analysis showed them to fall within two groups, whilst the majority were independently Poisson distributed, a smaller group, although otherwise tending to homogeneity, were all most abundant in one core which contained most fragments of hexactinellid sponge. The significance of such fragments in terms of the behavioural ecology of the species remain obscure. Possibly disparate factors are involved, ranging from browsing on epibionts, shelter, substratum for attachment, and possibly, as a projection from the bottom (causing local *de*-celeration in the bottom current and sedimentation of suspended particles) as sites of enhanced food supply and larval settlement (Jumars & Eckman, 1983). These authors emphasize how much this 'decidedly non-random species pattern . . . hinged critically on one core'. Even if difficult to detect, such rare spatial occurrences might be as important as similarly rare and difficult-to-detect temporal events as determinants of community structure (see Chapter 8).

At the level of subcores, patterns of species concordance or *discordance* in abundance per subcore were not clearly evident. Overall, concordance was demonstrated by Jumars (1975*a*) between species within the polychaete family Paraonidae, this possibly resulting from a second-order coactive effect as physical exclusion from bottom area occupied by *Tharyx* mudballs (Fig. 6.7). Furthermore, Thistle (1979*a*) found harpacticoid copepods covaried significantly with polychaete worms when the latter were combined into functional groups on the basis of feeding type and motility, the copepods tending to avoid sessile surface-deposit feeding worms.

An alternative approach is to apply a clustering technique, such as the statistic 'NESS' (number of expected species shared), in order to group species amongst the samples (see Chapter 9). This procedure was applied to species abundances occurring in a total of 80 box-cores taken in an ambitious box-core sampling programme in the equatorial E. Pacific; replicates from each station being pooled, with clusters of stations at three 2×2 sites (Fig. 6.8(*a*)). The resulting dendrogram (Fig. 6.8(*b*)) tends to reflect the spatial separation of the sites; the degree of within-site uniformity varying, and the apparent mosaic structure indicated, being interpreted as possibly related to underlying patterns of sedimentary variation (Hecker & Paul, 1979).

The lack of any indication of coherently 'typical' multispecies pattern

Fig. 6.7. The relationship between the numbers of 'mudballs' of the cirratulid *Tharyx luticastellus* and the numbers of shallow-burrowing paraonid polychaete individuals per 0.01 m² subcore from 1.23 km depth in the San Diego Trough; Md, median value: (*a*) total number of mudballs remaining after sample sieving; (*b*) only those mudballs still occupied by *Tharyx*. The absence of apparent correlation with mudballs still occupied by *Tharyx* supports the hypothesis of physical exclusion of paraonids by habitat structures, whose local density did not correspond closely with numbers of living *Tharyx*. (From Jumars, 1975*b*.)

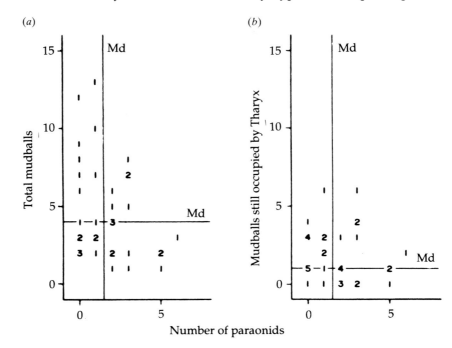

Number of paraonids

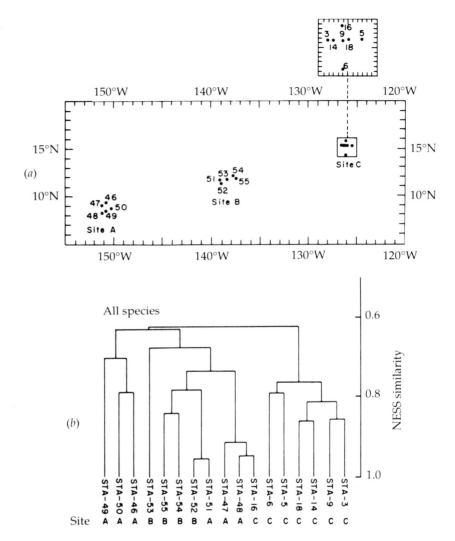

Fig. 6.8. Large-scale pattern from 80 box-core samples taken in the abyssal equatorial Pacific. (*a*) Chart of sites of three clusters of sample stations (numerals). (*b*) Dendrogram of site groups formed on the basis of all macrofauna retained from four to five replicate 0.25 m² cores per site, using Number of Expected Species Shared (NESS) similarity statistic. (From Hecker & Paul, 1979.)

even in areas avoiding obvious topographic complexity suggests that a daunting complexity in multispecies pattern exists in the deep sea. Clearly, in order to understand this, much more data on large and small-scale variations in the physico-chemical environment will need to be collected and correlated to faunal abundances. A study of multispecies pattern employing a variety of multivariate procedures to foraminiferan abundance in several subdivided 0.25 m² box-cores from the central N. Pacific begins to suggest what may be required. By means of multiple discriminant analysis, species clustering could be related to several biological and physical variables (Bernstein *et al.*, 1978). Although the results demonstrate relationships to metazoan functional types present in the same subcores, the nature of cause and effect remains obscure.

Furthermore, there is evidence for spatial heterogeneity of both living and dead benthic Foraminifera at such small scales, suggesting persistence of multispecies patch structure (Bernstein & Meador, 1979).

7

Abundance and size structure of the deep-sea benthos

There are two major variables that are clearly related to resource avail-ability in the deep-sea environment. First, the density (standing crop), expressed either as biomass, organic or carbon content, or numbers of individuals; and second the body size of individuals. With both, a large literature has demonstrated, or qualified, an inverse relationship to bathymetry along the depth gradient from the continental shelf to the abyss.

DENSITY

In this chapter we shall concentrate on quantitative investigations of the abundance of *benthic* life on and within the deep-sea bottom. This is because quantitative data on the purely *benthopelagic* fauna are very sparse. However, there are indications that biomass of gelatinous organ-isms, such as sea cucumbers, found swimming just off the bottom may, in places, be high (Childress *et al.*, 1989). We shall consider biomass of other benthopelagic organisms, such as large, swimming scavenging organ-isms, along with other megafauna later in the chapter.

Quantitative studies of the deep-sea benthos date from the 1950s with the cruise of the 'Galathea'. On this voyage a 0.2 m^2 Petersen grab was first used in the deep sea (Spärck, 1956*b*) and this followed upon many Russian deep-sea expeditions using the 0.25 m^2 'Okean' grab (Filatova, 1982). The Russian studies have underlined the positive relationship between pelagic and benthic productivity, and their results (Fig. 7.1) largely reinforce the general prediction that density of benthic life de-creases with depth and distance from shore, as well as from polar and temperate to tropical latitudes (Filatova, 1982). The crucial controlling factor is the dependence of benthic fauna on available food resources (Belyaev, 1966). We shall examine this proposition in the light of more recent sampling (much of it reviewed by Rowe, 1983) both in terms of size-related categories of the benthos, and in terms of its changing taxonomic composition.

SIZE SPECTRA

The separation of size categories in marine benthic communities dates from Mare (1942). Her pioneering work in the English Channel off Plymouth separated organisms into size-based categories. These were based on retention by different sieve mesh sizes in order to distinguish between a motile and epifaunal or burrowing (infaunal) macrofauna, and smaller, interstitial animals, designated the meiofauna, as well as the larval stages of the 'macrofaunal' groups. Later, the groups of larger animals living on the seabed large enough to be recognizable in seabed photographs were designated as the 'megafauna'. Although the names of these categories have been retained, the sieve-size divisions of Mare have had to be abandoned by deep-sea workers because only a small portion of 'macrofaunal' biota are retained on a 1 mm sieve as a result of the much smaller body size of deep-sea taxa. Hence, the sieve size employed by deep-sea workers to retain macrofauna has decreased to 0.42 mm, 0.297 mm, 0.250 mm or less. For the meiofauna the lower limit of 0.1 mm is now generaly taken as 62, 60, 40 or 30 μm (Hulings & Gray, 1971; Dinet et al., 1985).

We shall see later in this chapter in the section of Size Structure that these empirically separated size categories seem to correspond to distinct peaks in size-class spectra for the total benthic community in the deep sea. Furthermore, these peaks seem to correspond to functionally disparate groupings.

Fig. 7.1. Global distribution of benthic biomass (g m^{-2} wet weight) in the world's oceans mainly based on Russian grab sampling programmes. (From G. M. Belyaev et al., 1973.)

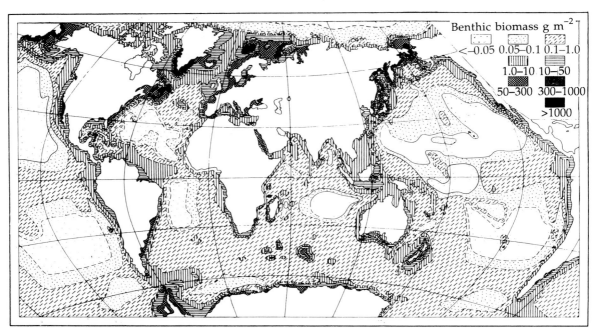

RELATIVE STANDING CROP OF SIZE-BASED CATEGORIES

Are these size-spectra peaks of roughly equal importance in terms of total biomass, or does one section of the benthos such as the macrofauna dominate the remainder? There are few data available that cover the total size range of benthic organisms in shallow water let alone the deep sea. One comprehensively studied area lies in the central N. Pacific. Here, not surprisingly, meiofauna and nanobiota dominate the fauna in numbers (0.3 and 99.7%, respectively), and also in terms of biomass (63.8 and 34.9%, respectively); while meiofauna are two orders of magnitude more numerous and have a greater biomass than macrofauna (Fig. 7.2). In contrast, macrofaunal biomass is greater than meiofaunal biomass in shallow water (Snider et al., 1984).

MEASURES OF STANDING CROP: BIOMASS OR NUMERICAL ABUNDANCE?

Rowe (1983) shows that estimates of macrofaunal biomass are far less affected than those of animal density in comparing data using sieves of 0.42 and 0.297 mm meshes or less, quite a high proportion of macrofaunal

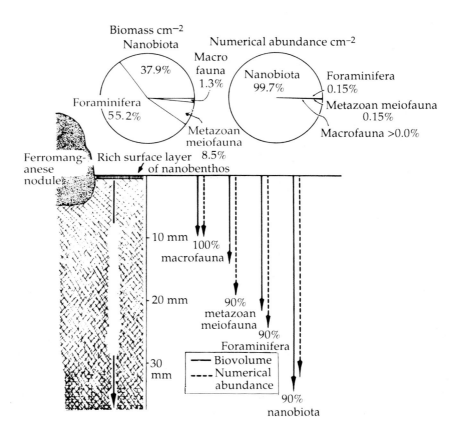

Fig. 7.2. Schematic representation of vertical distributions of various size groups of benthos in the central N. Pacific. It assumes that all organisms collected in the water overlying the core originated from the sediment. The diagram ignores the rare, larger macrofauna that will occur deeper than 10 mm into the sediment. (From Snider et al., 1984.)

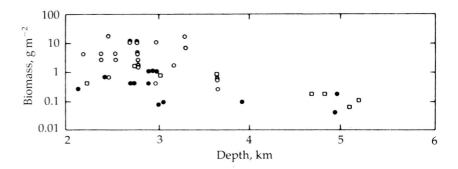

Fig. 7.3. Comparison of the wet weight biomass estimates in the N.W. Atlantic using 0.297 mm sieve (open squares), and 0.42 mm sieve (open and closed circles). The latter are distinguished because they were taken using different samplers, either an anchor dredge (filled circles) or a Birge–Ekman grab operated by DSRV 'Alvin'. Those indicated by open squares were taken by means of a grab respirometer. See Chapters 3 and 12 for descriptions of these gears. (From Rowe, 1983.)

individuals being retained by even a 0.5 mm sieve (Fig. 7.3). Most investigators now exclude from the macrofaunal assessment those animals, such as nematodes, harpacticoids and ostracods that might be retained by the sieve but generally regarded as 'meiofaunal' (Sanders *et al.*, 1965; Hessler & Jumars, 1974; Gage, 1977; Desbruyères *et al.*, 1980). Dinet *et al.* (1985) distinguish between the metazoan macrofauna *sensu stricto* that follows the latter practice in excluding nematodes, copepods and ostracods from the metazoan macrofauna *sensu lato* that includes *all* fauna retained by a 250 μm screen.

We emphasize that it is important to qualify estimates of biomass not only in terms of sieve size but also on which major taxa are sorted from the fauna. Such choices are made on pragmatic rather than on any taxonomic or phylogenetic grounds. The phylum Protozoa encompasses organisms as large as xenophyophores that, on the basis of size, are part of the megafauna; the komokiaceans and many agglutinating foraminiferans that are large enough to be regarded as macrofauna; other, more 'normal'-sized, calcareous foraminiferans are on a size basis grouped with the meiofauna; and, finally, sporozoan and ciliophoran protozoans that comprise the nanobiota (size range 2 to 42 μm). Furthermore, until a clearer relationship can be established between biomass and abundance from knowledge of size structure in different taxa and size categories of the fauna, quantitative data are best compared on the basis of both criteria. These should include non-destructive estimates of wet weight biomass that can be standardized against destructive measures of dry weight biomass, partitioning of organic components and elemental carbon, nitrogen and calorific content.

Rowe (1983) argues that, for the quantification of life on the deep-sea floor, the weight of living organisms, or biomass, is a more meaningful measure than the number of animals per unit area, although measures of mass and abundance do seem to follow the same trends (Fig. 7.4). However, one serious disadvantage of measures of biomass is that this mass can be measured in a variety of ways: wet or dry, and with or without skeletal elements such as shells, or even in terms of major organic constituents or as calorific content (Table 7.1). The protoplasm of unicells such as agglutinated foraminiferans, komokiaceans and xenophyophores may be inextricably coated with sediment particles or incorporate stored

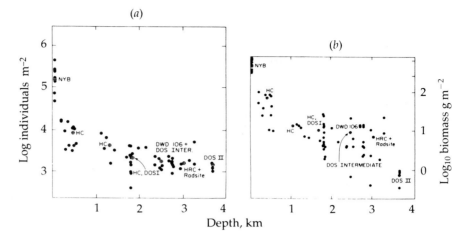

Fig. 7.4. The relationships of (a) number of macrofaunal animals and (b) wet weight biomass per square metre, to depth from various quantitative sampling sites (labels) in N.W. Atlantic. Solid circles are individual samples; open circles, averages from repeat-sampled stations. (From Rowe, Polloni & Haedrich, 1982.)

waste (stercomes) so that their wet or dry weight biomass is not directly comparable with that of other animals. Amongst metazoans there might be difficulties in comparing different taxa either within or between samples resulting from discrepancies between total mass, as might be estimated by wet weight biomass, and organic carbon content: taxa such as echinoderms having a relatively high calcium carbonate skeletal content but less organic carbon on a weight basis than other major taxa (Table 7.2).

An extreme example of this difficulty is provided by box-core samples from the Venezuelan Basin where hexactinellid sponges comprised more than an order of magnitude more wet weight biomass than the total remaining macrofauna, yet contribute a much smaller fraction of total organic carbon (Richardson & Young, 1987). On the other hand, because of the supposed depth dependence of mean body size, the number of individuals present will be more sensitive to the size of sieve mesh used in the investigation. This is why a plot of standing crop seems to decline

Table 7.1. *Measures of metazoan biomass (Rowe, 1983)*

Fresh wet weight	Weight after blotting excess liquid
Preserved wet weight	Weight as above after preservation
Dry weight	Weight after drying to constant weight at 60–90 °C
Dry weight with shells removed	As above, but with shells cut away or dissolved with acid
Ash-free dry weight	Weight loss on combustion at 500 °C
Elemental analysis of carbon or nitrogen	Elemental analyser on combustion
Partitioning of organic matter into lipid, carbohydrate and protein component	Chemical analysis of individual compounds
Calorific content	Heat production on ignition

Table 7.2. *Measures of biomass in different major metazoan taxa (Rowe, 1983)*

Organisms	% Carbon of wet weight	% Carbon of dry weight
Polychaetes	5.1%	40.6%
Crustaceans	3.7%	37.5%
Molluscs	4.1%	33.5%
Echinoderms	2.6%	26.1%
Macrobenthic infauna (polychaetes, amphipods and bivalves)	4.3%	37.5%
Average of all categories ($n = 19$)	3.4%	33.0%
Total number of animals: 5983	Total number of analyses: 99	

faster when expressed as number of individuals than wet-weight biomass (Fig. 7.4). Fragmentation of delicate animals sometimes makes it difficult to count certain organisms, such as branching komokiacian Foraminifera.

Another possible source of bias involved in comparing abundances rather than biomass can result from differences in age structure. Thistle, Yingst & Fauchald (1985) found a preponderance of subadult sizes (perhaps related to frequent sediment disturbance) amongst polychaetes and bivalves from the high energy HEBBLE area on the Nova Scotia rise. This, they suggested, might inflate estimates of standing crop based on faunal abundance compared to sites where adults dominate the assemblage. Similar bias could result from recruitment resulting from seasonal breeding when summertime samples might be numerically enhanced by large numbers of recently settled young (Lightfoot, Tyler & Gage, 1979; Gage *et al.*, 1980; Tyler *et al.*, 1982). Rowe (1983) points out that measures of biomass which will be of most relevance to considerations of ecosystem dynamics and energy flow, will require measurement of the fauna not only in terms of organic carbon and calorific content but as utilizable fat, carbohydrate and protein – as has been accomplished for some deep-sea holothurians (Sibuet & Lawrence, 1981; Walker, Tyler & Billett, 1987a,b). Rowe (1983) argues that, since most of the total biomass tends to be found in the less abundant, large individuals rather than in the more numerous smaller ones, biomass is a more dependable measure for estimating production and for comparing data from different studies and areas. However, this ignores bias resulting from our experience that biomass measurements are more variable than counts of number of animals, simply because they are markedly affected by the relatively rare occurrences of large-bodied animals in the necessarily relatively small size of quantitative samples (Gage, 1977).

GLOBAL AND REGIONAL VARIATIONS IN BIOMASS

Many parts of the world ocean have now been sampled using quantitative sampling devices that yield at least roughly comparable data. However, in relation to the immense area of the deep ocean, the areas where benthic biomass, or standing crop, has been characterized is still quite small. What's more, the area covered by the samples from each area is miniscule compared to the bottom area they purport to characterize; and variability in sampling caused by aggregated dispersion of benthic populations has barely been investigated (see Chapter 6). The total of 709 quantitative samples from which biomass is plotted against depth in Fig. 7.5 can be compared with the hundreds of thousands of seabed photographs that have been taken over the same period; for example, more than 80 000 bottom photographs were taken in the late 1970s of the ferromanganese nodule fields in the Clarion–Clipperton Fracture Zone of the north-eastern equatorial Pacific (Sorem *et al.*, 1979; Foell & Pawson, 1986). Yet the quantitative composition of the macro- and meiobenthos of this area has been characterized by just 15 box-cores 0.25 m^2 (G. D. F. Wilson & Hessler, 1987).

Nevertheless, for the macrofauna, the data from the summed quantitative samples (Fig. 7.5), most of which come from Russian grab sampling, do tend to confirm the proposition of decreasing biomass with increasing depth, indicating a clear trend for an exponential decrease along the depth gradient (Rowe 1971*a*). But the overall level of biomass (and the slope of any fitted regression of semilogarithmic plots) in subsets of these data from different localities varies on different continental margins (Fig. 7.6); being dependent on surface production (Rowe, 1971*a*; Rowe, Polloni

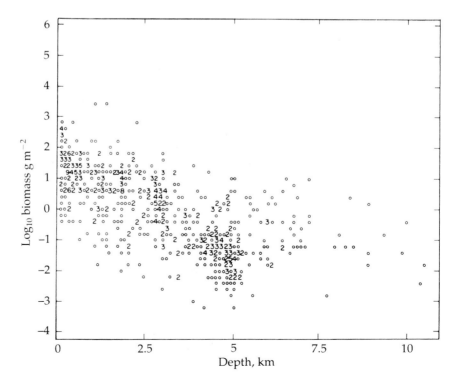

Fig. 7.5. Macrofaunal standing crop plotted against depth from 709 deep-sea quantitative samples from various sources, mostly Okean-grab, box-core, and anchor-dredge samples. A regression of these data yield the following regression: $\log_{10}$ biomass = 1.25–0.00039 (depth). (From Rowe, 1983.)

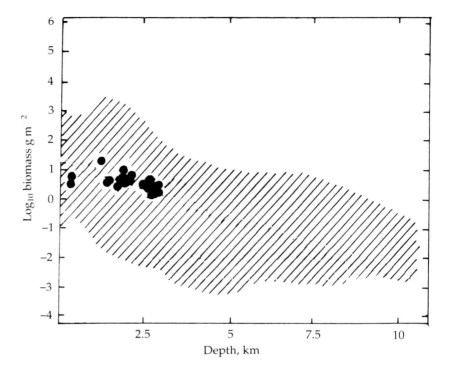

Fig. 7.6. Standing crop of macrofauna plotted against depth (closed circles) from samples taken with USNEL box corer from one area (the Rockall Trough), with standardized sample-processing procedure. Hatched area shows the spread of values plotted in Fig. 7.5. (J. D. Gage, unpublished data.)

& Horner, 1974), width of the continental shelf (Rowe & Haedrich, 1979) and latitude (Belyaev, 1966).

Similar trends seem to apply both to the meiofauna and megafauna (Haedrich *et al.*, 1980; Khripounoff *et al.*, 1980; C. R. Smith & Hamilton, 1983; Ohta, 1983; Rutgers van der Loeff & Lavaleye, 1986; Lampitt, Billett & Rice, 1986; Tietjen *et al.*, 1989).

CAUSES OF VARIATIONS IN BIOMASS

The conventional explanation for this overall trend is that, since the midwater and benthic community share the same ultimate food source, the scale and efficiency of utilization by midwater organisms and its rate of degradation by microorganisms, as particulate organic material (POM) sinks to the bottom, will determine the quantity ultimately available to the benthos. For example, packaging of material by zooplankton into fast-sinking faecal pellets will accelerate the sedimentation of material to the bottom (McCave, 1975). However, the efficiency in assimilation will determine the food value of the pellet to the benthos; during the spring bloom overfeeding by copepods might result in many ingested phyto-plankton cells remaining undigested. Such poor coupling of primary production to pelagic consumption might explain higher benthic biomass in high latitudes where, despite low average annual productivity levels, highly intense seasonally pulsed productivity may allow more organic matter to leak from the epipelagic and escape remineralization within the meso- and bathypelagic zones (Rowe, 1983; Vinogradova & Tseitlin, 1983).

Another argument relates biomass primarily to the influences of high coastal-zone productivity and terrestrial runoff which will diminish with increasing distance from land. An intensive comparison of a station sited near the Amazon cone in the W. equatorial Atlantic at 4.44 km depth with another more than 200 miles away at 4.84 km on the adjacent abyssal plain showed a close relationship of benthic biomass to downward particulate flux (Sibuet *et al.*, 1984). Slope upwelling, in enhancing surface productivity, leads to increased benthic abundance and biomass compared with equivalent depths elsewhere, but nevertheless decreases with increasing depth and distance from shore (Pfannkuche, Theeg & Thiel, 1983).

Effects of land runoff are particularly noticeable in enhanced terrigenous sedimentation near the mouths of major rivers carrying high loadings of suspended particulates, such as the Amazon (Sibuet *et al.*, 1984). In deep trenches sited near the continental land masses, macrobenthic standing crops of several grammes per square metre are found, rather than values of milligrammes that would be predicted from the regression (Bruun, 1957; Belyaev, 1966; Vinogradova *et al.*, 1974; Belyaev, 1989). Trenches appear to act as traps for coastal sediment and terrigenous plant detritus (Wolff, 1976; George & Higgins, 1979) that seems to fuel enhanced benthic production compared to adjacent abyssal areas further offshore. On the other hand, Rowe (1983) points out that *within* individual trenches, benthic standing crop decreases with depth at about the same rate as the general pattern indicating that similar processes of pelagic remineralization operate with increasing depth of the water column as elsewhere. Areas of regional upwelling against the continental margin fuelling high surface production is reflected in high benthic standing crop off N.W. Africa, but in some other areas such as off Chile and Peru, the very high surface productivity leads to anoxia characterized by a 'sulphide biome' in reducing conditions on the bottom (Thiel, 1982). Locally enhanced standing crop may occur at shallower depths in submarine canyons on the continental slope that can act as traps or funnels for detrital material from a coastal estuary or adjacent shelf area (Griggs *et al.*, 1969; Rowe *et al.*, 1982). However, in other canyons biomass may be the same or even lower than background levels (Rowe *et al.*, 1982; Houston & Haedrich, 1984). Such effects then start to grade into small-scale heterogeneity in organic input to the bottom such as the transient attractions of motile megafauna to large-lump foodfalls, or to phytodetrital detritus collecting in topographic lows on the seabed (Billett *et al.*, 1983; Lampitt, 1985*a*).

Areas experiencing strong near-bottom currents on the continental margin may be enriched beyond the expectation on the basis of depth and benthic standing crop at less energetic sites nearby (Gage, 1979; Thistle *et al.*, 1985). In shallower water, fishermen have long associated such areas with their best catches; the current-swept bottoms carrying organic matter in suspension encouraging a greater development of deposit-feeding benthic prey than on quieter, muddy areas (Murray & Hjort, 1912). Although organic productivity at the surface may be no higher than elsewhere, food available to a sessile or sedentary deposit feeder will be constantly replenished by resuspension, perhaps locally sedimented into a feeding pit (see Nowell, Jumars & Fauchald, 1984; Jumars *et al.*, 1990) or intercepted by suspension feeding. Perhaps even more importantly, the potential food source provided by microbial biomass seems to be enhanced in such high-energy areas (Baird *et al.*, 1985). A parallel can be drawn to similar findings of enhanced microbial activity and biomass in high energy compared to sheltered beaches (Novitsky & MacSween, 1989). Such conditions of frequent sediment resuspension mimic the constant stirring necessary for optimal culture of sediment micro-organisms in the laboratory.

The lowest densities of benthic biomass are found on the abyssal plains far from land, lying under the centre of oceanic gyres where surface productivity is very low. Typical of such areas are the central N. Pacific, the Sargasso Sea and Porcupine Abyssal Plain. Here at depths below 4.5 km macrofaunal abundances are about 100 animals m^{-1} weighing about 0.05 g m^{-1} (Hessler & Jumars, 1974; Rutgers van der Loeff & Lavaleye, 1986). Low benthic standing crop is also found where the deep water mass is much warmer than elsewhere, such as the Mediterranean (*c.* 13.56 °C) and the Red Sea (min. 21.56 °C), (Dinet *et al.*, 1973; Rowe, 1983; Thiel, 1979*b*; Thiel *et al.*, 1987). In these areas pelagic consumption seems to be enhanced. Although planktonic grazing effects are thought to be small in the Red Sea, this results in a high rate of degradation of organic matter in the warm water column, and, of what little is available at the bottom, much is lost for benthic production because of a high energy demand of temperature-related metabolism.

There are few good data on macrofaunal densities in relation to feeding type. However, Rex, Etter & Nimeskern (1990) show that the predatory neogastropods and opisthobranchs have a much steeper decline in density with increasing depth than gastropod taxa dominated by deposit feeders (archaeogastropods and mesogastropods), and suggest that members of higher trophic levels are more sensitive to energy loss between trophic levels in the benthic food chain.

BIOMASS TRENDS WITH MEGAFAUNA

For the megafauna, quantitative data are much more scarce. Although caught in large trawls, such organisms are too rare to be collected in numbers sufficient for quantitative estimation by quantitative samplers such as box-corers. For the larger epifauna such as holothurians and asteroids, quantitative estimates can be made from seabed photographs or manned submersible observations (Wigley & Emery, 1967; Barham *et al.*, 1967; Grassle *et al.*, 1975; Haedrich & Rowe, 1977; Ohta, 1983; Sibuet & Segonzac, 1985; Lampitt, Billett & Rice, 1986). However, these estimates ignore the possibly important contribution made by both the motile scavenging megafauna and by the megafaunal burrowers, that are occasionally taken by box corers (Gage, 1977); although attempts have been made to estimate their density from the large burrow and faecal traces visible in seabed photographs (Mauviel, Juniper & Sibuet, 1987). Nevertheless these estimates show the same phenomenon of decreasing density with increasing depth as displayed by macrofauna (Fig. 7.7). Although subject to bias in favour of less motile organisms, it is claimed that the megabenthos declines more rapidly than the smaller size groups with increasing depth and decreasing nutritional resources (Khripounoff *et al.*, 1980; Sibuet *et al.*, 1984; Sibuet & Segonzac, 1985).

Estimates of epifaunal biomass on rocky bottoms, except at hydro-thermal vents (see Chapter 15), are as yet unavailable.

For the highly motile scavenging megafauna, the poor relationship between the catches of trawls and density estimates from bottom photographs (Haedrich & Rowe, 1977; Rice *et al.*, 1979) have encouraged attempts to improve the quantitative interpretation of trawl catches, such as by acoustic tracking, odometer wheels, and cameras on trawls (Rice *et al.*, 1982), and by the more challenging but perhaps eventually more rewarding method of relating the estimated odour dispersion to the catch from baited traps (Desbruyères *et al.*, 1985; Rowe, Sibuet & Vangriesheim, 1986; Sainte-Marie & Hargrave, 1987). Density is estimated from the rates of appearance of the organism in relation to the estimated odour plume (Fig. 7.8). Such methods are in their infancy, estimates being heavily dependent on accurate knowledge of vertical eddy diffusivity and advection from bottom currents considered in relation to the M_2 tidal pulse. Amphipods, being the organisms first to arrive at bait, have the highest

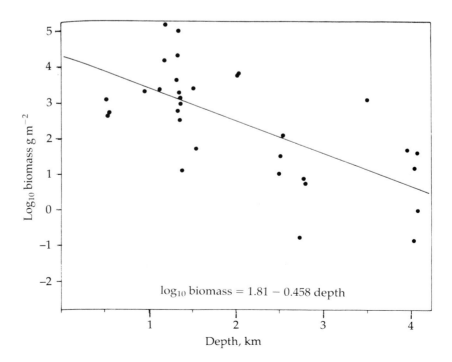

Fig. 7.7. Megabenthic standing crop in trawl hauls from the Porcupine Seabight plotted against depth. (From Lampitt *et al.*, 1986.)

$$\log_{10} \text{biomass} = 1.81 - 0.458 \text{ depth}$$

Log$_{10}$ biomass g m^{-2}

Depth, km

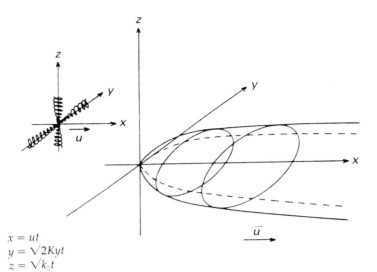

Fig. 7.8. Hypothetical domain of attractant produced from a carcase off the bottom according to a plume model. (From Rowe *et al.*, 1986.)

$$x = ut$$
$$y = \sqrt{2K_y t}$$
$$z = \sqrt{k_z t}$$

abundance, the mixed scavenging amphipod assemblage in the Demarara Abyssal Plain being estimated at 0.14–0.77 ind. 10^{-3} m²; about five times more than the estimate for a scavenging penaeid prawn. By means of this approach, the biomass of macrourids has been estimated at 24–29 kg ha^{-1} in the Bay of Biscay (Desbruyères *et al.*, 1985).

BIOMASS TRENDS FOR MEIOFAUNA

For the meiofauna, the data available on densities seem to show trends similar to the nutrient-dependent relationships shown by macrofauna (Thiel, 1975, 1979*a*; Shirayama, 1983). Although comparisons of meiofaunal and macrofaunal abundance from the same sampling programme are still few, they indicate that meiofaunal densities are roughly three or four orders of magnitude greater than for macrofauna (Shirayama, 1983; Sibuet *et al.*, 1984; Snider *et al.*, 1984; Rutgers van der Loeff & Lavaleye, 1986; Richardson & Young, 1987). Thiel's (1979*a*) claim that meiofaunal densities decrease more slowly with increasing depth than those of macrofauna, was not confirmed by Shirayama (1983) (Fig. 7.9). Pfannkuche (1985) found that meiofaunal densities decreased most rapidly between 0.5 and 1.5 km; from 2 to 4 km depth standing crop decreased only slightly. Both this and studies made in the bathyal Coral Sea Plateau off N.W. Australia (Alongi & Pichon, 1988) indicated that this depth-related decrease in metazoan meiofaunal biomass is significantly correlated to rate of detrital input. Concurrent measurements of meiofaunal biomass with those of near-bed flux of organic carbon and nitrogen are few, but indicate a highly significant positive relationship (Sibuet *et al.*, 1984; Rowe & Deming, 1985; Tietjen *et al.*, 1989); the work of Tietjen *et al.* (1989) indicating the importance of near-bed lateral transport of organic material to the benthic community, probably as nepheloids.

Other workers have used the quantity of sediment-bound chloroplastic

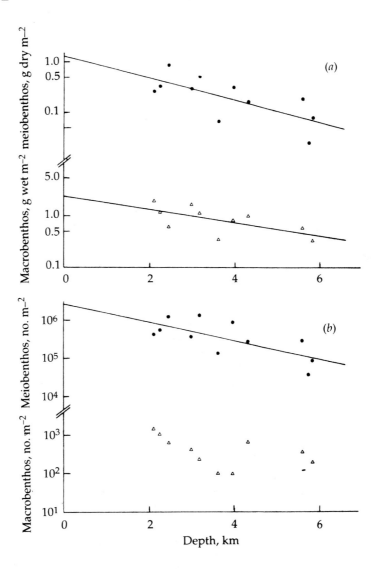

Fig. 7.9. Biomass (*a*) and standing crop (*b*) of meio- and macrobenthos in relation to depth in the western Pacific. The differences in slope of the regressions for each of the two size classes are not significant. (From Shirayama, 1983.)

pigments as an indirect indicator of rate of phytodetrital input. This was positively correlated with meiofaunal density at two sites in the N.E. Atlantic (Fig. 7.10) and in the Mediterranean (Soertaert & Heip, 1989). In the Coral Sea, as appears to be the case elsewhere in the deep sea, foraminifers and other protozoans *increase* in biomass with depth down the continental slope indicating they are better suited to exploit oligo-trophic conditions and hence dominate the food webs of the deep sea (Alongi, 1987).

Although meiofaunal nematodes show a decreasing size with increas-ing depth, they tend to be bigger deeper down in the sediment. However, this possibly reflects the greater motility of the larger sized animals allowing them to penetrate the more compact deeper sediment layers.

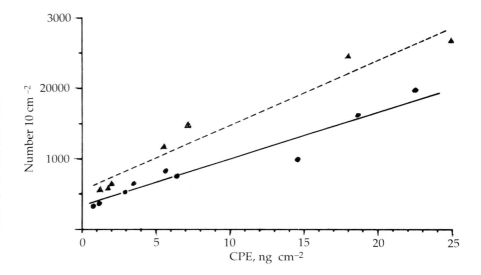

Fig. 7.10. Relationship between meiofaunal density and sediment-bound chloroplastic pigment equivalents (CPE) in the N.E. Atlantic in the Porcupine Seabight (filled circles and continuous line, regression: $y = 320 + 66.5x$, $r = 0.963$) and 35° N off N.W. Africa (filled triangles and pecked line, regression: $y = 555 + 91.3x$, $r = 0.967$). (From Pfannkuche *et al.*, 1983

A contrasting distribution of biomass is shown in shallow-water benthos, where biomass is skewed towards larger size categories (Mare, 1942; Jones, 1956; Fenchel, 1978; Schwinghamer, 1981, 1983).

SIZE STRUCTURE

The remarks in the previous section showing an increasing proportional role of animals of meiofaunal size in total benthic biomass has been ascribed to a trend towards decrease in average size of individuals of 'macrofaunal' taxa. Their size in oligotrophic areas of the deep sea has become '. . . so small that they are all of meiofaunal size' (Hessler, 1974). This idea seemed to be supported by the steeper slopes of regressions of biomass, compared to abundance, against depth in the Gulf of Mexico and off Peru (Rowe & Menzel, 1971; Rowe, 1971*a*). This apparent shift towards smaller organism size led Thiel (1975) to define the deep sea as a 'small organism habitat', and, partly in order to stimulate further investigation, made the proposition that 'With increasing depth and decreasing food concentration small organisms gain importance in total community metabolism'. We shall examine this notion in the light both of the occurrence of gigantism of certain taxa and, with respect to more recent data, consider it in relation to theoretical implications of organism size. Does both miniaturization and gigantism occur amongst deep sea fauna?

H. N. Moseley (1880) observed from the results of the 'Challenger' expedition that, while certain organisms appeared to be dwarfed by conditions of life in the deep sea, others attain 'gigantic proportions'. The well-documented occurrence of gigantism amongst certain taxa, such as scavenging amphipods, some isopods, and caridean shrimps such as *Acanthephyra*, particularly in oligotrophic areas, suggest that food limitation will by no means always lead to a dwarfed fauna. A concept that gigantism was linked to the metabolic effects of great hydrostatic pressure was developed in the late 1950s (Birstein, 1957). While this was expressed mainly by various crustacean taxa (Wolff, 1956a,b, 1962; Jones, 1969), examples have also been cited from other groups such as the giant hydroid *Branchiocerianthus* (see Chapter 4) and the isopod *Munnopsis* (Chapter 5). Such gigantism also has been linked to retarded sexual maturity and indeterminate growth (Wolff, 1962). While accepting that incidences of increased size occur, Madsen (1961b) concluded there is an overall trend to dwarfing related to food scarcity; body size having no relationship to hydrostatic pressure. This seems to be supported by the large body size of the exotic fauna found around hydrothermal vents (see Chapter 15). For the mainly megafaunal echinoderms and decapods trawled from the New England Slope, no such depth-related decrease in body size is evident; but for the benthopelagic fish in these and other trawl hauls from this area (Fig. 7.11) a positive ('bigger deeper') relationship of *increasing* body weight with depth is evident (Wenner & Musick, 1977; Polloni et al., 1979). However, this relationship appears to be much less well developed off Newfoundland (Snelgrove & Haedrich, 1987). Furthermore, macrofaunal samples collected along the New England transect, too, failed to show any depth-related trend in biomass when standardized to mean individual weight. Polloni et al. (1979) argued that the differing slopes of biomass and abundance regressions, against depth are subject to bias, such as the result of small sample size, which might exaggerate the importance of smaller, more numerous sizes as overall density decreases with increasing depth (reducing the chances of finding rarer, large organisms). They concluded that, notwithstanding a drop in

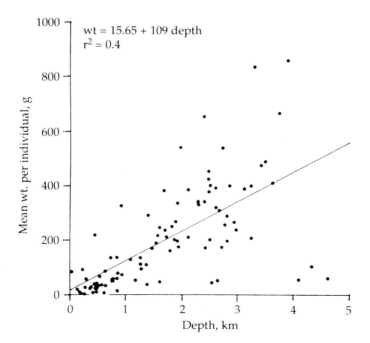

Fig. 7.11. Mean weight of benthopelagic fishes in relation to depth in the N.W. Atlantic. (From Polloni et al., 1979.)

food concentration of almost two orders of magnitude, there is no significant decline in mean macrofaunal organism size from 0.4–4 km depth. However, these findings do not deny a demonstrably much greater mean size of inshore macrobenthos (Gage, 1978).

For the meiobenthos, median size decreases with depth. This is ascribed to limited food availability with depth causing a rapid decrease in, mostly relatively large-sized, forms of meiofauna living in the surface layer of sediment (non-interstitial forms) whilst deeper living forms seem unaffected (Shirayama, 1983). Although the latter author found this relationship was reversed amongst nematodes both Pfannkuche (1985) and Soetaert & Heip (1989) found an increasing number of nematodes in the smaller size fractions with increasing depth. As for megafauna, a shallower slope in the rate of decline of megafaunal abundance versus biomass with depth reflects a decline in mean body weight with increasing depth (Lampitt et al., 1986). However, this decrease reflects changes in taxonomic composition.

Findings of both gigantism and dwarfism among deep-sea fauna might seem mutually exclusive in searching for a possible global influence. Clearly, there is no directly depth-related causation for small (or large) organism size, and Jumars & Gallagher (1982) remark that its causes remain open to speculation concerning both physiological and ecological mechanisms. In addition to possible causes for gigantism based on indeterminate growth and retardation in maturity, explanations in terms of adaptation to an optimal foraging strategy appear most attractive. Large size, as in scavenging amphipods, has been related to the need for high motility in locating sparsely dispersed food.

The presence of both relatively large, epifaunal 'vacuum cleaner' deposit feeders, exemplified by elasipod holothurians, and the dwarfed size of macrofaunal taxa, exemplified by tiny protobranchs such as *Microgloma*, has been related to intense natural selection towards divergent responses to scarcity in labile food particles in deep-sea sediment. On the one hand the large, but watery bodies of deposit-feeding holothurians, allow a greater gut volume (higher gut : body volume ratio), and hence longer gut residence times in order to allow more complete digestion with the help of gut bacteria (perhaps particularly of the more refractory organics) than could be achieved by an animal of meiofaunal size (Jumars et al., 1990). On the other hand, the body miniaturization of macrofaunal taxa permits the animal to select particles of greatest nutritional value on an individual basis. In fact these small animals may verge on macrophagy, where each potential food particle encountered is evaluated before ingestion (see Chapter 11 for further discussion of deposit feeding). However, in benthic biota, especially for infaunal species, size spectra in size classes of benthic biota are thought to be constrained by the physical characteristics of the sediment (Schwinghamer, 1981, 1983), or by life-history strategies of dominant taxa (Warwick, 1984). According to Schwinghamer's model, the three peaks on the biomass size spectrum are related to optimal sizes for three predominating lifestyles. Although only limited data have been analysed (Fig. 7.12), the model seems equally valid

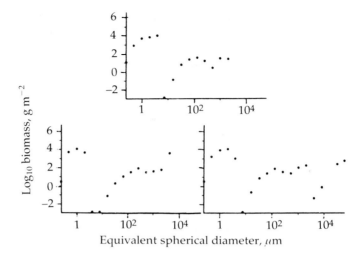

Fig. 7.12. Size spectra of organisms sampled by 0.25 m² box-corer from three positions on the abyssal plain off New England (depth range 4.5–5.85 km). (From Schwinghamer, 1985.)

in the deep-sea sediment community (Schwinghamer, 1985). The first peak at around 1 μm is related to microbiota attached to sediment particles; the second at 125–250 μm to the interstitial meiofauna; the third comprising the whole of the macrofauna that utilize the sediment as an integral unit. Although corresponding spectra for the larger size classes are lacking, the existence of a fourth peak at an equivalent spherical diameter from about 20 mm upwards is indicated by the size spectrum (Fig. 7.13) of organisms caught in trawlings with a fishing mesh of 4.5 mm (Lampitt et al., 1986). This confirms intuition in regarding the megafauna as a distinct functional group along with the micro-, meio- and macrofauna. The expression of these constraints is indicated by the low biomass values in the intervening troughs between peaks in the biomass-size spectrum. In some sediments these are separated by several orders of magnitude in biomass of size classes expressed in octaves (base 2 logarithms).

DETERMINANTS OF SIZE STRUCTURE

What can explain the existence at the supra-interstitial level (macro- and megafauna) of two opposing trends in the deep sea? On the one hand, towards the body-size miniaturization seen mainly amongst the deposit-feeding macrofauna; and on the other towards gigantism seen mainly amongst opportunist megafaunal scavengers (although also including some deposit and suspension feeders such as aspidochirote and elasipod holothurians, scalpellid barnacles and sorberacean tunicates). Clearly, these two peaks, and the intervening trough, representing these two functional groups on size-class spectra imply powerful polarizing pressures towards macrofaunal dwarfs and megafaunal giants.

In his stimulating book on the ecological implications of body size, Peters (1983) argues that, assuming equality of biomass amongst size classes, that the relative *importance* (in terms of rates of energy flow per unit of biomass) of individual animals and size classes declines with

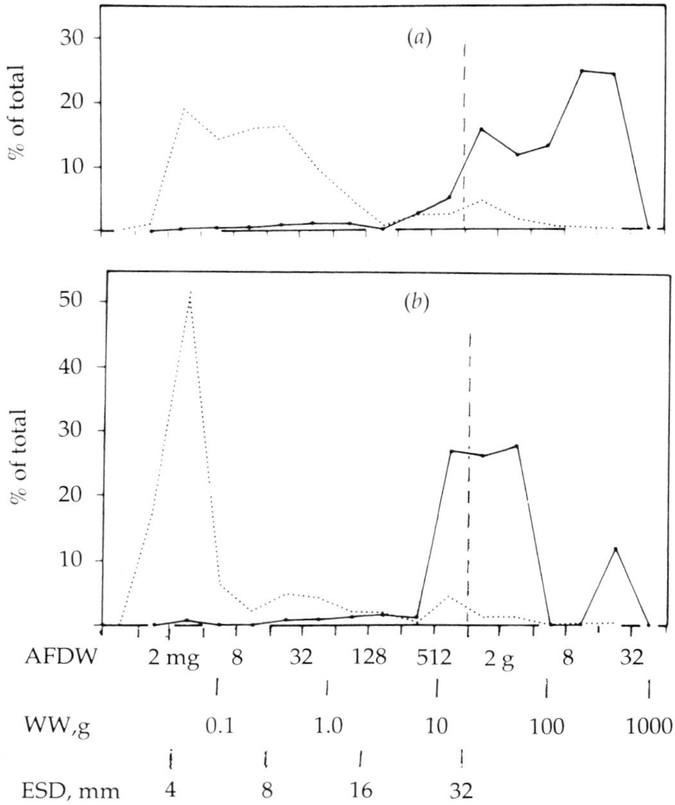

Fig. 7.13. Distribution of megafaunal biomass (ash-free dry weight, AFDW) and abundance, as percentage of total haul in trawlings from Porcupine Seabight, N.E. Atlantic. Pecked line at 1 g AFDW represents boundary between 'small' and 'large' species, allocated to size categories on mean weight of species in haul. Wet weight (WW) and equivalent spherical diameter (ESD) calculated using WW conversion factor of 17.5 × AFDW and specific gravity of wet specimens = 1. (From Lampitt *et al.*, 1986.)

increasing size; hence community processes will be dominated by smaller species, despite rough equivalence in standing crop. He points out that shifts in peaks in community size spectra to smaller animals affects mass specific rates, such as productivity/biomass ratios. Let us assume that the relationship of energy flow relations of deep-sea biota can be estimated fairly accurately (as they can from other ecosystems) from data on population density and individual body mass. Then such ratios would be expected to *increase* with decreasing body size. Given that the deep-sea ecosystem, like any other, supports only that amount of animal biomass that can be balanced from inputs from primary production and metabolic demands, then a shift to mean smaller body size implies that the total community biomass must be reduced. Communities dominated by smaller animals must, he claims, process energy and nutrients more rapidly and, hence, show more dramatic spatial and temporal changes in population size. Whilst lower biomass certainly applies to the deep-sea ecosystem, the latter assumption is contrary to the expectation, admittedly based as much on opinion than fact, of exceptionally *low* rates in secondary production in the deep sea. Although our knowledge of rates of secondary production are scant; it seems intuitively unlikely that these rates are any *faster*, as implied by Peters' model, in the deep sea than in the shallow-water benthic community where animal size, at least for the macrofauna, is larger.

Conversely, Brown & Maurer (1986) argue from analysis of the relationship of population density to body mass in several land taxa and communities, that several ecological advantages enable *larger* species (and larger individuals within species) to monopolize resources; this contradicting Peters' expectation that species of small body size use at least as large a proportion of resources within ecosystems as their larger relatives. Many terrestrial studies have demonstrated several advantages of bigger body size, and large size could enable scavenging amphipods or fish, for example, to maintain a wide foraging range to locate rare food-falls. Similarly, increasing size enables a deposit-feeding epifaunal holothurian to forage over a wide area; to have a larger gut capacity for bulk processing of sediment and to spend less energy per unit biomass on body maintenance and hence become more efficient at extracting usable energy from low-quality foods. Consequently, the same amount of available energy supports a greater biomass of a large species than of a small one. Large size has also been explained as an 'escape' from predation risk, an argument that is particularly applicable to a slow-moving epifaunal detrivore.

Why then, have large species not dominated the resource allocation in the deep sea? In situations where resources are particularly scarce, as in the most impoverished areas of the deep sea, perhaps the answer lies in the need for intraspecific encounters to ensure sexual reproduction. Amongst slow-moving deposit feeders, this necessitates a minimal density that can only be achieved by reduced body size (Rex, 1973; Gage, 1978). Certainly, large-bodied detritivores seem to be absent from the most oligotrophic bottoms; in these communities the large-bodied fauna seem to be either highly motile scavenging opportunists or predators.

The existence in these oligotrophic abyssal areas of suspension-feeders such as hexactinellid and demospongid sponges, and relatively large bodied agglutinating rhizopod protozoans such as komokiaceans and xenophyophores, might seem paradoxical. Lipps & Hickman (1982) suggest that such animals that build elaborate skeletal structures are 'caloric dwarfs' and can become abundant because they contain relatively little tissue or protoplasm, have slow growth rates and low metabolic requirements.

8
The diversity gradient

From the days of the 'Challenger' expedition, biological oceanographers had relied on intuition that the extreme physical conditions and impoverished nutritional input could be tolerated only by a small number of specialized forms of life. This concept was overturned in the 1960s after examination of bottom samples obtained by Howard Sanders and Robert Hessler at the Woods Hole Oceanographic Institution using the fine-meshed epibenthic sled (see Chapter 5) uncovered an astonishing richness in species of the smaller animals dwelling in the deep-sea sediments (Hessler & Sanders, 1967; Sanders & Hessler, 1969). These workers showed that the trend of decreasing diversity with increasing depth in species caught in relatively coarse meshed deep-sea trawls was an artefact resulting from the decreased density of individual animals and the small number of samples taken at great depths.

Also, such high species richness had not been predicted by theoretical ecologists. Environments that are seemingly spatial and temporally uniform, with few and low-grade nutritional sources, were thought to tend towards an equilibrium with just a few competing species (Hutchinson, 1953). We shall examine the literature that has attempted to explain this apparent anomaly. But first we must define the concept so that its measurement becomes tractable.

MEASUREMENT OF DIVERSITY

The term *diversity* is commonly used as a synonym for species richness, the number of *species* present in the community. The number of species may be expressed in terms of number of species within some higher taxon, usually the genus in order to provide information on the extent, and perhaps rate, of evolutionary radiation. However, diversity is usually simply quantified in terms of the total number of species occurring within the community, and estimated in terms of samples from that community. Leaving aside this and the taxonomic problem of deciding what constitutes a species in the deep sea (see Chapter 10), diversity is very difficult to quantify from samples. One reason for this is that the individuals and taxa may be patchily dispersed on the bottom at varying scales (see Chapter 6). Although the sampling swath of sled samplers might be thought to be less affected by at least small-scale patchiness, they are less efficient than box-corers at recovering the total fauna present (see Chapter 3), but the latter will be most affected by any decimetre pattern present.

The other reason why diversity is difficult to quantify from samples is because the numbers of species present in them depends not only on the number of organisms present in the community but also on the numerical distribution of these individuals amongst these species. A limited sample of n individuals from a community in which the population is divided amongst the S species will appear very much richer in species than that in a sample of the same number of individuals from another community in which n is very *un*evenly spread amongst the same number of species, i.e. in which one or a few species are markedly numerically dominant. Thus the concept of species diversity incorporates both the *number* of species (species richness) in the total community and the degree of *evenness* with which the individuals are distributed amongst these species, or 'dominance diversity' (Pielou, 1969, 1977; Peet, 1974).

Two methods have been widely used to estimate diversity in samples from the deep-sea community:

(a) Shannon-Weiner information function This expresses the information content, H, per individual in the sample:

$$H' = - \sum_{i=1}^{S} p_i \log p_i$$

where p is the fraction comprised by species i in the sample. The degree of Evenness, J, in the relative abundances of the species in the sample is expressed as $J' = H'/H'_{max}$.

(b) Rarefaction curves These avoid statistical shortcomings of such single-value estimators (which have unsatisfactory sampling properties that can result in biased estimates, see Bowman *et al.*, 1969, and W. Smith & Grassle, 1977). Most deep-sea workers have employed Hurlbert's (1971) expression, derived from the hypergeometric distribution, where the expected number of species in a random sample of animals taken at random, without replacement, from the community, is calculated as:

$$E(S_n) = \sum_{i=1}^{S} \left[1 - \frac{\dbinom{N-N_i}{n}}{\dbinom{N}{n}} \right], \qquad \text{for } n \leq N$$

where, $E(S_n)$ = number of species expected in a sample of n individuals taken from the community; where N = total number of individuals in the community; S = total number of species in the community; N_i = number of individuals of the ith species in that sample, and n = number of individuals in the hypothetical sample for which the number of species is estimated. An arithmetic plot, or 'rarefaction', of $E(S_n)$ versus n (Fig. 8.1) plots as a curvilinear interpolation from the actual number of species S observed in the sample of n individuals. (Actually, the interpolating procedure originally employed by Sanders (1968) slightly overestimates species richness, see Hurlbert, 1971; Simberloff, 1972.) Assuming that the proportion of the fauna comprised by each species is independent of location and is free to vary stochastically, then unbiased rarefactions of $E(S_n)$ can be derived from a set of contiguous individuals, such as in a box-core, or a summed set of these. Various methods of deriving confidence limits of $E(S_n)$ have been described (W. Smith & Grassle, 1977; Tipper, 1979; W. Smith, Grassle & Kravitz, 1979a; G. D. F. Wilson, 1987, unpublished data).

The evenness component of diversity expresses the rate at which the rarefaction curve approaches the asymptote. Counter-intuitively, curves generated from samples numerically dominated by a few species show a less steep rate of climb than those in which abundances are more evenly spread amongst the species (Fig. 8.1). In fact *Evenness* (or Dominance Diversity) is an important and useful parameter as it is recognized as responsive to *disturbance* (defined as any population-reducing effect) of the community (Platt & Lambshead, 1985; Lambshead & Platt, 1988). Evenness may be expressed as a plot of the cumulative contributions made by the species to total abundance, or as a ranking of the percentage abundance of species from the most to the least common, the so-called dominance diversity curves (Lambshead, Platt & Shaw, 1983; Shaw, Lambshead & Platt, 1983; R. G. Hughes, 1986). Another approach is the Ewen-Caswell 'neutral model'; this sensitive method is relatively sample-size dependent and generates a species-abundance distribution for a sample of given N and S assuming no interaction or competitive advantage between species (Caswell, 1976). Evenness is expressed as its deviation from this theoretical evenness.

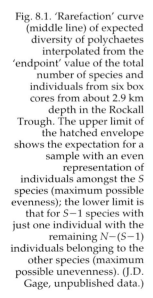

Fig. 8.1. 'Rarefaction' curve (middle line) of expected diversity of polychaetes interpolated from the 'endpoint' value of the total number of species and individuals from six box cores from about 2.9 km depth in the Rockall Trough. The upper limit of the hatched envelope shows the expectation for a sample with an even representation of individuals amongst the S species (maximum possible evenness); the lower limit is that for $S-1$ species with just one individual with the remaining $N-(S-1)$ individuals belonging to the other species (maximum possible unevenness). (J.D. Gage, unpublished data.)

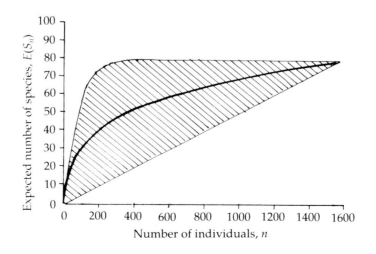

HOW MANY SPECIES ARE THERE?

The few data sets available from the deep sea that one might think are large enough to provide an answer to this question, fail to yield rarefaction, or species-area, curves that even approach the asymptote, i.e. where additional species will no longer be discovered by additional sampling. The largest body of good quantitative data was obtained during the early 1980s from the Atlantic slope off the United States. In 554 box-core samples (each of 900 cm^2) taken between 32° and 41° latitude N at depths down to 3 km, nearly 1600 different macrobenthic invertebrates were identified. Table 5.1 provides a breakdown of this metazoan diversity at one of these sites. At this site where 233 box-cores were taken along a 176-km long transect at 2.1 km depth, 798 infaunal species from 14 invertebrate phyla were found (Blake *et al.*, 1987; Maciolek *et al.*, 1987*a,b*; Grassle & Maciolek, unpublished). The rarefaction curves, or plots of species versus increasing area sampled, from these stations (Fig. 8.2) continue to rise steadily, as more samples are collected, the number of species recorded increases at a rate of about 25 m^{-2} suggesting that many more species are present in the community than have yet been sampled. Furthermore, in common with quantitative data from other deep-sea areas, no single species comprises more than 8% of the total individuals. The number of species increases along a depth contour more slowly than *across* depth contours. Albeit extrapolations to estimate the total number of species present from curves of expected numbers of species in samples from one area will grossly underestimate the real number present. The relative abundances of macrofauna shows a quite constant pattern in quantitative samples from the deep sea (Fig. 8.3); but these, nevertheless,

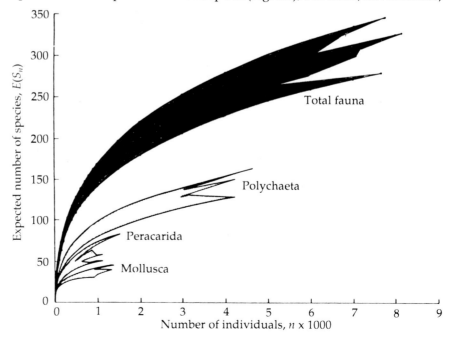

Fig. 8.2. Rarefaction curves (range only shown) of species richness amongst metazoan macrofauna off New England from 168 box-cores taken at approx. 2.1 km depth. (Modified from Maciolek *et al.*, 1987*b*.)

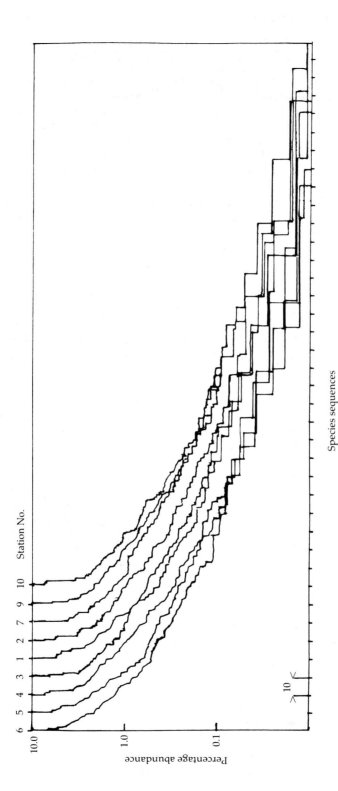

Fig. 8.3. Species abundance relationships amongst macrofauna in ten box-cores from the data shown in Fig. 8.2. The percentage abundance of species are ranked from the most common (left) to the least common (right) as species sequences. The nine stations are ordered by position along a transect along the 2.1 km depth contour. The intervals of 10 on the baseline are numbers of species. Each station has a curve representing a roughly similar distribution of individuals among species. (Modified from Grassle & Maciolek, unpublished observations.)

can only be fitted to the extreme right-hand tail of a lognormal distribution – which has been commonly employed in shallow-water studies as a theoretical model of the relationship of the number of species to individuals (R. G. Hughes, 1986). Hence, the lognormal is not very helpful in predicting the total pool of species present because the mode of the fitted distribution still lies well to left of the observed data, which then represents only one extreme tail of the distribution – even from 168 pooled box-cores! On the, still undemonstrated, assumption that the lognormal provides a reasonable fit, then 11 800 species are present in the particular community sampled at 2.1 km depth, while the deep sea as a whole '. . . probably contains millions of species' (Grassle & Maciolek, unpublished). As more of the deep-sea floor is sampled, the more its animal diversity seems to rival that of the richest terrestrial environments, the tropical rain forest (Grassle, Maciolek & Blake, 1990).

IS DIVERSITY SIMILAR IN DIFFERENT AREAS OF THE DEEP SEA?

As far as can be determined from the limited sampling so far undertaken, there is little similarity between species richness of deep-sea communities inhabiting different ocean basins. Rarefaction curves based on comparable data sets from the central N. Pacific indicate higher species richness

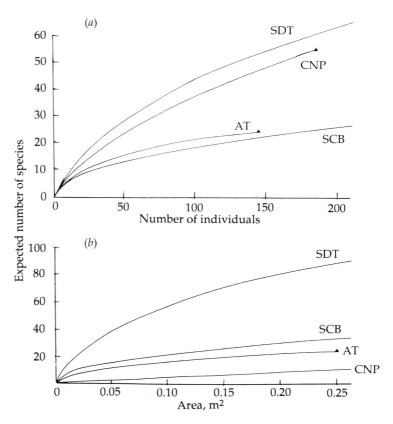

Fig. 8.4. Rarefaction curves for expected species diversity plotted against numbers of individuals (*a*) and area (*b*) for polychaete macrofauna in box cores from the San Diego Trough (SDT), Santa Catalina Basin (SCB), Central N. Pacific (CNP), and the Aleutian Trench (AT). (From Jumars & Hessler, 1976.)

than along the Gay Head–Bermuda Transect (Hessler, 1974; Hessler & Jumars, 1974). Even areas which are geographically close, may show wide differences in diversity. For example, box-cores from the bathyal San Diego Trough provided 314 species compared with only 162 species in the same number of box-cores from the nearby Santa Catalina Basin off California (Fig. 8.4), probably as a result of reduced oxygen levels (Jumars, 1976). Similarly, reduced diversity as a result of low oxygen conditions occurs on the continental slope under areas of upwelling and high surface productivity, such as Walvis Bay, S.W. Africa (Sanders, 1969). Physical stress, such as the catastrophic effect of sediment slumps and slides, as a result of the tectonic instability of trenches may explain why there are fewer species present there than on the adjacent abyssal plain (Fig. 8.4) (Jumars & Hessler, 1976).

Geologically recent geographic isolation may, however, explain the depressed richness in the Norwegian/Arctic and Mediterranean Seas. These are separated from the N. Atlantic by shallow sills, and their faunas share few species in common with the N. Atlantic. A similarly depressed diversity is found in the Sea of Japan and in the Red Sea whose faunas have developed recently in virtual isolation from those in the deep sea of the Pacific and Indian Oceans.

IS THERE A CONSTANT DOWNSLOPE GRADIENT IN RICHNESS?

Sanders & Hessler's (1969) results from samples taken with the anchor dredge and epibenthic sledge showed that the diversity of polychaetes and bivalves increased at depths below the continental shelf to levels comparable to those found on shallow tropical soft bottoms. Rex (1973, 1976) subsequently found that the diversity of gastropod molluscs in

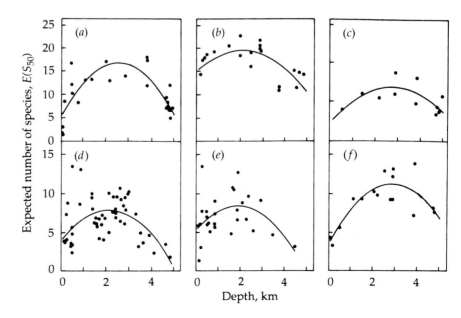

Fig. 8.5. Bathymetric patterns of expected species diversity. The points are values of the number of species expected in a random sample of 50 individuals, $E(S_{50})$ (a) gastropods; (b) polychaetes; (c) protobanch bivalves; (d) cumaceans; (e) invertebrate megafauna; (f) fish megafauna. The parabolas are regressions using a function of the form $Y = a + b.X^2$. (From Rex, 1981.)

these hauls also increased from the shelf down the slope but *decreased* with increasing distance out on to the abyssal plain (Fig. 8.5(*a*)). On the basis of a roughly similar pattern with polychaetes, cumaceans and bivalves (Fig. 8.5(*b*)–(*d*)), Rex (1981, 1983) claimed that this 'parabolic' response of species richness to the depth gradient applies to all macrofaunal taxa. Although in the extensive box-core sampling on the Atlantic slope of the U.S.A., richness is highest at 3 km depth off Cape Lookout, macrofaunal diversity was found to be highest at mid-slope depths (1.2–1.6 km) at two more northerly sites on the Atlantic margin of U.S.A. (Blake *et al.*, 1987; Maciolek *et al.*, 1987*a,b*). However, results from trawlings of megafaunal invertebrates and fish from the N.W. Atlantic (Fig. 8.5(*e*),(*f*)) also seem to show that maximum richness occurs at mid-slope depths rather than on the continental rise (Haedrich, Rowe & Polloni, 1980; Rex, 1981, 1983; Rowe, Polloni & Haedrich, 1982), and this is supported by results from the N.E. Atlantic (Sibuet, 1977; Paterson, Lambshead & Sibuet, 1985). But at 5–6 km depth in the central N. Pacific, macrofaunal diversity seems even higher than at bathyal depths (Fig. 8.4) (Hessler & Jumars, 1974).

However, it remains unclear to what extent these conclusions are affected by declining faunal density with depth (see Chapter 7) which will necessitate a commensurate increase in sampling effort at greater depths. Grassle (1989) found, from comparison of 'species density', plotted as the number of species against the density of individuals obtained from quantitative sampling from several different deep-sea localities, a remarkable *similarity* in richness at depths of 2.7–4.9 km (Fig. 8.6). Depressed richness was, however, shown up in sediments affected by hydrothermal activity (see Chapter 15).

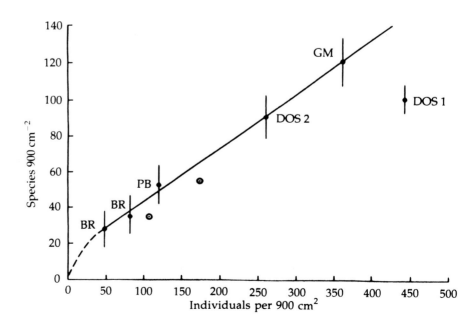

Fig. 8.6. Total numbers of species of metazoan macrofauna plotted against total numbers of individuals per 900 cm² from quantitative sampling on the same station, showing a linear relationship regardless of depth or location of sampling area (labels). DOS 1 is located in 1.8 km depth and DOS 2 in 3.9 km depth, both South of New England (N.W. Atlantic); BR refers to two sites on the northeast Bermuda Rise (4.6 and 4.9 km depth); PB is located in the Panama Basin at 3.9 km depth; GM is located at 2.7 km depth near the Galapagos Islands. (From Grassle, 1989.)

Decreased richness does seem to be a feature of deep ocean trenches (Jumars & Hessler, 1976; Filatova & Vinogradova, 1974; Vinogradova *et al.*, 1974; Belyaev & Mironov, 1977; Vinogradova, Zezina & Levenstein, 1978*b*; Shin, 1984).

EVENNESS IN DEEP-SEA SAMPLES

There are few data available on the distribution of relative abundance in samples from deep-sea communities. Using both past data sets, and the results of the extensive box-core sampling off New Jersey, Grassle & Maciolek (unpublished data) showed that the single most common species comprises only 7–8% of the total individuals, whilst the abundances of the next most abundant species makes up a quickly declining share of the total community. Amongst the vast majority of remaining species, 28% occur only once and nearly 11% only twice.

Grassle & Maciolek observed that the variance in occurrence between samples is high amongst the most common species, some of which are known to increase in response to disturbance. This suggests how, as in shallow water, the relative evenness of samples may reflect disturbance. In fact the least even samples of macrofauna in the deep sea have come from the HEBBLE area which is frequently disturbed by sediment eroding benthic storms, and from samples from echiuran faecal mounds. In these situations the most abundant species makes up 50–67% of the total community (Thistle *et al.*, 1985; C. R. Smith *et al.*, 1986).

PROCESSES IN FAUNAL DIVERSIFICATION

The question why there are so many species present in the deep sea has exercised many minds but the large literature on the subject, more often than not, reflects *opinion* based on inadequate or non-existent data. Because of the lack of consensus, we need to examine this thinking in some detail. We will conclude with recent thinking implicating the importance of disturbance.

LONG-TERM, EVOLUTIONARY AND SHORT-TERM, ECOLOGICAL MAINTENANCE COMPONENTS OF DIVERSITY

Discussion on deep-sea diversity has often confused phenomena on both evolutionary and ecological time scales, i.e. long-term or evolutionary diversity and the short-term processes maintaining diversity within the community. For a complete understanding of the species richness of biological communities as local assemblages of organisms, it is important to consider a *balance* of these two aspects. The former lead to processes of species formation, or speciation, and geographic dispersal (topics that we shall examine later in Chapter 10), against the latter processes, perhaps involving competitive exclusion, predation and stochastic variation, which may promote local extinction (Ricklefs, 1987). In other words, any complete explanation of high deep-sea diversity must look not only for influences of the physical or local biotic interactions in controlling the numbers of actually coexisting species, but also for the regional and historical processes which determine the number of species potentially able to be present in the community. These processes include unique events, such as those resulting from climatic change, and circumstances such as habitat area and geographic isolation, that will also profoundly influence local community structure. The water-transported availability of dispersal stages may well reduce the effect of physical isolating mechanisms in speciation, and the 'openness' of this environment (*sensu* Roughgarden, Iwasa & Baxter, 1985; Roughgarden, 1986) might well be important in the large numbers of rare species which contribute so greatly to local diversity in the deep sea (Grassle & Maciolek, unpublished).

Theories on the *maintenance* of high deep-sea benthic diversity have fallen into two groups: (*a*) explanations that stress *equilibrium* processes, such as resource or habitat partitioning, where adaptationally 'fine-tuned' species co-exist at densities near the carrying capacity of the environment, and (*b*) *disequilibrium* explanations which invoke local disturbance to produce a patchy habitat supporting populations at an early growth phase below carrying capacity, allowing species to persist without competitively excluding each other.

EQUILIBRIUM EXPLANATIONS

STABILITY–TIME HYPOTHESIS

Ideas of resource partitioning acting in concert with climatic stability as diversity controls in the deep sea were developed by Howard Sanders at Woods Hole Oceanographic Institution. In his classic comparative study of marine benthic diversity, Sanders (1968) suggested that physical stability in the deep-ocean environment has allowed extreme adaptational specialization to develop on the evolutionary time-scale amongst potentially competing species so that competitive interactions are minimized. The theory obtained support from a positive relationship between species diversity and perceived environmental stability on geological time-scales in soft sediments in a wide range of marine and fresh-water soft-bottom areas. Environmental stability leads to the development of a highly diverse community maintained by refined competitive interactions, or 'biological accommodation'. By contrast, when conditions are less predictable, physiological stress will favour tolerance to a wide range of physical conditions and hence prevent the high diversity resulting from evolutionary divergence into separate niches. This idea was later developed in terms of high diversity expressed in the degree of partitioning of trophic resources as a response to high stability in food resources: the most oligotrophic regimes in the deep sea should have higher diversity than more eutrophic areas, as species have to become evermore specialized in order to acquire sufficient food (Valentine, 1973). This seemed to be supported by the apparently higher species richness found amongst the macrobenthic taxa in the central N. Pacific than on the continental slope (Hessler, 1974). In the context of peracarids, such as isopods, Hessler & Thistle (1975) related this to morphological, behavioural and physiological adaptations to low food availability.

Chapter 2 shows that the deep sea can no longer be conceived as the physically stable and predictable environment previously assumed. Energetic boundary currents and the occurrence of benthic storms, which periodically erode, transport and re-deposit sediment, some occurring far out on the abyssal plain, are major sources of disturbance for the benthic community (J. Y. Aller, 1989). Furthermore, on the continental shelf, surface productivity may be high but subject to intense blooms that extend on to the upper slope, where they may lead to local extinctions amongst benthic detritus eaters (Margalef, 1969; Rex, 1976). Are the communities in these areas, which are known to experience frequent sediment-eroding disturbances, less diverse than those on more tranquil bottoms? Data provide conflicting support. On the one hand, the diversity of the harpacticoid copepods at the high-energy HEBBLE site does not seem to differ from the San Diego Trough, although abundances in samples taken as a storm ended were significantly lower than during an interlude between storms suggesting that the harpacticoid populations are affected by such disturbances (Thistle, 1983a, 1988). On the other hand, both agglutinated foraminifers, polychaetes and bivalves are considerably less diverse (Kaminski, 1985; Thistle et al., 1985).

Significantly, the high species dominance characteristic of disturbed, low-diversity inshore areas (Lambshead, Platt & Shaw, 1983) is evident at the HEBBLE site, one polychaete, *Paedampharete acutiseries,* making up 50–64% of the metazoan fauna.

At the *evolutionary* level, Abele & Walters (1979) pointed out that the much greater area of the deep sea would promote diversification simply because of the reduced chances of complete extinction of broadly distributed species, leading to the large numbers of rare species which characteristically contribute so much to local species richness (Osman & Whitlach, 1978). From the geological perspective, stability *or* habitat area may be important in regulating diversity: the fossil record shows steplike increases in diversity of offshore shelf benthic habitats while that inshore has remained constant. But, whether this difference is related to area, habitat heterogeneity, stability, or a combination of the three remains obscure (Bambach, 1977). Certainly, data on morphological evolution in plankton in the Atlantic suggest this is more rapid in low latitudes despite the smaller overall habitat areas there, implying that the more stable regime favours proliferation of new morphologies (Stehli et al., 1972). On the other hand, Haedrich (1985) found only a negative relationship between numbers of benthic megafauna and available habitat area on the continental slope and rise off New England. However, this relationship becomes positive if prey availability (expressed as infaunal macrobenthic biomass) is taken into account as well as habitat area, with numbers of megafaunal species at lower slope depths plotting above the regression, fitting in with the observations that species maxima occur at intermediate depths (see above).

Most other theories are concerned only with the processes involved in *maintenance* of high diversity in the deep sea.

HABITAT HETEROGENEITY

This approach sees spatial heterogeneity as more important than dietary specialization in the resource partitioning mechanisms leading to faunal diversification (Jumars, 1975b, 1976; Jumars & Gallagher, 1982; Jumars & Eckman, 1983). The highly developed, tiered complexity of the tropical rain forest, or the structural intricacy of a coral reef, results from biotic structure, and seems to have a first-order relationship to the rich diversity of fauna found in these habitats. From analysis of spatial segregation and concordance of spatial pattern of individuals with identifiable habitat

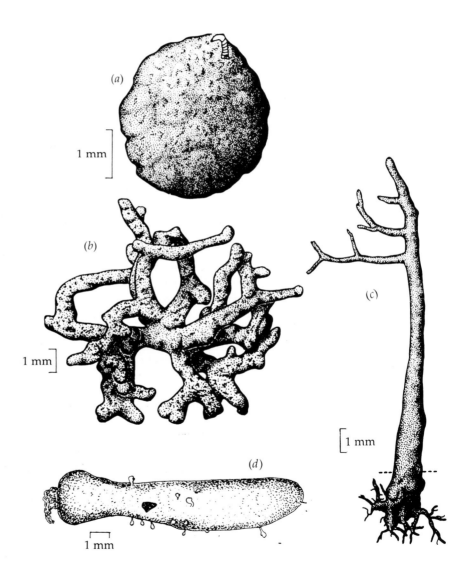

Fig. 8.7. Biogenic structures from the San Diego Trough thought to play a role in maintaining high species richness by providing habitat heterogeneity for small benthic animals: (a) empty sediment-agglutinated test of foraminifer *Orictoderma* sp. occupied by polychaete *Tharyx monilaris*; (b) reticular tubed ?xenophyophore; (c) bush-like 'rooted' ?xenophyophore. (d) faecal pellet-like structure 'fouled' with several small attached bryozoans and a single, triangular agglutinated foraminifer (other examples of such associations are illustrated in Figs 4.34, 4.48, 5.32(b) and 5.33(a), (b), (c). ((a)–(c) from Thistle, 1979a; (d) from Jumars, 1976.)

landmarks in the deep-sea sediment (see Chapter 14), much of this heterogeneity appears to be at the scale of the 'ambit' (sphere of influence) of individual organisms (Jumars, 1975b, 1976; Thistle, 1979b, 1983b). It includes such small-scale biogenic features as animal tubes, burrows or branching tests of agglutinating Foraminifera shown in Fig. 8.7.

In shallow water one would expect rapid obliteration of such effects as burrows and surface traces of an organism on its local environment from the physically energetic conditions and high rates of physical disturbance. Below the shelf-slope break, physical energy levels and rates of biological activity decrease so that the effects on their local environment persist long enough to provide distinct microhabitat patches. Such patches would, by isolating potential competitors and perhaps by providing refuges from predators, buffer against competitive exclusion and reduce the risk of extinction by predation, thereby leading to higher diversity (Menge & Sutherland, 1976). Hence, the sediment stability existing in the deep sea may permit microhabitat exploitation through either highly refined specialization or non-equilibrium processes (see below), or both. Jumars (1975b) cited as an example the apparent exclusion of a paraonid worm by cirratulid mudballs (discussed in Chapter 6) which may prevent the paraonid from feeding properly. Other examples cited by Thistle (1979b) and Jumars (1976) are shown in Fig. 8.7. Thistle & Eckman (1990) later investigated the importance of such structures as sources of patchiness by placing mudball 'mimics' on the bottom using the submersible 'Alvin' in order to see whether copepod species were, as previously shown from core samples, more abundant around mudballs than elsewhere (Thistle & Eckman, 1988). The results indicated two of the species to use the mudball as a habitat while a third used it as a refuge from predation.

Further examples are provided by agglutinated and komokiacean foraminiferans and xenophyophores, along with the tests of calcareous foraminiferans, which, as discussed in Chapters 4 and 5, have been found to provide refuge habitats for other Foraminifera and a wide variety of metazoans (Gooday, 1983, 1984; Gooday & Haynes, 1983; Gooday & Cooke, 1984). The latter are mostly sipunculans, but also include nematodes, polychaetes, various peracarid crustaceans, along with epizooic hydroids and ctenostomatous Bryozoa (Figs 4.34, 4.48, 5.34). To what extent such associations are obligatory is unknown, although a facultative relationship seems most likely; however, the abundance of such foraminifera or xenophyophore 'hosts' in bottom samples suggests that they make an important contribution to small-scale spatial structure in the sediment (Bernstein et al., 1978; Gooday, 1984). Furthermore, the positive concordance in distributions of living and dead individuals of certain foraminifers, suggests the patch structure may persist for several generations (Bernstein & Meador, 1979).

The biologically generated habitat heterogeneity found in the quiet areas investigated by Jumars, seems to be absent where deep seabeds are subjected to dynamic current regimes (Lonsdale & Hollister, 1979; Tucholke et al., 1985), but is present on the less energetic adjacent areas

(Swift, Hollister & Chandler, 1985). Can such conditions provide a test for the model in maintaining high diversity in the deep-sea sediments? There are again conflicting data. Although the association between organism-generated habitat heterogeneity and harpacticoid copepod distributions apparent in the relatively tranquil San Diego Trough was absent at the highly energetic HEBBLE site, this is not reflected in any difference in copepod diversity (Thistle, 1983b). On the other hand, the declining macrofaunal and megafaunal diversity on the continental rise from its mid-slope peak may be consistent with the Habitat Heterogeneity model since erosive bottom-current energy and unpredictibility in physical conditions (as exemplified by the HEBBLE study area) would prevent persistence of habitat microstructure.

DISEQUILIBRIUM EXPLANATIONS

Jumars & Gallagher (1982) point out that whatever mechanism prevents competitive exclusion in promoting high diversification needs also to explain how a higher diversity is maintained in the deep sea than in shallow water. The stability–time hypothesis most explicitly addresses this question by proposing finer resource partitioning owing to refined biological interactions, but provides little explanation for a peak in diversity on the continental slope. Theories proposing a bathymetric gradient in disturbance perhaps provide the most parsimonious explanation for the typically humpbacked diversity curve with increasing depth.

BIOLOGICAL DISTURBANCE

This derives from theories of predator control in maintaining high diversity in terrestrial and intertidal communities (Paine, 1966; Paine & Vadas, 1969; Harper, 1969; Connell, 1970; Dayton, 1971). Dayton & Hessler (1972) argued that widespread *disturbance* in the deep sea results from predation by large epibenthic and benthopelagic 'croppers', and by macrofauna cropping meiofauna. Disturbance would serve to depress abundances of competitors, so that resources would rarely be limiting, thus minimizing competitive interactions to allow co-existence of species sharing the same resources. The process will foster, not the highly specialized niches predicted by equilibrium theories, but a generalist lifestyle where diets are broad and overlapping. These include the large motile croppers such as benthopelagic fish whose diet will be broad and opportunistic (Haedrich & Henderson, 1974; Sedberry & Musick, 1978; Mauchline & J. D. M. Gordon, 1986), relying on sparse but unpredictable food items and carrion. They also include the larger epibenthic deposit feeders, such as elasipodid holothurians (such as those shown in Fig. 8.8), whose 'vacuum cleaning' strategy will ingest the superfical sediment along with its inhabitants. Clearly, such a mechanism operating to maintain high *short-term, disequilibrium* diversity cannot be extrapolated to large-scale differences which may owe more to *long-term*, or *evolutionary* processes, such as relative stability, age or area (Levinton, 1982).

Does the intensity of competition actually vary inversely with predation pressure? Amongst gastropods, numerical dominance, especially amongst deposit feeders, is most evident on the shelf and on the abyssal plain; there being a more even distribution of relative abundance at intermediate depths, perhaps because competition is countered by predation (Rex, 1973, 1976). Also, species-per-genus ratios (normalized to a common number of species) are lowest on the shelf, increase to a maximum on the continental rise, and decline again in the abyss (Fig. 8.9), suggesting that competitive displacement is least at intermediate depths (Rex & Warén, 1981; Rex, 1981, 1983). In shallow water, high frequencies of shell repair have been associated with co-evolved predator/prey relationships where snails have evolved shell architecture to deter potentially lethal predation. While such shell scars are common in the deep sea, they show no clear trend with depth. Additionally, since the likely predators of gastropods show generalist feeding strategies, such co-evolved relationships seem less developed in the deep sea than in shallow water (Vale & Rex, 1988).

Furthermore, a depth-related trend in competitive displacement does not explain the higher macrobenthic diversity observed in the oligotrophic central N. Pacific compared to the slope or to more eutrophic abyssal areas (Hessler, 1974). In the low-productivity mid-oceanic areas, far from

Fig. 8.8. Dense 'herd' of the elasipodid holothurian *Scotoplanes globosa* photographed from the bathyscaphe 'Trieste' on the floor of the San Diego Trough (*c* 1.2 km depth). Also visible (e.g. middle foreground) are specimens of the epifaunal brittle star *Ophiophthalmus normani*. It was from the indiscriminate sediment swallowing activity of such megafauna as *Scotoplanes* that the idea arose of constant cropping of macrofauna within the sediment which permits co-existence of many more potential competitors than would be supported in an undisturbed community. (From Barham *et al.*, 1967.)

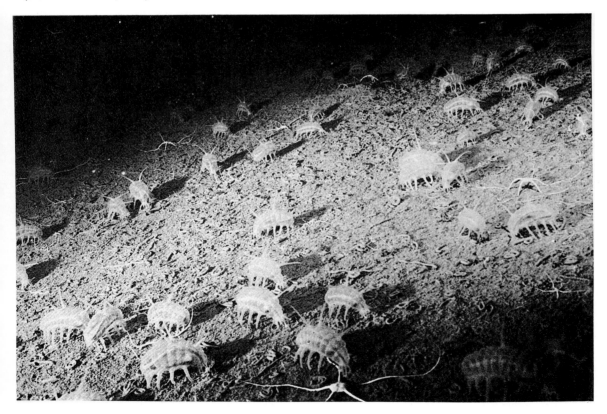

land, predatory species such as megafaunal croppers generally are absent presumably because the energetic cost of locating prey at such low densities precludes this lifestyle; the few potentially predatory species have adopted, trophically generalistic, scavenging and highly motile lifestyles (Hessler & Jumars, 1974).

With regard to the importance of habitat heterogeneity, Jumars & Gallagher (1982) argue that dietary generalism merely reflects food scarcity in the deep sea rather than being a corollary of disturbance-mediated disequilibrium. Furthermore, in these circumstances, the expectation would be greater habitat, rather than dietary, specialization. Undersaturation of habitat by competitors will result in *more* food being available to individuals, and hence encourage dietary specialization rather than the reverse predicted by disturbance.

Clearly, the implications of the habitat heterogeneity model conflict with those of disturbance which would claim that niche-partitioning opportunities are very limited in the homogeneity of the deep-sea sediment. Such persistent microscale patch structure is also inconsistent with the pervasive disturbance caused by non-selective megafaunal cropping which might be expected to result in patchiness at a larger scale.

Grassle & Sanders (1973) pointed out that, in such a heavily cropped community, the population structure of prey species should be dominated by younger stages. The limited data at their disposal suggested typical deep-sea life-history tactics of low fecundity, low rates of recruitment and growth, and high survivorship, seemingly inconsistent with biological disturbance. More recent studies (see Part IV) suggest that the life-history tactics and rate processes associated with deep-sea organisms are closer to those of shallow-water organisms than had previously been thought. More convincingly, Grassle & Sanders re-asserted the importance of competitive interactions, but argued that niche differentiation extended beyond diet. The physical stability might permit microhabitat specialization with local disturbances leading to a mosaic of successional

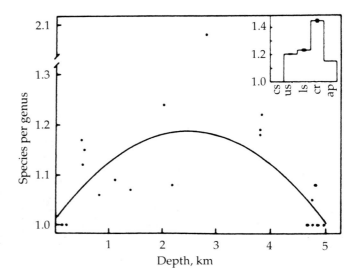

Fig. 8.9. Species-per-genus (S/G) ratios estimated as averages of 1000 random samples of $E(S_{68})$ individuals from whole samples, plotted against depth in the N.W. Atlantic. In fitting the curve, the topmost point is omitted. Inset shows expected S/G ratios for the continental shelf (cs), upper slope (us), lower slope (ls), and continental rise (cr) when their size is reduced to that of the abyssal plain (ap) having 23 species; each regional fauna representing the combined listings of the $E(S_{68})$ most abundant species found in stations occurring within the regions. (From Rex, 1983.)

stages, with certain species being adapted, perhaps to an early stage in succession, so that the high diversity could be maintained as a process of 'contemporaneous disequilibrium'.

The microscale pattern implied in the theory of Habitat Heterogeneity approximates the size and duration of the lifespans of individuals; and since the community is so diverse, stochasticity in the spatial pattern of organisms will be reflected in such interactions. The death or removal of an organism (such as a foraminiferan or harpacticoid copepod) by predation might create a gap disturbance by vacating its microhabitat, which might be occupied by a specimen of a different species: by reducing competition this will help to maintain diversity by co-existence through contemporaneous disequilibrium (Bernstein *et al.*, 1978; Thistle, 1979*b*; Rex, 1981). However, while a concept of microscale patches may be consistent with the idea of a temporal mosaic, there is no need to imply any deterministic successional sequence (Rex, 1981). As we shall see below, results from deep-sea recolonization experiments can be interpreted more easily as a stochastic process than as a deterministic succession.

INTERMEDIATE DISTURBANCE HYPOTHESIS

It has become recognized in recent years that the frequency of natural disturbance and rate of environmental change in tropical rainforests and coral reefs are often much faster than the rates of recovery from perturbations, so preventing the reaching of equilibrium. In the deep sea the equivalent of tropical storms which perturb rainforests and coral reefs might range from massive sediment resuspension resulting from sediment slumps or benthic storms, to small-scale lacunae resulting from deposit feeding or bioturbation. The previous discussion of non-equilibrium processes in diversification has assumed the same holds for the deep sea. Connell (1978) suggested that in tropical forests and coral reefs the highest diversity is maintained at *intermediate* scales of disturbance, resulting in a typical bell-shaped response of species richness along gradients of either predator intensity or disturbance frequency (Fig. 8.10);

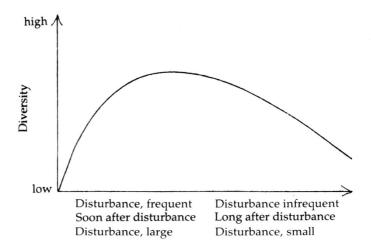

Fig. 8.10. 'Intermediate disturbance' hypothesis. (From Connell, 1978.)

and this theory has general application to the deep sea. In terms of successional dynamics, lateral immigration of motile animals or settlement by larval propagules will soon follow creation of an open space in the community. Initially, diversity will be low because the time for recolonization is short; only those potential immigrants within range or species happening to be producing propagules and within dispersal range will colonize. If disturbances continue, only those species, such as opportunists, capable of rapid response will make up the community. As the interval between, or the area of intensity of, disturbanced increases, diversity will also increase since more time is available for immigration and larval colonization from the background community; new species, previously excluded by their lower powers of dispersal and slower growth, can now reach maturity. But, as the interval between disturbances increases further, diversity will *decline* because of competitive interactions and exclusion. Clearly, high population growth rates will accelerate approach to equilibrium while lower rates will permit coexistence for a longer period. By population growth rates we include both the growth in size of individuals and the increase in numbers of individuals (Huston, 1979). Opportunists will typically have high potential rates ('*r*-selected' species of MacArthur & E. O. Wilson, 1967), whilst species whose populations are better fitted to compete and avoid predation so that they can develop close to the carrying capacity of the habitat will have lower rates ('*K*-selected' species).

Diversity inevitably will be low where food is so limiting that some species are excluded because they cannot grow or maintain sufficiently dense populations to allow sexual interaction; but Huston's (1979) model predicts that diversity will be highest at low growth rates, decreasing with increasing *r*. A 'break point' is suggested at very low growth rates where but a slight increase in growth rate will result in a rapid increase in diversity. The comparatively low diversity for the abyss is postulated to result from long periods between disturbances that can still permit the community to approach competitive equilibrium despite low growth rates – and consequently low rates of displacement.

However, as mentioned previously, the richness of macrofaunal taxa in samples from the most oligotrophic abyssal areas provide no indication of the depressed diversity expected (Hessler, 1974; Hessler & Jumars, 1974; G. D. F. Wilson & Hessler, 1987a; G. D. F. Wilson, 1987). The compensatory effects described by Huston (1979) may provide an answer to this conundrum. Where low population growth rates are associated with extremely low densities of individuals, competitive interactions will rarely have the opportunity to be expressed, hence permitting longer coexistence amongst competitors. This can be expected to apply more to the smaller, less motile or sessile animals than to the motile megafauna whose interactions are more frequent. It is also possible that differences in disturbance frequency arising from kinetic energy of mesoscale eddies transmitted to the benthic boundary (see Chapter 2) may apply to the ocean basins at different latitudes.

Although the potential for individuals to grow rapidly may not be so depressed in the deep sea as previously thought (see Chapter 13), growth and fecundity of deep-sea species probably remain low unless an unpredictable bonanza occurs so the population growth rate remains low and also densities of individuals remain low. Nevertheless, physical differences between deep sea and shallow water habitats may render both predation and competition more important in promoting diversification, i.e. make them less effective at eliminating deep-sea species.

The apparently bell-shaped curves in species richness down the depth gradient (Fig. 8.5) were cited by Huston (1979) to support his theory. High diversity is maintained on the continental rise and lower slope because rates of displacement are low and the approach to equilibrium is interrupted by the moderately high levels of predation disturbance found there (Fig. 8.11). A higher rate of population growth on the upper slope (as a consequence of higher productivity) would render predation less effective in preventing approach to equilibrium despite the high numbers of predators present. Conversely, on the abyssal plain, rates of population reduction by predation may be too low to prevent the community from approaching equilibrium, despite the low rate of population growth as a result of sparse food resources (Rex, 1981). Certainly, gastropod diversity seems to be correlated with both organism density and predator diversity (Rex, 1976). Alleviation of competition at lower trophic levels permits higher diversity that, in turn, provides greater potential for competitive partitioning of prey resources amongst predators: snail predators become more efficient by becoming more specialized in their choice of prey. Because of the loss of energy in transfer from one trophic level to the next,

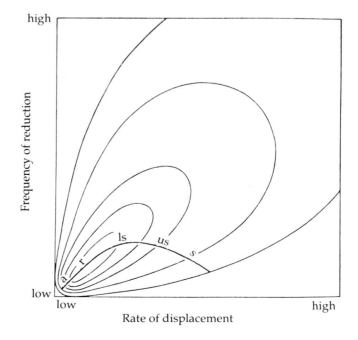

Fig. 8.11. Predictions of Huston's dynamic equilibrium model of species diversity for various combinations of the frequency (or magnitude) of population reduction and rate of competitive displacement. Contours show predicted diversity levels, with the highest values in the ellipsoid at bottom left. The curve plots the diversity expectation for rate of displacement and frequency of reduction from the shelf (s), upper slope (us), lower slope (ls) to the rise (r) and abyss (a). (Modified from Huston, 1979 and Rex, 1983.)

the number and relative biomass of intermediate levels in the pyramid is governed by the rate of production at the base. Hence, the diversifying feedback will be limited by this rate, and stability of primary production (since it affects the predictability of prey) which will ultimately limit the local expression of species diversity.

THE IMPORTANCE OF PATCH DYNAMICS

Ideas on the importance of patchiness in structuring deep-sea benthic communities have been developed by Fred Grassle at the Woods Hole Oceanographic Institution. This approach is derived from thinking related to spatial heterogeneity and disturbance (discussed above), but applied to a much smaller scale, and is related to the results from sediment-tray recolonization experiments (see below). In his approach to understanding deep-sea community structure, the kinds of colonizing species and the rates of population response at any particular area of the deep-sea bottom, are controlled by the kind of disturbance and the mosaic of background populations; this mosaic pattern being at least as important as the frequency of disturbance in maintaining high diversity (Grassle & Morse-Porteous, 1987; Grassle, Maciolek & Blake, 1990; Grassle & Maciolek, unpublished). Therefore, the important features of the deep-sea environment in maintaining high species richness are: (a) a patchiness in organic input against a background of low productivity; (b) sporadic, small-scale disturbance events occurring against a background of relatively constancy and (c) an 'open' marine system (*sensu* Roughgarden *et al.*, 1985) where there are no barriers to larval colonization over vast areas. Disequilibrium successional sequences seem to be as variable as the patches they are associated with. These may range from areas of complete or partial community reduction, perhaps resulting from various types and scales of predation, or bottom-current scour (Thistle *et al.*, 1985), to areas of local enrichment resulting from sources ranging, in turn, from large animal carcasses and macrophyte detritus to small patches of phytodetrital floc. They can also include biogenic structures ranging in size from biogenic microscale features (Fig. 8.7) to the large sediment casts and mounds resulting from bioturbation (e.g. C. R. Smith *et al.*, 1986) which themselves provide some organic enrichment. Each will become colonized by a unique subset of species resulting from random immigration and extinction in a naturally patchy environment (Osman & Whitlach, 1978), and particularly from randomness in availability of larvae derived from low-level, continuously or seasonally breeding, background populations. These will include opportunists which may normally exist at barely detectable background levels. Compared to terrestrial and shallow water habitats, these patches may be smaller and less common; but overall are more persistent owing to the much reduced rates of physical downgrading and burial from pelagic sedimentation. Certainly, the patches will be too rare to show up in random box-cores, yet are probably frequent enough to be evident in comparing trawl replicates.

TESTING NON-EQUILIBRIUM MODELS: EVIDENCE
FROM 'NATURAL' AND SEABED EXPERIMENTS

Evidence to test the relative importance of microhabitat specialization and contemporaneous disequilibrium in structuring deep-sea benthic communities faces several difficulties. What support is available from studies of spatial pattern and their concordance with the environmental landscape? Overall, the data (summarized in Chapter 6) show that although diversity-controlling processes can be identified at scales of 100 km to 10 cm, spatial segregation or discordance in species' abundances does not suggest that either a strong environmental mosaic or patch disturbance occurs at these scales. Rather, the evidence suggests that resources or habitat partitioning processes operate at scales of less than 0.01 m^2, and that the *environmental grain* recognized by the animal (either actively in terms of habitat selection or passively as a result of disturbance) approximates the microscale of its individual *ambit* (Jumars, 1976; Jumars & Eckman, 1983). However, there are formidable difficulties in identifying microhabitat heterogeneity in a remote environment which already presents problems in obtaining undamaged catches of organisms – let alone the fragile and transient phenomena associated with the activities of single animals.

Let us consider the high-energy HEBBLE area as a natural experiment to test the role of physical downgrading. If the benthic community is as diverse as those of more placid conditions then, under Huston's (1979) model, they might be expected to differ markedly in terms of rate of displacement (population growth rate). Although harpacticoid copepod communities from these two areas appear to show similar diversity, the polychaete community is less diverse (D. Thistle, personal communication). The age structure of macrobenthic taxa, such as bivalves, are dominated by juvenile sizes (Thistle *et al.*, 1985) which would lie on the exponential part of the growth curve. This suggests that rate of displacement may overall indeed be higher in these HEBBLE populations.

RECOLONIZATION EXPERIMENTS

This approach aims to mimic the creation of unpopulated patches created by disturbance on the deep-sea bed. These experiments, first conducted by biologists of the Woods Hole Oceanographic Institution on the continental margin off New England, have provided the first direct data on the role of non-equilibrium processes in controlling diversity and community structure.

Trays, each measuring 50 × 50 cm containing a 10-cm depth of deep-sea sediment (defaunated by freezing and thawing), were placed on the ocean floor at 1.76 km depth by the submersible 'Alvin' and recovered 2 or 26 months later after closure of a hinged lid (Grassle, 1977). Since this early experiment, various technical improvements have been made resulting in the development of Recolonization Tray Free Vehicles. These consist of a fibreglass framework, buoyed by glass spheres, but which sinks to the bottom when weighted by detachable ballast. The framework supports six polyethylene sediment trays ($30 \times 30 \times 7.5$ cm deep) covered by a fibreglass lid (Fig. 8.12(*a*)). The experiment is retrieved by acoustic command from the ship which actuates release of the ballast and automatic closure of the sediment-tray lids before the trays rise to the surface. The most recent modification to this design (Fig. 8.12(*b*)) incorporates a single circular sediment tray that fits flush into a streamlined surround designed to minimize alteration of flow characteristics over the experiment (Maciolek *et al.*, 1987*b*). (This is an important consideration when trying to simulate natural conditions for larval settlement from the boundary-layer plankton.) Another free-vehicle sediment tray design has been developed by French workers (Fig. 8.12(*c*)). In this apparatus the frame supports a rotating disc, each with four small 314 cm^2 chambers, which provide a total surface area of 0.5 m^2 (Desbruyères *et al.*, 1980).

The special faunas which colonize wood have been studied by simply setting out artificial 'wood islands' on the ocean floor which are either recovered by submersible or as a free vehicle.

With the addition of organic material to the tray sediment, the experiments have provided information on the significance of patchy organic inputs against a background of low productivity (Grassle, 1977; Levin & C. R. Smith, 1984; C. R. Smith, 1985*a*, 1986; Grassle & Morse-Porteous, 1987). These experiments in the N.W. Atlantic and others conducted off southern California have lasted from 2–59 months. The results (summarized in Table 8.1) show a greatly reduced rate of colonization by macrofau-

Table 8.1. *Deep-sea colonization on macrofauna using sediment trays (C. R. Smith & Hessler, 1987)*

Location	Depth (km)	Area (cm^2)	Deployment time (months)	Type of sediment
Northwest Atlantic	1.8	2500	2–26	Azoic indigenous sediment, caged and uncaged
				Glass beads with fish meal, caged
Northwest Atlantic	3.64	2500	2–59	Azoic indigenous sediment, and uncaged
				Glass beads with fish meal, caged and uncaged
				Indigenous sediment (untreated)
Northeast Atlantic	2.16	314	6–11	Azoic indigenous sediment
				Azoic shelf sediment
Northeast Atlantic	4.15	314	6–11	Azoic indigenous sediment
				Glass beads
				Glass beads enriched with bacteria, phytoplankton, or corn-meal agar
Eastern Pacific	1.3	2500	5	Azoic indigenous sediment
				Azoic indigenous sediment with ground kelp

Fig. 8.12. Sediment Tray Free Vehicles (STFVs); all consist of trays of experimental sediment that are exposed for varying lengths of time for natural colonization by fauna, and sealed prior to recovery to the surface by release systems operated by acoustic command (ac). (*a*) STFV (upper is side view; lower, plan) designed at the Woods Hole Oceanographic Institution: the array of six fibreglass sediment trays (st), each measuring 30 × 40 × 7.5 cm deep, with a fibreglass lid (li) to seal the trays before and after exposure on the seabed. During descent, the weight of the lid covers the trays which are then lifted clear of the mudbox when it bottoms as the guide rods (gr) are forced up (as shown in the drawing). On acoustic command from the ship the release (re) is unhooked from the expendable ballast (ew) allowing the buoyancy spheres (bs) to lift the trays to meet the lid, which seals the edge of each sediment tray with a silicone rubber gasket (ga). (*b*) Shows an improved design for minimizing hydrodynamic effects that possibly bias recolonization of the mudboxes shown in (*a*). This is achieved by a single circular sediment tray located in the centre of a large disc which slopes smoothly down at the sides; other labelling: lt, flashing light and radio beacon to aid recovery at the surface. (*c*) Rotating recolonization tray designed by IFREMER, Brest, with four small chambers in each rotating disc (only three are shown to improve clarity). The inset shows the sequence (I–III) where the spring-loaded (sp) disc is first allowed to rotate a quarter turn by corrosion of a (*continued*)

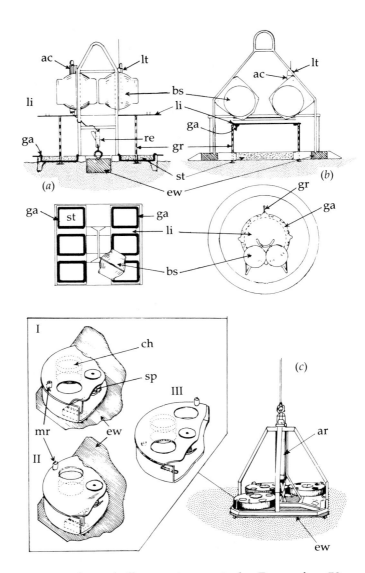

nal taxa compared to shallow water controls. Even after 59 months, neither the population densities nor the species richness matched those of the natural community (Grassle, 1977; Levin & C. R. Smith, 1984; Grassle & Morse-Porteous, 1987). The low rates of colonization seem surprisingly constant with varying substrata and depths (Fig. 8.13), but there were considerable variations in the species colonizing with no obvious seasonal effect (time of year of deployment or recovery). These colonists often are uncommon in the background community, the tray communities apparently still converging to natural conditions, even after 5 years! Certain species, mostly spionid, paraonid, capitellid and sigalionid polychaetes, brittle stars and myriotrochid holothurians, showed the most rapid increase in numbers, particularly after organic enrichment of

Fig. 8.12. *Continued*
magnesium release (mr)
which exposes (II) the
previously sealed (I)
chambers; the final quarter
turn sealing each chamber
again (III) being actuated by
release of the expendable
weight (ew) by the acoustic
release (ar) under command
from the ship. ((a) and (b)
modified from Maciolek *et
al.*, 1986; (c) modified from
Desbruyères *et al.*, 1980.)

the tray. The enrichment was by adding ground-up fish to artificial sediments of glass beads of similar particle size to natural sediment. In the unenriched trays, the colonization was usually by moderately, but not markedly, opportunistic, species; there was no overwhelming dominance by particular species, and the number of species present roughly showed a simple linear relationship to number of individuals present. However, amongst the early colonists were species of genera well known as opportunists in shallow water, such as the polychaetes *Capitella* and *Ophryotrocha* which were particularly abundant in the artificially enriched trays. Interestingly, high densities of *Ophryotrocha* were detected in some of Grassle's control box-cores which were naturally enriched with decomposing *Sargassum* lying on the seabed. This indicates that such opportunistic elements might sometimes lead the successional sequence of

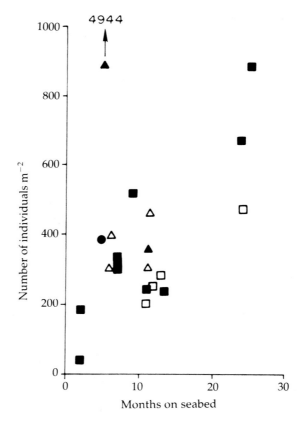

Fig. 8.13. Numerical density of animals in colonization trays, initially defaunated by freezing and thawing, and deployed for varying periods on the deep seabed from: 2.16 km in the N.E. Atlantic (closed triangles) with background macrofaunal densities of *c.* 2800 m^{-2}; 4.15 km in the N.E. Atlantic (open triangles) with background density of *c.* 3600 m^{-2}; 1.8 km depth in the N.W. Atlantic (closed squares) with background densities of *c.* 4900 m^{-2}; 3.64 km in the N.W. Atlantic (open squares) with background densities of *c.* 2900 m^{-2}; 1.3 km in the E. Pacific (closed circles) with background densities of *c.* 4100 m^{-2}. (From C. R. Smith & Hessler, 1987.)

recolonization in such patches with some organic enrichment in the deep sea, as assumed by non-equilibrium models; but there is, in general, a lack of any deterministic successional sequence in unenriched patches in soft-bottom communities (C. R. Smith & Hessler, 1987). Variability may also result from seasonal breeding of certain species with pelagic larvae (see Chapter 13) whose recruitment to the experimental sediment may only occur during limited periods.

In sediment trays screened with mesh to exclude predators there were sharp increases in some species particularly some of the more opportunistic species. This indicated that predation pressure may well play a role in regulating community structure. However, there was no evidence of one or more species gaining a monopoly of resources as a result of predation as might be predicted by Biological Disturbance.

Similar experiments undertaken in the Bay of Biscay, in which a variety of natural and artificial sediments were used (composed of either glass beads enriched with various organic material or agar), generally showed the same slow recolonization by macrofauna, meiofauna and microbiota (Desbruyères, Bervas & Khripounoff, 1980; Desbruyères et al., 1985). However, one deployment showed much higher rates of colonization dominated by the polychaetes *Prionospio* sp., *Ophryotrocha puerilis* and *Ophryotrocha* sp. (Desbruyères et al., 1980). However, this occurred when current-transported flocculent organic detritus was found in the experimental sediment, suggesting that the experimental sediment must possess or acquire the trophic conditions favourable for colonizing species. (Desbruyères et al., 1985). These results therefore are comparable to the differences seen in colonization pattern between enriched and unenriched conditions detected by Grassle & Morse-Porteous (1987).

Overall, the sediment trays provide little hint of the competitive interactions, or exclusion of species, that are assumed to be so important in Huston's (1979) model. However, such competition might be more important in ephemeral patches of organic enrichment where the very low diversity and high dominance by opportunists does suggest that competitive replacement, typical of successional dynamics, occurs (Grassle & Morse-Porteous, 1987).

NATURAL ORGANIC PATCHINESS

It is easy to see how falls of organic material, which besides macroalgae may include phytodetritus, seagrass, wood and carcases of large nektonic animals, might constitute important sources of organic heterogeneity in the deep sea. Such landmarks assume added importance with the decline in sedimentation of zooplankton faecal pellets and phytodetrital aggregates in more oligotrophic areas. Small nekton falls are rapidly consumed by scavengers (see Chapter 4) but seem to be of very rare occurrence. The even rarer larger falls (e.g. whole carcases) may persist much longer because they oversaturate the density of the community to process such a massive input. At bathyal depths these have been shown to produce a low-intensity disturbance of the natural bottom community by resus-

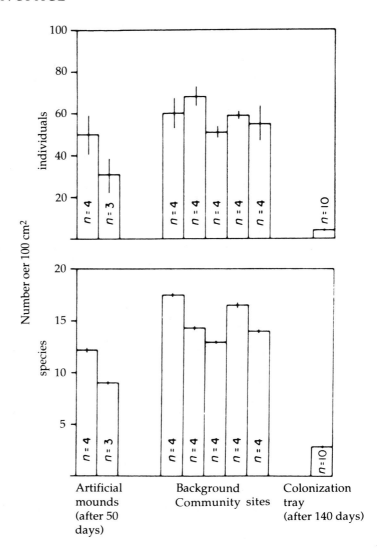

Fig. 8.14. Mean (± standard error) abundance (a) and species richness (b) of macrofauna from replicate 100 cm² core samples (n = number of samples) collected from two artificial mounds (left), five locations in the background community away from natural mounds (middle) and a colonization tray of pre-frozen sediment placed on the seabed for 140 days (right). The artificial mounds (10 cm high, 45 cm diameter, composed of subsurface sediment without macrofauna) simulated natural echiuran mounds at the 1.24 km study site in the eastern Pacific. (From C. R. Smith & Hessler, 1987.)

pending sediment, this reducing infaunal diversity and abundance. Unlike the sediment-tray experiments, there seems to be rapid colonization by *post*larval stages of background community dominants, such as a paraonid *Levinsenia* and the cirratulid *Chaetozone*, along with a 'rare' cumacean *Cumella*, indicating that these components of the infauna can rapidly exploit disequilibrium conditions (C. R. Smith, 1986). Pieces of waterlogged wood are more common near continental margins with big rivers and narrow shelves (see Chapter 11) and must be sufficiently abundant in order to maintain viable populations of deep-sea wood borers which are able to colonize rapidly (Turner, 1973, 1977). Such resources are too rare to detect by normal sampling, and yet overall are common enough to maintain stocks of rare specialist species which would otherwise be absent in the 'open' conditions of the deep-sea benthic environment.

Bioturbation by larger infauna (see Chapter 14) may provide a more frequent source of fine-scale disturbance which affects smaller infaunal benthos, and probably is also associated with some level of organic enrichment (Mauviel et al., 1987). In the Santa Catalina Basin, large sediment mounds generated by the 'convective' bioturbation of large burrowing worms are quickly recolonized by macrofauna (C. R. Smith et al., 1986). Artificial mounds excavated nearby by the submersible 'Alvin' were rapidly recolonized and within 50 days already contained 52–85% of the macrofaunal abundance and species richness of background community levels (Fig. 8.14). Sediment mixing is known to enhance microbial activity (Kristensen & Blackburn, 1987), so the rapid response was possibly associated with a local increase in organic availability. It remains unclear whether colonization of the new mound is by larval recruitment or immigration from surrounding sediment.

The seasonal deposition and subsequent resuspension of phytodetritus (Billett et al., 1983; Lampitt, 1985a; Rice et al., 1986) might also profitably be considered as a source of both temporal and spatial patchiness. Such material tends to collect in topographic lows (Lampitt, 1985a) and in relict burrow openings on the seabed (J. Y. Aller & R. C. Aller, 1986) either as it sediments or is moved around by near-bottom currents. The development of cyanobacteria-feeding foraminiferan populations on this floc (Gooday, 1988) suggests that the local enrichment in feeding conditions resulting from such phytodetrital patches may contribute to a successional mosaic (Gooday & Turley, 1990).

Community structure in samples from the high-energy HEBBLE area shows striking resemblance to the subadult or juvenile-dominated age structure of sediment-tray colonists (Thistle et al., 1985). The occasional episodes of erosive bottom currents during benthic storms constantly create defaunated patches, with enhanced microbial biomass that can be considered as local enrichment, that are colonized by meio- and macrofauna that take advantage of the increased microbial food availability to reach peak abundances during the quieter depositional periods between storms (J. Y. Aller, 1989). Similar physical disturbances also create faunally depauperate patches in energetic inshore sediments (Eagle, 1975). They may lead to a mosaic of patches being formed in which the patches are at different successional stages, hence a high diversity of smaller taxa may be maintained in these physically unstable and unpredictable conditions.

The disparity in recolonization rates between sediment tray experiments and more 'natural' disturbance, such as artificial mounds and food falls, has been discussed by C. R. Smith (1985b). Experiments in the intertidal showed that recolonization to 'plugs' of sediment raised off the bottom bears little resemblance to that in plugs set flush with the sediment, and where fauna accumulated at much faster rates, indicate that models of benthic infaunal colonization rates based on sediment-tray data may be heavily biased (C. R. Smith & Brumsickle, 1989).

CONCLUSIONS

We here depart from our usual practice in leaving the, possibly confused, reader to choose between conflicting explanations by making some general observations.

Clearly no one body of theory has been adequately tested either by direct observation or by artificial recolonization experiments. While the significance of competitive displacement implicit in non-equilibrium models is not easily tested, results from recolonization experiments indicate that competitive interactions are not as important as often imagined. Yet competitive interactions form a basic assumption of what we might call the *disequilibrium paradigm*. In futher investigation of the ideas of Grassle relating to disturbance, recolonization and patch dynamics, it will be important to resolve the disparity in colonization rates apparent between sediment trays and more 'natural' experiments monitoring patch dynamics, such as those of C. R. Smith and his co-workers. Such experiments remain technically difficult in the deep sea. Opportunities in the shape of natural disturbance of different sorts will present themselves as our knowledge of such perturbation improves with long-term monitoring of the deep ocean bed. Large-scale disturbance experiments to assess impacts of manganese nodule mining (see Chapter 16) also promise to provide valuable data. It is clear that any experiment will need to address the full range in type, scale, and persistence of such patch heterogeneity and hence certainly involve much effort and expense. Yet such an approach to understanding disequilibrium processes, along with a much improved understanding of the life history and population biology of individual species, promises to reward us with a far more certain understanding of processes involved in controlling deep-sea community structure.

9

Depth-related patterns in community composition

PATTERNS OF SPECIES REPLACEMENT WITH DEPTH

Since the time of the 'Challenger' Expedition it has been noticed that, whereas populations change almost imperceptibly over wide horizontal areas of the great ocean basins, their composition changes rapidly with depth down the continental margin. This represents part of one of the greatest environmental gradients on this planet: that related to the depth gradient on the sloping parts of the floor of the ocean. However, the causes of this pattern remain one of the most difficult and elusive problems faced by deep-sea ecologists. In contrast to the relative ease with which depth-related gradients in standing crop and in diversity can be measured as single variables (see Chapters 7 and 8), changes in species composition with increasing depth are much more difficult to parameterize, let alone explain. As pointed out in Part II which summarizes the deep-sea fauna, some (eurybathic) species have wide vertical distributions that extend from the abyss up to quite shallow water while other (stenobathic) species seem much more tightly zoned with respect to depth. Furthermore, there are few data on the depth-related distribution of the smaller animals.

MAJOR ZONES

Early studies related the major physiographical and hydrographical features of the continental margin to boundaries in major zones in the fauna down the depth gradient. The shelf break, which constitutes the major physiographical feature of the Earth's surface, marks the boundary between the shelf and the deep-sea fauna. In his classic *Les Profondeurs de la Mer* published in 1948 describing the deep-water faunal associations off western Europe, Edouard Le Danois was the first to clearly distinguish vertically zoned faunal associations that were subjectively related to physiography and sediment types found at different depths. He extended the concept of the 'mud-line' defined by John Murray (1895) as the upper limit for typical deep-sea conditions of soft, muddy bottom and faunal elements characteristic of such habitat, which off western Europe occurs at roughly 200 m depth just below the edge of the shelf. Elsewhere it may lie as deep as 500 m, or occur in a few metres depth close inshore in the fjord-like Scottish lochs. In Norway, the Sognefjorden, which exceeds 1.2 km in depth, despite its shallow sill, contains species characteristic of the deep sea below 1 km. Ekman (1953) suggested that the bathymetric boundary between hemipelagic (characterized by a high terrigenous mineral matter content, and reflecting offshore transport of organic material from shallow water) and pelagic sediments (where organic input is limited to that from the surface of the ocean), may constitute a less notional deeper zoogeographic boundary.

The classic synthesis on the *Zoogeography of the Sea* by Sven Ekman was published in 1953 (based on his original German text, *Tiergeographie des Meeres*, published in 1935). Ekman showed that it is impossible to define a universally applicable upper boundary for the deep-sea fauna. For example, the shelf off the Antarctic continent has been depressed by an ice cover much deeper than elsewhere, and there is no clear distinction between its fauna and that in deeper water (see Menzies *et al.*, 1973). Ekman described the trend, which he termed Equatorial Submergence, where many ubiquitous species which occur at bathyal or even abyssal depths at low latitudes, inhabit much shallower waters in the cold polar seas. This has been considered to be evidence for a long-standing view that colonization of the deep sea has been from polar seas, but also the deeply embedded, but still largely untested, view in the deep-sea literature of the overriding importance of temperature (Ekman, 1953; Bruun, 1956, 1957; Madsen, 1961b; Hansen, 1967), *vis-à-vis* of the hydrostatic pressure gradient (Knudsen, 1970), in determining bathymetric patterns in faunal zones.

Although there has been much variation in terminology, there is a prevailing concept of two major provinces, or depths zones. These are the slope or *bathyal* (or *archibenthal*) zone, a transitional fauna comprising species from both shallow and deep water, and the true deep-sea fauna characteristic of the *abyssal* zone; with latitudinally converging bathymetric limits towards low latitudes separating the two. Menzies *et al.* (1973), point out that there is greater faunal continuity between the shelf and slope faunas at high rather than at low latitudes. In turn, the bathyal fauna has greater faunistic continuity with the abyssal at *low* than at *high* latitudes: in the Antarctic it is barely distinguishable.

Deriving from Ekman (1953) a largely 'stenothermal' bathyal, or archibenthal, fauna is characteristic of the relatively stable regime existing below the depth of the seasonal thermocline. Ekman also identified the many, usually more 'eurythermal', elements which, although numerous, are sufficiently bathymetrically cosmopolitan to contribute little to faunistic characterization of vertical zones. Such species, although having their main centre of distribution on the slope, are those that may be found, as constituting 'archibenthal enclaves' in nearshore soft sediments (Ekman, 1953). The upper limit of the second, deeper zone was thought to lie roughly at 1 km, and extends on to the abyssal plain containing the abyssal fauna. Later authors have placed the upper limit of the abyssal fauna much deeper at depths varying from 1.8 to about 3 km depth, with either an intervening 'semiabyssal' zone (Le Danois, 1948) or a bathymetrically extended bathyal or archibenthal zone. The varying depth of the start of the true abyssal fauna is classically related to the temperature structure of the deep ocean, being placed roughly at the 4 °C isotherm (Bruun, 1956, 1957) or, more accurately, at the depth of the deepest, or permanent thermocline. Below this depth, light is completely absent and, it was believed, seasonal effects have completely disappeared, with temperatures virtually constant (usually between 1 and 2.5 °C, but much higher in the Mediterranean and Red Seas). A bathymetric narrowing in the bathyal zone from high to low latitudes (Menzies *et al.*, 1973) can be related to the diminishing effect of seasonal mixing and the shallowing of the permanent thermocline, and hence the upper boundary of the abyssal zone, towards the Equator. In polar seas the temperature structure results in a fauna on the continental shelf which is equivalent elsewhere to that of the bathyal, or archibenthal, zone containing fauna elsewhere found in abyssal depths. In the Arctic, Menzies *et al.* (1973) show that zonation within the abyssal province below corresponds well to water-mass structure which includes the submerged intrusion of warmer water from the Atlantic. Strong correlations of limits of the bathyal zone with water-mass structure have also been recognized elsewhere, e.g. off the eastern United States and Peru (Menzies *et al.*, 1973). The bathyal zone is essentially transitional, containing as it does elements from both the shelf above and the abyss below. Being intermediate in bathymetry, temperature range and sediment type explains the difficulty experienced by earlier workers to fix bathymetric boundaries on the slope. This is reflected in the term 'archibenthal zone of transition' of Menzies *et al.* (1973), who see it as sufficiently distinct in faunal composition to justify separation as a distinct zone only in the non-polar deep sea. These authors also provided a scheme for subdividing the abyssal zone, each subzone with a characteristic fauna, which can be related to differences in the physiographic, sedimentary and hydrographic environment.

Such zones have until recently remained largely notional, based as they are on somewhat subjective synthesis of records over wide areas. In recent years, one goal for deep-sea studies, especially in the N. Atlantic, has been to better define these zones by applying objective statistical procedures to data on both the physical and biological environment from intensive sampling designs along the depth gradient. It is important to be clear in the use of the term 'zonation' since, in the past, the term has been taken to imply either presence of step-like boundaries between areas of faunal homogeneity or a pattern of uniform change. Following Rex (1981) and Carney *et al.* (1983) we shall use the term to describe the, usually non-repeating, sequential pattern of species replacement measurable as changes in the overall rate of change in faunal composition, since this can embody both viewpoints.

STATISTICAL METHODS FOR ANALYSIS OF ZONATION

These have the aim of detecting underlying structure which can be related to environmental variables such as the depth gradient. There are essentially two approaches to the analysis of such data. The first approach employs multivariate methods. These, although having wide application, lack the rigour of mono- or bi-variate statistical methods whose function is to test specific hypotheses. Hence, they lack both a method of assessing statistical significance and a rationale permitting clear ecological interpretation, although the *pattern* generated by multivariate methods can be used to generate hypotheses that can be tested by statistical methods. All methods essentially involve calculation of an index of similarity, or 'distance', based on the degree of association. This may be measured between each possible pair of samples, in terms of their component species, or in terms of these species whose association is then considered in terms of their representation (that might be weighted in terms of their numerical abundance) in samples. For the purposes of describing bathymetric zonation, it can also be visualized as similarity values between all stations along the depth gradient (Fig. 9.1).

The three most widely applied in deep-sea studies of the many similarity statistics available are: (i) the Percent Similarity Coefficient (Whittaker & Fairbanks, 1958); (ii) the Bray–Curtis coefficient; (iii) the Normalized Expected Species Shared, or NESS, measure of similarity

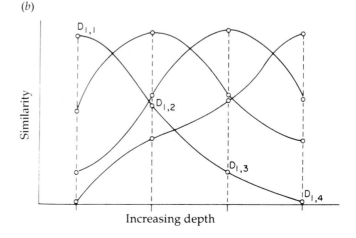

Fig. 9.1 (*a*) Matrix representation of values, $D_{i,j}$, of a similarity statistic between all possible pairs of samples, S, that in this case have been taken along the depth gradient. The next step would attempt to partition the similarity matrix through the application of sorting rules or formal mathematical procedures to produce clusters. (*b*) When plotted against depth the similarities form a normal curve around sample depth; with a non-repeating sequence. This model will give increasing dissimilarity with increasing depth interval between samples. (From Carney *et al.*, 1983.)

(Grassle & Smith, 1976). The latter is based on Hurlbert's (1971) expected number of species and similarly depends on taking random subsamples (the number of random subsamples is the sample size index, m, of a preset number of individuals from the original collection. The expected number of species shared in two random subsamples of m individuals is normalized by using the expected species shared in two random subsamples of m individuals within each collection. Because $2m$ individuals are required for the computation, m is normally about half the number of individuals in the smallest sample. The half-matrix of all possible sample pairings may then be clustered, the intensity of clustering depending on the combinatorial strategy chosen (Grassle, Sanders & W. Smith, 1979). A method based on the two-sample jackknife has been developed by W. Smith, Kravitz & Grassle 1979b) to obtain confidence intervals for the latter, and other similarity measures based on random samples.

This is usually followed by simplification of the matrix of similarities (Fig. 9.1(a)) by means of techniques of *classification*. This may simply be a rearrangement of the half-matrix to bring most similar values close together. However, the usual procedure is to show up groups of high similarity by means of a tree-like, hierarchical representation, or *dendrogram* (such as that shown in Fig. 9.5). The alternative is an ordering, or *ordination*, of the similarity matrix, as conceptualized in its simplest form in Fig. 9.1(b), although the similarity statistic employed must conform to the underlying geometric model. Both approaches are reviewed in Gauch, 1982, and Digby & Kempton, 1987. Classification suffers from the conceptual limitation of seeing pattern as discrete clusters (even when the faunal similarity between stations appears to be better described as a continuum). The usual aim is to produce a dendogram whose branching levels will depend on the relative similarity between the progressively larger agglomerations of the data. Furthermore, parameters of the sorting strategy employed may be varied to produce a result fitting in with the preconception of the investigator (Carney *et al.*, 1983).

The alternative method of ordination aims to represent sample and species association as faithfully as possible as a swarm of points in multidimensional space (e.g. Fig. 9.10). Being based on vector models, ordination is free of these criticisms of classification, but produces simplifications along linear axes that may be difficult to relate to observed environmental gradients, such as depth. Detrended Correspondence Analysis (Hill, 1979a; Hill & Gauch, 1980; Greenacre, 1984) has been the method most widely applied in deep-sea studies.

Clearly, for both classification or ordination methods to succeed, it is important that comparison is made between standard samples that are sufficiently large to minimize stochasticity in representation of the communities at the different stations. The latter must be sufficiently closely spaced to represent the pattern present, whether this be a gradient or discrete zones, or a combination of both that might embody changes in rate of change of continuum. Ideally, this is achieved by means of sample replicates whose within-site similarity should be greater than that with replicates from any other station. Replicates also should be closely spaced along the depth gradient. Unfortunately, few sample sets so far achieved from the deep-sea fully satisfy these demanding criteria.

Overall, ordination seems conceptually preferable to classification since it more accurately reflects the gradual nature of faunal change over the depth gradient.

The second approach to the analysis of zonation relies on accurate data on the vertical range of individual species. For example, using a photosled the density as well as distribution of easily recognized epifaunal species can be plotted along the depth gradient (Fig. 9.2). Furthermore, the overall depth-related pattern seems to be constant at different times of the year, even when the counts include motile species such as brittle stars (Fig. 9.3). Such information may also be available from intensively worked trawling transects where a large amount of data have been obtained at all depths along a section down the continental margin; such as that shown in Fig. 9.4. Curves showing the cumulative recruitment of new species encountered plotted against depth (e.g. Fig. 9.7) can be informative on the bathymetric rate of change of the fauna (Haedrich *et al.*, 1980; Gage *et al.*, 1985; Haedrich & Maunder, 1985). The coincidence-of-range method (Fig. 9.8) of Backus *et al.* (1965) further refines this

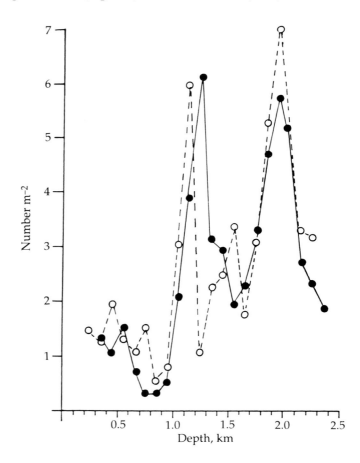

Fig. 9.2. Depth distributions of total megafauna from two photo-sled surveys off New England, N.W. Atlantic, taken at different times of the year. Open circles, Nov. 1984; closed circles, May l985. (From Maciolek *et al.*, 1987*b*.)

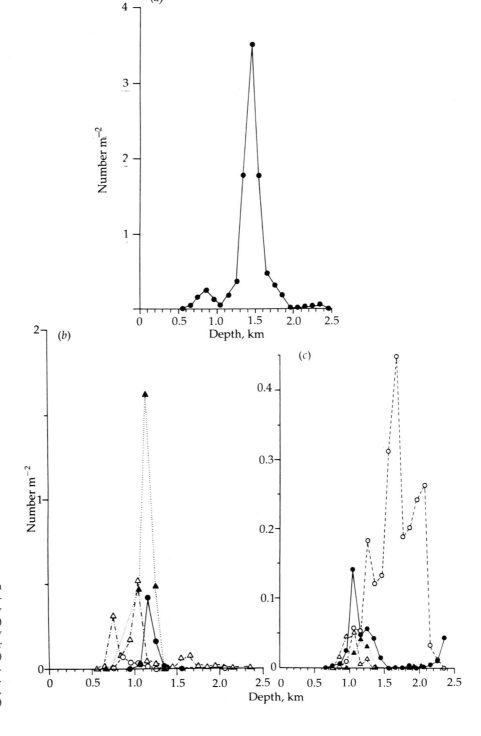

Fig. 9.3. Depth distribution of megafauna from photo-sled surveys off New England, N.W. Atlantic: (*a*) Xenophyophore, probably *Reticulammina*; (*b*) four species of gorgonian; (*c*) three species of pennatulid. Other details as for Fig. 9.2. (From Maciolek *et al.*, 1987*b*.)

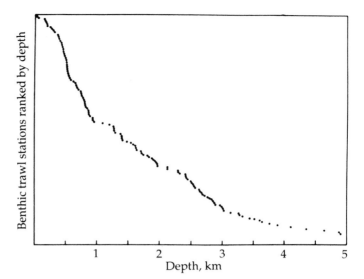

Fig. 9.4. Depth distribution of the trawl hauls off New England (N.W. Atlantic) that are shown classified in terms of their faunal similarity in Fig. 9.5. (From Haedrich *et al.*, 1980.)

approach, which is not dependent on measuring similarity between combinations of sample pairs along the depth gradient. Applied to benthic and benthopelagic fauna, it relies instead on data on the vertical range of species (that might have been obtained from a variety of gear) in order to measure the number of first and last occurrences of species – which are assumed to have characteristic ribbon-like zoned distributions along the depth contours (Haedrich, Rowe & Polloni, 1975; Gage *et al.*, 1985). Since these methods require comprehensive knowledge of vertical ranges of individual species, they can only be applied to groups of animals, such as echinoderms, that can be identified accurately as well as intensively investigated areas of the continental margin.

Clearly, in analysis of overall zonation patterns, both approaches are particularly sensitive to sampling gaps or differences in sampling intensity. With coincidence-of-range this results in artificially reducing the expectation of first and last occurrences; with multivariate analysis by reducing similarity of adjacent sample pairs.

DIFFERENCES IN SPECIES REPLACEMENT AMONGST TAXA AND FAUNAL GROUPS

Overall, the depth distributions of individual taxa show a wide range in pattern, varying from species found over a wide depth range to those restricted to a narrow band. Results from camera-sled transects in the N.W. Atlantic have documented some of the occurrence and density peaks along the depth gradient amongst sessile and slow-moving mega-fauna (Figs 9.2, 9.3). Although closely related megafaunal species over-lapped considerably in their depth ranges, each appear to show differing depth optima (Hecker, 1990).

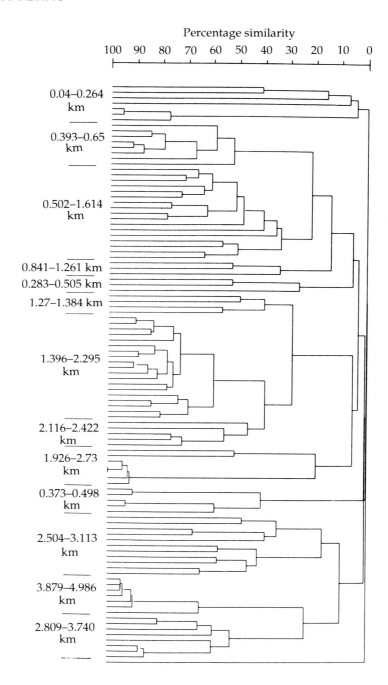

Fig. 9.5. Dendrogram of similarity of megafauna in trawl hauls taken at different depths on the continental slope and rise off New England, N.W. Atlantic. (From Haedrich *et al.*, 1980.)

Both multivariate analysis, including classification and ordination (Figs 9.5, 9.9, 9.10, 9.11) and downslope cumulative species recruitment and coincidence-of-range (Figs 9.6, 9.7, 9.8), of the megafaunal and bentho-pelagic faunas have provided evidence for the fairly sharp changes in rate

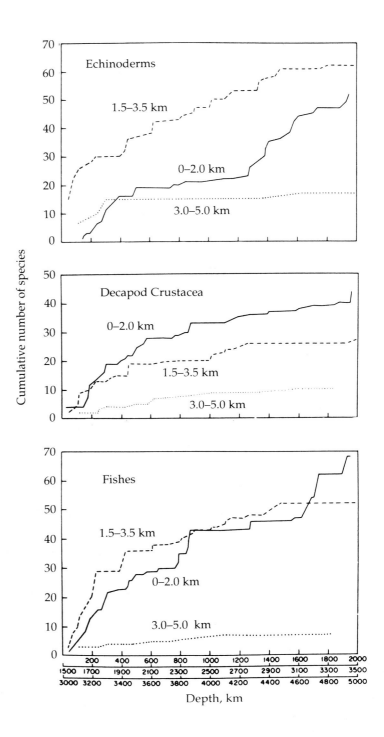

Fig. 9.6. Cumulative addition of species of major megafaunal and benthopelagic fauna in trawl hauls taken at different depths on the continental slope and rise off New England, N.W. Atlantic. (From Haedrich *et al.*, 1980.)

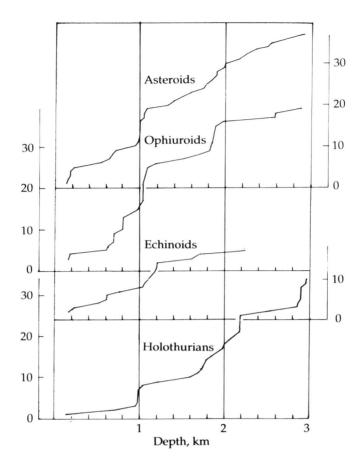

Fig. 9.7. Cumulative addition of species of the four main echinoderm groups in trawlings at different depths along the depth gradient in the Rockall Trough, N.E. Atlantic. (From Gage, 1986.)

of change in faunal composition implied in zonation (Haedrich *et al.*, 1980; Rowe, Polloni & Haedrich, 1982; Haedrich & Maunder, 1985; Gage *et al.*, 1985). At other sites, only weakly developed zonation was apparent, at least amongst benthopelagic fishes (Merrett & Marshall, 1981; Sulak, 1982; Snelgrove & Haedrich, 1987). But studies on the smaller animals generally suggest more gradual species replacement with depth (Fig. 9.12). Along the Gay Head–Bermuda transect, gastropods and cumaceans

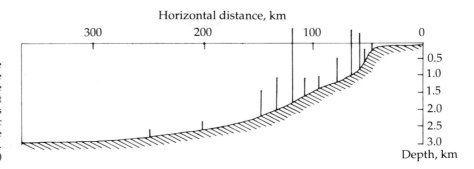

Fig. 9.8. Values of the coincidence-of-range statistic sensitive to the number of first and last occurrences of species along the bathymetric profile sampled in the Rockall Trough, N.E. Atlantic. (From Gage, 1986.)

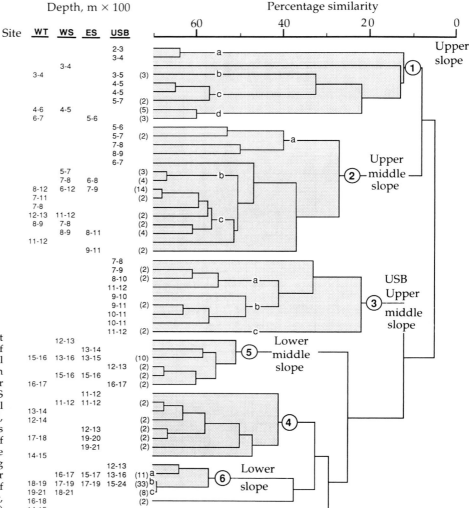

Fig. 9.9. Classification, at 100 m depth intervals, of similarity of megafaunal species identified from photosled tows along four transect sites, WT, WS, ES and USB, on the continental slope off New England, N.W. Atlantic. USB was located on the slope off Georges Bank, the remaining three being closer together further south on the slope S. of Cape Cod. (From Hecker, 1990.)

showed much narrower depth distributions than either brittle stars or polychaetes (Fig. 9.13), the higher overall levels of similarity for the latter being ascribed to eurybathic elements (Grassle, Sanders & W. Smith, 1979). These authors suggest that differences in intensity of zonation amongst macrofauna are closely related to the dispersal capabilities of species during their early development. However, considering only the continental slope and rise off New England, different macrofaunal groups show considerable fidelity in clustering indicating an overall zoned pattern strongly dominated by polychaetes, of: upper slope (0.58–1 km), lower slope (1.5–2 km), upper rise (3 km) and lower rise (3.5 km) associations that show no evidence of seasonal variability (Blake *et al.*, 1987).

Overall, the results from analysis of macro- and megafaunal transects worked at various locations in the Atlantic confirm the sharpest change in

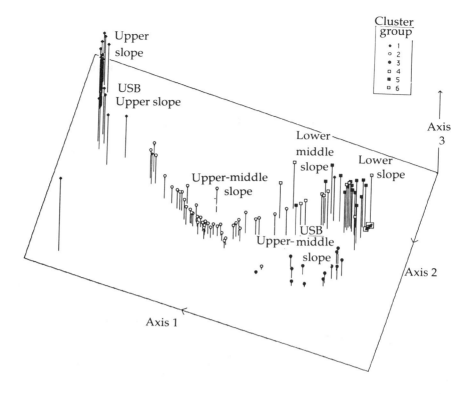

Fig. 9.10. Ordination by means of detrended correspondence analysis of the megafaunal species from the four transect sites off New England considered in 100 m depth intervals. Symbols represent clusters of intervals defined by classification shown in Fig. 9.9. The position of the cluster groups is shown plotted from their scores on the first three axes of the ordination. See Fig. 9.9 for explanation of the other labels. (From Hecker, 1990.)

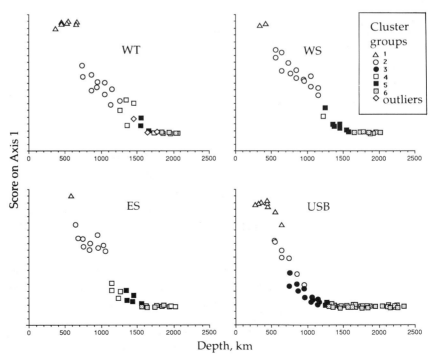

Fig. 9.11. Position of 100 m depth intervals on the first axis of correspondence analysis of megafauna plotted against the mean depth interval. Symbols represent clusters formed by classification. See Fig. 9.9 for explanation of the labels. (From Hecker, 1990.)

Fig. 9.12. Classification of macrofauna in Birge-Ekman box-cores from various sites along the continental slope and rise of the United States in the N.W. Atlantic. (From Rowe *et al.*, 1982.)

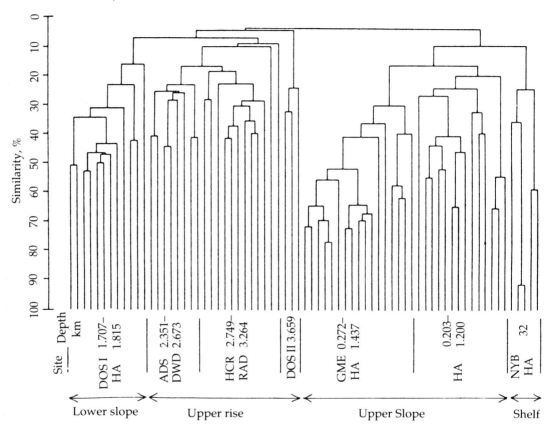

faunal composition occurs at the edge of the shelf, while the separation of a zone between 0.4 and 1 km depth is supported by results from the megafauna in this area (Sanders *et al.*, 1965; Grassle *et al.*, 1979; Haedrich *et al.*, 1975, 1980; Rex, 1981, 1983).

REGIONAL DIFFERENCES IN VERTICAL PATTERN

The published evidence for various macrofaunal and megafaunal groups indicates that the pattern of faunal change will vary considerably from area to area (Haedrich *et al.*, 1975, 1980; Grassle *et al.*, 1979; Rex, 1977; Gage, 1986). The extensive trawling and photographic transects along the continental margin of the United States show a general pattern of zonation with areas of sharp rates of change in faunal composition separating zones of much higher homogeneity at different sites (Menzies

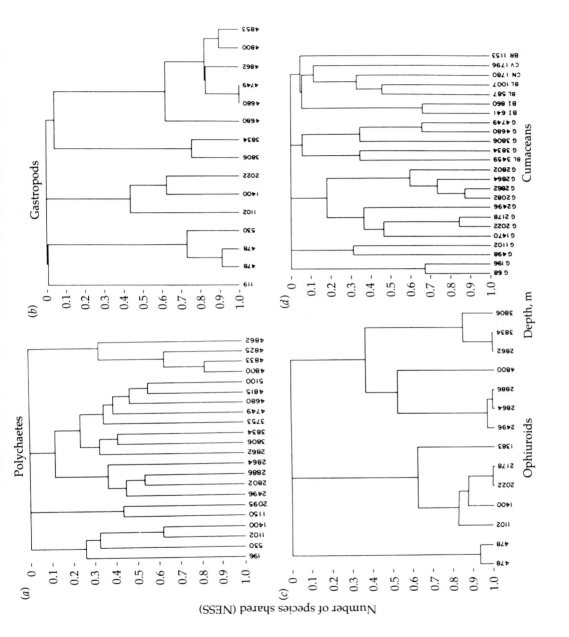

Fig. 9.13. Classification by NESS similarity of different macrofaunal taxa in epibenthic sled hauls from the Gay Head–Bermuda transect. (From Grassle, Sanders & W. Smith, 1979.)

et al., 1973; Haedrich *et al.*, 1975, 1980; Hecker *et al.*, 1983; Blake *et al.*, 1987; Hecker, 1990). While the exact depth boundaries may differ amongst the studies, discrepancies seem to roughly correspond to topographic and geological differences on the slope, as well as in the differing taxa emphasized by trawling and photo transects. The results from surveys including canyons show some deviations from the normal slope pattern. These reflect topographic differences and faunal elements thought to be indicative of canyon conditions. Overall, the studies show major changes in species composition, depending on transect site, at 0.4 to 0.6 km and at 1 km on the upper slope. There is another faunal discontinuity at the boundary between the middle and lower slope (1.4 to 1.6 km); with an intervening area of gradual change, that nevertheless involves the fauna changing completely about twice (Blake *et al.*, 1987; Maciolek *et al.*, 1987). The results from trawlings suggest an additional discontinuity at 2 km depth, with the fauna showing much greater homogeneity thereafter (Haedrich *et al.*, 1975, 1980). Step-like increments in rate of species recruitment (Fig. 9.6) from the very intensively worked transect in the N.W. Atlantic (see Fig. 9.4) reflect these changes in rate of change and have shown the much slower rate of faunal change on the rise into the abyss. A similar step-like pattern in species recruitment, together with peaks in the first and last occurrences of species of echinoderms (Figs 9.7, 9.8) occurs at 0.8 to 1.2 km and at about 1.8 km depth in the Rockall Trough, N.E. Atlantic (Gage, 1986). These trends agree with those reported by Sibuet (1977) from the Bay of Biscay, and are fundamentally similar to patterns from the N.W. Atlantic discussed above.

There are less data available from the Pacific. Off Oregon, ordination of epibenthic holothurians show a sharp shelf-edge transition but only a gradual change, with a complete replacement every 2 km (Carney & Carey, 1977); whilst peaks in rate of replacement amongst benthopelagic fish occur between 0.4 to 0.7 km coinciding with the Pacific oxygen minimum, whilst another peak occurs at 1.9 to 2.2 km (Pearcy, Stein & Carney, 1982).

The general conclusion from results of classification and ordination suggests that faunal zones may best be seen as areas of relatively slow faunal change separated by areas of more rapid faunal change.

CAUSES OF ZONATION PATTERN

As outlined above, until recently such discussion has focussed mainly on possible effects of physical factors, especially boundaries of physiological tolerance to temperature, and the influence of physiographic and hydrographic features of the continental margin. This approach dates from Murray & Hjort (1912) and is exemplified by Le Danois (1947) and Ekman (1953). However, even for the megafauna the data, unfortunately, are insufficient to test the validity of a global pattern responding to latitudinally related differences in physical factors such as the depth of the permanent thermocline. Furthermore, in any explanation for the causes of zonation it is necessary to explain why one subset of the fauna is markedly more tolerant to the varying conditions along the depth gradient than others. As more recent examples of the influence of more local factors, changes in sediment conditions, including sediment chemistry, have been implicated with zones of faunal change at the regional level, especially on the upper slope (Carey, 1965; Haedrich *et al.*, 1975; Southward & Dando, 1988); while the effect of deep boundary currents on larval dispersal and current-borne detrital food was considered important by Rowe & Menzies (1969).

With the epifaunal megafauna, some at least of the zonation observed seems to reflect changes in trophic strategies along a gradient in food and hydrodynamic energy; with a mixture of suspension and carnivores/scavengers on the upper slope, carnivores/scavengers alone on the middle slope, and a mixture of suspension feeders and deposit feeders on the lower slope and rise of the Atlantic continental margin of the United States. The availability of hard substrata, such as ice-rafted stones and boulders, may also restrict distributions of sessile species such as sponges and corals. However, some suspension feeders, such as certain coelenterates and the stalked crinoids, show very considerable vertical ranges. It has been suggested that these species simply take advantage of local conditions maintaining high levels of resuspended sediments (Carney *et al.*, 1983).

The generally high similarity amongst box-cores taken at widely spaced stations on the abyssal plain (Hessler & Jumars, 1974; Hecker & Paul, 1979) and the uniformity along deeper isobaths (Maciolek *et al.*, 1987*b*) are associated with a concept of an increasingly uniform environment with increasing depth (Rex, 1981).

Some recent studies have stressed the importance of biological interactions, particularly in determining differing rates of zonation; groups dominated by croppers and predators such as epibenthic gastropods being zoned more rapidly than infaunal deposit feeders (Rex, 1977). The absence of any obvious selection in food items shown in studies of the diet of deep-sea animals (see Chapters 4 and 5 and the section Feeding strategies in Chapter 11) suggests that competitive interactions for the same limited resource may be enhanced. This competition may be a prime structuring force in communities. Carney *et al.* (1983) point out that the appeal of perceiving competitive interactions and predation as important factors in determining zonation patterns results from our inability to relate the patterns occurring below 1 km depth to physiological factors and because of the recognition of such ecological phenomena in maintaining the narrow zonation in the rocky intertidal. Indeed, such competitive and predatory interactions are assumed to be of fundamental importance in disequilibrium explanations for high deep-sea diversity (see Chapter 8). Such processes may operate in the spike-like peaks in abundance of individual epifaunal taxa (Figs 9.2, 9.3). However, a progression from description to prediction of faunal zonation patterns faces considerable difficulties resulting from the complexity of the multispecies analysis necessary.

One approach adopted by Rex (1977) derives from Terborgh's (1971) theory of distributions on environmental gradients. In this model the data on the distribution of species along a gradient, such as terrestrial elevation or bathymetry, are used to find evidence for competitive resource partitioning along the resource or physiological gradient. Here each species might be expected, in the absence of interspecific effects, to vary randomly about its optimum. Where resources vary in line with the gradient, competition would be absent and species' ranges will overlap extensively resulting in gradual changes in rate of species replacement. Competitive interactions between species will result in a serial partitioning of the resource along the gradient where competitive exclusion at the boundaries will give rise to much sharper rates of change (Fig. 9.14). Coincidence of boundaries amongst several taxa will result in major faunal discontinuities.

In applying this theory to data from the Gay Head–Bermuda transect, Rex (1977) found that the rate of faunal change was dependent on the group of organisms analysed, with megafauna changing most rapidly and infaunal polychaetes the slowest (Fig. 9.15). This result fitted in with notions that taxa at higher levels on the food chain will be less subject to predatory reduction in their populations and hence experience more

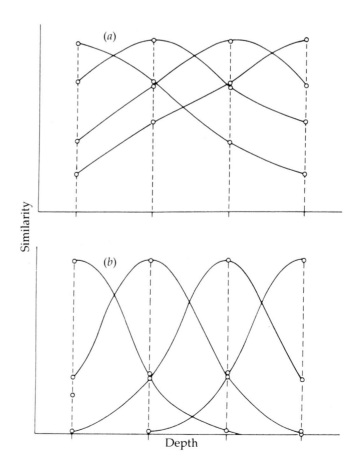

Fig. 9.14. Theoretical similarities of species plotted against depth with: (a) variable resources and minimal interspecific competition and (b) shared resources resulting in competitive interaction between species. (From Carney et al., 1983.)

Fig. 9.15. Similarity values plotted against depth for different faunal groups trawled off New England, showing differing rate of change. Upper curve; fishes showing a relatively low rate of change, contrast with megafaunal invertebrates (lower curve) which show the highest rate of change; possibly reflecting differing motility or trophic grouping. Predatory gastropods (triangles) fall between these two extremes. (From Carney *et al.*, 1983.)

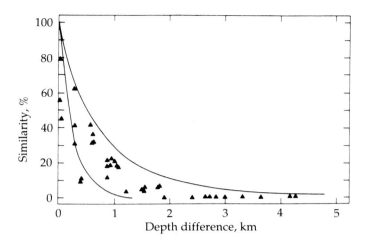

competitive crowding on the gradient (Menge & Sutherland, 1976). However, this explanation may be too simplistic as elsewhere megafaunal holothurians showed the slowest rate of change compared with polychaetes and amphipods (see Carney *et al.*, 1983).

Perhaps the most comprehensive data are available for benthopelagic fishes. However, analysis of the available data from the N. Atlantic do not produce repeatable patterns other than those reflecting the occurrence of two widespread and abundant species, *Synaphobranchus kaupi* at slope depths and *Coryphaenoides (Nematonurus) armatus* on the continental rise. Communities identified from analysis within a survey area cannot be identified elsewhere. Haedrich & Merrett (1990) therefore believe that, at least for fishes, the concept of zonation, or of communities, has no value in the deep sea.

To conclude, we cannot but agree with Carney *et al.* (1983) who, in their review of the subject of zonation in the deep sea, suggest that our future understanding of vertical zonation will benefit from viewing any pattern as the result of several processes operating at both evolutionary and ecological timescales. Whilst analysis of total faunal patterns can be instructive in formulating ideas, it can also obscure a complex pattern that requires to be seen and analysed as the sum of the range and adaptations of individual species considered at a local level.

10

Zoogeography, speciation and the origin of the deep-sea fauna

HORIZONTAL DISTRIBUTIONS IN THE DEEP SEA

Deriving from the monotony of the fauna from abyssal basins in trawlings undertaken world-wide during the pioneering voyage of the 'Challenger', the first conception of the zoogeography of the deep sea was of a single province, sharing many species with cosmopolitan distributions. Although this view was supported by Bruun (1957), other workers have perceived some differentiation of the abyssal into four zoogeographic zones, the Atlantic, Indo-Pacific, Arctic and Antarctic (Ekman, 1953). The extensive global sampling investigations of Russian workers has been summarized in English by Vinogradova (1959, 1962a,b, 1979). She found only 15% of species occurring in more than one ocean and only 4% being found in all of them. These conclusions follow the philosophy of an essentially unified fauna for the abyssal and hadal zones; whilst recognizing substantial differentiation has occurred in different oceanic regions, particularly those corresponding to topographic boundaries such as trenches (Fig. 10.1).

For the N. Atlantic, these conclusions were essentially similar to those of Mortensen (1907), and are more or less supported by zoogeographic analyses of collections from the 'Galathea' expedition (Kirkegaard, 1954; Wolff, 1962; Levi, 1964; Millar, 1970). Other schemes developed from the 'Galathea' sampling differ only with respect to the major faunistic connections (Madsen, 1961b; Hansen, 1967, 1975; Knudsen, 1979). Other, more complex, schemes have been developed subdividing Ekman's zones into further subareas and provinces with species having quite narrow ranges separated by topographic barriers (Clark, 1962) or mainly related to the origin and temperature structure of deep-water masses (Menzies *et al.*, 1973). More recent workers have considered species distributions in relation both to plate tectonics and deep-water circulation, as well as bathymetry (see below); while the dispersal abilities of differing modes of larval development seem to be of subsidiary importance (Schein-Fatton, 1988).

Fig. 10.1. Zoogeographical divisions of the abyssal and hadal zones of the world ocean. Boundaries between I, regions; II, subregions; III, abyssal provinces; IV, hadal provinces. 1, Pacific/N. Indian deep-sea region: 1A, Pacific subregion; $1A_1$, W. Pacific province; $1A_2$, E. Pacific province; A/J, Aleutian–Japan hadal province; PH, Philippine; M, Mariana; B/N, Bougainville–New Hebrides; T/K, Tonga–Kermadec; P/CH, Peru–Chile hadal provinces. 1B, N. Indian subregion; J, Java hadal province. 2, Atlantic deep-sea region: 2A, Arctic subregion; 2B, Atlantic subregion; $2B_1$, N. Atlantic abyssal province; R, province of Romanche Trench. 3A, Antarctic-IndoPacific subregion: $3B_1$, Indian Ocean abyssal province; $3B_2$, Pacific abyssal province; S/A, South Atlantic hadal province. (From N. G. Vinogradova, 1979.)

The notion of a distinct fauna of deep-ocean trenches is shown from the results of mainly Russian trawlings (Zenkevitch & Birstein, 1956; Belyaev, 1966, 1989; Bruun, 1957). These show a higher percentage of species of amphipods, polychaetes, bivalves, echiurids and holothurians and a lower percentage of sea stars, echinoids, sipunculids and brittle stars, and especially non-actinian and scyphozoan coelenterates, bryozoans, cumaceans and fishes, than in the surrounding abyss; whilst decapod crustaceans are completely absent. The Russian work also highlighted the marked numerical and species dominance of the fauna by holothurians, polychaetes, bivalves, isopods, actinians, amphipods and gastropods, in that order; the mass occurrences of single holothurian species being particularly characteristic. These results, along with the bathymetric uniformity in frequency of occurrences at different depth levels and the similarity in these frequencies and in qualitative composition from one trench to another, led Wolff (1960, 1970) to propose a distinct hadal, or ultra-abyssal, zone. This was thought to show both a high degree of differentiation and species endemism (up to about 75% in some Pacific trenches), although this becomes insignificant at the generic level. Other work suggests that much of the differentiation is at the level of subspecies, and that other endemics exist at much lower densities, and therefore much less obviously, in the surrounding abyssal (Hansen, 1975).

In considering the eurybathic species, some of which we have seen in Chapters 4 and 5 having bathymetric ranges that span the bathyal to the hadal zones, Vinogradova (1962a, 1969, 1979) was able to distinguish differing vertical ranges of mainly megabenthic species. The coelenterates are most eurybathic, next to sipunculids, barnacles and other crustaceans, whilst the proportion is much reduced amongst sponges, isopod crustaceans, pogonophores and echinoderms.

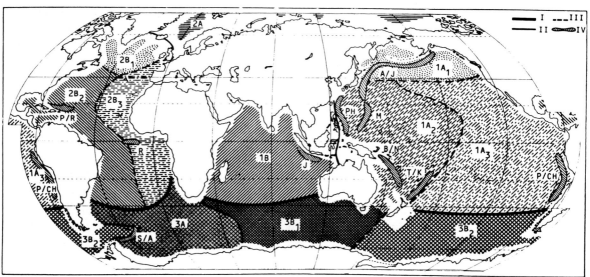

Ekman (1953) also first demonstrated a different pattern of horizontal range amongst the fauna on the slope with distributions tending to *increase* rather than decrease as one ascends the continental margin. Although opposed by data from sea stars (Madsen, 1961*b*; Sibuet, 1979), E. C. Southward (1979) maintained from pogonophoran distributions in the Atlantic that only lower slope species were geographically widespread, whilst both abyssal and upper-slope species were more restricted in horizontal range. Ekman's idea was developed by later workers (Pasternack, 1964; Vinogradova, 1969*b*; Menzies *et al.*, 1973; Kucheruk, 1976) who recognized a bathymetrically narrow but globally wide-ranging, ribbon-like distribution of certain bathyal species such as the echinoderms *Ophiomusium lymani* and *Scotoplanes globosa*. Menzies *et al.* (1973) linked this phenomenon to dispersal of larval stages by deep boundary currents. Divergences in such currents, occurring on the Atlantic slope of N. America off Cape Lookout, the Grand Banks off Newfoundland and off the eastern coast of Japan, have been proposed as zoogeographical barriers to horizontal distribution of certain groups (Cutler, 1975; Hansen, 1975; Haedrich & Maunder, 1985).

However, the idea of an essentially widely distributed fauna in the ocean basins, resulting from the absence of barriers and a confluence of the ocean floor, has been supported from comparisons at generic and higher level where distributions tend to have a global uniformity. For example, of the 143 genera of isopods known from the deep Pacific, only 9 have not been found in the Atlantic; such results demonstrating that, in contrast to shallow water or on land, the environment in the deep sea is sufficiently homogeneous that adaptations and lifestyles represented by taxonomic levels as low as genera can exist everywhere (Hessler & G. D. F. Wilson, 1983). Even the physically and hydrographically isolated basins discussed below largely conform to this homogeneity at generic level.

Because there remain many problems in the objective recognition of taxa at the lowest levels of species and genera (see below), it is still unclear whether the high species richness, discussed in Chapter 8 amongst the smaller benthic animals, is associated with a proportionately high number of taxa at generic and higher level, compared to shallow water. However, the information available, in general, suggests a much higher ratio of species-per-genus than amongst shallow-water faunas.

SPECIATION AND ZOOGEOGRAPHY IN THE DEEP SEA

Hypotheses of speciation in the deep sea mainly derive from study of zoogeographic processes. Such processes are fundamental to any understanding of depth-related changes in diversity and faunal composition. However, such considerations are relatively recent. The view little more than two decades ago was of a deep sea impoverished in species owing to its demanding conditions for life; an environment where, because of the presumed constancy in conditions, evolution has proceeded much more slowly than in shallow water (Carter, 1961). This view had kept alive the old idea of the deep sea as a refuge for species long extinct elsewhere (Zenkevitch & Birstein, 1960), or its fauna being derived mainly from the adjacent shelf (Bruun, 1957; Menzies *et al.*, 1973). The discovery of high species richness in the deep sea (see Chapter 8), together with careful taxonomic studies, now prompts a view of the deep sea as a site of prolific speciation, and perhaps the place of origin of higher-level taxa (Hessler & G. D. F. Wilson, 1983).

PROBLEMS IN UNDERSTANDING SPECIATION

Theoretical studies on speciation have been well developed amongst terrestrial faunas where geneological relationships are better understood than in the sea. Such relationships remain unknown for deep-sea faunas. In a recent review of speciation in the deep sea G. D. F. Wilson & Hessler (1987*a*) point out that this weakens any inference of speciation from zoogeographic data alone and may overlook the underlying genetic mechanism. Consideration of such mechanisms requires knowledge of the population genetics of species. While genetic polymorphism has been studied in some species (see below), few of these studies have focussed on genetic differences between localities.

WHAT CONSTITUTES A SPECIES?

Another major problem of the zoogeographic approach to understanding speciation is the problem of what constitutes a species; this being shared with other studies dependent on consistent and coherent criteria for delimiting species in a poorly known fauna such as that in the deep sea. As the large and demographically comprehensive collections of particular taxa from the wide-ranging sampling programmes of the 1960s and 1970s have been studied, subtle differences in morphology, indicative of prolific speciation, have been apparent (Fig. 10.2). One problem has been that the broadness of the concept of what constitutes a species seems often to depend on the apparent breadth of its distribution, a perception perhaps coloured by underlying assumptions of the lack of isolating barriers and global uniformity in the environment. The assessment of how much significance to put on morphological variation in separating species is subjective, some workers being less conservative than others in decisions on whether to ascribe varietal, subspecific or specific rank to variation that, in the past, was often analysed in very small collections of specimens. For example, Hansen (1975) in his monograph on the elasipod holothurians of the 'Galathea' expedition recognized only two species amongst geographical variants of the elasipod holothurian *Scotoplanes*, with most of the variation being encompassed by the presumably cosmopolitan species *S. globosa*. In this, he was perhaps, quite justifiably, influenced by their large, buoyant eggs and their known powers of swimming and drifting, particularly in juveniles (see Chapter 13), offering wide dispersal possibilities by currents. However, Russian work has since split the species into five, each with more restricted regional distributions (Gebruk, 1983). A similarly conservative philosophy has

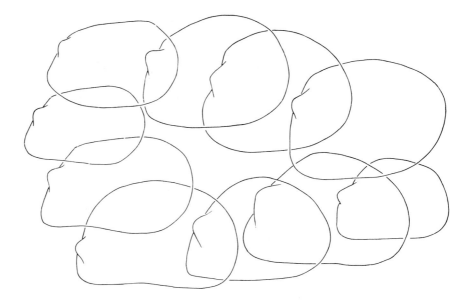

Fig. 10.2. Shell outlines of ten (unnamed) species belonging to the mytilid bivalve genus *Dacrydium* from the Atlantic Ocean. Most are restricted to one ocean basin within a narrow depth range. (From Allen, 1979.)

usually been applied to many other taxa (Kirkegaard, 1954; Madsen, 1961*a*; Knudsen, 1970) where a wholly appropriate reluctance to ascribe specific rank to variants has been adopted until more or better material is available. Consequently, this has led to many supposedly widespread species being 'split' in the course of time as collecting methods at sea have improved and sample sizes increased, and criteria other than morphological differentiation have been considered.

Approaches such as examination of biochemical variability has in shallow-water fauna revealed many cases of sibling (outwardly very similar or identical) species, particularly amongst polychaetes, e.g. Clark (1977); J. P. Grassle & Grassle (1977). Examples cited by G. D. F. Wilson & Hessler (1987*a*) include the macrourid fish *Coryphaenoides (Nematonurus) armatus* which, from studies on electrophoretic and morphometric variability (Wilson & Waples, 1983, 1984), seems to include geographically circumscribed races. Amongst invertebrates with supposedly widespread distributions, the quill worm *Hyalinoecia tubicola* may be a complex of morphologically similar species (Grassle *et al.*, 1975); while the isopod *Eurycope complanata*, previously thought to range widely in the N. Atlantic, has been split into 12 species each with a restricted distribution (G. D. F. Wilson, 1983*a*).

Other studies have found a high degree of endemism within ocean basins. This has been particularly marked amongst peracarid crustaceans where species' distributions may be restricted both geographically and vertically (Barnard, 1961, 1962; Wolff, 1962; G. D. Wilson, 1983*a,b*; Holdich & Bird, 1985; N. S. Jones, 1985; and for polychaetes, Hartman & Fauchald, 1971).

As more powerful techniques for distinguishing species become available to deep-sea taxonomists, many more species with 'cosmopolitan' distributions will be shown to be groups of related species with relatively restricted distributions (Grassle & Maciolek, unpublished data).

SPECIATION AND GENETIC VARIABILITY IN RELATION TO THE DEPTH GRADIENT

Environmental gradients are perceived as important in providing the opportunities for the selective pressures that drive speciation. We have seen in previous chapters that depth-related gradients in standing crop, body size, species richness and community composition are steepest in the bathyal zone on the continental slope. G. D. F. Wilson & Hessler (1987a) suggest that proximity to variability associated with the surface layers of the ocean, variability in topography and down-slope processes and the presence of energetic boundary currents will provide enhanced opportunities for speciation, perhaps operating in concert with the processes implicated in diversity maintenance that were discussed in Chapter 8. However, studies on genetic heterogeneity in taxa found over fairly wide bathymetric limits, such as the cosmopolitan, lower continental slope brittle star, *Ophiomusium lymani*, and the gastropod *Bathybembix bairdi*, could not clearly correlate heterozygosity to the depth gradient (Doyle, 1972; Siebenaller, 1978a). In fact, *O. lymani*, along with three species of sea star, appears to show only a modest degree of genetic polymorphism, whilst another sea star, *Nearchaster aciculosus*, shows much higher levels, yet *O. lymani* has a much wider zoogeographic range than any of the sea stars (Ayala & Valentine, 1974; Valentine, Hedgecock & Barr, 1975). However, since the proportion of heterozygotes in *O. lymani* tended to be lower than expected from the laws of genetics, Murphy, Rowe & Haedrich (1976) suggest that populations may be genetically isolated along the brittle star's ribbon-like range. Selection pressures will be weakest at the centre of the species' range where conditions are optimal and its fitness greatest; the relaxed selection pressure permitting greater genetic variability. However, nearer its limits, selection pressure will be more intense, the population perhaps being maintained by propagules from nearer the range optimum. This will tend to eliminate much variability, resulting in maximal homozygosity amongst outliers.

The notion of phenotypic uniformity amongst peripherally isolated populations is central to the Founder Principle (Mayr, 1963). This describes the establishment of a new population from a small subset of the original population carrying only a small fraction of the total genetic variation of the parent population. This principle should have wide application in possible 'leapfrog' patterns in geographic variation amongst the large-scale distributions of the deep sea. This may be particulary important along the continental slope where continuity is interrupted by canyon topography and population-reducing downslope processes such as sediment slides (Almaça, 1983) and on seamounts. However, on the shallower (< 1 km summit depth) seamounts, there are roughly equal number of local (endemic) to widespread/cosmopolitan species of megafauna, while deeper ones are typically dominated by widespread/cosmopolitan species (R. R. Wilson & Kaufmann, 1987).

Although many deep-sea invertebrates accord with the expectation of showing a high level of genetic variability (Gooch & Schopf, 1972; Siebenaller, 1978a), others, such as elasipod holothurians show very low levels (Bisol, Costa & Sibuet, 1984). Data from benthopelagic fish also show low heterozygosity, this being interpreted as suggesting pressure insensitivity at the biochemical level (Siebenaller, 1978b, 1984; Siebenaller & Somero, 1978a,b).

The frequency of species formation and extinction has been linked to the environmental tolerances of species; the expectation being that eurytopic species would survive longer than stenotopic species with similar dispersal ability. However, the restricted bathymetric range of many deep-sea invertebrates may rather reflect limited opportunities for dispersal or emigration than stenotopy. The successful transplantation from 0.4 km depth in the Antarctic of specimens of the barnacle *Bathylasma corolliforme* (normal depth range 0.1–1.5 km) to 25 and 40 m depth where they survived at least 2 yr and produced larvae (Dayton, Newman & Oliver, 1982), suggests that assumptions of stenotopy from a narrow distributional range may be unjustified. Furthermore, feeding data provided for different taxa in Chapters 4 and 5 and summarized in Chapter 11, suggest broad rather than narrow dietary preferences in both fish and invertebrates. The few data on other habitat requirements, such as choice of substratum, also suggest eurytopy. For example, the catholic requirements of the genetically polymorphic, arctic sea star *Ctenodiscus* (Shick, Taylor & Lamb, 1981) imply similar eurytopy in widely distributed deep-sea echinoderms that are also genetically polymorphic.

DISPERSAL AND ISOLATION IN SPECIATION

The importance of mode of larval dispersal on species richness amongst different taxa already has been discussed in Chapter 8. Assuming extinction rates are constant and occur randomly among species, mode of dispersal in regulating gene flow can be related to their propensity to form new species. Sanders & Grassle (1971) contrasted the relatively low species richness of deep-sea brittle stars, many of which have planktotrophic early development, with peracarids that brood their young with no free-living larval stage. However, many deep-sea invertebrates have the intermediate, lecithotrophic, mode of development where the free-swimming, non-feeding larva is pelagic (presumably near the bottom) for a limited (but unknown) period of time. It is also likely that present range (whether wide or limited) and the dispersal abilities of the adult, whether by swimming or drifting in the water column as with many deep-sea elasipod and aspidochirote holothurians (Hansen, 1975; Pawson, 1982; Billett *et al.*, 1985; Ohta, 1985), will also be important in determining rates of dispersal. But the relationship between dispersal and the gene flow that might control speciation is not necessarily direct. G. D. F. Wilson & Hessler (1987a) point out that taxa, such as isopods, with direct development, include both cosmopolitan families endemic to the deep sea, which must therefore be specifically adapted to deep-sea conditions, and widely distributed genera, indicating wide dispersal before sufficient differentiation had occurred to justify recognition as separate genera. Such findings support the notion of the absence of absolute barriers to gene flow in promoting speciation. There is little evidence to the contrary. However, David (1983) provides one example from morphometric differences between populations of the echinoid *Pourtalesia jeffreysi* on either side of the mid-oceanic ridge in the Norwegian Sea (Fig. 10.3) which, he suggests, reflects incipient speciation in a species whose lecithotrophic reproduction (Harvey & Gage, 1984) limits gene flow between the two populations.

Another factor encouraging speciation may be the low population densities of deep-sea animals. G. D. F. Wilson & Hessler (1987*a*) estimate that, assuming random spatial pattern, an average-sized (*c.* 1-mm long) animal will be separated from its nearest neighbour of the same species by

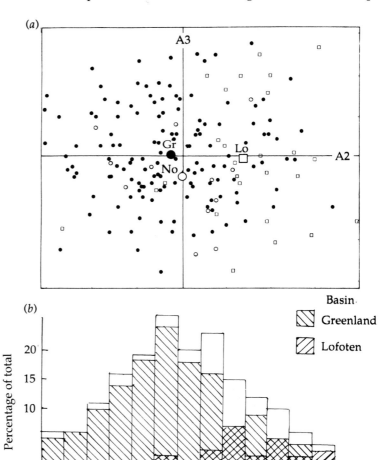

Fig. 10.3. Morphometric analysis of measurements of tests of 175 specimens of the irregular echinoid *Pourtalesia jeffreysi* from three basins in the Norwegian Sea, by means of Principal Components Analysis. Gr, Greenland Basin; Lo, Lofoten Basin; No, Norwegian Basin. (*a*) Projection of axes 2 and 3; (*b*) histograms of scores on 2nd axis from individuals from each of the three basins. Unhatched area, totals. (From David, 1983.)

1318 body lengths in the very oligotrophic equatorial eastern Pacific. By reducing the rate of gene flow through the population, such low densities are thought to encourage divergence amongst conspecific 'demes', or local and more or less isolated units of populations (see Carter, 1961).

Clearly, an important priority for future research will be an expansion of studies of geographic variation by means of both morphometric and electrophoretic methods applied to the full range of deep-sea fauna. Such data applied in combination with detailed cladistic analysis of monophyletic lineages, or 'clades', along with improved knowledge of life-history biology, will permit testing of hypotheses on processes of speciation and on the origin and maintenance of diversity in the deep sea.

THE ORIGIN OF THE DEEP-SEA FAUNA

The place of deep-sea animals in the evolutionary history of marine taxa has been debated since the middle of the nineteenth century. It was predicted from dredge finds of stalked crinoids such as *Rhizocrinus lofotensis* from the deep, fjordic coast of Norway that an even more archaic fauna would be found at greater depths; and this notion was one of the ideas inspiring the 'Challenger' expedition (see Chapter 1). Despite the lack of support from the results of the voyage, this idea persisted and has periodically been rejuvenated by isolated discoveries, such as that of the primitive mollusc *Neopilina* (see Chapter 5); although Menzies & Imbrie (1955) pointed out that more examples of archaic taxa could be found in shallow water. Furthermore, the dominance of ancient forms such as the protobranch bivalves is likely to be related to their generalist deposit-feeding lifestyle that is well suited to the food-poor sediments in deep water (J. A. Allen, 1983). The representation of the more recently evolved suspension-feeding eulamellibranchs that dominate in shallow water has been shown to be more likely the result of eulamellibranchs being poorly suited to feeding conditions prevailing in the deep sea. It is not suggested that present deep-sea protobranchs have persisted there for this length time, but that it is more likely they have radiated from immigrants from shallower water (Clarke, 1961; J. A. Allen, 1979, 1983). In the case of echinoderm taxa, it has been suggested that bathyal forms are the most primitive, while those in the abyssal and hadal zones are more recently evolved (Madsen, 1961*b*; Hansen, 1975).

In the absence of a clear fossil record of unequivocally deep-sea fauna (except from Foraminifera – see below), two opposing ideas on the origin of the deep-sea fauna have been put forward: (1) evolution within the deep sea; and (2) migration from shallow water. The latter has, as its basis, the hypothesis that the fauna was populated through emigration from centres of origin in shallow water at high latitudes (Dahl, 1954; Wolff, 1960; Kussakin, 1973; Menzies *et al.*, 1973) where the important environmental barrier of temperature would not present a barrier between shallow and deep water. This *submergence* argument superficially seems most likely for groups that are highly diverse in the deep sea, such as isopods, since, although component families have their centre of abundance in the deep sea, many have representatives in cold, shallow waters at high latitudes. Hessler & Thistle (1975) and Hessler, G. D. F. Wilson & Thistle (1979) instead argue that these cold shallow areas have been colonized from deeper waters (high latitude *emergence*): because (i) the centre of generic and species diversity lies in the deep sea resulting in typical 'spindle'-shaped depth distributions; (ii) where phylogeny has been worked out, the most primitive species or genera in families reside in deep water; (iii) the complete absence of eyes in deep-sea families (where presumably they have been lost since they confer no selective advantage), and their absence also in confamilial species living in shallow, high latitudes. In evolution, once lost, complex structures such as eyes are not regained.

Until the advent and general acceptance of the theory of plate tectonics, there was little certain information available on changes in the deep-sea environment. Today, results from deep-sea drilling and micropalaeontology, particularly from the foraminiferans (summarized by Douglas & Woodruff, 1981) allow documentation of major changes in both the composition and depth of faunal associations. We now know that as recently as the Middle Miocene (16 Ma) a 10 °C cooling of the deep-ocean water mass occurred. This probably resulted in massive faunal extinctions, and precipitated a change in deep-sea oceanography to the modern glacial mode. This was characterized by development of polar ice caps, and associated intensified circulation of the deep water mass having its main site of formation in polar oceans, particularly the Antarctic (see Chapter 2).

Owing to potential faunal pathways and biological similarities between the deep sea and the Antarctic (see Lipps & Hickman, 1982), the histories of their faunas has been thought likely to be closely linked, this contributing to the view that the deep-sea fauna has its origin in the shallow Antarctic (Wolff, 1960; Menzies *et al.*, 1973). Furthermore, from careful analysis of the deep-sea molluscan distribution and taxonomy, Clarke (1962) concluded that this fauna was probably derived by invasions from adjacent shallow water all over the world. A careful examination of the distribution and phylogeny of a restricted taxa, the isopod family Ilyarachnidae, suggests, conversely, that this family has originated and radiated *within* the deep sea and then emerged to diversify in the Antarctic owing to the absence of competing decapod crustaceans (Hessler & Thistle, 1975). In their assessment of the available information from the microfossil record from both deep-sea Foraminifera and Antarctica, Lipps & Hickman (1982) conclude that elements of both faunas have accumulated by several processes, with the majority of species having originated in place. A far smaller proportion have migrated between the two regions in one direction or the other, with probably fewer still migrating into the deep sea from other areas, such as the Arctic which could have exported species only since the Pleistocene.

THE FAUNA OF ISOLATED BASINS

Owing to its physical isolation by shallow sills from other deep-sea areas, and the outflowing pattern of deep-water circulation (see Chapter 2), the deep fauna of both the Arctic Ocean–Norwegian Sea and Mediterranean Sea is strongly characterized by endemic elements (Ekman, 1953; Dahl, 1979; Bouchet & Warén, 1979b; Sibuet, 1979). Bouchet & Warén suggest, from the Arctic mollusc fauna, an affinity with the old N. Pacific fauna that lived in the Polar Basin before disconnection from the modern Pacific by formation of the Bering Strait. However, most opinion sees it more likely that the bulk of the fauna of the Arctic basins consists of comparatively recent immigrants from the adjacent shelves (Dahl, 1972, 1979; Dahl *et al.*, 1976; Just, 1980; Hessler & G. D. F. Wilson, 1983).

Endemism amongst the fauna of the deep Mediterranean basins is similarly seen only at specific level. This reflects both the recentness of transgressive events (influx of the ocean), allowing re-invasion and an evolutionary source in local shallow waters. Because of the nearly isothermal conditions, typically bathyal species extend into quite shallow water (Ekman, 1953; Peréz, 1982; Fredj & Laubier, 1985).

The Red Sea is an even younger basin whose connection with the deep sea is still only a narrow sill separating it from the Indian Ocean. Its 'abyssal' faunal, like that of the similarly almost landlocked Sea of Japan, has no endemic elements. Both faunas are thought to be composed entirely of eurybathic elements from the adjacent Indian or Pacific Oceans, some of which have descended from the shelf area down to a depth of 3.5 km in the Sea of Japan (Ekman, 1953).

HOW OLD IS THE DEEP-SEA FAUNA?

The fossil evidence eliminates any notion of a single age of the deep-sea fauna. Clearly, this together with evidence from studies of deep-sea sediments indicates that, over at least the past 100 million years, the deep sea has been far from the stable, unchanging environment previously perceived (Streeter & Shackleton, 1979; Caralp, 1987). Madsen (1961b) has reviewed the affinities between modern and fossil forms in the abyssal, concluding that present-day species belong to families differentiated in the Mesozoic, but to higher groups in the Palaeozoic. Amongst the Foraminifera, while certain components seem to have been present for a long period of time, there have been several periods of diversification or change in the assemblage (Streeter, 1973). At the generic level, the fauna includes both an ancient late Cretaceous-early Tertiary, and a later Tertiary, element the apparently ancient fauna is not made up of the relics previously imagined, their morphological similarity to ancient fossils most probably being the result of convergent evolution (Lipps & Hickman, 1982). Therefore, modern foraminiferan species composition, like that of other marine taxa, was established relatively recently, certainly since the beginning of the Miocene (22 Ma).

Part IV   *Processes: patterns in time*

Because of its remoteness and inaccessibility for direct measurements, it is far easier to study the distribution of fauna on the ocean floor and to record the *results* of their various activities than it is to study the *processes* from which these patterns in space arose. In particular, data on the *rates* of any biological process are sparse and difficult to obtain. The traditional view of the deep sea has become one of a low-activity ecosystem where biota subsist on low levels of available food. This perception has resulted from the extremely low densities of organisms and the low levels of organic material of very poor nutritive value available for them as food. Furthermore, the low numbers of microorganisms in deep-sea sediments have suggested rates of microbial activity to be exceptionally low. This view seemed to be dramatically confirmed by the 'Alvin' lunches – when the food left in the flooded submersible was found to be well preserved on its recovery from the deep-sea bed one year later. The concept of exceptionally low rates of growth and turnover of the animal populations has become deeply embedded as a consequence of radiometric estimates of around 100 yr for the age of large specimens of the small deep-sea bivalve *Tindaria callistiformis*.

In this section we shall see that this view is being challenged by new findings from the deep sea by our most recently won data on a variety of biological processes, from respiration to reproduction, and feeding mechanisms to bioturbation of the sediment. These include unexpectedly rapid phytodetrital sedimentation from the surface and suggestions of rapid microbial utilization of 'new' primary production on the deep-sea bed. Furthermore, there are data showing seasonal breeding and indicating rates of demographic processes amongst larger animals more typical of shallow-water populations.

Data on a wide variety of biological rate processes at the deep-sea benthic boundary have been reviewed by Gage (in press). However, even if it is possible to infer some steps of the biologically mediated processes from the data presently available, we lack a clear overall picture of these processes and how they relate to each other. This need has been recognized as one of the most urgent areas to address in current research programmes.

11

Food resources, energetics and feeding strategies

SOURCES OF FOOD

Possibly the most important limiting factor in deep-sea ecology is food availability. All production in the deep sea, except at hydrothermal vents (see Chapter 15), is fuelled, either directly or indirectly, by the import of organic matter to the bottom, the major part consisting of 'new' production sinking from the process of carbon production by photosynthesis in the euphotic zone. This dependency on organic import make it an *allochthonous*, rather than *autochthonous* (such as the hydrothermal vents), system. Rowe & Staresinic (1979) and Rowe (1981) have outlined the pathways by which the various forms of organic matter, as a food source, enter the deep sea (Fig. 11.1). Particulate Organic Matter (POM) includes both large food-falls, consisting of animal carcasses along with terrigenous and coastal plant debris, as well as fine particulate organic matter mostly from planktonic animals, including faecal pellets and moults, and phytoplankton. In addition, sediments, particularly those in reducing conditions, have been found to contain a relatively large fraction of Dissolved Organic Matter (DOM). This, it has been argued, also constitutes a significant food source for some biota.

LARGE FOOD-FALLS: ANIMAL CARCASES

These include the bodies of large vertebrates such as marine mammals and fish, and large invertebrates such as squid. In an early review of the characteristics of the deep-sea environment, Bruun (1957) suggested the importance of the sinking of whale and shark remains as a food source, although no direct observations were available at that date. The first indirect evidence came from Isaacs & Schwartzlose (1975) using fish carcasses as bait set up on the bottom with a recording camera. While this provided the first photographic evidence of the rapidity with which bait attracted large scavenging organisms, a few years earlier Forster (1964)

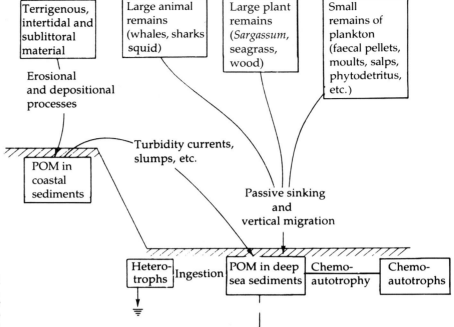

Fig. 11.1. Conceptual model of the potential sources, transport and sinks for organic matter to the deep sea. (Slightly modified from Rowe & Staresinic, 1979.)

had shown the rapidity with which baits are taken by scavenging fish on long-lines set on the continental slope.

Rowe & Staresinic (1979) noted that a large carcase had never been observed on the deep-sea floor in 50 000 seabed photographs on file at the Woods Hole Oceanographic Institution, and in numerous dives in 'Alvin'. This led Stockton & DeLaca (1982) to conclude that large food-falls are rare events. However, there does now exist a growing body of evidence for the presence of large carcases on the bottom. For example, Heezen & Hollister (1971) show a photograph of the skeleton of a seal at 600 m whilst Jannasch (1978) reports the occurrence of half a porpoise carcase at 3.65 km depth in the N.W. Atlantic. Furthermore, in a visual survey using 'Alvin', C. R. Smith (1985) found one large carcase (c. 2 kg) and four small carcases (mean weight c. 50 g) per 8100 m^2 in the bathyal Santa Catalina Basin. Later, in 1987, he discovered the remains of a 20-m long blue or fin whale, and estimated that the average distance between whale carcases might be of the order of only 8 km (C. R. Smith *et al.*, 1989).

Although large food-falls are a source of concentrated organic matter their occurrence is aperiodic and unpredictable, except where they may occur seasonally and predictably under the migration routes of some fish species (Tyler, 1988). That large food-falls are important is not in question as the emplacement of carcases in the deep sea elicits a rapid response from scavenging species such as amphipods, ophiuroids and fish (see below). Also the indirect evidence of stomach content analysis of a variety of invertebrates and fish suggests they consume these large food-falls. C.

R. Smith (1985, 1986) was the first to attempt to quantify this food as an energy source for deep-sea benthos, suggesting it provides 11% of the benthic community respiration requirement.

Whole-animal food-falls occur on a smaller scale when blooms of macroplanktonic species die and sink to the bottom. Moseley (1880) carried out some experiments with salps demonstrating how rapidly they could sink. More recent evidence comes from studies of the vertical migration of salps and the observation of salp remains at the seabed in the N.W. Atlantic (Weibe *et al.*, 1979; Caccione, Rowe & Malahoff, 1978). Similar observations of scyphomedusae have also been made (Jumars, 1976). Stockton & DeLaca (1982) noted that, although the scyphomedusae are scavenged by ophiuroids, there was no evidence that the salps were utilized in the same way.

LARGE FOOD-FALLS OF PLANT ORIGIN

Moseley (1880) commented on the amount of vegetable matter and debris such as leaves, branches and fruits brought up by trawls from the 'Challenger'. He noted that the fruits were still fresh and full of animals feeding on the flesh. A little later Agassiz (1888) had found orange and mango leaves, sugar cane and nutmeg in samples from *c.* 3 km depth and subsequently postulated that rapidly sinking animal and plant remains were an important food source for the deep-sea benthos (C. R. Smith, 1985). Wolff (1979, 1980) reviews the occurrence and possible utilization by animals of plant remains in the deep sea.

MACROALGAE AND SEAGRASS

Although coastal macroalgae and seagrass fragments have often been encountered in sediment traps and on the seabed, and such fragments are often important in detrital food chains in shallow water, their contribution to deep-sea POM has often been discounted (Menzies *et al.*, 1967; Menzies & Rowe, 1969; Schoener & Rowe, 1970). Debris from seagrass such as *Thalassia* may arrive as a result of uprooting during seasonal tropical storms and being carried offshore where it sinks. We have noticed seagrass debris occurring in samples and bottom photographs within the Lisbon and Setubal canyon systems that probably originated from coastal lagoons and estuaries near the head of the canyons. Debris of perennial macroalgae occurs adjacent to coral reefs in the bathyal Coral Sea Plateau (Alongi, 1990), and is also thought to provide a significant input in the Weddell Sea in the Southern Ocean where it may modulate the intense but short seasonal pulse in energy input to the benthos from primary production that is typical of high latitudes (Reichardt, 1987).

There are many observations indicating that deep-sea epifaunal deposit-feeders ingest macroalgal, seagrass and terrestrial plant detritus, including wood (Mortensen, 1935, 1938; Wolff, 1979, 1980; Pawson, 1982). Surprisingly, analysis of the ratios of the stable carbon isotopes ^{13}C to ^{12}C (that are supposed to 'fingerprint' nutritional sources) indicates that at least some of this material may be metabolized directly by sea urchins despite constituting a food source very low in nitrogen, and which decomposes very slowly on the deep-sea floor (Suchanek *et al.*, 1986). It remains possible that the guts of some of these sea urchins support nitrogen-fixing bacteria that in shallow water are known to contribute to the nutritional value of otherwise nitrogen-poor food value (Guerinot & Patriquin, 1981).

SARGASSUM

This pelagic macrophyte is found in considerable quantities on the ocean floor in the Sargasso and Caribbean Seas, the Gulf of Mexico and in the Central Pacific, and is a constant, although patchy, source of organic material in the N.W. Atlantic (Grassle & Morse-Porteous, 1987). Healthy *Sargassum* may be transported into the deep sea by wind-induced Langmuir circulation (D. L. Johnson & Richardson, 1977). If the wind is strong enough (> 25 knots) the Langmuir cells may extend to a depth of 100 m. This is the critical depth for the rapid collapse of the gas vesicles of *Sargassum* and if this occurs the seaweed becomes negatively buoyant and continues to sink; deposition on to the seafloor taking about 40 h. In the Sargasso Sea it would appear that these criteria are satisfied during the winter months suggesting there may be a seasonal input to the deep sea.

TERRESTRIAL PLANT REMAINS

Their occurrence in deep-sea trawlings was noted by several of the great oceanographic expeditions up to the 'Galathea'. Branches and twigs from trees are most common followed by pieces of wood, bark and fruits. Wolff (1979) reviews records of animals using such material as a substratum or shelter. Few of these organisms listed by Wolff are thought able to ingest wood and macrophyte material directly. However, wood forms a significant food source for wood-boring bivalves in the deep sea (Knudsen, 1961; Turner, 1973). Bacteria are thought responsible for the breakdown of cellulose in the stomach of the closely related wood-boring shipworm *Teredo*, which may also support nitrogen-fixing bacteria. Whether a similar gut microflora exists in deep-sea Xylophagainae seems likely but untested. These molluscs convert the wood to faecal pellets that are eaten by detritus feeders; and as the wood disintegrates the boring molluscs are preyed upon if alive and scavenged if dead. Wood may be found regularly (Rowe & Staresinic, 1979) or rarely (Grassle & Morse-Porteous, 1987) in deep-sea samples. Although unpredictable in occurrence at small scales, it does seem to be most common in deep-sea basins and trenches associated with island arcs such as in the E. and W. Indies, and areas with massive fluvial export (e.g. Alongi, 1990). Its appearance in the deep sea may be tied to the rainy season in the tropics or the spring runoff in temperate latitudes where food is brought down to the sea by rivers, becomes waterlogged, and sinks to the sea floor (Turner, 1973).

One of the main differences between faunal and macrophyte remains in the deep sea is the persistence of the latter. Stockton & DeLaca (1982) suggest that the quality of organic matter in the animal remains is more readily available as a food source to scavenging species, so that its scarcity only reflects rapid utilization. Conversely, the predominance of cellulose in macrophyte remains results in more resistance to digestive attack, but also a low nitrogen content. It requires specialized modes of feeding involving slow microbial fermentation to deal with the organic material of such plant remains and they therefore persist longer.

In general terms, these large food-falls provide not only an energy substrate to the deep sea, but their presence at the deep-sea bed also influences the structure of the benthic community by causing spatial heterogeneity owing to highly localized energy enrichment (Stockton & DeLaca, 1982; C. R. Smith, 1985, 1986).

TRANSPORT BY TURBIDITY CURRENTS

Turbidity currents are thought often to be characterized by high levels of organic matter (Keller *et al.*, 1973). Such downslope processes are considered important transporters of organic material to the deep sea as evidenced by seagrass wrapped around submarine cables and buried seagrass and wood fragment in cores from trenches and basins (see Wolff, 1979, for references), but the extent of this input is difficult to quantify. The best-documented example is off the N.W. United States where turbidity currents are relatively common. Here, the numbers of animals living in the Cascadia Channel are four times greater than those living on the nearby Cascadia Abyssal Plain (Griggs, Carey & Kulm, 1969).

PARTICULATE ORGANIC MATTER FROM THE EUPHOTIC ZONE

Our knowledge of the downward flux of this material, its quality, quantity and periodicity, has been obtained mostly within the 1970s and 1980s. The use of sediment traps (Honjo *et al.*, 1980; Honjo & Doherty, 1988; Simpson, 1982) and deep-sea bed photography (Lampitt & Burnham, 1983; Honjo *et al.*, 1984) has shown that this downward flux can be traced into water deeper than 4 km; and in some areas of the world ocean it appears as a seasonally predictable pulse. The data collected to date have been reviewed by Angel (1984), Fowler & Knauer (1986), Deuser (1986) and Alldredge & Silver (1988).

The vertical flux of particulate organic material consists of three main types: amorphous aggregates, faecal pellets and moults.

AMORPHOUS AGGREGATES (MACROFLOCS OR MARINE SNOW)

This is flocculent material probably derived from a variety of sources including the gelatinous bodies of pelagic fauna such as salps and discarded 'houses' of larvaceans, and aggregated diatoms (Angel, 1984; Smetacek, 1985; Alldredge & Silver, 1988; Alldredge & Gotschalk, 1989). This marine snow is recognized as an important site of production/decomposition processes and a habitat for bacteria and microzooplankton (Fowler & Knauer, 1986). The bacteria associated with these aggregates are carried into deeper water (Lochte & Turley, 1988) but their role in particle decomposition is still unclear. Free-living bacteria may be the principal mediators of particle degradation, breaking them into fine non-sinking particles at the expense of fast-sinking ones (Cho & Azam, 1988). As the aggregates sink from the euphotic zone they scavenge particles such as algal cells and small faecal pellets thus accelerating their sinking rate (Kranck & Milligan, 1988). Also found in these aggregates are trace metals, inorganic nutrients, proteins, carbohydrates and lipids (Fowler & Knauer, 1986).

FAECAL PELLETS

These come in a variety of shapes and sizes depending on the organism that produced them, and are well reviewed by Fowler & Knauer (1986). At one end of the scale are loose, amorphous aggregates resembling macro-flocs, such as those produced by salps, and which are thought to be quite important in the downward flux of carbon in some areas (Iseki, 1981). At the other end are dense tightly packed pellets some of which, especially those produced by microcrustaceans, are bounded by a chitinous peritro-phic membrane and this is important in determining the 'halflife' of the pellet. These membrane-bound pellets are more likely to reach the seabed intact than unbound ones. However, the unbound faecal pellets produced by midwater fish are known to arrive at the seabed almost undegraded. In doing so, these faecal pellets transport their nutrients and other elements virtually intact. The composition of faecal pellets is highly diverse and includes phytoplankton cells and gut microflora and it has been suggested that these are more important in the degradation of the pellet than bacteria colonizing the pellet externally (Gowing & Silver, 1983). Besides organic components, faecal pellets contain relatively heavy inorganic particles and these ballast the pellets and aid their sinking. Although these pellets may sink under their own weight, there is evidence that material consumed by organisms near the surface is voided at depth after downward migration. This process is likely to occur in the top 1.5 km of water where vertical migration is known to occur (Rowe & Staresinic, 1979), but below this point passive sinking is the dominant mechanism taking pellets to the deep-sea bed.

MOULTS

The dominant fraction in large particle flux consists of dead, intact organisms and hard parts of plankton. This is particularly evident where significant seasonal blooms in zooplankton occur. Pelagic moults probably degrade within a few days and will rarely reach the deep-sea bed, although there is some tantalizing evidence suggesting that moults, presumably produced by deep-water populations, are relatively abundant in the BBL (see Fowler & Knauer, 1986). Although the data are limited, there is evidence that crustacean (euphausid) moults are rich in nitrogen with traces of carbohydrate (Angel, 1984).

RATE, DEGRADATION AND NUTRITIVE VALUE OF PARTICULATE FLUX TO THE DEEP-SEA BED

For many years it was assumed that all particulate material sinks very slowly. However, McCave (1975) suggested the sinking rate of particles could be more rapid owing to the formation of aggregates. In the last ten years there has been a significant increase in our knowledge of this vertical flux of POM and attempts have been made to quantify the flux as well as determining how this energy source is utilized at the deep-sea bed (see Chapter 12). The main questions posed are: (*a*) how rapidly does this material reach the deep-sea bed? (*b*) how much survives degradation during descent? (*c*) is it of nutritive value to the deep-sea benthos?

Data collected at a sediment trap at 3.8 km depth in the Sargasso Sea serve as a quantitative and qualitative illustration of the flux of material from surface waters to the sea bed (Deuser, 1986). Although surface production is > 100 mg m^{-2} d^{-1} the flux to the bottom varies from 17.7 to 60 mg m^{-2} d^{-1} depending on season (Fig. 11.2). This material is composed of both organic and inorganic components. The inorganic carbonate fraction constitutes 50 to 75% of the total flux whilst the organic matter constitutes 4 to 5% (Deuser, 1986). This organic matter is composed of sugars and amino acids which show a seasonality in their vertical flux in relation to that of total organic matter (Ittekkot *et al.*, 1984). These authors have identified and quantified the dominant sugars as glucose, galactose and mannose and the dominant amino acids as glycine, aspartic acid and glutamic acid associated with this flux. Similar data are available for the Panama Basin (Honjo, 1982; Ittekkot *et al.*, 1984).

Besides the sinking of aggregates and faecal pellets, whole microscopic organisms sink to the deep-sea bed, some of it from seasonal blooms in surface waters. The sinking of planktonic Foraminifera that bloom in surface waters contributes much to the organic matter content of deep

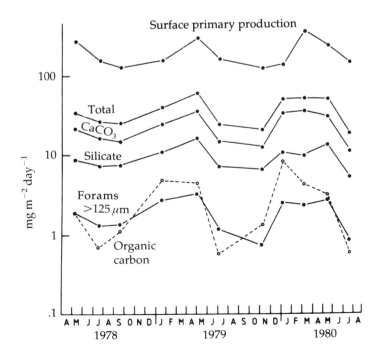

Fig. 11.2. Seasonal changes in the total and component fluxes of particulate matter collected in a sediment trap at 3.2 km depth in the Sargasso Sea in relation to surface primary production. (From Deuser *et al.*, 1981.)

water (see Thunnell & Reynolds, 1984; Deuser, 1987) and may be a significant seasonal food source for scaphopod molluscs (Davies, 1987).

In the North Pacific, the flux of diatoms and silicoflagellates to the deep-sea bed has a seasonal component (Takahashi, 1986, 1987). It seems likely that this downward flux of phytoplankton is aided by mucous secretions that cause aggregations of the cells (Smetacek, 1985; Kranck & Milligan, 1988). In the northern Indian Ocean an increased particle flux rate has been related to a seasonal monsoon (Nair et al., 1989).

In the N.E. Atlantic, the downward flux of phytoplankton has been photographed reaching the seabed at various depths down to 4 km in the Porcupine Seablight (Lampitt, 1985a). Surface produced plankton starts arriving at the seabed in late June, reaches a maximum in late July and declines during August (Figs 11.3, 11.4). The diatoms associated with the vertical flux in this region were Thalassionema nitzschoides, Nitzschia seriata and N. delicatissima, species typical of production in surface waters over this site. Analysis of this phytodetritus material has shown that the organic carbon content varied from 0.56% to 1.28% (Rice et al., 1986). These values are low when compared to those of Deuser (1986) (see above). The C/N ratio increased from 9.0 at 1 km to 23.6 at 4.5 km suggesting a greater degree of degradation at the greater sample depths. Even if this material does not appear to be very nutritious, deep-sea megabenthic organisms have been observed feeding on it (Lampitt, 1985b; P. A.Tyler, personal observations). A similar, greenish gelatinous phytodetritus has been found at about 4.5 km depth on the Porcupine Abyssal Plain (Theil et al., 1988). The fast sinking aggregates probably form by drifting phytoplankton-containing mucus flake becoming loaded by entangled phaeodrian cells (Radiolaria) and their faecal pellets (Riemann, 1989). The trophic significance of this markedly seasonal pulse of fast-sedimenting organic particles (Deuser & Ross, 1980; Deuser et al., 1981; Honjo, 1982, 1984; Betzer et al., 1984) that appear to be related to the appearance on the seabed of very mobile, patchy, easily re-suspended phytodetrital floc after the spring bloom in the N.E. Atlantic (Billett et al., 1983; Lampitt, 1985a; Rice et al., 1986) remains unclear. This topic, along with the cause of its gradual disappearance through the summer, is the subject of much current research (summarized below). The results are starting to suggest that this huge input of organic matter has great significance to deposit-eating benthos. Certainly, analysis of gut contents indicates that this material is utilized as food by deposit-feeding echinoderms, sipunculans and actinians (Thiel et al., 1988).

Elsewhere, a blanketing flocculent layer on the deep sea bed has been observed composed of material altered to a mainly inorganic composition, perhaps the residue of degraded phytodetritus, that is similar in organic content to the superficial sediment below (Fowler & Knauer, 1986; Reimers & Wakefield, 1989).

Recently it has become evident that there are two distinct classes of particles in the water column, suspended and sinking (Karl, Knauer & Martin, 1988). The suspended particles contribute most of the standing stock of POM and have the greater bacterial populations. Microbial activity associated with the sinking POM decreases with depth, and thus stands a greater chance of reaching the seabed undegraded (Karl *et al.*, 1988; Cho & Azam, 1988). The conclusion drawn by Karl *et al.*, 1988) that sinking POM makes a poor habitat for bacterial growth is contradicted by the vigorous microbial activity which rapidly develops once the phyto-detritus reaches the seabed (Lochte & Turley, 1988). Possibly it is only after the material has reached the seabed that it is colonized by specialized barophilic heterotrophs, and these are the organisms that are responsible for its degradation rather than the cyanobacteria also observed associated with it (Suess, 1988).

In shallow water, the response of the benthic community to the fallout of organic matter from surface production can be immediate (Graf *et al.*, 1983). Organic particulates are colonized by a range of zooflagellates, amoebae, ciliates, and small metazoans such as turbellarians, nematodes and rotifers, which all feed on the bacterial and fungal microflora associated with organic detritus (see review by Fenchel, 1978). Recent research suggests that in the deep sea similar food chains may exist; the phytodetritus being colonized by a variety of prokaryote microorganisms (Lochte & Turley, 1988; Turley & Lochte, 1990) which are consumed by certain elements of the benthic allogromiid, textulariid and rotaliinid foraminiferan community – and by nematodes, all of which seem to rapidly proliferate in the phytodetritus (Gooday, 1988; Turley, Lochte & Patterson, 1988; Gooday & Lambshead, 1989; Patterson, 1990). The foraminifers, at least, are consumed by larger fauna such as scaphopod molluscs and holothurians which seem to selectively graze phytodetritus-rich surface sediment (Davies, 1987; Billett *et al.*, 1988).

The rates and significance of these processes have been well reviewed, in the context of responses to other food inputs, by Gooday & Turley (1990). Furthermore, there is now evidence to show that the response of the benthic community may be as rapid in the deep sea as it is in shallow water. Measurements of chlorophyll *a* in the sediment rose sharply in early June after a pulse of faecal-pellet sedimentation on the Vøring Plateau in the Norwegian Sea. This was accompanied by swift rise in sediment ATP and heat production, which are indicators of benthic (mainly microorganism) production and energy flow, respectively; with an overall response of less than 8 days! (Graf, 1989). Furthermore, this study indicated that the effect was as quickly transmitted deep into the sediment, probably as a result of the feeding activities of sipunculans.

An opposing view was taken by Pearcy & Stuiver (1983) who inter-preted their ^{14}C data showing a decline of the radioisotope in organic material down to 5.18 km depth in the N.E. Pacific as indicating that rapidly sinking particles from the euphotic do *not* constitute the principal source of dietary organic carbon for deep-sea fishes and large benthic invertebrates. Instead, they argued that the 'large and nutritious' par-ticles that sink into the deep sea consist of 'aged' carbon, with an average residence time in the deep sea of about 18–35 yr, derived mainly from recycling of non-refractory carbon by mesopelagic animals. However, their interpretation has been challenged by Williams, Druffel & K. L.

Fig. 11.3. Examples of photographs from a 'Bathysnap' record, with frames taken every 8 h, at 4.025 km depth in the Porcupine Seabight (N.E. Atlantic) showing the first appearance (*a*) and (*continued*)

Smith (1987) who conclude that the ^{14}C gradient in Dissolved Inorganic Carbon (DIC) in the surface mixed layer, combined with the chronological age of the midwater organisms themselves, are primarily responsible for the decrease in biocarbon ^{14}C, so that the principal source of dietary carbon for deep-sea biota is from rapidly sinking organic detritus along with active, animal-mediated, downward transport of living carbon. A

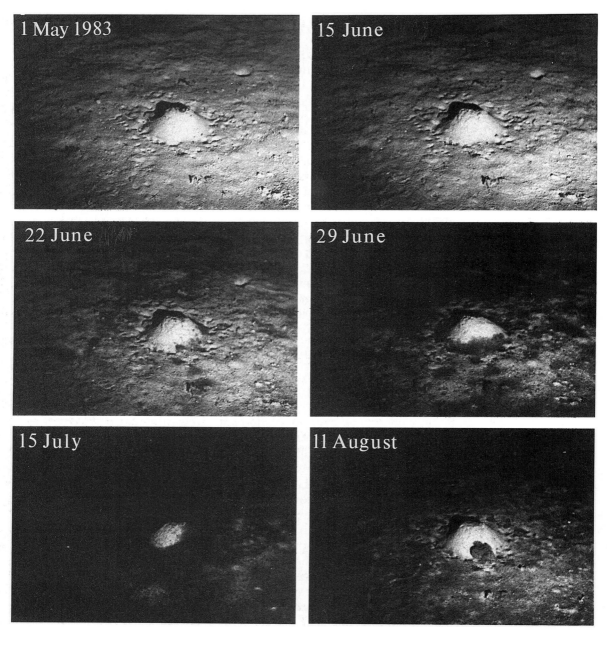

subsequent build-up and re-deposition (*b*)–(*e*) of phytodetrital 'fluff' on the seabed around a mound. The last photograph (*f*) shows this detrital carpet disappearing at the end of the summer. (Courtesy Dr R. S. Lampitt, Institute of Oceanographic Sciences.)

cautionary note has been sounded by K. L. Smith *et al.* (1989) concerning the data for *downward* vertical flux. In an experiment to collect *upward* flux they noted that the upward flux 1.2 km above the seabed (water depth 5.8 km) was 66.7% of the concurrently measured downward flux. This upward flux consisted of eggs, larvae and possibly carcases, suggesting such upward flux to be a significant component of carbon and nitrogen cycling in the open ocean. Furthermore, this buoyant matter may act as a means of recycling lipid-rich material back to the surface (Grimalt *et al.*, 1990).

CONCLUSIONS ON IMPORTANCE OF PARTICULATE FLUX

Something like 1–3% of surface organic primary production reaches the abyssal seabed by a variety of pathways. Much of it sinks at a rate of 100 m d^{-1} and so forms a suitable food source in terms of its composition for the deep-sea benthos. Most of the sinking POM in the worlds oceans will form a suitable substrate for heterotrophic bacterial activity. Some of the POM (possibly most of it), is converted to bacterial tissue thus making otherwise refractory organic matter available to suspension and deposit feeding organisms, especially at the deep-sea floor. Only a small fraction of organic matter is not utilized either by microbes or metazoans and becomes incorporated into the sedimentary record. Cole *et al.* (1987) suggest that 50 to 85% of the organic carbon reaching the deep-sea floor is remineralized within one year. The remainder is believed to have a residence time between 15 and 150 yr in the surface sediment (Emerson *et al.*, 1985) compared to 0.3 to 3.0 yr in the water column (Gardner *et al.*, 1983). The implications of such pulsed food input on the activity of the larger organisms is considered in Chapters 12 and 13 on metabolic and reproductive seasonality in the deep sea.

The data suggest that the availability of particulate food in the deep sea is generally a significant limiting factor, despite periodic and seasonal large influxes of organic material. Thus feeding strategies have evolved that compensate for this unpredictability in the food supply.

Fig. 11.4. Seasonal variability in amount of phytodetritus on the seabed at 4.025 km depth in the Porcupine Seabight (N.E. Atlantic) quantified from the film density (measured by input meter) of frames taken by 'Bathysnap'. Vertical bars represent degree of resuspension, subjectively ranked on a scale of 1 to 5, in individual photographs which were taken once every 512 min. (From Lampitt, 1985*a*.)

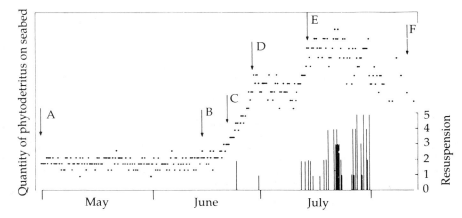

DISSOLVED ORGANIC MATTER (DOM)

DOM is a food source (reviewed by Williams, 1975) which is produced in the deep sea as a result of bacterial action, metabolic processes in metazoans, and dissolved products being released during the decay of organisms after death. Dissolved Organic Carbon (DOC) is also thought to act as an odour plume which attracts scavenging species to carrion.

Recent analyses have suggested that concentrations of DOM are at least double those previously measured. There are questions to be answered about the methodology used, but if such values are correct then the implications are quite startling. For example, the dissolved organic carbon pool exported from the euphotic zone will amount to about twice the pool of CO_2 in the atmosphere, and will be about twice that of the carbon pool in terrestrial plants (Toggweiler, 1988). It certainly constitutes the highest concentrations of organic matter in the sea. DOM is composed of two major fractions. The first consists of compounds which are metabolized rapidly by heterotrophic activity and are maintained at threshold levels. The second, and largest, fraction includes the more refractory dissolved organics which are not so readily metabolized. However, Toggweiler (1988) suggests that there is a fraction of high molecular weight compounds which have a much faster turnover than the *c.* 6000 yr old fraction previously known – which includes high molecular weight polymers such as lignins, humic acids and proteins.

Concentrations of DOM in the interstitial water of deep-sea sediments are approximately ten times those found in the overlying water column (Tanone & Handa, 1980), but, unlike the DOM found in overlying waters, much of the interstitial DOM is identifiable. Free amino acids can attain concentrations of 5.6 mg l^{-1} and free sugars 0.4 mg g^{-1} dry weight of sediment (Southward & Southward, 1982). The role of these compounds in the nutrition of deep-sea animals is open to much speculation, but it is known that free amino acids are taken up by certain shallow-water invertebrate taxa. It is believed that uptake of dissolved organic matter contributes at least partially to the energy requirements of the Pogonophora (Southward & E. C. Southward, 1982), although there is considerable interest in the proportion of organic material contributed by symbiotic chemosynthetic bacteria (Southward *et al.*, 1981, 1986). Only in *Siboglinum ekmani* does mean uptake of DOC seem able to contribute all the energy requirement of the adult. Most other pogonophores examined have an energy requirement deficit of up to 70% (Southward & Southward, 1982). These authors have estimated that the uptake of DOC by the seastar *Plutonaster* and the polychaete *Tharyx* provides 30% of their energy requirements. The solitary coral *Thecopsammia* and the polychaete *Hyalinoecia* collected from depths of 1 to 1.8 km have been maintained without food, in waters containing a high level of DOM, for prolonged periods (George, 1981). The ascothoracian barnacles which are internally parasitic on deep-sea seastars probably live on DOM. It would appear that the organisms most likely to exploit DOC are those with soft bodies and a large surface area/body volume ratio, such as sponges and suspension feeding coelenterates.

FEEDING STRATEGIES

In our review of the fauna of the deep-sea benthic boundary in Part II (Chapters 4 and 5) we have encountered many different strategies in feeding, many of which are associated with particular taxa. These include the usual categories of suspension feeders, deposit feeders, herbivores, carnivores and scavengers, often associated with specialized morphologies, but attempts to generalize are complicated by flexibility in feeding habits shown by some species. For example, spionid polychaetes (which are abundant in the deep sea in inshore waters) hold their two mucous-clad palps up in an erect helical coil to entrap particles in currents, but, in quieter conditions, the same palps are used for deposit feeding (Taghorn, Nowell & Jumars, 1980). But the chief difficulty in categorizing deep-sea animals into the feeding guilds to be described below, is the sparsity in direct evidence of the resources utilized by each species. Categorization into feeding type is by analogy with better known relatives in shallower water, sometimes supported by analyses of morphology and examination of gut contents.

Two trends are apparent from Chapters 4 and 5:

(i) Suspension feeders markedly decrease in overall importance with increasing depth. Most abyssal taxa are deposit feeders, which on morphological evidence can be further subdivided into subsurface and surface-deposit feeders (Fig. 11.5). There is a trend indicated in Chapter 4, for taxa which are normally suspension feeders in shallow water, to have evolved carnivorous or possibly deposit-feeding habits in the abyss. It is only in regions of the deep sea with exceptionally high productivity, such as hydrothermal vents (see Chapter 15), or high

Fig. 11.5. Surface-deposit feeding by the shallow-water, mud dwelling spionid *Malacoceros*; the paired, ciliated feeding palps (fp) select particles as they explore the sediment surface. The worm lives in a mud-tube within the sediment. Deep-sea spionids probably feed in a similar manner, although they will rarely live at such high density as depicted; this foraging strategy becoming increasingly unable to provide resources at a rate sufficient to meet metabolic demands as food supplies become more sparse with increasing depth and distance from land. (Drawing courtesy Dr T. H. Pearson, SEAS Ltd., Oban.)

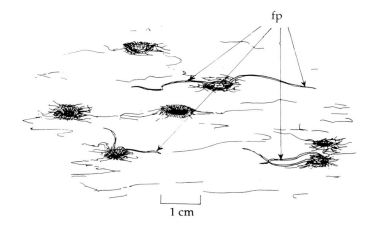

1 cm

bottom current flow that suspension feeders become prominent.

(ii)   Despite this discernible evolution away from dependence on the utilization of suspended particles, there is a second trend for specialist carnivores to become increasingly scarce with increasing depth. The low density of prey must make this lifestyle increasingly unprofitable in relation to effort. However carnivory seems to be retained as an option by the guild of omnivorous scavengers which become more important with depth (see Chapter 4). Amongst this fauna one can perceive a trend not only towards increased size but increased motility (Fig. 11.6), with a concomitant progressive loss in the less-motile scavenging species (such as brittle stars): with descent into the abyss, the scavenging fauna is composed of a few highly specialized, and highly motile, specialists, such as the giant amphipods.

Owing to the absence of photosynthetic production, herbivores similar to those in shallow water would be thought to be absent. Yet the presence of relatively fresh planktonic plant cells and macroalgal, seagrass and wood fragments on the seafloor does not mean that their usual food source is completely absent at depth. In fact, there appear to be a whole suite of deep-sea species adapted to exploit such ephemeral resources, the best studied of which are those utilizing wood (Turner, 1977). Amongst deposit feeders, sessile surface deposit feeding, where the animal extends tentacles or feeding palps over the sediment from a more or less permanent tube or burrow usually predominates, but becomes noticeably less predominant in more oligotrophic basins (Young *et al.*, 1985). At the middle of oligotrophic, mid-oceanic gyres it appears that few if any animals are able to make a living on resources within reach of one tube or burrow, and motility becomes the rule (Jumars & Fauchald, 1977).

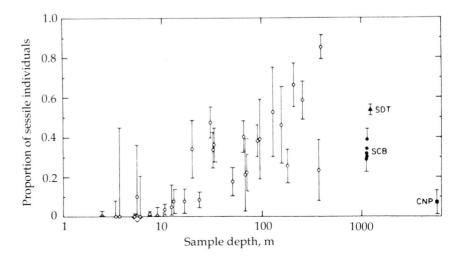

Fig. 11.6. Proportion of sessile polychaetes plotted against depth offshore from southern California. SDT, San Diego Trough; SCB, Santa Catalina Basin. Bars indicate 95% confidence intervals. (From Jumars & Fauchald 1977.)

SUSPENSION FEEDING

FEEDING METHODS

These fauna collect suspended particles from the water using a variety of methods as described for the different taxa in Part II. The chemical similarity in food source and hydrodynamic and physical constraints (Jørgensen, 1966) have resulted in evolutionary convergence in many of the feeding mechanisms. Passive particle interception exploiting current shears is achieved by a series of fibres, ranging from the outstretched arms of ophiacanthid brittle stars and of isocrinid sea lilies, the tentacles of coelenterates and ectoprocts, and the branchial basket of ascidians by no means are limited to simple sieving; direct interception of particles following flow streamlines around fibres being hydrodynamically the most likely mode of capture (Rubenstein & Koel, 1977). Active interception is seen in bivalves whose often complicated ciliary mechanisms associated with mucus both permit selectivity in particle feeding and generate the current of water needed to make the mechanism mechanically more efficient. Tentacular structures associated with mucus production to help entrap particles occur amongst coelenterates and echinoderms. The former still have stinging nematocysts which kill small, live plankton and provide a continuity between carnivory and suspension feeding. This is particularly evident in the deep sea where, at least in the abyss, generally more hydrodynamically tranquil conditions provide severely limited opportunities for feeding on resuspended organic detritus.

RELATIONSHIP TO BOTTOM CURRENTS

Overall, suspension feeding is much less important in the deep sea than in energetic coastal habitats. However, there are many observations in the deep-sea literature indicating that typical deep-sea suspension feeding taxa are numerous where topographic features enhance bottom currents. Examples include marginal areas experiencing energetic boundary currents that will enhance particulate flux to filter feeders (e.g. Gage *et al.,* 1983) and seamounts (e.g. Genin *et al.,* 1986). The detailed camera-sled surveys on the continental slope off the eastern seaboard of the U.S.A., have clearly shown this relationship between the occurrence of larger suspension feeding epifaunal species and topographic features which generate enhanced background current activity. Generally, carnivore/scavengers and suspension feeders predominate on the upper slope of the eastern seaboard, suspension feeders dominate mid-slope, and deposit feeders on the lower slope and abyss. However, where the boundary current impinges on the upper rise, a predominantly suspension-feeding fauna occurs (Blake *et al.,* 1987; Maciolek *et al.,* 1987*a,b*). However, amongst 'suspension-feeding' species are many which are capable of taking small live prey such as colonial coelenterates, corals and anemones. Almost nothing is known of the size spectra or the nutritive value of the particles taken by deep-sea suspension feeders. It would be particularly interesting to learn more of the nutritive quality of particles carried by currents in areas of deep sea with strong flow regimes. Although it has been thought that microbial films may be abraded during sediment transport (Jumars & Nowell, 1984), other work indicates that resuspended particles carry a richer microbial flora than that present on deposited particles (Baird *et al.*, 1985).

DEPOSIT FEEDING

NUTRITIONAL SOURCES FOR DEPOSIT FEEDERS

The deep-sea sediment comprises a complex mixture dominated by inert mineral grains of both terrigenous and pelagic origin. But, unlike shallow water deposits, its organic content is very low, both in dissolved and particulate organic matter, hence it contains very sparse populations of free-living microorganisms (Sorokin, 1978; Jannasch & Wirsen, 1973; Deming & Colwell, 1982; Tabor *et al.*, 1982). Levels of chemoautotrophic production are estimated to occur at barely detectable levels of around $0.01–0.1$ mg organic carbon m^{-2} yr^{-1} (Rowe & Staresinic, 1979). Furthermore, what little POM ordinarily is present has probably already been recycled through the alimentary tracts of midwater animals, and is likely to be highly refractory, consisting mostly of structural organic material such as scleroproteins from the moulted casts of planktonic crustaceans. Despite what seems to be an exceptionally poor food source, deposit feeders flourish, albeit at lower densities, in the deep sea and have turnover rates that seem to be within the range of those in shallow water (see Chapter 13).

This apparent paradox may be resolved once the significance of microbial activity and bacteria-based food-chains based on the fast-sedimenting organic particulates (considered above under Sources of Food) and the importance of symbiotic relationships between microbes and metazoan hosts is more completely assessed. Certainly, emerging data reviewed above on fast-sinking organic particles indicates that it would be a mistake to assume that the food of deposit feeders results solely from a slow and continuous rain of the more refractory residual particles remaining from the pelagic consumers above. Rather, the supply may be pulsed into 'downpours' of labile material that has sunk rapidly from the surface layers. We know also from measurements of dynamic hydrographic regimes involving frequent sediment resuspension (see Chapter 2) that this deposition may be subject to active lateral transport, particularly near the ocean basin margins and over topographic barriers such as seamounts, and carry with it microorganisms and small and larval metazoans (J. Y. Aller, 1989).

CHARACTERISTICS OF DEPOSIT FEEDING

Many of the problems inherent in deposit feeding differ only in degree from problems of suspension feeding. In shallow water many species are known to switch facultatively from one feeding regime to the other, and some may even feed simultaneously by both means (Meadows & Reid, 1966; Hughes, 1969; Rasmussen, 1973; Taghorn *et al.*, 1980; Pohlo, 1982; Dauer, 1983).

All deposit feeders bulk process sediment through the alimentary tract. In shallow water, each day a sediment feeder typically processes an amount of sediment equivalent to its own body weight. Data on weight-specific feeding rates amongst deep-sea species are not as yet available, but they seem likely to fall within the range of values from 0.4 to 45–120 mg ingested sediment mg^{-1} body wt tabulated by Lopez & Levinton (1987) from shallow water. Shallow-water bivalves attain high rates of sediment processing by prior sorting and rejection of unsuitable particles as pseudofaeces; deep-sea protobranchs also possess large labial palps which in shallow-water species perform the initial processing (Allen, 1978). The distance between faeces ejected by large epifaunal holothurians, and the absence of tracks or sediment removal led Heezen & Hollister (1971) to suggest that only the very surface film of sediment is skimmed off by such deposit feeders; and this is supported from analyses of stomach contents (Sibuet *et al.*, 1984; Billett *et al.*, 1988). Similarly the spoke-like feeding traces made by echiuran worms (see Chapter 5), and the morphology of the feeding palps of polychaetes, suggests that only the most recently sedimented material is taken by the more sedentary deposit feeders. Billett *et al.* (1988) show that as well as degradation of labile plant pigments during passage through the gut of epibenthic holothurians, the detrital composition on the sediment surface matches that of its foregut closely, even when phytodetrital cover on the seabed is patchy. This suggests that these sluggish animals are effective in feeding on patches of new detritus.

The mechanics of particle selection by tentaculate deposit feeders, such as polychaetes, is modelled by Jumars, Self & Nowell (1982), who concluded that particle size selection in tentaculate deposit feeders is a function mainly of the adhesive strength of the mucus on the tentacle, and may not be associated with any specific morphological adaptations. Mucus adhesion may also account for any ability to preferentially select coated over uncoated particles, rather than any behavioural response (Taghorn, 1982).

As in shallow water, the foraging patterns of many deep-sea deposit feeders seem to reflect a dependence on sediment transport (Jumars & Nowell, 1984; Jumars *et al.*, 1990). Horizontal transport may particularly favour the utilization of newly-deposited detrital floc. Selection of this material by buried macrofaunal deposit feeders may be achieved in strong flow conditions by means of shallow feeding pits rather than from extension of feeding tentacles or palps illustrated in Fig. 11.5. The pits effectively capture material in bedload transport and will enhance rates of local deposition of suspended particles. In areas where the flow regime is much quieter, large-bodied epifaunal deposit feeders, such as holothurians, may become favoured. Their motility allows them to gather the most nutritious surface material effectively, while their large bulk provides a large gut capacity and deters predation.

The consequences of episodic flux of particles have barely been considered by deep-sea biologists, despite the rapidly accumulating data (summarized earlier in this Chapter) of rapid utilization of phytodetritus. Furthermore, there are now data relating phytodetritus availability to gut contents in samples, taken at different times of the year, of the deep-sea deposit-feeding sea urchin (*Echinus affinis* which grazes this material directly on the seabed (L. S. Campos, personal communication). Jumars *et al.* (1990) suggest that larger burrowers, such as sipunculan worms, which are known to rapidly transport material deep into the sediment, hence prevent it being sequestered by smaller, surface-living heterotrophs. Similarly, echiuran worms may hoard organic material gathered from the surface by packaging it into relatively large faecal pellets for feeding on later. These have been observed as little piles or as part of the burrow lining. It is not known whether some chemical agent or the size of the pellets themselves deter utilization by other organisms; but Jumars *et al.* (1990) surmise that as the organs for excreting nitrogenous waste are located in close proximity to the anus, this suggests deliberate enrichment in order to encourage growth of bacteria to make the pellets more nutritious.

THE IMPORTANCE OF BACTERIA

The concept of such microbial 'gardens' (Hylleberg, 1975) derives from the observation in shallow water that organic particles that are stripped of attached microbiota during digestion within the guts of larger animals are quickly recolonized by microorganisms and fungi. A similar process occurs after defaecation so that a repeated transfer of microbial biomass to deposit feeders occurs (Newell, 1965; and references in Lopez & Levinton, 1987). However, this concept has been challenged by studies showing that too little bacterial biomass is ingested to supply the carbon requirements of inshore macrofauna (see Kemp, 1987 for references). This difficulty might be thought to apply even more strongly to the deep sea, where microbial degradation in deep-sea sediments has been regarded as too low to meet energy demands of benthic animals. However, recent observations suggest that the fresh, surface-derived organic material, such as the bodies of coccolithophorids and associated macroaggregates of phytodetritus, is rapidly decomposed at the sediment surface within one year, and that input of these particles is enough to account for all benthic respiration (Gardner, Hinga & Mara, 1983; Cahet & Sibuet, 1986; Rowe & Deming, 1985; Cole, Honjo & Erez, 1987; Lochte & Turley, 1988). Even if activity and turnover of barotolerant bacteria associated with these particles is greater than has been thought, it seems more likely that microbial food chains involving prokaryotes and other microbiota, along with small metazoans, are important as food resources for deposit feeders (Gooday, 1988). The degradation of refractory particles by barophilic symbiotic bacteria within the gut of deep-sea invertebrates is also important (see Jannasch & Taylor, 1984 for references). Pelletization of faeces and pseudofaeces, by preventing them from being reingested, might similarly encourage development of enhanced microbial biomass within the gut (Allen & Sanders, 1966; Levinton, 1979). Similar effects might well also result from mucus secretion and the physical disturbance of the microenvironment of bacteria by burrowers (Yingst & Rhoads, 1980; Aller, 1982).

Bacteria are both highly digestible and nutritious compared with most other particulate organic particles in the sediment. Along with diatoms, protozoans and nematodes, they may provide essential proteinaceous nutritional requirements which cannot be met by the animal itself (Phillips, 1984). In shallow water, repeated studies of the relative nutritive value of microbiota and nonliving organic matter have supported the view that before organic matter in sediment becomes available to deposit feeders it must be converted into bacterial biomass. Hence, deposit feeders are not feeding on organic detritus so much as the microbial populations that it supports.

The results on the deep-sea sediment of such massive scales of bulk feeding by deposit feeders in an environment of low rates of sedimentation is the intense reworking or bioturbation of the sediment (considered in Chapter 14) and has considerable importance when trying to understand geochemical cycles, and interpreting the geological record represented by the sediment.

HIGHER LINKS IN DEEP-SEA FOOD CHAINS

As will be clear from data in the systematic review of deep-sea animals in Part II, organisms specialized to feed on a narrow range of prey or other dietary items seems to be rare in the deep sea. The best-known examples of such dietary specialists are found amongst gastropod molluscs and wood-boring bivalves. On the other hand most large, roving organisms such as macrourid fish or decapod crustaceans seem to be able to take a wide variety of prey, including carrion. However, information on trophic connections in deep-sea food chains remain tantalizingly sparse and of poor quality: for example those benthopelagic fish which have swim bladders, are deformed on recovery by the swim bladders everting their stomach contents back out of their mouths. The stomachs of scavenging crustaceans are often found full, but their gastric mills grind everything into an unidentifiable soup. However, despite these difficulties, careful analysis of stomach contents with identifiable remains, has highlighted the apparent lack in selectivity of predatory species, especially fish (Pearcy & Ambler, 1974; Sedberry & Musick, 1978; Mauchline & Gordon, 1984, 1985) and brittle stars (Litvinova & Sokolova, 1971; Pearson & Gage, 1984). The benthopelagic macrourid fishes seem to feed on multi-species patches, and four types of feeding strategy may be distinguished (Mauchline & Gordon, 1986). The future use of sophisticated biochemical techniques for dietary analysis in deep-sea food-web analysis has considerable potential as was indicated by a preliminary study using cross-reacting antisera (Feller, Zagursky & Day, 1985). Uncontaminated homogenized tissue extracts of a phylogenetically wide range of organisms obtained from shallow water were injected into rabbits so that antisera could be obtained from them. These antisera make it possible to detect microgram amounts of specific antigen proteins from organisms identifiable to major taxa level by means of immunoassay. This pioneering study identified the presence of antigenic proteins from holothurian, anemone, gastropod, decapod and foraminiferan prey from the gut contents of grenadiers, *Coryphaenoides (Nematonurus) armatus* that visually appeared to consist only of a fluid containing parasites, crustacean exoskeletons and gastropod opercula; demonstrating the importance of benthic predation in these animals.

12

Metabolic processes: microbial ecology, and organism and community respiration at the deep-sea bed

MICROBIAL ECOLOGY: APPROACH AND PROBLEMS

The first observations of bacterial populations in the deep sea were made in 1882 and 1883 during the cruises of the 'Travailleur' and 'Talisman' (Certes, 1884). Although observations continued to be made, no data became available on rates of deep-sea bacterial metabolism until the early 1950s. Morita & Zobell (1955) and Zobell and Morita (1957) demonstrated that bacterial activity in deep-sea sediments was very low. This was not thought surprising as the low temperature, high pressure and low nutrient levels known to occur in the deep sea did not present a particularly favourable milieu for bacterial growth. All bacterial activity in the deep sea (with the exception of chemosynthesis which is limited to hydrothermal vents and sulphide-rich cold seeps – see Chapter 15) is heterotrophic, requiring an energy source in the form of organic matter ultimately derived from surface production.

In the last 20 years there has been a great effort in understanding the bacterial ecology of the deep sea. This effort was stimulated by two unrelated events. The first was the accidental sinking of the submersible 'Alvin'. The submersible was swamped by a wave on launching. The crew escaped but left behind their lunch which consisted of bouillon, bologna sandwiches and apples. When 'Alvin' was recovered one year later, the scientists were amazed to find the food was still in good condition (see photograph in Jannasch, 1978) within the flooded pressure sphere, but it soon rotted even in a refrigerator at atmospheric pressure (Jannasch *et al.*, 1970). The second major event was the discovery of hydrothermal vents. Here the energy cycle is driven by the oxidation of sulphide ions in the vent water by the chemosynthetic bacterial population which fix carbon dioxide to produce organic matter which becomes available to the metazoan populations (Jannasch, 1984). Similar communities using methane as the energy sources have now been discovered in a number of locations.

The advances in our understanding of bacterial ecology in the deep sea have occurred mostly as a result of technological advances including the use of submersibles for *in situ* studies and the development of pressure vessels in which bacteria can be cultured in the laboratory at deep-sea pressures (Jannasch *et al.*, 1973; Jannasch & Wirsen, 1973; Yayanos, 1979). These are used in concert with measurement of microbial activity using ^{14}C labelled substrate, and, more recently, radiolabelled nucleotides by measurement of nucleic acid synthesis, in conjunction with direct counts of bacterial numbers using epifluorescence microscopy (Alongi, 1990).

There have been a number of recent reviews of microbial ecology in the deep sea (Nealson, 1982; Jannasch & Wirsen, 1983; Jannasch & Taylor, 1984) as well as a number of reviews on the effect of hydrostatic pressure on microbial metabolism (Landau & Pope, 1980; Marquis & Matsumura, 1978).

In this first section of Chapter 12 let us examine the bacterial ecology of deep-sea sedimentary material and review attempts to determine how these bacteria control rates of organic matter cycling at the deep-sea bed. Generally, bacteria in the surficial sediments of the deep sea are heterotrophs requiring an organic energy source and oxygen to produce energy as ATP in the oxidative phosphorylation cycle. The exceptions are the chemosynthetic bacteria found at hydrothermal vents, cold seeps and within reducing sediments. As we have seen in Chapter 2, oxygen is rarely limiting in the deep sea, but the organic matter content of deep-sea sediments may be very low (< 0.5%). Jannasch & Taylor (1984) presented a scheme of growth curves in response to hydrostatic pressure (Fig. 12.1) which was used by Deming (1986) to define a terminology. *Barosensitive* bacteria are those that die at relatively low pressures (< 200 atm). *Barotolerant* bacteria are those that can grow at pressures of 400 atm (occasionally to 600 atm) but grow best at 1 atm. This group contains most bacteria tested from aquatic and terrestrial habitats (Deming, 1986). *Barophilic* bacteria are those that grow optimally under elevated hydrostatic pressure (Zobell & Johnson, 1949). Those which function exclusively at high pressures and die at low pressure are referred to as *obligate barophiles* (Zobell & Morita, 1957). Deming (1986) reports that, although a wide variety of barophiles have been isolated in recent years, only two strains of obligate barophiles, both from hadal samples, have been isolated.

In the deep sea it has long been predicted that free-living bacteria in the

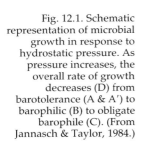

Fig. 12.1. Schematic representation of microbial growth in response to hydrostatic pressure. As pressure increases, the overall rate of growth decreases (D) from barotolerance (A & A') to barophilic (B) to obligate barophile (C). (From Jannasch & Taylor, 1984.)

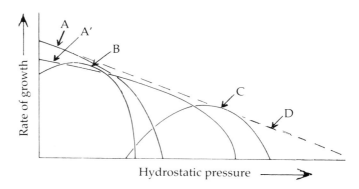

sediment were likely to be barotolerant, whereas the bacteria found in the guts of deep-sea organisms would be barophilic. The main problem this hypothesis presented was that experimental growth studies are difficult to conduct *in situ* and relied on endpoint determinations that could not be subjected to rigorous statistical analysis. Removing bacteria from their natural environment may modify their growth responses, although replicate samples could be used to increase statistical validity. Yayanos *et al.* (1981) had demonstrated that it was possible to isolate bacterial populations from the deep sea as long as the temperature of the sample was not raised and the sample was recompressed as quickly as possible after retrieval and inoculation.

Wirsen & Jannasch (1983) highlight the main questions facing deep-sea microbiology. They ask: (*a*) what is there? (*b*) how many are there? and (*c*) what are they doing and how rapidly are they doing it? As standard bacterial techniques are difficult to operate at several kilometres depth in the deep sea, research into this area of deep-sea ecology has presented some unique technical problems. Various workers have attempted to solve these technical problems by three main methods:

(i)   *In situ* studies using natural populations of bacteria manipulated by the use of 'Alvin' or by free vehicles or 'landers'.

(ii) Laboratory based studies, especially on board ship, in which natural populations of bacteria are recovered at low temperature and after inoculation are recompressed to ambient temperature and pressure. The benefits of this method are that it is more easily manageable and replicates can be carried out.

(iii) Isolation of deep-sea bacteria after decompression/recompression, the identification of strains, and the subjection of these strains to rigorous microbial techniques (Yayanos *et al.*, 1979; Jannasch & Wirsen, 1984).

BACTERIA IN DEEP-SEA SEDIMENTS

The early expeditions to the Pacific demonstrated low bacterial activity in the red clays and *Globigerina* oozes of the abyssal plains, but a higher population of bacteria in the sediments of oceanic trenches (Morita, 1979). In both cases the bacterial growth rate was found to be very slow. From samples taken in the Weber Deep off the Philippines at a depth of 7.25 km controls of a sulphate-reducing bacterium showed no growth over a 3-y period at 1 atm and 5 °C whilst it took *one year* for there to be positive signs of sulphate reduction in the culture at 5 °C and 715 atm (Zobell & Morita, 1957).

The *in situ* approach to understanding these bacterial processes has been pioneered by Jannasch and Wirsen at the Woods Hole Oceanographic Institution. These workers have used the submersible 'Alvin' for manipulative experiments supplemented by the use of experimental apparatus on free vehicles (Fig. 12.2). They started from the hypothesis that bacterial activity in the deep-sea sediments was very low. In an early

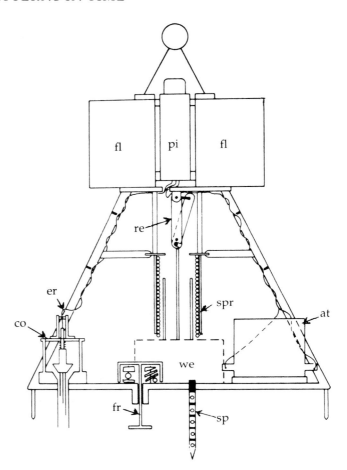

Fig. 12.2. Diagram of 'pop-up' free vehicle for deep-sea microbial studies. fl, syntactic foam flotation; pi, acoustic pinger housing with batteries and electronic timer; re, release hook; spr, spring; we, weight; co, core unit; er, electrocorrosive release for automated sample injection; fr, fouling rack; sp, sediment poker; at, amphipod trap. (From Jannasch & Wirsen, 1983.)

experiment at 1.83 km off New England, Jannasch & Wirsen (1973) exposed enriched media (0.1% starch, 0.033% agar or 0.1% gelatin) together with wood, paper towels and thalli of the alga *Ulva* to the sediments on the deep-sea floor. The media were left exposed for 51 weeks while sterile controls were kept at 4 °C in the laboratory. At the same time, inoculations of varying concentrations of labelled mannitol, sodium acetate, sodium glutamate and casamino acids were deposited for a 14-week period at 1.83 km. These samples from 1.83 km were supplemented by water samples taken at 200 m during the descent of 'Alvin' but incubated on the seabed. The laboratory incubations of the deep water samples at atmospheric pressure were metabolized 17.5 to 125 times faster than the *in situ* incubations. On the seafloor, even after 51 weeks, the changes in the dry weight of the hard substrates was not significant and there was no measurable degradation. The labelled substrate experiments produced rates which were three orders of magnitude lower in the *in situ* samples than in the controls incubated at 1 atm. Jannasch & Wirsen (1973) concluded that, even with the enrichment of deep sediments, there was no significant increase in the activity of the indigenous microflora over a 1-yr period.

Since these early experiments, Jannasch and his co-workers have refined their techniques using free vehicles (Jannasch & Wirsen, 1983; Wirsen & Jannasch, 1986) and isolating deep-sea bacteria in the absence of decompression (Jannasch, Wirsen & Taylor, 1982) as well as testing these isolates for pressure adaptation (Jannasch & Wirsen, 1984). In their free vehicle study Wirsen & Jannasch (1986) set up incubation at various depths from 2.6 to 5.33 km in the western Atlantic with a control at 12 m depth in Buzzards Bay near Woods Hole. ^{14}C-labelled glucose, acetate, glutamate and trimethylamine were injected in sediment cores at 2, 4 and 7 cm below the surface. Incubation times varied from 3 to 38 days with controls incubated at 1 atm and *in situ* temperature. The experimental data showed that the rate of microbial transformation decreased (*a*) with increasing water depth; and (*b*) with increasing depth into the sediment layer. However, the controls at 1 atm did not reflect this pattern suggesting the deep-sea populations of bacteria were a mixture of barotolerant and barophilic strains in various proportions (Jannasch & Taylor, 1984). Wirsen & Jannasch (1986) note that the main barophilic response was in the trimethylamine-injected cores which indicated to them that there may be a substrate specificity with respect to pressure. From this study it was concluded that maximum free-living microbial activity was in the very surface layers of the sediments where the sedimenting particles contain elevated concentrations of organic matter. The activity at the sediment interface was an order of magnitude higher than in the water column immediately above, or the sediment a few centimetres below.

The approach adopted originally by Zobell & Morita (1957) and refined by Deming and Colwell and their co-workers has been to collect natural populations from the deep sea using corers, and in the laboratory incubating the bacteria in various substrates at *in situ* (sample collection depth) pressure and temperature. Schwarz & Colwell (1975) presented some of the earliest observations using the more refined approach. They obtained sediment by gravity corer from 7.75 and 8.13 km depth in the Puerto Rico Trench. Sediment from the top 2 cm of the core diluted with sterile artificial seawater, was cultured with an added ^{14}C-labelled amino acid mixture containing glutamic acid, alanine and leucine. These cultures were immediately recompressed to *in situ* pressures on board ship and incubated for up to 6 mo. Controls were incubated at atmospheric pressure. Their results indicate that the uptake of amino acid was 55 times slower in the samples at pressure than in the controls at 1 atm, and CO_2 respiration was decreased 45 times. These data supported the theory that deep-sea sediment bacterial metabolism and biosynthesis was greatly reduced (Schwarz & Colwell, 1975).

In a later study Tabor *et al.* (1982) cultured microbial populations from the deep-sea sediment surface collected by box-coring in the S.E. (4.3 to 5.24 km depth) and N.W. (3.5 km) Atlantic Ocean. The inoculation procedure was similar to that of Schwarz & Colwell (1975) using ^{14}C-labelled glutamate or acetate. In a parallel experiment, the gut contents of an amphipod and holothurian were treated in the same way (see below). The results from the sediment experiment suggested bacterial uptake of the labelled compound was slower at pressure than in the controls at 1 atm, but that the rate was within the 95% confidence limits of the control suggesting substrate utilization was not significantly different at 1 atm or *in situ* pressure. For the first time, evidence had been found which contradicted the hypothesis of low activity in deep-sea bacterial populations. The parallel experiments on the gut contents of deep-sea metazoans showed that bacteria in these environments grew better at pressure than at 1 atm suggesting they were truly barophilic.

This study of deep-sea sediment bacteria has been extended by Deming & Colwell (1985) and Deming (1985) to cover samples from 4.12 and 4.715 km in the Bay of Biscay, 4.47 and 4.85 km on the Demerara Abyssal Plain (off Brazil) and in the N.W. Atlantic at 1.85 km depth.

Deming & Colwell (1985) obtained sediment samples from the Demerara Abyssal Plain using a box-corer. In addition, sinking particles were collected in sediment traps moored 7 to 200 m off the bottom. The bacterial populations were incubated with ^{14}C-labelled glutamic acid at 3 °C and 440 or 480 atm for 5 days and controls were maintained at 1 atm. The level of enrichment of glutamic acid was kept at a level $< 10\%$ above the natural level as excessive additional substrate was believed to suppress bacterial activity under pressure. Data from both the analyses of seabed sediment and from the particles in the sediment trap suggested that substrate incorporation was *enhanced* by *in situ* pressures when compared with 1 atm. This detection of a barophilic response of free-living bacterial was attributed to the short incubation period and the non-enriching concentrations of added substrate (Deming & Colwell, 1985). These data led the authors to conclude that there is '... a population of indigenous barophilic bacteria, rather than barosensitive immigrants that dominate in the turnover of the naturally low levels of glutamic acid in the deep-sea sediments examined'. Deming (1985) conducted a series of identical experiments in the Bay of Biscay and in the Hatteras Abysssal Plain. However, at both sites there was no significant growth of bacteria on any natural substrate except on one sample of sediment from the Hatteras Abyssal Plain that had been enriched with chitin and in which a barophilic response was observed. In contrast, the sedimentary particles collected by sediment trap 10 m above the seabed at these sites contained bacteria that showed a barophilic response. In more recent work in the N.E. Atlantic, Turley *et al.* (1988) incubated at 450 atm water directly overlying the undisturbed sediment collected from 4.5 km depth using the multiple corer (see Chapter 3) and enriched with sterilized phytodetritus obtained from shallow water. This resulted in a rapidly developing, barophilic microbial population which included a bacterivorous microflagellate as well as bacteria. Similar results showing a relatively barophilic response were obtained by Alongi (1990) in cultures from sediments with fresh macroalgal detritus in the Coral and Solomon Seas.

It is apparent from these two types of approach, the *in situ* experiment and the onboard incubation of bacteria under pressure after decompression, that there is some equivocation in the interpretation of the results. There is no doubt that bacteria are present in deep-sea sediments that respond 10 to 1000 times slower than shallow-water populations. Maximum bacterial activity occurs at the sediment surface and decreases into the water column and with depth into the sediment. The failure to stimulate deep-sea bacterial growth by artificially enriching deep-sea sediments suggests that these deep-sea bacteria are barotolerant, but it is possible that the enrichment may have been too great. Certainly, experiments with low levels of enrichment (as performed by Deming, 1985, and Turley *et al.*, 1988) seem to induce a *barophilic* response. Although these ambiguities have yet to be resolved, it is likely that the bacterial community in deep-sea sediments will prove to be a mixture of barotolerant and barophilic bacteria. Barotolerant strains are found at very low levels of nutrient whilst barophilic strains are associated with highly localized areas of nutrient enrichment, such as sinking faecal pellets and phytodetritus.

It is this association of barophilic bacteria with local increases in substrate concentration that suggests that both hydrothermal vent bacteria and those associated with the guts of deep-sea invertebrates may be barophilic.

GUT BACTERIA

Zobell & Morita (1957) were the first to suggest that there may be an abundance of barophilic bacteria in the guts of deep-sea animals. Early evidence for increased bacterial activity in this milieu was indirect. Hessler *et al.* (1978) examined preserved gut smears of amphipods caught in baited traps and noted the high concentration of bacterial cells which far exceeded the bacterial counts found in associated deep-sea sediments. Jannasch *et al.* (1976) had found barotolerant bacteria in the guts of fish, echinoderms and Crustacea whilst Ohwada *et al.* (1980) isolated 46 strains of barotolerant bacteria from the guts of various macrofauna from the deep Atlantic Ocean. Their observations suggested that the barotolerance of bacteria increased in samples of macrofauna with depth. At more or less the same time, other workers were isolating these barotolerant bacteria from gut contents. Yayanos *et al.* (1979) isolated a barophilic bacterium from the rotted remains of amphipods from 5.7 km depth. These bacteria could have arisen from the gut contents or body wall of the amphipods or from the seawater; but it was evident that they grew optimally at *c.* 500 atm, close to the pressure at which they were collected.

The first observations of barophilism in intestinal bacteria were given by Schwarz *et al.* (1976) who showed that bacteria from the gut of an amphipod, when cultured for 5 weeks under enrichment and at pressure, grew more rapidly than controls at 1 atm. Yayanos *et al.* (1981) and Yayanos & Dietz (1983) isolated bacteria from an amphipod collected at 10.5 km depth in the Mariana Trench. In culture at 1035 atm these bacteria had a doubling time of 33 h, an optimal doubling time of 25 h at 690 atm, but at 350 atm failed to grow.

Jannasch *et al.* (1980) and Jannasch & Wirsen (1983) determined the metabolic rate of the intestinal flora of scavenging deep-sea amphipods by trapping them in free-fall traps and feeding them, *in situ*, with radio-labelled bait or bait substitute. This technique has been applied at a variety of depths from 1.41 to 5.33 km in the western Atlantic. Non-accessible bait was used to enhance the attraction of the scavenging amphipods. On recovery of the traps, amphipods that had consumed the labelled bait were fractionated using cold and hot trichloracetic acid (TCA), for low molecular weight sugars and amino acids, and polysaccharides and nucleic acids respectively; ethanol, for peptides and long chain amino acids; and ether (for lipids). Each fraction was read on a scintillation counter. Although the results are equivocal, some major trends are identified (Wirsen & Jannasch, 1983). Within a few days of exposure microbial transformations were taking place, although the transfer of radiolabelled material to the amphipod tissue took longer. The cold TCA fraction contained the highest amount of label suggesting a very active microbial population although there is the possibility that this is confused with the early stages of lipogenesis. However, the former suggestion is supported by the high recovery of radiolabel in the polysaccharide/nucleic acid fraction in one deployment suggesting a rapid increase in microbial biomass. Wirsen & Jannasch (1983) conclude by noting that their results support the developing view that the gut tracts of deep-sea scavengers offer sites of increased, and possibly, barophilic microbial activity.

During this period, French microbiogists were isolating bacteria from the guts of deep-sea echinoderms (Bensoussan *et al.*, 1979, 1984; Ralijona & Bianchi, 1982). Bensoussan and his co-workers noted that Gram-negative rods dominated in the echinoderm guts (of *Solaster* sp. and *Pseudostichopus villosus*) whilst Gram-negative cocci dominated in the sediments. The gut microflora was less diversified than the sediment microflora but concentrations in the echinoderms were 50 times higher than that of the sediment. Altogether, 28 strains were isolated from *Solaster*; 22 strains from *Pseudostichopus* and 80 strains from the sediment. Phenotypic analysis based on 139 features indicated that some of the bacterial groups are unique to the gut of either *Solaster* or *Pseudostichopus* or to the sediment. Some groups are found in the guts of both echino-derms. The data suggest that the microflora in the digestive tracts of deep-sea animals differs from sediment microflora. Lastly, all three environments (asteroid gut, holothurian gut and sediment) had high diversity indices.

A rigorous experimental approach to the problem of barophilic growth of bacteria from the guts of deep-sea amphipods and holothurians has been taken by J. Deming and her co-workers. Remember that amphipods are scavengers feeding on carcasses in the deep sea whilst holothurians are selective deposit feeders whose gut contents contain higher levels of organic carbon and nitrogen than the surrounding sediment (Khripou-noff & Sibuet, 1980).

In amphipods, two distinct groups were observed (Deming *et al.*, 1981). One had large numbers of viable bacteria in their guts (4×10^7

to 2×10^9 g^{-1}) whilst the second had significantly fewer (1.6×10^4 to 4×10^5 g^{-1}) but still higher than in the local sediment (0.8×10^2 to 2×10^4 g^{-1}). 150 strains of bacteria were isolated of which 75% proved to be obligate psychrophiles. Later Deming (1986) proved these bacteria to be true barophiles that could only survive in nutrient-rich environments.

The data presented for the gut microflora of holothurians suggest a doubling time of 11 h at 430 atm compared with 4 h at 1 atm. Although not a true barophilic response, the difference in doubling times is not significant and compares well with the 4 to 13 h doubling time reported for barophilic bacteria by Yayanos *et al.* (1979). By contrast, growth of the transitory sediment bacteria in the holothurian gut was inhibited by *in situ* pressure giving a doubling time of 36 h.

In a subsequent study of the gut microflora of *Pseudostichopus*, *Deima* and *Psychropotes* from > 4 km depth on the Demerara Abyssal Plain Deming & Colwell (1982) showed that the gut contents of these species contained 1.5 to 3 times the number of bacteria compared to the surrounding sediment. Lowest counts were in the foregut (site of main digestion) whilst bacterial counts increased 3 to 10 times in the hindgut. Gram-negative rods were found associated with the digestive epithelium. By testing the response of these bacteria from the hindgut to ^{14}C-labelled glutamic acid, noting the response to yeast extract and using epifluorescent microscopy, these authors found elevated activity at ambient pressure (Fig. 12.3). Deming & Colwell (1982) concluded that these bacteria transformed any organic matter in sediments ingested by the holothurian and thus were 'important participants in nutrient recycling in the deep-

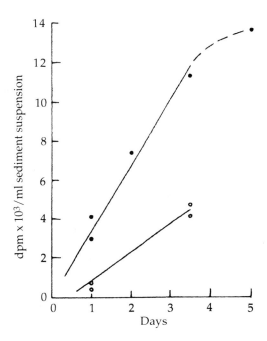

Fig. 12.3. Total microbial utilization (uptake and incorporation plus respiration) of ^{14}C-glutamic acid in the hindgut contents of the deep-sea holothurian *Psychropotes* sp. after incubation at 3 °C and 1 atm (upper) and 440 atm (lower). (From Deming & Colwell, 1982.)

sea benthos'. It is possible also that metabolites released by the bacteria provided additional nutrition for the host.

If we compare bacterial metabolism in different niches in the deep sea, we can interpret some microbial ecological strategies (Deming, 1986). First, substrate availability distinguishes the two major types of microbial habitat. The concentration of organic matter in deep-sea sediments is limiting, even though it receives a rain of particulate organic matter ranging from faecal pellets to whole carcasses. Free-living bacteria in these sediments, although barophilic, have evolved towards *oligotrophy* in which they grow slowly but efficiently in carbon-limited habitats. There-fore attempting to isolate them on artificially enriched substrates would result in minimal success (Deming, 1986).

The second major habitat is within the guts of deep-sea metazoans where the organic contents are much higher, either as a result of the host scavenging on carrion or by selective deposit feeding. In this niche, bacteria have evolved towards *copriotrophy*, growing rapidly *only* when presented with an enriched source of organic substrate (Deming, 1986). In these cases pressure stimulates total microbial substrate utilization and they are true barophiles.

Although there is still much research to be carried out into deep-sea microbial ecology, a study by Rowe & Deming (1985) has attempted to determine the quantitative role of bacteria in the turnover of organic carbon in deep-sea sediments. Their data are based on bacterial activity for sediments and sediment traps in the Demerara Abyssal Plain and the Bay of Biscay (see above). The composite inputs and losses are summar-ized in Fig. 12.4. In both the surface and subsurface biota *c.* 90% of the carbon input is lost to respiration. Of the carbon input, a very small proportion is accumulated in the sediment and the remainder is used for growth and reproduction by metazoans or bacteria. The latter category is estimated as consuming between 13 and 30% of the total organic carbon input. The total budget for organic carbon at the deep-sea bed is thus in the order of 9.4 mg C m^{-2} d^{-1} (3.4 g C m^{-2} yr^{-1}) which corresponds (see below) to the values of Sediment Community Oxygen Consumption for similar depths (Smith & Hinga, 1983).

There is still much to be learned about the ecology of deep-sea bacteria. Much of the current effort is concentrated on understanding microbial production at hydrothermal vents (see Chapter 15). However, in other parts of the deep sea, small-scale variations are being understood espe-cially in response to sedimenting particles; but we know very little of the temporal variability of bacterial turnover of organic matter at the deep-sea bed, especially in relation to the, now demonstrable, seasonal flux of organic matter from the surface production to the deep-sea bed.

METABOLIC PROCESSES

During the last ten years there has been a rapid increase in our under-standing of the key physiological processes of respiration and repro-

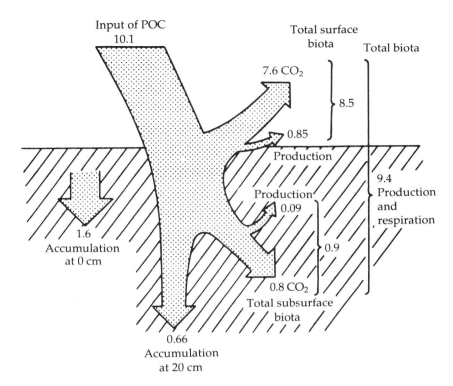

Fig. 12.4. Schematic representation of averages of the input and fate of organic carbon inferred from sediment trap and core samples from two sites (4.4 km and 4.8 km depth) on the Demerara Abyssal Plain and one site (4.1 km depth) in the Bay of Biscay. The numbers represent averages of carbon flux in mg $m^{-2} d^{-1}$. (From Rowe & Deming, 1985.)

duction in deep-sea organisms. However, even as late as 1983 Somero, Siebenaller & Hochachka commented that very little was known of the metabolic adaptations of benthic invertebrates to the deep-sea environment. We shall in this second section consider only respiration.

Respiration may be measured at the organism level or at the population level (sediment community oxygen consumption). The methods employed to measure respiration *in situ* have been devised mainly by K. L. Smith and his colleagues at the Scripps Institution of Oceanography. These have been developed as sophisticated free vehicles (see below).

In most cases the respiration rate, and thus the energy demand, of the organism is measured over a relatively short period (usually in h). By contrast, to understand the reproductive processes in deep-sea benthic invertebrates, a long-term sampling programme (> 1 yr) is required that obtains samples at regular intervals so that any changes, if present, in any reproductive cycle can be perceived. Owing to logistic and financial constraints, these types of study are rare, but, as we shall see, there are data from time-series sampling programmes in the San Diego Trough off California and from the Rockall Trough in the N.E. Atlantic.

The traditional way to measure energy demand is to determine the oxygen consumption of individuals and from these data extrapolate the energy requirement of the total population. In the deep sea, owing to the varying size of the organisms and the remoteness of the environment, it is possible to measure the respiratory rate at individual organism level only for megabenthos and fish. Smaller organisms, particularly the macro- and meiofauna, have to be treated as a community and their respiration measured at population level. By measuring the respiratory rate of deep-sea organisms their energy demand (g C m^{-2} yr^{-1}) can be calculated and thus annual energy budgets can be constructed for deep-sea populations as we know both the energy input and consumption (excluding reproduction and growth). However, these estimates assume a constancy in rate of consumption that, as we shall see later from respiratory data obtained at different times of the year, is more illusory than real.

RESPIRATION IN INDIVIDUAL ANIMALS

This has been measured *in situ* using the Fish Respirometer (Fig. 12.5(*a*)). The apparatus is either placed on the seabed and monitored from a submersible, or operated as a free vehicle. Fish are lured into the acrylic chambers with bait that is automatically removed once a fish enters. Movements of any trapped fish are recorded by an array of acoustic sensors in the wall of the trap. The trap can perform two functions. If the entrance is closed by a mesh screen only the effect of starvation can be determined. If the acrylic doors are closed, the trap acts as a benthic respirometer and oxygen variations are measured by polarographic

Table 12.1. *Respiration rates in individual species in the deep sea*

Species	Depth (km)	Oxygen consumption (ml h^{-1} mg^{-1} wet weight)	Reference
Echinodermata			
Ophiophthalmus normani	1.3	26–45	Smith, 1983
Ophiomusium lymani	1.23	50	Smith, 1983
Ophiomusium armigerum	3.65	23–30	Smith, 1983
Crustacea			
Paralicella caperesca	3.68	210–980	Smith & Baldwin, 1982
Orchomene sp.	1.3	20–660	Smith & Baldwin, 1982
Eurythenes gryllus	0.01–3.25	60–64*	George, 1979*a*
Parapagurus pilosimanus	1.0	9–20*	George, 1979*a*
Polychaetes			
Hyalinoecia artifex	0.8–1.6	2*	George, 1979*b*
Fish			
Coryphaenoides acrolepis	1.23	2.7–3.7	Smith, 1978
Coryphaenoides acrolepis	2.76	3.1	Smith, 1978
Eptatretus deani	1.23	2.7–3.22	Smith & Hessler, 1974
Sebastolobus altivelis			
adult	1.3	2.7–3.22	Smith & Brown, 1983
juvenile	1.3	26.6–34.4	Smith & Brown, 1983

*Laboratory measurements on animals recompressed from trawl samples.

oxygen sensors, and excretion products, by withdrawal by syringe (Smith & Baldwin, 1983).

The respiratory rates, measured *in situ* mostly for a variety of deep-sea megafauna and benthopelagic fish are summarized in Table 12.1. In the brittle stars *Ophiophthalmus normani*, *Ophiomusium lymani* and *O. armigerum* the respiration rate is very similar irrespective of depth (1.23 to 3.65 km) at between 23 and 50 μl h^{-1} g^{-1} wet weight (Smith, 1983). These data are comparable to those of shallow-water ophiuroids suggesting that depth is not an important parameter regulating the consumption of oxygen. However, the respiration rate of the holothurian *Scotoplanes globosa* from 1.3 km is considerably lower at between 4 and 15 μl h^{-1} g^{-1} wet weight. This, however, is comparable to the consumption rates in shallow-water holothurians.

Other data have been obtained from experiments on specimens recompressed after recovery from bathyal depths. But the low rates of oxygen consumption measured may well have resulted from the drastic changes in pressure and temperature they experienced during capture. In a study of the respiration of 11 benthic crustaceans recovered using a thermally insulated cod-end Childress *et al.* (1990) could show no significant relationship between oxygen consumption and depth when the data were adjusted to take into account a moderate degree of metabolic dependency on temperature. In deep-sea scavenging amphipods the respiratory rate appears to remain relatively constant (60–64 μl g^{-1} h^{-1}) over a wide pressure range, but increases rapidly especially when excited by food odour (George, 1979a). In *Paralicella caperesca* from 3.65 km the respiratory rate rose from 20 to 660 μl g^{-1} h^{-1} wet weight when excited by food odour and, for the more shallow-living *Orchomene* sp., it rose from 210 to 980 μl g^{-1} h^{-1} wet weight (Smith & Baldwin, 1982). These elevated levels could be maintained for up to 8 h.

These data suggest a variety of adaptational traits have evolved in deep-sea megafauna. George (1981) suggests that two main groups occur: (i) those with a low oxygen uptake; (ii) those with a high oxygen uptake. Typical of the first group are *Scotoplanes* and *Hyalinoecia* which move over the sediment surface relatively slowly ingesting organic matter as they go as they have a continuous low energy demand. The second group is represented by swimming crustaceans such as scavenging amphipods which need to respond rapidly to availability of food whilst conserving energy between meals. Smith & Baldwin (1982) suggest that, between periods of feeding, the amphipods enter a state of torpor to prevent starvation when the respiratory rate is lowered and the amphipod utilizes high energy reserves such as lipid. In this state, the amphipod must be responsive to any food odour which, if sensed, elicits a rapid response of a homing search and feeding activity, with a greatly increased respiration rate, fuelled by utilizing reserves such as glycogen.

Data on respiration rates in fish are given in Table 12.1 (Smith & White, 1982). The first successful attempt to measure *in situ* the respiration rate in a motile deep-sea fish was at a depth of 1.23 km in the San Diego Trough (Smith & Hessler, 1974). They noted that the respiration rate in *Coryphae-*

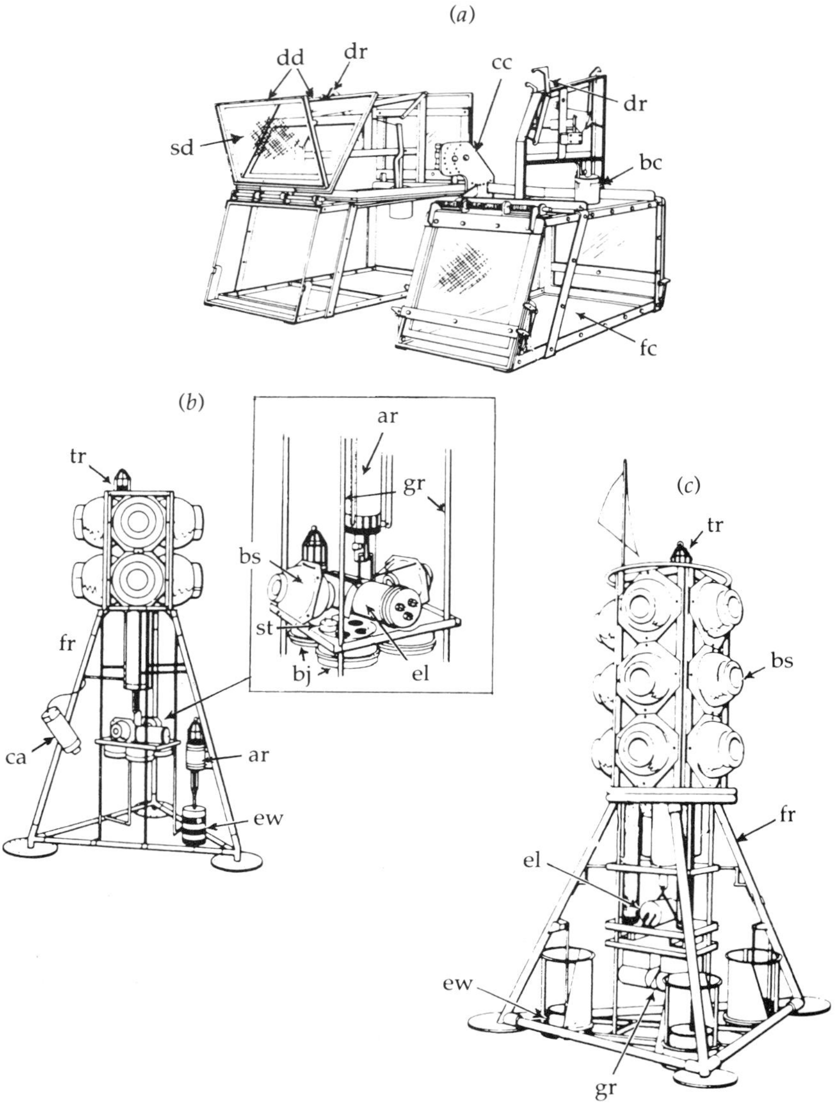

Fig. 12.5. *In situ* respirometers used by K. L. Smith and co-workers. (*a*) Dual fish trap respirometer which can be operated either by submersible or as a free vehicle. It is clamped to a wire (cc) at various altitudes above the bottom. Each chamber can trap a fish attracted to the bait cannister (bc) inside by means of a spring-loaded double door (dd) release system. This is triggered via a lever system (dr) by the submersible's manipulator arm from which the whole operation can be monitored visually. The volume of the fish chamber (fc) is 53.7 l. Changes in dissolved oxygen inside the chamber are continuously recorded. By separating the fish from bait by the screen door (sd), respiration under conditions of starvation can be measured. (*b*) and (*c*) are two free vehicle respirometers (FVRs) designed for measuring oxygen uptake by the benthic community. In (*b*) a bell jar respirometer consisting of four side-by-side plastic tubes, capped at one end (bj), are inserted into the sediment leaving 5–10 cm of overlying water. Oxygen consumption by the sediment community is measured by a polarographic electrode with a stirring motor (st). Release of the weighted bell jar unit (shown in inset) along guide rods (gr) and, at the end of the experiment, release of the expendable descent weight (ew) is effected by an acoustic command release system (ar). Other labels: bs, buoyancy spheres; fr, metal supporting tripod frame; ca, monitoring camera; el, pressure housing for electronic control and recording; tr, transducer of acoustic command system. (*c*) The

(continued)

noides acrolepis and *Eptatretus deani* was significantly lower than related shallow-water species. Measurement of the respiration rate of *Coryphaenoides (Nematonurus) armatus* from 3.65 km depth showed a very similar rate (2.7 to 2.3 μl g^{-1} h^{-1}) to that of its congener *C. acrolepis* from 1.23 km (Smith, 1978a). In *Sebastolobus altivelis*, the respiration rate was 2.7 to 3.2 μl g^{-1} h^{-1} although the juvenile of this species had a rate an order of magnitude greater (Table 12.1) (Smith & Brown, 1983). These authors also noted that the juvenile respiration rate was 1.5 to 1.8 times higher during the night than during the day. All these fish are benthopelagic and thus spend some of their time above rather than on the seabed. The low

free-vehicle grab respirometer (FVGR) is able, additionally, to retrieve the enclosed sediment sample at the end of the experiment. Four modified Ekman grabs (gr) ($21 \times 21 \times 30$ cm) possess spring-loaded jaws that can penetrate 30 cm, enclosing 441 cm^2 of sediment surface. A top plate slides down on guide rods to seal the top of the grabs with a silicone gasket. Oxygen consumption is otherwise measured as in the FVR. Respiration is monitored over a period of 1 to 5 days before the grabs are commanded to close and the FVGR is recalled by release of the descent weights. (From Smith & White, 1982.)

respiration rate in deep-sea fish may be the result of a similar selective pressure as seen in the amphipods where there is increased metabolic activity during location of food and feeding but, during the quiescent period, the fish rest on the bottom using minimal energy.

RESPIRATION AT THE COMMUNITY LEVEL

Data are available on the respiration rate of those organisms that inhabit the benthic boundary layer, such as zooplankton close to the seafloor, and of all the organisms living on and within the bottom sediment (the Sediment Community Oxygen Consumption, or SCOC).

(i) Benthic Boundary Layer (BBL) Respiration K. L. Smith (1982) measured the respiration rate of the benthic boundary layer community at various levels (1, 5, 10 and 50 m) above the deep-sea floor using *in situ* methods. Generally oxygen consumption decreased with distance above the sea bed (Table 12.2). The integrated macrozooplankton oxygen consumption for the full 50 m BBL was 1575 μl m^{-1} d^{-1} which was equivalent to only 3% of the SCOC in the same area (see below). Data from 3.85 km depth in the Panama Basin (Smith *et al.*, 1986) give the integrated macrozooplankton oxygen consumption as 111 μl m^{-1} d^{-1} over the 50 m BBL. This is equivalent to the use of 0.05 mg C m^{-2} d^{-1} by the macrozooplankton. Over the same depth increment, the bacterioplankton incorporation and respiration rate accounted for 1.25 mg C m^{-2} d^{-1} (Smith *et al.*, 1986).

(ii) Sediment Community Oxygen Consumption (SCOC) At the sediment–water interface, the SCOC has been measured *in situ* in a variety of deep-sea areas using various modifications of the Sediment Community Respirometer (Fig. 12.5(*b*)), a free vehicle devised by K. L. Smith at the Scripps Institution of Oceanography. Although data on sediment respiration previously had been obtained on decompressed samples, it was from these *in situ* determinations that the first accurate data of deep-sea community respiration (Table 12.1) were obtained (reviewed by Smith & White, 1982; Smith & Hinga, 1983). This apparatus is a development of a bell-jar respirometer. The equipment is operated as a free vehicle supported by a tripod frame on which are mounted two side-by-side plastic cylinders. Each is capped at one end and inserted into

Table 12.2. *Respiration in the Benthic Boundary Layer and deep water*

Site	Depth (km)	Oxygen consumption (ml h^{-1} mg^{-1} wet weight)	Reference
Macrozooplankton (mainly copepods)	3.8	0.24	Smith *et al.*, 1986
BBL zooplankton	1.3	0.24–0.49	Smith *et al.*, 1986
Paracalliosoma coecus	1.1	40–50	Childress, 1975

the sediment, leaving 5–10 cm of overlying water enclosed. The rate at which dissolved oxygen is depleted in the water provides the measure of 'community respiration'. Alternatively, release of radioisotope markers can be made to follow take-up and release of nutrients by the microbial community in the seabed. Details of the centrally located bell-jar unit are shown in the inset to Fig. 12.5(b). On top of the tripod is the flotation package, and the apparatus is made negatively buoyant for deployment by about 300 kg of ballast. Recovery is effected by release of this ballast on acoustic command from the ship stationed above.

The Free Vehicle Grab Respirometer (FVGR) shown in Fig. 12.5(c) represents an evolutionary development of that described above. It is equipped with four stainless steel grabs, modified as respirometer chambers, that are able to retrieve the enclosed sediment at the end of the experiment. This sophisticated free vehicle measures both sediment community oxygen consumption and nutrient release *in situ*, and re-covers a sediment sample for analysis of both the contained fauna and sediment chemistry.

Although additional data are available from other locations, it is possible to compare supply and demand of energy as data on particle flux is available at these sites.

The first results of *in situ* oxygen uptake by a deep-sea community, obtained using the Sediment Community Respirometer, are from 1.85 km depth in the N.W. Atlantic Ocean (Smith & Teal, 1973). They noted oxygen uptake was two orders of magnitude less than that in shallow water. To prove this was biological, and not chemical, oxygen demand, the sediments were treated with formalin after which there was no measurable oxygen uptake. Continued studies at a variety of depths in the N.W. Atlantic demonstrated that SCOC decreases with depth from 1.31 ml O_2 m^{-2} h^{-1} at 1.345 km to 0.02 ml O_2 m^{-2} h^{-1} at 5.2 km depth (Smith, 1978b; Smith *et al.*, 1978). Low values of SCOC have also been determined in the N.E. Atlantic (Patching, Raine & Barnett, 1986). Although other parameters influence the oxygen consumption, depth is the most important contributing 83.1% of the variation (Smith & Hinga, 1983). A second variable is the flux of POC to the seabed which decreases both with depth and distance from the shore. The percentage POC flux utilized by SCOC also decreases with depth. However, as there is not a build-up of organic matter in the sediment, the POC flux not used in SCOC must be utilized by other organisms, or be exported laterally (Smith & Hinga, 1983).

In the Gulf of Mexico and the Bahamas region, SCOC is considerably higher than in the N.W. Atlantic, being 3.1 ml O_2 m^{-2} h^{-1} at 2 km depth decreasing to 0.69 ml O_2 m^{-2} h^{-1} at 3.45 km (Table 12.3). The high rates of SCOC in the Tongue of the Ocean may be a response to its proximity to land (Smith & Hinga, 1983). However, even the high fluxes of POC in this area (Table 12.3) are insufficient to fuel the SCOC, suggesting there is a substantial import of organic material. This is likely to be in the form of seagrass or other macroscopic plants, as this material has been observed at the seafloor in this region (Rowe & Staresinic, 1979).

Table 12.3. *Sediment Community Oxygen Consumption (SCOC)*

Station	Depth (km)	SCOC, measured (ml O_2 m^{-2} h^{-1})	SCOC (l O_2 m^{-2} yr^{-1})	SCOC per yr (g C m^{-2} yr^{-1})	POC flux (g C m^{-2} utilized yr^{-1})	% POC flux
N. Atlantic						
77DE	1.35	1.31	11.48	5.25	5.4	97
DWD	2.2	0.46	4.03	1.84	6.4	29
ADS	2.75	0.35	3.07	1.4	2.3	61
HH	3.0	0.2	1.75	0.8	2.3	35
DOS2	3.65	0.21	2.1	0.96	4.2	23
NN	5.08	0.07	0.61	0.28	0.7	40
MM	5.2	0.02	0.18	0.08	0.4	11
Gulf of Mexico						
77FG	6.75	2.95	25.84	11.81	2.6	
TOTO	2.0	3.1	27.16	12.41	2.1	
76B	3.45	0.69	6.04	2.77		
N. Pacific						
AA26	1.193	2.22	19.45	8.75	9.8	91
SDT	1.23	2.4	21.02	9.67	9.8	99
SCB	1.3	2.54	22.25	10.21	5.4–21.3v	
C66	3.815	2.28	19.97	9.19	9.8	94
F	4.4	0.7	6.13	2.81	0.2–5.4v	
G	4.9	0.29	2.54	1.17	0.2–0.6v	
CNP	5.9	0.13	1.14	0.52	0.4v	

v = seasonally variable.
From Smith & Hinga, 1983, and Smith, 1987.

In the N. Pacific, the first data came from 1.23 km in the San Diego Trough where the SCOC was 2.4 ± 0.1 ml m^{-2} h^{-1} (Smith, 1974). In a more ambitious study Smith, Laver & Brown (1983) determined the SCOC at a series of stations right across the North Pacific. SCOC

Fig. 12.6. Schematic representation of the percentage utilization of the total sedimenting particulate organic matter by the sediment community, plankton, and benthopelagic fauna of the benthic boundary at 3.65 km depth in the N.W. Atlantic. (From Smith & White, 1982.)

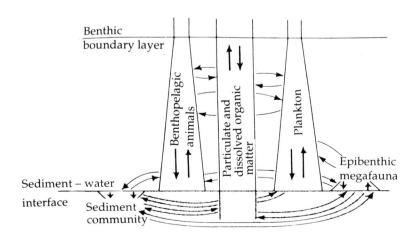

decreases with both depth and distance from the shore (Table 12.3). The data suggest (Smith & Baldwin, 1984b; Smith, 1987) that the SCOC in this region has a seasonal component, and that this seasonality may be related to the seasonal productivity and flux of POC in the overlying waters. However, Smith (1987) concludes that only 59% of the variability in SCOC may be attributed to the vertical flux of POC. Furthermore, variations in SCOC, measured from a free-vehicle grab respirometer, and of POC, measured concurrently from moored sediment traps, show no apparent synchrony or phasing (Smith, 1989). Thus a *direct* coupling of POC and SCOC remains unconfirmed.

Attempting to balance the supply and use of energy at the deep-sea bed is fraught with difficulty. Smith & White (1982) attempted to determine how much of the supply of organic carbon is utilized at the sea bed. Their data (Fig. 12.6) suggested 23% was used by SCOC, 4% by the plankton and 15% by benthopelagic animals. If we assume 2% is used by the mobile megafauna, this still leaves 70% of the supplied organic matter unaccounted for. To this apparent reservoir must be added large food-falls, such as animal carcasses and plant debris, and dissolved organic carbon. On the debit side, besides respiration, carbon may be stored as somatic tissue or exported into the water as sexual products. Eggs contain high-energy lipids and may be a significant sink of carbon. Understanding this balance is fundamental to our comprehension of energy flows in the deep-sea ecosystem.

13

Reproduction, recruitment and growth of deep-sea organisms

ASSUMPTIONS AND PREDICTIONS

Until recently, some of the least understood biological processes in the deep ocean have been those associated with the mode of reproduction, growth and survivorship of deep-sea organisms and the demography of their populations. Early observations of sexuality, gonad development and brooding were made as brief comments in the major taxonomic works whilst information on recruitment and growth was non-existent. The sampling programmes of the early deep-sea expeditions aimed at wide spatial coverage to give descriptive information rather than long-term sampling designs at fixed stations. Hence reproductive development could not be followed through its various stages from initiation to maturity – as is routinely done in shallow-water and intertidal species (Giese & Pearse, 1974), nor could the recruitment and subsequent growth of discrete cohorts be assessed. Our knowledge of these processes in deep-sea invertebrates and fish still remains scanty.

On the basis of the constant temperature regime of the deep ocean, Orton (1920) predicted that deep-sea species would not undergo the seasonal periodicities in breeding shown by their relatives in shallower water subject to annual changes in water temperature, but, instead, breeding would take place year-round.

Another prediction concerned the mode of early development of deep-sea organisms. In shallow water most marine invertebrates produce vast numbers of tiny eggs that hatch into characteristic planktonic larvae which feed in water and are dispersed by water currents. These eventually settle on to the bottom metamorphosing from the planktonic form to a juvenile form of the adult. The great Danish marine biologist Gunnar Thorson (1950), in reviewing the reproduction and larval ecology of marine bottom invertebrates, predicted that deep-sea species will always have relatively low fecundity, with little or no pelagic development. He considered that parallels existed between the conditions prevailing in the deep sea and in Polar Seas where the pelagic phase of development is partially or totally curtailed. The difficulties of such tiny forms migrating the several kilometres to and from the surface layers, combined with the energetic cost to the parent of producing the copious larvae necessary to make a hazardous journey, would rule out early development in the surface waters as a viable reproductive strategy in the deep sea.

REPRODUCTIVE STRATEGIES IN THE DEEP SEA

Early development in the water by means of swimming or free-floating larvae is termed *indirect* development. In his classical scheme, Thorson (1946, 1950) distinguished those species with a free-swimming feeding larvae (*planktotrophy*) from those having larvae which are free-swimming but are unable to feed independently and so subsist on stored food reserves (*lecithotrophy*). In *direct* development, the fertilized egg or zygote develops directly into a juvenile form of the adult, omitting any larval stage and subsequently metamorphosis. Recently, a more fundamental difference has been identified in whether the larva is able to feed or not; this separates planktotrophy from other strategies which are often difficult to distinguish as being either lecithotrophic or direct (Strathmann, 1978; Jablonski & Lutz, 1983). These strategies have contrasting benefits. Evolutionary selection trades one advantage, such as wide dispersion against another, such as the energetic cost to the parent of producing propagules. Species with planktotrophic development produce a large number of eggs which favours high variability and chance mutation, but mortality is extremely high (thought to exceed 99% in shallow water) of both eggs and larvae in the plankton through either predation or starvation. The survivors, however, provide a dispersal phase in the animal's life history, and because of their variability are more likely to include the set of characteristics which allow colonization of new environments. Conversely, in species with non-planktotrophic early development, they produce fewer eggs with a greater energetic investment per egg to ensure the chance of attainment of adulthood is maximized. The extreme adaptation is seen in those species which either brood their young or development is within encapsulated eggs (usually attached to the bottom) providing protection also for the developing embryo (Fig. 5.24). But although survivorship may be greater, dispersal is necessarily more limited than among planktotrophic larvae. Dispersion will be greatest with free-swimming, lecithotrophic larvae which generally are smaller, and hence can be produced in greater numbers than the propagules of direct developers. For those lecithotropic larvae, culturing experiments suggest that mortality is particularly high at metamorphosis when there is a switch from the planktonic mode of feeding to the adult mode. Lecithotrophic early development predominates amongst deep-sea bivalves (Ockelmann, 1965; Knudsen, 1970; Scheltema, 1972).

Another prediction is that the deep sea is an environment with low rates of biological activity. This has been based on the results of *in situ* studies conducted in the light of the 'Alvin' lunches during the 1970s (see Chapter 12) on respiration of sediment, microbial communities and fish. The expectation that growth rates amongst deep-sea animals would be similarly depressed (Grassle & Sanders, 1973) was reinforced by the results of radiometric dating on the small bivalve *Tindaria callistiformis* that suggested the largest specimens were around 100 yr old (Turekian *et al.*, 1975). This has been related to typical life-history traits of small brood size, and observed age structures which are dominated by older individuals (Grassle & Sanders, 1973; Sanders, 1979). Such traits were linked by Sanders to the supposed development of a 'biologically accommodated' community consisting of species each with a narrow microhabitat specialization and hence permitting coexistence within a high-diversity community (see Chapter 8); the assumption of high stability of the ecosystem in time is basic to Sanders's concept.

Do the data now available on the reproduction and life histories of various deep-sea benthic taxa fulfil these predictions? In answering this question we shall examine the special life-history problems posed by the deep-sea environment. The organism needs to procreate itself successfully given the limitations of resources available and the constraints imposed (and opportunities provided) by its physical environment. These factors will certainly include low food availability, which will restrict the scale of reproductive production, and low population densities which will pose problems in cross-fertilization. These physical factors may also include the occurrence of (occasionally highly energetic) bottom currents that provide opportunities for dispersal of demersal larvae, and perhaps of older benthic stages.

REPRODUCTION AND RECRUITMENT IN DEEP-SEA INVERTEBRATES

COELENTERATES

The limited evidence available from deep-sea anthozoans serves to illustrate the potential for variability in reproduction. The zooanthid *Epizoanthus* is epizoic on the hermit crab *Parapagurus pilosimanus*; its egg production takes place in a similar way to shallow-water zoanthids (Muirhead *et al.*, 1986), but continues throughout the year. The egg size suggests the larva is planktonic. The anemones *Paracalliactis stephensoni* and *Phelliactis robusta* reproduce seasonally only in April–May of each year and a larva is the dispersal stage (Van Praet & Duchateau, 1984; Van Praet, personal communication). There is a paradox that both continuous and seasonal reproduction is found amongst deep-sea invertebrates, and this will recur again and again when reviewing evidence from the other invertebrate groups.

POLYCHAETES

Although polychaetes dominate the deep-sea infauna, there are very few studies of their reproductive biology. Hartman & Fauchald (1971), concluded that polychaetes from along the Gay Head–Bermuda Transect were year-round breeders. The only seasonal study of a deep-sea polychaete, the flabelligerid *Fauveliopsis glabra,* taken in a five-sample study over 1 yr in the San Diego Trough (Rokop, 1974), supported this conclusion.

The evidence of early life history and growth rates from recolonization tray experiments is based on larval stages dispersed by currents rather than lateral migration by swimming or crawling adults although this is likely to occur with 'errant' forms such as scale worms, and possibly even some 'sedentary' forms such as ampharetids (Desbruyères *et al.*, 1985). Bearing this bias in mind, the recolonization results suggest that reproduction in a wide variety of families, of 'sedentary' species including Capitellidae, Spionidae, Dorvilleidae, Paraonidae, Hesionidae, Cirratulidae and Sabellidae, is by water-borne dispersal stages. Assuming that worms are indeed colonizing the trays as larvae growth is quite rapid; the opportunistic *Capitealla* spp. attain maturity in about 1 yr (Grassle, 1977; Grassle & Morse-Porteous, 1987; Grassle, Sanders & W. Smith, 1979; Desbruyères *et al.*, 1980, 1985; Levin & Smith, 1984).

CRUSTACEA

The deep-sea Crustacea have a variety of reproductive types. Peracarids (isopods, amphipods, cumaceans and tanaids) are direct developers since they brood their eggs and young until they develop to a juvenile form of the adult. It was in the deep-sea isopods and amphipods that George & Menzies (1967, 1968) first suggested a reproductive seasonality. However, data based on a comparison of the percentage of the brooding females amongst samples of a species of the asellote genus *Ilyarachna* sp. taken in August and December from the Gay Head–Bermuda transect (Sanders & Hessler, 1969*a*) were not consistent with reproductive seasonality. Also tanaids from this transect, Gardiner (1975) included young stages and females with marsupia (brood pouches) throughout the year in some species, again indicating continuous reproduction with a lack of seasonality. Rokop (1977*b*) re-examined the data of George & Menzies and agreed with the evidence for seasonal reproduction in the isopod *Storthyngura birsteini.* He considered the evidence for seasonal reproduction in other species to be highly tenuous. In contrast, Harrison (1988) analysed a long-term series of samples of isopods from 2.9 km depth in the Rockall Trough and concluded that there is seasonal variation in breeding intensity with a significantly higher proportion of females brooding in the winter months (25%) compared to the summer months (5%). Furthermore, there were more newly released juveniles present in the samples taken in the summertime (also coinciding with maxima in numbers of young in bivalves and echinoderms, see below).

There are few data on the development of deep-sea peracarids. From a single unusually large sample of the cumacean *Leucon jonesi* from about 1.5 km depth off Surinam, Bishop (1982) described the growth of early moult stages or *instars*. Growth of the early instars was typically much more rapid than those later. As in shallow-water populations, females are iteroparous (have multiple broods) with a resting instar allowing development of the oocytes, between carrying broods of 6–12 young. Thurston (1979) observed polymodality in body-size frequencies amongst scavenging lyssiannasid amphipods from the N.E. Atlantic, which he interpreted as resulting either from seasonal breeding, or from ecdysial (moult) growth stages. However, there was no evidence for any trend in recruitment/breeding in an extensive sampling programme for the giant species *Eurythenes gryllus* in the Pacific (Baldwin & Smith, 1987). The recurrent peaks in the size range correspond to successive moult stages and the geometric growth increment in successive instars is clearly seen (Ingram & Hessler, 1987) in the size data of *E. gryllus* (Fig. 13.1). Females grow larger and have more instars than males. Like other amphipods, they are probably iteroparous with a resting instar between each brood after maturity is reached. Brooding females are unknown amongst

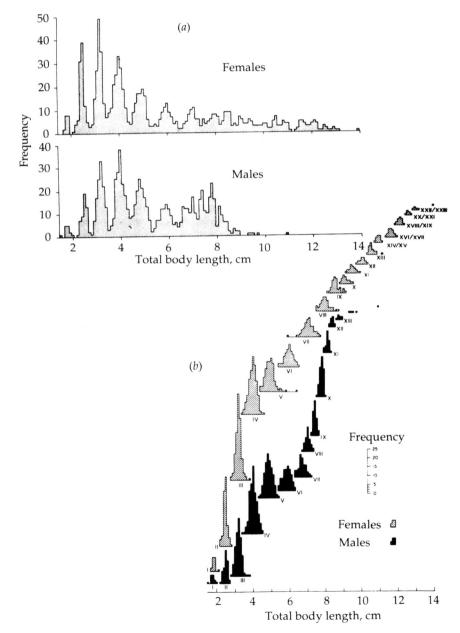

Fig. 13.1. (*a*) Total body-length frequencies of males and females of *Eurythenes gryllus*. (*b*) Individual instars, separated from the total size frequency distribution. (From Ingram & Hessler, 1987.)

scavenging amphipods, so estimates of fecundity have been based on oocyte counts. These vary between 70 and 185. However, in some species the oocyte counts decrease after development of secondary sexual characteristics. This suggests resorption occurs rather than seasonal breeding (Thurston, 1979; Hessler *et al.*, 1978; Ingram & Hessler, 1987). Juveniles appear to pass rapidly through the early instars, but, as they grow older, the length of the intermoult period increases. Assuming recruitment is continuous, this explains why fewer of the first few instars are caught than later ones.

Relatively little is known of reproduction in the larger deep-sea crustaceans. Ahlfeld (1979) examined seasonally disparate samples of *Parapagurus pilosimanus, Catapaguroides microps, Munidopsis rostrata* and *Nematocarcinus ensifer* concluding that some reproductive activity occurs throughout the year, as all four species showed periodic increases in breeding intensity. *Parapagurus pilosimanus* from the Blake Plateau, has asynchronous year-round breeding activity, but spawning is highly synchronous in winter (George, 1981). In the N.E. Atlantic, *P. pilosimanus* breeds throughout the year with no evidence of reproductive seasonality. In the bathyal spider crab *Dorhynchus thomsoni* there is a distinct reproductive cycle (Hartnoll & Rice, 1985). Although the pattern of egg carrying and larval development is similar to that in shallow-water species, incubation of the eggs would appear to take 8–9 months. The larvae of deep-sea crabs are not well known although Williamson (1982) has identified the larva of *Dorhynchus thomsoni* whilst Perkins (1973) and Sulkin & van Heukelem (1980) report the 'typical' decapod larval stage found in the deep-sea red crab *Chaceon quinquedens*. Reproduction in the commercially exploited species *Geryon maritae* from the upper continental slope off S.W. Africa suggests that there is no reproductive seasonality and the details of its gametogenic biology suggest considerable similarity to its shallow-water congeners (Melville-Smith, 1987). Year-round reproduction is found in the polychelids *Stereomastis nana* and *S. sculpta* (Wenner, 1978). In these species it is only the largest females that carry the eggs. Wenner (1980) describes reproduction in the penaeid *Benthesicymus bartletti* but, owing to the limited data, could not determine whether breeding was continuous or seasonal.

MOLLUSCS

The reproduction of deep-sea molluscs has received more attention than the previous taxa. Most of the available evidence concerns the protobranch bivalves and prosobranch gastropods. Ockelmann (1965) surveyed types of early development amongst shallow-water bivalves in the N.E. Atlantic, relating this to the morphology of the larval shell, or prodissoconch. He stated that lecithotrophic development predominates among deep-sea bivalves, and that direct development and brood protection are rare, 58% of the bathyal bivalves from the Indian Ocean showing evidence of lecithotrophic development (Knudsen, 1967, 1970). Knudsen (1979) summarizing the known data on development concluded that, in 60% of bathyal species (excluding species of the specialized wood-boring subfamily Xylophagainae), development is lecithotrophic and in 30% it is direct. At abyssal depths, these proportions are 70–75% and 15%, respectively (again excluding Xylophagainae which appear to show brood protection). In shallow water, planktotrophic (pelagic) development predominates, the most marked change in mode of reproduction occurs between the sublittoral and bathyal zones. Deep-sea bivalves tend to have smaller gonads than those of shallow-water forms; R. Scheltema (1972) traced a depth-related gradient in decreasing fecundity derived in counts of ripe eggs in the gonads of seven *Nucula* spp. The gonad of the tiny deep-sea nuculid *Microgloma* contains only two eggs, the lowest number yet found in any bivalve (Sanders & Allen, 1973).

Rokop (1974, 1979) analysed the reproductive cycle of four species in the San Diego Trough: *Nuculana pontonia*, *Nucula darella*, *Tindaria cervola* and *Bathyarca* sp. In all four, reproduction was year-round, confirming R. Scheltema's (1972) suggestion that breeding is always continuous in deep-sea bivalves. However, in the protobranch bivalves *Yoldiella jeffreysi* (Fig. 13.2) and in *Ledella pustulosa*, from 2.9 km depth in the Rockall Trough (Lightfoot *et al.*, 1979), the gametogenic cycle is distinctly seasonal. The maximum egg size observed suggests development is lecithotrophic rather than planktotrophic. Jablonski & Lutz (1983) suggest that the diminutive size of most deep-sea molluscs necessitates the adoption of a non-planktotrophic mode of larval development, because

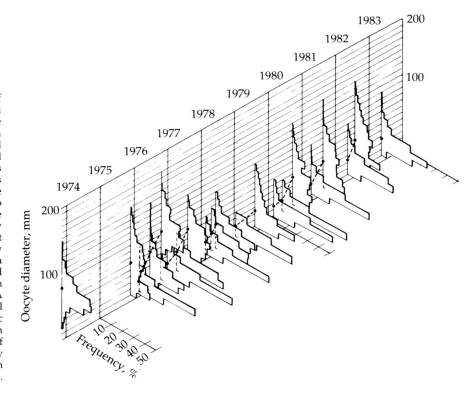

Fig. 13.2. Size frequencies of oocytes in the gonads of a protobranch bivalve *Yoldiella jeffreysi*: from 2.9 km depth in the Rockall Trough to show seasonal breeding. Filled circles represent mean diameters for each sample and are joined by pecked lines to indicate the seasonal cycle in oogenesis, initiated early in the year, with most active vitellogenesis (yolky development of egg) in summer, and concluded with release of ripe eggs in early winter/spring. A parallel cycle in seasonal spermatogenic development occurs in males, with 'spawnout' of both sexes probably occurring synchronously in the population.

they would be physically incapable of producing sufficient planktotrophic larvae per brood to ensure successful recruitment.

Deep-sea species of the wood-boring Xylophagainae have a very specialized lifestyle that may include seasonal reproduction. Experimental wood blocks placed on the abyssal seabed are rapidly colonized. The juveniles grow rapidly, mature early and have a high reproductive rate. The planktonic larval stage is prolonged which maximizes their chance of locating more wood. Meanwhile, the adults are consuming their habitat and die once it is finished. Turner (1973, 1977) postulated that, because import of wood to the sea is seasonally associated with periods of heavy rain, the larval release may be seasonal; the peak varying geographically.

Larvae of deep-sea bivalves rarely occur in the plankton. Allen (1983) mentions observations of bivalve larvae in the surface plankton of the Atlantic. Lamellibranch larvae were taken at 1.8–2 km depth near the Kurile–Kamchatka Trench (Mileikovsky, 1968). We have taken shelled larvae, probably of several protobranch species, from deeply towed plankton hauls in the Rockall Trough.

GASTROPODS

Fertilization in gastropods is usually internal; otherwise reproductive patterns in the prosobranch gastropods are similar to those found in the protobranch bivalves. Reproduction occurs year-round in the abyssal mesogastropod *Benthonella tenella*; the oocyte size/frequency histograms showing no seasonal differences (Rex, Van Ummersen & Turner, 1979). Its larval shell indicates a prolonged planktotrophic existence. Successful recruitment may follow cues provided by episodic food falls which trigger settlement and stimulate rapid growth through the early stages when juvenile mortality is highest. They suggested that this fits in with the life-history models of Murphy (1968) and Schaffer (1974) which predict selective advantage for longevity and iteroparity to be associated with the life-history traits shown by *Benthonella*, although such traits may not be typical of abyssal species as a whole. However, similar reproductive features are seen in the neogastropod *Colus jeffreysianus* and in the trochid *Calliotropis ottoi* from the N.E. Atlantic. Gametogenesis is a continuous process throughout the year and all the stages of oogenic development are found in each follicle of the ovary, whilst the size of the ripe egg suggests direct early development in both species (Colman *et al.*, 1986a; Colman & Tyler, 1988).

Observation of the early shell morphology in adult deep-sea gastropods can, as in bivalves, give much information on the mode of early development. Species with planktotrophic development have a larval shell, or *dissoconch* (found at the very apex of the adult shell), which is narrow, multispiral, usually brown in colour, and has a distinct ornate sculpture. It is possible, clearly to distinguish *protoconch I* (embryonic shell) and *protoconch II* (larval shell) (Fig. 13.3). In species with non-planktonic development, the larval shell is large, bulbous, paucispiral (few spirals), single-coiled and unsculptured.

These parameters have been used by a number of authors to determine the reproductive mode of deep-sea prosobranchs (Bouchet, 1976a,b; Bouchet & Warén, 1982; Rex & Warén, 1982; Colman *et al.*, 1986b). The data suggest that planktotrophic development in prosobranch snails increases with depth. At depths < 1 km, less than 25% of species have planktotrophic development whilst deeper than 4 km over 50% had planktotrophic development (Rex & Warén, 1982). Planktotrophic veliger larvae of two common deep-sea prosobranch snails *Benthomangelia macro* and *Benthonella tenella* have been collected from the N.E. Atlantic and Mediterranean (Richter & Thorson, 1974; Bouchet, 1976b; Bouchet & Warén, 1979a), the adults of which live between 2 and 4 km depth. The astonishing implication that such tiny larvae migrate over such a depth range is supported by evidence from significant differences in the stable oxygen isotope values between the larval and adult shells. This suggests the larval shell was formed in the warmer surface waters as the isotopic $^{18}O : {^{16}O}$ ratio in precipitated calcite is directly related to temperature (Bouchet & Fontes, 1981; Killingley & Rex, 1985). Similar analyses of the shell of lecithotrophic species show no disparity in oxygen isotope ratios between larval and adult shell indicating that such larvae stay at the

Fig. 13.3. Scanning electron micrograph of the larval shell of the deep-sea prosobranch gastropod *Amphissa acutecostata* (fam. Columbellidae) showing features typical of planktotrophic early development. PI, protoconch I (embryonic shell); PII, protoconch II (larval shell); SR, sinusigerous riblet of adult shell (T). Scale bar = 0.1 mm. (From Colman, 1987.)

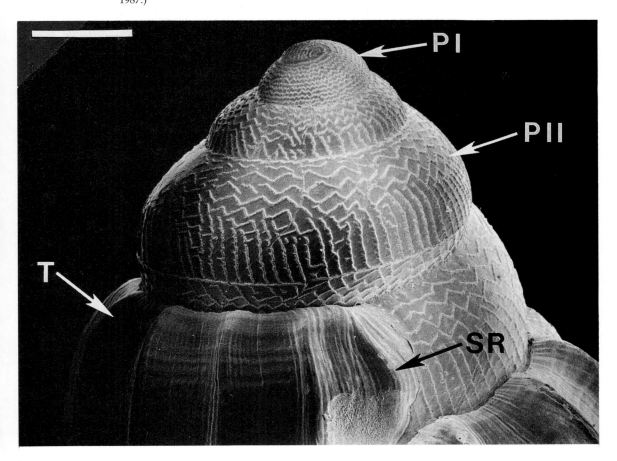

bottom. Bouchet (1976*a*) suggests a bioenergetic advantage of exploitation of phytoplankton as food along with benefit of dispersal by surface water currents. The selective advantages in such a pattern is now inferred to occur in 30–43% of prosobranch gastropods in the N. Atlantic (Bouchet & Warén, 1979*b*; Colman, Tyler & Gage, 1986*b*).

Most of the remaining species appear to have an encapsulated early development on the bottom (Fig. 5.24).

OTHER MOLLUSCS

Evidence from sediment tray colonization experiments indicate that juveniles of the worm-like aplacophoran mollusc, *Prochaetoderma yongei* become adult in only 2 months, and reach sexual maturity in 1 yr (A. H. Scheltema, 1987). Although gametogenesis is asynchronous, there appear to be periods of increased recruitment and ripe individuals, but whether this is true seasonality is unknown.

Amongst the Scaphopoda, *Cadulus californicus* has been examined in detail (Rokop, 1974, 1977*a*). At bathyal depths in the San Diego Trough, this species showed a seasonal reproductive cycle in which there was synchrony of gamete development, and spawning occurred between July and October. There is some evidence that scaphopods from the Rockall Trough breed seasonally, in relation to variation in the ratio of intake of planktonic and benthic foraminiferans in their diet (Davies, 1987).

BRACHIOPODS

In the articulate species *Frieleia halli* from the San Diego Trough, Rokop (1977*a*) found seasonal reproduction, with spawning occurring between January and April. However, in explaining these seasonal phenomena, Rokop suggested that the cycle might be a result of a vertical distribution of the population extending from shallow into deep water, or possibly that the reproductive cycle is synchronized by tidal phenomena.

ECHINODERMS

The most complete suite of reproductive data is available for echinoderms, probably because they are cosmopolitan and large-sized. To date, we have examined various aspects of the reproductive biology of over 40 species in samples from 0.5 to 5.4 km depth. The great Danish zoologist, Theodor Mortensen, in his comprehensive monographs of echinoderms, published from the early years of this century right up to the 1950s, regularly commented on the reproductive condition of the specimens, that included deep-sea species, he was examining. However, it was from material collected along the Gay Head–Bermuda transect that the first detailed observations of reproductive patterns in deep-sea echinoderms were made. Initially, Schoener (1968) used differences in population size structure to suggest a seasonal input of postlarvae to the adult population of *Ophiura ljungmani* and *Ophiomusium lymani*. These data were supplemented by an examination of egg size and number in five species of deep-sea ophiuroid. Schoener (1972) associated the small eggs and high fecundity of *Ophiura ljungmani* with indirect development to a pelagic larval stage, whilst the larger egg size and lower fecundity in the remaining species suggested direct development. Rokop (1974) in his 1-yr time series from the San Diego Trough noted no evidence of any seasonal reproductive variation in the brittle star *Ophiophthalmus normani*.

The largest suite of data has come from the Scottish Marine Biological Association's time-series sampling programme in the Rockall Trough undertaken during the 1970s and 1980s. Using both this material and that from samples taken by the U.K. Institute of Oceanographic Sciences in the N.E. Atlantic, a detailed analysis of the reproductive biology of a large number of echinoderms has been made by Tyler and co-workers (Tyler, 1986). It is evident from these observations that there are three main types of reproductive pattern in deep-sea echinoderms.

(i) *'Continuous' reproduction*   This is the dominant reproductive pattern in deep-sea echinoderms. In the females, it is typified by the production of relatively few large eggs (600 μm to 3.4 mm diameter) which are well supplied with yolk. Oocyte size/frequency counts suggest there is a large reserve of small previtellogenic oocytes ($< 300\ \mu$m) in the ovary (Fig. 13.4(a)). Some of these undergo vitellogenesis and develop to the maximum size. In many of the species there is evidence of (a) recycling of unspent oocytes and (b) occasional 'nurse oocytes' in which an oocyte grows to a certain size and then breaks down presumably to provide energy for oocytes developing through to the maximum size.

This pattern of continuous production is seen in many ophiuroid species, the echinothuriid sea urchins and most of the holothurians examined. Most of these echinoderm species have separate sexes (gonochorism) except for the simultaneous hermaphrodite *Parorhiza pallens* and the protandric hermaphrodite *Ophiacantha bidentata* (Tyler & Gage, 1982a).

In the majority of gonochoric species the males are in a state of continuous maturity, with the exception of males in the holothurian family Deimatidae in which spermatogenesis has not been observed (Tyler & Billett, 1988). This ensures that the male is ripe on a chance encounter with a ripe female. In this pattern we imply that development is direct although the fertilized egg may be dispersed in the water column above the seabed. There is some evidence of pelagic dispersal of juveniles in the elasipod *Psychropotes* as young of this species have been taken in plankton tows up to 3 km above the seabed (Grieg, 1921; Billett *et al.*, 1985; Tyler & Billett, 1988). Although we have assumed that this direct development takes place demersally within the benthic boundary layer (Tyler & Gage, 1984a) a number of experiments with echinothuriids suggest that the eggs of *Phormosoma placenta* and *Araeosoma fenestratum* are capable of floating right up to the sea surface in under two days where presumably the higher temperature will enable more rapid development (Young & Cameron, 1987; Cameron, McEuen & Young, 1988).

Surprisingly, there have been very few observations of brooding in deep-sea echinoderms, even in groups such as the asteroid family

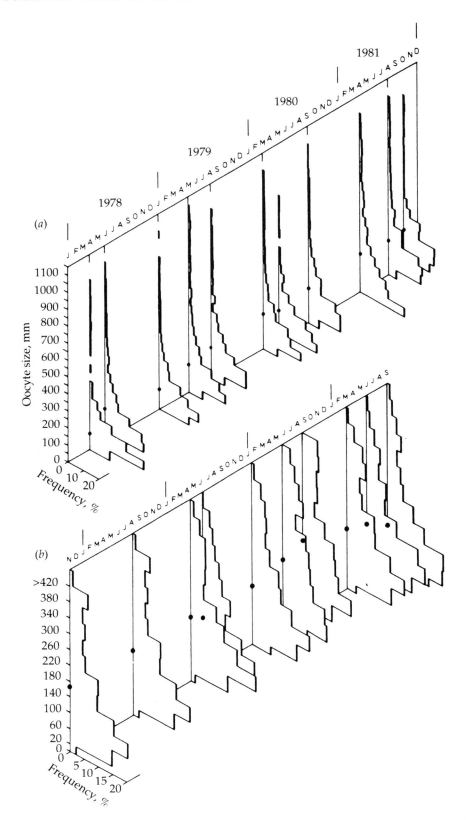

Fig. 13.4. Oocyte size/
frequencies in species
showing non-seasonal
pattern in gametogenesis:
(a) sea star *Hymenaster
membranaceus*; (b) brittle star
Ophiomusium lymani. Both
from 2.2 km depth repeat
station in the Rockall
Trough. Other details as in
Fig. 13.2. (From Tyler, 1986.)

Pterasteridae in which all other known species brood. Only in the holothurian *Oneirophanta mutabilis affinis* has intra-ovarian brooding been described (Hansen, 1968).

(ii) *Intermediate development* This pattern is seen in very few deep-sea echinoderms and is best described in the cosmopolitan ophiuroid *Ophiomusium lymani*. This species has an intermediate egg size (*c*. 420 μm) and an intermediate fecundity (*c*. 10^4 eggs per individual) but examination of the oocyte size/frequency data shows no evidence of gametogenic seasonality (Fig. 13.4(*b*)). In shallow-water ophiuroids with these reproductive parameters, an abbreviated larva is usually found (Hendler, 1975). However, no pelagic larva of any sort has been observed for *Ophiomusium* although the early postlarva has been described by Schoener (1967). In an examination of the population structure of this species from the N.E. Atlantic, Gage & Tyler (1982) have shown a seasonal pulse in recruitment of postlarvae to the adult population (see Fig. 13.6(*b*)). In the absence of any apparent seasonality in the production of gametes (Gage & Tyler, 1982), we must assume that mortality of new recruits must vary at different times of the year, perhaps related to seasonal deposition of fresh particulate organic matter from the surface production.

(iii) *Seasonal reproduction* This unexpected reproductive pattern was first proposed for deep-sea echinoderms by Schoener (1968) after her examination of the population structure of ophiuroids collected at different times of the year along the Gay Head–Bermuda transect. In a more detailed data set from between 1 and 2.9 km in the N.E. Atlantic, we have unequivocal evidence of seasonal reproduction in three echinoderm species and circumstantial evidence for a further five. The characteristics that identify these species are small eggs (*c*. 100 μm maximum diameter), high fecundity, synchrony of gamete development and a distinct seasonal reproductive cycle. Although the fine detail varies slightly between species, the main seasonal features are: (*a*) the initiation of gametogenesis in the Spring of each year (except in *Echinus affinis* where it occurs in November/December); (*b*) active vitellogenesis during the Summer months and early Autumn; (*c*) a spawnout in the early Spring of each year.

These features have been observed in the ophiuroid *Ophiura ljungmani*, the asteroid *Plutonaster bifrons* and the echinoid *Echinus affinis* (Fig. 13.5) (Tyler *et al.*, 1982; Tyler, 1986, 1988). In *Ophiura ljungmani* this seasonal breeding is reflected in a marked influx of juvenile stages to the population that are very conspicuous in summertime epibenthic sled samples in the Rockall Trough (Fig. 13.6(*a*)) (Lightfoot *et al.*, 1979). The pattern remains the same for all species of *Echinus* from shallow to deep water in the N.E. Atlantic (Gage *et al.*, 1986). The asteroid *Dytaster insignis* has a similar pattern to *Plutonaster*, and the reproductive cycle of the upper bathyal brittle star *Ophiocten gracilis* also appears to be highly seasonal. In this last species, the seasonality is confirmed by means of the gametogenic biology, polymodal disc-size frequencies and also by the occurrence of its larva *Ophiopluteus ramosus* in surface plankton tows taken in

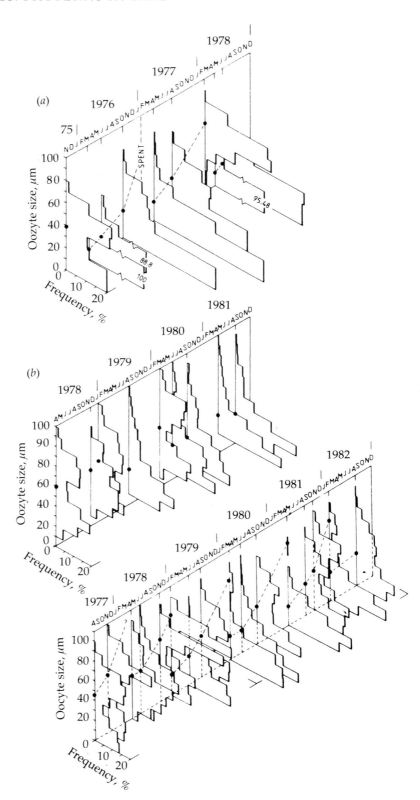

Fig. 13.5. Oocyte size/ frequencies in seasonally reproducing echinoderms from a 2.2 km depth repeat station in the Rockall Trough: (*a*) brittle star *Ophiura ljungmani*; (*b*) sea star *Plutonaster bifrons*; (*c*) sea urchin *Echinus affinis*. Other details as in Fig. 13.2. (From Tyler, 1986.)

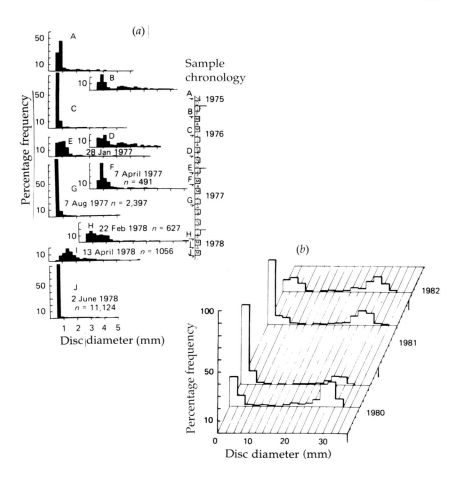

Fig. 13.6. Size frequency histograms of brittle stars: (a) *Ophiura ljungmani* from 2.9 km; (b) *Ophiomusium lymani* (from 2.2 km repeat station) to show pattern of summertime recruitment of juveniles in the Rockall Trough. ((a) Modified from Gage & Tyler 1981b.)

the Spring (Geiger, 1963; Semenova *et al.*, 1964; Tyler & Gage, 1982b; Gage & Tyler, 1982). Postlarval *Ophiocten gracilis* have been taken in the late Spring in plankton hauls and are recruited to the benthos shortly afterwards (Gage & Tyler, 1981a). In an elegant approach, using the 'Johnson Sealink II' submersible, Young & Cameron (1989) have cultured larvae of the bathyal *Linopneustes longispinus* at atmospheric pressure and temperatures from 5° to 25 °C. They showed this species had a similar development to shallow-water echinoderms, developing best at 10° to 15 °C. This suggests that these planktotrophic larvae rely on food resources occurring deeper than the photic zone.

In the deep-sea ophiuroids the number of arm segments present in pelagic postlarvae has been used as a guide to the type of early development. In those undergoing direct or abbreviated development there are rarely more than two arm segments present, whereas those undergoing indirect development have up to ten arm segments to each arm whilst still in the plankton (Schoener, 1967, 1969).

The breeding of deep-sea echinoderms provide good examples of

Fig. 13.7. Population size structure of seasonally breeding brittle stars from epibenthic sled hauls taken within a few days of each other during summer at different depths in the Rockall Trough. The disc-size frequencies show a differing proportion of larger sizes that probably reflects decreasing survivorship of young away from the centre of distribution: (*a*) upper-abyssal/lower bathyal species *Ophiura ljungmani*; (*b*) upper bathyal species *Ophiocten gracilis*. (From Gage & Tyler, 1982*b*.)

wasteful dispersal of larvae that accompanies planktotrophy, a phenomenon long known from shallow water. We have shown that, at certain times of the year, there is a marked influx of juveniles to the adult population of deep-sea echinoids and ophiuroids at different depths in the Rockall Trough. The size structure of samples indicates that survivors of juveniles settling in their normal depth zone grow to adult size; but, outside their established depth zone, the size structure (Fig. 13.7(*a*),(*b*)) indicates rapidly increasing mortality away from the centre of distribution, with little or no survival to adult size (Gage & Tyler, 1982).

CONTROLS IN SEASONAL BREEDERS

For there to be seasonal reproduction in deep-sea species there must be some exogenous factor controlling the development of the gonad and its spawning. We suggest that the sinking from the surface of seasonally produced organic matter (see Chapter 11) forms a food source for developing larvae in the plankton; and when it reaches the seabed

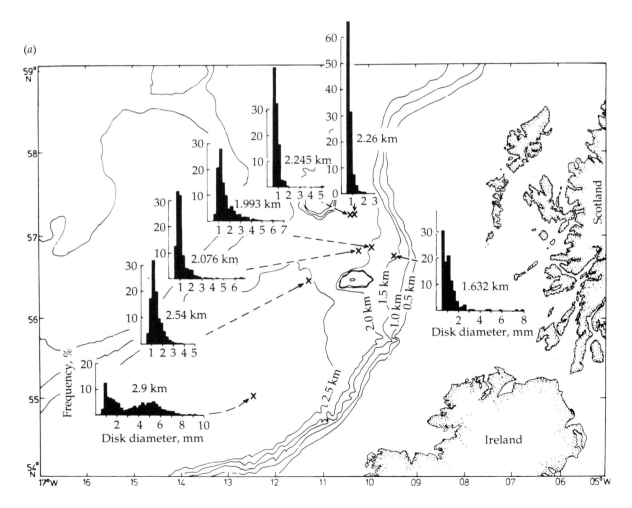

provides a nutritional source to fuel vitellogenic development in the adults and the growth of newly settled young. Although the appearance of this material at the seabed (Fig. 11.3) coincides with the onset of vitellogenesis, we do not know what factor(s) initiate gametogenesis or stimulate spawning except that, in the species examined, spawning is coincident with the period of maximum eddy kinetic energy in the N.E. Atlantic (Dickson *et al.*, 1982). Tyler & Gage (1984*b*) speculated that currents resulting from such vorticity transmitted to the bottom may carry pheromones triggering spawning amongst a ripe population, but evidence, at present, is lacking.

From these data of invertebrate reproduction we may conclude there is no particular pattern that may be classified as typical of the deep sea. Selective pressures have led to a variety of successful reproductive patterns.

MATING AND BREEDING AGGREGATIONS

As in shallow water, with most deep-sea invertebrates the sexes are separate (gonochorism) with external fertilization of released eggs and

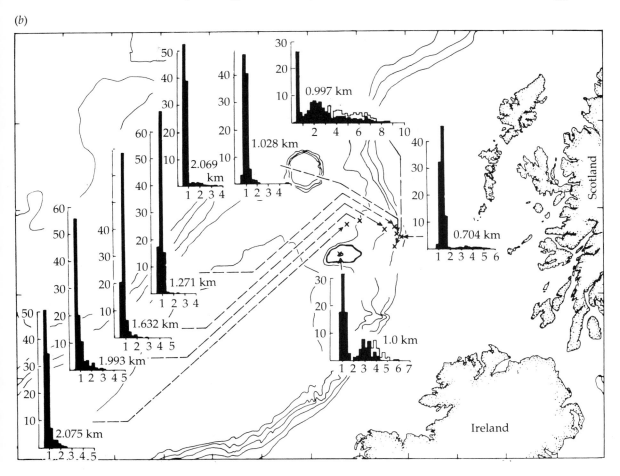

(b)

sperm. However, in some taxa, such as gastropod molluscs, the eggs are fertilized internally by sperm introduced and stored in the body of the female, whilst some other molluscs are hermaphrodites. Clearly, herma-phoditism will be of benefit in an ecosystem where the low numerical density makes locating a mate difficult or even improbable, but this is offset by the problems of self-fertilization and inbreeding. Consequently, the gonads of hermaphrodites usually change from one sex to another rather than ripening simultaneously.

From the distribution data of individual species, we know that, for many species, population density is low and that mating must be opportunistic when a female and male meet. These chance encounters will benefit from the female and male being as ripe as possible for as long as possible. Hence, in most deep-sea invertebrates, a few eggs are produced at a time and are resorbed if they are not spawned. Two mechanisms may aid successful fertilization. In seasonally breeding species, eggs and sperms in all individuals are produced at more or less the same time, released, and external fertilization takes place.

The problem of finding a mate may also be overcome in the aggre-gations seen from manned submersibles and in deep-sea photographs (see Chapter 6), which may represent a social breeding activity as much as a herding for more efficient grazing or a response to patchy food. The aggregations observed in the sea urchin *Phormosoma placenta* (Grassle *et al.*, 1975) and in the holothurian, *Kolga hyalina* (Fig. 6.2) (Billett & Hansen, 1982) may represent breeding aggregations, as at other times the popu-lations are quite dispersed. However, there is no photographic evidence of any mass spawning event in these species and this suggestion must remain speculative. In bathyal depths off the Bahamas, C. M. Young (personal communication) has shown that the deep-sea echinoids *Cidaris blakei* and *Stylocidaris lineata* pair prior to spawning. Although only about 50% of the pairings were male/female, this would appear to be a strategy to aid successful fertilization.

REPRODUCTION IN DEEP-SEA BENTHIC FISH

Much of the information on reproduction in deep-sea fish has arisen from studies not specifically dedicated to this end but as comments in taxono-mic or distributional studies (see Merrett & Marshall, 1981; Merrett & Domanski, 1985; Merrett & Saldanha, 1985). As in the invertebrates, there appears to be a variety of reproductive patterns. Unfortunately long-term observations of deep-sea benthopelagic fish populations are rare, and thus most data on reproduction are specific time observations. The main information concerns fecundity, sexuality and development amongst species of the dominant family amongst benthopelgic fishes, the Mac-rouridae. These have assumed some commercial fishing importance, particularly by the Russians. In general, fecundity is not related to depth, and both gonochoric species, such as the Liparidae and Zoarcidae, and hermaphroditic species, such as the Chlorophthalmids, are found (Mead *et al.*, 1964; Sulak, 1977). However, the Liparidae have large eggs and relatively low fecundities (Stein, 1980), and may be mouth brooders (Wenner, 1979), and probably take up a benthic lifestyle very soon or immediately after hatching. In the Zoarcidae and Chlorophthalmids, the eggs develop on the seabed. This typifies the variability of reproductive strategies in deep-sea fish. Data on early life history are sparse or absent, but the slope dwelling synaphobranchid eels have long been known, from the larval stages, to breed in the Sargasso Sea.

In the N.E. Atlantic there have been some studies in which reproduction forms an important element of the ecological study. There is evidence for both continuity of breeding, and seasonal breeding in different species, from the same site, but also evidence that geography affects the breeding strategy (Gordon, 1979; Gordon & Duncan, 1987; Merrett, 1987). Merrett (1987) examined reproduction in a number of species from north and south of 40° N in the N.E. Atlantic. Those from the 'southern' assemblage have low fecundity and, in the three dominant species, the ovary contains three generations of oocytes. This strategy is interpreted as an adaptation to the oligotrophic, less seasonal environment south of 40° N. In the 'northern' assemblage, fecundity is higher, the eggs in the ovary are all in the same stage of development and appear to be spawned simultaneously in February to April. This strategy is adapted to the eutrophic seasonal conditions in the waters north of 40° N (Merrett, 1987). From the 'northern' assemblage Gordon (1979) summarized the data of timing of seasonal reproduction to that date, whilst breeding information on macrourids from the N. Pacific are summarized by Stein and Pearcy (1982), who also estimate average fecundities ranging from about 2.6×10^4 to 2.5×10^6. Many species appear to breed seasonally, but at differing times of the year. For example, the N. Atlantic macrourid *Nezumia aequalis* has a spawning season lasting from April to October whereas *Trachyrhynchus murrayi* and the morid *Lepidion eques* appear to spawn between March and May. Gordon & Duncan (1987) also reported seasonal spawning of *Coryphaenoides guentheri* from 2.2 km depth in April and May. In the Liparidae, which have a wide depth distribution in the deep sea, Stein (1980) found that species spawning throughout the year are primarily abyssal, whilst bathyal species included species showing spawning periodicities.

One problem in understanding seasonality in deep-sea fish reproduction is that the spawning season is not synchronous between species and thus cannot necessarily be related to the spring plankton bloom as seen in the deep-sea invertebrates, unless young stages are able to feed on secondary production in the euphotic zone. However, in motile organisms that are widely dispersed at low densities, there will be powerful advantages in populations synchronizing reproductive development in order to maximize the reproductive value of interspecific encounters.

Although macrourid eggs are spawned and fertilized near the bottom, they incorporate an oil globule to make them buoyant. Early development as pelagic larvae is thought to take place above the seasonal thermocline, with subsequent descent during later development to the benthic boundary (Merrett, 1986).

GROWTH RATES OF DEEP-SEA ORGANISMS

MOLLUSCS

In their influential paper, Turekian *et al.* (1975) employed the innovatory technique of radiometric dating to age the shell of the protobranch bivalve *Tindaria callistiformis.* This study has done as much as any other to support the still-pervasive view of exceptionally low growth rates amongst deep-sea organisms. Specimens were obtained at 3.8 km depth from the Gay Head–Bermuda transect located in the N.W. Atlantic. Activities of the naturally occurring radioisotope ^{228}Ra (halflife 5.75 yr) were measured in four different size fractions of the shell. Although showing considerable scatter, the results (Fig. 13.8) were thought not inconsistent with these relatively tiny specimens reaching reproductive maturity at about 50 yr, and an estimated age for the largest specimens of 100 yr (albeit with a 95% confidence interval of ±76 yr)! It is worth our while examining how this result was obtained and what assumptions are incorporated into this radiometric chronology. The ^{228}Ra activity in any size fraction is given by the amount of mass (as a cubic function of length) weighted for the decay of ^{228}Ra in each mass increment since the mass, including the ^{228}Ra, was added. The expression used to estimate the activity of ^{228}Ra at the time collected from the bottom incorporates a growth-rate function where the time relationship to change in mass was derived from pronounced sculptural rings on the shell. These, however, are not necessarily laid down at the regular time intervals assumed. Similar sculptural rings on the slow-growing inshore bivalve *Astarte* appear to be formed at increasingly longer time intervals with increasing age (Trutschler & Samtleben, 1987), and cannot be taken as age markers. Jumars & Gallagher (1982) caution against inferring that slow individual

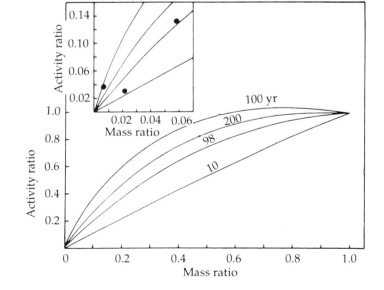

Fig. 13.8. ^{228}Ra activity ratio (^{228}Ra activity in individual *Tindaria callistiformis* of a given size fraction normalized to that of the largest size fraction) plotted (filled circles in upper inset) against mass ratio (mass of individual of a given size fraction normalized to that of the largest size fraction). Curves are calculated for various ages of the oldest animal. (From Cochran, 1982.)

and population growth rates are characteristic of the deep sea. Indeed, it has become clear from studies of shell banding, tagging and radiometric dating that certain shallow water bivalves may survive to ages in excess of 100 yr (Jones *et al.*, 1987; Thompson, Jones & Dreibelbis, 1980; Forster, 1981; Turekian *et al.*, 1979; Breen & Shields, 1983).

From the varying size structure shown in samples of protobranch bivalves that we have taken through the year from the Rockall Trough time series, it is possible to infer that juvenile growth is fairly rapid (Fig. 13.9). This interpretation is reinforced by the presence of a ring-like pattern reflecting growth checks, rather than shell sculpture, on the shell (Fig. 13.10) of some of those showing seasonal breeding; although we cannot yet be certain that these checks are not caused by the seasonal breeding cycle. The merging and stacking of the adult frequencies make analysis of cohort structure difficult by means of classical techniques. But it is possible to fit a model embodying a growth rate whose initial bounds are estimated from the movement of juvenile modes of the two species showing seasonal breeding, *Ledella pustulosa* and *Yoldiella jeffreysi*, along

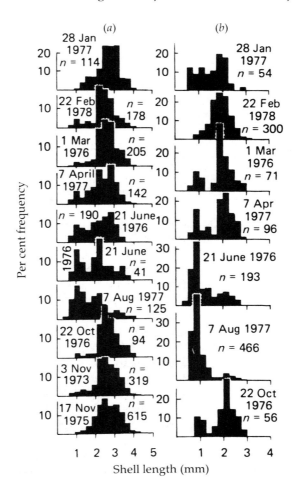

Fig. 13.9. Shell-length frequencies of (*a*) *Ledella pustulosa* and (*b*) *Yoldiella jeffreysi* in epibenthic sled samples from the 2.9 km depth Permanent Station in the Rockall Trough. The samples, which were taken at different times between 1973 and 1978, are arranged as a 'composite year' to show the recruitment of smallest sizes to the populations during summer. (From Gage, 1985.)

Fig. 13.10. Shell of specimen of *Ledella pustulosa* from 2.9 km depth in the Rockall Trough showing growth banding assumed to represent annual growth checks. The specimen, collected in summer, is thought to have an age of about 4 yr.

with an appropriate survivorship function. The fit of an optimized model with 8 yr classes to the observed shell-size frequencies for *Ledella pustulosa* is shown in (Fig. 13.11). Such models suggest that growth and mortality amongst these species may not be markedly different from those of populations of inshore species.

Deminucula cancellata appears to remain reproductively active throughout the year so that growth analysis of movement of age-marked cohorts resulting from annual breeding cannot be applied to this species. However, specimens recovered from a sediment tray deployed for 26 months in the N. Atlantic had almost attained reproductive maturity (Grassle, 1977). Assuming colonization occurred by means of a water-borne larva, a growth to this size (2 mm) must have occurred within this period (Grassle & Morse-Porteous, 1987). Furthermore, in the Rockall Trough, recruitment appears to be annually pulsed, as in the brittle star *Ophiomusium* (Fig. 13.5(*b*)), so that a growth model can be developed based on annual recruitment waves into a frequency distribution.

Similarly, fast growth rates of larger bodied protobranchs whose bathymetric range extends into bathyal depths from shallower water have been estimated from analysis of shell-growth banding (Hutchings & Haedrich, 1984; Gilkinson *et al.*, 1986).

The only non-bivalve mollusc for which there are good data on growth is the aplacophoran *Prochaetoderma yongei*. A. H. Scheltema (1987) showed from sediment tray recolonisation experiments (see Chapter 8) that this small species grows to adult size within 2 months and attains sexual maturity within 1 yr. Despite this, repopulation of a disturbed area by this essentially opportunistic species may still require about 10 yr owing to its low fecundity and lack of synchrony in egg production.

COELENTERATES

Estimates of the growth rates in deep-sea solitary corals from the S. Atlantic have also been made by means of radiometric techniques (Coch-

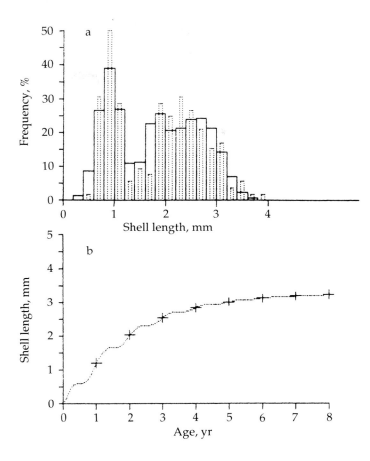

Fig. 13.11. (*a*) Expected frequencies of demographic model (open bars) with eight year classes, embodying growth curve shown in (*b*) and a mortality of 43% of each year class per year, fitted to observed shell-size frequencies (narrow dotted bars) of *Ledella pustulosa* from 2.9 km in the Rockall Trough. (*b*) Von Bertalanffy growth curve (with seasonally varying rate) of the fitted model with parameter values given in Table 13.1.

ran, 1982). Activities of ^{228}Ra were measured in different size fractions of the population. Growth curves were fitted to plots of the change in total ^{228}Ra in different sized corals against their mass, by approximating the skeletal growth as growth of a cone. The two alternative growth models, one assuming constant *linear* increments, and the other, more reasonably, assuming constant *volume* increments give estimates of an age of approximately 60 or 6 yr for the largest specimen (Fig. 13.12). Some support for the latter interpretation was obtained from a further analysis using another naturally occurring radioisotope, ^{210}Pb, with a different halflife (22.3 yr) that showed little change between size fractions.

BRACHIOPODS

Examination of the shell of the inarticulate brachiopod *Pelagodiscus atlanticus* shows clear growth banding, which, on the assumption of an annual periodicity in growth, indicate a lifespan of 3 to 6 yr (Fig. 13.13), with maturity being reached in either the first, second or third year of life (Zezina, 1975). A similarly fast rate of growth is hypothesized for the articulate species *Macandrevia africanum* from analysis of growth-line structure in the shell in specimens from 3 km deep in the tropical S.

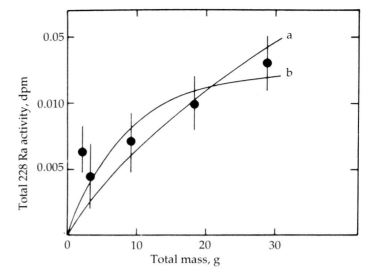

Fig. 13.12. Total ^{228}Ra activity in a deep-sea solitary coral as a function of coral mass from specimens in different size fractions. Curves are best-fit model calculations of activity versus mass for growth functions of (*a*) constant length rate and (*b*) constant volume rate. (From Cochran, 1982.)

Atlantic. It is thought large specimens may reach an age of 12 to 14 yr (Laurin & Gaspard, 1988).

CRUSTACEANS

Bishop (1982) was able to analyse the relative growth of the cumacean *Leucon jonesi* from instar-related peaks in size frequencies of a large sample. However, these data lack the time scale necessary to calculate a growth rate in absolute time units. The only estimate of absolute growth rates amongst deep-sea Crustacea has been obtained from size frequencies of the giant scavenging amphipod *Eurythenes gryllus* trapped in the central N. Pacific (Ingram & Hessler, 1987). These authors interpret a shift in a peak in instar abundance as reflecting growth of a dominant year class or cohort during the 1 yr interval between sampling (possibly

Fig. 13.13. Analysis of growth banding on shells of brachiopod *Pelagodiscus atlanticus*: (*a*) lateral view of shell showing shell diameters (d) subscripted by their corresponding age (*t*) in years that are plotted in (*b*): Ford–Walford plot of shell measurements with fitted regression indicating fit to Von Bertalanffy growth function. The intercept with the pecked line of zero growth denotes the shell size at the theoretical growth asymptote of maximum growth. Filled circles, observed shell diameters; crosses, theoretical size for the fitted growth function. (From Zezina, 1976.)

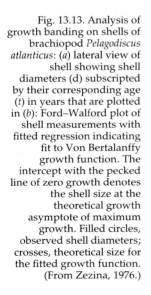

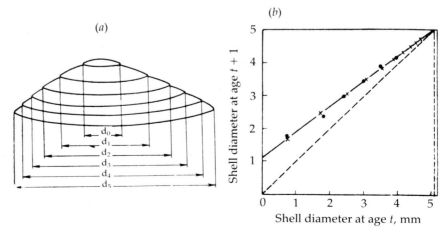

related to an El Niñõ event occurring in 1976). Using this, and an assumption that body size and growth rate in crustaceans are related to age, Ingram & Hessler estimate female *E. gryllus* mature at about 8.8 yr, by which time they have attained a length of about 7 cm and thereon have multiple broods. The smaller-sized males are thought to mature at 4 yr, resulting in an overall male/female ratio of 3 : 1.

ECHINODERMS

The seasonally pulsed recruitment resulting from annual breeding amongst common species of brittle stars and echinoids in the Rockall time series has allowed us to apply classical methods of analysis of size frequencies where the growth of age marked cohorts can be followed along the size axis of frequency distributions in a sample time series. In the brittle star *Ophiura ljungmani*, the growth of juvenile sizes can be followed after recruitment although the decreasing numbers in each age class along with variability in individual growth does not permit cohorts to be recognized into adulthood. However, the growth curves plotted from the time series suggested a pattern of seasonal growth (Tyler & Gage, 1980; Gage & Tyler, 1981*b*). Although not apparently showing seasonal spawning, the annual pattern in recruitment in the larger brittle star *Ophiomusium lymani* permitted a similar approach to be applied (Gage & Tyler, 1982). In contrast to *Ophiura ljungmani*, the *Ophiomusium lymani* population in Rockall is dominated by adult sizes (indicating much less severe mortality in later life); but because these sizes form a large, virtually unimodal, peak, this confounded attempts to dissect the size structure into the cohorts that could be traced from the pulsed recruitment of the relatively fast-growing juveniles (see Fig. 13.5(*b*)).

Computer models developed to understand the growth and survivorship of the populations of this species world-wide indicate that the large adult peak of the Rockall population may comprise a stack of a large number of overlapping year classes (Fig. 13.14). This implies a low mortality amongst adult brittle stars in the Rockall Trough which is thought to be related to rather low population density. Analysis of populations in the San Diego Trough, where the numbers of adults relative to smaller sizes is more modest, but where the population exists at much higher densities, suggests a much lower adult survivorship. Gage (1982) suggests that this may result from greater competition for resources. Ring-like growth zones which have recently been discovered in the skeletal arm ossicles of both *Ophiura ljungmani* (Fig. 13.15) and *Ophiomusium lymani* (Fig. 13.16) provide independent support for these models of the population dynamics developed for both species (Gage, 1990). Similar growth banding within the stalk ossicles has been used to age specimens of the sea lillies *Annacrinus wyvillethomsoni* and *Bathycrinus carpenteri*. By assuming an annual period, perhaps related to nutritive flux, the oldest specimen of both species was estimated to be from 10 to 15 yr old (Roux, 1977; Duco & Roux, 1981).

Comparison of the size structure of *Ophiura ljungmani* in the time series suggested interannual variation in year-class strength, perhaps related to

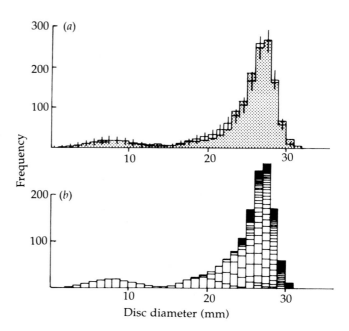

Fig. 13.14. Frequencies of demographic model (open bars) developed for frequencies (stippled bars) observed in population of brittle star *Ophiomusium lymani* at the 2.2 km depth repeat station in the Rockall Trough: (*a*) observed frequencies and summed model frequencies with 95% confidence intervals; (*b*) model frequencies showing stacking of expected frequencies for the component year classes of the model, with a mortality of 10% per year.

differences in early survivorship of recruits (Fig. 13.17). This phenomenon seems to be a feature of the common deep-sea sea urchin *Echinus affinis* whose variable size structure in space and time makes analysis of size frequencies unrewarding. However, the time-series approach in the Rockall Trough has allowed us to follow the postlarval growth of newly recruited urchins to the population for a short time before they disappeared from the samples. A growth curve fitted to these data showed good agreement with analysis of growth zones detected in the skeletal plates (Figs 13.18(*a*), 13.19(*a*)) of this urchin (Gage & Tyler, 1985). Such bands are well known in urchins from shallow water, where there is good evidence that they reflect an annual period in growth rate; adult *E. affinis* were thought to be up to 28 yr old. These sea urchins seem to grow considerably more slowly and to live longer than congeners on the upper slope and in shallow-water (Gage, Tyler & Nichols, 1986). A markedly uneven representation of ages amongst the population is thought to reflect interannual cycles in recruitment success, but the cause of such variability (as in shallow-water populations) remains unknown. Growth zones have also been analysed in the irregular sea urchins *Echinosigra phiale* (Fig. 13.18(*b*)) and *Hemiaster expergitus* from the same station. The results (Fig. 13.19(*b*)) suggest a faster growth occurs in these burrowing species than in *Echinus affinis* (Gage, 1987). Assuming that the ring-like pattern in the plates of the test reflect an annual period in skeletal growth, we can be more certain that the growth rings on deep-sea urchins are laid down annually throughout their lives and not just after adulthood is reached (as a result of diversion of resources into gametogenesis and spawning) since the irregular species show no seasonal periodicity in

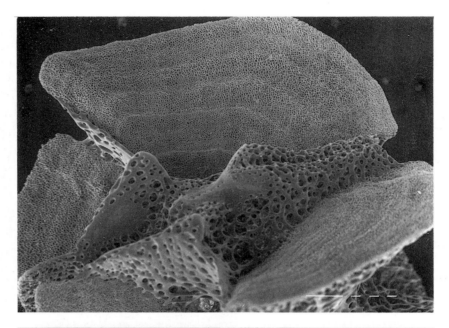

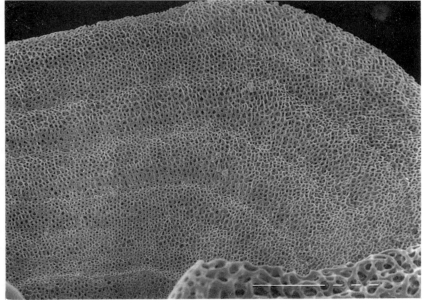

Fig. 13.15. Scanning electron micrographs of arm ossicles of the deep-sea brittle star *Ophiura ljungmani* from 2.9 km depth in the Rockall Trough: (*a*) oblique view of whole ossicle showing pattern of growth banding on the flange-like inter-ossicle muscle attachments; (*b*) detail showing changes in density of trabecular microstructure corresponding to the rings which are thought to reflect a pattern of annual checks in skeletal growth rate. (From Gage, 1990.)

gametogenesis (Harvey & Gage, 1984), and in any case these rings are clearly present on the test of juvenile sizes.

GROWTH OF DEEP-SEA FISHES

Knowledge of the age structure and growth of shelf fishes has tradition-ally derived from analysis of modal periodicities in size frequencies

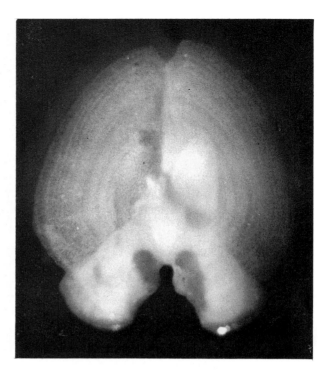

Fig. 13.16. Light photomicrograph of arm ossicle of brittle star *Ophiomusium lymani* after treatment to show up the numerous, closely spaced growth rings present. The large number and fine spacing of these tend to corroborate the demographic model developed from study of disc-size frequencies. (From Gage, 1990.)

deriving from annual recruitment pulses and from 'reading' growth rings in skeletal elements such as otoliths and scales. Despite similar growth-ring structure being known from deep-sea benthopelagic macrourids since the early years of this century (Murray & Hjort, 1912; Farran, 1924; Ranou, 1975; Wilson, 1982), information on age structure and recruitment (reviewed by Gordon, 1979) is still sparse. Rannou (1976) arrived at an estimate of population age structure by separating age classes from modes in the population size structure, and from frequencies of otolith

Fig. 13.17. Disc-size frequencies of the deep-sea brittle star *Ophiura ljungmani* from time series of samples from the Rockall Trough showing pattern of interannual change in overall size structure; the older sizes present in the earlier samples are absent in the later ones. (From Gage & Tyler, 1981*b*.)

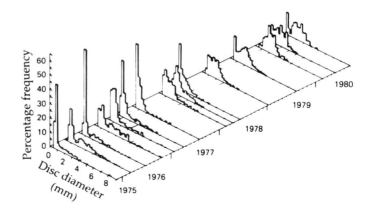

(a)

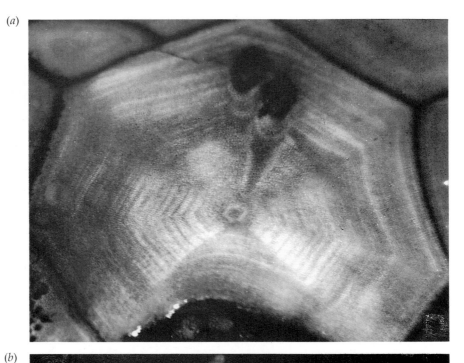

(b)

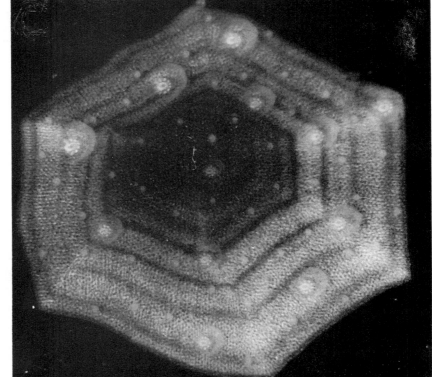

Fig. 13.18. Growth banding in skeletal plates of deep-sea sea urchins from 2.2 km depth in the Rockall Trough: (a) regular urchin *Echinus affinis* (an exceptionally large specimen of 50 mm test diameter from which approximately 27 rings were counted); (b) irregular urchin *Echinosigra phiale* (specimen measuring 36 mm test length).

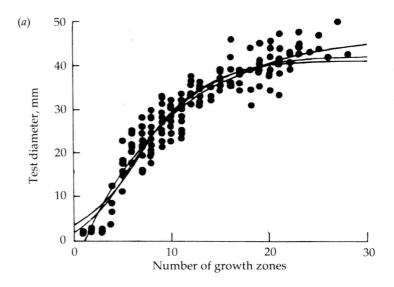

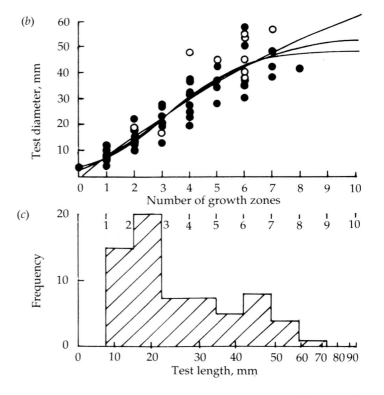

Fig. 13.19. Growth curves fitted to counts of sea urchin growth rings (examples of which are shown in Fig. 13.18) from a 2.2 km depth repeat station in the Rockall Trough: (a) *Echinus affinis*; (b) *Echinosigra phiale*. Assuming that the rings reflect a seasonally varying skeletal growth rate, then the counts can be read as age in years; (c) shows the age structure of the *Echinosigra phiale* population from the frequencies of these ages in the summed samples from the repeat station. ((a) Modified from Gage & Tyler, 1986; (b) and (c) modified from Gage, 1987.)

growth rings in *Nezumia sclerorhynchus* (Fig. 13.20). Furthermore, studies of otolith microstructure have revealed a pattern of much finer rings in specimens in the abyssal macrourids *Coryphaenoides (Nematonurus) armatus variabilis* and *C. (N.) yaquinae* that resemble the daily growth increments of shallow-water fish (R. R. Wilson, 1988). However, in the absence of any possible light-determined periodicity, their causation and true period remains speculative. The growth curves derived from the, assumed annual, period of the major otolith growth rings of macrourids in general are typical of the rather asymptotic form of those of shallow-water bony fish, indicating fish grow steadily throughout a lifetime of less than 10 to more than 30 yr (Gordon, 1979; Wilson, 1982; Sahrhage, 1986; Bergstad & Isaken, 1987). However, work on two non-macrourid bathyal species that are commercially exploited, the orange roughy *Hoplostethus atlanticus*, and the sablefish *Anoplopoma fimbria* (see Chapter 16) indicates that natural populations contain large numbers of very old fish (up to 70 yrs old in the case of *A. fimbria*) that are barely increasing in size at all (Beamish & Chilton, 1982; Merrett, 1989).

Gordon (1979) reviews data from size measurements of the commercially fished macrourid *Coryphaenoides rupestris* and other species of this genus, along with *C. (Nematonurus) armatus*, indicating a downslope migration with increasing age. After reaching reproductive size, *C. rupestris* are then found over the full depth range with a partial depth segregation of sexes. Size-related depth segregation has been suggested to be related to increased foraging efficiency required in deeper water where food is less plentiful (Polloni *et al.*, 1979). However, this idea is

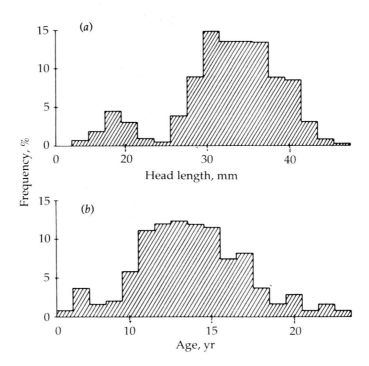

Fig. 13.20. (*a*) Size-frequencies and (*b*) age-frequencies from counts of otolith growth rings, for the macrourid *Nezumia sclerorhynchus* from the eastern Mediterranean (bathymetric range 0.3–3.0 km). (From Jumars & Gallagher, 1982 based on data of Rannou, 1976.)

rejected by Stein & Pearcy (1982) who favour an explanation related to relaxed competition for food in the water column compared to the bottom.

RATES OF SECONDARY PRODUCTION ON THE DEEP-SEA BED

Although the available data clearly are too sparse to allow any meaningful approach to estimates of turnover rates amongst the total community of the benthic boundary, it is possible to make estimates for individual species, and perhaps even for sections of the community assuming that values of demographic parameters are roughly comparable. The rate of turnover of a species' population is conveniently expressed as the ratio between its annual Production and Biomass, or P : B ratio, this ratio being markedly affected by age and size structure as determined by its life-history traits. Populations whose size structure is dominated by relatively fast-growing juveniles will show a higher rate of production in relation to its biomass than one consisting mostly of the older, relatively slow-growing adults. Generally, there is a significant correlation between annual P : B ratios and the lifespan of organisms (Robertson, 1979). By calculating ratios of a few key species, estimates of production of other species have been made in shallow water using knowledge of their life history and standing crop (Sanders, 1956).

Is such an approach possible in the deep sea? Probably not at present as information is available only for isolated species from widely separated areas. This approach dates from the analysis by Zezina (1975) of the brachiopod *Pelagodiscus atlanticus* for the Gay Head–Bermuda transect. The ratio of production to biomass (P : B ratio) in this animal was estimated at 0.3–0.42; values which fall within the range of turnover values estimated from inshore benthos (summarized by Robertson, 1979). However, this estimate does not take into account reproductive production.

The data on fecundity and egg size given by Lightfoot *et al.* (1979) for the annually breeding bivalves *Ledella pustulosa* and *Yoldiella jeffreysi* in the Rockall Trough has been used by Rowe (1983) to arrive at an estimate of annual reproductive production for these populations in the Rockall Trough, which comprise a significant fraction of total macrobenthic standing crop. By estimating that half of macrobenthos at this site made a similar reproductive investment, Rowe arrived at a figure for the ratio of reproductive production : biomass for the total macrobenthos of 0.03. We may extend this estimate to cover *total* (somatic plus reproductive) annual production in four of the numerically dominant bivalves at the Rockall permanent station at 2.9 km depth. These estimates were obtained using demographic models developed mainly by tracking size modes resulting from seasonal recruitment in a time series of samples, such as those shown in Fig. 13.9 for *Ledella pustulosa* and *Yoldiella jeffreysi*, and corroborated by shell-growth lines, and other information if available. Table 13.1 gives details of this model and the calculations of wet weight production,

Table 13.1. *Demographic (a) and production (b) models for the protobranch bivalve* Ledella pustulosa *from the Rockall Permanent Station (2.9 km depth)*

(a)

Year class	Time, t (yr)	Mean shell length, L (mm)	S.D. (mm)	Number in yr class	Total number of survivors
1	0.40	0.49	0.23	1000	1000
2	1.40	1.60	0.23	648	1648
3	2.40	2.28	0.23	420	2068
4	3.40	2.68	0.23	272	2340
5	4.40	2.93	0.23	176	2516
6	5.40	3.08	0.24	114	2630
7	6.40	3.17	0.26	74	2704
8	7.40	3.22	0.32	48	2752

Where length L at time t, $L(t) = L_\infty (1 - e^{-K(t - t_0)})$, and K is the von Bertalanffy growth coefficient.

Survivorship function $Z = 0.43$, where $Z = 1 - e^{-z}$ and the dispersion (S.D.) of each year class increases following an asymptotic function equivalent to that for the means.

(b)

Year class	Time, t (yr)	Mean weight (mg)	Weight increment (mg)	Total weight (mg)	Cumulative weight (mg)
1	0.40	0.01	0.01	14.76	14.76
2	1.40	0.53	0.51	342.17	356.93
3	2.40	1.51	0.99	635.79	992.72
4	3.40	2.48	0.97	674.84	1667.56
5	4.40	3.23	0.75	568.74	2236.30
6	5.40	3.74	0.52	427.39	2663.69
7	6.40	4.08	0.34	301.80	2965.49
8	7.40	4.29	0.21	205.73	3171.22

For sample (dotted frequencies) shown in Fig. 13.12 where $n = 163$, biomass = 277.09 mg (calculated from a power curve function describing the relation of net weight to shell length), annual wet weight production is 187.85 mg; a Production to Biomass (P : B) ratio of 0.68.

and P : B ratio (turnover rate of the population) that were made from it for this protobranch species.

Estimates for *Yoldiella jeffreysi* (P : B ratio, 0.78), *Malletia cuneata* (1.03) and *Deminucula cancellata* (0.94) from the 2.9 km deep Permanent Station in the Rockall Trough were calculated from similar models (J. D. Gage, unpublished). Corroboration of rates of growth and mortality which were incorporated into the models on which these estimates were based, was, as for *Ledella pustulosa*, obtained from shell growth lines, size-related mortality from the size distribution of dead shells; and, in the case of *Deminucula cancellata*, data from sediment tray recolonization experiments (Grassle & Morse-Porteous, 1987). These estimates of turnover fall within the range of those typical of molluscs from shallow water (see, e.g. Sanders, 1956; Rachor, 1976; Robertson, 1979).

IS THERE A CHARACTERISTIC LIFE-HISTORY 'STRATEGY' FOR DEEP-SEA ORGANISMS?

This chapter has considered the admittedly often sparse and incomplete data from various deep-sea taxa. It is already clear that the predictions (outlined at the beginning of this chapter) on the reproduction and larval ecology of deep-sea organisms will have only limited application.

With respect to seasonality, the expectation of a lack of seasonal periodicities in breeding clearly has not proved valid. This suggests the presence of a powerful selective advantage in synchrony of reproductive effort. In an environment that now seems much more likely to experience a significant, seasonally pulsed, input of 'new' organic material with associated biota, a synchrony in the processes of gametogenetic development and recruitment of young to the bottom will be of high selective value. We might ask why do more species not show such reproductive seasonality? The answer may be that more species may show seasonal recruitment than might be inferred from study of gametogenic development. Although difficult to quantify from the low numbers collected, our observations from the Rockall Trough time series suggest that some echinoderms other than *Ophiomusium lymani* show a summertime peak in recruitment, despite the absence of a synchronized gametogenic periodicity in the population. Such a 'strategy' suggests a wasteful, if low-level, reproductive production at other times of the year. As in shallow water, such wasteful production is normally associated with planktotrophy, where larvae are subject to dispersal to unsuitable depths or areas (e.g. Gage & Tyler, 1982). It is interesting that none of the species showing seasonal breeding appear to show the, sometimes, global distributions of some of those species where ripe oocytes are apparently available year-round, such as *Ophiomusium lymani*. Clearly, there is a need for more data on the reproductive seasonality over the full geographical range of species, particularly those found also at low latitudes where seasonal inputs may be less well developed or have different timing.

The prediction that pelagic development is nearly or totally suspended in the deep sea (Thorson, 1950) has also been found to conflict with recent data demonstrating true planktotrophy amongst deep-sea benthic invertebrates. Indeed, the occurrence of planktotrophy is surprising from considerations of the energetic cost and risks involved in migration through the deep-sea water column. However, the apparent absence of planktotrophy in any species of less than about 5 mm maximum body dimension strongly suggests that the energetic cost of producing enough eggs to ensure recruitment restricts this mode of early development to large-sized species. The dominance of non-pelagic, lecithotrophic early development in many non-crustacean taxa suggests that the saving in production of eggs, in a strategy that nevertheless retains some ability for water-born dispersal, is a powerful trait that might be traded off only by an opposing one of at least equal selective value. That even the energetic effort involved in producing lecithotrophic eggs has a significant 'cost' to the animal is indicated from the declining fecundity of protobranch congeners down the depth gradient (R. S. Scheltema, 1972). Nevertheless, lecithotrophy remains as the single overriding element of the life-history strategy of deep-sea biota, largely confirming the prediction mentioned at the beginning of this section. However, in this study of the deep-sea snail *Benthonella*, Rex *et al.* (1979) emphasizes that 'The deep sea is a complex and varied environment' where 'It may be no more meaningful to speak of a typical deep-sea reproductive strategy than it would be to typify a single shallow water or terrestrial strategy'.

The prediction that extremely slow growth rates prevail amongst deep-sea organisms seems, at least, a gross oversimplification. The data reviewed above show that, where comparisons of closely related biota are possible, very often those found deepest show the lowest fecundity, slowest rate of growth, and a greater concomitant longevity; yet the data considered overall show that such low reproductive production, slow growth and great age are by no means the general rule in the deep sea.

14
Animal–sediment relations in the deep sea

BIOTURBATION

Charles Darwin (1881) first established the importance of burrowing land animals, such as earthworms, in the mixing of the uppermost layer of the soil. A similar mixing effect may be seen on coastal mud-flats resulting from the activities of burrowing animals, such as the lugworm *Arenicola*, which creates a micro-landscape of pits and volcano-like faecal mounds (Fig. 14.1) as a result of its sediment swallowing lifestyle. In recent years it has been shown that the activities of the benthos of shallow soft bottoms profoundly affect sediment properties and processes (Johnson, 1971; Rhoads, 1974; Rhoads & Boyer, 1982; R. C. Aller, 1982; Meadows & Tufail, 1986).

In the deep sea, because benthic standing stock may be several orders of magnitude less than in productive inshore areas, and individual benthic animals are generally of much smaller size, it might seem that such effects will be of only minor importance. Furthermore, it has been thought that rates of biological processes are much lower in the deep sea. Against this, it can be argued that deposit-eating forms dominate by far over suspension feeders and may be adapted towards more complete utilization of organic materials (e.g. longer guts). Because of decreasing hydrodynamic energy and rate of sedimentation, there should also be less frequent re-suspension of sediment and hence less disruption of biogenic structure; and, because of the low rates of sedimentation, such biogenic structure should persist much longer than in shallow water (Rowe, 1974). Hence, all-in-all, it might be thought that their effects can be considered much reduced, or even discounted, in considerations of the geochemical equilibria and diagenesis of minerals at the benthic boundary.

Purely from visual evidence, the homogeneous sediment bottoms of stagnant basins such as the Cariaco Trench and the Black Sea, and under upwelling areas of high pelagic productivity (where oxygen is totally consumed and the bottom sediment is lifeless), show a marked contrast with those where benthic fauna are found (Fig. 14.2). This indicates that bottom organisms play a significant role in restructuring and altering the sediment. We shall examine the evidence, from seabed photographs and analysis of cores, showing that biogenic alteration of sediments is indeed important down to the greatest depths.

For geologists, an understanding of biogenic structures resulting from bioturbation characteristic of the deep sea might provide useful markers of past environments. Such palaeoenviromental indicators can aid not only the interpretation of ancient depositional conditions (Ekdale, 1985), but, having been subjected to postdepositional processes as well, can be of use in the study of diagenesis (change from recent seafloor deposit to consolidated hard rock). Furthermore, it is being realized that such processes taking place over the vastness of the deep ocean bottom are of significance in understanding global biogeochemical equilibria in the cycling of major elements such as carbon, and hence in maintaining the conditions for life on our planet.

LEBENSSPUREN, OR TRACES

The term *lebensspuren* (German, life traces) describes the physical manifestations of benthic animals in sediments. They are also known simply as traces. It is estimated from seabed photographs that roughly 7% of the

Fig. 14.1. Underwater photograph (*c.* 1 m^2) of intertidal sediment in a Scottish sealoch showing bioturbation by the lugworm *Arenicola* for comparison with Fig. 14.2.

Fig. 14.2. Bioturbated seabed at 2 km depth in the Rockall Trough (N.E. Atlantic) (covering *c.* 1 m²) showing abundant mounds and burrows, along with fine projecting structures and other microstructure (possibly including tubes of polychaetes and/or agglutinated foraminifers). (Courtesy Dr A. J. Southward, Marine Biological Association, Plymouth.)

sediment surface on the continental slope is visibly disturbed by traces and about half this value in the abyss (Laughton, 1963). However, this estimate only relates to traces visible in photographs covering a square metre or more (Fig. 14.3). At the microscale revealed by close-up photographs covering just a few square centimetres (Fig. 14.4(a),(b)) an even more dynamic landscape, indicating almost continuous disturbance is evident.

In terms of behaviour of the animal, several categories of lebensspuren may be separated (Seilacher, 1953):

(i) *Resting traces* These are imprints of animals that were stationary (Figs 14.3, 14.7(f)).

(ii) *Crawling traces* These are often characterized by a displaced 'bow-wave' of sediment (Fig. 14.5(a),(b)) and sometimes also decorated with the imprints of locomotory organs, such as holothurian podia (Fig. 14.7(a),(b),(h),(j),(k)).

(iii) *Feeding structures* Examples are pellets formed from faeces or pseudofaeces by deposit-ingesters (Figs 8.8, 14.7(d)).

(iv) *Grazing traces* – delicate marks on the sediment surface (Fig. 14.7(b),(j),(l),(n),(o)).

Fig. 14.3. The ploughing trail visible, interrupted by star-shaped resting traces, was evidently made by the sea star *Plutonaster bifrons* visible, half-buried, at middle right. The photograph was taken on 1 July 1979 at 1.95 km depth in the Porcupine Seabight (N.E. Atlantic) when the seabed was overlain by a layer of phytodetritus. (Courtesy Dr A. L. Rice, Institute of Oceanographic Sciences.)

(v) *Dwellings* – habitats such as burrows or tubes (Figs 14.1, 14.2, 14.6(*a*),(*b*), 14.8(*a*)–(*g*), 14.9(*a*)–(*i*)).

Clearly, these categories have different effects on the physical characteristics of the sediment, some being more ephemeral than others. Crawling is the most transient, and most destructive of previous physical and biogenic structure, and hence results in considerable sediment mixing. Resting and Feeding Traces are more permanent resulting in less mixing; while Dwellings, whilst reflecting more permanent biogenic structure (resulting in well-known 'mottling' effects in the stratigraphy of the sediment), have limited sediment mixing effect.

Geologists, who have long studied structures interpreted as fossil traces in sedimentary rocks, refer to the different types as *Ichnogenera*; these occurring in characteristic assemblages, or *ichnofacies*. It is only in recent years that, by study of similar structures in modern sediments, some of these can be related to traces produced by known organisms living in the deep sea (e.g. Ekdale & Berger, 1978).

The advent of deep-sea photography, deep-diving submersibles and efficient box-corers has shown that such traces are commonplace, even

Fig. 14.4. Small-scale biogenic relief on the sediment surface in the Rockall Trough; each photograph covers about 0.035 m² and shows the wealth of fine structure created by animals of macrofaunal dimensions: (*a*) 2.0 km depth lower Hebridean Slope showing the two arm tips of an *Ophiomusium lymani* and between them the digestive tract showing through the transparent body wall of a very small elasipodid holothurian; (*b*) 1.2 km depth upper Hebridean slope, with abundant microrelief including (middle bottom) light-coloured recently excavated sediment surrounding a small burrow, and many projecting structures that may include polychaete tubes and soft-walled agglutinated foraminifers and komokiacea. (Courtesy Dr A. J. Southward, Marine Biological Association, Plymouth.)

though only a minority of seabed photographs or cores show large animals present. Lebensspuren are, in fact, the principal cause of small-scale heterogeneity both on, and within, the deep ocean floor.

FORMATION OF LEBENSSPUREN

In all except the most energetic of marginal areas, deposition dominates over erosion and the resulting water-saturated muds and oozes are loosely compacted, with a high water content (60–90%) and a bearing capacity from 25 down to 5 g cm^{-2}. Such a consistency is easily marked and disturbed, yet once marked will not quickly smooth itself; tracks of the submersible 'Alvin' and heavy towed bottom gear persist from one

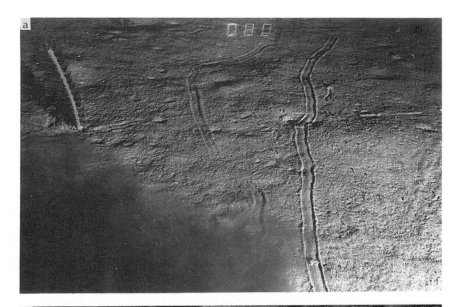

Fig. 14.5. Crawling trails from the continental slope off S.W. Ireland. (*a*) Double-ridged trail made by the neogastropod *Troschelia berniciensis* at 0.98 km depth; (*b*) irregular ploughing trails made by the irregular sea urchin *Spatangus raschi* at 0.92 km depth. (Courtesy Dr A. L. Rice, Institute of Oceanographic Sciences.)

year to the next (Rowe, 1974; Grassle *et al.*, 1975). Furthermore, bearing capacities are sufficient that the usually rather watery bodies of deep-sea animals will not sink into the ooze and need to excavate in order to penetrate the mud. Sedimentation rates vary from 0.1–0.2 cm kyr^{-1} on the red-clay oligotrophic mid-plate basins and up to 20 cm kyr^{-1} on the continental slope. This compares with rates inshore of several cm per year in fjords and estuaries. Hence, it used to be speculated that some of these

Fig. 14.6. Mounds: (*a*) large crater mound at 3.921 km depth off Cap Blanc (N.W. Africa); (*b*) Volcano mounds at 0.4 km depth on the upper slope off Ireland. These probably were made by the burrowing sea cucumber, *Molpadia blakei*. The large-polyped coelenterates are the pennatulid *Kophobelemnon stelliferum*. Numerous small brittle stars are visible on the sediment surface. (Courtesy Dr A. L. Rice, Institute of Oceanographic Sciences.)

traces are hundreds of years old, particularly those tracks and mounds that are many centimetres in height and depth which, it might be supposed, are particularly persistent.

Imprints made by a variety of fauna have been interpreted from photographs and observations from submersibles of the deep-sea floor all over the world ocean (Laughton, 1963; Ewing & Davis, 1967; Heezen & Hollister, 1971; Hollister, Heezen & Nafe, 1975; Ekdale & Berger, 1978; Mauviel & Sibuet, 1985; Young *et al.*, 1985). Discrete tracks are formed by certain echinoderms, arthropods or certain fish, such as morids or tripod

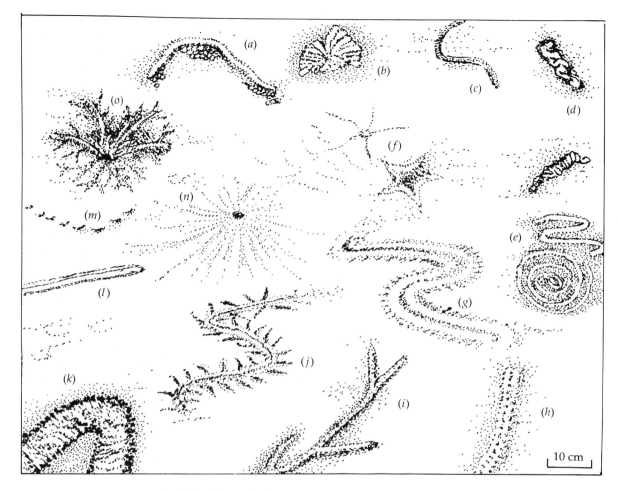

Fig. 14.7. Drawings of different kinds of superficial trace and their probable origin (in parentheses): (a) smooth meandering ridge – sometimes, as drawn, with faecal(?) balls associated with them (unknown origin); (b) rosette, or 'spokes' – radial markings from a burrow opening (surface-deposit feeding polychaete or echiuran); (c) simple groove – can be straight or sinuous (actinian, mollusc?); (d) faecal coils, or 'knots' (holothurian casts); (e) coil-and-loops (lophenteropneust); (f) brittle star (upper) and sea

(continued)

fish where the body is raised off the bottom in 'walking' or probing the bottom (Figs 4.26, 4.30). Although crabs may leave a characteristic series of puncture-like prints, the echinoderms are responsible for most of the large and prominent tracks and trails visible. Brittle stars may produce a series of partial body impressions giving a feathery 'pinnate' trail (such as those that are visible near the animal photographed in Fig. 4.1), whilst both brittle stars and sea stars may leave clearer body impressions after a stationary period half-buried in the ooze between periods ploughing through the surface layer (Fig. 14.3). However, by far the majority of tracks are made by elasipod sea cucumbers, such as *Benthogone* shown in Fig. 4.13; the number and arrangement of its 'walking' podia resulting in characteristic tracks composed of lateral rows of shallow holes. Grooves and ridges are made by animals that crawl on, or just beneath, the surface. The megafaunal echinoderms, especially the larger, aspidochirote holothurians, which lack large 'walking' podia, move on a creeping sole, and epifaunal polychaetes such as *Hyalinoecia* seem to be responsible for most grooves and ridges visible in photographs. Other furrows are

star resting traces – arm marks from previous movement by the brittle star lead to the resting trace; (*continued*) (*g*) double plough furrows, sometimes 'crenulated' (irregular echinoids); (*h*) four-row 'treaded' track with closely spaced inner paired impressions and an outer row of impressions (track of elasipodid holothurian such as *Benthodytes* or *Paelopatides*) (*i*) branched ridge – ridge with lateral branches (unknown origin); (*j*) pinnate ('herringbone') trail (fish?); (*k*) 'tread trail' track – straight or sinuous, with lateral perforations (track of sea star?); (*l*) double furrow – two ridges separated by a groove (elasipodid *Psychropotes*); (*m*) discontinuous groove – a succession of small perforations – sometimes paired, or several parallel rows (fish, decapod crustacean); (*n*) fine-rayed rosette, or 'spokes,' surrounding burrow (polychaete?); (*o*) branched rosette surrounding burrow (bivalve, sipunculid, polychaete?). (Redrawn and modified from Ewing & Davis, 1967; Heezen & Hollister, 1971; Kitchell *et al.*, 1978*b*; Mauviel & Sibuet, 1985 and Young *et al.*, 1985.)

excavated by irregular echinoids (Fig. 14.5(*b*)) that move in meandering paths, partially, or almost completely, buried in the ooze in eutrophic areas. Some benthopelagic fish may also be able to excavate plough-like furrows with their shovel-shaped mouths, while Mauviel & Sibuet (1985) give a photograph of a macrourid fish with its head buried in the ooze in the Bay of Biscay.

Because the amount of nutriment in the form of bacteria and other organic particles is so small, great quantities of sediment must be ingested for deposit feeders to make a living in the deep sea. Deming & Colwell (1982) estimated that 100 g of sediment may pass through the digestive tract of a holothurian per day; whilst C. R. Smith *et al.* (1986) estimated, from the density of faecal mounds produced by echiurans in the Santa Catalina Basin of California, that these worms are processing sediment at the rate of around 1500 ml m^{-2} yr^{-1}. This faecal, or pseudo-faecal, material of deposit feeders is commonly seen on the sediment surface and represents re-worked sediment perhaps little altered in physical properties from the bottom deposit. Some, however, may be nutritious enough, perhaps as a result of microbial growth, to be actively foraged, such as the faecal casts of the holothurian *Benthogone* shown in a Bathysnap record from the Porcupine Seabight that after 22 days was eaten within one hour by *Echinus affinis* (Lampitt, 1985*b*).

The enigmatic coils and loops made by lophenteropneusts (Fig. 4.15(*b*)) are common features of the bottom in parts of the deep ocean, particularly in the Southern Ocean and S. Pacific. Other rope-like loops and coils of faeces (which are shown littering the seafloor in Fig. 8.8) are ejected periodically by holothurians which skim off a bacteria-rich surface film of sediment estimated at less than 1 mm thick.

Mounds, often associated with burrows (Figs 14.6(*a*), 14.9(*a*),(*d*),(*e*),(*h*)) are without doubt the most common infaunal trace, forming the dominant decimetre-scale topography of the deep-sea floor in nearly all deep-sea environments (Heezen & Hollister, 1971; C. R. Smith *et al.*, 1986). They result from a variety of biological sources and mechanisms (Hollister, Heezen & Nafe, 1975; Young *et al.*, 1985), but typically are formed of faecal material from megafaunal deposit feeders, such as burrowing echiuroids and enteropneusts. Those of enteropneusts are associated with single or multiple burrow openings which may surround the base of the mound (Fig. 14.9(*d*)) (Mauviel *et al.*, 1987). Other burrows may surmount a mound like a volcano (Figs 14.6(*a*),(*b*), 14.9(*a*)). Burrow openings unassociated with mounds (Fig. 14.8(*a*),(*e*)) seem to be much more rare but occasionally occur in clusters, or crater fields (Fig. 14.9(*b*)). A particular type of 'gashed' mound (Fig. 14.9(*c*)) probably results from the retraction of typically abyssal species of echiuran worms living in the blindly-ending horizontal limb of their 'L'-shaped burrow (Fig. 14.10), the opening of which (surrounded by a typical rosette of grazing marks, see Fig. 4.16(*d*)) is always close by (Vaugelas, 1989).

Manipulative experiments using the hydraulic 'claw' of DSRV 'Alvin' at 1.24 km depth in the Santa Catalina Basin off California have shown just how rapidly such mounds are formed; echiuran mounds (produced

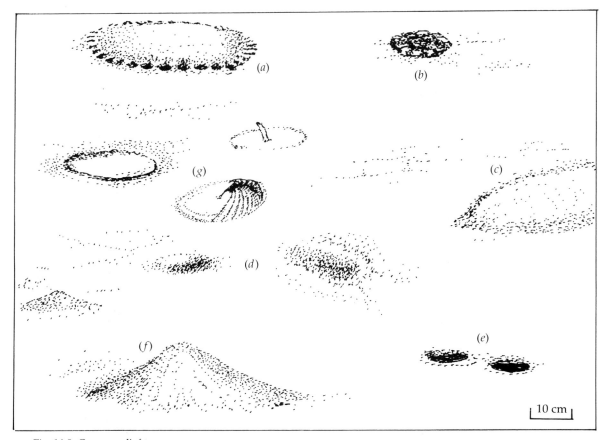

Fig. 14.8. Convex relief traces (probable origin in parentheses): (*a*) ring of burrows – 'fairy rings' (unknown origin); (*b*) floc-filled burrow (unoccupied burrow); (*c*) low mound (unknown origin); (*d*) shallow depression and craters (polychelid crustacean, actinian?); (*e*) simple large burrows (burrowing polychaete, crustacean?); (*f*) smooth cones and mounds (unknown but probably multiple origin); (*g*) deep or shallow circular grooves – some can be seen to be scribed by a gorgonian such as *Primnoa* (see Fig. 4.43*b*), others with a central upright tube are thought to resuit from the activity of (*continued*)

by usually shallower living species that live in 'U'-shaped burrows) over which fine glass beads had been sprinkled by the submersible 'Alvin' were cored 50 days later showing the beads buried 1–3 cm down (C. R. Smith *et al.*, 1986). Such rates of faecal deposition are around 1000 times higher than long-term rates of sediment accumulation in this area!

Feeding traces, as distinct from those caused by locomotion or faecal ejections, are more rare. The rosette-like pattern (referred to above) formed by the feeding proboscis of burrowed echiuran worms has been described in Chapter 4 (Fig. 4.16(*d*)). However, such spoke-like traces (Fig. 14.7(*b*),(*n*),(*o*)) may be formed by other worms such as polychaetes.

A morphological classification of deep-sea lebensspuren, mainly based on that of Mauviel & Sibuet (1985), which is based mainly on megafaunal traces photographed in the N.E. Atlantic, and that of Young *et al.* (1985), based on lebensspuren in the Caribbean Sea, is given in Figs 14.7–9 with a summary of their origin as far as is known. Table 14.1 lists the morpho-types of Young *et al.* (1985) and relates them to lebensspuren figured in the present work.

polychaete feeding palps, such as the oweniid *Myriochele*. (Drawn from photographs and drawings in Ewing & Davis, 1967; Heezen & Hollister, 1971; Mauviel & Sibuet, 1985 and Young *et al.* 1985.)

Table 14.1. *Classification of lebensspuren morphotypes of Young* et al. *(1985) related to those figured in Figs 14.6–8 and elsewhere*

Morphotype	Figure no.	Probable origin
Motile (originating from grazing deposit feeder)		
Faecal coil	Fig. 14.7(*d*),(*e*)	elasipod and aspidochirote holothurian
Three-lobed plough	Figs 14.7(*g*), 14.5(*b*)	spatangoid sea urchin
Smooth plough	Fig. 14.7(*h*)	aspidochirote holothurian
Treaded plough		echinoid?
Crenulated plough		echinoid?
Smooth meandering ridge	Fig. 14.7(*a*)	unknown surface burrower
Broken meandering ridge		?
Meandering groove	Fig. 14.5(*a*)	mainly mollusc
Elongated groove	Fig. 5.25(*b*)	mainly mollusc
Pinnate	Fig. 14.7(*j*)	bottom-feeding fish?
'Borrow pit'		fish (rays?)
Depression	Fig. 14.8(*d*)	various, including polychelid crustacean
Sedentary (originating from Dwelling or Resting Trace)		
Smooth round	Fig. 14.2	various burrowed megafauna
Clumped-lumped mound	Figs 14.9(*c*), 14.10	echiuran worm?
Rayed mound	Fig. 14.9(*f*)	xenophyophore *Psammetta*
Pitted mound	Fig. 14.9(*d*)	enteropneust worm
Cone	Figs 14.6(*b*), 14.9(*a*)	molpadid holothurian
Vertical tube	Fig. 14.2	polychaete worm
Horizontal tube		polychaete *Abyssoclymene*
Burrow	Fig. 14.8(*e*)	various invertebrates and fish
Circular groove	Fig. 14.8(*g*)	oweniid polychaetes
Circular ridge	Fig. 14.8(*g*)	and gorgonians
Rosette	Figs 4.16(*d*), 11.5 14.7(*b*),(*n*),(*o*)	various burrowing deposit feeders
Star	Figs 14.3, 14.7(*f*)	Porcellanasterid and other sea stars

OPTIMAL FORAGING THEORY AND TRACES

In searching for markers of environmental conditions in ancient depositional environments, sedimentary geologists have been attracted to the idea of using the geometric form of trace fossils, assumed to result from the preserved faecal or locomotory traces of deposit-feeding benthic animals, as indicators of bathyal or abyssal depths. It has been postulated that, in eutrophic, shallow seas, the conservation of energy is not critical, allowing deposit-feeding animals to forage inefficiently, leaving an apparently random pattern of criss-crossing traces and frequent encounters between individuals. Conversely, in the food-limited (oligotrophic) conditions of the deep sea an efficient utilization of resources by sediment 'skimmers' becomes crucial in order to conserve energy. This results in

Fig. 14.9. Complex relief: (a) Volcano mound (*Molpadia blakei* – burrowed subsurface deposit feeding); (b) 'crater fields' – often associated with irregular mounds (enteropneusts?); (c) 'clumped' mound, mound broken up into irregular clumps or smooth lumps (echiuran?); (d) 'cone and crater ring' – pitted mound (enteropneust); (e) large humped, sometimes arched, burrow or depression and, small humped depression (shallow excavations may be feeding craters of fish; deeper, arched excavations may be burrows of crab *Geryon*); (f) rayed mound (xenophyophore *Psammetta*); (g) 'crater rows' – aligned 'volcanoes' (unknown origin); (h) mound with adjacent burrow – mound can be up to 30 cm high and the adjacent pit up to 1–2 m wide and 30 cm deep (unknown origin – see also Fig. 14.6(a)); (i) double burrows within a shallow bordered pit (unknown origin). (Redrawn from Mauviel & Sibuet, 1985 and from photographs in Ewing & Davis, 1967; Young *et al.*, 1985.)

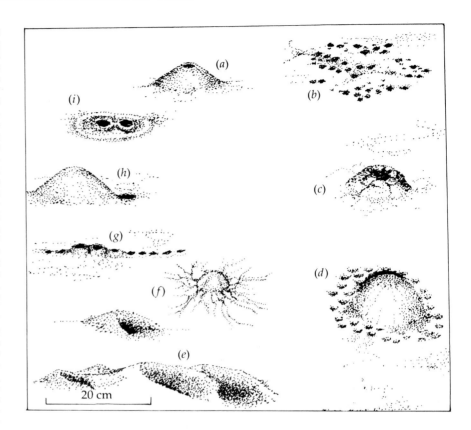

highly organized foraging strategies aimed at minimizing crossing recently grazed areas, such as the complex spiral or looping tracks which we have seen made by lophenteropneusts (Seilacher, 1967a,b).

Computer simulation has indicated that such apparently complex feeding patterns can, in fact, result from quite simple behavioural modification where avoidance of crossing will result in both spiral and looping foraging strategies (Raup & Seilacher, 1969; Papentin, 1973). This 'foraging paradigm' has now been rigorously tested by examining the occurrence and relative geometric complexity of traces visible in seabed photographs from different depths and productivity regimes in the present-day deep ocean (Kitchel *et al.*, 1978a,b; Kitchell, 1979). Not only did the results (Fig. 14.11) fail to show any clear bathymetric gradient in supposed complexity, from simple scribble-like traces, through meanders or loops, to spirals and complex double spirals; but the diversity of such complex feeding trails was much higher in the Antarctic than in the Arctic, despite the higher surface productivity in the Southern Ocean.

Furthermore, along the depth gradient, both looping meanders and spirals were found to peak in occurrence at around 3–3.5 km depth. Although such traces might provide good indication of such intermediate depths, clearly their presence or absence cannot be taken as a definitive indication of depth. Kitchel *et al.* (1978b) argued that the presence or

Fig. 14.10 Feeding activity of a burrowed abyssal echiuran worm showing probable mode of formation of 'gashed' mound illustrated in Fig. 14.9(c). The drawings depict the stages in the feeding activity with Stage 1 showing the extended feeding proboscis (pr) that forms the characteristic 'rosette' pattern of spokes (sp) radiating from the central burrow opening (bo). Stage 2 shows the proboscis partially retracted and no longer visible from the surface. Stage 3 shows the worm fully retracted with its swollen body pushing up the sediment to produce the tension-gashed mound at the edge of the spoke rosette on the sediment (a similarly disturbed area of sediment is shown near the echiuran spoke trace in Fig. 4.16(d)). (After Vaugelas, 1989.)

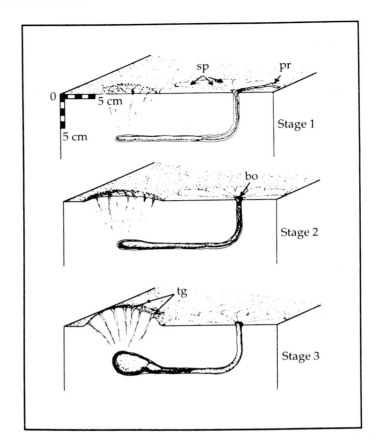

absence of surface-grazing organisms probably exerts a greater influence on trace diversity than depth or food supply.

However, it would be a mistake to reject, because of this, the utility of optimal foraging theory in understanding trophic processes in the deep ocean. It has been assumed in the past that the food supply of deposit feeders is, to all intents and purposes, homogeneously dispersed on the seabed, albeit at low levels; given the low densities of animals the deposit feeder might as well forage in a straight line since this would be no less efficient than a spiral or looped meander. However, there are some indications that this might not necessarily be the case. Non-random foraging traces might be expected to more efficiently exploit small-scale patches in distribution of detrital food, as shown in the patchy distribution of recently deposited phytodetrital floc (such as that visible in Fig. 14.3) after the spring bloom (Billett et al., 1983; Rice et al., 1986). In this context it is interesting that spiral-burrowing intertidal polychaetes have been reported to turn more tightly on encountering food-rich sediment (Risk & Tunnicliffe, 1978). However, another advantage of maximizing the resources in a circumscribed area as shown by spirals and meanders might be to minimize predation risk. Ohta (1984) points out that the poor

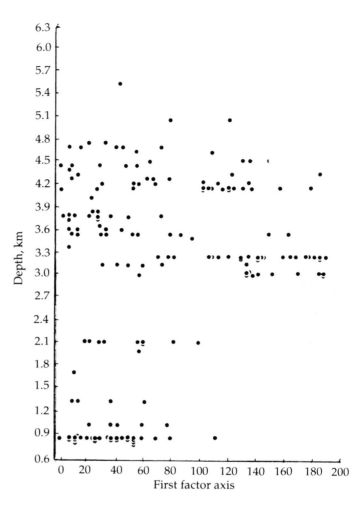

Fig. 14.11. Morphological complexity in trace fossils plotted against depth. The horizontal axis is a principal-components analysis measure of 'randomness,' which decreases to the right. Maximum randomness is exemplified by the criss-crossing plough furrows made by spatangoid sea urchins (e.g. Fig. 14.4(*b*)). Minimum randomness is shown by spirals, coils and loops (e.g. Figs 14.6(*f*), 4.14(*b*). Multiple circles represent more than one score of the same value. No significant correlation is evident between bathymetry and the degree of randomness. (From Kitchell, 1979.)

relationship of this behaviour with depth may be reflected by our limited understanding of the relationship of biomass, and the availability of food, to depth, which seems not to show the simple inverse proportionality often assumed (see Chapter 7). Large local differences in food availability may alter community structure and relative dominance of feeding type (Sokolova & Pasternak, 1964). Kitchell (1979) concluded that, although the bathymetric stratification of ecological interactions may in fact represent a gradient in exchange processes, the presence and abundance of foraging traces is largely species specific rather than related to depth. Ohta (1984) points out that one should be careful to compare like with like; for example, comparisons of surface grazing efficiency should be made only from grazing traces; and these should be limited to similar behavioural types avoiding excessively wide or within too narrow spectra of environmental gradients. In interpreting behavioural patterns reflected in traces, increased complexity is not necessarily the consequence of behavioural efficiency, i.e. foraging optima. Behaviour reflected in traces will be genetically imprinted and hence not sufficiently plastic to allow much response to nutritional gradients (Ohta, 1984).

These conclusions receive support from analysis of lebensspuren in relation to organism functional type in seabed photographs from the Venezuelan Basin in the Caribbean (Young *et al.*, 1985). Although densities of traces and megafauna were not correlated, their relative diversities were. Trace density was highest where most could be ascribed to sedentary, rather than motile, deposit feeders, the former dominating on the more oligotrophic sediment. This suggests that the locomotory activity of motile deposit feeders tends to smooth out such microrelief on the deep seabed (Brundage *et al.*, 1967; Rowe *et al.*, 1974; Rowe, 1974; Paul *et al.*, 1978; Thorndike *et al.*, 1982; Gardner, Sullivan & Thorndike, 1984). Traces may also be selectively eaten, such as the holothurian faecal cast, referred to earlier, that was consumed within one hour by a foraging sea urchin.

Furthermore, recent data indicate that bottom currents might quite quickly smooth down even the most massive features. And, even in relatively tranquil areas, it now seems likely that the activity of other animals will also gently erase such traces. In order to be preserved as a trace fossil, such biogenic structure will not only have to avoid ingestion and current-smoothing at the surface, but also the obliterating effect of sediment mixing, or bioturbation, both before and after burial.

The dynamics of trace concentrations (defined as the fraction of seabed covered by tracks and trails) have been considered by Wheatcroft, C. R. Smith & Jumars (1989) who develop a model of trace dynamics in relation to the density and composition of motile epibenthic megafauna, and microscale roughness of the sediment surface. For example, in the Santa Catalina Basin (1.3 km depth) owing to high sediment roughness, trace production is low despite the abundant epibenthic megafauna. However, in the energetic HEBBLE area (4.8 km depth) a much smoother sediment surface results in trace production by most epifaunal taxa; but the very abundant and active infauna produce high rates of sediment mixing and thus low trace residence times and concentrations (5% of bottom area). Wheatcroft *et al.* (1989) conclude on the basis of this and previous data that, regardless of mechanism of trace destruction, traces are ephemeral structures with lifespans measured in days and weeks, rather than months and years as previously thought (Mauvial & Sibuet, 1985). Coupled with high rates of near-surface mixing within the sediment, this suggests that the preservation of lebensspurren as trace fossils may be more exceptional than has been previously thought.

WITHIN-SEDIMENT EFFECTS

In the deep-sea, as in shallow water the lifestyle of burrowers, such as worms and bivalves, is evidently related to protection from predation rather than better access to food, since their diet largely remains focussed on the rich surface film. Unlike high-energy shallow bottoms where much high-grade organic material gets buried, there would seem little incentive for deep-sea forms to feed beyond this food-rich interface. Relatives of deep-feeding forms in shallow water, such as the maldanid worm *Clymenella* which, in intertidal sediments, creates feeding voids at depth (Rhoads, 1974) may have a different lifestyle. For example, Young *et al.* (1985) concluded from seabed photographs and from the occurrence of specimens in trawl hauls that the deep-sea maldanid *Abyssoclymene annularis* inhabits large tubes on the sediment surface. Therefore, this species, at least, would appear not to feed at depth in the sediment. However, deposit-feeding holothurians, such as the molpadid *Molpadia blakei*, will be surface feeding from the similarity of the volcano-like cones that it very probably excavates (see Figs 14.6(*b*), 14.9(*a*)) to those of its coastal congener *M. oolitica* whose feeding mechanism was studied by Rhoads & Young (1971). Furthermore, this holothurian locally may be very abundant in the deep sea (Sibuet, 1977). Other even deeper burrowing forms may exist in the deep sea. We have found piles of faecal pellets in diverticulae of large-diameter tubes 20–30 cm deep within box-cores from the Rockall Trough. In inshore muds, similar burrows have been found to result from the activities of a suite of deep-burrowing mega-fauna. These include callianassid decapod crustaceans, some burrowing as deep as 3–5 m below the surface (Pemberton *et al.*, 1976; Frey, Howard & Pryor, 1978), and with burrows up to 10 cm in diameter (Chapman & Rice, 1971), and an assortment of burrowing, or burrow-living, fish (Atkinson, 1986). However, the majority of the burrowed fauna are so small as to be confined to the top few centimetres. Even the largest volcano-like mounds created by, for example, the faecal ejections of large echiurans result from surface-feeding activity. The origin of some of the largest burrows and holes in the sediment surface, such as the aligned volcanoes shown in Fig. 14.9(*g*) remains enigmatic. By analogy with the complex burrow structures created by decapod crustaceans, such as callianassid crustaceans and fish living in coastal muds, we can speculate on a parallel complexity beneath the deep-sea bed.

Another important exception to the dependency of deep-sea organisms to the surface film of the sediment is found amongst the Pogonophora. These gutless worms can burrow more than 40 cm deep into the highly organic sediments of submarine canyons to tap layers rich in reduced compounds required by the bacterial symbionts on which they depend for nutrition (Southward & Dando, 1988).

GEOLOGICAL SIGNIFICANCE OF BIOTURBATION

From the point of view of the geologist interested in trying to reconstruct ancient sedimentary environments from the signals in the stratigraphic record, bioturbation, or benthic mixing, affects the sediment profile in four main ways: (i) production of trace fossils from secondary structures; (ii) mechanical and/or chemical alteration of the sediment; (iii) filtering or smearing primary stratigraphical signals; and (iv) influencing sediment stability and erosion.

In shallow water, bioturbation is known to enhance geochemical fluxes as well as lead to abundant trace-fossil structure in sediment profiles and to influence sediment stability and erosion (Meadows & Tufail, 1986). Because of the reduced standing crop and supposed low rate of metabolic activity of the benthos in the deep sea, the expectation might be that such effects are much reduced or absent. The opposite appears to be the case. The particle mixing leads to blurred resolution in microfossil dating of deep-sea sediments by lengthening and overlapping of indicator fossil horizons for discrete past time intervals (Berger & Heath, 1968). It also creates a wealth of persistent secondary structures, or traces, within the sediment of whose biological origin we are mostly ignorant. Mixing can also profoundly affect chemical diagenesis of sediments (R. C. Aller, 1982); the chemical layering (detectable as often abrupt changes in Rh or Eh potentials) found in aquatic environments, with an oxidizing zone a few millimetres thick at the interface and overlying a much thicker zone of reducing conditions.

DEPTH OF MIXING

Although much can be gained from seabed photographs on the effects of biota on the sediment and the interpretaton of trace fossils, quantitative data on biogenic mixing, or re-working, requires study of core samples of the sediment. A realization that such processes have had a significant effect even in the abyss dates from Bramlette & Bradley (1942). Evidence of mixing has been detected at least 40 cm below the surface. In sediments with a bed graded by slumping, the amount of reworking can be estimated from the degree of bed disturbance (Piper & Marshall, 1969). Estimates have also been made from 'impulse' sources such as microtektites and bomb-produced plutonium (Guinasso & Schink, 1975). However, such bedding planes are unusual and rare in deep-sea sediments.

Methods employing dating using naturally occurring and cosmogenic radionuclides with continuous inputs date from the French/American Mid-Ocean Undersea Study (FAMOUS) on the Mid-Atlantic Ridge area in the 1970s. Here, undisturbed cores retaining an intact sediment/water interface were taken using the submersible 'Alvin'. The half-lives of these radionuclides cover a range from tens to thousands of years. If the decay rate (as indicated by halflife) is comparable to the rate at which it is incorporated into the sediment, e.g. ^{210}Pb (halflife 22 yr), there should be a gradient in concentration near the sediment–water interface (Fig. 14.12(b)); a longer-lived nuclide, such as ^{14}C (halflife 5.7 ky) behaves more like a stable tracer with, to all intents, a constant activity in the mixed layer, the profile only showing linear increase in age with increasing depth, *below* the mixed layer (Fig. 14.12(a)). The rate of mixing is fast enough for a homogeneous concentration in ^{14}C but sufficiently slow that there is a gradient in concentration of ^{210}Pb. Furthermore, from the ^{210}Pb profile, we can rather crudely deduce that the top 8 cm must be reworked completely in at least 5 halflives of ^{210}Pb (= 100 yr) for there to be an excess of ^{210}Pb at all depths in the mixed zone. Such data provide the opportunity to develop a model of this system in order to obtain a more exact estimate. The best known are *diffusion models* first developed by

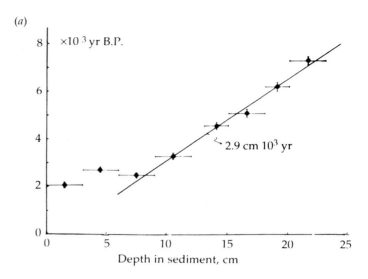

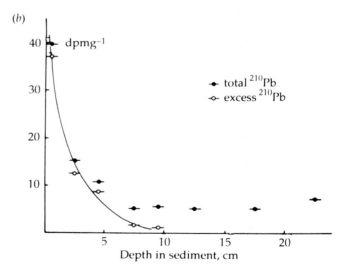

Fig. 14.12. Particle-mixing profiles as measures of within-sediment bioturbation from a core taken on the Mid-Atlantic Ridge: (a) ^{14}C ages plotted as a function of depth in sediment. The constancy in age in the top 8 cm delimits the 'mixed layer'; the linear increase below 8 cm corresponds to a sediment accumulation rate of 2.9 cm M yr $^{-1}$. This pattern is produced by continuous bioturbation to 8 cm depth with essentially no mixing below; (b) ^{210}Pb activity as a function of depth in sediment. Excess ^{210}Pb (total ^{210}Pb activity – ^{226}Ra activity) is distributed to 8 cm. The particle mixing coefficient for this sample is estimated at 6×10^{-9} cm^2 s^{-1}. Other details as for (a). (From Cochran, 1982.)

Goldberg & Koide (1962) where the mixing of particles is assumed to resemble eddy diffusion in liquids.

^{14}C and ^{210}Pb profiles can only be measured in carbonate oozes, and in the red clay areas of the Pacific, the activity of ^{230}Th, which has a long halflife and is effectively scavenged by sedimenting particles, has been measured instead. In further modifications of this approach the assumption of a uniformly mixed layer has been replaced with functions of linear or exponential decrease with depth, or of randomized mixing, and with a time- as well as depth-dependency in nuclide concentration.

The results of such studies show that the summed activity of burrowing macrofauna may result in a layer of biogenically mixed sediment down to a depth (apparently unrelated to rate of sediment deposition) of from 6 to 15 cm. Particle mixing coefficients measured from shallow water are about six orders of magnitude higher than these values from the deep sea. Are such differences in rate of biological reworking related to the decreasing amount of benthic biomass down the depth gradient, to low temperatures or to differences in magnitude of mixing by different sorts of organism? Since the latter two variables might equally well apply to shallow-water environments, they seem less useful as potential correction terms than biomass, which seems to account for most of the enormous range in values from the coastal to deep-sea sediments (Matisoff, 1982). Such comparability, incidentally, provides some indication that rates of reworking activity, and, hence we might infer, rates of other biological processes such as growth, might not be so different from those in shallow water. However, evaluation of bioturbation using ^{210}Pb with ^{32}Si or $^{239+240}$Pu yield markedly different estimates of mixing; the faster mixing rate of Pu perhaps being related to the possibility that particular tracers are associated with particles of differing size. Selectivity in ingestion of particles by bioturbating organisms, perhaps reflecting the differing food values of tracer-associated particles, will invalidate any assumpton that particles behave in similar ways in bioturbation (DeMaster, 1979; Stordal *et al.*, 1985; Swinbanks & Shirayama, 1986*b*).

Tests of such models with shallow-water animals shows that diffusion models adequately describe mixing by reworking by an amphipod, but not the directional, 'conveyer-belt' mode of deposit feeding by an oligochaete (Robbins *et al.*, 1978). Clearly, in the deep sea, diffusion models fail to take into account the effect of locally concentrated mixing and directional transport by larger deposit feeders (Boudreau, 1986*a,b*). For example, profiles of $^{234\text{excess}}$Th (halflife 24 days, but which remains detectable in the sediment for around 100 days) in the cores of echiuran mounds taken by C. R. Smith *et al.* (1986), along with time-lapse photographs of the surface of the mound, show that mound formation leads to rapid and episodic turnover of local areas of the sediment. These authors estimate that the top 10 cm of sediment off southern California can be turned over by echiurans alone in about 70 yr – equivalent to a sediment particle passing through an echiuran gut, on average, about ten times before its permanent burial. Hence, although spatially rare, such megafaunal burrowers are likely to have dramatic effects on sediment mixing depths and diagenetic processes.

Furthermore, a model of homogeneous mixing in the upper layer can not explain subsurface maxima in both ^{210}Pb and $^{239+240}$Pu profiles from cores (Somayajulu *et al.*, 1983; Rutgers van de Loeff & Lavaleye, 1986). The latter authors suggest that a net transport downwards occurs to the level of the maxima which they suggest result from the conveyer belt feeding of sipunculids that make up 28% (equivalent to 8 worms m^{-2}) of macrofaunal standing crop at this site; these sipunculids alone being calculated to turn the sediment over three times before it is buried. These anomalies are supported by the sparse data available on the vertical distribution of smaller infauna within the sediment. As if to underline the dangers of applying single techniques to estimate benthic mixing, Swinbanks & Shirayama (1986) relate a marked subsurface peak in ^{210}Pb at 2–3 cm depth to the vertical distribution of the infaunal xenophyophore *Occultammina profunda* which concentrates ^{210}Pb, originally ingested with food obtained from the surface, in the stercomes (faecal bodies) that occupy much of the body of these organisms. The resulting hot-spots in ^{210}Pb in the sediment may have a significant effect on the geochemical balance of ^{210}Pb in the sediment, and hence on data utilizing the ^{210}Pb profile to estimate biogenic particle mixing in the deep ocean sediments.

Meiofauna are thought to be concentrated in the most superficial layer of sediment (Thiel, 1972b; Coull *et al.*, 1977; Dinet & Vivier, 1977; Vivier, 1978), and although nematodes and foraminiferans have been found on occasion to much greater depths within the sediment, 99% of meiofaunal individuals occur in the surface 12 cm (Shirayama, 1984b; Swinbanks & Shirayama, 1984); whilst macrobenthic organisms, too, are concentrated in the top-most layer of the sediment (Hessler & Jumars, 1974; Jumars, 1978; Shirayama & Horikoshi, 1982). The available data suggest that peracarid crustaceans and protobranch bivalves are generally restricted to the upper 3 cm whilst polychaetes and other worm-like taxa extend to deeper strata.

We have found from dissecting box-cores that larger worm-like animals such as large polychaetes, sipunculids such as *Sipunculus norvegicus*, and echiurans burrow down to at least 15 cm. Numerous fine, vertical burrows constructed by the sipunculid *Golfingia* have been found to extend to at least 50 cm on the Norwegian continental slope (Romero-Wetzel, 1987), and similar fine deep burrows have been found elsewhere, perhaps made by different organisms, some extending down more than 2 m from the sediment surface (Thomson & J. B. S. Wilson, 1980; Wetzel, 1981; Weaver & Schultheiss, 1983). We have already referred above to the depth of burrows of Pogonophora, and, although not surface feeders, they probably also contribute to deep sediment mixing. Although the densities of such deep burrowers may be much lower than the smaller bioturbating infauna nearer the sediment surface, they must be considered the principal cause of bioturbation below the upper few centimetres.

X-radiographs of box-core slices confirm these general results and show a variety of burrow structures, including vertical, U-shaped, spiral and branching types (Pye, 1980; Yingst & R. C. Aller, 1982; Rutgers van der Loeff & Lavaleye, 1986). Although Pye (1980) notes that the maximum number of burrows occurred 3 cm below the surface on the continental slope off Scotland, intense biogenic activity may have homogenized the sediment nearer the interface with the overlying water, as in some sections from the HEBBLE area off Nova Scotia examined by Yingst & Aller (1982). In other HEBBLE radiographs, the uppermost 2–3 cm layer, criss-crossed by small burrows, shows as the most intensely reworked area, these being replaced by larger and predominatingly horizontally orientated burrows at depth in all sections. Clearly, the bioturbated zone extends well beyond the 'mixed' zone of radiometric profiling, and hence studies of deep-sea bioturbation need to combine radiometric with X-radiographic profiling.

EFFECTS OF BIOTURBATION ON SEDIMENT GEOCHEMISTRY AND DIAGENESIS

In shallow water, geochemical fluxes of inorganic ions, and eventual sediment diagenesis, can be dramatically modified by the enhanced porosity and increase in reactive surfaces resulting from the micro-environments associated with the burrows, tubes and irrigatory activities of burrowing organisms (R. C. Aller & Yingst, 1978; Anderson & Meadows, 1978; Gust & Harrison, 1981; R. C. Aller, 1982). The sparse available data from the deep sea indicates that bioturbation is at least as important as in shallow water in promoting biogeochemical heterogeneity in the sediment. Meadows & Tait (1985) measured Eh, heterotrophic microbial biomass (estimated by 'plating' – counting numbers of colony-forming units on solid culture medium) and the geotechnical parameter, sediment shear strength (reflecting sediment compaction and reworking) along vertical and horizontal profiles of box-cores from the Rockall Trough. They detected significant heterogeneity associated with burrows occurring to a depth of $c.$ 33 cm within the sediment. Meadows & Tait also showed that microbial biomass at the sediment surface, and the maximum slope of the Eh profile, decreases with increasing water depth. More information is badly needed on the relationship of microbial densities to hydrodynamic energy, particularly regimes involving periodic sediment resuspension. In their studies at the highly energetic HEBBLE site on the Nova Scotia Rise, J. Y. Aller & R. C. Aller (1986) show that both occupied and relict burrows influence sediment chemistry and the distribution of sediment biota. They found sediment ATP (adenosine triphosphate) concentration, and counts using epifluorescence microscopy, as a direct measure of bacterial biomass, together with counts of meiofaunal abundances, were significantly greater around burrows of the macrofaunal ampharetid polychaete worm *Amphicteis* (see Fig. 5.4(*a*) and elsewhere, Figs 14.13, 14.14). Increased concentrations of ATP (reflecting high rates of microbial turnover or activity) despite reduced density of bacterial numbers within feeding pits of macrofauna such as *Amphicteis* suggests a possible 'gardening' of microbes. Here, the worm encourages microbial growth for consumption as food, in a way parallel to that thought to occur in some shallow and intertidal species (Aller & Yingst, 1985). J. Y. Aller & R. C. Aller (1986) suggest that relict burrows can trap fresh organic detrital flux from the surface; this acting as a localized energy substrate for microbial degradation in an otherwise food-poor medium. As found in intertidal sediments (Reise, 1981), numbers of meio- and macrofauna, particularly nematodes and foraminifera, increase around such burrows, perhaps responding to the enhanced microbial populations. Remobilization of the redox-sensitive metals, iron and manganese in the sediment in and around burrow structures reflects this enhanced microbial activity near both filled and unfilled burrows. J. Y. Aller & R. C. Aller (1986)

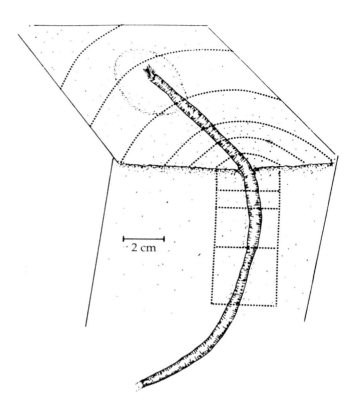

Fig. 14.13. Tube of ampharetid polychaete *Amphicteis* sp. in a box-core from the HEBBLE area (N.W. Atlantic) showing radial and vertical sampling zones around it. The dotted area around the upper end of the occupied tube shows the worm's feeding pit (see also Fig. 5.3(*a*) showing life position and feeding mechanism of ampharetid). (From J. Y. Aller & R. C. Aller, 1986.)

2 cm

estimate that 34% of the seafloor area has been affected by such sediment burrows at the HEBBLE area.

In oligotrophic mid-ocean areas of the equatorial Pacific a distinct three-layer burrow stratigraphy can be observed in calcareous ooze: a superficial, homogeneous-appearing, 'monotonic' layer overlying a middle, 'mottled layer' where fossil burrows are colour-enhanced, and an underling 'faded layer' being distinguished by much fainter or absent traces (Berger *et al.*, 1979; Swinbanks & Shirayama, 1984). X-radiographs of the upper layer reveal numerous infilled burrows, suggesting intense bioturbation. It has long been known that metallic ions dissolved in sediment pore-water are precipitated around burrows as a result of burrow irrigation by infauna, and Swinbanks & Shirayama show that the layering is caused primarily by microvariations in solid phase manganese and iron, resulting from bioturbation and redox diagenesis, in and around filled-in burrows. It has been suggested that manganese diagenesis within such sediments is mainly regulated by biological activity as reflected in gradients measured *in situ* in respiratory uptake by meiobenthos (Shirayama & Swinbanks, 1986). Bioturbation therefore results in a marked heterogeneity in vertical profiles of these metals in deep-sea pelagic ooze.

Southward & Dando (1988) suggest that the large concentrations of pogonophores in the highly organic sediment of submarine canyons may

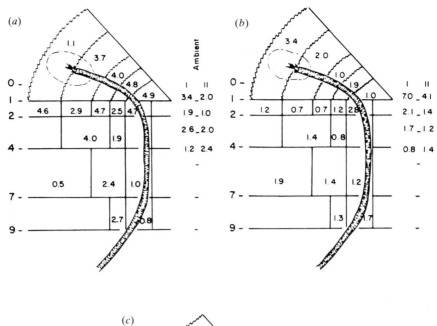

Fig. 14.14. Vertical and horizontal distributions of (a) bacteria; (b) total sediment ATP; and (c) total meiofauna and nematodes around tube of *Amphicteis* sp. depicted in Fig. 14.13. (From J. Y. Aller & R. C. Aller, 1986.)

locally diminish the net diagenesis of sulphur as a result of the activity of their sulphur-oxidizing symbiotic bacteria.

EFFECTS OF ORGANISMS ON SEDIMENT STABILITY

Benthic organisms may be classified into functional groups according to their effects, both direct and indirect, on sediment stability (see reviews by Woodin & Jackson, 1979; Woodin, 1983). In shallow water, dense beds of marine grass or sessile fauna, which project above the sediment, surface, act to stabilize the bed by enhancing settlement of fine particles (see Nowell, Jumars & Eckman, 1981; Eckman, 1987 and references cited therein). Sedentary tube-burrowers, such as amphipods and polychaetes, may form mats at high densities that stabilize sediment by reducing resuspension and erosion.

Although similar effects by animals are possible in the deep sea, they are rarely sufficiently crowded to make this likely. Rather, isolated projecting organisms such as pennatulids or worm tubes may cause local scour and eventual sediment destabilization as isolated surface roughness (Eckman, 1979, 1983; Luckenbach, 1986). Where they are abundant, both the constant reworking of fine particles by motile, deposit-feeders such as protobranch molluscs, and the sediment disturbance caused by their movements and by digging predators such as benthopelagic fish may create a pelletized surface layer of high water content that is easily resuspended and eroded (Rhoads & Young, 1970; McLellan, 1977; Hecker, 1982; Bender & Davis, 1984), while a similar effect may well result from large deposit-feeding infauna, such as echiurans, that deposit pelletized faecal mounds on the sediment. However, mucus-binding of sediment particles on the seafloor by microbes (Filatova, 1982; Tufail, 1987), which are well developed on deep-sea bottoms experiencing high currents (Baird et al., 1985) may act to stabilize the bed (Eckman, Nowell & Jumars, 1981).

On steep slopes and in canyons, the intense bioturbation caused by dense assemblages of burrowing benthic fauna benefiting from enhanced sedimentation is thought to cause sediment instability and eventual slumping on the steepest slopes, whilst resuspension of superficial sediment by epifauna, such as the crabs *Geryon* and *Chaceon*, may contribute to nepheloids and downslope transport of material (Dillon & Zimmerman, 1970; Stanley, 1971; Hecker, 1982; Malahoff et al., 1982).

Part V *Parallel systems and anthropogenic effects*

As if to underline how little of the deep ocean has been explored, deep-sea scientists were astounded by the unexpected discovery in 1977 of a remarkable assemblage of large-sized, bizarre-looking creatures entirely different in life-style from the fauna of the rest of the deep sea as it had become (and largely remains) known. This fauna constituted concentrations of biomass (ranging from 10 to 70 kg m^{-2} wet weight) many orders of magnitude greater than that supported by the deep-sea floor nearby. These clearly productive, but isolated, faunal 'oases' consist of giant-size bivalved molluscs and strange red-plumed tubeworms clustering around the newly discovered hydrothermal vents at 2.8 km depth on the Galapagos Rift, a spreading centre in the equatorial eastern Pacific. What's more surprising is that these creatures subsist on organic matter originating, not from the sun-driven photosynthetic production going on at the surface of the ocean, but from chemosynthetic microbes, some of them living as symbionts within their body tissues that use as energy-providing substrates inorganic chemicals such as sulphur derived from the bowels of the earth.

There have been many more recent discoveries of similar faunas associated with other forms of submarine seepage, along with a realization of similarities with biochemical systems in biota within the reducing conditions of highly organic sediments, where energy is obtained by utilizing electron acceptors other than oxygen. This has suggested that such faunas may have much closer links to ancestral conditions for life on Earth before the development of our oxygenated atmosphere than to the more 'usual' inhabitants of the deep oceans.

These 'parallel' systems have generated an enormous amount of enquiry, much of it making use of the capabilities of deep-diving submersibles in conjunction with transponder navigation (see Chapter 3) to locate a circumscribed, small area on the bottom and to carry out precisely controlled sampling and experimental manipulations on the deep-sea bed. Because of the pace and intensity of research, this chapter can only provide a limited, and certainly quickly dated, account of the biology of these unique habitats.

The final chapter briefly reviews the present and potential use of the deep sea by Man. Although vast in area, its inaccessibility has, until recent years, deterred active exploitation of the living and mineral resources associated with the deep-sea bed. However, pressures from increasing population growth and the depletion of resources and assimilative capacity for wastes on the continental shelf are forcing an increasing interest in the deep sea. Insidiously, this increasing interest encompasses not only the potential (though almost certainly limited) living resources, but also a view of the deep-sea bed as a convenient repository of Man's most noxious wastes.

15

Deep-sea hydrothermal vents and cold seeps

HYDROTHERMAL VENTS

THE EASTERN PACIFIC VENTS

The existence of hydrothermal vents was first suspected in the eastern Pacific from records of hot-water 'spikes' and bottom photographs of giant bivalves made by the towed instrument system Deep Tow in 1976 on the Galapagos Rift (Lonsdale, 1977*a,b*). The presence of primordial gases, particularly helium isotopes, from water samples, provided evidence that these hot springs were heated by molten rock below the seabed. But the extraordinary nature of the associated vent fauna was revealed soon after to dumbfounded observers in the manned submersible 'Alvin' (Corliss & Ballard, 1977; Corliss *et al.*, 1979). This vent field is situated on the Galapagos Rift lying almost on the Equator between the Galapagos spreading centre and nearby Galapagos Islands, off the coast of Ecuador (Fig. 15.1). Active vents with associated fauna were discovered at 2.5 km depth on the basaltic rock bottom formed from fresh lava flows running along a 1–2 km stretch of ridge formed along the Rift Valley axis of this relatively slowly separating spreading centre. This forms part of the sometimes branching but continuous, global system of mid-oceanic ridges (Fig. 15.2).

Although such vent communities were initially regarded as isolated and rare phenomena, a quickening pace of exploration has found similar communities to be associated with nearly all areas of tectonic activity that have been investigated in the deep Pacific and Atlantic (see below). These include vents not only associated with spreading centres, but also subduction zones, fracture zones and back-arc basins (spreading centres associated with subduction processes in deep trenches). In the Pacific Ocean, for example, hydrothermal vent fields, with a similarly luxuriant fauna, were discovered in roughly similar depths between 11 and 13° N and 21° N on the East Pacific Rise off Mexico, which include high-temperature 'black smokers' (Ballard, van Andel & Holcomb, 1982;

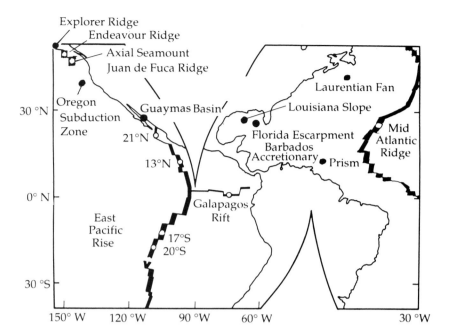

Fig. 15.1. Locations of the hydrothermal vent and seep communities discovered in the eastern Pacific and Atlantic. (Modified from Grassle, 1986.)

CYAMEX Scientific Team, 1981; Ballard, Hekinian & Francheteau, 1984); in the Guaymas Basin in the Gulf of California (Grassle, 1985); on the Juan de Fuca and Explorer Ridges off the State of Washington and British Columbia (Canadian American Seamount Expedition, 1985; Crane *et al.*, 1985; Tunnicliffe *et al.*, 1985); south of the Equator at 20° S along the Galapagos spreading centre (Francheteau & Ballard, 1983); along the subduction zone off the E. coast of Japan; and along the back-arc spreading centres in the Mariana Trough near the Mariana Trench (Hessler, Lonsdale & Hawkins, 1988) and in the Lau and North Fiji Basins,

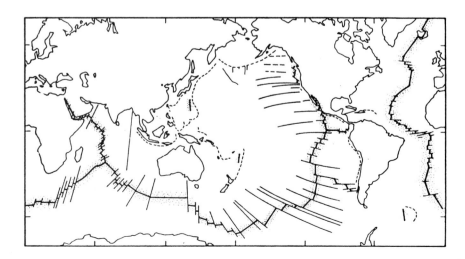

Fig. 15.2. The global pattern in oceanic ridge spreading centres.

W. and E. of Fiji, respectively (Auzende & Honza, 1988). It has been thought likely that along active ridge areas, vent fields may occur about every kilometre or less (Crane & Ballard, 1980). The locations of eastern Pacific (and Atlantic) sites known to us are shown in Fig. 15.1.

THE HYDROTHERMAL VENT COMMUNITY

Although considerable differences in the relative abundances of the fauna at different vent sites have been observed, the animals of the E. Pacific hydrothermal vents are characterized by large bivalved clams and mussels and brightly coloured vestimentiferan tubeworms. In the absence of 'smoker' chimneys of precipitated minerals which are formed only at the hottest vents, the light colour of bivalve shells and crabs standing out against the black basaltic rock provide the best markers to submersible observers for the vent fields. These are seldom larger than 60 m across (Fig. 15.3). Other sites may appear 'dead' with only scattered bivalve shells. The differences in development of different faunal elements noted from site to site have been related to differences in vent flow rate or water chemistry (Desbruyères *et al.*, 1982; Hessler, Smithey & Keller, 1985; Fustec, Desbruyères & Juniper, 1987; Hessler *et al.*, 1988*b*). The out-of-this-world appearance and rich concentration of biomass, reaching 8.5 kg weight wet m^{-2} at lower temperature vents, but only averaging 2–4 kg wet weight m^{-2} at the hottest vents (200–360° C) on the East Pacific Rise (Fustec, Desbruyères & Laubier, 1988), at these 'oases' of life provide submersible observers with a stark contrast with the relative barrenness of adjacent hard substrata in the deep ocean.

Fig. 15.3. Artist's representation of the exploration by the submersible 'Nautile' of the hydrothermal vent community associated with 'black smoker' chimneys made up of precipitated sulphides, and the more diffuse, lower temperature flow from 'white smokers' surrounded by the tangled tubes of alvinellid worms. (Drawing courtesy Violaine Martin, IFREMER, Brest.)

The best-understood areas are those known longest and most re-visited, these having yielded the most information on the composition, structure, mode of life, and also rate of change, of the vent community. Including the communities of brine and cold seeps, they consist of nearly 160 new species, belonging to at least 16 previously unknown families of invertebrate. These new names are used in this chapter, but space prevents providing references to the source descriptions; the most recent listing, compiled by Torben Wolff, of species endemic to hydrothermal vent, giving the taxonomic authority and other details, appeared in the unpublished 'Deep-Sea Newsletter' for December 1985. Black and white photographs of organisms of vents and cold seeps are often unsatisfactory. However, excellent colour photographs of vent organisms have been published in a number of semi-popular articles, such as Anonymous (1979), Laubier & Desbruyères (1984); Hessler (1981) and Hessler, Lonsdale & Hawkins (1988). Furthermore, an excellent recognition manual with coloured illustrations of each species has been compiled by Segonzac (1987). Grassle (1986) provides a good review of the biology of hydrothermal vents, while the reviews by Laubier (1989) and Southward (1989) also cover the ecology of the similar communites found associated with cold seeps and reducing sediments. Other good, but more detailed, sources of information on the hydrothermal vent communities can be found in the volumes edited by M. L. Jones (1985), Childress (1988) and Laubier (1988).

Already, fossil analogues of vent communities have been recognized indicating that forms of life such as the worms along with other fauna in a low-diversity community lived associated with active sulphide mineralization as far back as the Lower Carboniferous, at least 350 mya (Banks, 1985; Haymon & Koski, 1985; Bitter, Scott & Schenk, 1990).

PHYSICAL CONDITIONS AND PERSISTENCE OF VENT COMMUNITIES

Hydrothermal activity along mid-oceanic ridges results from the fissures and fractures formed in fresh ridge-crest basalt as it cools and is rifted apart providing conduits for the circulation of cold bottom water into the underlying crust. The circulating seawater penetrates to depths of a few kilometres, reacting chemically with hot basalt at temperatures in excess of 300 °C, and emerges as hot springs on the ocean floor. The hydrothermal fluid either flows as warm (5–250 °C) diffuse emissions from cracks and crevices in the basaltic rock, as high-temperature (270–380 °C) black smoker chimneys formed of precipitated minerals or from sometimes lower temperature, but still very hot, 'white smokers', from which the fluid escapes as a cloudy plume (Fig. 15.3) of high flow rate (max. 1–5 m s^{-1}). The rising plume soon mixes so that most vent creatures live at close to the temperature of the ambient water mass (c. 2 °C). Vivid proof that such vents and their associated community are transient and variable phenomena is provided by accumulations of dead, giant bivalve shells (see Fig. 15.4(c)) which, since they are known to persist for only about 15 yr before being dissolved, must indicate quite recent change in conditions (Ballard, van Andel & Holcomb, 1982; Turner & Lutz, 1984; Lutz, Fritz & Rhoads, 1985). The geophysical and geochemical evidence suggests short bursts of hydrothermal activity occur lasting decades or less. On a shorter timescale of days down to seconds, temperature records from amongst the vent communities show erratic and rapid fluctuations suggesting that the animals are subject to large changes in their chemical environment (Tunnicliffe *et al.*, 1985; K. S. Johnson, Childress & Beehler, 1988). Within the lifetime of an active vent, fluctuating conditions are evidenced from studies of ring-like variations in shell microstructure analogous to the growth rings in shallow water bivalves, and from differences observed in the fauna on return visits to vent sites (Hessler & Smithey, 1983; Laubier & Desbruyères, 1984; Hessler, Smithey & Keller, 1985; Grassle, 1985; Fustec, Desbruyères & Juniper, 1987; Hessler *et al.*, 1988).

ENERGY SOURCES

The energy source sustaining such lush oases was initially a mystery, but several indications after the early exploring expeditions to the Galapagos Rift pointed to a primarily non-photosynthetic source of organic carbon to vent organisms. By 1980 it was realized that it is the intense growth of chemoautotrophic bacteria, using sulphur-containing inorganic compounds as an oxidizing substrate, in the hydrothermal fluid deep within the porous lava that supports these colonies of large, fast-growing vent animals (Jannasch & Wirsen, 1979; Jannasch & Mottl, 1985; Cavanaugh, 1985). Even more surprising was the discovery that the most numerous and conspicuous organisms have developed symbiotic relationships with chemoautotrophic bacteria (Cavanaugh *et al.*, 1981; Felbeck, 1981). As a consequence these megafauna dominate the primary production in the vent community (Jannasch, 1985; K. S. Johnson *et al.*, 1986). Such chemosynthesis of organic carbon from elemental carbon dioxide and methane contrasts with photosynthesis where the source of energy is light from the sun rather than that derived from chemical oxidations. Similar chemoautotrophic reactions go on, for example, within the reducing conditions of the black subsurface layer in highly organic sediments where the supply of oxygen has been used up; and where similar symbioses have been found in burrowing macrofauna (Felbeck *et al.*, 1981; Southward *et al.*, 1981; Cavanaugh, 1985; Southward, 1986). However, it is only at hydrothermal vents and other seepage areas (see below) that the combination of heat and the ready supply of reduced inorganic substrates to an interface with oxygenated water combine with the metabolic diversity of bacteria to permit production of metazoan animals on such a lavish scale (Fig. 15.3).

   Besides occurring in symbiotic association within the gills and other tissues of bivalves and vestimentiferan worms, there is a rich community of free-living bacteria including the *Beggiatoa*-like forms that may form the conspicuous web-like mats on any hard surface, including the shells and tubes of animals. In the Guaymas Basin, where they comprise the dominant organism of the vent site, patches of *Beggiatoa* mats covering the anoxic, black sediment, may reach 3–4 m in diameter and 3 cm thick. In laboratory culture, these mats show a chemoautotrophic metabolism (Jannasch, Nelson & Wirsen, 1989). Within the warm sediment, sulphur-reducing bacteria flourish, some tolerating temperatures greater than 100 °C. Futhermore, methanogenic archaebacteria have been isolated from Guaymas Basin sediment that were growing at more than 110 °C (Huber *et al.*, 1989). Within the hydrothermal plume, or immediately above, bacterial densities of the order of 10^3 cells ml^{-1} have been measured on Galapagos vents (Jannasch & Wirsen, 1979; Karl *et al.*, 1980; Cartiss *et al.*, 1979); but elsewhere in the plume only about 20% of the growing cells have been found to be chemosynthetic; whilst just above, the free-living bacteria are virtually all heterotrophs (Naganumi, Otsuki & Seki, 1989). It is thought likely that the untold billions of such highly efficient transformers of energy must generate a predominant part of the biomass of warm deep-sea vents (Naganumi *et al.*, 1989). Microbial production of the low temperature (10 °C) vents on the Galapagos Rift is thought to be 2–3 times that of photosynthetic production at the surface in the same region (Karl *et al.*, 1980).

(*a*)

Fig. 15.4. (*a*) The giant vent clam *Calyptogena magnifica* of the E. Pacific hydrothermal vents shown aligned along fissures in the basalt at 21° N where they will be bathed with a slow outflow of warm vent fluid;

continued

THE FAUNA OF HYDROTHERMAL VENTS OF THE EASTERN PACIFIC

MOLLUSCS

In contrast to the small size of most deep-sea bivalves are two giant-sized species, the clam-like *Calyptogena magnifica* (family Vesicomyidae) (Fig. 15.4) and a mussel *Bathymodiolus thermophilus* (family Mytilidae) (Fig. 15.5) which occur in dense clusters around vents. These species may exist in enormous densities, the biomass of *B. thermophilus* exceeding 10 kg m^{-2} in one vent area (Hessler & Smithey, 1983), and give the eastern Pacific vent fauna its distinctive appearance to observers from submersibles, prompting names such as 'Mussel Bed' and 'Clambake' for individual vent sites in the Galapagos Rift. Both bivalves are crevice-living, *C. magnifica* being found (Fig. 15.4(a)) only where there is at least slightly elevated temperatures indicating emission of hydrothermal fluid. However, isolated individuals of *B. thermophilus* occur on open rock surfaces,

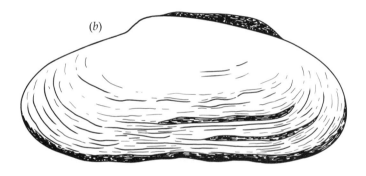

(b)

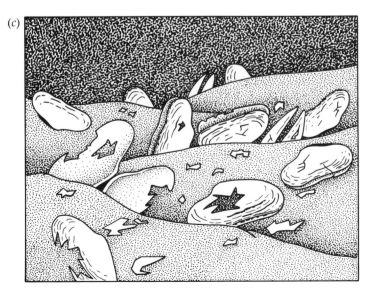

(c)

(b) living individual of *Calyptogena magnifica*, which can attain 25 cm in length; (c) dead, dissolving shells of *Calyptogena* lying in areas where vent emission has ceased. (Drawings courtesy Violaine Martin, IFREMER, Brest; (c) modified slightly.)

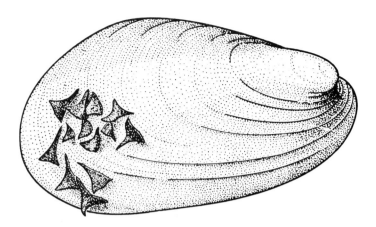

Fig. 15.5. Shell of *Bathymodiolus thermophilus* showing the basal attachment of byssal attachments of other individuals. (Drawing courtesy Violaine Martin, IFREMER, Brest.)

attached by byssal threads secreted by the foot, but never far from vent openings. *Calyptogena magnifica* possess a large foot that is normally inserted into the crevice, but they have been observed using the foot to change station on the bottom. Both species possess symbiotic bacteria within their gills, those in *Calyptogena* making up to 75% of the gill tissue (Stahl *et al.*, 1984). It is now clear that these microbial sulphide-reducing symbionts, by fixing carbon dioxide, provide for the nutrition of their bivalve hosts. Like other hosts of chemoautotrophic bacterial symbionts, their dependence on redox reactions restricts them to the areas of interface between ambient oxygenated seawater and the hydrothermal fluid where reduced sulphide and perhaps methane chemicals are present. At the Rose Garden *Calyptogena magnifica* are found in areas with relatively low flux of hydrothermal fluid, and gain exposure to reducing compounds by the insertion of the well-vascularized foot into cracks carrying the flow. Vent water is undetectable around the siphons and it is thought that individuals take up sulphide through the foot and oxygen and inorganic carbon through their gills (Fisher *et al.*, 1988a).

Bathymodiolus thermophilus contains abundant microbial symbionts within its gill, but the role of these bacteria in the nutrition of their host remains poorly understood, and their importance has been questioned by Fisher *et al.* (1987). Since these mussels retain a functional mouth and gut, it is thought they can ingest bacteria by filter feeding and, furthermore, may derive at least part of their food from particles derived from the euphotic zone. But, clearly its much reduced gut indicates that this nutritional source is secondary to that from its symbiotic microbes. Furthermore, even if filter feeding, it requires higher concentrations of suspended food than are to be found away from the vents (Le Pennec & Prieur, 1984; Le Pennec, Prieur & Lucas, 1985; Hessler *et al.*, 1988b; and reviews by Fisher, in press; Somero, Anderson & Childress, in press). Variable and usually much lower levels in activities of enzymes associated with chemosynthesis within gill tissues of *B. thermophilus* compared to either *Calyptogena* or the tubeworm *Riftia* are thought to reflect reduced dependence on bacterial symbionts and explain why the mussels can thrive over the wider range of conditions (Fisher *et al.*, 1988b).

More than 30 species of limpet-like gastropod have recently been recorded from around hydrothermal vents, and these have been tentatively assigned to eight different familes in seven superfamilies (McLean, 1988), including a new family of cocculiniform limpets. They occur, grazing on microbes, either on the bare rock surfaces, on sulphide mounds or chimneys, or on the surfaces of larger sessile organisms such as vestimentiferan worms or mussels. Most species are known from the more southerly Pacific sites, but those known from other vents seem to be different species. Other vent molluscs include new species of gastropods with coiled shells (reviewed by Warén & Bouchet, 1989), an unidentified whelk-like turrid gastropod, a pectinid bivalve *Bathypecten vulcani*, and new species of the worm-like Aplacophora.

WORMS

Perhaps the single organism giving the eastern Pacific vent community its surrealistic quality is the red-plumed, tube-dwelling worm *Riftia pachyptila* (Fig. 15.6). This animal has presented the biggest puzzle to zoologists trying to decode from its morphology and anatomy its correct place in the classificatory system of the animal world. Their long, permanent tubes are attached deep within crevices. Lacking mouth or gut, they clearly show affinity to the similarly gut-less, but usually thread-sized, phylum Pogonophora. They are related to species of large but apparently rare obturate (plumed) pogonophorans (family Lamellibrachiidae) from the deep sea. The first, *Lamellibrachia barhami* was discovered in the 1960s from the Californian Continental Borderland, and other species subsequently have been found characteristic of areas of cold seepage (Hecker, 1985). With *Riftia* these species are placed in the class Vestimentifera. The genus *Riftia* has been placed in its own family, Riftiidae, while species of the superficially similar large, plumed genus *Ridgeia*, found considerably further north on the Juan de Fuca Ridge, forms another new family, Ridgeiidae, that seems to have closer affinity to lamellibrachiids. M. L. Jones (1985*a,b*) puts them all in a related but separate phylum to the Pogonophora, the Vestimentifera, comprising at least eight known species. Lacking a digestive system, vestimentiferans obtain their nutriment through the richly vascularized, leaf-like branchial lamellae, or gills, that are attached at the base to form a plume-like structure (Fig. 15.7), the blood vessels containing haemoglobin allowing a tolerance to varying oxygen tensions in the water. As in *Calyptogena* and *Bathymodiolus*, the body of the worm carries an enormous number of symbiotic sulphur-oxidizing, carbon-fixing bacteria. These bacteria contribute up to half its weight, but are probably capable of supplying most of the worm's metabolic needs. The need for uptake of oxygen, sulphide and carbon dioxide from the water underscores the need for the worm to live in well-mixed conditions (Felbeck, 1985). *Riftia* also has the ability to withstand prolonged anoxic conditions, caused by short-term variations in vent flow, by regulation of oxygen consumption. Nevertheless, Tunnicliffe, Garrett & Johnson (1990) found that about half the population of *Ridgeia*, recorded over many days with a time-lapse camera, were retracted at any

Fig. 15.6. The community at 13° N investigated by French scientists, showing a mass of the large vestimentiferan *Riftia pachyptila*, accompanied by numerous *Bathymodiolus*, crabs, *Munidopsis* and fish in close proximity. (Drawing courtesy Violaine Martin, IFREMER, Brest.)

one time. Since extended tube worms suffer a high mortality rate from predation by fish and from periodic collapse of the sulphide chimneys on which they are attached, this behaviour may be necessary to reduce predation risk and maintain their tubes despite their need of the dissolved sulphide in the vent flow. Many other animals, including mussels, the shrimp *Alvinocaris*, a sea anemone and species of limpet including *Neomphalus*, live amongst *Riftia* tubes, whilst *Calyptogena* lives in crevices away from the vestimentiferans.

The polychaete worms include the large 'Pompei worm' *Alvinella pompejana* (Fig. 15.8(*a*)), now classified in the new family Alvinellidae, are characteristic of the hotter vents at 13° and 21° N. The worms typically live in large honeycomb-like tube masses (Fig. 15.8(*b*)) which form a snowball-like edifice around vent openings and on the walls of white smokers where hydrothermal fluid issues at about 150 °C, and have also been seen on the sulphide chimney walls of 350 °C black smokers. Microorganisms, attached externally to dendritically branched appendages of the posterior parapodia, live in a symbiotic association with the

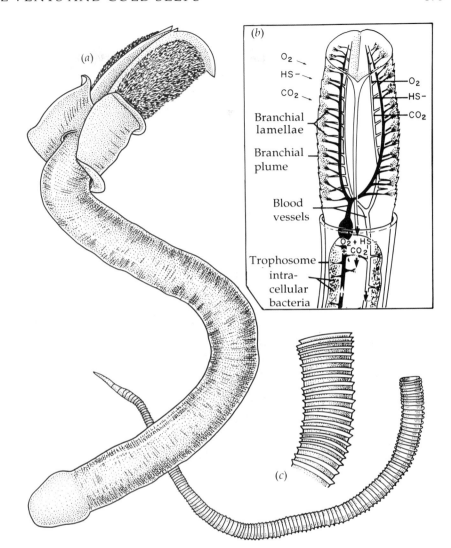

Fig. 15.7. (*a*) *Riftia pachyptila* extracted from its tube, along with (*b*) a fragment of its tube and (*c*) the tubes of the 'Jericho' worm *Tevnia jerichonana*. Inset shows gas exchange between the surrounding water and the endosymbiotic bacteria contained within the trophosome of *Riftia*, and circulation of blood within the branchial filaments and pinnules scattered over the leaf-like branchial lamellae, that form the characteristic, bright-red elongate 'plume'. (Drawing by Violaine Martin, IFREMER, Brest.)

worm. They are likely to provide a good part of the worm's food supply, either by direct ingestion of bacteria through the mouth using the tentacles, or across the highly vascularized posterior epidermis from dissolved organic compounds produced by the bacteria (Desbruyères & Laubier, 1980). Other polychaetes, classified in the genus *Paralvinella* also occur but lack epibiotic bacteria, and are probably deposit feeders. All these worms seem to be able to tolerate the exceptionally high temperature found closest to the vent where temperatures of 285 °C have been measured (Grassle, 1986). Another polychaete that can be very abundant at vent sites are limey-tubed suspension feeding serpulids, the new species *Laminatubus alvini* and *Protis hydrothermica* sometimes forming a continuous zone around the vent field at the Galapagos Rift (Hessler &

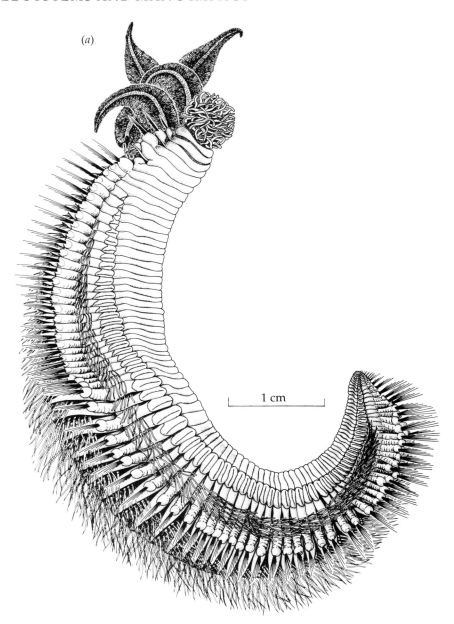

Fig. 15.8. (*a*) 'Pompeii' worm *Alvinella pompejana* showing the small number of segments and the long dorsal papillae.
continued

Smithey, 1983). Other polychaetes include several polynoid worms (scaleworms), such as *Branchipolynoe symmytilida*, which lives, perhaps semi-parasitically, within the mantle cavity of about a third of the *Bathymodiolus* population, and several new species belonging to the families Spionidae, Eunicidae, Dorvilleidae, Nereidae, Phyllodocidae and Maldanidae; most of the latter being deposit-feeding forms found in the sediment deposited at vent sites (Blake, 1985; Desbruyères *et al.*, 1985).

(b)

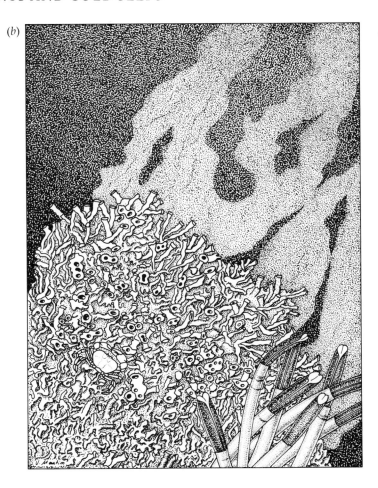

(b) White smoker at the 'Pogonord' site at 13° N surrounded by a massive tubeworm colony of *Alvinella*, amongst which moves the large crab *Cyanograea*; at lower right some tubes of the vestimentiferan *Riftia pachyptila*. (Drawing courtesy Violaine Martin, IFREMER, Brest.)

Light-coloured worms draped over the rock at the Galapagos vents became known as spaghetti worms and were later identified as a new species, genus and family of the phylum Enteropneusta, *Saxipendium coronatum*. It is not known for certain how these unusual worms feed, but since the posterior end lying over the rock leaves the anterior end drifting freely in the water, they may be suspension feeders (Grassle, 1986). It is possible they are distantly related to the epifaunal lophenteropneusts of abyssal deep-sea sediments described in Chapter 4.

CRUSTACEANS

Amongst benthic species, hydrothermal vents have yielded a new and primitive genus of stalked scalpellid barnacle, representing a relic of the Mesozoic (Newman, 1979), and of leptostracan and isopod peracarids. However, decapod crustaceans make up the most conspicuous crustacean fauna. They include remarkable new forms of scavenging and carnivorous brachyuran classified in the genera *Bythograea* and *Cyanograea* (Fig. 15.9(a),(b)), the former two species tending to nestle within

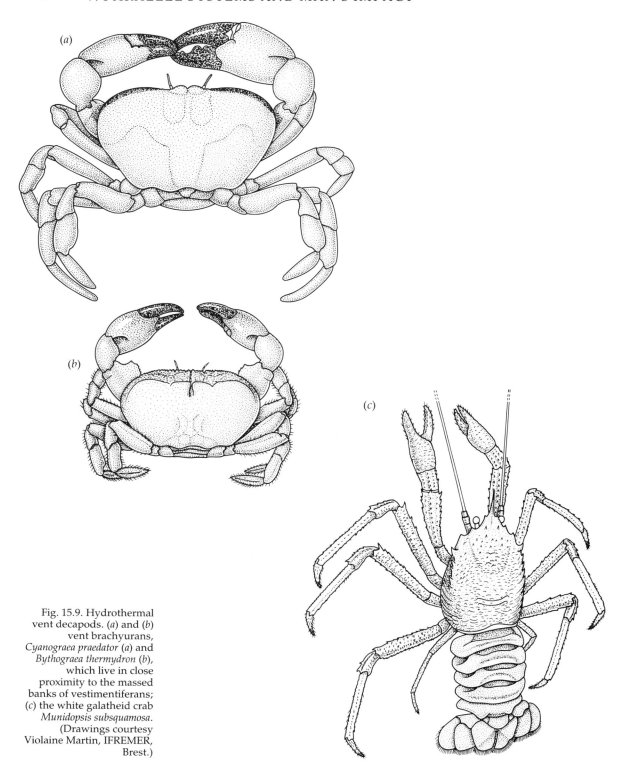

Fig. 15.9. Hydrothermal vent decapods. (*a*) and (*b*) vent brachyurans, *Cyanograea praedator* (*a*) and *Bythograea thermydron* (*b*), which live in close proximity to the massed banks of vestimentiferans; (*c*) the white galatheid crab *Munidopsis subsquamosa*. (Drawings courtesy Violaine Martin, IFREMER, Brest.)

vestimentiferan and mussel clumps, while the latter, as a predator on *Alvinella* has a more restricted distribution. A new species and genus of caridean shrimp (family Breseliidae), named *Alvinocaris lusca*, swarms over *Riftia* or *Bathymodiolus* at densities up to 112 m^{-2} at the Galapagos Rift (Williams & Chace, 1982). However, it has not so far been found elsewhere, although a related species has been found in enormous concentrations at 'black smokers' in the Atlantic and in the Marianas Trough (see below). Other decapods found at vent sites include both new species and forms known from similar depths elsewhere in the deep sea, such as *Munidopsis subsquamosa* (Fig. 15.9(*c*)). Although often observed, this seems to be because it prefers the open spaces where it is easily seen rather than by existing at high densities around the vents. It still remains unknown whether the new species are unique to vents or are simply too rare to have been collected from non-vent areas. In practical terms, changes in density of *Bythograea* and *Munidopsis* accurately track the occurrence of vents and can aid in their location using submersibles and remotely controlled cameras (Van Dover, Franks & Ballard, 1987).

(*a*)

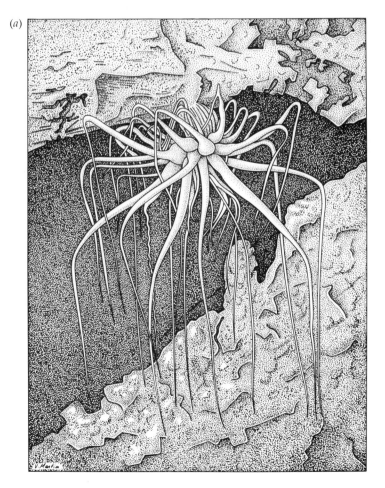

Fig. 15.10. Vent sea anemones: (*a*) a large, so far uncollected and therefore undescribed species, whose tentacles, 1 m in length, are orientated into the current;

continued

(b)

(b) another large anemone, *Actinostola callosi* surmounting a lava pillar along with several mushroom-like demospongid sponges *Caulophacus cyanae* and *Munidopsis subsquamosa*. (Drawings courtesy Violaine Martin, IFREMER, Brest.)

COELENTERATES

Little is known of the representatives of this phylum (Grassle, 1985), mostly because they are difficult to identify. However, anemones (mostly species belonging to the families Actinostolidae and Hormathiidae) have been observed sometimes to be abundant enough to form an unbroken carpet at the Galapagos Rift, and they also occur in abundance around the edge of vents in the Marianas and N. Atlantic (see below). They may also reach an impressive size, occasional large sea anemones up to 1.5 m in length having been found at 13° N (Fig. 15.10). Other coelenterates include the strange-looking Galapagos 'dandelion' living on the periphery of vents which has been identified as a new genus of siphonophore, *Thermopalia taraxaca*.

BENTHOPELAGIC COMMUNITY

Swarms of copepods and other zooplankton, including free-swimming larvae, have been observed over vent plumes. At one site, copepod

Fig. 15.11. The small zoarcid
fish *Thermarces cerberus*,
common at both 13° and 21°
N. (Drawing courtesy
Violaine Martin, IFREMER,
Brest.)

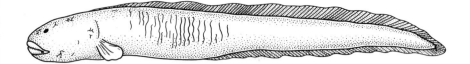

swarms composed of one new, presumably vent-specific, species *Isaacsi-
calanus paucisetus* reached densities of 920 individuals m^{-2} and dry weight
biomass of 133 mg m^{-2} (Smith, 1985b). Such small-scale patchy development of monospecific populations are most probably related to locally
high microbial densities associated with 'collapsed pit'-type vents. At a
larger scale, zooplanktonic biomass, more than an order of magnitude
higher than might be predicted at this depth must be responding to
microbial enrichment from the vent fluids (Berg & Van Dover, 1987;
Wiebe *et al.*, 1988). Ambient water currents and convection cells in the
immediate vicinity of vents may also raise local zooplanktonic biomass by
an entrainment mechanism (Lonsdale, 1977b; Enright *et al.*, 1981). In
contrast to the 'normal' benthopelagic zooplankton which is dominated
by copepods, benthopelagic zooplankton over vents is depleted of such
elements and enriched with respect to larval and juvenile stages of
benthic vent species which differ from site to site in accordance with the
nature and development of the benthic community (Berg & Van Dover,
1987).

Surprisingly, few fish have been found to be associated with hydrothermal vents; and those seen are difficult to catch from the submersible.
The eelpouts (family Zoarcidae) *Thermarces cerberus* (Fig. 15.11) and *T.
andersoni* are probable endemics at the eastern Pacific vents, but a pink
coloured new species of bythitid fish, *Bythites hollisi*, frequently hovered,
head down and with undulating tail, within the warm-water plume at the
Galapagos and 11° and 13° N vents, and is the only species thought to be
an obligatory vent inhabitant (Cohen, Rosenblatt & Moser, 1990). Other
species have been seen, and a few identified, belonging to four other
familes, but it is doubtful whether these are truly endemic to the
hydrothermal vent habitat.

FUNCTIONING OF THE HYDROTHERMAL VENT COMMUNITY

FEEDING

Lonsdale (1977b) proposed two possible nutritional sources supporting
these dense concentrations of large-sized animals: material brought in by
advection from the surrounding deep-sea area by the rising hydrothermal plume, and bacterial chemosynthesis. The first source was
quickly ruled out as inadequate to support the huge standing stock and
apparently rapid turnover of vent organisms. In general, planktonic
biomass about 100 m above the vent field is little enhanced compared to

nearby non-vent areas (Wiebe *et al.*, 1988), despite the occurrence of planktonic swarms in the immediate vicinity of the plume (see above). This indicates that a diversity of bacterial communities, many of them chemoautotrophs obtaining their energy from the oxidation of reduced sulphur and other compounds, must lie at the base of the food chains of vent biota. As we have seen, intimate symbiotic relationships of micro-organisms within the body tissues or on the skin of their invertebrate host are well developed in the most successful and characteristic organisms associated with hydrothermal vents so that 'normal' particulate feeding mechanisms have become unnecessary.

The dependence of these invertebrates on chemosynthetic bacteria is clearly indicated by analysis of the stable isotope ratios of elements such as carbon and nitrogen in their body tissues. In particular, the ratio $^{13}C/^{12}C$, $\delta^{13}C$, reflects the age of the carbon utilized in the food chain, that originating from chemosynthesis being characteristically lower in ^{13}C compared to the 'new' carbon produced by photosynthesis (Felbeck *et al.*, 1981; Rau, 1985).

Since the existence of bacterial symbionts was established by Cavanaugh *et al.* (1981) and the chemoautotrophic nature of the relationship determined by Felbeck (1981), we still know little of these bacteria (see review by Prieur, Jeanthon & Jacq, 1988) and of the mechanisms developed by their hosts for tolerating the high temperatures and toxic chemicals of vent emissions (see review by Somero *et al.*, in press). Nevertheless, the immense numbers of free-living bacteria that are aggregated as particles in the vent emissions and on living and non-living surfaces provide a potent food source for a host of suspension- and deposit-feeding vent animals, whose bodies in turn, provide food for predatory and scavenging species.

RESPIRATION AND GROWTH RATES

In situ measurements of respiration, CO_2 incorporation and substrate utilization indicate very high rates of microbial metabolism (Karl *et al.*, 1980; Jannasch & Wirsen, 1979; Jannasch, 1983; Jannasch & Mottl, 1985). Respiration rates of vent megafauna are also high and at least comparable to those expected in shallow water (Mickel & Childress, 1982; Childress & Mickel, 1982, 1985; Arp, Childress & Fisher, 1984; Smith, 1985*a,b*). Furthermore, because of the relatively short persistence of vents (varying from several years to several decades), and because food resources and predation pressure appear to be far from limiting we would expect that such organisms are able to quickly colonize new areas and make rapid growth. Radiometric dating by Turekian *et al.* (1979), using the ^{238}U and ^{232}Th decay series present in shell-growth horizons of *Calyptogena magnifica*, indicate an age of around 7 yr for the 22 cm specimen analysed (Fig. 15.12). Another approach roughly corroborated this result by file-notching the growing valve edge of *Bathymodiolus thermophilus*; recoveries 9 months later had put on significant growth, the age of the oldest mussels being estimated at 19 plus or minus 7 yr from a fitted von Bertalanffy growth curve (Rhoads *et al.*, 1982). Yet another approach was

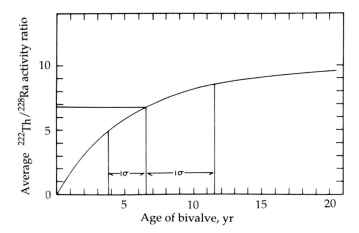

Fig. 15.12. Growth curve for *Calyptogena magnifica* derived from $^{222}\text{Th}/^{228}\text{Ra}$ activity ratio. The measured average value of the ratio, 0.68 (± 1 standard deviations shown as vertical lines to age axis), corresponds to an age of around 7 yr for the 22 cm long bivalve analysed. (From Turekian *et al.*, 1981.)

to determine a growth curve based on rates of shell dissolution in *Calyptogena magnifica*; the results indicating the largest (*c.* 24 cm long) specimens from the Galapagos Rift to be about 20 years old (Turner & Lutz, 1984; Lutz, Fritz & Rhoads, 1985), although similar estimates on specimens from 21° N show a slightly slower growth rate (Roux, Rio & Fatton, 1985; Lutz, Fritz & Cerrato, 1988). In this species, maturity is reached at about 4 years when they are around 12 cm long.

From such data has come realization that these geochemically based communities of organisms show rates of biological production comparable to the highest known in the marine environment.

LIFE-HISTORY TACTICS

Because of their ephemeral habit in an environment of abundant food, there has been selection for large size to maximize fecundity in a limited time (Grassle, 1986). Surveys indicate vents are usually less than 10 km apart while vent fields may be spaced as much as 100 km along the Juan de Fuca Ridge (Crane *et al.*, 1985). Such isolation implies the need to develop efficient means for recolonization at a rate on the same order as the generation time of the vent species. However, Grassle (1986) points out that the time span of hydrothermal activity along a whole segment of ridge crest is likely to take several generations. Within-generation dispersal over vast distances may not, after all, be such an important requirement for survival. Hence, the finding that most vent species have lecithotrophic, rather than planktotrophic early development (Lutz, Jablonski & Turner, 1984; Berg, 1985; Turner, Lutz & Jablonski, 1985; E. C. Southward, 1988; Cary, Felbeck & Holland, 1989; McHugh, 1989) is less surprising (see Chapter 13 for discussion of these modes of larval development). Only the mussel *Bathymodiolus*, the shrimp *Alvinocaris*, some decapods, and the enteropneust *Saxipendium* possess the small egg size and high fecundity associated with planktotrophy; although the lipid-rich eggs of *Riftia pachyptila* are also small and numerous and may well also have a limited pelagic early development (Cary *et al.*, 1989). This fits in with the observation from repeat visits to the Galapagos vent fields of the apparently slow rate that mussels replace *Riftia*, only later coming to dominate the community. This is because, unless planktonic larvae can settle immediately, recruitment will have to come from other vent sites (Hessler *et al.*, 1988*b*).

However, transport by little-known, cold deep currents make generalizations derived from shallow water on the relationship of larval type to dispersal ability difficult to apply (Grassle, 1986); but despite the large distances separating vent areas, many characteristic species are present at all of the sites studied in the eastern Pacific. Hence, the free-swimming larvae of a number of these species may have a dispersal capability sufficient to maintain chains of far-flung populations through stepwise larval dispersal (Lutz, 1988). Furthermore, Warén & Bouchet (1989) suggest that many species may be able to delay settlement for months at a time. Experimental recruitment panels deployed at various sites on the E. Pacific Rise and Galapagos Rift show broad size ranges in postlarval or juvenile populations of polychaete, molluscs and barnacle species colonizing the slate panels, indicating intermittent or continuous recruitment occurs at vent sites (Van Dover, Berg & Turner, 1988). Certainly, larvae and postlarval forms of bivalves, gastropods, polychaetes and crustaceans associated with vents have been collected at 100–200 m above the Guaymas Basin vent field, indicating that postlarvae may play an important role in dispersing vent species (Wiebe *et al.*, 1988). Polymodal size frequencies in large samples of the alvinellid polychaete *Paralvinella palmiformis* from the Juan de Fuca Ridge vents suggests that recruitment is episodic, perhaps resulting from discrete (possibly synchronized) breeding in the population; although in its congener, *P. pandorae*, continuous reproduction seems more likely (McHugh, 1989).

THE LIFE CYCLE OF VENT COMMUNITIES

There has been a growing conviction that, to properly understand the natural history of deep-sea hydrothermal vents, it is necessary to study them through time. This has resulted in an increasing emphasis on repeat visits to the longest and best-described sites. The fast rate of change is evidenced from the commonly seen beds of dead vesicomyid shells that from shell dissolution rates must have died within the last 15–25 yr (Killingley *et al.*, 1980; Lutz *et al.*, 1985). French work on the E. Pacific Rise at 13° N detected varying changes after 2 yr; the most marked change was detected at the vent field named 'Pogonord' from substratum collapse leading to the death of a *Riftia* clump, while elsewhere *Riftia* had been replaced by *Alvinella*, but elsewhere recruitment of *Riftia* was evident (Fustec *et al.*, 1987). Revisits by 'Alvin' to the 'Rose garden' vent field on the Galapagos Rift 5 and 8 yr after its initial discovery in 1979 has provided evidence of more substantial faunal change (Childress (ed.), 1988; Hessler *et al.*, 1988*b*). From a supposition that the vent in 1979 was at a relatively early stage of development, a rough sequence of community change has emerged. Initially, the vent is colonized by species hosting autotrophic bacteria such as vestimentiferans, clams and mussels, along with filter feeding species settling around the periphery where they can benefit from particles falling out from the plume. Both vestimentiferans and the filter feeders then decline as sulphide concentration and/or water flux diminishes, but the bivalve populations, especially mussels, persist or even expand. Biological interaction might also contribute to the observed decline of tubeworms. This may come about as a result of either competition with mussels which can more effectively remove sulphide from the fluid or by the rapidly growing individual mussels physically altering the flow pattern of vent water so that it is diverted from the plumes of the vestimentiferans (Johnson et al., 1986, 1988; Childress, 1988). Furthermore, decreasing vent flow, or increasingly effective filtration by mussels becoming less dependent on chemosynthesis, may explain the decline in filter-feeding species such as anemones, serpulids, siphonophores and enteropneusts (Berg & Van Dover, 1987).

SPECIATION

Vents may be considered as ephemeral, biogeographic islands to their endemic faunas. The potentially restricted gene flow is particularly important in consideration of speciation. Clearly, the species of each 'island' need to be able to colonize the new ones or else become extinct. Studies on genetic variation in vent species clearly indicate great potential in understanding genetic isolation and speciation in the deep ocean. Some information on *Bathymodiolus* has emerged which indicates little genetic differentiation between two Galapagos sites 8 km apart, but considerable differences when these sites are compared with mussels 2200 km away at the 13° N site (J. P. Grassle, 1985). However, the cause of faunal differences between vent sites cannot easily separate between differences in dispersal ability and ecological differences between sites. However, with increasing separation the proportions of species may differ considerably, and entirely new kinds of animals may be present. Those species that disappear usually are replaced by a closely related form. Such 'congeneric replacement' may explain differences in morphology of *Riftia* at the various sites in the eastern Pacific. Inherent low genetic variability in *R. pachyptila* may explain the limited genetic divergence evident from studies of alloenzymic variability in populations from various sites from the Galapagos Rift and at 21° N (Bucklin, 1988).

The mid-ocean spreading centres form a continuous network throughout the oceans; there are many branches but few gaps (Fig. 15.2). Even the recently discovered vent communities of the N. Atlantic spreading centres (see below) are part of this continuum, being linked to the E. Pacific Rise via the mid-ocean ridges extending across the S. Pacific south of Australia, across the Indian Ocean and around southern Africa. Although plate tectonics results in a changing pattern of mid-ocean ridges over millions of years, new ones are always extensions from existing ridges, providing the fauna with a route for colonization. Presently isolated sections, such as the Juan de Fuca and Explorer Ridges (now separated from the E. Pacific Rise by the San Andreas Fault) are separated by more than 2500 km from the vent communities to the south. Genetic exchange between the two areas being no longer possible, the faunas have diverged as result of isolation from about 35 Ma (Hessler *et al.*, 1988*b*; Tunnicliffe, 1988). The discovery of similar faunas associated with cold seeps (see below) also reinforces this view that such biota constitute a separate faunal system of global scale. A degree of isolation is thought also to explain differences in the vent fauna discovered from 'Alvin' in 1987 in the Mariana Trough in the western Pacific (a back-arc spreading centre bordering the subduction zone of the Mariana Trench) but isolated from the midocean ridge system. Here a vent-type fauna very different in character to those of the E. Pacific occurs (Hessler *et al.*, 1988). The community is dominated by a sessile barnacle, allied to those of shallow water, but of a species that is the most primitive known living today (Newman & Hessler, 1989), and by limpets; but also with new elements including a large, hairy-shelled gastropod whose enlarged gills are packed with sulphur-oxidizing chemoautotrophic bacteria filling about 40% of the snail's body volume. This symbiotic relationship indicates that this gastropod occupies the ecological role of giant bivalves and tubeworms at other hydrothermal vents. Other fauna include a new congener of the bresiliid shrimp *Rimicaris* found on the Mid-Atlantic Ridge (see below). An abundance of large sea anemones on the periphery of the vents bears striking resemblance to the Atlantic vents, whilst other fauna, including *Bathymodiolus* and *Alvinella* seem to be congeners of species in the eastern Pacific.

Taxonomic comparisons between the northern Juan de Fuca Ridge and East Pacific Rise vents suggest rates of speciation have been low, the Juan de Fuca Ridge possessing an endemic assemblage of generally lower diversity than that found on the East Pacific Rise (Tunnicliffe, 1988). Furthermore, the apparent absence, in a recently discovered midplate hydrothermal system associated with a volcanic seamount off Hawaii, or any development of communities of large-sized biota characterizing other hydrothermal vents (Karl *et al.*, 1988) suggests that complete isolation from the global system of plate formation and destruction may be important in the initial establishment of such colonies.

VENT COMMUNITIES IN THE ATLANTIC

Along the Mid-Atlantic Ridge active hydrothermal vents with associated vent fauna have been discovered at 3.6–3.7 km depth (Fig. 15.1); some associated with hot 'black smokers' and sulphide chimneys (Detrick *et al.*, 1986; Rona *et al.*, 1986). In both areas, along with bacterial mats, there are enormous swarms of two species of a new family (Bresiliidae) of large caridean shrimp, named *Rimicaris exoculata* and *R. chacei* (Williams & Rona, 1986), along with sessile, translucent anemones. These shrimps ingest sulphide particles from 350 °C black smoker chimneys from which they appear to graze associated free-living microorganisms (Van Dover *et al.*, 1988*b*). Although lacking 'normal' eyes, *R. exoculata* possesses a pair of large dorsal organs containing visual pigment that are thought to detect the hot water plumes as low-level black-body radiation (Van Dover *et al.*, 1989).

But overall, compared with the eastern Pacific, the fauna is less varied; in particular, bivalve molluscs seem rare and tubeworms apparently absent.

COMMUNITIES ASSOCIATED WITH OTHER SUBMARINE SEEPAGE

Similar assemblages of animals have been found which are at least partially dependent on autotrophic production associated with seafloor emission of dissolved reducing substances, not necessarily related to tectonic activity. These various submarine seepages in the deep and shallow seas are reviewed by Hovland & Judd (1988) who include speculations on their significance to physical and chemical oceanography and biological production. Excluding those associated with tectonic activity which we have already considered, they are of three main types: hydrocarbon (petroleum), groundwater, and seepages that include material from the Earth's mantle. Similar animals also have been observed by biologists in 'Alvin' to be associated with the oily bones of the intact remains of a whale lying on the bottom in the 1.24 km deep Santa Catalina Basin off California (C. R. Smith *et al.*, 1989).

HYDROCARBON SEEPS

Areas of hydrocarbon seepage and methane hydrate deposits (identifiable as acoustic blanking, or 'wipeout zones' on seismic records, or as bubble plumes emanating from the bottom) are of common occurrence in the Gulf of Mexico (Kennicutt II *et al.*, 1988). In shallow depths natural gas seepage points are linked to bacterial mats on fishing banks indicating enhanced benthic productivity. On the continental slope, such as the upper continental slope off Louisiana (Fig. 15.1), hydrocarbon seepage is associated with chemosynthetic benthic communities comprised of a fauna taxonomically comparable to that of the hydrothermal vents of the Pacific, but lacking the temperature anomalies typical of the latter. The community includes the vestimentiferan tubeworm *Lamellibrachia*, the vesicomyid bivalves *Calyptogena ponderosa* and *Vesicomya cordata*, and the large *Bathymodiolus*-like mytilid, *Pseudomiltha* sp. with similarly fleshy gills, along with other bivalves previously known from non-seep areas, including *Acesta bullesi* and *Lucinoma atlantis* (Kennicutt II *et al.*, 1985a,b, 1988; Brooks *et al.*, 1985; Turner, 1985). The bivalves *Calyptogena* and *Vesicomya* occur, along with dead shells, in dense aggregations on the seabed and are able to plough through the sediment surface, perhaps responding to gradients in pore-water sulphides and hydrocarbons (Rosman, Boland & Baker, 1987).

The composition of seep faunal communities in the Gulf of Mexico is complex. The density of mussels correlates significantly to water–

methane levels, while tubeworm cover correlates with sediment–hydrocarbon loading. At least five basic assemblages are recognizable, these including not only mussel beds, clam beds and tubeworm clumps, but also epifaunal brachiopod/solitary coral assemblages and gorgonian fields. These may overlap spatially and have some shared dependence on the chemosynthetic processes discussed below. Furthermore a chemical environment very similar to that off Louisiana, and also supporting endosymbiont-containing bivalves, has recently been found at 0.42–0.6 km depth on the northern Californian Slope (Kennicutt II *et al.*, 1988; 1989).

Bubble plumes from methane hydrate deposits within the sediment are probably of widespread occurrence on the continental margin. One site at 0.77 km depth in the Sea of Okhotsk, west of Paramushir Island in the Kuril Islands was investigated by Russian scientists using a submersible. The bubble plumes from pits and funnels in the methane-saturated and highly reduced sediment is associated with lush populations of a large (up to 20 cm) bivalve similar to *Conchocele* and an ampharetid-like polychaete worm, apparently containing symbiotic chemosynthetic sulphur-oxidizing bacteria (Zonenshayn *et al.*, 1987).

Methane bubble plumes are known to be associated with similar 'pockmark' features on soft, cohesive shelf sediments in the northern North Sea (Hovland & Thomsen, 1989). Although active pockmarks are associated with concentrations of organisms such as bivalves and euphausiids, unlike the deep-water sites, these seem to be species known from the background community.

Experiments have demonstrated for the first time in a living mussel (*Pseudomiltha*), from the hydrocarbon seep community in the Gulf of Mexico, the oxidative uptake of methane carbon. This seems to be undertaken by means of endocellular methanotrophic bacteria located in the swollen gill tissue of the mytilid (Childress *et al.*, 1986; Brooks *et al.*, 1987; Fisher *et al.*, 1987; Cary, Fisher & Felbeck, 1988); whilst Cavanaugh *et al.* (1987) report similar bacteria from gill tissue of mussels from the Florida Escarpment (see below). Although a symbiosis with these gill microbes that are able to utilize methane rather than hydrogen sulphide seems likely to be important in the nutrition of these mussel populations, and may even satisfy the mussels' carbon needs, an input from suspension feeding again cannot be ruled out. Interestingly, the discovery of methanotrophic symbiosis in Pogonophora indicates that a similar mode of nutrition occurs elsewhere amongst animals living in low-oxygen habitats such as highly organic reducing sediments where methane might be expected to be produced (Schmaljohan & Flügel, 1987). However, the high oxygen demand of such methanotrophic symbionts may well have restricted their occurrence (Childress & Fisher, 1988).

GROUNDWATER SEEPS

In the Gulf of Mexico, cold sulphide, and methane-enriched, water seeps from the passive continental margin in 3.266 km depth at the base of the steep slope of the porous limestone of the Florida Escarpment (Fig. 15.1)

Fig. 15.13. Diagrammatic representation of the seepage areas from the base of the Florida Escarpment. A jointed limestone underwater cliff lies to the right and the abyssal sediment at left, with seepage represented as stippled areas. Bacterial mats (be) lie in the centre of the seepage; the beds of mussels (mu) are restricted to the sediment. Clumps of tube worms (tw) live both on the sediment and in fissures in the wall of the escarpment. Horizontal scale about 5 m. (From Paull *et al.*, 1984.)

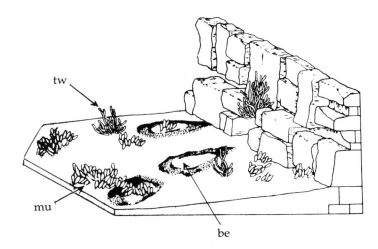

where it meets the relatively impermeable hemipelagic clay of the Missis-sipi Fan. This source supports a dense faunal assemblage, associated with a bacterial mat on the sediment surface, that is 20–30 m wide and at least 1.5 km long (Paull *et al.*, 1984; Hecker, 1985). The community (Fig. 15.13) consists of large mussels up to 19 cm long and a vestimentiferan worm named *Escarpia laminata*. Both animals are apparently supported by chemoautrophic symbiotic bacteria; stable isotope analysis indicating that the living tissues of both *E. laminata* and the mussels contain carbon predominantly derived from oxidation of fossil populations (Cary *et al.*, 1989; Paull *et al.*, 1989). Other epifaunal organisms include the vesico-myid, *Calyptogena*, galatheid crabs, serpulid worms, anemones, stoloni-ferous soft corals, brittle stars, turrid and limpet-like gastropods and shrimps making up a community remarkably similar in composition to that of the E. Pacific hydrothermal vents.

TECTONIC SUBDUCTION ZONE SEEPS

These differ from the hydrothermal vents where the seeping medium is warmed by the close proximity of molten rock. At subduction zones, oceanic crust lies well below the sediment as it is subducted below overlying continental crust along tectonically active continental margins. As a consequence, seepage associated with these areas is more diffuse, and lower in temperature, and is typically rich in dissolved methane.

The first such subduction seep was discovered in the eastern Pacific off Oregon where vent-type fauna including species of *Lamellibrachia* and large vesicomyid bivalves (probably *Vesicomya gigas*) have been dredged from the sediment and where fluids are suspected to seep from rock fissures lying beneath the sediment blanket (Suess *et al.*, 1985; Kulm *et al.*, 1986). Dense concentrations of *Vesicomya gigas* have also been obtained at 2 km depth from sediments in the southern trough of the Guaymas Basin in the Gulf of California where thick *Beggiatoa*-like bacterial mats coat sulphide, and hydrocarbon-saturated, sediment (Grassle *et al.*, 1985).

Here the fluid has to pass through 200–400 m of sediment before reaching the surface as seepage only a few degrees above ambient bottom temperature (2 °C); but in places it emerges as hot springs of up to 350 °C.

JAPANESE SUBDUCTION ZONES

Dense benthic communities dominated by *Calyptogena* clam colonies associated with a lithodid (stone) crab *Paralomis* were found in 1984–85 by the Japanese submersible 'Shinkai 2000' at around 0.8–1.1 km depth in Sagami Bay off Tokyo. The crabs were observed to feed on the blackened sediment in the area probably associated with a cold seepage. Similar assemblages were seen by the new deeper diving French submersible 'Nautile' in 1985 in the course of Franco-Japanese submersible explorations at many of the 50 or so sites of cold, sediment porewater seeps discovered at 3.86–6 km depth in the subduction zones of the trenches off the E. coast of Japan (Bourlegue *et al.,* 1985; Cadet *et al.,* 1985; Laubier, Ohta & Sibuet, 1986; Le Pichon *et al.,* 1987; Ohta & Laubier, 1987). The occurrence of groupings of dead, dissolving *Calyptogena* shells suggests that, like hydrothermal vents, such cold seeps are ephemeral and cyclic. The supporting cast of animals varies from site to site but includes serpulid worms and sea anemones attached to dead shells, motile galatheid crabs and swimming holothurians such as *Peniagone,* along with a large-sized caprellid amphipod. The presence of symbiotic bacteria similar to those of *C. magnifica* in the gills of the two new species of *Calyptogena* present suggest an active sulphur metabolism as the primary energy source, perhaps with sulphides being absorbed by the foot in the sediment and transported to the symbiotic bacteria in the gills via the blood (Fiala-Médioni & Le Pennec, 1988). However, unlike *Calyptogena magnifica* from the hydrothermal vents which is entirely reliant on bacterial symbionts to provide its nutritional needs, these *Calyptogena* species in the subduction-zone sediments seem to retain functional, albeit reduced, digestive tracts. These contain particulate matter including phytoplankton debris, so that such material probably contributes to its nutritional input (Le Pennec & Fiala-Médioni, 1988). Interestingly, of the four species of *Calyptogena* collected at the seeps, up to three were found at the same seep area. Although some limited motility of *Calyptogena* was observed by Ohta & Laubier (1987), which possibly permits migration to new sites nearby, the colony-like groupings of dead shells suggest this is insignificant and that most mortality occurs as a result of old age or the limited duration of active seepage (Juniper & Sibuet, 1987).

Other non-bivalve species seem to represent opportunistic aggregations of omnivorous, deposit- and suspension-feeding species. These are responding to local areas of food enrichment, in the shape of the flesh and organic debris produced by the *Calyptogena* colonies and possibly free-living chemosynthetic microbial productivity in the peripheral sediment. The sites may be subjected to weak porewater seepage, too low to support *Calyptogena,* but providing organically enriched conditions for deposit feeders such as tubicolous polychaetes and *Peniagone* (Juniper & Sibuet, 1987).

It is interesting that the protobranch bivalve *Solemya* found at the Oregon subduction zone, and the lucinacean *Lucinoma* found on the Louisiana Slope, both belong to genera and families with species known elsewhere to harbour symbiotic bacteria in areas that are not likely to be sites of seepage, such as highly organically enriched sediments resulting in anaerobic reducing conditions rich in sulphides and free sulphur, such as seagrass beds and sewage outfalls (Cavanaugh, 1985; Felbeck, 1983; Fisher & Hand, 1984). Furthermore, bivalve families such as the Lucinidae and Thyasiridae include species harbouring symbiotic bacteria in their gills which are most probably sulphur-oxidizing autotrophs (Dando & Southward, 1986), but living in reducing sediments with sometimes barely detectable levels of free sulphide (E. C. Southward, 1986). Clearly, such symbiotic systems along with the development there of extensive microbial chemosynthesis indicate a possible common origin with those associated with tectonic activity.

OTHER DEEP-SEA SEEPAGE SITES

Vent-type organisms have also been observed, by means of deep-sea photography, associated with cold seeps at 1–2.2 km depth just E. of Barbados in the southern termination of the Barbados accretion wedge (Fig. 15.1). (This consists of the material that accumulates before a plate is pushed under another.) Here a 'mud volcano' exists, consisting of an oval crater about 1 km across from whose centre hot, fluidized mud slowly flows upward (providing an escape route for water trapped between the colliding American and Caribbean plates off the W. Indies). The seep community consists of a discontinuous area of colonies dominated by large *Bathymodiolus* and small vesicomyid bivalves with long clusters of vestimentiferan worms up to 2 m long, along with periodic dead-shell accumulations, on a bottom made up of indured mud covered with a ferruginous bacterial mat overlying a carbonate cement (Jollivet *et al.*, 1990).

Dense vent-type communities have also been discovered in 1986 at 3.84–3.89 km depth by observers in 'Alvin' on the Laurentian Fan (Fig. 15.1) on the S.E. Canadian continental margin (Mayer *et al.*, 1988). The community includes vesicomyid and thyasirid bivalves, gastropods, pogonophorans, galatheid crabs and other epifaunal taxa, along with powdery, filamentous bacterial mats covering gravel waves on the seabed, created during the passage of the turbidity current following the 1929 earthquake (see Chapter 2). It seems likely that these communities have become established since 1929, sustained by chemoautotrophic production utilizing reduced compounds present in deep sediments eroded by the current.

THE ORIGIN OF THE VENT-TYPE FAUNA

The taxonomic similarity of cold-seep and hydrothermal vent faunas indicate a common origin and evolutionary history. Indeed, Hecker (1985) suggests that the greater longevity of sites of seepage makes them more likely as the habitats from which the ancestors of these animals may have originally evolved. However, their very fundamental differences from the fauna of the surrounding deep sea suggests an origin from a different source. Their taxonomic similarities to the fauna of reducing sediments and similar adaptations to the toxic sulphide environment, along with microbial symbioses, strongly suggest a common origin of this 'parallel' deep-sea fauna. In fact, many species are now known to occur in a range of reducing habitats in the deep sea, and their occurrence on such ephemeral habitats as a whale skeleton suggests that such oily carcasses (estimated to occur at a density of very roughly one every 300 km^{-2}) may be important 'stepping stones' for the dispersal of deep-sea animals that depend on chemosynthesis (C. R. Smith et al., 1989). Despite the wide diversity of vent biota some sorts, such as sponges, hydroids, corals, gorgonians, antipatharians, bryozoa and echinoderms, that are elsewhere abundant on rocky areas are conspicuous by their absence (although some brittle stars occur at the periphery of vents). Perhaps such taxa are somehow intolerant of physical or chemical conditions at vents (Hessler & Smithey, 1983). Certain taxa are known to be more sensitive than others to metals in hydrothermal fluid: concentrations of a wide suite of metallic species have been found in the gills of Calyptogena that would normally be toxic in shallow-water bivalves (Roesijadi & Crecelius, 1984). The lack of a well-developed vascular system, present in annelid and vestimentiferan worms, crustaceans and molluscs, might also put certain groups at a disadvantage in an environment of markedly varying oxygen supply; the small anemones being the exceptions that prove the rule as actinians are known to be tolerant of anoxic conditions (Sassman & Mangum, 1972). The absence of encrusting colonial coelenterates, such as corals and bryozoans, might be a result of their asexual mode of growth; the lifetime of vents being too short to provide the competitive advantage they enjoy, for example on coral reefs by smothering and inhibiting settlement of competitors (Grassle, 1986). Furthermore, they may be at a distinct disadvantage in lacking motility or even any ability to reorientate their feeding surfaces. Even the bivalves are able to move in order to relocate themselves, Calyptogena by means of a very long foot and Bathymodiolus by means of secretion of byssal threads.

For deep-sea biologists, the discovery of such large-sized and fast-living organisms has finally laid to rest the idea that the increasing pressure and decreasing temperature down the depth gradient alone limit the activity of forms of life in the deep sea. In a wider perspective, such anaerobic chemosynthetic bacterial systems that operate on a global scale in parallel to those depending on photosynthesis may provide insights into conditions and pathways for the origin of life on Earth. Because of the geographical continuity and temporal persistence of spreading centres, despite the constant process of birth, growth and eventual extinction, ocean vents are thought to be an ancient feature of the ocean bottom (Malahoff, 1985). Hence these faunas may well be older than those of the deep sea more familiar to us. Because of this, there has arisen a hypothesis that submarine hot springs were the site for the synthesis of organic compounds leading to the first living organisms on Earth (Corliss, Baross & Hoffman, 1981; Nisbet, 1987). However, Miller &

Bada (1988) argue that such carbon sources exposed to high temperature (exceeding 300 °C) under strongly reducing conditions are unfavourable for the synthesis of biological polymers in aqueous solution. Nevertheless, it is perhaps salutary to ponder that, in the event of the eventual extinction of photosynthetically dependent oceanic and terrestrial life by a nuclear winter, such 'parallel' systems might provide the only hope for continuity of life on this planet.

16
Anthropogenic impacts: Man's effects on the deep sea

The world ocean, with a volume of 137×10^6 km^3, is the largest ecosystem on Earth, and has been used for a variety of purposes by Man for millenia. Many of mankind's uses of the sea are innocuous. Sea routes are still very important for transportation and an important source of food. However, since the industrial revolution it has increasingly become a repository of waste. Owing to its volume and physical properties, the dilution effects are enormous, and, as a result of its chemistry and biology, there is a built-in capacity to recycle much of the deposited waste.

Because of its vast volume and area, the influence of the world ocean on world climate is profound. The phytoplankton of the surface layers regenerate atmospheric oxygen and act as a buffer for CO_2, thus moderating any 'greenhouse' effect. It is the maintenance of this global balance that emphasizes the importance of keeping the integrity of the ocean and not contaminating it to such a level that its 'natural' functions are impaired. However, we must be careful, when considering the disposal of waste, to define what is contamination and what constitutes pollution. GESAMP (1982) defined contamination as 'the introduction of substances into the marine environment which alters the concentration and distribution of substances within the ocean'. Pollution is defined as 'the introduction by Man, directly or indirectly, of substances or energy into the marine environment, resulting in such deleterious effects as harm to living resources, hazards to human health, hindrance to marine activities including fisheries, impairment of quality for use of seawater and reduction of amenities'.

Of necessity, much of Man's exploitation of the ocean has been confined to a relatively narrow band round the coast or on the continental shelf. Exploitation of this zone has been direct or indirect. Although a thorough review of shallow water exploitation is well beyond the scope of this book, it is worth noting some of the main influences for comparison with deep-sea exploitation.

Direct exploitation of the continental shelf includes a wide variety of fisheries and pharmaceuticals, hydrocarbon, placer (superficial ore containing sediment), carbonate, sand and gravel extraction as well as the disposal of sewage sludge, dredge spoil, industrial and medical waste. In addition, these shallow seas have been used for aquaculture, desalination plants, defence, and wave energy-producing programmes.

Indirect contamination of the marine environment can be via the atmosphere or by rivers along which a variety of chemicals including pesticides, SO_2, chlorinated fluorocarbons, radioactive fallout and heavy metals reach the sea.

Much of this waste is retained in shelf waters. In many cases the amount discharged is within the assimilative, or carrying, capacity of the environment, but in a number of cases this contamination becomes pollution (*sensu* GESAMP, 1982). With this background in mind, we can consider what, if any, impact these contaminants have on the deep-sea benthic ecosystem.

As outlined above, the continental shelf has been extensively exploited by Man. In direct contrast, the vast area of the deep-sea floor is the ecosystem least exploited by our species. There is a limited fishery for deep-sea animals (fish and invertebrates) but much of this is still in an exploratory stage. There is also a growing interest in the industrial potential of thermophilic bacteria found at hydrothermal vents. There has been considerable interest in the mining of manganese nodules and other minerals from the deep-sea floor. However, any exploitation of the deep-sea bed is likely to be expensive as ships have to be maintained at sea and the technology developed to raise minerals from very deep water.

It is the very remoteness of the deep sea, both physically and psychologically, which makes it attractive for another anthropogenic influence – the disposal of waste: waste which, for political or safety reasons, is unsuitable for disposal on land or coastal waters, especially where contaminants in the waste may be recycled back to Man.

For both harvesting and waste disposal management, plans have to be developed to utilize the ocean and there is the ever-present problem of conflict of interest that maritime law is trying to clarify. In this chapter, we assess the impact of (*a*) the exploitation of the natural resources in the deep sea and (*b*) the disposal of Man's waste on the ecology of deep-sea organisms.

EXPLOITATION OF NATURAL DEEP-SEA RESOURCES

LIVING RESOURCES

Compared to the continental shelf, the living resources of the deep sea have been exploited to only a very limited extent. This is a function of (*a*) poor knowledge of deep-sea fishery stocks, especially their life history biology (which may make them unsuitable for exploitation); (*b*) low densities of most species; (*c*) the cost of harvesting this wild stock, especially in relation to the investment involved; and (*d*) worries about the sustainability of stocks so remote from their source of primary production.

Amongst deep-sea living resources, the fish present the most exploitable stock, although species of the deep-sea crab *Chaceon* (formerly in the genus *Geryon*), which lives near the shelf break on the upper slope (see Chapter 4), have been taken commercially since 1973 (Wigley & Theroux, 1975; Melville-Smith, 1987). The exploitation of deep-living fish (see Chapter 4), in the main, is still in the assessment stage. A number of slope dwelling and deep mid-water species are trawled in different parts of the world ocean.

The best known of exploited deep-sea fish are the roundnose grenadier *Coryphaenoides rupestris* and the roughhead grenadier *Macrourus berglax*. The stocks of these macrourids are fished mainly by the Soviet fishing fleet in the Arctic and Northwestern Atlantic. The catch, which peaked at 83 800 tonnes a year in the period 1967–78, has been declining ever since, but whether this has been caused by too-intensive fishing or perhaps as the result of long-term cooling of water masses, is still unclear (Atkinson *et al.*, 1982; Savvatimsky, 1987). Data on the distribution, population age structure and life-history biology of these rattails in the northern N. Atlantic is given by Sahrhage (1986), Bergstad & Isaksen (1987) and Bergstad (in press). At abyssal depths the macrourid species *Coryphaenoides (Nematonurus) armatus* and *C. (N.) yaquinae* have been estimated from a population density of about 200 fish km^{-2} to have a global biomass of around 150×10^6 tonnes, which is equivalent to the total annual world commercial fish catch! (I. G. Priede, personal communication).

Around New Zealand and Australia, the orange roughy, *Hoplostethus Atlanticus* (family Trachicthyidae), a benthopelagic fish occurring on the continental slope in many parts of the world, is fished from stocks over seamounts and the Chatham Rise at 0.75 to 1 km where trawlers can sometimes catch 50 tonnes an hour (Merrett, 1989). Although taken as a food source, this species has high levels of wax esters in the muscle and these oils and waxes are used in cosmetics, pharmaceuticals, and in high grade lubricants. These oils have proved a good substitute for sperm whale oil (Wilson, 1982; Merrett & Wheeler, 1983; Lester *et al.*, 1988). The total catch in the mid-1980s was about 42 000 tonnes a year, but there are fears that the stock, comprising mostly large, old fish, may be in decline.

There is also a long-standing fishery in the Pacific for the sablefish, or blackcod, *Anoplopoma fimbria*, which occurs on the upper slope all round the Pacific to 1.5 km, and where it is taken by otter trawl and multihook setlines. This is the only deep-sea fish for which estimates of stock age structure from 'reading' the growth lines in skeletal elements such as scales and otoliths have been validated from recoveries of marked fish that had been released back into the wild. The fish had been 'tagged' some years previously by means of an injection of the antibiotic tetracycline (which leaves a characteristic fluorescent mark at the growing edge of the bones and scales of the fish). The results, which may well also apply to other species where an expansion in fishing is contemplated, indicate the stock includes a number of old, but very slowly growing fish that are much older (in this case a maximum age of approximately 40 yr old) than indicated from counts of otolith growth rings (Beamish & Chilton, 1982).

This indicated that the stock could become quickly depleted of large fish, so that a sustained fishery would not be viable unless carefully regulated.

In the Atlantic there has been a long-standing fishery for the scabbard-fish, *Aphanopus carbo,* using long-lines from small boats fished at depths of 0.75–1 km depth off Madeira. This fish is common in deep water elsewhere in the N.E. Atlantic but is not taken commercially.

It is always possible that pressure will be brought to bear to harvest more of these living resources in the deep sea. However, as most of the potentially commercial stocks occur on the continental slope, they lie within the 200-mile Exclusive Economic Zone (EEZ) of a particular coastal state – which may, or may not, have the will or the necessity to harvest the resource.

Interest in the biotechnological potential of deep-sea thermophilic bacteria has developed quite recently. The ability for natural mass growth of a mat-forming sulphur-reducing *Beggiatoa*-like organism found at the Guaymas Basin vent field (see Chapter 15) has been pointed out by Jannasch *et al. (*1989). Furthermore, a thermophilic bacterial methanogen, isolated from the same site, may have a general significance in the formation of oil at high temperatures and pressures (Huber *et al.,* 1989).

NON-LIVING RESOURCES

The deep sea contains extensive deposits of commercially desirable minerals in various forms. The most well known of these are the ferro-manganese nodules (rich in Co, Ni and Mn) found on the abyssal plains of all oceans (Heath, 1982). In addition to nodules, metalliferous sediments (rich in Zn, Cu, Au, Ag, Co) are found in the Red Sea deep sea (Nawab, 1984) and in massive sulphide deposits found along the mid-ocean ridges (rich in Zn, Cu and Fe) (Francheteau *et al.,* 1979; Bonatti, 1983; Malahoff, 1985). Although similar deposits are found on land, they are not always accessible because of political considerations. What is particularly significant about these deposits is that they contain the so-called 'strategic minerals' which have been argued as essential to the defence industry of many countries. Aside from any environmental constraints, the initial argument has been as to the necessity of mining the deep-sea deposits. This discussion is beyond the scope of this book and the case for and against is argued by Pendley (1982) and Clark (1982).

The environmental impact of deep-sea mining is, however, of great significance as these deposits can cover about 75% of the abyssal central N. Pacific. Here, they typically cover 20–40% of the sediment surface (for excellent photographs, see Heezen & Hollister, 1971). The Clarion–Clipperton Fracture Zone in the Pacific is an area particularly rich in manganese nodules containing the highest concentrations of Co, Ni and Cu (Ross, 1980). What is of concern to us in the context of the biota of the deep sea is that the disturbance created by their collection may profoundly modify the ecology of the environment. In this chapter our discussion is based on the effects of manganese nodule and metalliferous sediment mining, as the exploratory phase of this kind of exploitation is further advanced than other types of deep-sea mining.

Techniques for collecting manganese nodules in water > 3 km are discussed by Smale-Adams & Jackson (1978). Four sorts of systems have been proposed (Fig. 16.1). These include (*a*) a series of buckets dragged over the seabed; (*b*) a remote vehicle crawling over the seabed scooping up nodules which are then passed up as slurry to the mother ship; or (*c*) a remote controlled miner which gathers nodules and deposits them on a semi-submersible platform. In his popular article, Knecht (1982) comments that the mining process will have a detrimental effect on deep-sea benthic ecosystems (Ozturgut *et al.*, 1981; Jumars, 1981; Curtis, 1982). The environmental impact will occur in two phases: first, during the collection of the nodules and, second, during the discharge of tailings from the mother ship.

Ozturgut *et al.* (1981) provide some of the best evidence of the immediate impact of nodule mining on the deep-sea bed. The main effect will be a

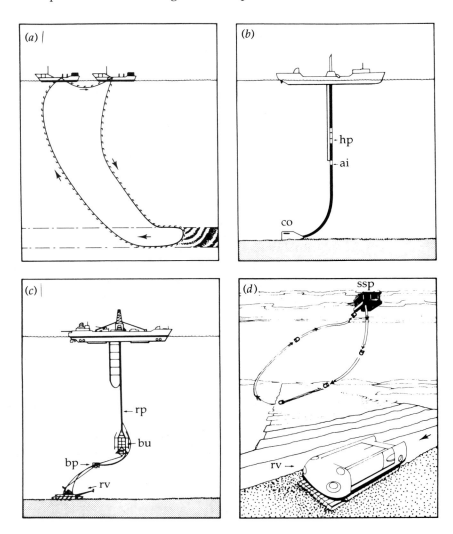

Fig. 16.1. Systems proposed for mining manganese nodules from the abyssal seabed in the Pacific: (*a*) continuous bucket system; (*b*) pump system utilizing compressed air injection (ai) and hydraulic pumps (hp), or an electric pump mounted on the collector (co); (*c*) and (*d*), remote-controlled vehicles, either tethered (*c*) or autonomous (*d*) collector vehicles (rv) that crawl along the bottom scooping up and crushing nodules that in (*c*) are passed as a slurry up a buoyed pipe (bp) to an intermediate station, or buffer (bu), which passes them up to the ship via a rigid pipe (rp). The French concept shown in (*d*) includes a fleet of miner vehicles operating a banded pattern on the seabed, each gathering nodules and depositing them at a semisubmersible platform (ssp) before swooping down again for another load. (After Knecht, 1982.)

result of collector disturbance which removes the nodules, sediment and fauna to a depth of 'several centimetres'. Sedimentary material is pushed to the side of the collector as observed in shallow water dredging. The collector retains the nodules but discharges the remaining sediment and fauna as a suspension onto the surrounding seabed where it forms a thick blanket. The benthic plume produced by the passage of the collector has a sediment concentration 3 to 75 times that of the background suspension. Fine material will be transported downstream in the benthic boundary layer (see Chapter 2). This benthic plume may persist for some days and be transported > 10 km from the collection site (Ozturgut *et al.*, 1981). Curtis (1982) gives perspective to these events by noting that, to retain 1000 tonnes of nodules, a disturbance of 4000 tonnes of sediment is necessary.

To most observers this would suggest a devastating effect on the deep-sea benthos. Although there is evidence of annual recruitment in deep-sea populations (see Chapter 13), the few experiments conducted on recolonization in the deep-sea (Grassle, 1987; Desbruyères *et al.*, 1980; Grassle & Morse-Porteous, 1987) suggest a very slow rate in the re-establishment of the natural benthic community (see Chapter 8). Even if the so-called 'banded pattern' of nodule collection is used, recolonization will potentially take many years and there could be economic pressure to collect every available nodule in an area. Perhaps the only benthic fauna likely to benefit in the short term are the scavengers which will be presented with an increased food supply in the form of animals injured during mining (Jumars, 1981). On a more optimistic note, Jumars (1981) has suggested that a low level of mining activity may increase species diversity by allowing opportunistic species to take up residence in the collector tracks thus supplementing the community not affected by mining. These suggestions are supported by a recent study by G. D. F. Wilson & Hessler (1987), who sampled a small-scale test mining site five years after use and compared it to a control (non-mined) site. They suggested that, immediately after mining, there was an unknown (but potentially measurable) effect on the fauna; but after five years the community had recovered enough that they observed no measurable difference in the fauna at the two sites at the sampling scale used. They concluded that such small-scale test mining had no lasting impact on the deep-sea benthos; but they refused to predict the effect of full-scale mining on the benthic community. Jumars (1981) believed that large-scale mining will have a dramatic local detrimental effect and decrease species diversity.

The physical disturbance may be modified by toxic trace elements released by both collection and processing of the nodules. In addition to the infauna in the sediment, the fauna attached to the nodules itself will be damaged severely (Mullineaux, 1987). The Deep Ocean Mining Environmental Study (DOMES), suggested '(sea) surface discharge of mining waste may result in long-term exposure of marine biota to heavy metals'. Food chain accumulation can magnify this effect, but data are still lacking. However, Ozturgut *et al.* (1981) are in no doubt that, as a result of manganese nodule mining: (*a*) the benthos in the path of the collector will be destroyed; (*b*) nearby benthic organisms will be smothered by settling suspended sediment; (*c*) physiological activities will be modified; and (*d*) that microbial and chemical activity in the lower water column will be changed owing to the suspended material. The suggestion that mining activities are analogous to natural 'catastrophies' such as ash falls or turbidity currents fails to realize that fauna in more unstable areas are modified to disturbance, whereas, in the areas where Mn nodules are mined, such natural disturbance may be highly unusual and the fauna thus more susceptible to environmental perturbations (Jumars, 1981).

The first large-scale experiment to assess the environmental impact used a 8 m wide multiple plough that was towed by the ship to disturb an area of about 8 km^2 in 4.15 km of water S. of the Galapagos Islands in 1989. This German study has only just begun at the time of writing, but future biological monitoring will assess the degree and area of disturbances, and the time taken for the test area to recover to its previous state. This experiment promises to yield information not only of direct relevance to impact assessment of nodule mining, but also of fundamental importance to our understanding of the rôle of disturbance to maintaining the rich diversity of smaller animals living on the deep ocean bed (see Chapter 8).

Recovery of metalliferous sediments in the deeper parts of the Red Sea does not present such an acute environmental problem, as the benthic fauna of the deep Red Sea is exceptionally limited (Thiel, 1979*b*). However, in a preliminary study, Abu Gideiri (1984), has suggested that, even if the discharge of mining tailings is restricted to depths greater than 1.1 km in the Red Sea, at least 2 to 4% of the total seabed below 1.5 km depth will become azoic, although he considered the proportion unaffected would be sufficient to maintain the local species diversity in this area. Abu Gideiri (1984) was concerned also that the benthic fauna would be contaminated by toxic metals associated with the sinking seston from epipelagic and mesopelagic ecosystems. However, the particle size in the Red Sea brines are < 10 μm and will hardly sink at all, thus likely to persist for months or years in the water column, and there subject to basin-wide advection.

Massive sulphide deposits develop as a result of hydrothermal activity (Francheteau *et al.*, 1979). Although the hydrothermal vents have a magnificant fauna (see Chapter 15), active vents are ephemeral and exploitation of the minerals will take place after the extinction of the vent and its community.

WASTE DISPOSAL TO THE DEEP-SEA BED

In the absence of any global policy to reduce the production of waste, pressure to use the deep sea as a repository for waste that ranges from harmless to highly dangerous to Man is growing, owing to political and logistic constraints on terrestrial and coastal environments currently used. Land waste disposal is limited and the near shore waters and the continental shelf, recipient of much waste at present, are important resources of food. They are also limited in area. These factors have led Man to consider the vast unused area that occupies two-thirds of the Earth's surface and apparently contributes virtually nothing to his well-being. Consequently, increasing pressure is being placed on the deep sea as the final repository of unwanted and often dangerous waste. The deep ocean certainly does have a massive assimilative capacity, and certain wastes may find their final resting place here.

On a relatively minor level, anthropogenic waste has been thown into the deep sea since Man started crossing the oceans. Man-made artefacts are found quite regularly in deep-sea photographs (see Heezen & Hollister, 1971) and occasionally form suitable substrates for sessile organisms. Sunken ships (by accident or design), litter the deep-sea floor, the most celebrated being the 'Titanic' recently discovered and photographed on the deep seabed in the N.W. Atlantic. Even after 75 years at 3.0 km depth, very few encrusting animals are found. The age of coal-burning steam-ships was very short (the mid 1800s to the 1940s), yet a remarkable amount of clinker is found in deep-sea samples. Kidd & Huggett (1981), on examining epibenthic sled hauls, found clinker dominating the rock debris and our own hauls on the slope off Lisbon (Portugal), which is a major sea lane, were full of clinker. However, this is waste disposal on a small scale, and has not had a deleterious effect on deep-sea benthic fauna.

On a larger scale, the proximal deep ocean is being used to dispose of:

(i)   dredge spoil
(ii)   sewage sludge
(iii) pharmaceuticals and industrial wastes
(iv)   low level radioactive waste

The disposal of waste into the marine environment is controlled by the 'Convention on the Prevention of Marine Pollution from Dumping of Wastes and other Matter', better known as the 'London Dumping Convention'. This has been in force since 1975 and provides a legal framework (involving 57 countries) to regulate dumping at sea (NEA, 1985).

Deep ocean disposal of dredge spoil   The dredging of marine waterways to the world's major ports is essential to keep open the economic arteries which maintain a nation's wealth. The only review of deep ocean disposal of dredge spoil is by Pequegnat (1983). In this review he considers the social and economic cost of land disposal against sea disposal. His hypothesis is that the deep ocean is capable of assimilating the estimated $< 76 \times 10^6$ m^3 of dredge material with minimal environmental impact. This claim is supported by the ability of the ocean to assimilate considerably higher sediment inputs in the form of turbidity currents and similar events.

If the dredge spoil is carried out to deep water, it will sink naturally.

Much of the very fine material will remain in suspension, almost indefinitely, within the permanent thermocline, and only the coarser material will reach the deep-sea floor. During descent, any change in pH, redox potential or salinity, will absorb or desorb trace materials.

At the deep-sea floor, the sinking sediment produces a bottom cloud and a mound. The bottom cloud, being composed of particles, will give a density surge outwards from the site of bottom contact. As a result of mixing, this cloud is diluted and any associated organic matter is colonized and utilized by heterotrophic bacteria. Dredge spoil is only an environmental problem when heavily contaminated with heavy metals and oil. This contamination precludes dredge spoil from the Hudson, Rhine and Mersey rivers being used for land reclamation.

In one of the very few field studies of the disposal of dredge spoil in offshore waters, Pequegnat (1983) reports the principal ecological effects on the slope organisms was a reduction in species diversity, numbers and biomass. However, within a relatively short time, species diversity and numbers had regained pre-dump levels, although biomass remained depressed. Pequegnat (1983) suggests that, even after major disposal, recolonization of any area may be rapid and cites Turner's (1973) study of the colonization of wood panels (see Chapters 5 and 13). However, the more apposite long-term recolonization studies by Grassle (1977), and Grassle & Morse-Porteous (1987), have shown that defaunated deep-sea sediments take a long time to recolonize. It is possible that the disposal of marine dredge spoil will have a minimal impact on the deep-sea benthos if spread over a large area and time scale, and may well form an acceptable alternative site to land disposal.

Deep ocean disposal of sewage sludge   For many years, especially in coastal communities, it has been policy to discharge treated and untreated sewage directly into the seas. This has led to eutrophication in enclosed areas with a consequent deoxygenation of the water and subsequent detrimental effect on natural benthic populatons. If sewage is treated, there is still the sewage sludge residue, which may contain elevated levels of Cd, Cu, Pb, Hg, Zn and polychlorinated biphenols. These are frequently discarded to the marine environment, especially in nearshore waters or on the continental shelf. Although the importance of separating domestic and industrial sewage is now being recognized, there are now strong pressures to scale down, or discontinue, dumping of sewage on the continental shelf.

As an alternative, the deep sea has been proposed as a possible discharge area for sewage sludge. Off the New England coast, municipal waste from the New York/New Jersey area is now being discharged at a site just beyond the shelf edge in water depths of about 2.7 km (Walker & Paul, 1989). It is argued that sewage has a nutritional value, in terms of fats and proteins, very similar to that of marine detritus (Vaccaro *et al.*, 1981). At present, this form of waste disposal in the deep ocean is still in the exploratory phase but may assume an increasing importance in the future. As we are understanding the natural vertical flux of organic matter to the deep sea (see Chapter 11), it may soon be possible to predict the amount of disposed sludge and the rate at which it will reach the seabed in a particular area. From our knowledge of the present levels of organic matter actually reaching the seabed and its relationship to benthic standing crop (see Chapter 7), it will be possible roughly to predict changes such as biomass increases that may result. Some preliminary calculations by Angel (1988) suggest that sewage sludge could be discharged directly into the deep-sea benthic boundary layer (*c.* the bottom 50 m) using a drain hose from a surface vessel (Fig. 16.2). 10^6 m^3 of sludge (the annual production of the United Kingdom) would cover an area of 600 km^2. In the N.E. Atlantic, the renewal rate of bottom water is thought sufficient to oxidize 150.1^6 tonnes of sewage sludge per year.

The limited evidence available suggests that these two forms of waste disposal into the deep sea may be relatively innocuous under controlled conditions. However, the next two forms of waste disposal have the potential to seriously modify the ecology of deep-sea benthic organisms.

Industrial waste disposal to the deep-sea bed   It is rarely appreciated that many of the everyday manufactured goods we take for granted, as well as modern therapeutic drugs, may be produced at the expense of a toxic

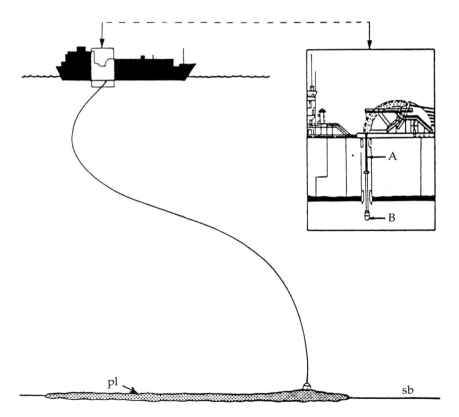

Fig. 16.2. Method proposed by a U.K. company for sewage sludge disposal to the deep ocean. The large tanker discharges sludge via a 45 cm hose to the benthic boundary layer at about 4 km depth where it results in a localized near-bed plume (pl) overlying the seabed (sb). Inset labelling: A, drain hose; B, discharge nozzle. (From Angel, 1988.)

waste byproduct. So far we have dealt with waste within the assimilative capacity of the ocean and of a not dissimilar quality to material naturally entering the ocean. Industrial wastes discharged into the ocean have no natural analogues and the ocean has greater difficulty in recycling them. Such exotic chemicals will accumulate on the seabed with a possible detrimental effect on deep-sea benthos. This aspect of deep ocean waste disposal has been examined thoroughly by Simpson *et al.* (1981). They present data from the Puerto Rico dumpsite in the Puerto Rico Trench and from the 106 mile deepwater dumpsite off the N.E. coast of the United States. Although data from the Puerto Rico dumpsite are limited, the material consisted of pharmaceutical waste including penicillin. Although discharged into the water column, it is possible that penicillin has a detrimental effect on bacterial populations associated with sinking particulates and this increases the POM entering the deep sea. However, this effect is believed to be minimal.

The field studies at the deep-water dumpsite (DWD106) in the N.W. Atlantic (Pearce *et al.*, 1979; Simpson *et al.*, 1981) involved the disposal of various types of waste including both high acid and high alkali, Cr, V, phenol and organo-phosphorus pesticides. Much of the waste was in liquid form and is dispersed initially by the passage of the discharging ship. The accumulation of waste was between the sea surface and the pycnocline. The latter structure may prevent waste reaching the deep-sea floor (Simpson *et al.*, 1981). It may be possible that toxic elements and compounds are adsorbed on to particles which sink to the deep-sea floor and are incorporated into the benthic food chain. In an earlier study, Pearce *et al.* (1979) showed that this waste had no obvious impact on the community structure or heavy metal burdens in the benthic macrofauna. It would seem that, at present, the level of this type of waste disposal is very low and the impact on the benthos at DWD106 minimal.

Radioactive waste disposal in the deep ocean   Of all the discussions of disposal in any environment, the disposal of radioactive waste has generated most emotion. Fortunately, there has been a rational scientific debate on the capacity of the deep ocean to assimilate radioactive waste. Our aim here is to synthesize a brief review of the diverse literature that examines both the effects of that disposal that has taken place and future effects of these long-lived nuclides. In any study of the environmental effect of the disposal of radioactive waste in the deep sea, the effect on benthic organisms is secondary to determining any potential routes by which the radioactive material can get back to Man. The main sources of radionuclides in the sea are weapons testing, nuclear accidents and the direct disposal of low level nuclear waste. In this section we have tried to concentrate on the effects of radionuclides on the fauna of the benthic boundary layer, but, of necessity, one has to consider the wider concept of the deep-sea ecosystem in relation to radioactive waste disposal. The overall capacity for the oceans to absorb radioactive waste is reviewed by Needler & Templeton (1981).

NATURAL RADIONUCLIDE LEVELS IN THE DEEP SEA

For many years it has been widely known that there are elevated levels of radionuclides in the deep-sea sediments (Svedrup, Johnson & Fleming, 1942; Menzies, 1965). Radiolarian oozes have a radium content of 14×10^{-12} g g^{-1} compared to 0.3×10^{-12} g g^{-1} in nearshore sediments (Menzies, 1965). More recently, Woodhead & Pentreath (1983) have estimated dose rates to deep-sea organisms from the natural background. Their data show that the concentration of uranium and thorium in deep-sea sediments is inversely related to the calcium carbonate concentration. Thus the red clays have a higher natural radionuclide content than globigerina ooze. Woodhead & Pentreath (1983) suggest that only ^{230}Th and ^{226}Ra are in excess in the deep-sea sediments when compared with terrestrial rocks and that this excess alpha and beta radiation is likely to affect the microfauna and meiofauna in the sediment and the guts of sediment-swallowing benthic species. In general, the other radionuclides are not significantly different from levels in shallow-water sediments. In addition to radionuclides in sediment, there are enhanced levels of naturally occurring ^{210}Po in the guts of mid-water organisms (Cherry & Heyraud, 1982; Heyraud et al., 1988).

ARTIFICIAL ENHANCEMENT OF RADIONUCLIDES IN THE DEEP SEA – WEAPONS TESTING AND NUCLEAR ACCIDENTS

It is well established that radionuclides from nuclear weapons testing are found in deep-sea sediments (Livingston & Anderson, 1983). As early as 1963, Osterberg et al. (1963) noted the elevated levels of ^{95}Zr, ^{95}Nb, ^{141}Ce and ^{144}Ce in the holothurians Paelopatides and Stichopus from 2.8 km depth off the coast of Oregon. All these radionuclides have short half-lives (maximum of 282 days for ^{144}Ce), suggesting the transport from the surface to deep sea was more rapid than has been previously supposed. The mechanism of this rapid vertical transport has been provided by sediment trap studies (see Chapter 11). Examination of the radionuclides associated with POM collected in sediment traps shows that POM is capable of scavenging plutonium and americium and transporting these elements to the deep sea (Livingston & Anderson, 1983; Fowler et al., 1983). Unexpected evidence of this rapid vertical flux of scavenged radionuclides was presented by the Chernobyl nuclear accident (Buesseler et al., 1987; Fowler et al., 1987). By chance, Fowler and his co-workers had a sediment trap moored at 200 m depth over 2.2 km of water near Calvi, Corsica between 13 April and 21 May 1986, timed to sample over a series of 6.25 day periods. The nuclear accident occurred on 26 April 1986 and fallout entered the sea near Calvi on 4–5 May. On retrieval and examination, the data indicated that the main pulse of radionuclide reached the trap some seven days after the peak fallout, suggesting a sinking rate of 29 m d^{-1}. This vertical flux of radionuclides was confirmed by traps set in the North Sea (Kempe & Nies, 1987) and in the Black Sea (Buesseler et al., 1987). This rapid sinking was a result of the uptake of radionuclide by plankton and the production of faecal pellets that sink rapidly. These serendipitous data confirm the importance of faecal pellets in rapidly transporting radionuclides from surface layers to great depths where they may be taken up by benthic organisms.

ARTIFICIAL ENHANCEMENT OF RADIONUCLIDES IN THE DEEP SEA – WASTE DISPOSAL

Initial impressions suggest that the deep sea is an attractive proposition for the disposal of radioactive waste. It is remote, dilution factors are enormous, and disposal is relatively cheap. The main form of nuclear wastes are:

(i) alpha emitters – usually associated with nuclear fuel processes and have the most densely ionizing radiation, e.g. americium and plutonium.

(ii) beta emitters – four main sources are found (NEA, 1985): (a) plutonium from reprocessing nuclear fuel; (b) routine power plant operations produce ^{90}Sr, ^{137}Cs; (c) industrial and academic research, e.g. ^{14}C and ^{124}I mainly as laboratory rubbish; (d) redundant nuclear plant.

(iii) tritium waste (^3H) usually in the form of labelled compounds used in medicines or research.

At present only low level radioactive waste has been discharged at deep-sea dump sites. This waste disposal is highly regulated and carefully monitored. In the N.E. Atlantic there is a dumpsite at approx. 46° N, 17° W which has received packaged, low-level nuclear waste for over 20 years. The results of site monitoring and modelling of future disposal based on these results are reviewed by the Nuclear Energy Agency (NEA) (1985). Although this document examines the effects of radionuclides on marine organisms, it is primarily concerned with tracing potential pathways from the deep-sea dump back to Man.

Using the N.E. Atlantic Dumpsite (NEADS) as a case study, the wastes being disposed of are low-level wastes from nuclear power stations and scientific and medical work. All the material is packaged in steel drums or concrete containers which provide shielding and prevent waste escape.

NEADS has been in existence since 1967 and the current site is a rectangle 45° 59′ to 46° 10′ N by 16° to 17° 30′ W. The main features which resulted in the selection of this site are that it is too deep for trawling (> 2000 m), it is free of undersea cables, relatively near the land (thus avoiding costly steaming), yet sufficiently far from the continental margin to be unaffected by downslope processes such as turbidity currents. The mean depth is 4.4 km and the sediment in the area is 350 to 370 m thick consisting of marl facies. Owing to the nature of the BBL, it might be thought that waste released at the dumpsite will enter a narrow zone above the bottom only. However, recent work on the effect on BBL hydrodynamics by propagation of eddy vorticity to the deep-sea bed (see Chapter 2) suggests that, in the long term, it is unwise to assume that dissolved waste released into the BBL will be trapped permanently in a narrow zone above the bottom. The natural fauna at the NEAD site is relatively depleted and consists of coelenterates, polychaetes, cirripedes, brachiopods, bivalves, ophiuroids, holothurians and tunicates (NEA, 1985). A dummy drum has been in place at the site for over three years, and during this period no organisms have attached themselves to it, suggesting a paucity of potential fouling organisms in this area.

RADIONUCLIDES AND THE BENTHIC FAUNA AT NEADS

Evidence for the occurrence of a wide range of radionuclides from the dumpsite area suggest that the short-lived radionuclides found in the local invertebrates originated as fallout from the atmospheric testing of nuclear weapons whereas there were no significant differences in radionuclide content between NEADS and a control site. However, a single exception was the anemone *Chitoanthus abyssorum*, in which the levels of ^{90}Sr and ^{137}Cs increased between 1966 and 1980 possibly owing to a waste container leakage.

Experimental uptake by shallow-water organisms of sediment from the NEADS site has been studied by Vangenechten *et al.* (1983). These authors noted that the uptake of ^{241}Am was more rapid in the polychaete *Hermione hystrix* than in the isopod *Cirolana borealis* or the bivalve *Venerupis decussata,* suggesting that, if available, this radionuclide is bioavailable.

There are still unknown factors that may affect the activity and transport of radionuclides at the dumpsite. The effect of bioturbation on radionuclide mobility and the effect of radionuclides on genetics and physiological processes, including reproduction, are still unclear.

However, the question of the potential transfer of radionuclides back to Man is better understood. The evidence suggests radionuclides can enter the deep sea (by particle flux) more easily than they can leave it; but over a long time period (and some half-lives are very long), a possible transfer mechanism may achieve completion. The NEADS study (NEA, 1985) concluded that it was highly unlikely that any such material could be transported through the food chains and reach Man in any dose more than a number of orders of magnitude lower than the permitted dose of 1 mSv yr^{-1}.

All the evidence to date has considered the disposal of low level radioactive waste. The next phase would have been the disposal of intermediate and high-level waste by embedding the waste containers deep in the sediment (Freeman *et al.,* 1984). Some of the implications of accidental exposure to the benthos are considered by Hessler & Jumars (1977, 1979). Although there has been an active research programme concerning the technology and environmental effects of high-level radioactive waste disposal, political pressures at the time of writing (1989) have halted the programme for the disposal of radioactive waste in the deep sea.

Thus the deep sea can be classified along with the other great wilderness areas of the Earth, and exploitation of its resources should not be attempted until we fully understand the natural history and ecology of this complex ecosystem.

References

Abele, L. G. & Walters, K. (1979). Marine benthic diversity: a critique and alternative parameters. *Journal of Biogeography*, **6**, 115–26.

Abu Gideiri, Y. B. (1984). Impacts of mining on central Red Sea environment. *Deep-Sea Research*, **31A**, 823–31.

Agassiz, A. (1888). *Three Cruises of the United States Coast and Geodetic Survey Steamer 'Blake'*. 2 vols. London: Sampson Low, Marston, Searle & Rivington.

Ahlfeld, T. E. (1977). A disparate seasonal study of reproduction of eight deep-sea megainvertebrate species from the NW Atlantic Ocean. Unpublished Ph.D. Thesis, Florida State University, 105 pp.

Åkesson, B. (1961). Some observations on *Pelagosphaera* larvae (Sipunculoidea). *Galathea Report*, **5**, 7–17.

Aldred, R. G., Thurston, M. H., Rice, A. L. & Morley, D. R. (1976). An acoustically monitored opening and closing epibenthic sledge. *Deep-Sea Research*, **23**, 167–74.

Aldred, R. G., Riemann-Zurneck, K., Thiel, H. & Rice, A. L. (1982). Ecological observations on the deep-sea anemone *Actinoscyphia aurelia*. *Oceanologica Acta*, **2**, 389–95.

Alldredge, A. L. & Gotschalk, C. C. (1989). Direct observations of mass flocculations of diatom blooms: characteristics, settling velocities and formation of diatom aggregates. *Deep-sea Research*, **36A**, 159–73.

Alldredge, A. L. & Silver, M. W. (1988). Characteristics, dynamics and significance of marine snow. *Progress in Oceanography*, **20**, 41–82.

Allen, J. A. (1958). On the basic form and adaptations to habitat in the Lucinacea (Eulamellibranchia). *Philosophical Transactions of the Royal Society of London*, Series B, **241**, 421–84.

(1978). Evolution of the deep sea protobranch bivalves. *Philosophical Transactions of the Royal Society of London*, Series B, **284**, 387–401.

(1979). The adaptations and radiation of deep-sea bivalves. *Sarsia*, **64**, 19–27.

(1983). The ecology of the deep-sea Mollusca. In *The Mollusca*, Vol. 6, ed. W. D. Russell-Hunter, pp. 29–75. London: Academic Press.

(1985). The recent Bivalvia: their form and evolution. In *The Molluscs*, Vol. 10, *Evolution*, eds E. R. Trueman & M. R. Clarke, pp. 337–403. Orlando: Academic Press.

Allen, J. A. & Morgan, R. E. (1981). The functional morphology of Atlantic deep-water species of the families Cuspidaria and Poromyidae (Bivalvia): an analysis of the evolution of the septibranch condition. *Philosophical Transactions of the Royal Society of London*, Series B, **294**, 413–546.

Allen, J. A. & Sanders, H. L. (1966). Adaptations to abyssal life as shown by the bivalve *Abra profundorum*. *Deep-Sea Research*, **13**, 1175–84.

(1973). Studies on deep-sea Protobranchia (Bivalvia); prologue and the Pristiglomidae. *Bulletin of the Museum of Comparative Zoology of Harvard College*, **145**, 237–62.

Allen, J. A. & Turner, J. F. (1974). On the functional morphology of the family Verticordiidae (Bivalvia) with descriptions of a new species from the abyssal Atlantic. *Philosophical Transactions of the Royal Society of London*, Series B, **268**, 401–536.

Allen, J. R. L. (1970). *Physical Processes of Sedimentation*. London: Unwin University Books.

Aller, J. Y. (1989). Quantifying sediment disturbances by bottom currents and its effect on benthic communities in a deep-sea western boundary zone. *Deep-Sea Research*, **36A**, 901–34.

Aller, J. Y. & Aller, R. C. (1986). Evidence for localized enhancement of biological activity associated with tube and burrow structures in deep-sea sediments at the HEBBLE site, western North Atlantic. *Deep-Sea Research*, **33A**, 755–90.

Aller, R. C. (1982). The effects of macrobenthos on chemical properties of marine sediment and overlying water. In *Animal–Sediment Relations: the Biogenic Alteration of Sediments*, eds P. L. McCall & M. J. S. Tevesz, pp. 53–102. New York: Plenum Press.

Aller, R. C. & Yingst, J. Y. (1978). Biogeochemistry of tube-dwellings: a study of the sedentary polychaete *Amphitrite ornata*. *Journal of Marine Research*, **36**, 201–54.

(1985). Effects of the marine deposit-feeders *Heteromastus filiformis* (Polychaeta), *Macoma balthica* (Bivalvia), and *Tellina texana* (Bivalvia) on averaged sedimentary solute transport, reaction rates, and microbial distributions. *Journal of Marine Research*, **43**, 615–45.

Almaça, C. (1982). Marine slides and allopatric speciation. In *Marine Slides and Other Mass Movements*, eds S. Saxov & J. K. Nieuwehuis, pp. 325–34. New York: Plenum Press.

Alongi, D. M. (1987). The description and composition of deep-sea microbenthos in a bathyal region of the western Coral Sea. *Deep-Sea Research*, **34A**, 1245–54.

(1990). Bacterial growth rates, production and estimates of detrital carbon utilization in deep-sea sediments of the Solomon and Coral Seas. *Deep-Sea Research*, **37A**, 731–46.

Alongi, D. M. & Pichon, M. (1988). Bathyal meiobenthos of the western Coral Sea: distribution and abundance in relation to microbial standing stocks and environmental factors. *Deep-Sea Research*, **35A**, 491–503.

Alton, M. S. (1966). Bathymetric distribution of sea stars (Asteroidea) off the northern Oregon coast. *Journal of the Fisheries Research Board of Canada*, **23**, 1673–714.

Ambler, J. W. (1980). Species of *Munidopsis* (Crustacea, Galatheidae) occurring off Oregon and in adjacent waters. *Fishery Bulletin*, **78**, 13–34.

Anderson, R. C. & Meadows, P. C. (1978). The importance of diffusive permeability of animal burrow linings in determining marine sediment chemistry. *Journal of Marine Research*, **41**, 299–322.

Andrew, N. L. & Mapstone, B. D. (1987). Sampling and the description of spatial pattern in marine ecology. *Oceanography and Marine Biology: an Annual Review*, **25**, 39–90.

Angel, M. V. (1984). Detrital organic fluxes through pelagic ecosystems. In *Flows of Energy and Materials in Marine Ecosystems*, ed. M. J. Fasham, pp. 475–516. London: Plenum Press.

  (1988). The deep-ocean option for the disposal of sewage sludge. *The Environmentalist*, **8(1)**, 19–26.

Angel, M. V. & Baker, A. de C. (1982). Vertical distribution of the standing crop of plankton and micronekton at three stations in the Northeast Atlantic. *Biological Oceanography*, **2**, 1–30.

Angel, M. V., Fasham, M. J. R. & Rice, A. L. (1981). Marine biology needed to assess the safety of a program of disposal of high-level radioactive waste in the ocean. In *Marine Environment Pollution*, Vol. 2. *Mining and Dumping*, ed. R. A. Geyer, pp. 297–312. Amsterdam: Elsevier.

Anikouchine, W. A. & Sternberg, R. N. (1973) *The World Ocean: An Introduction to Oceanography*. Englewood Cliffs, New Jersey: Prentice-Hall.

Anonymous (1979). Strange world without sun. *National Geographic Magazine*, **156**, 680–8.

Armi, L. & Millard, R. C. (1976). The bottom boundary layer in the deep ocean. *Journal of Geophysical Research*, **81**, 4983–90.

Arnaud, F. & Bamber, R. N. (1987). The biology of Pycnogonida. *Advances in Marine Biology*, **24**, 1–96.

Arp, A. J., Childress, J. J. & Fisher, C. R. (1984). Metabolic and blood gas transport characteristics of the hydrothermal vent bivalve. *Calyptogena magnifica*. *Physiological Zoology*, **57**, 648–62.

Atkinson, D. B., Bowering, W. R., Parsons, D. G., Horsted, S. A. & Minet, J. P. (1982). A review of the biology and fisheries for roundnose grenadier, Greenland halibut and northern shrimp in Davis Strait. *NAFO Scientific Council Studies*, **3**, 7–27.

Atkinson, R. J. A. (1986). Mud-burrowing megafauna in the Clyde Sea Area. *Proceedings of the Royal Society of Edinburgh*, **90B**, 351–61.

Ayala, F. J. & Valentine, J. W. (1974). Genetic variability in the cosmopolitan deep-water ophiuran *Ophiomusium lymani*. *Marine Biology*, **27**, 51–7.

Băcescu, M. (1985). Apseudoidea (Crustacés, Tanaidacea). In *Peuplements Profonds du Golfe de Gascogne*, eds L. Laubier & C. Monniot, pp. 435–40. Brest: Institut Français de Recherche pour l'Exploitation de la Mer.

Backus, R. H. (1966). The 'pinger' as an aid to deep trawling. *Journal du Conseil Permanent International pour Exploration de la Mer*, **30**, 270–7.

Backus, R. H., Mead, G. L., Haedrich, R. L. & Ebeling, A. W. (1965). The mesopelagic fishes collected during cruise 17 of the R/V Chain, with a method for analyzing faunal transects. *Bulletin of the Museum of Comparative Zoology, Harvard*, **134**, 139–58.

Baird, B. H., Nivens, D. E., Parker, J. H. & White, D. C. (1985). The biomass, community structure, and spatial distribution of the sedimentary microbiota from a high-energy area of the deep sea. *Deep-Sea Research*, **32A**, 1089–99.

Baldwin, R. J. & Smith, K. L. (1987). Temporal variation in the catch rate, length, color and sex of the necrophagous amphipod *Eurythenes gryllus* from the central and eastern North Pacific. *Deep-Sea Research* **34A**, 425–39.

Ballard, R. D. (1975). Photography from a submersible during project FAMOUS. *Oceanus*, **18**, 31–9.

  (1982). Argo and Jason. *Oceanus*, **25**, 30–5.

Ballard, R. D., van Andel, T. H. & Holcomb, R. T. (1982). The Galapagos Rift at 86° W: 5. Variations in volcanism, structure, and hydrothermal activity along a 30-kilometer segment of the rift valley. *Journal of Geophysical Research*, **87**, 1149–61.

Ballard, R. D., Hekinian, R. & Francheteau, J. (1984). Geological setting of hydrothermal activity at 12°50′ N on the East Pacific Rise: A submersible study. *Earth and Planetary Science Letters*, **69**, 176–86.

Bambach, R. K. (1977). Species richness in marine benthic assemblages throughout the Phanerozoic. *Paleobiology*, **3**, 152–7.

Bandel, K. & Leich, H. (1986). Jurassic Vampyromorpha (dibrachiate cephalopods). *Neues Jahrbuch für Geolologie und Paläontologie. Monatshefte*, **1986**, 129–48.

Bandy, O. (1965). The pinger as a deep water grab control. *Undersea Technology*, **6**, 36.

Banks, D. A. (1985). A fossil hydrothermal worm assemblage from the Tynagh lead-zinc deposit in Ireland. *Nature, London*, **313**, 128–31.

Barham, E., Ayer, N. J. & Boyce, R. E. (1967). Megabenthos of the San Diego Trough: photographic census and observations from the bathyscaphe Trieste. *Deep-Sea Research*, **14**, 773–84.

Barnard, J. L. (1961). Gammaridean Amphipoda from depths of 400 to 6000 meters. *Galathea Report*, **5**, 23–128.

  (1962). South Atlantic abyssal amphipods collected by R. V. Vema. Abyssal Crustacea. *Vema Research Series (Columbia University, New York)*, **1**, 1–78.

  (1969). The families and genera of marine gammaridean Amphipoda. *Bulletin of the U.S. National Museum*, **271**, 1–535.

(1971). Gammaridean Amphipoda from a deep-sea transect off Oregon. *Smithsonian Contributions to Zoology*, No. 61, 86 pp.

(1973). Deep-sea Amphipoda of the Genus *Lepechinella* (Crustacea). *Smithsonian Contributions to Zoology*, No. 133, 30 pp.

Barnard, J. L. & Hartman, O. (1959). The sea bottom off Santa Barbara, California: biomass and community structure. *Pacific Naturalist*, **1**, 6.

Barnard, J. L. & Ingram, C. L. (1986). The supergiant amphipod *Alicella gigantea* Chevreux from the North Pacific Gyre. *Journal of Crustacean Biology*, **6**, 825–39.

Barnes, A. T., Quetin, L. B., Childress, J. J. & Pawson, D. L. (1976). Deep-sea macroplanktonic sea cucumbers: suspended sediment feeders captured from deep submergence vehicle. *Science, Washington*, **194**, 1083–5.

Barnett, P. R. O., Watson, J. & Connelly, D. (1984). The multiple corer for taking virtually undisturbed samples from shelf, bathyal and abyssal sediments. *Oceanologica Acta*, **7**, 399–408.

Barnett, V. (1974). *Elements of Sampling Theory*. London: English Universities Press.

Bartsch, G. M. (1988). Deep-sea halacarids (Acari) and descriptions of new species. *Journal of Natural History*, **22**, 811–21.

Beamish, R. J. & Chilton, D. E. (1982). Preliminary evaluation of a method to determine the age of sablefish (*Anopoploma fimbria*). *Canadian Journal of Fisheries and Aquatic Sciences*, **39**, 277–87.

Belyaev, G. M. (1966). Bottom Fauna of the Ultra-abyssal of the World Ocean. Moscow: Institute of Oceanology, USSR Academy of Sciences (in Russian, translated by Israel Program for Scientific Translations, Jerusalem 1972).

(1970). Ultra-abyssal holothurians of the genus *Myriotrochus* (order Apoda, fam. Myriotrochidae). *Trudỹ Instituta Okeanologii*, **86**, 458–88 (in Russian).

(1989). *Deep-sea Oceanic Trenches and their Fauna*. Moscow: Institute of Oceanology, USSR Academy of Sciences (in Russian).

Belyaev, G. M. & Mironov, A. N. (1977). Bottom fauna of the West Pacific deep-sea trenches. *Trudỹ Instituta Okeanologii*, **108**, 7–24 (in Russian, English summary).

Belyaev, G. M. & Vilenkin, B. Y. (1983). Species diversity of the bottom fauna in deep-sea trenches. *Okeanologyia*, **23**, 150–4 (in Russian, English summary).

Belyaev, G. M., Vinogradova, N. G., Levenshyteyn, N. G., Pasternak, F. A., Sokolova, M. N. & Filatova, Z. A. (1973). Distribution patterns of deep-water bottom fauna related to the idea of the biological structure of the ocean. *Oceanology*, **13**, 114–20 (English translation of *Okeanologiya*).

Bender, K. & Davis, W. R. (1984). The effect of feeding by *Yoldia limatula* on bioturbation. *Ophelia*, **23**, 91–100.

Bensoussan, M. G., Scoditti, P.-M. & Bianchi, A. J. M. (1979). Étude comparative des potentialités cataboliques de microflores entériques d'échinodermes et des sédiments superficiels prelevées en milieu abyssal. *Compte rendu hebdomadaire des séances de l'Académie des sciences, Paris* (Série D), **289**, 437–40.

(1984). Bacterial flora from echinoderm guts and associated sediment in the abyssal Vema Fault. *Marine Biology*, **79**, 1–10.

Berg, C. J. (1985). Reproductive strategies of mollusks from abyssal hydrothermal vent communities. *Bulletin of the Biological Society of Washington*, **6**, 185–97.

Berg, C. J. & Van Dover, C. L. (1987). Benthopelagic macrozooplankton communities at and near deep-sea hydrothermal vents in the eastern Pacific Ocean and Gulf of California. *Deep-Sea Research*, **34A**, 379–401.

Berger, W. H., Bé, A. W. H. & Vincent, E. (eds) (1979/81). Oxygen and carbon isotopes in Foraminifera. *Palaeogeography, Palaeoclimatology, Palaeoecology*, **33** (1/3), 1–277.

Berger, W. H., Ekdale, A. A. & Bryant, P. P. (1979). Selective preservation of burrows in deep-sea carbonates. *Marine Geology*, **32**, 205–30.

Berger, W. H. & Heath, G. R. (1968). Vertical mixing in pelagic sediments. *Journal of Marine Research*, **26**, 134–43.

Berger, W. H., Vincent, E. & Thierstein, H. R. (1981). The deep-sea record: major steps in Cenozoic ocean evolution. *Special Publications. Society of Economic Paleontologists and Mineralogists, Tulsa*, **32**, 489–504.

Bergstad, O. A. (1990). Distribution, population structure, growth and reproduction of the roundnose grenadier *Coryphaenoides rupestris* (Pisces: Macrouridae) in the deep waters of the Skagerrak. *Marine Biology*, **107**, 25–39.

Bergstad, O. A. & Isaksen, B. (1987). Deep-water resources of the Northeast Atlantic: distribution, abundance and exploitation. *Fisken og Havet*, 1987(3), 1–56.

Berner, R. A. (1976). The benthic boundary layer from the point of view of a geochemist. In *The Benthic Boundary Layer*, ed. I. N. McCave, pp. 33–55. New York: Plenum Press.

Bernstein, B. B. & Meador, J. P. (1979). Temporal persistence of biological patch structure in an abyssal benthic community. *Marine Biology*, **51**, 179–83.

Bernstein, B. B., Hessler, R. R., Smith, R. & Jumars, P. A. (1978). Spatial distribution of benthic Foraminifera in the central North Pacific. *Limnology and Oceanography*, **23**, 401–16.

Betzer, P. R., Showers, W. J., Laws, E. A., Winn, C. D., DiTullio, G. R. & Kroopnick, P. M. (1984). Primary productivity and particle fluxes on a transect of the equator at 153° West in the Pacific Ocean. *Deep-Sea Research*, **31A**, 1–11.

Bianchi, A. J., Bianchi, M., Scoditti, P. M. & Bensoussan, M. G. (1979). Distributions des populations bactériennes hétérotrophes dans les sédiments et les tractus digestifs d'animaux benthiques recueilles dans la faille Vema et les plaines abyssales du Demerara et de la Gambie. *Vie Marine*, **1**, 7–12.

Billett, D. S. M. Deep-sea holothurians. *Oceanography and Marine Biology: an Annual Review* (in press).

Billett, D. S. & Hansen, B. (1982). Abyssal aggregations of *Kolga hyalina* Danielssen and Koren (Echinodermata: Holothuroidea) in the northeast Atlantic Ocean. *Deep-Sea Research*, **29A**, 799–818.

Billett, D. S. M., Hansen, B. & Huggett, Q. (1985). Pelagic Holothurioidea (Echinodermata) of the northeast Atlantic. In *Echinodermata*, eds B. F. Keegan & D. S. O'Connor, pp. 399–411. Rotterdam: Balkema.

Billett, D. S. M., Lampitt, R. S., Rice, A. L. & Mantoura, R. F. C. (1983). Seasonal sedimentation of phytoplankton to the deep-sea benthos. *Nature, London*, **302**, 520–2.

Billett, D. S. M., Llewellyn, C. & Watson, J. (1988). Are deep-sea holothurians selective feeders? In *Echinoderm Biology*, eds R. D. Burke, P. V. Mladenov, P. Lambert & R. L. Parsley, pp. 421–9. Rotterdam: Balkema.

Bird, G. J. & Holdich, D. M. (1985). A remarkable tubicolous tanaid (Crustacea: Tanaidacea) from the Rockall Trough. *Journal of the Marine Biological Association of the United Kingdom*, **65**, 563–72.

Birstein, Y. A. (1957). Certain peculiarities of the ultra-abyssal fauna at the example of the genus *Storthyngura* (Crustacea Isopoda Asellota). *Zoologicheskii Zhurnal*, **36**, 961–85 (in Russian, English summary).

Birstein, Y. A. & Zarenkov, N. A. (1970). On the bottom decapods (Crustacea, Decapoda) of the Kurile-Kamchatka region. *Trudy̆ Institut Okeanologii*, SSSR, **86**, 420–6 (in Russian, translated by Israel Program for Scientific Translations, Jerusalem 1972).

Bishop, J. D. D. (1981). A revised definition of the genus *Epileucon* Jones (Crustacea, Cumacea) with descriptions of species from the deep Atlantic. *Philosophical Transactions of the Royal Society of London*, Series B, **291**, 353–409.

(1982). The growth, development and reproduction of deep-sea cumaceans (Crustacea: Peracarida). *Zoological Journal of the Linnaean Society*, **4**, 359–80.

Bisol, P. M., Costa, R. & Sibuet, M. (1984). Ecological and genetic survey of two deep-sea holothurians: *Benthogone rosea* and *Benthodytes typica*. *Marine Ecology – Progress Series*, **15**, 275–81.

Bitter, P. H., Scott, S. D. & Schenk, P. E. (1990). Early carboniferous low-temperature hydrothermal vent communities from Newfoundland. *Nature, London*, **344**, 145–8.

Blake, J. A. (1985). Polychaeta from the vicinity of deep-sea geothermal vents in the eastern Pacific. I. Euphrosinidae, Phyllodocidae, Hesionidae, Nereidae, Glyceridae, Dorvilleidae, Orbiniidae and Maldanidae. *Bulletin of the Biological Society of Washington*, **6**, 67–101.

Blake, J. A., Hecker, B., Grassle, J. F., Brown, B., Wade, M., Boehm, P.

D., Baptiste, E., Hilbig, B., Maciolek, N., Petrecca, R., Ruff, R. E., Starczak, V. & Watling, L. (1987). Study of Biological Processes on the U.S. South Atlantic Slope and Rise. Phase 2. Final Report prepared for U.S. Department of the Interior Mineral Management Service, Washington, D.C., 414 pp. + Appendices A–M.

Bodin, P. (1968). Copépodes harpacticoides des étages bathyal et abyssal du Golfe de Gascogne. *Mémoires du Muséum National d'histoire naturelle, Paris*, Série A, Zoologie, **55(1)**, 1–107.

Bonatti, E. (1983). Hydrothermal metal deposits from the Oceanic Rifts: A classification. In *Hydrothermal Processes at Seafloor Spreading Centres*, eds P. A. Rona, K. Bostrom, L. Laubier & K. L. Smith Jr, pp. 491–502. Plenum Press.

Bone, Q. & Roberts, B. L. (1969). The density of elasmobranchs. *Journal of the Marine Biological Association of the United Kingdom*, **49**, 913–37.

Booth, D. A. & Gage, J. D. (1980). On minimizing warp payout in deep-sea trawling. Unpublished report. Dunstaffnage Marine Research Laboratory, Scottish Marine Biological Association.

Bouchet, P. (1976*a*). Mise en évidence d'une migration de larves véligères entre l'étage abyssal et la surface. *Comptes rendu hebdomadaire des séances de l'Académie des sciences, Paris (Sér. D)*, **283**, 821–4.

(1976*b*). Mise en évidence de stades larvaires planctoniques chez des Gastéropodes Prosobranches des étages bathyal et abyssal. *Bulletin du Museum National d'histoire naturelle, Paris (Sér. 3)*, No. 400, Zoologie, **277**, 947–71.

Bouchet, P. & Fontes, J-C. (1981). Migrations verticales des larves de Gastéropodes abyssaux: arguments nouveaux à l'analyse isotopique de la coquille larvaire et postlarvaire. *Comptes rendu hebdomadaire des séances de l'Académie des sciences, Paris*, **292**, 1005–8.

Bouchet, P. & Warén, A. (1979*a*). Planktotrophic larval development in deep water gastropods. *Sarsia*, **64**, 37–40.

(1979*b*). The abyssal molluscan fauna of the Norwegian Sea and its relation to other faunas. *Sarsia*, **64**, 211–43.

(1980). Revision of the Northeast Atlantic bathyal and abyssal Turridae (Mollusca: Gastropoda). *Journal of Molluscan Studies, Supplement* **8**, 1–116.

(1985). Revision of the northeast Atlantic bathyal and abyssal Neogastropoda excluding Turridae (Mollusca, Gastropoda). *Bollettino Malacologico, Supplemento* **1**, 122–296.

(1986). Revision of the northeast Atlantic bathyal and abyssal Aclididae, Eulimidae, Epitonidae (Mollusca, Gastropoda). *Bollettino Malacologico, Supplemento* **2**, 288–576.

Boudreau, B. P. (1986*a*). Mathematics of tracer mixing in sediments: I. Spatially dependent, diffusive mixing. *American Journal of Science*, **226**, 161–98.

(1986*b*). Mathematics of tracer mixing in sediments: II. Nonlocal mixing and biological conveyer-belt phenomena. *American Journal of Science*, **286**, 199–238.

Bouma, A. H. (1969). *Methods for the Study of Sedimentary Structures*. New York: John Wiley.

Bourlegue, J., Le Pichon, X. & Iiyama, J. T. (1985). Prévision des tremblements de terre dans la région de Tokai (Japon). *Compte rendus hebdomadaires des séances de l'Académie des sciences, Paris (Sér. II)*, **16**, 1217–19.

Bourne, D. W. & Heezen, B. C. (1965). A wandering enteropneust from the abyssal Pacific, and the distribution of 'spiral' tracks on the sea floor. *Science, Washington*, **150**, 60–3.

Bowman, K. O., Hutcheson, K., Odum, E. P. & Shenton, L. R. (1969). Comment on the distribution of indices of diversity. In *Statistical Ecology*, Vol. 3, eds G. P. Patil, E. C. Pielou & W. E. Waters, pp. 315–59. Pennsylvania State University Press.

Bowman, T. E. & Manning, R. B. (1972). Two arctic bathyal crustaceans: the shrimp *Bythocaris cryonesus* new species, and the amphipod *Eurythenes gryllus*, with *in situ* photographs from Ice Island T-3. *Crustaceana*, **23**, 187–201.

Bramlette, M. N. & Bradley, W. H. (1942). Lithology and geological interpretations. *In Geology and Biology of North Atlantic Deep-sea Cores*. U.S. Geological Survey Professional Paper 196, 34 pp.

Breen, P. A. & Shields, T. L. (1983). Age and size structure in five populations of geoduck clam (*Panope generosa*) in British Columbia. *Canadian Technical Report of Fisheries and Aquatic Sciences*, no. 1169, 62 pp.

Briggs, K. (1985). Deposit feeding by some deep-sea megabenthos from the Venezuela Basin: selective or non-selective. *Marine Ecology – Progress Series*, **21**, 127–34.

Brooks, J. M., Kennicutt II, M. C., Birdigare, R. R. & Fay, R. R. (1985). Hydrates, oil seepage, and chemosynthetic ecosystems on the Gulf of Mexico slope. *EOS*, **66**, 106.

Brooks, J. M., Kennicutt II, M. C., Fisher, C. R., Macko, S. A., Cole, K., Childress, J. J., Bidigare, R. R. & Vetter, R. D. (1987). Deep-sea hydrocarbon seep communities; evidence for energy and nutritional carbon sources. *Science, Washington*, **238**, 1138–42.

Brown, J. H. & Maurer, B. A. (1986). Body size, ecological dominance and Cope's rule. *Nature, London*, **324**, 248–50.

Brundage, W. L., Buchanan, C. L. & Patterson, R. B. (1967). Search and serendipity. In *Deep-Sea Photography*, ed. J. B. Hersey, pp. 75–87. Baltimore: Johns Hopkins Press.

Bruun, A. F. (1937). Contributions to the life histories of the deep sea eels: Synaphobranchidae. *Dana Report*, No. 9, 31 pp.
    (1956). The abyssal fauna: its ecology, distribution and origin. *Nature, London*, **177**, 1105–8.
    (1957). Deep sea and abyssal depths. *Geological Society of America Memoir*, **67(1)**, 641–72.

Bucklin, A., Wilson, R. R. & Smith, K. L. (1987). Genetic differentiation of seamount and basin populations of the deep-sea amphipod *Eurythenes gryllus*. *Deep-Sea Research*, **34A**, 1795–810.

Buesseler, K. O., Livingston, H. D., Honjo, S., Hay, B. J., Manganini, S. J., Degens, E., Ittekkot, V., Izdar, E. & Konuk, T. (1987). Chernobyl radionuclides in a Black Sea sediment trap. *Nature, London*, **329**, 825–8.

Burnett, B. R. (1973). Observations of the microfauna of the deep-sea benthos using light and scanning electron microscopy. *Deep-Sea Research*, **20**, 413–17.

(1977). Quantitative sampling of microbiota of the deep-sea benthos. I. Sampling techniques and some data from the abyssal central North Pacific. *Deep-Sea Research*, **24**, 781–9.

(1979). Quantitative sampling of microbiota of the deep-sea benthos. II. Evaluation of technique and introduction to the biota of the San Diego Trough. *Transactions of the American Microscopical Society*, **98**, 233–42.

(1981). Quantitative sampling of microbiota of the deep-sea benthos. III. The bathyal San Diego Trough. *Deep-Sea Research*, **28A**, 649–63.

Burnett, B. R. & Nealson, K. H. (1981). Organic films and microorganisms associated with manganese nodules. *Deep-Sea Research*, **28A**, 637–45.

Busby, R. F. (1977). Unmanned submersibles. In *Submersibles and their Use in Oceanography and Ocean Engineering*, ed. R. A. Geyer, pp. 23–59. Amsterdam: Elsevier.

Butman, C. A. (1987). Larval settlement of soft-sediment invertebrates: the spatial scales of pattern explained by active habitat selection and the emerging role of hydrodynamical processes. *Oceanography and Marine Biology: an Annual Review*, **25**, 113–65.

Caccione, D. A., Rowe, G. T. & Malahoff, A. (1978). Submersible investigation of the outer Hudson submarine canyon. In *Sedimentation in Submarine Canyons, Fans and Trenches*, eds D. J. Stanley & G. Kelling, pp. 42–50. Stroudsberg, Pennsylvania: Dowden, Hutchinson & Ross.

Cadet, J. P., Kobayashi, K., Aubouin, J., Boulegue, J., Dubois, J., Von Huene, R., Jolivet, L., Kanazawa, T., Kasahara, J., Suyehiro, K., Lallemand, S., Nakamura, Y., Pautot, G., Suyehiro, K., Tani, S., Tokuyama, H. & Yamazaki, T. (1985). De la fosse de Japon à la fosse des Kouriles: premiers résultats de la campagne océanographique franco-japonaise Kaiko (leg III). *Compte rendus hebdomadaires des séances de l'Académie des sciences, Paris (Sér. II)*, **5**, 287–96.

Cahet, G. & Sibuet, M. (1986). Activité biologique en domains profond: transformations biochemique *in situ* de composés organiques marqués au carbone—14 à l'interface eau-sédiment par 2000 m de profondeur dans le Golfe de Gascogne. *Marine Biology*, **90**, 307–15.

Cairns, S. D. (1982). Antarctic and subantarctic Scleractinia. *Antartic Research Series*, **34**, 74 pp.

Calvert, S.E. (1978). Geochemistry of oceanic ferromanganese deposits. *Philosophical Transactions of the Royal Society of London, Series A*, **290**, 43–73.

Cameron, J. L., McEuen. F. S. & Young, C. M. (1988). Floating lecithotrophic eggs from the bathyal echinothuriid sea urchin *Araeosoma fenestratum*. In *Echinoderm Biology*, eds R. D. Burke, P. V. Mladenov, P. Lambert & R. L. Parsley, pp. 177–80. Rotterdam: Balkena.

Canadian American Seamount Expedition. (1985). Hydrothermal vents on an axis seamount of the Juan de Fuca ridge. *Nature, London*, **313**, 212–14.

Caralp, M.-H. (1987). Deep-sea circulation in the northeastern Atlantic over the past 30000 years: the benthic foraminiferal record. *Oceanologica Acta*, **10**, 27–40.

Carey, A. G. (1965). Preliminary studies on animal–sediment interrelationships off the central Oregon coast. *Transactions of the Joint Conference of Ocean Scientists and Engineers*, **1**, 100–10.

(1972). Food sources of sublittoral, bathyal and abyssal asteroids in the northeast Pacific. *Ophelia*, **10**, 35–47.

Carey, A. G. & Hancock, D. R. (1965). An anchor-box dredge for deep-sea sampling. *Deep-Sea Research*, **12**, 983–4.

Carlgren, O. (1956). Actinaria from depths exceeding 6000 meters. *Galathea Report*, **2**, 9–16.

Carman, K. R., Sherman, K. M. & Thistle, D. (1987). Evidence that sediment type influences the horizontal and vertical distribution of nematodes at a deep-sea site. *Deep-Sea Research*, **34A**, 45–53.

Carney, R. S. & Carey, A. G. (1977). Distribution pattern of holothurians on the northeastern Pacific (Oregon, U.S.A.) continental shelf slope, and abyssal plain. *Thallasia Jugoslavica*, **12**, 67–74.

Carney, R. S., Haedrich, R. L. & Rowe, G. T. (1983). Zonation of fauna in the deep sea. In *The Sea*, Vol 8, ed. G. T. Rowe, pp. 371–98, New York: Wiley-Interscience.

Carpenter, W. B., Jeffreys, J. W. & Thomson, W. (1870). Preliminary report of the scientific exploration of the deep sea in H.M. surveying-vessel 'Porcupine', during the summer of 1869. *Proceedings of the Royal Society of London*, **18**, 397–492.

Carter, G. S. (1961). Evolution in the deep sea. In *Oceanography*, ed. M. Sears, pp. 229–38. Washington, D.C.: American Association for the Advancement of Science.

Cartwright, N. G., Gooday, A. J. & Jones, A. R. The morphology, internal organization, and taxonomic position of *Rhizammina algaeformis* Brady, a large agglutinated deep-sea foraminifer. *Journal of Foraminiferal Research*, **19**, 115–25.

Cary, C., Fry, B., Felbeck, H. & Vetter, R. D. (1989). Multiple resources for a chemoautotrophic community at a cold water brine seep at the base of the Florida Escarpment. *Marine Biology*, **100**, 411–18.

Cary, S. C., Felbeck, H. & Holland, N. D. (1989). Observations on the reproductive biology of the hydrothermal vent tube worm *Riftia pachyptila*. *Marine Ecology Progress Series*, **52**, 89–94.

Cary, S. S., Fisher, C. R. & Felbeck, H. (1988). Mussel growth supported by methane as a sole carbon and energy source. *Science, Washington*, **240**, 78–80.

Caswell, H. (1976). Community structure: a neutral model analysis. *Ecological Monographs*, **46**, 327–54.

Cavanaugh, C. M. (1983). Symbiotic chemoautotrophic bacteria in marine invertebrates from sulphide-rich habitats. *Nature, London*, **302**, 58–61.

  (1985). Symbiosis of chemoautotrophic bacteria and marine invertebrates from hydrothermal vents and reducing sediments. *Bulletin of the Biological Society of Washington*, **6**, 373–88.

Cavanaugh, C. M., Gardiner, S. L., Jones, M. L., Jannasch, H. W. & Waterbury, J. B. (1981). Procaryotic cells in the hydrothermal vent tubeworm, *Riftia pachyptila* Jones: possible chemoautotrophic symbionts. *Science, Washington*, **213**, 340–2.

Cavanaugh, C. M., Levering, P. R., Maki, J. S., Mitchell, R. & Listrom, M. E. (1987). Symbiosis of methylotrophic bacteria and deep-sea mussels. *Nature, London*, **325**, 348.

Cavanie, A. & Hyacinthe, J. L. (1976). Étude du courant et de la marée a la limite du plateau continental d'après les mesures effectuées pendant la campagne Golfe de Gascogne 1970. *Rapports Scientifique et Technical CNEXO*, **32**, 1–41.

Cedhagen, T. (1988). Position in the sediment and feeding of *Astrorhiza limicola* Sandahl, 1857 (Foraminifera). *Sarsia*, **73**, 43–7.

Certes, A. (1884). Sur la culture, à labrides germes atmosphériques, des eaux et des sédiments rapportés par les expéditions du Travailleur et Talisman. *Comptes rendu hebdomadaire des séances l'Académie des sciences, Paris*, **98**, 690–3.

Chapman, C. J. & Rice, A. L. (1971). Some direct observations on the ecology and behaviour of the Norway lobster *Nephrops norvegicus*. *Marine Biology*, **10**, 321–9.

Chardy, P. (1979). Structure of deep-sea Asellota assemblages in the Bay of Biscay; relationships with the environment. *Ambio Special Report*, **6**, 79–82.

Charmasson, S. S. & Calmet, D. P. (1987). Distribution of scavenging Lysianassidae amphipods *Eurythenes gryllus* in the northeast Atlantic: comparison with studies held in the Pacific. *Deep-Sea Research*, **34A**, 1509–23.

Cherbonnier, G. & Sibuet, M. (1972). Résultats scientifiques de la campagne Noratlante: astéroides et ophiurides. *Bulletin du Muséum national d'histoire naturelle, Paris (Sér. 3) Zoologie*, No. 76, 1333–94.

Cherry, R. D. & Heyraud, M. (1982). Evidence of high natural radiation doses in certain mid-water oceanic organisms. *Science, Washington*, **218**, 54–56.

Childress, J. J. (1976). The respiratory rates of midwater crustacea as a function of depth of occurrence and relation to the oxygen minimum layer off southern California. *Comparative Biochemistry and Physiology*, **50A**, 787–99.

(ed.) (1988). Hydrothermal vents: A case study of the biology and chemistry of a deep-sea hydrothermal vent of the Galapagos Rift. *Deep-Sea Research*, **35**, Nos 10/11A, 1677–849.

(1988). Biology and chemistry of a deep-sea hydrothermal vent on the Galapagos Rift; the Rose Garden in 1985. Introduction. *Deep-Sea Research*, **35A**, 1677–80.

Childress, J. J., Cowles, D. L., Favuzzi, J. A. & Mickel, T. J. (1990). Metabolic rates of benthic deep-sea decapod crustaceans decline with increasing depth primarily due to the decline in temperature. *Deep-Sea Research*, **37A**, 929–49.

Childress, J. J. & Fisher, C. R. (1988). The methanotrophic symbiosis in a hydrocarbon seep mussel. Fifth Deep-Sea Biology Symposium, June 26th–July 1st 1988, Brest: Institut Français de Recherche pour l'Exploitation de la Mer.

Childress, J. J., Fisher, C. R., Brooks, J. M., Kennicutt, M. C., Bidigare, R. & Anderson, A. E. (1986). A methanotrophic marine molluscan (Bivalvia, Mytilidae) symbiosis: mussels fueled by gas. *Science, Washington*, **233**, 1306–8.

Childress, J. J., Gluck, D. L., Carney, R. S. & Gowing, M. M. (1989). Benthopelagic biomass distribution and oxygen consumption in a deep-sea benthic boundary layer dominated by gelatinous organisms. *Limnology and Oceanography*, **34**, 913–30.

Childress, J. J. & Mickel, T. J. (1982). Oxygen and sulfide consumption rates of the vent clam *Calyptogena pacifica*. *Marine Biology Letters*, **3**, 3–79.

Childress, J. J. & Mickel, T. J. (1985). Metabolic rates of animals from the hydrothermal vents and other deep-sea habitats. *Bulletin of the Biological Society of Washington*, **6**, 249–60.

Cho, B. C. & Azam, F. (1988). Major role of bacteria in biogeochemical fluxes in the ocean interior. *Nature, London*, **332**, 441–3.

Clark, J. P. (1982). The nodules are not essential. *Oceanus*, **25**, 18–21.

Clark, R. B. (1977). Reproduction, speciation and polychaete taxonomy. In *Essays on Polychaetous Annelids*, eds D. K. Reish & K. Fauchald, pp. 477–501. Los Angeles: Alan Hancock Foundation Special Publications.

Clarke, A. H. (1962). On the composition, zoogeography, origin and age of the deep-sea mollusk fauna. *Deep-Sea Research*, **9**, 291–306.

Cliff, A. D. & Ord, J. K. (1973). *Spatial Autocorrelation*. London: Pion.

Cochran, J. K. (1982). The use of naturally occurring radionuclides as tracers for biologically related processes in deep-sea sediments. In *The Environment of the Deep-Sea*, eds W. G. Ernst & J. G. Morin, pp. 55–72. Englewood Cliffs, New Jersey: Prentice-Hall.

Cohen, D. M., Rosenblatt, R. H. & Moser, H. G. (1990). Biology and description of a bythitid fish from deep-sea thermal vents in the tropical eastern Pacific. *Deep-Sea Research*, **37A**, 267–83.

Cole, J. J., Honjo, S. & Erez, J. (1987). Benthic decomposition of organic matter at a deep-water site in the Panama Basin. *Nature, London*, **327**, 703–4.

Colman, J. G. & Tyler, P. A. (1988). Observations on the reproductive biology of the deep-sea trochid *Calliostoma otteri* (Philippi). *Journal of Molluscan Studies*, **54**, 239–42.

Colman, J. G., Tyler, P. A. & Gage, J. D. (1986a). The reproductive biology of *Colus jeffreysianus* (Gastropoda: Prosobranchia) from 2000 m in the N.E. Atlantic. *Journal of Molluscan Studies*, **52**, 45–54.

  (1986b). Larval development of the deep-sea gastropods (Prosobranchia: Neogastropoda) from the Rockall Trough. *Journal of the Marine Biological Association of the United Kingdom*, **66**, 951–65.

Comita, P. B., Gagosian, R. B. & Williams, P. M. (1984). Suspended particulate organic material from hydrothermal vent waters at 21° N. *Nature, London*, **307**, 450–3.

Conan, G., Roux, M. & Sibuet, M. (1981). A photographic survey of a population of the stalked crinoid *Diplocrinus (Annacrinus) wyvillethomsoni* (Echinodermata) from the bathyal slope of the Bay of Biscay. *Deep-Sea Research*, **28A**, 441–53.

Connell, J. H. (1970). A predator–prey system in the marine intertidal region. 1. *Balanus glandula* and several predatory species of *Thais*. *Ecological Monographs*, **40**, 49–78.

  (1978). Diversity in tropical rain forests and coral reefs. *Science, Washington*, **199**, 1302–9.

Cook, D. G. (1970). Bathyal and abyssal Tubificidae (Annelida, Oligochaeta) from the Gay Head–Bermuda transect, with descriptions of new genera and species. *Deep-Sea Research*, **17**, 973–81.

Cooper, L. H. N. (1952). The physical and chemical oceanography of the waters bathing the continental slope of the Celtic Sea. *Journal of the Marine Biological Association of the United Kingdom*, **30**, 465–509.

Corliss, J. B. & Ballard, R. D. (1977). Oases of life in the cold abyss. *National Geographic Magazine*, **152**, 441–53.

Corliss, J. B., Baross, J. A. & Hoffman, S. E. (1981). An hypothesis concerning the relationship between submarine hot springs and the origin of life on Earth. In *Proceedings 26th International Geological Congress, Geology of Oceans Symposium, Paris, July 7–17, 1980*, pp. 59–69. Paris.

Corliss, J. B., Dymond, J., Gordo, L. I., Edmond, J. M., von Herzen, R. P., Ballard, R. D., Green K., Williams, D., Bainbridge, A., Crane, K. & van Andel, T. H. (1979). Submarine thermal springs on the Galapagos Rift. *Science, Washington*, **203**, 1073–83.

Corner, E. D. S., Denton, E. J. & Forster, G. R. (1969). On the buoyancy of some deep-sea sharks. *Proceedings of the Royal Society, Series B*, **171**, 415–29.

Coull, B. C. (1972). Species diversity and faunal affinities of meiobenthic Copepoda in the deep sea. *Marine Biology*, **14**, 48–51.

Coull, B. C., Ellison, R. L., Fleeger, J. W., Higgens, R. P., Hope, W. D., Hummon, W. D., Rieger, R. M., Sterrer, W. E., Thiel, H. & Tietjen,

J. H. (1977). Quantitative estimates of the meiofauna from the deep sea off North Carolina, USA. *Marine Biology*, **39**, 233–40.

Craib, J. S. (1965). A sampler for taking short undisturbed marine cores. *Journal du Conseil*, **30**, 34–9.

Crane, K., Aikman, F., Embley, R. Hammond, S. & Malahoff, A. (1985). The distribution of geothermal fields on the Juan de Fuca Ridge. *Journal of Geographical Research*, **90**, 727–44.

Crane, K. & Ballard, R. D. (1980). The Galapagos Rift at 86° W: 4. Structure and morphology of hydrothermal fields and their relationship to the volcanic and tectonic processes of the Rift Valley. *Journal of Geographical Research*, **85**, 1443–54.

Crosnier, A. & Forest, J. (1973). Les crevettes profondes de l'Atlantique oriental tropical. *Faune Tropicale*, **19**, 1–409.

Culliney, J. B. & Turner, R. D. (1976). Larval development of the deep-water wood boring bivalve, *Xylophaga atlantica* Richards (Mollusca, Bivalvia, Pholadidae). *Ophelia*, **15**, 149–61.

Curry, G. B. (1983). Ecology of the recent deep-water rhynchonellid brachiopod *Cryptopora* from the Rockall Trough. *Palaeogeography, Palaeoclimatology, Palaeoecology*, **44**, 93–102.

Curtis, C. (1982). The environmental aspects of deep ocean mining. *Oceanus*, **25**, 31–36.

Cutler, E. B. (1975). Zoogeographical barrier on the continental slope off Cape Lookout, North Carolina. *Deep-Sea Research*, **22**, 893–901.

Cutler, E. B. & Cutler, N. J. (1987). Deep-water Sipuncula from the eastern Atlantic Ocean. *Sarsia*, **72**, 71–89.

CYAMEX Scientific Team: Francheteau, J., Needham, H. D., Choukroune, P., Juteau, T., Seguret, M., Ballard, R. D., Fox, P. J., Normark, W. R., Carranza, A., Cordoba, D., Guerrero, J. & Rangan, C. (1981). First manned submersible dives on the East Pacific Rise at 21° N (Project Rita): general results. *Marine Geophysical Research*, **4**, 345–79.

Dahl, E. (1954). The distribution of deep-sea Crustacea. In *On the Distribution and Origin of the Deep Sea Bottom Fauna. International Union of Biological Sciences*, Ser. B, **16**, 43–8.

(1972). The Norwegian Sea deep water fauna and its derivation. *Ambio Special Report*, **2**, 19–24.

(1979). Amphipoda Gammaridea from the deep Norwegian Sea. A preliminary report. *Sarsia*, **64**, 57–60.

Dahl, E., Laubier, L., Sibuet, M. & Stromberg, J.-O. (1976). Some quantitative results on benthic communities of the deep Norwegian Sea. *Astarte*, **9**, 61–79.

Dando, P. R. & Southward, A. J. (1986). Chemoautotrophy in bivalve molluscs of the genus *Thyasira*. *Journal of the Marine Biological Association of the United Kingdom*, **66**, 915–29.

Darwin, C. R. (1881). *The Formation of Vegetable Mould through the Action of Worms, with Observations on their Habits*. London: John Murray.

Dattagupta, A. K. (1981). Atlantic echiurans. Part I. Report on twenty-two species of deep-sea echiurans of the North and the South Atlantic Ocean. *Bulletin du Muséum national d'histoire naturelle. Paris. (Sér. 3)*, No. 2, *Zoologie*, 353–78.

Dauer, D. M. (1983). Functional morphology and feeding behaviour of *Scololepis squamata* (Polychaeta: Spionidae). *Marine Biology*, **77**, 279–85.

David, B. (1983). Isolement géographique de populations benthique abyssales: les *Pourtalesia jeffreysi* (Echinoidea, Holasteroida) en Mer de Norvège. *Oceanologica Acta*, **6**, 13–20.

Davies, G. D. (1987). Aspects of the biology and ecology of deep-sea Scaphopoda. Unpublished PhD Thesis, Heriot Watt University, Edinburgh, 194 pp.

Dayton, P. K. (1971). Competition, disturbance and community organization: the provision and subsequent utilization of space in a rocky intertidal community. *Ecological Monographs*, **41**, 351–89.

Dayton, P. K. & Hessler, R. R. (1972). Role of biological disturbance in maintaining diversity in the deep sea. *Deep-Sea Research*, **19**, 199–208.

Dayton, P. K., Newman, W. A. & Oliver, J. S. (1982). The vertical zonation of the deep-sea Antarctic acorn barnacle, *Bathylasma corolliforme* (Hoek): experimental transplants from the shelf into shallow water. *Journal of Biogeography*, **9**, 95–109.

De Broyer, C. & Thurston, M. H. (1987). New Atlantic material and redescription of the type specimens of the giant abyssal amphipod *Alicella gigantea* Chevreux (Crustacea). *Zoologica Scripta*, **16**, 335–50.

DeLaca, T. E., Karl, D. & Lipps, J. H. (1981). Direct use of dissolved organic carbon by agglutinated benthic foraminifera. *Nature, London*, **289**, 287–9.

DeMaster, D. (1979). The marine silica and Si budgets. Unpublished PhD Thesis, Yale University.

Deming, J. W. (1985). Bacterial growth in deep-sea sediment trap and boxcore samples. *Marine Ecology – Progress Series*, **25**, 305–12.

(1986). Ecological strategies of barophilic bacteria in the deep ocean. *Microbiological Sciences*, **3**, 205–11.

Deming, J. W. & Colwell, R. R. (1982). Barophilic bacteria associated with the digestive tract of abyssal holothurians. *Applied and Environmental Microbiology*, **44**, 1222–30.

(1985). Observations of barophilic microbial activity in samples of sediment and intercepted particulates from the Demerara Abyssal Plain. *Applied and Environmental Microbiology*, **50**, 1002–6.

Deming, J. W., Tabor, P. S. & Colwell, R. R. (1981). Barophilic growth of bacteria from intestinal tracts of deep-sea invertebrates. *Microbial Ecology*, **7**, 85–94.

Desbruyères, D., Bevas, J. Y. & Khripounoff, A. (1980). Un cas de colonisation rapide d'une sédiment profond. *Oceanologica Acta*, **3**, 285–91.

Desbruyères, D., Crassous, P., Grassle, J., Khripounoff, A., Reyss, D., Rio, M. & Van Praet, M. (1982). Données écologiques sur un nouveau site d'hydrothermalisme actif de la ride du Pacifique oriental. *Compte rendus de l'Académie des sciences, Paris (Sér. III)*, **295**, 489–94.

Desbruyères, D., Deming, J., Dinet, A. & Khripounoff, A. (1985). Réactions de l'écosystème benthique profond aux perturbations: nouveaux résultats expérimentaux. In *Peuplements Profonds du Golfe de Gascogne*, eds L. Laubier & C. Monniot, pp. 121–42. Brest: Institut Français de Recherche pour l'Exploitation de la Mer.

Desbruyères, D., Gaill, F., Laubier, L. & Fouquet, Y. (1985). Polychaetous annetids from hydrothermal vent ecosystems: an ecological overview. *Bulletin of the Biological Society of Washington*, **6**, 103–16.

Desbruyères, D. & Laubier, L. (1980). *Alvinella pompejana* gen. sp. nov., Ampharetidae aberrent des sources hydrothermales de la ride Est-Pacifique. *Oceanologica Acta*, **3**, 267–74.

Detrick, R. S., Honorez, J., Adamson, A. C., Brass, G. W., Gillis, K. M., Humphris, S. E., Mevel, C., Meyer, P. S., Petersen, N., Rautenschlein, M., Shibata, T., Staudigel, H., Wooldridge, A. & Yamamoto, K. (1986). Mid-Atlantic bare-rock drilling and hydrothermal vents. *Nature, London*, **321**, 14–15.

Deuser, W. G. (1986). Seasonal and interannual variations in deep water particle fluxes in the Sargasso sea and their relation to surface hydrography. *Deep-Sea Research*, **33A**, 225–46.

(1987). Seasonal variation in isotopic composition and deep-water fluxes of the tests of perennially abundant planktonic forams of the Sargasso sea. Results from the sediment trap collections and their palaeoceanographic significance. *Journal of Foraminiferan Research*, **17**, 14–27.

Deuser, W. G. & Ross, E. H. (1980). Seasonal change in the flux of organic carbon to the deep Sargasso Sea. *Nature, London*, **283**, 364–5.

Deuser, W. G., Ross E. H. & Anderson, R. F. (1981). Seasonality in the supply of sediment to the deep Sargasso Sea and implications for the rapid transfer of matter to the deep ocean. *Deep-sea Research*, **28A**, 495–505.

Dickinson, J. J. (1978). Faunal composition of the gammarid Amphipoda (Crustacea) in two bathyal basins of the California continental borderland. *Marine Biology*, **48**, 367–72.

Dickinson, J. J. & Carey, A. G. (1978). Distribution of gammarid Amphipoda (Crustacea) on Cascadia Abyssal Plain (Oregon). *Deep-Sea Research*, **25**, 97–106.

Dickson, R. R. (1983). Global summaries and intercomparisons: flow statistics from long-term current meter moorings. In *Eddies in Marine Science*, ed. A. R. Robinson, pp. 278–353. Berlin: Springer-Verlag.

Dickson, R. R., Gould, W. J., Griffiths, C., Medler, K. J. & Gmitrowicz, E. M. (1986). Seasonality in currents of the Rockall Trough. *Proceedings of the Royal Society of Edinburgh*, **88B**, 103–25.

Dickson, R. R., Gould, W. J., Gurbutt, P. A. & Killworth, P. D. (1982). A seasonal signal in the ocean currents to abyssal depths. *Nature, London,* **295**, 193–8.

Dickson, R. R. & Hughes, D. G. (1981). Satellite evidence of mesoscale eddy activity over the Biscay abyssal plain. *Oceanologica Acta,* **4**, 43–6.

Digby, P. G. N. & Kempton, R. A. (1987). *Multivariate Analysis of Ecological Communities.* London: Chapman and Hall.

Diggle, P. J. (1983). *Statistical Analysis of Spatial Point Patterns.* London: Academic Press.

Dillon, W. P. & Zimmerman, H. B. (1970). Erosion by biological activity in two New England submarine canyons. *Journal of Sedimentary Petrology,* **40**, 542–7.

Dinet, A. (1979). A quantitative survey of meiobenthos in the deep Norwegian Sea. *Ambio Special Report,* **6**, 75–7.

Dinet, A., Desbruyères, D. & Khripounoff, A. (1985). Abondance des peuplements macro- et meio-benthiques: répartition et stratégie d'échantillonage. In *Peuplements Profonds du Golfe de Gascogne,* ed. L. Laubier & C. Monniot, pp. 121–42. Brest: Institut Français de Recherche pour l'Exploitation de la Mer.

Dinet, A., Laubier, L., Soyer, J. & Vitellio, P. (1973). Résultats biologique de la campagne Polymede. II. Le meiobenthos abyssal. *Rapport et procès-verbaux des réunions. Commission internationale pour l'exploration scientifique de la Mer Méditerranée,* **21**, 701–4.

Dinet, A. & Vivier, M.-H. (1977). Le meiobenthos abyssal du Golfe de Gascogne. I. Considérations sur les données quantitatives. *Cahiers de Biologie Marine,* **18**, 85–97.

  (1979). Le meiobenthos abyssal du Golfe de Gascogne. II. Les Peuplements de Nématodes et leur diversité spécifique. *Cahiers de Biologie Marine,* **20**, 9–123.

Dobzhansky, T., Ayala, F. J., Stebbins, G. L. & Valentine, J. W. (1977). *Evolution.* San Francisco: Freeman.

Douglas, R. & Woodruff, F. (1981). Deep-sea benthic Foraminifera. In *The Sea,* Vol. 7, ed. C. Emiliani, pp. 1233–8. New York: John Wiley.

Doyle, R. W. (1972). Genetic variation in *Ophiomusium lymani* (Echinodermata) populations in the deep sea. *Deep-Sea Research,* **19**, 661–4.

  (1979). Ingestion rate of a selective deposit feeder in a complex mixture of particles: testing the energy optimization hypothesis. *Limnology and Oceanography,* **24**, 867–74.

Duco, A. & Roux, M. (1981). Modalités particulières de croissance liées au milieu abyssal chez les Bathycrinidae (Échinodermes, Crinoïdes pédoncules). *Oceanologica Acta,* **4**, 389–93.

Eagle, R. A. (1975). Natural fluctuations in a soft bottom benthic community. *Journal of the Marine Biological Association of the United Kingdom,* **55**, 865–78.

Eckman, J. A. (1979). Small-scale patterns and processes in soft-substratum, intertidal community. *Journal of Marine Research*, **37**, 437–57.

(1983). Hydrodynamic processes affecting benthic recruitment. *Limnology and Oceanography*, **28**, 241–57.

(1987). The role of hydrodynamics in recruitment, growth, and survival of *Argopecten irradians* (L.) and *Anomia simplex* (D'Orbigny) within seagrass meadows. *Journal of Marine Biology and Ecology*, **106**, 165–91.

Eckman, J. A., Nowell, A. R. M. & Jumars, P. A. (1981). Sediment destabilization by animal tubes. *Journal of Marine Research*, **39**, 361–74.

Eckman, J. A. & Thistle, D. (1988). Small-scale spatial pattern in meiobenthos in the San Diego Trough. *Deep-Sea Research*, **35**, 1565–78.

Eittreim, S., Thorndike, E. M. & Sullivan, L. (1976). Turbidity distribution in the Atlantic Ocean. *Deep-Sea Research*, **23**, 115–27.

Ekdale, A. A. (1985). Paleoecology of the marine endobenthos. *Palaeogeography, Palaeoclimatology, Palaeoecology*, **50**, 63–81.

Ekdale, A. A. & Berger, W. H. (1978). Deep-sea ichnofacies: modern organism traces on and in pelagic carbonates of the western equatorial Pacific. *Palaeogeography, Palaeoclimatology, Palaeoecology*, **23**, 263–78.

Ekman, S. (1953). *Zoogeography of the Sea*. London: Sidgwick & Jackson.

Eleftheriou, A. & Holme, N. A. (1984). Macrofaunal techniques. In *Methods for the study of Marine Benthos*, eds. N. A. Holme & A. D. McIntyre, pp. 140–216. Oxford: Blackwell Scientific Publications.

Ellett, D. J., Edwards, A. & Bowers, R. (1986). The hydrography of the Rockall Channel – an overview. *Proceedings of the Royal Society of Edinburgh*, **88B**, 61–81.

Ellett, D. J. & Martin, J. H. A. (1973). The physical and chemical oceanography of the Rockall Channel. *Deep-Sea Research*, **20**, 585–625.

Ellett, D. J. & Roberts, D. (1973) The overflow of Norwegian Sea deep water across the Wyville Thomson Ridge. *Deep-Sea Research*, **20**, 585–625.

Elliott, J. M. (1977). *Some Methods for the Statistical Analysis of Samples of Benthic Invertebrates*. Scientific Publication No. 25. Ambleside, Cumbria: Freshwater Biological Association.

Emerson, S., Fischer, K., Reimers, C. & Heggie, D. (1985). Organic carbon dynamics and preservation in deep-sea sediments. *Deep-Sea Research*, **32A**, 1–22.

Emig, C. C. (1985). Distribution et synécologie des fonds à *Gryphus vitreus* (Brachiopoda) en Corse. *Marine Biology*, **90**, 139–46.

(1987). Offshore brachiopods investigated by submersible. *Journal of Experimental Marine Biology and Ecology*, **108**, 261–73.

Enright, J. T., Newman, W. A., Hessler, R. R. & McGowan, J. A. (1981). Deep-ocean hydrothermal vent communities. *Nature, London*, **289**, 219–21.

Epp, D. & Smoot, N. C. (1989). Distribution of seamounts in the North Atlantic. *Nature, London*, **337**, 254–7.

Erseus, C. (1985). Distribution and biogeography of Oligochaeta. In *Peuplements Profonds du Golfe de Gascogne*, eds L. Laubier & C. Monniot, pp. 365–7. Brest: Institut Français de Recherche pour l'Exploitation de la Mer.

Ewing, M. & Davis, R. A. (1967). Lebensspuren photographed on the ocean floor. In *Deep-Sea Photography*, ed. J. B. Hersey, pp. 259–94. Baltimore: Johns Hopkins Press.

Fager, E. W. (1972). Diversity: a sampling study. *American Naturalist*, **106**, 293–310.

Farran, G. P. (1924). Seventh report on the fishes of the Irish Atlantic slope. The macrurid fishes (Coryphaenoididae). *Proceedings of the Royal Irish Academy*, **36B**, 91–148.

Fauchald, K. & Jumars, P. A. (1979). The diet of worms: a study of polychaete feeding guilds. *Oceanography and Marine Biology: an Annual Review*, **17**, 193–284.

Felbeck, H. (1981). Chemoautotrophic potential of the hydrothermal vent tubeworm *Riftia pachyptila* Jones (Vestimentifera). *Science, Washington*, **203**, 1073–83.

(1983). Sulfide oxidation and carbon fixation by the gutless clam *Solemya reidi*: An animal–bacteria symbiosis. *Journal of Comparative Physiology*, **152**, 3–11.

(1985). CO_2 fixation in the hydrothermal vent tube worm *Riftia pachyptila* (Jones). *Physiological Zoology*, **58**, 272–81.

Felbeck, H., Childress, J. J. & Somero, G. N. (1981). Calvin–Benson cycle and sulphide oxidation enzymes in animals from sulphide-rich habitats. *Nature, London*, **293**, 291–3.

Felbeck, H. & Somero, G. N. (1982). Primary production in deep-sea hydrothermal vent organisms: roles of sulfide-oxidizing bacteria. *Trends in Biochemical Research*, **7**, 201–4.

Feller, R. J., Zagursky, G. & Day, E. A. (1985). Deep-sea food-web analysis using cross-reacting antisera. *Deep-Sea Research*, **32A**, 488–97.

Fenchel, T. M. (1975a). Factors determining the distribution patterns of mud snails (Hydrobiiae). *Oecologia, Berlin*, **20**, 1–17.

(1975b). Character displacement and coexistence in mud snails (Hydrobiidae). *Oecologia, Berlin*, **20**, 19–32.

(1978). The ecology of the micro- and meiobenthos. *Annual Review of Ecology and Systematics*, **9**, 99–121.

Fiala-Médioni, A. & Le Pennec, M. (1988). Structural adaptations in the gill of the Japan subduction zone bivalves (Vesicomyidae) *Calyptogena phaseoliformis* and *Calyptogena lauberi*. *Oceanologica Acta*, **11**, 185–92.

Filatova, Z. A. (1982). On some problems of the quantitative study of deep-sea bottom fauna. *Trudy Instituta Okeanologii*, **117**, 5–18 (English translation by Institute of Oceanographic Sciences, Translation No. 179, 1984).

Filatova, Z. A. & Vinogradova, N. G. (1974). Bottom fauna of the South Atlantic deep-sea trenchs. *Trudy Instituta Okeanologii*, **98**, 141–56 (in Russian, English summary).

Firth, R. W. & Pequegnat, W. E. (1971). Deep-sea lobsters of the families Polychelidae and Nephropidae (Crustacea, Decapoda) in the Gulf of Mexico and Caribbean Sea. Texas A & M Research Foundation, Reference 71–11T, 103 pp.

Fisher, C. R. Marine environments and their chemolithautotrophic symbionts. *Reviews in Aquatic Sciences* (in press).

Fisher, C. R., Childress, J. J., Arp, A. J., Brooks, J. M., Distel, D. L., Dugan, J. A., Felbeck, H., Fritz, L. W., Hessler, R. R., Johnson, K. S., Kennicutt II, M. C., Lutz, R. A., Macko, S. A., Newton, A., Powell, M. A., Somero, G. N. & Soto, T. (1988*a*). Variation in the hydrothermal vent clam *Calyptogena magnifica*, at the Rose Garden vent on the Galapagos spreading centre. *Deep-Sea Research*, **35A**, 1811–31.

Fisher, C. R., Childress, J. J., Arp, A. J., Brooks, J. M., Distel, D., Favuzzi, J. A., Felbeck, H., Hessler, R. R., Johnson, K. S., Kennicutt II, M. C., Macko, S. A., Newton, A., Powell, M. A., Somero, G. N. & Soto, T. (1988*b*). Microhabitat variation in the hydrothermal vent mussel *Bathymodiolus thermophilus* at the Rose Garden vent on the Galapagos Rift. *Deep-Sea Research*, **35A**, 1769–88.

Fisher, C. R., Childress, J. J., Oremland, R. A. & Bidigare, R. R. (1987). The importance of methane thiosulfate in the metabolism of the bacterial symbionts of two deep-sea mussels. *Marine Biology*, **96**, 59–71.

Fisher, M. & Hand, C. (1984). Chemoautotrophic symbionts in the bivalve *Lucina floridana* from seagrass beds. *Biological Bulletin. Marine Biological Laboratory, Woods Hole, Mass.*, **167**, 445–59.

Foell, E. J. & Pawson, D. L. (1986). Photographs of invertebrate megafauna from abyssal depths of the north-eastern equatorial Pacific Ocean. *Ohio Journal of Science*, **86**, 61–8.

Forster, G. R. (1964). Line-fishing on the continental slope. *Journal of the Marine Biological Association of the United Kingdom*, **44**, 277–284.

(1981). A note on the growth of *Arctica islandica*. *Journal of the Marine Biological Association of the United Kingdom*, **61**, 817.

Fowler, S. W., Ballestra, S., La Rose, J. & Fukai, R. (1983). Vertical transport of particulate-associated plutonium and americium in the upper water column of the Northeast Pacific. *Deep-Sea Research*, **30A**, 1221–33.

Fowler, S. W., Buat-Menard, P., Yokoyama, Y., Ballastra, S., Holm, E. & Huu Van Nguyen (1987). Rapid removal of Chernobyl fallout from Mediterranean surface waters by biological activity. *Nature, London*, **329**, 56–58.

Fowler, S. W. & Knauer, G. A. (1986). Role of large particles in the transport of elements and organic compounds through the oceanic water column. *Progress in Oceanography*, **16**, 147–94.

Francheteau, J. & Ballard, R. D. (1983). The East Pacific rise near 21° N,

13° N and 20° S: Inferences for a long-strike variability of axial processes of the Mid-Ocean Ridge. *Earth and Planetary Science Letters*, **64**, 93–116.

Francheteau, J., Needham, H. D., Choukroune, P., Juteau, T., Seguret, M., Ballard, R. D., Fox, J. P., Normark, W., Carranza, A., Cordoba, D., Guerrero, J., Rangin, C., Bougault, H., Cambon, P. & Hekinian, R. (1979). Massive deep-sea sulphide ore deposits discovered on the East Pacific Rise. *Nature, London*, **227**, 523–8.

Fredj, G. & Laubier, L. (1985). The deep Mediterranean benthos. In *Mediterranean Marine Ecosystems*, eds M. Moriatou-Apostolopoulou & V. Kiortsis, pp. 109–45. New York: Plenum Press.

Freeman, T. J., Murray, C. N., Francis, T. J. G., McPhail, S. D. & Schultheiss, P. J. (1984). Modelling radioactive waste disposal by penetrator experiments in the abyssal Atlantic Ocean. *Nature, London*, **310**, 130–3.

Frey, R. W., Howard, J. D. & Pryor, W. A. (1978). *Ophiomorpha*: its morphologic, taxonomic, and environmental significance. *Palaeogeography, Palaeoclimatology, Palaeoecology*, **23**, 199–229.

Fujita, T. & Ohta, S. (1988). Photographic observations of the life style of a deep-sea ophiuroid *Asteronyx loveni (Echinodermata)*. *Deep-Sea Research*, **35A**, 2029–43.

Fujita, T., Ohta, S. & Oji, T. (1987). Photographic observations of the stalked crinoid *Metacrinus rotundus* Carpenter in Surugu Bay, Central Japan. *Journal of the Oceanographical Society of Japan*, **43**, 333–43.

Fustec, A., Desbruyères, D. & Juniper, S. K. (1987). Deep-sea hydrothermal vent communities at 13° N on the East Pacific Rise: microdistribution and temporal variations. *Biological Oceanography*, **4**, 99–164.

Fustec, A., Desbruyères, D. & Laubier, L. (1988). Biomass estimates of animal communities associated with deep-sea hydrothermal vents near 13° N/EPR. *Oceanologica Acta* (spec. Vol.) **8**, 15–21.

Gage, J. D. (1975). A comparison of the deep-sea epibenthic sledge and anchor-box dredge samplers with the van Veen grab and hand coring by divers. *Deep-Sea Research*, **22**, 693–702.

(1977). Structure of the abyssal macrobenthic community in the Rockall Trough. In *Biology of Benthic Organisms*, eds B. F. Keegan, P. O. Ceidigh & P. J. S. Boaden, pp. 247–60. Oxford: Pergamon.

(1978). Animals in deep sea sediments. *Proceedings of the Royal Society of Edinburgh*, **76B**, 77–93.

(1979). Macrobenthic community structure in the Rockall Trough. *Ambio Special Report*, **6**, 43–6.

(1982). Age structure in populations of the deep-sea brittle star *Ophiomusium lymani*: a regional comparison. *Deep-Sea Research*, **29A**, 1505–86.

(1986). The benthic fauna of the Rockall Trough: regional distribution and bathymetric zonation. *Proceedings of the Royal Society of Edinburgh*, **88B**, 159–74.

(1987). Growth of the deep-sea irregular sea urchins *Echinosigra phiale* and *Hemiaster expergitus* in the Rockall Trough (N.E. Atlantic Ocean). *Marine Biology*, **96**, 19–30.

(1990). Skeletal growth markers in the deep-sea brittle stars *Ophiura ljungmani* and *Ophiomusium lymani*. *Marine Biology*, **104**, 427–35.

Biological rates in the deep sea: a perspective from studies on processes at the benthic boundary layer. *Reviews in Aquatic Sciences* (in press).

Gage, J. D. & Billett, D. S. M. (1986). The family Myriotrochidae Théel (Echinodermata: Holothurioidea) in the deep Northeast Atlantic Ocean. *Zoological Journal of the Linnaean Society*, **88**, 229–76.

Gage, J. D., Billett, D. S. M., Jensen, M. & Tyler, P. A. (1985). Echinoderms of the Rockall Trough and adjacent areas. 2. Echinoidea and Holothurioidea. *Bulletin of the British Museum, Natural History, (Zoology)*, **48**, 173–213.

Gage, J. D., Lightfoot, R. H., Pearson, M. & Tyler, P. A. (1980). An introduction to a sample time-series of abyssal macrobenthos: methods and principle sources of variability. *Oceanologica Acta*, **3**, 169–76.

Gage, J. D., Pearson, M., Billett, D. S. M., Clark, A. M., Jensen, M., Paterson, G. L. J. & Tyler, P. A. (1985). Echinoderm zonation in the Rockall Trough (NE Atlantic). In *Proceedings of the Fifth International Echinoderm Conference, Galway 24–29 September 1984*, eds B. F. Keegan & B. D. S. O'Connor, pp. 31–6. Rotterdam: Balkema.

Gage, J. D., Pearson, M., Clark, A. M., Paterson, G. L. J. & Tyler, P. A. (1983). Echinoderms of the Rockall Trough and adjacent areas. I. Crinoidea, Asteroidea and Ophiuroidea. *Bulletin of the British Museum, Natural History, (Zoology)*, **45**, 263–308.

Gage, J. D. & Tyler, P. A. (1981*a*). Non-viable seasonal settlement of larvae of the upper bathyal brittlestar *Ophiocten gracilis* in the Rockall Trough abyssal. *Marine Biology*, **64**, 153–61.

(1981*b*). Reappraisal of age composition, growth and survivorship of the deep-sea brittle star *Ophiura ljungmani* from size structure in a time series from the Rockall Trough. *Marine Biology*, **64**, 163–72.

(1982). Growth and reproduction in the deep-sea brittlestar *Ophiomusium lymani* Wyville Thomson. *Oceanologica Acta*, **5**, 73–83.

(1985). Growth and recruitment of the deep-sea urchin *Echinus affinis*. *Marine Biology*, **90**, 41–53.

Gage, J. D., Tyler, P. A. & Nichols, D. (1986). Reproduction and growth of *Echinus acutus* var. *norvegicus* and *E. elegans* on the continental slope off Scotland. *Journal of Experimental Marine Biology and Ecology*, **101**, 61–83.

Gardiner, L. F. (1975). The systematics, postmarsupial development, and ecology of the deep-sea family Neotanaidae (Crustacea: Tanaidacea). *Smithsonian Contributions to Zoology*, No. 170, 265 pp.

Gardner, W. D. (1989). Baltimore Canyon as a modern conduit of sediment to the deep sea. *Deep-Sea Research*, **36A**, 323–58.

Gardner, W. D., Hinga, K. R. & Marra, J. (1983). Observations on the degradation of biogenic material in the deep ocean with implications on accuracy of sediment trap fluxes. *Journal of Marine Research*, **41**, 195–214.

Gardner, W. D., Sullivan, L. G. & Thorndike, E. M. (1984). Long-term photographic, current, and nephelometer observations of manganese nodule environments in the Pacific. *Earth and Planetary Science Letters*, **70**, 95–109.

Gauch, H. G. (1982). *Multivariate Analysis in Community Ecology*. Cambridge University Press.

Gebruk, A. V. (1983). Abyssal holothurians of the genus *Scotoplanes* (Elasipoda, Elpidiiae). *Zoologicheskii Zhurnal*, **62**, 1359–70 (in Russian, English summary).

Geiger, S. R. (1963). *Ophiopluteus ramosus* between Iceland and Newfoundland. *Nature, London*, **198**, 908–9.

Genin, A., Dayton, P. K., Lonsdale, P. F. & Spiess, F. N. (1986). Corals on seamount peaks provide evidence of current acceleration over deep-sea topography. *Nature, London*, **332**, 59–61.

George, J. D. & George, J. J. (1979). *Marine Life. An Illustrated Encyclopaedia of Invertebrates in the Sea*. London: Harrap.

George, R. Y. (1979a). What adaptive strategies promote immigration and speciation in deep-sea environment. *Sarsia*, **64**, 61–5.

(1979b). Behavioral and metabolic adaptation of polar and deep-sea crustaceans: a hypothesis concerning physiological basis for evolution in cold adapted crustaceans. *Bulletin of the Biological Society of Washington*, **3**, 283–96.

(1981). Functional adaptations of deep-sea organisms. In *Functional Adaptations of Deep-sea Organisms*, eds F. J. Vernberg & W. B. Vernberg, pp. 280–332. Academic Press.

(1985). Basal and active metabolic rates of deep-sea animals in relation to pressure and food ration. In *Proceedings of the 19th European Marine Biology Symposium*, ed. P. E. Gibbs, pp. 173–82, Cambridge: University Press.

George, R. Y. & Higgins, R. P. (1979). Eutrophic hadal benthic community in the Puerto Rico Trench. *Ambio Special Report*, **6**, 51–8.

George, R. Y. & Menzies, R. J. (1967). Indication of cyclic reproductive activity in abyssal organisms. *Nature, London*, **215**, 878.

(1968). Further evidence for seasonal breeding cycles in the deep-sea. *Nature, London*, **220**, 80–1.

Gerdes, D. (1990). Antarctic trials of the multi-box corer, a new device for benthos sampling. *Polar Record*, **26**, 35–8.

GESAMP (1982). Scientific criteria for the selection of waste disposal sites at sea. *Reports and Studies*, No. 16, 1–60. Vienna: International Atomic Energy Agency.

Geyer, R. A. (ed.) (1977). *Submersibles and their use in Oceanography and Ocean Engineering*. Amsterdam: Elsevier.

Ghiorse, W. C. & Hirsch, P. (1982). Isolation and properties of ferromanganese-depositing budding bacteria from Baltic Sea ferromanganese concretions. *Applied and Environmental Microbiology*, **43**, 1464–72.

Giere, O. & Pfannkuche, O. (1982). Biology and ecology of marine Oligochaeta, a review. *Oceanography and Marine Biology: an Annual Review*, **20**, 173–308.

Giese, A. C. & Pearse, J. S. (1974). Introduction: general principles. In *Reproductive Ecology of Marine Invertebrates*, eds A. C. Giese & J. S. Pearse. New York: John Wiley.

Gilkinson, K. D., Hutchings, J. A., Oshel, P. E. & Haedrich, R. L. (1986). Shell microstructure and observations on internal banding patterns in the bivalves *Yoldia thraciaeformis* Storer, 1838, and *Nuculana pernula* Müller, 1779 (Nuculanidae), from a deep-sea environment. *The Veliger*, **29**, 70–7.

Goldberg, E. D. & Koide, M. (1962). Geochronological studies of deep-sea sediments by the ionium/thorium method. *Geochimica et Cosmochimica Acta*, **26**, 417–50.

Gooch, J. L. & Schopf, T. J. M. (1972). Genetic variability in the deep-sea: relation to environmental variability. *Evolution*, **26**, 545–52.

Gooday, A. J. (1983). *Primitive Foraminifera and Xenophyophorea in IOS epibenthic sledge samples from the Northeast Atlantic*. (I.O.S. Report No. 156.) Wormley, Surrey: Institute of Oceanographic Sciences.

(1984). Records of deep-sea rhizopod tests inhabited by metazoans in the north-east Atlantic. *Sarsia*, **69**, 45–53.

(1986a). Soft-shelled Foraminifera in meiofaunal samples from the bathyal northeast Atlantic. *Sarsia*, **71**, 275–87.

(1986b). Meiofaunal foraminiferans from the bathyal Porcupine Seabight (northeast Atlantic): size structure, standing stock, taxonomic composition, species diversity and vertical distribution in the sediment. *Deep-Sea Research*, **33A**, 1345–73.

(1988). A response by benthic Foraminifera to the deposition of phytodetritus in the deep sea. *Nature, London*, **332**, 70–3.

Gooday, A. J. & Cook, P. L. (1984). Komokiacean foraminifers (Protozoa) and paludicelline ctenostomes (Bryozoa) from the abyssal northeast Atlantic. *Journal of Natural History*, **18**, 765–84.

Gooday, A. J. & Haynes, J. R. (1983). Abyssal foraminifers, including two new genera, encrusting the interior of *Bathysiphon rustica* tubes. *Deep-Sea Research*, **30A**, 591–614.

Gooday, A. J. & Lambshead, P. J. D. (1989). Influence of seasonally deposited phytodetritus on benthic foraminiferal populations in the bathyal northeast Atlantic: the species response. *Marine Ecology – Progress Series*, **58**, 53–67.

Gooday, A. J. & Turley, C. M. (1990). Responses by benthic organisms to inputs of organic material to the ocean floor: a review. *Philosophical Transactions of the Royal Society of London*, Series A, **331**, 119–38.

Gordon, I. (1955). Crustacea Decapoda. *Report of the Swedish Deep-Sea Expedition*, 2, Zoology, Fasc. **2 (19)**, 237–45.

Gordon, J. D. M. (1979). Seasonal reproduction in deep-sea fish. In *Cyclic Phenomena in Marine Plants and Animals*, eds E. Naylor & R. G. Hartnoll, pp. 223–30. Oxford: Pergamon Press.

(1986). The fish populations of the Rockall Trough. *Proceedings of the Royal Society of Edinburgh*, **88B**, 191–204.

Gordon, J. D. M. & Duncan, J. A. R. (1985). The ecology of the deep-sea benthic and benthopelagic fish on the slopes of the Rockall Trough, northeastern Atlantic. *Progress in Oceanography*, **15**, 37–69.

(1987). Deep-sea bottom-living fishes at two repeat stations at 2200 m and 2900 m in the Rockall Trough, northeastern Atlantic Ocean. *Marine Biology*, **96**, 309–25.

Gould, W. J. & McKee, W. D. (1973). Vertical structure of semi-diurnal tidal currents in the Bay of Biscay. *Nature, London*, **244**, 88–91.

Gould-Somero, M. (1975). Echiura. In *Reproduction in Marine Invertebrates*, Vol. III, eds A. C. Giese & J. S. Pearse, pp. 277–311. New York: Academic Press.

Gowing, M. M. & Silver, M. W. (1983). Origins and microenvironments of bacteria mediating fecal pellet decomposition in the sea. *Marine Biology*, **73**, 7–16.

Gowing, M. M. & Wishner, K. F. (1986). Trophic relationships of deep-sea calanoid copepods from the benthic boundary layer of the Santa Catalina Basin, California. *Deep-Sea Research*, **33A**, 939–61.

Graf, G. (1989). Benthic-pelagic coupling in a deep-sea benthic community. *Nature, London*, **341**, 437–9.

Graf, G., Schulz, R., Peinert, R. & Meyer-Reidl, L. A. (1983). Benthic response to sedimentation events during autumn to spring at a shallow-water station in the western Kiel Bight. *Marine Biology*, **77**, 235–46.

Grant, W. D., Williams, A. J. & Gross, T. F. (1985). A description of the bottom boundary layer at the HEBBLE site: Low-frequency forcing, bottom stress and temperature structure. *Marine Geology*, **66**, 219–41.

Grasshoff, M. (1982). Die Gorgonaria, Pennatularia und Antipatharia des Tiefwassers der Biscaya (Cnidaria, Anthozoa). Ergebnisse der franzosischen Expeditionen Biogas, Polygas, Geomanche, Incal, Noratlante und Fahrte der Thalassa. *Bulletin du Museum national d'histoire naturelle, Paris (Sér. A)*, **3**, 731–66.

(1985). Die Gorgonaria, Pennatularia und Antipatharia. In *Peuplements Profonds du Golfe de Gascogne*, eds L. Laubier & C. Monniot, pp. 299–310. Brest: Institut Français de Recherche pour l'Exploitation de la Mer.

Grassle, J. F. (1977). Slow recolonization of deep-sea sediment. *Nature, London*, **265**, 618–19.

(1980). *In situ* studies of deep-sea communities. In *Advanced Concepts in Ocean Measurement*, eds F. P. Diemer, F. J. Vernberg & D. Z. Mirkes, pp. 321–32. University of South Carolina Press.

(1985). Hydrothermal vent animals: distribution and biology. *Science, Washington*, **229**, 713–17.

(1986). The ecology of deep-sea hydrothermal vent communities. *Advances in Marine Biology*, **23**, 301–62.

(1989). Species diversity in deep-sea communities. *Trends in Ecology and Evolution*, **4**, 12–15.

Grassle, J. F., Brown-Leger, L. S., Morse-Porteous, L., Petreca, R. & Williams, I. (1985). Deep-sea fauna of sediments in the vicinity of hydrothermal vents. *Bulletin of the Biological Society of Washington*, **6**, 411–28.

Grassle J. F., Maciolek N. J. & Blake J. A. (1990). Are deep-sea communities resilient? In *The Earth in Transition: Patterns and Processes of Biotic Impoverishment*, ed. Woodwell G. M., pp. 384–59. New York: Cambridge University Press.

Grassle, J. F. & Morse-Porteous, L. S. (1987). Macrofaunal colonization of disturbed deep-sea environments and the structure of deep-sea benthic communities. *Deep-Sea Research*, **34A**, 1911–50.

Grassle, J. F. & Sanders, H. L. (1973). Life histories and the role of disturbance. *Deep-Sea Research*, **20**, 643–59.

Grassle, J. F., Sanders, H. L., Hessler, R. R., Rowe, G. T. & McLennan, T. (1975). Pattern and zonation: a study of the bathyal megafauna using the research submersible *Alvin*. *Deep-Sea Research*, **22**, 643–59.

Grassle, J. F., Sanders, H. L. & Smith, W. (1979). Faunal changes with depth in the deep-sea benthos. *Ambio Special Report*, No. 6, 47–50.

Grassle, J. F. & Smith, W. (1976). A similarity measure sensitive to the contribution of rare species and its use in investigation of variation in marine benthic communities. *Oecologia, Berlin*, **25**, 13–22.

Grassle, J. P. (1985). Genetic differentiation in populations of hydrothermal vent mussels (*Bathymodiolus thermophilus*) from the Galapagos Rift and 13° N on the East Pacific Rise. *Bulletin of the Biological Society of Washington*, **6**, 429–42.

Grassle, J. P. & Grassle, J. F. (1977). Sibling species in the marine pollution indicator *Capitella* (Polychaeta). *Science, Washington*, **192**, 567–9.

Green, R. H. (1979). *Sampling Design and Methods for Environmental Biologists*. New York: Wiley-Interscience.

Greenacre, M. J. (1984). *Theory and Applications of Correspondence Analysis*. London: Academic Press.

Grieg, J. A. (1921). Echinodermata. *Report on the Scientific Results of the 'Michael Sars' North Atlantic Deep Sea Expedition, 1910*, 3(2), 1–47.

Griffin, D. J. G. & Brown, D. E. (1975). Deepwater decapod Crustacea from eastern Australia: Brachyuran crabs. *Records of the Australian Museum*, **30**, 248–71.

Griffin, D. J. G. & Tranter, H. A. (1986). Some majid spider crabs from the deep Indo-west Pacific. *Records of the Australian Museum*, **38**, 351–71.

Griggs, G. B., Carey, A. G. & Kulm, L. D. (1969). Deep-sea sedimentation and sediment fauna interaction in Cascadia Channel and on Cascadia Abyssal Plain. *Deep-Sea Research*, **16**, 157–70.

Griggs, R. W. (1972). Orientation and growth form of sea fans. *Limnology and Oceanography*, **17**, 185–92.

Gross, T. F., Williams, A. J. & Nowell A. R. M. (1988). A deep-sea sediment transport storm. *Nature, London*, **331**, 518–21.

Guennegan, Y. & Rannou, M. (1979). Semidiurnal rhythmic activity in deep-sea benthic fishes in the Bay of Biscay. *Sarsia*, **64**, 113–16.

Guerinot, M. L. & Patriquin, D. G. (1981). The association of N_2-fixing bacteria with sea urchins. *Marine Biology*, **62**, 197–207.

Guinasso, N. L. & Schink, D. R. (1975). Quantitative estimates of biological mixing rates in abyssal sediments. *Journal of Geophysical Research*, **80**, 3032–4.

Gust, G. & Harrison, J. T. (1981). Biological pumps at the sediment-water interface: a mechanistic evaluation of the alpheid shrimp *Alpheus mackavi* and its irrigation pattern. *Marine Biology*, **64**, 71–8.

Haeckel, E. (1889). Report on the deep-sea Keratosa. *Report on the Scientific Results of the voyage of H.M.S. Challenger during the years 1873–76. Zoology*, **32**, 1–92.

Haedrich, R. L. (1974). Pelagic capture of the epibenthic rattail *Coryphaenoides rupestris*. *Deep-Sea Research*, **21**, 977–9.

  (1985). Species number–area relationship in the deep sea. *Marine Ecology – Progress Series*, **24**, 303–6.

Haedrich, R. L. & Henderson, N. R. (1974). Pelagic food of *Coryphaenoides rupestris*. *Deep-Sea Research*, **21**, 739–44.

Haedrich, R. L. & Maunder, J. E. (1985). The echinoderm fauna of the Newfoundland continental slope. In *Proceedings of the Fifth International Echinoderms Conference, Galway, 24–29 September 1984*, eds B. F. Keegan & B. D. S. O'Connor, pp. 37–45. Rotterdam: Balkema.

Haedrich, R. L. & Merrett, N. R. (1988). Summary atlas of deep living demersal fishes in the North Atlantic Basin. *Journal of Natural History*, **22**, 1325–62.

  (1990). Little evidence for faunal zonation or communities in the deep sea demersal fish faunas. *Progress in Oceanography*, **24**, 239–50.

Haedrich, R. L. & Rowe G. T. (1977). Megafaunal biomass in the deep-sea. *Nature, London*, **269**, 141–2.

Haedrich, R. L., Rowe, G. T. & Polloni, P. (1975). Zonation and faunal composition of epibenthic populations on the continental slope south of New England. *Journal of Marine Research*, **33**, 191–212.

  (1980). The megabenthic fauna in the deep sea south of New England, USA. *Marine Biology*, **57**, 165–79.

Hansen, B. (1956). Holothurioidea from depths exceeding 6000 meters. *Galathea Report*, **2**, 33–54.

  (1967). The taxonomy and zoogeography of the deep-sea holothurians in their evolutionary aspects. *Studies in Tropical Oceanography, Miami*, **5**, 480–501.

(1968). Brood protection in the deep-sea holothurian *Oneirophanta mutabilis* Théel. *Nature, London*, **217**, 1062–3.

(1972). Photographic evidence of a unique type of walking in deep-sea holothurians. *Deep-Sea Research*, **19**, 461–2.

(1975). Systematics and biology of the deep-sea holothurians. *Galathea Report*, **13**, 1–262.

Hansen, B. & Madsen, F. J. (1956). On two bathypelagic holothurians from the South China Sea. *Galathea Report*, **2**, 55–9.

Hanson, L. C. & Earle, S. A. (1987). Submersibles for scientists. *Oceanus*, **30**, 31–8.

Hargrave, B. T. (1984). Sinking of particulate matter from the surface water of the ocean. In *Heterotrophic Activity in the Sea*, eds J. E. Hobbie & P. J. le B. Williams, pp. 155–78.

(1985). Feeding rates of abyssal scavenging amphipods *(Eurythenes gryllus)* determined *in situ* by time-lapse photography. *Deep-Sea Research*, **32A**, 443–50.

Hargreaves, P. M. (1984). The distribution of Decapoda (Crustacea) in the open ocean and near-bottom over an adjacent slope in the northern North-east Atlantic Ocean during autumn 1979. *Journal of the Marine Biological Association of the United Kingdom*, **64**, 829–57.

Harper, J. L. (1969). The role of predation in vegetational diversity. *Brookhaven Symposia in Biology*, **22**, 48–62.

Harrison, K. (1987). Deep-sea asellote isopods of the north-east Atlantic: the family Thambematidae. *Zoologica Scripta* **16**, 51–72.

(1988). Seasonal reproduction in deep-sea Crustacea (Isopoda: Asellota). *Journal of Natural History*, **22**, 175–97.

(1989). Are deep-sea asellote isopods infaunal or epifaunal? *Crustaceana*, **56**, 317–19.

Hartman, O. (1965). Deep-water benthic polychaetous annelids of New England to Bermuda and other North Atlantic areas. *Allan Hancock Foundation Publications*, **28**, 1–378.

Hartman, O. & Fauchald, K. (1971). Deep-water benthic polychaetous annelids off New England to Bermuda and other North Atlantic areas. Part II. Allan Hancock *Monographs in Marine Biology*, **6**, 1–327.

Hartnoll, R. G. & Rice, A. L. (1985). Further studies on the biology of the deep-sea spider crab *Dorhynchus thomsoni*: instar sequence and the annual cycle. In *Proceedings of the 19th European Marine Biology Symposium*, ed. P. E. Gibbs, pp. 231–41. Cambridge: University Press.

Harvey, R. & Gage, J. D. (1984). Observations on the reproduction and postlarval morphology of pourtalesiid sea urchins in the Rockall Trough area (N.E. Atlantic). *Marine Biology*, **82**, 181–90.

Hassack, E. & Holdich, D. M. (1987). The tubicolous habit amongst the Tanaidacea (Crustacea, Peracarida) with particular reference to deep-sea species. *Zoologica Scripta*, **16**, 223–33.

Haymon, R. M. & Koski, R. A. (1985). Evidence of an ancient hydrothermal vent community, fossil worm tubes in Cretaceous sulfide deposits of the Samail Ophiolite, Oman. *Biological Bulletin of the Society of Washington*, **6**, 57–65.

Hayward, P. J. (1978). The morphology of *Euginoma vermiformis* Jullien (Bryozoa Cheilostomata). *Journal of Natural History*, **12**, 97–106.

(1981). The Cheilostomata of the Deep Sea. *Galathea Report*, **15**, 21–68.

(1985). A summary of the Bryozoa. In *Peuplements Profonds du Golfe de Gascogne*, eds L. Laubier & C. Monniot, pp. 385–90. Brest: Institut Français de Recherche pour l'Exploitation de la Mer.

Heath, G. R. (1982). Deep-sea ferromanganese nodules. In *The Environment of the Deep-Sea*, eds W. G. Ernst & J. G. Morin, pp. 105–53. Englewood Cliffs, New Jersey: Prentice-Hall.

Hecker, B. (1982). Possible benthic fauna and slope instability relationships. In *Marine Slides and Other Mass Movements*, ed. S. Saxov & J. K. Nieuwenhuis, pp. 335–47. New York: Plenum Press.

(1985). Fauna from a cold sulfur-seep in the Gulf of Mexico: comparison with hydrothermal vent communities and evolutionary implications. *Bulletin of the Biological Society of Washington*, **6**, 465–73.

(1990). Variation in megafaunal assemblages on the continental margin south of New England. *Deep-Sea Research*, **37A**, 37–57.

Hecker, B., Logan, D. T., Gandarillas, F. E. & Gibson, P. R. (1983). Megafaunal assemblages in Lydonia Canyon, Baltimore Canyon, and selected slope areas. In *Canyon and Slope Processes Study*, vol. 3, pp. 1–140. Final Report for the U.S. Department of the Interior, Minerals Management Service Contract 14–12–001–29178.

Hecker, B. & Paul, A. Z. (1979). Abyssal community structure of the benthic infauna of the Eastern Equatorial Pacific: DOMES sites A, B, and C. In *Marine Geology and Oceanography of the Pacific Manganese Nodule Province*, eds J. L. Bischoff & D. Z. Piper, pp. 83–112. New York: Plenum Press.

Heezen, B. C. & Hollister, C. D. (1971). *The Face of the Deep*. New York: Oxford University Press.

Heip, C., Vincx, M. & Vranken, G. (1985). The ecology of marine nematodes. *Oceanography and Marine Biology: an Annual Review*, **23**, 399–489.

Heirtzler, J. R. & Grassle, J. F. (1976). Deep-sea research by manned submersibles. *Science, Washington*, **194**, 294–9.

Hendler, G. (1975). Adaptational significance of the patterns of ophiuroid development. *American Zoologist*, **15**, 691–715.

Hepper, B. T. (1971). Notes on *Geryon tridens* (Decapoda, Brachyura) from west of Ireland. *Journal of Natural History*, **15**, 343–8.

Hersey, J. B. (1967). *Deep-Sea Photography*. Baltimore: Johns Hopkins Press.

Hessler, R. R. (1970). The Desmosomatidae (Isopoda, Asellota) of the Gay Head–Bermuda transect. *Bulletin of the Scripps Institution of Oceanography*, **15**, 1–185.

(1974). The structure of deep benthic communities from central oceanic waters. In *The Biology of the Oceanic Pacific*, ed. C. B. Miller, pp. 79–93. Oregon State University Press.

(1981). Oasis under the sea – where sulphur is the staff of life. *New Scientist*, **92**, No. 1283, 741–7.

Hessler, R. R., Ingram, C. L., Yayanos, A. A. & Burnett, B. R. (1978). Scavenging amphipods from the floor of the Philippine Trench. *Deep-Sea Research*, **25**, 1029–47.

Hessler, R. R., Isaacs, J. D. & Mills, E. W. (1972). Giant amphipod from the abyssal Pacific Ocean. *Science, Washington*, **175**, 636–7.

Hessler, R. R. & Jumars, P. A. (1974). Abyssal community analysis from replicate box cores in the central North Pacific. *Deep-Sea Research*, **21**, 185–209.

(1977). Abyssal communities and radioactive waste disposal. *Oceanus*, **20**, 41–6.

(1979). The relation of benthic communities to radioactive waste disposal in the Deep-Sea. *Ambio Special Report*, **6**, 93–6.

Hessler, R. R., Lonsdale, P. & Hawkins, J. (1988a). Patterns on the ocean floor. *New Scientist*, **117**, No. 1605, 47–51.

Hessler, R. R. & Sanders, H. L. (1967). Faunal diversity in the deep sea. *Deep-Sea Research*, **14**, 65–78.

Hessler, R. R. & Smithey, W. M. (1983). The distribution and community structure of megafauna at the Galapagos Rift hydrothermal vents. In *Hydrothermal Processes at Seafloor Spreading Centers*, eds P. A. Rona, K. Bostrom, L. Laubier & K. L. Smith, NATO Conference Series IV, pp. 735–70. New York: Plenum Press.

Hessler, R. R., Smithey, W. M., Boudrias, M. A., Keller, C. H., Lutz, R. A. & Childress, J. J. (1988b). Temporal change in the megafauna at the Rose Garden hydrothermal vent (Galapagos Rift: eastern tropical Pacific). *Deep-Sea Research*, **35A**, 1681–709.

Hessler, R. R., Smithey, W. M., & Keller, C. H. (1985). Spatial and temporal variation of giant clams, tube worms and mussels at deep-sea hydrothermal vents. *Bulletin of the Biological Society of Washington*, **6**, 411–28.

Hessler, R. R. & Strömberg, J.-O. (1989). Behavior of janiroidean isopods (Asellota) with special reference to deep-sea genera. *Sarsia*, **74**, 145–59.

Hessler, R. R. & Thistle, D. (1975). On the place of origin of deep-sea isopods. *Marine Biology*, **32**, 155–65.

Hessler, R. R. & Wilson, G. D. F. (1983). The origin and biogeography of the malacostracan crustaceans in the deep sea. In *Evolution, Time and Space: the Emergence of the Biosphere*, eds R. W. Sims, J. H. Price & P. E. S. Whalley, pp. 227–54. London: Academic Press.

Hessler, R. R., Wilson, G. D. & Thistle, D. (1979). The deep-sea isopods: a biogeographic and phylogenetic overview. *Sarsia*, **64**, 67–76.

Heyraud, M., Domanski, P., Cherry, R. D. & Fasham, M. J. R. (1988). Natural tracers in dietry studies : data for ^{210}Po and ^{210}Pb in decapod shrimp and other pelagic organisms in the northeast Atlantic Ocean. *Marine Biology*, **97**, 507–19.

Hickman, C. S. (1981). Selective deposit-feeding by the deep-sea archaeogastropod *Bathybembix aeola*. *Marine Ecology – Progress Series*, **6**, 339–42.

(1983). Radular patterns, systematics, diversity, and ecology of deep-sea limpets. *The Veliger*, **26**, 73–92.

(1984). Composition, structure, ecology, and evolution of six cenozoic deep-water mollusc communities. *Journal of Paleontology*, **58**, 1215–34.

Hicks, G. R. F. & Coull, B. C. (1983). The ecology of marine meiobenthic copepods. *Marine Biology and Oceanography: an Annual Review of*, **21**, 67–175.

Hill, M. O. (1979*a*). DECORANA – *A FORTRAN Program for detrended correspondence analysis and reciprocal averaging*. Ithaca, New York: Cornell University.

(1979*b*). TWINSPAN – *A FORTRAN Program for arranging Multivariate data in an ordered two-way table by classification of the individuals and attributes*. Ithaca, New York: Cornell University.

Hill, M. O. & Gauch, H. G. (1980). Detrended correspondence analysis, an improved ordination technique. *Vegetatio*, **42**, 31–43.

Holdich, D. M. & Bird, G. (1985). A preliminary report on dikonophoran tanaids (Crustacea) from the Bay of Biscay. In *Peuplements Profonds du Golfe de Gascogne*, eds L. Laubier & C. Monniot, pp. 441–7. Brest: Institut Français de Recherche de l'Exploitation du Mer.

Holdich, D. M. & Jones, J. A. (1983). *Tanaids: Keys and Notes for the Identification of the Species*. Synopses of the British Fauna (New Series), eds D. M. Kermack & R. S. K. Barnes, No. 27. London: Cambridge University Press.

Hollister, C. D., Heezen, B. C. & Nafe, K. E. (1975). Animal traces on the deep-sea floor. In *The Study of Trace Fossils*, ed. R. W. Frey, pp. 493–510. New York: Springer.

Hollister, C. D. & McCave, I. N. (1984). Sedimentation under deep-sea storms. *Nature, London*, **309**, 220–5.

Hollister, C. D., Nowell, A. R. M. & Jumars, P. A. (1984). The dynamic abyss. *Scientific American*, **250**, 42–53.

Holme, N. A. & Willerton, P. F. (1984). Position fixing of ship and gear. In *Methods for the Study of Marine Benthos*, eds N. A. Holme & A. D. McIntyre, pp. 27–40. Oxford: Blackwell Scientific Publications.

Holthius, L. B. (1974). The lobsters of the superfamily Nephropsidea of the Atlantic Ocean. *Bulletin of Marine Science*, **24**, 67–76.

Honjo, S. (1982). Seasonality and interaction of biogenic and lithogenic particulate flux at the Panama Basin. *Science, Washington*, **218**, 883–4.

Honjo, S., Connell, J. F. & Sachs P. L. (1980). Deep Ocean Sediment Trap; Design and function of PARFLUX Mark II. *Deep-Sea Research*, **27A**, 745–53.

Honjo, S. & Doherty, K. W. (1988). Large aperture time-series sediment traps; design objectives, construction and application. *Deep-Sea Research*, **35A**, 133–49.

Honjo, S., Doherty, K. W., Agrawal, Y. C. & Asper, V. L. (1984). Direct optical assessment of large amorphous aggregates (marine snow) in the deep ocean. *Deep-Sea Research*, **31A**, 67–76.

Houston, K. A. & Haedrich, R. L. (1984). Abundance and biomass of macrobenthos in the vicinity of Carson Canyon, northwest Atlantic Ocean. *Marine Biology*, **82**, 301–5.

Hovland, M. & Judd, A. G. (1988). *Seabed Pockmarks and Seepages*. London: Graham & Trotman.

Hovland, M. & Thomsen, E. (1989). Hydrocarbon-based communities in the North Sea, *Sarsia*, **74**, 29–42.

Huber, R., Kurr, M., Jannasch, H. W. & Stettler, K. O. (1959). A novel group of abyssal methanogenic archaebacteria (*Methanopyrus*) growing at 110° C. *Nature, London*, **342**, 833–4.

Huggett, Q. J. (1987). Mapping of hemipelagic versus turbiditic muds by feeding traces observed in deep-sea photographs. In *Geology and Geochemistry of Abyssal Plains*, eds P. P. E. Weaver & J. Thomson, pp. 105–12 (Geological Society Special Publications No. 31). Oxford: Blackwell Scientific Publications.

Hughes, R. G. (1986). Theories and models of species abundance. *American Naturalist*, **128**, 879–99.

Hughes, R. N. (1969). A study of feeding in *Scrobicularia plana*. *Journal of the Marine Biological Association of the United Kingdom*, **49**, 805–23.

Hulings, N. C. & Gray, J. S. (1971). A Manual for the Study of Meiofauna. *Smithsonian Contributions to Zoology*, **28**, 1–79.

Hurlbert, S. H. (1971). The nonconcept of species diversity: a critique and alternative parameters. *Ecology*, **52**, 577–86.

Huston, M. (1979). A general hypothesis of species diversity. *American Naturalist*, **113**, 81–101.

Hutchings, J. A. & Haedrich, R. A. (1984). Growth and population structure in two species of bivalves (Nuculanidae) from the deep sea. *Marine Ecology – Progress Series*, **17**, 135–42.

Hutchinson, E. (1953). The concept of pattern in ecology. *Proceedings of the Academy of Natural Sciences, Philadelphia*, **105**, 1–12.

Hylleberg, J. (1975). Selective feeding by *Abarenicola pacifica* with notes on *Abarenicola vagabunda* and a concept of bacterial gardening. *Ophelia*, **14**, 113–37.

Ingram, C. L. & Hessler, R. R. (1983). Distribution and behavior of scavenging amphipods from the central North Pacific. *Deep-Sea Research*, **30A**, 683–706.

(1987). Population biology of the deep-sea amphipod *Eurythenes gryllus*. *Deep-Sea Research*, **34A**, 1889–910.

Isaacs, J. D. (1969). The nature of oceanic life. *Scientific American*, **175**, 636–7.

Isaacs, J. D. & Schwartzlose, R. A. (1975). Active animals of the deep-sea floor. *Scientific American*, **233**, 85–91.

Iseki, K. (1981). Particulate organic matter transport to the deep sea by salp fecal pellets. *Marine Ecology – Progress Series*, **5**, 55–60.

Ittekkot, V., Deuser W. G. & Degens D. G. (1984). Seasonality in the flux of sugars, amino acids and amino sugars to the deep ocean: Sargasso Sea. *Deep-Sea Research*, **31A**, 1057–69.

Ivanov, A. V., (1963). *Pogonophora*. London: Academic Press.

Jablonski, D. & Lutz, R. A. (1983). Larval ecology of marine benthic invertebrates: palaeobiological implications. *Biological Reviews*, **58**, 21–90.

Jannasch, H. W. (1978). Experiments in deep-sea microbiology. *Oceanus*, **21**, 50–7.

(1979). Chemosynthetic primary production at East Pacific sea floor spreading centers. *Bioscience*, **29**, 228–32.

(1983). Microbial processes at deep sea hydrothermal vents. In *Hydrothermal Processes at Seafloor Spreading Centers*, eds P. A. Rona, K. Bostrom, L. Laubier & K. L. Smith. NATO Conference Series IV, 677–709. New York: Plenum Press.

(1984). Chemosynthesis: the nutritional basis for life at deep-sea vents. *Oceanus*, **27**, 73–8.

(1985). The chemosynthetic support of life and the microbial diversity at deep-sea hydrothermal vents. *Proceedings of the Royal Society of London*, Series B, **225**, 277–97.

Jannasch, H. W., Cuhel, R. L., Wirsen, C. O. & Taylor, C. D. (1980). An approach for *in situ* studies of deep-sea amphipods and their microbial gut flora. *Deep-Sea Research*, **27A**, 867–72.

Jannasch, H. W., Eimhjellen, K., Wirsen, C. O. & Farmanfarmaian, A. (1970). Microbial degradation of organic matter in the deep-sea. *Science, Washington*, **171**, 672–5.

Jannasch, H. W. & Mottl, M. J. (1985). Geomicrobiology of deep-sea hydrothermal vents. *Science, Washington*, **229**, 717–25.

Jannasch, H. W., Nelson, D. C. & Wirsen, C. O. (1989). Massive natural occurrence of unusually large bacteria (*Beggiatoa* sp.) at a hydrothermal deep-sea vent site. *Nature, London*, **342**, 834–6.

Jannasch, H. W. & Taylor, C. D. (1984). Deep-Sea Microbiology. *Annual Review of Microbiology*, **38**, 487–514.

Jannasch, H. W. & Wirsen, C. O. (1973). Deep-Sea Microorganisms: *In situ* response to nutrient enrichment. *Science, Washington*, **180**, 641–3.

(1979). Chemosynthetic primary production of East Pacific seafloor spreading centers. *BioScience*, **29**, 592–8.

(1983). Microbiology of the Deep Sea. In *The Sea*, Vol. 8, ed. G. T. Rowe, pp. 231–59. New York: Wiley-Interscience.

(1984). Variability of pressure adaptation in deep sea bacteria. *Archives of Microbiology*, **139**, 281–8.

Jannasch, H. W., Wirsen, C. O. & Taylor, C. D. (1976) Undecompressed microbial populations from the deep sea. *Applied and Environmental Microbiology*, **32**, 360–7.

(1982). Deep-sea bacteria: isolation in the absence of decompression. *Science, Washington*, **216**, 1315–17.

Jannasch, H. W., Wirsen, C. O. & Winget, C. L. (1973). A bacteriological pressure-retaining deep-sea sampler and culture vessel. *Deep-Sea Research*, **20**, 661–4.

Jensen, P. (1987). Feeding ecology of free-living aquatic nematodes. *Marine Ecology – Progress Series*, **35**, 187–96.

(1988). Nematode assemblages in the deep-sea benthos of the Norwegian Sea. *Deep-Sea Research*, **35A**, 1173–84.

Johnson, D. L. & Richardson P. L. (1977). On the wind-induced sinking of *Sargassum*. *Journal of Experimental Marine Biology and Ecology*, **28**, 255–67.

Johnson, K. S., Beehler, C. L., Sakamoto-Arnold, C. M. & Childress, J. J. (1986). *In situ* measurements of chemical distributions in a deep-sea hydrothermal vent field. *Science, Washington*, **231**, 1139–41.

Johnson, K. S., Childress, J. J. & Beehler, C. L. (1988). Short-term temperature variability in the Rose Garden hydrothermal vent (Galapagos Rift: eastern tropical Pacific). *Deep-sea Research*, **35A**, 1711–44.

Johnson, R. G. (1971). Animal–sediment relations in shallow water benthic communities. *Marine Geology*, **11**, 93–104.

Jollivet, D., Faugeres, J.-C., Griboulard, R., Desbruyères, D. & Blanc, G. (1990). Composition and spatial organization of a cold seep community on the South Barbados accretionary prism: tectonic, geochemical and sedimentary context. *Progress in Oceanography*, **24**, 25–45.

Jones, D. S., Thompson, I. & Ambrose, W. (1978). Age and growth rate determinations for the Atlantic surf clam *Spisula solidissima* (Bivalvia: Mactracea), based on internal growth lines in shell cross sections. *Marine Biology*, **47**, 63–70.

Jones, M. L. (ed.) (1985). Hydrothermal vents of the eastern Pacific: an overview. *Bulletin of the Biological Society of Washington*, **6**, 1–545.

(1985*a*). On the Vestimentifera, new phylum: six new species, and other taxa, from hydrothermal vents and elsewhere. *Bulletin of the Biological Society of Washington*, **6**, 117–58.

(1985*b*). Vestimentiferan pogonophorans: their biology and affinities. In *The Origins and Relationships of the Lower Invertebrates*, eds S. C. Morris, J. D. George, R. Gibson & H. M. Platt, pp. 327–42. Oxford: Clarendon Press.

Jones, N. S. (1956). The fauna and biomass of a muddy sand deposit off Port Erin, Isle of Man. *Journal of Animal Ecology*, **25**, 217–52.

(1969). The systematics and distribution of Cumacea from depths exceeding 200 meters. *Galathea Report*, **10**, 99–180.

(1985). Distribution of the Cumacea. In *Peuplements Profonds du Golfe de Gascogne*, eds L. Laubier & C. Monniot, pp. 429–33. Brest: Institut Français de Recherche pour l'Exploitation de la Mer.

(1986). The Cumacea (Crustacea) of the INCAL cruise. *Proceedings of the Royal Society of Edinburgh*, **88B**, 306–7.

Jones, N. S. & Sanders, H. L. (1972). Distribution of Cumacea in the deep Atlantic. *Deep-Sea Research*, **19**, 737–45.

Jørgensen, C. B. (1966). *Biology of Suspension Feeding*. Oxford: Pergamon Press.

Jumars, P. A. (1975*a*). Methods for measurement of community structure in deep-sea macrobenthos. *Marine Biology*, **30**, 245–52.

(1975*b*). Environmental grain and polychaete species' diversity in a bathyal community. *Marine Biology*, **30**, 253–66.

(1976). Deep-sea species diversity: does it have a characteristic scale? *Journal of Marine Research*, **34**, 217–46.

(1978). Spatial autocorrelation with RUM (Remote Underwater Manipulator): vertical and horizontal structure of a bathyal benthic community. *Deep-Sea Research*, **25**, 589–604.

(1981). Limits in predicting and detecting benthic community responses to manganese nodule mining. *Marine Mining*, **3**, 213–29.

Jumars, P. A. & Eckman, J. (1983). Spatial structure within deep-sea benthic communities. In *The Sea*, Vol. 8, ed. G. T. Rowe, pp. 399–451, New York: Wiley-Interscience.

Jumars, P. A. & Fauchald, K. (1977). Between-community contrasts in successful polychaete feeding strategies. In *Ecology of Marine Benthos*, ed. B. C. Coull, pp. 1–20. Columbia, South Carolina: University of South Carolina Press.

Jumars, P. A. & Gallagher, E. D. (1982). Deep-sea community structure: three plays on the benthic proscenium. In *The Environment of the Deep Sea*, eds W. G. Ernst & J. G. Morin, pp. 217–55. Englewood Cliffs, New Jersey: Prentice-Hall.

Jumars, P. A. & Hessler, R. R. (1976). Hadal community structure: implications from the Aleutian Trench. *Journal of Marine Research*, **34**, 547–60.

Jumars, P. A., Mayer, L. M., Deming, J. W., Baross, J. A. & Wheatcroft, R. A. (1990). Deep-sea deposit-feeding strategies suggested by environmental and feeding constraints. *Philosophical Transactions of the Royal Society of London*, Series A, **331**, 85–101.

Jumars, P. A. & Nowell, A. R. M. (1984). Fluid and sediment dynamic effects on marine benthic community structure. *American Zoologist*, **24**, 885–97.

Jumars, P. A., Self, R. F. L. & Nowell, A. R. M. (1982). Mechanics of particle selection by tentaculate deposit-feeders. *Journal of Experimental Marine Biology and Ecology*, **64**, 47–70.

Jumars, P. A., Thistle, D. & Jones, M. D. (1977). Detecting two-dimensional spatial pattern in biological data. *Oecologia, Berlin*, **28**, 109–23.

Juniper, S. K. & Sibuet, M. (1987). Cold seep benthic communities in Japan subduction zones: spatial organization, trophic strategies and evidence for temporal evolution. *Marine Ecology – Progress Series*, **40**, 115–26.

Just, J. (1980). Abyssal and deep bathyal Malacostraca (Crustacea) from the Polar Sea. *Videnskabelige Meddeleser fra Dansk Naturhistorisk Forening*, **142**, 161–77.

Kaminski, A. (1985). Evidence for control of abyssal agglutinated foraminiferal community structure by substrate disturbance: results from the HEBBLE area. *Marine Geology*, **66**, 113–31.

Karl, D. M., Knauer, G. A. & Martin, J. H. (1988). Downward flux of particulate organic matter in the ocean: a particle decomposition paradox. *Nature, London*, **332**, 438–41.

Karl, D. M., McMurtry, G. M., Malahoff, A., & Garcia, M. O. (1988). Loihi Seamount, Hawaii: a mid-plate volcano with a distinctive hydrothermal system. *Nature, London*, **335**, 532–5.

Karl, D., Wirsen, C. & Jannasch, H. (1980). Deep-sea primary production at the Galapagos hydrothermal vents. *Science, Washington*, **207**, 1345–7.

Kaufmann, R. S., Wakefield, W. W. & Genin, A. (1989). Distribution of epibenthic megafauna and lebensspuren on two central North Pacific seamounts. *Deep-Sea Research*, **36A**, 1863–96.

Keller, G. H., Lambert, D., Rowe, G. T. & Staresnic, N. (1973). Bottom currents in the Hudson Canyon. *Science, Washington*, **180**, 181–3.

Kemp, P. F. (1987). Potential impact on bacteria of grazing by macrofaunal deposit-feeder, and the fate of bacterial populations? *Marine Ecology – Progress Series*, **36**, 151–61.

Kennicutt II, M. C., Brooks, J. M. & Bidigare, R. R. (1985). Hydrocarbon seep communities : four years of study. *Oceanography*, **1 (2)**, 44–5.

Kennicutt II, M. C., Brooks, J. M., Bidigare, R. R., Denoux, G. J. (1988). Gulf of Mexico hydrocarbon seep communities – 1. Regional distribution of hydrocarbon seepage and associated fauna. *Deep-Sea Research*, **35A**, 1639–51.

Kennicutt II, M. C., Brooks, J. M., Bidigare, R. R., Fay, R. R., Wade, T. L. & McDonald, T. J. (1985). Vent-type taxa in a hydrocarbon seep region on the Louisiana slope. *Nature, London*, **317**, 351–3.

Kennicutt II, M. C., Brooks, J. M., Bidigare, R. R., McDonald, S. J., Adkinson, D. L. & Macko, S. A. (1989). An upper slope 'cold' seep community: Northern California. *Limnology and Oceanography*, **34**, 635–40.

Kempe, S. & Nies, H. (1987). Chernobyl nuclide record from a North Sea sediment trap. *Nature, London*, **329**, 828–831.

Kerr, R. A. (1980). A new kind of storm beneath the sea. *Science, Washington*, **208**, 484–6.

Kerr, S. R. (1974). Theory of size distribution in ecological communities. *Journal of the Fisheries Research Board of Canada*, **31**, 1859–62.

Khripounoff, A., Desbruyères, D. & Chardy, P. (1980). Les peuplements benthiques de la faille VEMA: donées quantitatives et bilan d'énergie en milieu abyssal. *Oceanologica Acta*, **3**, 187–98.

Khripounoff, A. & Sibuet, M. (1980). La nutrition d'échinodermes abyssaux. I. Alimentation des holothuries. *Marine Biology*, **60**, 17–26.

Kidd, R. B. & Huggett, Q. J. (1981). Rock debris on abyssal plains in the

NE Atlantic : A comparison of epibenthic sledge hauls and photographic surveys. *Oceanologica Acta*, **4**, 99–104.

Killingley, J., Berger, W. H., MacDonald, K. C. & Newman, W. A. (1980). $^{18}O/^{16}O$ variations in deep-sea carbonate shells from the Rise hydrothermal field. *Nature, London*, **287**, 218–21.

Killingley, J. S. & Rex, M. A. (1985). Mode of larval development in some deep-sea gastropods indicated by oxygen–18 values of their carbonate shells. *Deep-Sea Research*, **32A**, 809–18.

Kirkegaard, J. B. (1954). The zoogeography of the abyssal Polychaeta. In *On the Distribution and Origin of the Deep Sea Bottom Fauna. International Union of Biological Sciences, Series B*, **16**, 40–3. Naples.

(1956). Benthic Polychaeta from depths exceeding 6000 meters. *Galathea Report*, **2**, 63–78.

(1980). Abyssal benthic polychaetes from the northeast Atlantic Ocean, southwest of the British Isles. *Steenstrupia*, **6**, 81–98.

(1983). Bathyal benthic polychaetes from the N.E. Atlantic Ocean, S.W. of the British Isles. *Journal of the Marine Biological Association of the United Kingdom*, **63**, 593–608.

Kitchell, J. A. (1979). Deep-sea foraging pathways: an analysis of randomness and resource exploitation. *Paleobiology*, **5**, 107–25.

Kitchell, J. A., Kitchell, J. F., Clark, D. L. & Dangeard, L. (1978a). Deep-sea foraging behavior: its bathymetric potential in the fossil record. *Science, Washington*, **200**, 1289–91.

Kitchell, J. A., Kitchell, J. K., Johnson, G. L. & Hunkins, K. L. (1978b). Abyssal traces and megafauna: comparison of productivity, diversity and density in the Arctic and Antarctic. *Paleobiology*, **4**, 171–80.

Klein, H. (1988). Benthic storms, vortices, and particle dispersion in the deep West European Basin. *Deutches Hydrographisches Zeitschrift*, **40**, Jahrgang 1987, Heft 3, 87–102.

Knecht, R. W. (1982). Deep ocean mining. *Oceanus*, **25**, 3–11.

Knudsen, J. (1961). The bathyal and abyssal Xylophaga (Pholadidae, Bivalvia). *Galathea Report*, **5**, 163–209.

(1967). The deep-sea Bivalvia. *Scientific Reports of the 'John Murray' Expedition 1933–1934*, **11**, 23–243.

(1970). The systematics and biology of abyssal and hadal Bivalvia. *Galathea Report*, **11**, 7–241.

(1979). Deep-sea bivalves. In *Pathways in Malacology*, eds S. van der Spoel, A. C. van Bruggen & J. Lever, pp. 195–224. 6th International Congress Unitas Malacologica Europaea, Amsterdam, Netherlands, August 15–20, 1977. Utrecht: Bohn, Scheltema & Holkema.

Koltun, V. M. (1970). Sponge fauna of the northwestern Pacific from the shallows to hadal depths. *Trudy Instituta Okeanologii*, **86**, 165–221 (in Russian).

Kramp, P. L. (1956). Hydroids from depths exceeding 6000 meters. *Galathea Report*, **2**, 17–20.

(1959). *Stephanoscyphus* (Scyphozoa). *Galathea Report*, **1**, 173–85.

Kranck, K. & Milligan, T. G. (1988). Macroflocs from diatoms: *in situ* photography of particles in Bedford Basin, Nova Scotia. *Marine Ecology – Progress Series*. **44**, 183–9.

Kristensen, E. & Blackburn, T. H. (1987). The fate of organic carbon and nitrogen in experimental marine sediment systems: Influence of bioturbation and anoxia. *Journal of Marine Research*, **45**, 231–57.

Kucheruk, N. V. (1976). Polychaete worms of fam. Ampharetidae from the deep part of the Alaska Bay. *Trudy̆ Instituta Okeanologii*, **99**, 91–101 (in Russian, English summary).

Kuhnelt, T. (1976). *Soil Biology*. London: Faber and Faber.

Kullenberg, B. (1951). On the shape and length of the cable during a deep-sea trawling. *Report of the Swedish Deep-Sea Expedition*, II, *Zoology* **(2)**, 29–44.

Kulm, L. D., Suess, E., Moore, J. C., Carson, B., Lewis, B. T., Ritger, S. D., Kadko, D. C., Thornburg, T. M., Embley, R. W., Rugh, W. D., Massoth, G. J., Langseth, M. G., Cochrane, G. R. & Scamman, R. L. (1986). Oregon subduction zone venting, fauna, and carbonates. *Science, Washington*, **231**, 561–6.

Kussakin, O. G. (1973). Peculiarities of the geographical and vertical distribution of marine isopods and the problem of deep-sea fauna origin. *Marine Biology*, **23**, 19–34.

Lagardère, J. P. (1985). Biogéographie et composition taxonomique du peuplement abyssal de Mysidacés. In *Peuplements Profonds du Golfe de Gascogne*, eds L. Laubier & C. Monniot, pp. 425–8. Brest: Institut Français de Recherche pour l'Exploitation de la Mer.

Lambshead, P. J. D. & Platt, H. M. (1988). Analyzing disturbance with the Ewens/Caswell neutral model: theoretical review and practical assessment. *Marine Ecology – Progress Series*, **43**, 31–41.

Lambshead, P. J. D., Platt, H. M. & Shaw, K. M. (1983). The detection of differences among assemblages of marine benthic species based on an assessment of dominance and diversity. *Journal of Natural History*, **17**, 859–74.

Lampitt, R. S. (1985a). Evidence for the seasonal deposition of detritus to the deep-sea floor and its subsequent resuspension. *Deep-Sea Research*, **32A**, 885–97.

(1985b). Fast living on the ocean floor. *New Scientist*, **105**, No. 1445, 37–40.

Lampitt, R. S. & Billett, D. S. M. (1984). Deep-sea echinoderms: a time and motion study. In *Proceedings of the Fifth International Echinoderm Conference, Galway, 24–29 September 1984*, eds Keegan, B. F. & O'Connor, B. D. S., p. 160. Rotterdam: Balkema.

Lampitt, R. S., Billett, D. S. M. & Rice, A. L. (1986). Biomass of the invertebrate megabenthos from 500 to 4100 m in the northeast Atlantic Ocean. *Marine Biology*, **93**, 69–81.

Lampitt, R. S. & Burnham, M. P. (1983). A free-fall time-lapse camera and current meter system "Bathysnap" with notes on the foraging behaviour of a bathyal decapod shrimp. *Deep-Sea Research*, **30A**, 1009–17.

Lampitt, R. S., Merrett, N. R. & Thurston, M. H. (1983). Inter-relations of necrophagous amphipods, a fish predator, and tidal currents in the deep sea. *Marine Biology*, **74**, 73–8.

Lampitt, R. S. & Paterson, G. L. J. (1988). The feeding behaviour of an abyssal sea anemone from *in situ* photographs and trawl samples. *Oceanologica Acta*, **10**, 455–61.

Land, J. van der (1985). Abyssal *Priapulus* (Vermes, Priapulida). In *Peuplements Profonds du Golfe de Gascogne*, eds L. Laubier & C. Monniot, pp. 379–383. Brest: Institut Français de Recherche pour l'Exploitation de la Mer.

Landau, J. V. & Pope, D. H. (1980). Recent advances in the area of barotolerant protein synthesis in bacteria and implications concerning barotolerant and barophilic growth. *Advances in Aquatic Microbiology*, **2**, 49–76.

Laubier, L. (1986). *Des Oasis au Fond des Mers*, Paris: Le Rocher.

(ed.) (1988). Biology and ecology of the hydrothermal vents [Conference Proceedings, Institut Océanographique, Paris, 4–7 November 1985.] *Oceanologica Acta*, (spec. Vol.) **8**, 233 pp.

(1989). Écosystèmes benthiques profonds et chimiosynthèse bactérienne: sources hydrothermales et suintements froids. In *Océanologie: Actualité et Prospective*, ed. M. M. Denis, pp. 61–99. Marseilles: Centre d'Océanologie de Marseille.

Laubier, L. & Desbruyères, D. (1984). Les oasis du fond des oceans. *La Recherche*, **15**, 1506–17.

Laubier, L., Martinais, J. & Reyss, D. (1972). Deep-sea trawling using ultrasonic techniques. In *Barobiology and the Experimental Biology of the Deep Sea*, ed. R. W. Brauer, pp. 175–96. University of North Carolina Press.

Laubier, L., Ohta, S. & Sibuet, M. (1986). Découverte de communautes animales profundes durant la campagne franco-japonaise Kaiko de plongées dans les fosses de subduction autour du Japon. *Compte rendus hebdomadaires des séances de l'Académie des sciences, Paris*, **302**, 25–9.

Laughton, A. S. (1963). Microtopography. In *The Sea*, Vol. 3, ed. M. N. Hill, pp. 437–472. New York: Wiley-Interscience.

Laurin, B. & Gaspard, D. (1988). Variations morphologique et croissance du brachiopode abyssal *Macandrevia africana* Cooper. *Oceanologica Acta*, **10**, 445–54.

Laver, M. B., Olsson, M. S., Edelman, J. L. & Smith, K. L. (1985). Swimming rates of scavenging deep-sea amphipods recorded with a free vehicle video camera. *Deep-Sea Research*, **32A**, 1135–42.

Le Danois, E. (1948). Les Profondeurs de la Mer. Paris: Payot.

Le Pennec, M. & Fiala-Medioni, A. (1988). The role of the digestive tract of *Calyptogena lauberi* and *Calyptogena phaseoliformis*, vesicomyid bivalves of the subduction zones of Japan. *Oceanologica Acta*, **11**, 193–9.

Le Pennec, M. & Prieur, D. (1984). Observations sur la nutrition d'un Mytilidae d'un site hydrothermal actif de la dorsal du Pacific oriental. *Compte rendus hebdomadaires des séances de l'Académie des sciences, Paris*, **298**, 493–8.

Le Pennec, M., Prieur, D. & Lucas, A. (1985). Studies on the feeding of a hydrothermal-vent mytilid from the East Pacific Rise. In *Proceedings of the Nineteenth European Marine Biology Symposium*, ed. P. E. Gibbs, pp. 159–66. Cambridge University Press.

Le Pichon, X., Iiyama, T., Chamley, H., Charvet, J., Favre, M., Fujimoto H., Furuta, T., Ida, Y., Kagami, H., Lallemant, S., Leggett, J., Murata, A., Okada, H., Rangin, C., Renard, V., Taira, A. & Tokuyama, H. (1987). The eastern and western ends of Nankai trough: results of box 5 and box 7 Kaiko survey. *Earth and Planetary Science Letters*, **83**, 199–213.

Lee, J. J. (1980). Nutrition and physiology of Foraminifera. In *Biochemistry and Physiology of Protozoa*, Vol. 3, eds M. Levandowsky & S. M. Hutner, pp. 43–66. London: Academic Press.

Leeder, M. R. (1985). *Sedimentology: Processes and Product*. London: Allen & Unwin.

Lemche, H. (1957). A new living deep sea mollusc of the Cambro-Devonian Class Monoplacophora. *Nature, London*, **179**, 413–16.

Lemche, H., Hansen, B., Madsen, F. J., Tendal, O. S. & Wolff, T. (1976). Hadal life as analyzed from photographs. *Videnskabelige Meddelelser fra Dansk Naturhistorisk Forening*, **139**, 263–336.

Lemche, H. & Wingstrand, K. G. (1959). The anatomy of *Neopilina galatheae* Lemche, 1957 (Mollusca Tryblidiacea). *Galthea Report*, **3**, 9–72.

Leonard, A. B., Strickler, J. R. & Holland, N. D. (1988). Effects of current speed on filtration during suspension feeding in *Oligometra serripinna* (Echinodermata: Crinoidea). *Marine Biology*, **97**, 111–25.

Lester, R. J. G., Sewell, K. B., Barnes, A. & Evans, K. (1988). Stock discrimation of the orange roughy, *Hoplostethus atlanticus*, by parasite analysis. *Marine Biology*, **99**, 137–43.

Levi, C. (1964). Spongaires des zones bathyale, abyssale et hadale. *Galathea Report*, **7**, 63–112.

Levin, L. A., DeMaster, D. J., McCann, L. D. & Thomas, C. L. (1987). Effects of giant protozoans (class: Xenophyophorea) on deep-seamount benthos. *Marine Ecology – Progress Series*, **29**, 99–104.

Levin, L. A. & Smith, C. R. (1984). Response of background fauna to disturbance and enrichment in the deep sea: a sediment tray experiment. *Deep-Sea Research*, **31A**, 1277–85.

Levin, L. A. & Thomas, C. L. (1989). The influence of hydrodynamic regime on infaunal assemblages inhabiting carbonate sediments on central Pacific seamounts. *Deep-Sea Research*, **36A**, 1897–915.

Levinton, J. S. (1979). Deposit-feeders, their resources, and the study of resource limitation. In *Ecological Processes in Coastal and Marine Systems*, ed. R. J. Livingstone, pp. 117–41. New York: Plenum Press. (1982). *Marine Ecology*. Englewood Cliffs, New Jersey: Prentice-Hall.

Lightfoot, R., Tyler, P. A. & Gage, J. D. (1979). Seasonal reproduction in deep-sea bivalves and brittlestars. *Deep-Sea Research*, **26A**, 967–73.

Lincoln, R. J. (1985). Deep-sea asellote isopods of the north-east Atlantic: the family Haploniscidae. *Journal of Natural History*, **19**, 655–95.

Lincoln, R. J. & Boxshall, G. A. (1983). Deep-sea asellote isopods of the north-east Atlantic: the family Dendrotionidae and some new ectoparasitic copepods. *Zoological Journal of the Linnear Society*, **79**, 279–318.

Lipps, J. H. (1983). Biotic interrelations in benthic foraminifera. In *Biotic Interactions in Recent and Fossil Benthic Communities*, eds M. J. S. Tevesz & P. L. McCall, pp. 331–76. New York: Plenum Press.

Lipps, J. H. & Hickman, C. S. (1982). Origin, age and evolution of Antarctic and deep-sea faunas. In *The Environment of the Deep Sea*, eds W. G. Ernst & J. G. Morin, pp. 324–56. Englewood Cliffs, New Jersey: Prentice-Hall.

Littler, M. M., Littler, D. S., Blair, S. M. & Norris, J. N. (1985). Deepest known plant life discovered on an uncharted seamount. *Science, Washington*, **227**, 57–9.

Litvinova, N. M. & Sokolova, M. N. (1971). Feeding of deep-sea ophiuroids of the genus *Amphiophiura*. *Okeanologija*, Moscow, **11** (in Russian. English translation by Russian Translation Board of the American *Geophysical Union*, pp. 240–7).

Livingston, H. D. & Anderson, R. F. (1983). Large particle transport of plutonium and other fallout radionuclides to the deep ocean. *Nature, London*, **303**, 28–231.

Lochte, K. & Turley, C. M. (1988). Bacteria and cyanobacteria associated with phytodetritus in the deep sea. *Nature, London*, **333**, 67–9.

Loeblich, A. R. & Tappan, H. (1984). Suprageneric classification of the Foraminiferida (Protozoa). *Micropaleontology*, **30**, 1–70.

Lonsdale, P. (1977*a*). Deep-tow observations at the mounds abyssal thermal field, Galapagos Rift. *Earth and Planetary Letters*, **36**, 92–110.

(1977*b*). Clustering of suspension-feeding macrobenthos near abyssal hydrothermal vents at oceanic spreading centers. *Deep-Sea Research*, **24**, 857–63.

Lonsdale, P. & Hollister, C. D. (1979). A near bottom traverse of Rockall Trough: hydrographic and geologic inferences. *Oceanologica Acta*, **2**, 91–105.

Lopez, G. R. & Levinton, J. S. (1987). Ecology of deposit-feeding animals in marine sediments. *The Quarterly Review of Biology*, **62**, 235–60.

Lu, C. C. & Roper, C. F. E. (1979). Cephalopods from deep-water Dumpsite 106 (Western Atlantic): vertical distribution and seasonal abundance. *Smithsonian Contributions to Zoology*, **288**, 1–36.

Luckenbach, M. W. (1986). Sediment stability around animal tubes: the roles of hydrodynamic processes and biotic activity. *Limnology and Oceanography*, **31**, 779–87.

Lutz, R. A. (1988). Dispersal of organisms at deep-sea hydrothermal vents: a review. *Oceanologica Acta* (Spec. Vol.) **8**, 23–9.

Lutz, R. A., Fritz, L. W. & Cerrato, R. M. (1988). A comparison of bivalve (*Calyptogena magnifica*) growth at two deep-sea hydrothermal vents in the eastern Pacific. *Deep-Sea Research*, **35A**, 1793–810.

Lutz, R. A., Fritz, L. W. & Rhoads, D. C. (1985). Molluscan growth at deep-sea hydrothermal vents. *Bulletin of the Biological Society of Washington*, **6**, 199–210.

Lutz, R. A., Jablonski, D. & Turner, R. D. (1984). Larval development and dispersal at deep-sea hydrothermal vents. *Science, Washington*, **226**, 1451–1453.

MacArthur, R. H. & Wilson, E. O. (1967). *The Theory of Island Biogeography*. Princeton, New Jersey: Princeton University Press.

MacGinitie, G. E. & MacGinitie, N. (1968). *Natural History of Marine Animals*. New York: McGraw-Hill.

Maciolek, N., Grassle, J. F., Hecker, B., Boehm, P. D., Brown, B., Dade, B., Steinhauer, W. G., Baptiste, E., Ruff, R. E., Petrecca, R. (1987*a*). Study of biological processes on the U.S. mid-Atlantic slope and rise. Final Report prepared for U.S. Dept. of the Interior, Minerals Management Service, Washington, D.C. 20240, 310 pp.

Maciolek, N., Grassle, J. F., Hecker, B., Brown, B., Blake, J. A., Boehm, P. D., Petrecca, R., Duffy, S., Baptiste, E. & Ruff, R. E. (1987*b*). Study of biological processes on the U.S. North Atlantic slope and rise. Final Report prepared for U.S. Dept. of the Interior, Minerals Management Service, Washington, D.C. 20240, 362 pp.

Macurda, D. N. & Mayer, D. L. (1976). The morphology and life habits of the abyssal crinoid *Bathycrinus aldrichianus* Wyville Thomson and its paleontological implications. *Journal of Paleontology*, **50**, 647–67.

Maddocks, R. F. & Steineck, P. L. (1987). Ostracoda from experimental wood-island habitats in the deep-sea. *Micropaleontology*, **33**, 318–55.

Madsen, F. J. (1961*a*). The Porcellanasteridae. A monographic revision of an abyssal group of sea-stars. *Galathea Report*, **4**, 33–176.

(1961*b*). On the zoogeography and origin of the abyssal fauna. *Galathea Report*, **4**, 177–218.

Malahoff, A. (1985). Hydrothermal vents and polymetallic sulfides of the Galapagos and Gorda/Juan de Fuca Ridge Systems and of submarine volcanoes. *Bulletin of the Biological Society of Washington*, **6**, 19–42.

Malahoff, A., Embley, R. W. & Fornari, D. J. (1982). Geomorphology of Norfolk and Washington Canyons and the surrounding continental slope and upper rise as observed from DSRV ALVIN. In *The Ocean Floor*, Bruce Heezen commemorative volume, eds R. A. Scrutton & M. Talwani, pp. 97–111. London: John Wiley.

Mann, C. R., Coote, A. R. & Garner, D. K. (1973). The meridional distribution of silicate in Western Atlantic Ocean. *Deep-Sea Research*, **20**, 791–801.

Manning, R. B. & Struhsaker, P. (1976). Occurrence of the Caribbean stomatopod *Bathysquilla microps*, off Hawaii, with additional records for *B. microps* and *B. crassispinosa*. *Proceedings of the Biological Society of Washington*, **89**, 439–50.

Mantyla, A. W. & Reid, J. L. (1983). Abyssal characteristics of the world ocean waters. *Deep-Sea Research*, **30A**, *805–33*.

Mare, M. (1942). A study of a marine benthic community with special reference to the microorganisms. *Journal of the Marine Biological Association of the United Kingdom*, **25**, 517–54.

Margalef, R. (1969). Diversity and stability: a practical proposal and a model of interdependence. *Brookhaven Symposia in Biology*, **22**, 25–37.

Marquis, R. E. & Matsumura, P. (1978). Microbial life under pressure. In *Microbial Life in Extreme Environments*, ed. D. J. Kushner. New York: Academic Press.

Marshall, N. B. (1973). Family Macrouridae. In *Fishes of the Western North Atlantic*. Memoir, Sears Foundation for Marine Research, No. 1, part 6, pp. 496–665.

(1979). *Developments in Deep-Sea Biology*. Poole, Dorset: Blandford Press.

Marshall, N. B. & Bourne, D. W. (1967). Deep-sea photography in the study of fishes. In *Deep-Sea Photography*, ed. J. B. Hersey, pp. 251–7. Baltimore: Johns Hopkins Press.

Marshall, N. B. & Merrett, N. R. (1977). The existence of a benthopelagic fauna in the deep-sea. In *A Voyage of Discovery: G. Deacon 70th Anniversary Volume*, ed. M. Angel, pp. 483–97. Oxford: Pergamon Press.

Matisoff, G. (1982). Mathematical models of bioturbation. In *Animal Sediment Relations: the Biogenic Alteration of Sediments*, ed. P. L. McCall & M. J. S. Tevesz, pp. 289–330. New York: Plenum Press.

Mauchline, J. & Gordon, J. D. M. (1984). Diets and bathymetric distributions of the macrourid fish of the Rockall Trough, northeastern Atlantic. *Marine Biology*, **81**, 107–21.

(1985). Trophic diversity in deep-sea fish. *Journal of Fish Biology*, **26**, 527–35.

(1986). Foraging strategies in deep-sea fish. *Marine Ecology – Progress Series*, **27**, 227–38.

Mauviel, A., Juniper, S. K. & Sibuet, M. (1987). Discovery of an enteropneust associated with a mound-burrows trace in the deep sea: ecological and geochemical implications. *Deep-Sea Research*, **34A**, 329–35.

Mauviel, A. & Sibuet, M. (1985). Répartition des traces animales et importance de la bioturbation. In *Peuplements Profonds du Golfe de Gascogne*, eds L. Laubier & C. Monniot. Campagnes Biogas. Brest: Institut Français de Recherche pour l'Exploitation de la Mer.

Mayer, L. A., Shor, A. N., Clarke, J. H. & Piper, D. J. (1988). Dense biological communities at 3850m on the Laurentian Fan and their relationship to the deposits of the 1929 Grand Banks earthquake. *Deep-Sea Research*, **35A**, 1235–46.

Mayr, E. (1963). *Populations, Species and Evolution*. Cambridge, Massachusetts: Harvard University Press.

McCartney, M. S. & Talley, L. D. (1984). Warm-to-cold conversion in the northern North Atlantic Ocean. *Journal of Physical Oceanography*, **14**, 922–35.

McCave, I. N. (1975). Vertical flux of particles in the ocean. *Deep-Sea Research*, **22**, 491–502.

McHugh, D. (1989). Population structure and reproductive biology of two sympatric hydrothermal vent polychaetes, *Paralvinella pandorae* and *P. palmiformis*. *Marine Biology*, **103**, 95–106.

McIntyre, A. D. (1969). Ecology of marine benthos. *Biological Bulletin*, **44**, 245–90.

McLean, J. H. (1988). New archaeogastropod limpet families in the hydrothermal vent community. *Malacological Review, Supplement* 4, 85–7.

McLellan, T. (1977). Feeding strategies of the macrourids. *Deep-Sea Research*, **24**, 1019–36.

Mead, G. W., Bertelson, E. & Cohen, D. M. (1964). Reproduction among deep-sea fishes. *Deep-Sea Research*, **11**, 569–96.

Meadows, D. S. & Reid, A. (1966). The behaviour of *Corophium volutator* (Crustacea: Amphipoda). *Journal of Zoology*, **150**, 387–99.

Meadows, P. S. & Tait, J. (1985). Bioturbation, geotechnics and microbiology at the sediment-water interface in deep-sea sediments, In *Proceedings of the Nineteenth European Marine Biology Symposium*, ed. P. E. Gibbs, pp. 191–9. Cambridge University Press.

Meadows, P. S. & Tufail, A. (1986). Bioturbation, microbial activity and sediment properties in an estuarine ecosystem. *Proceedings of the Royal Society of Edinburgh*, **90B**, 129–42.

Meincke, J., Siedler, G. & Zenk, W. (1975) Some current observations near the continental slope off Portugal. *Meteor. Forschungsergebnisse*, **16A**, 15–22.

Melville-Smith, R. (1987). The reproductive biology of *Geryon maritae* (Decapoda, Brachyura) off South West Africa/Namibia. *Crustaceana*, **53**, 259–75.

Menge, B. A. & Sutherland, J. P. (1976). Species diversity gradients: synthesis of the roles of predation, competition, and temporal heterogeneity. *American Naturalist*, **110**, 351–69.

Menzies, R. J. (1959). *Priapulus abyssorum*, new species, the first abyssal priapulid. *Nature, London*, **184**, 1585–6.

(1965). Conditions for the existence of life on the abyssal sea floor. *Oceanography and Marine Biology: an Annual Review*, **3**, 195–210.

(1973). Biological history of the Mediterranean Sea with reference to the abyssal benthos. *Rapports et procès-verbaux des réunions Commission internationale pour l'exploration scientifique de la Mer Méditerranée, Paris*, **21** (9), 717–23.

Menzies, R. J., George, R. Y. & Rowe, G. T. (1973). *Abyssal Environment and Ecology of the World Oceans*. New York: Wiley-Interscience.

Menzies, R. J. & Imbrie, J. (1955). On the antiquity of the deep-sea bottom fauna. *Oikos*, **9**, 192–201.

Menzies, R. J. & Rowe, G. T. (1969). The distribution and significance of detrital turtle grass *Thallasia testudinum*, on the deep-sea floor off North Carolina. *International Revue gesampten Hydrobiologia*, **54**, 217–22.

Menzies, R. J., Zanefield, J. S. & Pratt, R. M. (1967). Transported turtle grass as a source of enrichment of abyssal sediments off North Carolina. *Deep-Sea Research*, **14**, 111–12.

Merrett, N. R. (1986). Macrouridae of the eastern North Atlantic. *Fiche d'Identification du Plancton*, Fiche No. 173/174/175, 14 pp.

(1987). A zone of faunal change in assemblages of abyssal demersal fish in the eastern North Atlantic: A response to seasonality in production? *Biological Oceanography*, **5**, 137–51.

(1989). Fishing around in the dark. *New Scientist*, No. 1653, **121**, 50–4.

Merrett, N. R. & Domanski, P. A. (1985). Observations on the ecology of deep-sea bottom-living fishes collected off Northwest Africa. II. The Moroccan slope (27–34 N) with special reference to *Synaphobranchus kaupi* Johnson, 1982. *Biological Oceanography*, **3**, 349–99.

Merrett, N. R. & Marshall, N. B. (1981). Observations on the ecology of two deep-sea bottom-living fishes collected off northwest Africa (08°N–27° N). *Progress in Oceanography*, **9**, 185–244.

Merrett, N. R. & Saldanha, L. (1985). Aspects of the morphology and ecology of some unusual deep-sea eels (Synaphobranchidae, Derichthyidae and Nettastomatidae) from the eastern North Atlantic. *Journal of Fish Biology*, **27**, 719–47.

Merrett, N. R. & Wheeler, A. (1983). The correct identification of two trachichthyid fishes (Pisces, Berycomorphi) from the slope fauna west of Britain with notes on the abundance and commercial importance of *Hoplostethus atlanticus*. *Journal of Natural History*, **17**, 569–73.

Messing, C. G. (1985). Submersible observations of deep-water crinoid assemblages in the tropical western Atlantic. In *Echinodermata*, eds B. F. Keegan & B. D. S. O'Connor, pp. 185–93. Rotterdam: Balkema.

Meyer, D. L. (1982). Food and feeding mechanisms: Crinozoa. In *Echinoderm Nutrition*, eds M. Jangoux & J. M. Lawrence, pp. 25–55. Rotterdam: Balkema.

Mickel, T. J. & Childress, J. J. (1982). Effects of temperature, pressure, and oxygen concentration on the oxygen consumption rate of the hydrothermal vent crab *Bythograea thermydron* (Brachyura). *Physiological Zoology*, **55**, 199–207.

Mileikovsky, S. A. (1968). Distribution of pelagic larvae of bottom invertebrates of the Norwegian and Barents Sea. *Marine Biology*, **1**, 161–7.

Millar, R. H. (1965). Evolution in ascidians. In *Some Contemporary Studies in Marine Science*, ed. H. Barnes, pp. 519–34. London: Allen & Unwin.

(1970). Ascidians, including specimens from the deep sea, collected by the Vema and now in the American Museum of Natural History. *Journal of the Linnaean Society* (Zoology), **49**, 99–159.

Miller, J. E. & Pawson, D. L. (1990). Swimming sea cucumbers (Echinodermata: Holothuroidea): a survey, with analysis of swimming behavior in four bathyal species. *Smithsonian Contributions to the Marine Sciences*, No. 35, 18 pp.

Miller, S. L. & Bada, J. L. (1988). Submarine hot springs and the origin of life. *Nature, London*, **334**, 609–11.

Mills, E. L. (1983). Problems of deep-sea biology: an historical perspective. In *The Sea*, Vol. 8, ed. G. T. Rowe, pp. 1–79. New York: Wiley-Interscience.

Mironov, A. N. (1975). Mode of life of the pourtalesiid sea-urchins (Echinoidea: Pourtalesiidae). *Trudy̆ Instituta Okeanologii*, **103**, 281–8 (in Russian, English summary).

Monniot, C. (1979). Adaptations of benthic filtering animals to the scarcity of suspended particles in deep water. *Ambio Special Report*, **6**, 73–4.

Monniot, C. & Monniot, F. (1975). Abyssal tunicates: an ecological paradox. *Annales de l'Institute Océanographique Paris*, **51**, 99–120.

(1978). Recent work on the deep-sea tunicates. *Oceanography and Marine Biology: an Annual Review*, **16**, 181–228.

Monniot, F. (1979). Faunal affinities among abyssal Atlantic basins. *Sarsia*, **64**, 93–6.

Moore, D. A. (1973). *Marine Chartwork and Navaids*. Sevenoaks, Kent: Kandy Publications.

Morita, R. Y. (1979). Current status of the microbiology of the deep-sea. *Ambio Special Report*, **6**, 33–6.

Morita, R. Y. & Zobell, C. E. (1955). Occurrence of bacteria in pelagic sediments collected during the Mid-Pacific Expedition. *Deep-Sea Research*, **3**, 66–73.

Mortensen, T. (1907). Echinoidea (Part 2). *Danish Ingolf Expedition*, **4(2)**, 1–200.

(1927). *Echinoderms of the British Isles*. London: Oxford University Press.

(1933). Ophiuroidea. *Danish Ingolf Expedition*, **4(8)**, 1–121.

(1935). A Monograph of the Echinoidea, II. Copenhagen: Reitzel.

(1938). On the vegetarian diet of some deep-sea echinoids. *Annotations zoologicae japonenses*, **17**, 225–8.

Moseley, H. N. (1880). Deep-sea dredgings and life in the deep sea. *Nature, London*, **21**, 543–7, 569–72, 591–3.

Moskalev, L. I. & Galkin, S. V. (1986). Investigations of the fauna of submarine upheavals during the 9th trip of the research vessel 'Academic Mstislav Keldysh'. *Zoologichesky Zhurnal*, **65**, 1716–21 (in Russian, English summary).

Muirhead, A., Tyler, P. A. & Thurston, M. H. (1986). Reproductive biology and growth of the genus *Epizoanthus* in the NE Atlantic. *Journal of the Marine Biological Association of the United Kingdom*, **66**, 131–43.

Mullineaux, L. S. (1987). Organisms living on manganese nodules and crusts: distribution and abundance at three North Pacific sites. *Deep-Sea Research*, **34A**, 165–84.

(1988). The role of settlement in structuring a hard-substratum community in the deep sea. *Journal of Experimental Marine Biology and Ecology*, **120**, 247–61.

(1989). Vertical distributions of the epifauna on manganese nodules : implications for settlement and feeding. *Limnology and Oceanography*, **34**, 1247–62.

Murina, V. V. (1984). Ecology of Sipuncula. *Marine Ecology – Progress Series*, **17**, 1–7.

Murphy, G. I. (1968). Pattern in life history and the environment. *American Naturalist*, **102**, 390–404.

Murphy, L. S., Rowe, G. T. & Haedrich, R. L. (1976). Genetic variability in deep-sea echinoderms. *Deep-Sea Research*, **23**, 339–48.

Murray, J. (1895). A summary of the scientific results obtained at the sounding, dredging and trawling stations of H.M.S. 'Challenger'. *Report on the Scientific Results of the Voyage of H.M.S. Challenger during the years 1873–76*, Summary of Results, **2**, 1–1608.

Murray, J. & Hjort, J. (1912). *The Depths of the Ocean*. London: MacMillan.

Murray, J. & Renard, A. F. (1891). Report on the deep-sea deposits. *Report on the Scientific Results of the Voyage of H.M.S. Challenger during the years 1873–76*, Deep-Sea Deposits, 1–525.

Murray, J. W. (1973). *Distribution and Ecology of Living Foraminiferids*. New York: Crane, Russak & Co.

Murray, J. W. (1988). Neogene bottom water-masses and benthic Foraminifera in the NE Atlantic Ocean. *Journal of the Geological Society of London*, **145**, 125–32.

Nair, R. R., Ittekkot, V., Manganini, S. J., Ramaswamy, V., Hakke, B., Degens, E. T., Desai, B. N. & Honjo, S. (1989). Increased particle flux to the deep ocean related to Monsoons. *Nature, London*, **338**, 749–51.

Nardin, T. R., Hein, F. J., Gorsline, D. S. & Edwards, B. D. (1979). A review of mass movement processes, sediment and acoustic characteristics, and contrasts in slope and base-of-slope systems versus canyon-fan-basin floor systems. *Special Publications of the Society of Economic Paleontologists and Mineralogists*, Tulsa, **27**, 61–73.

Naganuma, T., Otsuki, A. & Seki, H. (1989). Abundance and growth rates of bacterioplankton community in hydrothermal vent plumes of the North Fiji Basin. *Deep-Sea Research*, **36A**, 1379–90.

Nawab, Z. A. (1984). Red Sea mining: A new era. *Deep-Sea Research*, **31A**, 813–822.

NEA (1985). *Review of the continued suitability of the dumping site for radioactive waste in the north-east Atlantic*. Paris: Nuclear Energy Agency, Organisation for Economic Co-operation and Development.

Neale, J. W. (1985). The incidence and distribution of cladoceran platycopine and podocopine Ostracoda in certain BIOGAS and INCAL samples taken from the deeper waters of the N.E. Atlantic. In *Peuplements Profonds du Golfe de Gascogne*, eds L. Laubier & C. Monniot, pp. 413–17. Brest: Institut Français de Recherche pour l'Exploitation de la Mer.

Nealson, K. H. (1978). The isolation and characterization of marine bacteria which catalyze manganese oxidation. In *Environmental Biogeochemistry and Geomicrobiology*, Vol. 3, ed. W. E. Krumbein, pp. 847–58. Ann Arbor, Michigan: Ann Arbor Science.

(1982) Bacterial ecology of the deep-sea. In *The Environment of the Deep-Sea*, ed. W. G. Ernst & J. G. Morin, pp. 179–216. Englewood Cliffs, New Jersey: Prentice-Hall.

Newell, R. C. (1965). The role of detritus in the nutrition of two marine deposit feeders, the prosobranch *Hydrobia ulvae* and the bivalve *Macoma balthica*. *Proceedings of the Zoological Society of London*, **144**, 25–45.

Newman, W. (1971). A deep-sea burrowing barnacle (Cirripedia: Acrothoracica) from Bermuda. *Journal of Zoology, London*, **165**, 423–9.

Newman, W. A. (1979). A new scalpellid (Cirripedia); a Mesozoic relic living near an abyssal hydrothermal spring. *Transactions of the San Diego Society of Natural History*, **19(11)**, 153–67.

Newman, W. A. & Hessler, R. R. (1989). A new abyssal hydrothermal verrucomorphan (Cirripedia: Sessilia): The most primitive living sessile barnacle. *Transactions of the San Diego Society of Natural History*, **21(16)**, 259–73.

Nisbet, E. G. (1987). *The Young Earth. An Introduction to Archaean Geology*. Winchester, Massachusetts: Allen & Unwin.

Novitsky, J. A. & MacSween, M. C. (1989). Microbiology of a high energy beach sediment: evidence for an active and growing community. *Marine Ecology – Progress Series*, **52**, 71–5.

Nowell, A. R. M. & Jumars P. A. (1984). Flow environments of aquatic benthos. *Annual Review of Ecology and Systematics*, **15**, 303–28.

Nowell, A. R. M., Jumars, P. A. & Eckman, J. E. (1981). Effects of biological activity on the entrainment of marine sediments. *Marine Geology*, **42**, 133–53.

Nowell, A. R. M., Jumars, P. A. & Fauchald, K. (1984). The foraging strategy of a subtidal and deep-sea deposit feeder. *Limnology and Oceanography*, **29**, 645–9.

Nozaki, Y., Cochran, J. K., Turekian, K. K. & Keller, G. (1977). Radiocarbon and Pb-210 distribution in submersible-taken deep-sea cores from Project FAMOUS. *Earth and Planetary Sciences Letters*, **34**, 167–73.

Ockelmann, K. W. (1965). Development types in marine bivalves and their distribution along the Atlantic Coast of Europe. In *Proceedings of the First European Malacological Congress, London 1962*, eds L. R. Cox & J. Peake, 25–35.

Odhner, N. H. (1960). Brachiopoda. *Reports of the Swedish Deep-Sea Expedition*, 2(Zool.) **23**, 402–6.

Ohta, S. (1983). Photographic census of large-sized benthic organisms in the bathyal zone of Suruga Bay, central Japan. *Bulletin of the Ocean Research Institute*, University of Tokyo, No. 15, 244 pp.

(1984). Star-shaped feeding traces produced by echiuran worms on the deep-sea floor of the Bay of Bengal. *Deep-Sea Research*, **31A**, 1415–32.

(1985). Photographic observations of the swimming behaviour of the deep-sea pelagothuriid holothurian *Enypniastes* (Elasipoda, Holothurioidea). *Journal of the Oceanographical Society of Japan*, **41**, 121–33.

Ohta, S. & Laubier, L. (1987). Deep biological communities in the subduction zone of Japan from bottom photographs during 'Nautile' dives in the Kaiko project. *Earth and Planetary Science Letters*, **83**, 329–42.

Ohwada, K., Tabor, P. S. & Colwell R. R. (1980). Species composition and barotolerance of gut microflora of deep-sea benthic macrofauna collected at various depths in the Atlantic Ocean. *Applied and Environmental Microbiology*, **40**, 746–55.

Oliver, G. & Allen, J. A. (1980*a*). The functional and adaptive morphology of the family Limopsidae (Bivalvia: Arcoida) from the Atlantic. *Philosophical Transactions of the Royal Society of London, Series B*, **291**, 77–125.

(1980*b*). The functional and adaptive morphology of the deep-sea species of the Arcacea (Mollusca: Bivalvia) from the Atlantic. *Philosophical Transactions of the Royal Society of London*, Series B, **291**, 6–76.

Orton, J. H. (1920). Sea temperature, breeding and distribution in marine animals. *Journal of the Marine Biological Association of the United Kingdom*, **12**, 339–66.

Osman, R. W. & Whitlach, R. B. (1978). Patterns of species diversity: fact or artifact? *Paleobiology*, **4**, 41–54.

Osterberg, C., Carey, A. G. & Curl, H. (1963). Acceleration of sinking rates of radionuclides in the ocean. *Nature, London*, **200**, 1276–7.

Ozturgut, E., Lavelle, J. W. & Burns, R. E. (1981). Impacts of manganese nodule mining on the environment : Results from pilot-scale mining tests in the north equatorial Pacific. In *Marine Environmental Pollution*, 2, *Dumping and Mining*, ed. R. A. Geyer, pp. 437–74, Amsterdam: Elsevier Oceanography Series.

Paine, R. T. (1966). Food-web complexity and species diversity. *American Naturalist*, **100**, 65–75.

Paine, R. T. & Vadas, R. L. (1969). The effects of grazing by sea urchins, *Strongylocentrotus* spp., on benthic algal populations. *Limnology and Oceanography*, **14**, 710–19.

Papentin, F. (1973). A Darwinian evolutionary system III. Experiments on the evolution of feeding patterns. *Journal of Theoretical Biology*, **39**, 431–45.

Parulekar, A. H., Harkantra, S. N., Ansari, Z. A. & Matondkar, S. G. P. (1982). Abyssal benthos of the central Indian Ocean. *Deep-Sea Research*, **29A**, 1531–7.

Pastnernak, F. A. (1964). The deep-sea pennatularians and antipatharians obtained by R/S "Vitjaz" in the Indian Ocean and the resemblance between the faunas of the pennatularians of the Indian Ocean and the Pacific. *Trudy Inst. Okeanologie*, **69**, 183–215 (in Russian, English summary).

(1977). Antipatharia. *Galathea Report*, **14**, 157–64.

Patching, J. W., Raine, R. C. T. & Barnett, P. R. O. (1986). An investigation into the causes of small scale variation in sediment community oxygen consumption in the Rockall Trough. *Proceedings of the Royal Society of Edinburgh*, **88B**, 281–90.

Paterson, G. L. J., Lambshead, P. J. D. & Sibuet, M. (1985). The Ophiuroidea fauna of the Bay of Biscay. In *Peuplements Profonds du Golfe de Gascogne*, eds L. Laubier & C. Monniot, pp. 491–507. Brest: Institut Français de Recherche pour l'Exploitation de la Mer.

Patterson, D. J. (1990). *Jakela libera* (Ruinan, 1938), a heterotrophic flagellate from deep oceanic sediments. *Journal of the Marine Biological Association of the United Kingdom*, **70**, 381–93.

Paul, A. Z. (1973). Trapping and recovery of living deep-sea amphipods from the Arctic Ocean floor. *Deep-Sea Research*, **20**, 289–90.

(1976). Deep-sea bottom photographs show that benthic organisms remove sediment cover from manganese nodules. *Nature, London*, **263**, 50–1.

Paul, A. Z., Thorndike, E. M., Sullivan, L. G., Heezen, B. C. & Gerard, R. D. (1978). Observations of the deep-sea floor from 202 days of time-lapse photography. *Nature, London*, **272**, 812–14.

Paull, C. K., Hecker, B., Commeau, R., Freeman-Lynde R. P., Neuman, C., Corso, W. P., Golubic, S., Hook, J. E., Sikes, J. E. & Curray, J. (1984). Biological communities at the Florida Escarpment resemble hydrothermal vent taxa. *Science, Washington*, **226**, 965–7.

Paull, C. K., Martens, C. S., Chanton, J. P., Neumann, A. C., Coston, J., Jull, A. J. T. & Toolin, L. J. (1989). Old carbon in living organisms and young $CaCO_3$ cements from abyssal brine seeps. *Nature, London*, **342**, 166–8.

Pawson, D. L. (1976). Some aspects of the biology of deep-sea echinoderms. *Thalassia Jugoslavica*, **12**, 287–93.

(1982). Deep-sea echinoderms in the Tongue of the Ocean, Bahama Islands: a survey, using the research submersible Alvin. *Australian Museum Memoir*, **16**, 129–45.

(1985). *Psychropotes hyalinus*, new species, a swimming elasipod sea cucumber (Echinodermata: Holothuroidea) from the north central Pacific Ocean. *Proceedings of the Biological Society of Washington*, **98**, 523–5.

(1986). *Peniagone leander* new species, an abyssal benthopelagic sea cucumber (Echinodermata: Holothuroidea) from the eastern Central Pacific Ocean. *Bulletin of Marine Science*, **38**, 293–9.

Pearce, J., Caracciolo, L. J., Grieg, R., Wenzloff, D. & Steimle, F. Jr. (1979). Benthic fauna and heavy metal burdens in marine organisms and sediments of a continental slope dumpsite off the northeast coast of the United States (Deepwater Dumpsite 106). *Ambio Special Report*, no. 6, 101–4.

Pearcy, W. G. & Ambler, J. W. (1974). Food habits of deep-sea macrourid fishes off the Oregon coast. *Deep-Sea Research*, **21**, 745–59.

Pearcy, W. G., Stein, D. L. & Carney, R. (1982). The deep-sea benthic fish fauna of the Northeastern Pacific ocean on Cascadia and Tufts Abyssal Plains and adjoining continental slopes. *Biological Oceanography*, **1**, 375–428.

Pearcy, W. G. & Stuiver, M. (1983). Vertical transport of carbon-14 into deep-sea food webs. *Deep-Sea Research*, **30A**, 427–40.

Pearson, M. & Gage, J. D. (1984). Diets of some brittle stars in the Rockall Trough. *Marine Biology*, **82**, 247–58.

Peet, R. K. (1974). The measurement of species diversity. *Annual Review of Ecology and Systematics*, **5**, 285–307.

Pemberton, G. S., Risk, M. J. & Buckley, D. E. (1976). Supershrimp: deep bioturbation in the Strait of Canso, Nova Scotia. *Science, Washington*, **192**, 790–1.

Pendley, W. P. (1982). The U.S. will need seabed minerals. *Oceanus*, **25**, 12–21.

Pequegnat, L. H. (1970*a*). Deep-sea caridean shrimps with descriptions of six new species. In *Contributions on the Biology of the Gulf of Mexico*, ed. F. A. Chace, pp. 59–124. (Texas A & M University Oceanographic Studies, vol. 1.) Houston: Gulf Publishing.

(1970*b*). Deep-water brachyuran crabs. In *Contributions on the Biology of the Gulf of Mexico*, ed. F. A. Chace, pp. 171–205. (Texas A & M University Oceanographic Studies, vol. 1.) Houston: Gulf Publishing.

Pequegnat, W. E. (1983). Some aspects of deep ocean disposal of dredged material. In *Wastes in the Ocean*, Vol. 2, eds D. R. Kester, B. H. Ketchum, I. N. Duedall & P. K. Park, pp. 229–52. New York: John Wiley.

Pequegnat, W. E. & Pequegnat, L. H. (1970). Deep-sea anomurans of superfamily Galatheoidea with descriptions of two new species. In *Contributions on the Biology of the Gulf of Mexico*, ed. F. A. Chace, pp. 125–70. (Texas A & M University Oceanographic Studies, vol. 1.) Houston: Gulf Publishing.

Pequegnat, W. E., Pequegnat, L. H., Firth, R. W., James, B. M. & Roberts, T. W. (1971). Gulf of Mexico deep sea fauna. Decapoda and Euphasiacea. In *Serial Atlas of the Marine Environment*, ed. W. Webster, pp. 1–12. New York: American Geographical Society.

Perez, J.-M. (1982). Major benthic assemblages. In *Marine Ecology*, ed. O. Kinne, Chap. 8, pp. 373–522. Chichester: John Wiley.

Perkins, H. C. (1973). The larval stages of the deep-sea red crab, *Geryon quinquedens* Smith, reared under laboratory conditions (Decopoda: Brachyrhyncha). *Fisheries Bulletin*, **71**, 69–82.

Peypouquet, J. P. (1980). Les relations Ostracodes-profondeur. Principles applicables pendant le Cenozoic. *Bulletin de l'Institut de Géologie du Bassin d'Aquitaine*, **28**, 13–28.

Peypouquet, J. P. & Benson, R. (1980). Les Ostracodes actuels des bassins du Cap et d'Angola: distribution bathymétrique en fonction de l'hydrologie. *Bulletin de l'Institut de Géologie du Bassin d'Aquitaine*, **28**, 5–12.

Peters, R. H. (1983). *The Ecological Implications of Body Size*. Cambridge: University Press.

Pfannkuche, O. (1985). The deep-sea meiofauna of the Porcupine Seabight and abyssal plain (NE Atlantic): population structure, distribution, standing stock. *Oceanologica Acta*, **8**, 343–53.

Pfannkuche, O., Theeg, R. & Thiel, H. (1983). Benthos activity, abundance and biomass under an area of low upwelling off Morocco, Northwest Africa. *Meteor Forschungsergebnisse.*, **36**, 85–96.

Phillips, N. W. (1984). Role of different microbes and substrates as potential suppliers of specific, essential nutrients to marine detritivores. *Bulletin of Marine Science*, **35**, 283–98.

Pielou, E. C. (1960). A single mechanism to account for regular, random and aggregated populations. *Journal of Ecology*, **48**, 575–84.

  (1969). *An Introduction to Mathematical Ecology*. New York: Wiley-Interscience.

  (1977). *Mathematical Ecology*. New York: Wiley-Interscience.

Pierce, F. E. (1974). *Wire Ropes for use in the Marine Environment*. IOS Report No. 2. Wormley, Godalming: Institute of Oceanographic Sciences.

Pinhorn, A. T. (1976). Living marine resources of Newfoundland-Labrador: Status and Potential. Department of the Environment (Canada), Fisheries and Marine Science. Bulletin 194, 18–25.

Piper, D. J. W. & Marshall, N. F. (1969). Bioturbation of holocene sediments on La Jolla deep-sea fan, California. *Journal of Sedimentary Petrology*, **39**, 601–6.

Platt, H. M. & Lambshead, P. J. D. (1985). Neutral model analysis of patterns of marine benthic species diversity. *Marine Ecology – Progress Series*, **24**, 75–81.

Platt, T. & Denman, K. (1977). Organization in the pelagic ecosystem. *Helgolander wissenshaftliche Meeresuntersuchungen*, **30**, 575–81.

Pohlo, R. (1982). Evolution of the Tellinacea (Bivalvia). *Journal of Molluscan Studies*, **48**, 245–56.

Polloni, P., Haedrich, R. L., Rowe, G. T. & Clifford, C. H. (1979). The size-depth relationship in deep ocean animals. *Internationale Revue der gesamten Hydrobiogie*, **64**, 39–46.

Por, F. D. (1965). La faune des Harpacticoides dans les vases profondes de la côté d'Israel – une faune panbathyale. *Rapport et Procès-*

Verbaux des réunions Commision internationale pour l'exploration scientifique de la Mer Méditerranée, **18** (2), 159–62.

Preston, A. (1983). Deep-sea disposal of radioactive wastes. In *Wastes in the Ocean*, eds P. K. Park, D. R. Kester, I. W. Duedall & B. H. Ketchum, pp. 107–22. New York: John Wiley.

Priede, I. G. & Smith, K. L. (1986). Behaviour of the abyssal grenadier, *Coryphaenoides yaquinae*, monitored using ingestible acoustic transmitters in the Pacific Ocean. *Journal of Fish Biology*, **29** (Supplement A), 199–206.

Priede, I. G., Smith, K. L. & Armstrong, J. D. (1990). Foraging behavior of abyssal grenadier fish: inferences from acoustic tagging and tracking in the North Pacific Ocean. *Deep-Sea Research*, **37A**, 81–101.

Prieur, D., Jeanthon, C. & Jacq, E. (1988). Les communautes bacteriennes des sources hydrothermales profondes du Pacific Oriental. *Vie et Milieu*, **37**, 149–164.

Pye, M. I. A. (1980). Studies of burrows in Recent sublittoral fine sediments off the west coast of Scotland. Unpublished PhD Thesis, University of Glasgow.

Rachor, E. (1976). Structure, dynamics and productivity of a population of *Nucula nitidosa* (Bivalvia, Protobranchiata) in the German Bight. *Bericht der Deutschen Wissenschaftlichen Kommission für Meeresforschung*, **24**, 296–331.

Ralijona, C. & Bianchi, A. (1982). Comparaison de la structure et des potentialités métaboliques des communautés bactériennes du contenu du tractus digestif d'holothuries abyssales et du sédiment environnant. *Bulletin du Centre d'études et de recherche scientifique Biarritz*, **14**, 199–214.

Rannou, M. (1975). Données nouvelles sur l'activité reproductive cycliques des poissons benthique bathyaux et abyssaux. *Compte rendu hebdomadaire des séances de l'Académie des sciences, Paris* (Sér. D), **281**, 1023–5.

(1976). Age et croissance d'un poisson bathyal: *Nezumia sclerorhynchus* (Macrouridae Gadiforme) de la Mer d'Alboran. *Cahiers de Biologie Marin*, **17**, 413–21.

Rasmussen, E. (1973). Systematics and ecology of the Isefjord marine fauna (Denmark). *Ophelia*, **11**, 1–495.

Rau, G. H. (1989). $^{13}C/^{12}C$ and $^{15}N/^{14}N$ in hydrothermal vent organisms: ecological and biogeochemical implications. *Bulletin of the Biological Society of Washington*, **6**, 243–7.

Raup, D. & Seilacher, A. (1969). Fossil foraging behaviour: computer simulation. *Science, Washington*, **166**, 994–5.

Reichardt, W. T. (1987). Burial of Antarctic macroalgal debris in bioturbated deep-sea sediments. *Deep-Sea Research*, **34A**, 1761–70.

Reid, J. L. & Lynn, R. J. (1971). On the influence of the Norwegian-Greenland and Weddell Seas upon the bottom waters of the Indian and Pacific Oceans. *Deep-Sea Research*, **18**, 1063–88.

Reid, R. G. B. & Reid, A. M. (1974). The carnivorous habit of members of the septibranch genus *Cuspidaria* (Mollusca: Bivalvia). *Sarsia*, **56**, 47–56.

Reidenauer, J. A. & Thistle, D. (1985). The tanaid fauna of the deep North Atlantic where near-bottom current velocities are high. *Oceanologica Acta*, **8**, 355–60.

Reineck, H. E. (1963). Der Kastengreifer. *Natur und Museum*, **93**, 102–108.

Reiners, C. E. & Wakefield, W. W. (1989). Flocculation of siliceous detritus on the sea floor of a deep Pacific seamount. *Deep-Sea Research*, **36A**, 1841–61.

Reise, K. (1981). High abundance of small zoobenthos around biogenic structures in tidal sediments of the Waden Sea. *Helgoländer Meeresuntersuchungen*, **34**, 413–25.

Renard, V. & Allenau, J. P. (1979). SEABEAM, multi-beam echo-sounding in Jean Charcot. *International Hydrographic Review*, **56**, 35–67.

Rex, M. A. (1973). Deep-sea species diversity: decreased gastropod diversity at abyssal depths. *Science, Washington*, **181**, 1051–3.

(1976). Biological accommodation in the deep-sea benthos: comparative evidence on the importance of predation and productivity. *Deep-Sea Research*, **23**, 975–87.

(1977). Zonation in deep-sea gastropods: the importance of biological interactions to rates of zonation. In *Biology of Benthic Organisms*, eds B. F. Keegan, P. O'Ceidigh & P. J. S. Boaden, pp. 521–30. Oxford: Pergamon Press.

(1981). Community structure in the deep-sea benthos. *Annual Review of Ecology and Systematics*, **12**, 331–53.

(1983). Geographical patterns of species diversity in the deep-sea benthos. In *The Sea*, Vol. 8, ed. G. T. Rowe, pp. 453–72. New York: John Wiley.

Rex, M. A. & Boss, K. J. (1973). Systematics and distribution of the deep sea gastropod *Epitonium (Ecclisseogyra) nitidum. Nautilus*, **87**, 93–8.

Rex, M. A., Etter, R. J. & Nimeskern, P. W. (1990). Density estimates for deep-sea gastropod assemblages. *Deep-Sea Research*, **37A**, 555–69.

Rex, M. A. & Warén, A. (1981). Evolution in the deep-sea: taxonomic diversity of gastropod assemblages. In *Biology of the Pacific Ocean Depths*. Proceedings of the XIV Pacific Science Congress (Khabarovsk, August 1979). Vladivostok: Academy of Sciences of the USSR, Far East Science Center, Institute of Marine Biology (in Russian, English summary).

(1982). Planktotrophic development in deep-sea prosobranch snails from the western North Atlantic. *Deep-Sea Research*, **29A**, 171–84.

Rex, M. A., Van Ummerson, C. A. & Turner, R. A. (1979). Reproductive pattern in the abyssal snail *Benthonella tenella* (Jeffreys). In *Reproductive Ecology of Marine Invertebrates*, ed. S. E. Stancyk, pp. 173–88. University of South Carolina Press.

Reyss, D. (1973). Distribution of Cumacea in the deep Mediterranean. *Deep-Sea Research*, **20**, 1119–23.

Rhoads, D. C. (1974). Organism–sediment relations on the muddy sea floor. *Oceanography and Marine Biology: an Annual Review*, **12**, 263–300.

Rhoads, D. C. & Boyer, L. F. (1982). The effects of marine benthos on physical properties of sediments: a successional perspective. In *Animal-Sediment Relations: the Biogenic Alteration of Sediments*, eds P. L. McCall & M. J. S. Tevesz, pp. 3–52. New York: Plenum Press.

Rhoads, D. C., Lutz, R. A., Cerrato, R. M. & Revelas, E. C. (1982). Growth and predation activity at deep-sea hydrothermal vents along the Galapagos Rift. *Journal of Marine Science*, **40**, 503–16.

Rhoads, D. C. & Young, D. K. (1970). The influence of deposit-feeding organisms on sediment stability and community trophic structure. *Journal of Marine Research*, **28**, 150–78.

(1971). Animal–sediment relations in Cape Cod Bay, Massachusetts. II. Reworking by *Molpadia oolitica* (Holothuroidea). *Marine Biology*, **11**, 255–61.

Rice, A. L. (1981). The abdominal locking mechanism in the deep-sea shrimp genus *Glyphocrangon* (Decapoda, Glypocrangonidae). *Crustaceana*, **40**, 316–19.

(1986). *British Oceanographic Vessels 1800–1950*. London: The Ray Society.

(1987). Benthic transect photography. In *Great Meteor East: a Biological Characterization*, pp. 144–8. Institute of Oceanographic Sciences, Deacon Laboratory, Report No. 248.

Rice, A. L., Aldred, R. G., Billett, D. S. M. & Thurston, M. H. (1979). The combined use of an epibenthic sledge and deep-sea camera to give quantitative relevance to macrobenthos samples. *Ambio Special Report*, no. 6, 59–72.

Rice, A. L., Aldred, R. G., Darlington, E. & Wild, R. A. (1982). The quantitative estimation of the deep-sea megabenthos: a new approach to an old problem. *Oceanologica Acta*, **5**, 63–72.

Rice, A. L., Billett, D. S. M., Fry, J., John, A. W. G., Lampitt, R. S., Mantoura, R. F. C. & Morris, R. J. (1986). Seasonal deposition of phytodetritus to the deep-sea floor. *Proceedings of the Royal Society of Edinburgh*, **88B**, 265–79.

Rice, A. L. & Thurston, M. H. (1988). Dense aggregations of an hexactinellid sponge in the Porcupine Seabight (Abstract). Fifth Deep-sea Biology Symposium, June 26th–July 1st 1988. Brest: Institut Français de Recherche pour l'Exploitation de la Mer.

Richards, K. J. (1982). Modelling the benthic boundary layer. *Journal of Physical Oceanography*, **12**, 428–39.

(1984). The interaction between the bottom mixed layer and mesoscale motions in the ocean: a numerical study. *Journal of Physical Oceanography*, **14**, 754–68.

(1990). Physical processes in the benthic boundary layer. *Philosophical Transactions of the Royal Society of London*, Series A, **331**, 3–13.

Richardson, M. & Young, D. K. (1987). Abyssal benthos of the

Venezuela Basin, Carribean Sea: standing stock considerations. *Deep-Sea Research*, **34A**, 145–64.

Richardson, P. L. (1985). Average velocity and transport of the Gulf Stream near 55° W. *Journal of Marine Research*, **43**, 83–111.

Richter, G. & Thorson, G. (1974). Pelagische Prosobranchier–Larven des Golfes von Neapel. *Ophelia*, **13**, 109–85 (English summary).

Ricklefs, R. E. (1987). Community diversity: Relative roles of local and regional processes. *Science, Washington*, **235**, 167–71.

Riemann, F. (1983). Biological aspects of deep-sea manganese nodule formation. *Oceanologica Acta*, **6**, 303–11.

(1989). Gelatinous detritus aggregates on the Atlantic deep-sea bed. Structure and modes of formation. *Marine Biology*, **100**, 533–9.

Risk, M. J. & Tunnicliffe, V. J. (1978). Intertidal spiral burrows – *Paraonis fulgens* and *Spiophanes wigleyi* in the Minas Basin, Bay of Fundy. *Journal of Sedimentary Petrology*, **48**, 1287–92.

Robbins, J. A., McCall, P. L., Fisher, J. B. & Krezoski, J. R. (1978). Effect of deposit feeders on migration of ^{137}Cs in lake sediments. *Earth and Planetary Science Letters*, **36**, 325–33.

Roberts, T. W. & Pequegnat, W. E. (1970). Deep-water decapod shrimps of the family Penaeidae. In *Contributions on the Biology of the Gulf of Mexico*, ed. F. A. Chace, pp. 21–58. (Texas A & M University Oceanographic Studies, vol. 1) Houston: Gulf Publishing.

Robertson, A. I. (1979). The relationship between annual production: biomass ratios and lifespans for marine macrobenthos. *Oecologia, Berlin*, **38A**, 193–202.

Roesijadi, G. & Crecelius, E. A. (1984). Elemental composition of the hydrothermal vent clam *Calyptogena magnifica* from the East Pacific Rise. *Marine Biology*, **83**, 155–61.

Rogers, A. (1974). *Statistical Analysis of Spatial Dispersion*. London: Pion.

Rokop, F. J. (1974). Reproductive patterns in deep-sea benthos. *Science, Washington*, **186**, 743–5.

(1977a). Seasonal reproduction of the brachiopod *Frieleia halli* and the scaphopod *Cadulus californicus* at bathyal depths in the deep-sea. *Marine Biology*, **43**, 237–46.

(1977b). Patterns of reproduction in the deep-sea benthic crustaceans: a re-evaluation. *Deep-Sea Research*, **24**, 683–91.

(1979). Year round reproduction in deep-sea bivalve molluscs. In *Reproductive Ecology of Marine Invertebrates*, ed. S. E. Stancyk, pp. 189–98. University of South Carolina Press.

Romero-Wetzel, M. B. (1987). Sipunculans as inhabitants of very deep, narrow burrows in deep-sea sediments. *Marine Biology*, **96**, 87–91.

(1989). Branched burrow-systems of the enteropneust *Stereobalanus canadensis* (Spengel) in deep-sea sediments of the Vöring-Plateau, Norwegian Sea. *Sarsia*, **74**, 85–9.

Rona, P. A., Klinkhammer, G., Nelsen, T. A., Trefry, J. H. & Elderfield, H. (1986). Black smokers, massive sulphides and vent biota at the Mid-Atlantic Ridge. *Nature, London*, **321**, 33–7.

Roper, C. F. E. (1969). Systematics and zoogeography of the world wide bathypelagic squid *Bathyteuthis* (Cephalopoda: Oegopsida). *Bulletin of the US Natural History Museum*, **291**, 1–210.

Roper, C. F. E. & Brundage, W. L. (1972). Cirrate octopods with associated deep-sea organisms: new biological data based on deep benthic photographs (Cephalopoda). *Smithsonian Contributions to Zoology*, **121**, 46 pp.

Roper, C. F. E. & Young, R. E. (1975). Vertical distribution of pelagic cephalopods. *Smithsonian Contributions to Zoology*, **209**, 1–51.

Rosman, I., Boland, G. S. & Baker, J. S. (1987). Epifaunal aggregations of Vesicomyidae on the continental slope off Louisiana. *Deep-Sea Research*, **34A**, 1811–20.

Ross, D. A. (1980). *Opportunities and Uses of the Ocean*. Berlin: Springer-Verlag.

Roughgarden, J. (1986). A comparison of food-limited and space-limited animal competition communities. In *Community Ecology*, ed. J. Diamond & T. J. Case, pp. 492–515. New York: Harper and Row.

Roughgarden, J., Iwasa, Y. & Baxter, C. (1985). Demographic theory for an open marine population with space-limited recruitment. *Ecology*, 54–67.

Roux, M. (1975). Les Crinoides pédoncles (Échinodermes) de l'Atlantique N.E.: inventaire, écologie et biogéographie. In *Peuplements Profonds du Golfe de Gascogne*, eds L. Laubier & C. Monniot, pp. 479–89. Brest: Institut Français de Recherche pour l'Exploitation de la Mer.

(1977). Les Bourgueticrinina (Crinoidea) recuillis par la 'Thalassa' dans le golfe de Gascogne: anatomie comparée des pédoncles et systematique. *Bulletin du Muséum national de histoire naturelle (Zoologie), Paris, Série 3*, **426**, 425–84.

(1982). De la biogéographie historique des océans aux reconstutions paléobiogéographiques: tendances et problèmes illustres par des examples pris chez les échinodermes bathyaux at abyssaux. *Bulletin de la Société Géologique de France, Paris, Série 7*, **24**, 907–16.

(1987). Evolutionary ecology and biogeography of recent stalked crinoids as a model for the fossil record. In *Echinoderm Studies*, Vol. 2, eds M. Jangoux & J. M. Lawrence, pp. 1–53. Rotterdam: Balkema.

Roux, M., Rio, M. & Fatton, E. (1985). Clam growth and thermal spring activity recorded by shells at 21° N. *Bulletin of the Biological Society of Washington*, **6**, 211–21.

Rowe, G. T. (1971a). Benthic biomass and surface productivity. In *Fertility of the Sea*, Vol. 2, ed. J. D. Costlow. New York: Gordon and Breach.

(1971b). Observations on bottom currents and epibenthic populations in Hatteras Submarine Canyon. *Deep-Sea Research*, **18**, 569–81.

(1974). The effects of the benthic fauna on the physical properties of deep-sea sediments. In *Deep-Sea Sediments: Physical and Mechanical Properties*, ed. A. L. Inderbitzen, pp. 381–400. New York: Plenum Press.

(1981). The deep-sea ecosystem. In *Analysis of Marine Ecosystems*, ed. A. R. Longhurst, pp. 235–67. London: Academic Press.

(1983). Biomass and production of the deep-sea macrobenthos. In *The Sea*, Vol. 8, ed. G. T. Rowe, pp. 97–121. New York: Wiley-Interscience.

Rowe, G. T. & Clifford, C. H. (1973). Modifications of the Birge-Ekman box corer for use with SCUBA or deep submergence vehicles. *Limnology and Oceanography*, **18**, 172–5.

Rowe, G. T. & Deming, J. W. (1985). The role of bacteria in the turnover of organic carbon in deep-sea sediments. *Journal of Marine Research*, **43**, 925–50.

Rowe, G. T. & Haedrich, R. L. (1979). The biota and biological processes of the continental slope. In *Continental Slopes*, eds O. Pilkey & L. Doyle, pp. 49–59. Tulsa, Oklahoma: Society of Economic Petrologists and Mineralogists Special Publication no. 27.

Rowe, G. T., Keller, G., Edgerton, H., Staresinic, N. & MacIlvaine, J. (1974). Time-lapse photography of the biological reworking of sediment in Hudson Canyon. *Journal of Sedimentary Petrology*, **44**, 549–52.

Rowe, G. T. & Menzel, D. W. (1971). Quantitative benthic samples from the Deep Gulf of Mexico with comments on the measurement of deep-sea biomass. *Bulletin of Marine Science*, **21**, 556–66.

Rowe, G. T. & Menzies, R. J. (1967). Use of sonic techniques and tension readings as improvements in abyssal trawling. *Deep-Sea Research*, **14**, 271–4.

(1968). Deep bottom currents off the coast of North Carolina. *Deep-Sea Research*, **15**, 711–19.

(1969). Zonation of large benthic invertebrates in the deep-sea off the Carolinas. *Deep-Sea Research*, **16**, 531–7.

Rowe, G. T., Merrett, N., Shepherd, J., Needler, G., Hargrave, B. & Marietta, M. (1986). Estimates of direct biological transport of radioactive waste in the deep-sea with special reference to organic carbon budgets. *Oceanologica Acta*, **9**, 199–208.

Rowe, G. T., Polloni, P. & Haedrich, R. L. (1982). The deep-sea macrobenthos on the continental margin of the northwest Atlantic Ocean. *Deep-Sea Research*, **29A**, 257–78.

Rowe, G. T., Polloni, P. T. & Horner, S. G. (1974). Benthic biomass estimates from the northwestern Atlantic Ocean and the northern Gulf of Mexico. *Deep-Sea Research*, **21**, 641–50.

Rowe, G. T. & Sibuet M. (1983). Recent advances in instrumentation in deep-sea biological research. In *The Sea*, Vol. 8, ed. G. T. Rowe, pp. 81–95. New York: John Wiley.

Rowe, G. T., Sibuet, M. & Vangriesheim, A. (1986). Domains of occupation of abyssal scavengers inferred from baited cameras and traps on the Demerara Abyssal Plain. *Deep-Sea Research*, **33A**, 501–22.

Rowe, G. T. & Staresinic, N. (1979). Sources of organic matter to the deep-sea benthos. *Ambio Special Report*, **6**, 19–24.

Rubenstein, D. I. & Koehl, M. A. R. (1977). The mechanisms of filter feeding: some theoretical considerations. *American Naturalist*, **111**, 981–94.

Rutgers van der Loeff, M. M. & Lavaleye, M. S. S. (1986). *Sediments, Fauna and the Dispersal of Radionuclides at the N.E. Atlantic Dumpsite for Low-Level Radioactive Waste*. Texel: Netherlands Institute for Sea Research.

Sahrhage, D. (1986). Wirtschaftlich wichtige Grenadierfische des Nordatlantiks. *Mitteilungen aus dem Institut für Seefischerei der Bundesforschungsansalt für Fischeri, Hamburg*. Nr. 37, 81 pp.

Saidova, K. M. (1970). Benthic foraminifers of the Kurile Kamchatka region. *Trudy Instituta Okeanologii*, **86**, 134–61 (in Russian).

Saint-Laurent, M. de (1985). Remarques sur la distribution des crustacés décapodes. In *Peuplements Profonds du Golfe de Gascogne*, eds L. Laubier & C. Monniot, pp. 469–78. Brest: Institut Français de Recherche pour l'Exploitation de la Mer.

Sanders, H. L. (1956). Oceanography of Long Island Sound, 1952–1954. The biology of marine bottom communities. *Bulletin of the Bingham Oceanographic Collection, Yale University*, **15**, 345–414.

(1968). Marine benthic diversity: a comparative study. *American Naturalist*, **102**, 243–82.

(1969). Benthic marine diversity and the stability–time hypothesis. *Brookhaven Symposia on Biology*, **22**, 71–81.

(1977). Evolutionary ecology and deep sea benthos. *Academy of Natural Sciences of Philadelphia*, Special Publications, **12**, 223–34.

(1979). Evolutionary ecology and life history patterns in the deep sea. *Sarsia*, **64**, 1–7.

Sanders, H. L. & Allen, J. A. (1973). Studies on the deep sea Protobranchia (Bivalvia); the prologue and the Pristiglomidae. *Bulletin of the Museum of Comparative Zoology*, **145**, 237–62.

(1985). Studies on deep-sea Protobranchia (Bivalvia); the family Malletiidae. *Bulletin of the British Museum (Natural History), Zoology*, **49**, 195–238.

Sanders, H. L. & Grassle, J. F. (1971). The interactions of diversity, distribution and mode of reproduction among major groupings of the deep-sea benthos. *Proceedings of the Joint Oceanographic Assembly* (Tokyo, 1970), S6–7, 260–2.

Sanders, H. L. & Hessler, R. R. (1969). Ecology of the deep-sea benthos. *Science, Washington*, **163**, 1419–24.

Sanders, H. L., Hessler, R. R. & Hampson, G. R. (1965). An introduction to the study of the deep-sea benthic faunal assemblages along the Gay Head–Bermuda transect. *Deep-Sea Research*, **12**, 845–67.

Sassman, C. & Mangum, C. M. (1972). Adaptation to environmental oxygen levels in infaunal and epifaunal sea anemones. *Biological Bulletin, Marine Biological Laboratory, Woods Hole*, **143**, 657–78.

Savvatimsky, P. I. (1987). Changes in species composition of trawl catches by depth on the continental slope from Baffin island to northeastern Newfoundland. *NAFO Scientific Council Studies*, **11**, 43–52.

Scarabino, V. (1979). Les Scaphopodes bathyaux et abyssaux de l'Atlantique sudoccidental (Systématique, distribution, adaptations). Nouvelle classification pour l'ensemblage de la Classe. Thèse de Doctorat en Océanologie, Université d'Aix-Marseille II, Marseilles, France.

Schaffer, W. M. (1974). Selection for optimal life histories: the effects of age structure. *Ecology*, **55**, 291–303.

Schein-Fatton, E. (1988). Relations between the bathymetric range of Pectinidae (Bivalvia) and their dispersal in the deep sea (Abstract). Fifth Deep-Sea Biology Symposium, June 26th–July 1st 1988, Brest: Institut Français de Recherche pour l'Exploitation de la Mer.

Scheltema, A. H. (1981). Comparative morphology of the radulae and alimentary tracts in the Aplacophora. *Malacologia*, **20**, 361–83.

(1985*a*). The aplacophoran family Prochaetodermatidae in the North American Basin, including *Chevroderma* n.g. and *Spathoderma* n.g. (Mollusca; Chaetodermomorpha). *Biological Bulletin of the Marine Biological Laboratory, Woods Hole*, **169**, 484–529.

(1985*b*). The genus *Prochaetoderma* (Aplacophora, Mollusca): initial account. In *Peuplements profonds du Golfe de Gascogne*, ed. L. Laubier & C. Monniot, pp. 391–6. Brest: Institut Français de Recherche pour l'Exploitation de la Mer.

(1987). Reproduction and rapid growth in a deep-sea aplacophoran mollusc, *Prochaetoderma yongi*. *Marine Ecology – Progress Series*, **37**, 171–80.

Scheltema, R. (1972). Reproduction and dispersal of bottom dwelling deep-sea invertebrates: A speculative summary. In *Barobiology and Experimental Biology of the Deep Sea*, ed. R. W. Bauer, pp. 58–68. University of North Carolina Press.

Schick, J. M., Edwards, K. C. & Dearborn, J. H. (1981). Physiological ecology of the deposit-feeding sea star *Ctenodiscus crispatus*: ciliated surfaces and animal-sediment interactions. *Marine Ecology – Progress Series*, **5**, 165–84.

Schick, J. M., Taylor, W. F. & Lamb, A. N. (1981). Reproduction and genetic variability in the deposit feeding sea-star *Ctenodiscus crispatus*. *Marine Biology*, **63**, 51–66.

Schlichting, H. (1968). *Boundary-layer Theory*, 6th ed. New York: McGraw-Hill.

Schmaljohan, R. & Flügel, H. J. (1987). Methane oxidizing bacteria in pogonophora. *Sarsia*, **72**, 91–8.

Schoener, A. (1967). Post-larval development in five deep-sea ophiuroids. *Deep-Sea Research*, **14**, 645–60.

(1968). Evidence for reproductive periodicity in the deep-sea. *Ecology*, **49**, 81–7.

(1969). Atlantic ophiuroids: some post larval forms. *Deep-Sea Research*, **16**, 127–40.

(1972). Fecundity and possible mode of development of some deep-sea ophiuroids. *Limnology and Oceanography*, **17**, 193–9.

Schoener, A. & Rowe, G. T. (1970). Pelagic *Sargassum* and its presence among the deep-sea benthos. *Deep-Sea Research*, **17**, 923–5.

Schriever, G. (1986). Distribution and ecology of Cletodidae (Crustacea, Copepoda) at the Iceland–Faroe Ridge from 290 m to 2500 m water depth. In *Proceedings of the Second International Conference on Copepoda, Ottowa, Canada, 13–17 August 1984*, eds G. Schriever, H. K. Schminke & C.-t. Shih, pp. 448–58. Ottawa: Syllogeus No. 58 National Museums of Canada, National Museum of Natural Sciences.

Schroder, C. J., Scott, D. B., Medioli, F. S., Bernstein, B. B. & Hessler, R. R. (1988). Larger agglutinated Foraminifera: comparison of assemblages from North Pacific and western North Atlantic (Nares Abyssal Plain). *Journal of Foraminiferal Research*, **18**, 25–41.

Schulenberger, E. & Barnard, J. L. (1976). Amphipods from an abyssal trap set in the North Pacific Gyre. *Crustaceana*, **31**, 241–58.

Schulenberger, E. & Hessler, R. R. (1974). Scavenging abyssal benthic amphipods trapped under oligotrophic central north Pacific gyre waters. *Marine Biology*, **28**, 185–7.

Schutt, C. & Ottow, J. C. G. (1978). Distribution and identification of manganese-precipitating bacteria from noncontaminated ferromanganese nodules. In *Environmental Geochemistry and Geomicrobiology*, Vol. 3, ed. W. Krumbein, pp. 869–78. Ann Arbor, Michigan: Ann Arbor Science.

Schwarz, J. R. & Colwell, R. R. (1975). Heterotrophic activity of deep-sea sediment bacteria. *Applied Microbiology*, **30**, 639–49.

Schwarz, J. R., Yayanos, A. A. & Colwell, R. R. (1976). Metabolic activities of the intestinal microflora of deep-sea invertebrates. *Applied and Environmental Microbiology*, **31**, 46–8.

Schwinghamer, P. (1981). Characteristic size distribution of integral benthic communities. *Canadian Journal of Fisheries and Aquatic Science*, **38**, 1255–63.

(1983). Generating ecological hypotheses from biomass spectra using causal analysis: a benthic example. *Marine Ecology – Progress Series*, **13**, 151–66.

(1985). Observations on size-structure and pelagic coupling of some shelf and abyssal benthic communities. In *Proceedings of the Nineteenth European Marine Biology Symposium*, ed. P. G. Gibbs, pp. 347–59. Cambridge: University Press.

Sedberry, G. R. & Musick, J. A. (1978). Feeding strategies of some demersal fishes of the continental slope and rise off the mid-Atlantic coast of the USA. *Marine Biology*, **44**, 357–75.

Segonzac, M. (1987). Manuel servant a la reconnaissance du faune marine profonde (2000 a 3000 m) des zones hydrothermales du Pacifique Est. /Rapport IFREMER/CENTOB. Limited distribution.

Seibold, E. & Berger, W. H. (1982). *The Sea Floor*. Berlin: Springer-Verlag.

Seilacher, A. (1953). Studien zur palichnologie. I. Uber die methoden der palichnologie. *Neues Jahrbuch der Geologie und Palaontologie*, **96**, 421–52.

(1967a). Fossil behavior. *Scientific American*, **217**, 72–80.

(1967b). Bathymetry of trace fossils. *Marine Geology*, **5**, 413–28.

Semenova, T. N., Mileikovsky, S. A. & Nesis, K. N. (1964). The morphology, distribution and seasonal incidence of the ophiuroid larva of *Ophiocten sericium* (Forbes) in the northwest Atlantic, Norwegian Sea and Barents Sea. *Okeanologiya*, **4**, 669–83 (in Russian).

Shaw, K. M., Lambshead, P. J. D. & Platt, H. M. (1983). Detection of pollution-induced disturbance in marine benthic assemblages with special reference to nematodes. *Marine Ecology – Progress Series*, **11**, 195–202.

Sheldon, R. W. (1969). A universal grade scale for particulate materials. *Proceedings of the Geological Society of London*, no. 1659, 292–5.

Sheldon, R. W. & Parsons, T. R. (1967). A continuous size spectrum for particulate matter in the sea. *Journal of the Fisheries Research Board of Canada*, **24**, 909–15.

Shepard, F. P. & Dill, R. F. (1966). *Submarine Canyons and Other Sea Valleys*. Chicago: Rand McNally.

Shin, P. K. S. (1984). Structure of the hadal macrobenthic infauna in the Japan Trench. *Asian Marine Biology*, **1**, 107–14.

Shirayama, Y. (1983). Size structure of deep-sea meio- and macrobenthos in the western Pacific. *Internationale Revue der gesamten Hydrobiologie*, **68**, 799–810.

(1984a). The abundance of deep sea meiobenthos in the Western Pacific in relation to environmental factors. *Oceanologica Acta*, **7**, 113–21.

(1984b). Vertical distribution of meiobenthos in the sediment profile in bathyal, abyssal and hadal deep sea systems of the Western Pacific. *Oceanologica Acta*, **7**, 120–9.

Shirayama, Y. & Horikoshi, M. (1982). Vertical distribution of smaller macrobenthos and larger meiobenthos in the sediment profile in the deep-sea system of Suruga Bay (Central Japan). *Journal of the Oceanographical Society of Japan*, **38**, 273–80.

Shiriyama, Y. & Swinbanks, D. D. (1986). Oxygen profiles in deep-sea calcareous sediment calculated on the basis of measured respiration rates of deep-sea meiobenthos and its relevance to manganese diagenesis. *La Mer*, **24**, 75–80.

Sibuet, M. (1977). Répartition et diversité des échinodermes en zone profonde dans le Golfe de Gascogne. *Deep-Sea Research*, **24**, 549–63.

(1979). Distribution and diversity of asteroids in Atlantic abyssal plains. *Sarsia*, **64**, 85–92.

Sibuet, M. & Lawrence, J. M. (1981). Organic content and biomass of abyssal holothuroids (Echinodermata) from the Bay of Biscay. *Marine Biology*, **65**, 143–7.

Sibuet, M., Monniot, C., Desbruyères, D., Dinet, A., Khripounoff, A.,

Rowe, G. & Segonzac, M. (1984). Peuplements benthiques et caractéristiques trophiques du milieu dans la plaine abyssale Demerara dans l'océan Atlantique. *Oceanologica Acta*, **7**, 345–58.

Sibuet, M. & Segonzac, M. (1985). Abondance et répartition de l'épifaune mégabenthique. In *Peuplements Profonds du Golfe de Gascogne*, eds L. Laubier & C. Monniot, pp. 143–56. Brest: Institut Français de Recherche pour l'Exploitation de la Mer.

Siebenaller, J. F. (1978*a*). Genetic variation in deep-sea invertebrate populations: the bathyal gastropod *Bathybembix bairdii*. *Marine Biology*, **47**, 265–75.

(1978*b*). Genetic variability in deep-sea fishes of the genus *Sebastolobus* (Scorpaenidae). In *Marine Organisms: Genetics, Ecology, and Evolution*, ed. B. Battaglia & J. Beardmore, pp. 95–122. New York: Plenum Press.

(1984). Pressure-adaptive differences in NAD-dependent dehydrogenases of congeneric marine fishes living at different depths. *Journal of Comparative Physiology*, **154(B)**, 443–8.

Siebenaller, J. F. & Hessler, R. R. (1977). The Nannoniscidae (Isopode, Asellota: *Hebefustis* n. gen. and *Nannoniscoides* Hansen. *Transactions of the San Diego Society of Natural History*, **19**, 17–43.

Siebenaller, J. F. & Somero, G. N. (1978*a*). Pressure-adaptive differences in lactate dehydrogenases of congeneric fishes living at different depths. *Science, Washington*, **201**, 255–7.

(1978*b*). Pressure-adaptive differences in the binding and catalytic properties of muscle-type (M4) lactate dehydrogenases of shallow—and deep-living marine fishes. *Journal of Comparative Physiology*, **129**, 295–300.

Sieg, J. (1986). Distribution of the Tanaidacea: synopsis of the known data and suggestions on possible distribution patterns. In *Crustacean Biogeography*, ed. R. H. Gore & K. L. Heck, pp. 165–93. Boston: Balkema.

(1988). Why do we find so many tanaidaceans in the deep sea? (Abstract). Fifth Deep-Sea Biolology Symposium, June 26th–July 1st 1988. Brest: Institut Français de Recherche pour l'Exploitation de la Mer.

Silvert, W. & Platt, T. (1978). Energy flux in the pelagic ecosystem: a time-dependent equation. *Limnology and Oceanography*, **23**, 813–16.

Simberloff, D. (1972). Properties of the rarefaction diversity measurement. *American Naturalist*, **106**, 414–18.

Simpson, D. C., O'Connor, T. P. & Park, P. K. (1981). Deep-ocean dumping of industrial wastes. In *Marine Environmental Pollution*, Vol. 2 (Mining & Dumping), ed. R. A. Geyer, pp. 379–400. Elsevier.

Simpson, W. R. (1982). Particulate matter in the oceans – sampling methods, concentration, size distribution and particle dynamics. *Oceanography and Marine Biology: an Annual Review*, **20**, 119–72.

Smale-Adams, K. B. & Jackson, G. O. (1978). Manganese nodule mining. *Philosophical Transactions of the Royal Society of London*, Series A, **290**, 125–33.

Smetacek, V. S. (1985). The role of sinking in diatom life-history cycles: ecological, evolutionary and geological significance. *Marine Biology*, **84**, 239–51.

Smith, C. R. (1985*a*). Food for the deep sea: utilization, dispersal and flux of nekton falls at the Santa Catalina Basin floor. *Deep-Sea Research*, **32A**, 417–42.

(1985*b*). Colonization studies in the deep sea: are results biased by experimental design? In *Proceedings of the Nineteenth European Marine Biology Symposium*, ed. P. E. Gibbs, pp. 183–90. Cambridge: Cambridge University Press.

(1986). Nekton falls, low-intensity disturbance and community structure of infaunal benthos in the deep sea. *Journal of Marine Research*, **44**, 567–600.

Smith, C. R. & Brumsickle, S. J. (1989). The effects of patch size and substrate isolation on colonization modes and rates in an intertidal sediment. *Limnology and Oceanography*, **34**, 1263–77.

Smith, C. R. & Hamilton, S. C. (1983). Epibenthic megafauna of a bathyal basin off southern California: patterns of abundance, biomass, and dispersion. *Deep-Sea Research*, **30A**, 907–28.

Smith, C. R. & Hessler, R. R. (1987). Colonization and succession in deep-sea ecosystems. *Trends in Ecology & Evolution*, **2**, 359–63.

Smith, C. R., Jumars, P. A. & DeMaster, D. J. (1986). *In situ* studies of megafaunal mounds indicate rapid sediment turnover and community response at the deep-sea floor. *Nature, London*, **323**, 251–3.

Smith, C. R., Kukert, H, Wheatcroft, R. A., Jumars, P. A. & Deming, J. W. (1989). Vent fauna on whale remains. *Nature, London*, **341**, 27–8.

Smith, K. L. (1974). Oxygen demands of the San Diego Trough sediments: an *in situ* study. *Limnology and Oceanography*, **19**, 939–44.

(1978*a*). Metabolism of the abyssopelagic rattail *Coryphaenoides armatus* measured *in situ*. *Nature, London*, **274**, 362–4.

(1978*b*). Benthic community respiration in the NW Atlantic Ocean: *in situ* measurements from 40 to 5200 m. *Marine Biology*, **47**, 337–47.

(1982). Zooplankton of the bathyal benthic boundary layer: *In situ* rates of oxygen consumption and ammonium excretion. *Limnology and Oceanography*, **27**, 261–471.

(1983). Metabolism of two dominant epibenthic echinoderms measured at bathyal depths in the Santa Catalina Basin. *Marine Biology*, **72**, 249–56.

(1985*a*). Deep-sea hydrothermal vent mussels: nutritional state and distribution at the Galapagos Rift. *Ecology*, **66**, 1067–80.

(1985*b*). Macrozooplankton of a deep sea hydrothermal vent: *in situ* rates of oxygen consumption. *Limnology and Oceanography*, **30**, 102–10.

(1987). Food energy supply and demand: a discrepancy between particulate organic carbon flux and sediment community oxygen consumption in the deep sea. *Limnology and Oceanography*, **32**, 201–20.

(1989). Short time series measurements of particulate organic carbon flux and sediment community oxygen consumption in the North Pacific. *Deep-Sea Research*, **36A**, 1111–19.

Smith, K. L., Alexandrou, D. & Edelman, J. L. (1989). Acoustic detection and tracking of abyssopelagic animals: description of an autonomous split-beam acoustic array. *Deep-Sea Research*, **36A**, 1427–41.

Smith, K. L. & Baldwin, R. J. (1982). Scavenging deep-sea amphipods: effects of food odor on oxygen consumption and a proposed metabolic strategy. *Marine Biology*, **68**, 287–98.

(1984a). Vertical distribution of the necrophagous amphipod, *Eurythenes gryllus*, in the North Pacific: spatial and temporal variation. *Deep-Sea Research*, **31A**, 1179–96.

(1984b). Seasonal fluctuations in deep-sea sediment community oxygen consumption: central and eastern North Pacific. *Nature, London*, **307**, 624–6.

Smith, K. L. & Brown, N. O. (1983). Oxygen consumption of pelagic juveniles and demersal adults of the deep-sea fish *Sebastolobus altivelis*, measured at depth. *Marine Biology*, **76**, 325–32.

Smith, K. L., Carlucci, A. F., Williams, P. M., Henrichs, S. M., Baldwin, R. J. & Graven, D. B. (1986). Zooplankton and bacterioplankton of an abyssal benthic boundary layer: *in situ* rates of metabolism. *Oceanologica Acta*, **9**, 47–55.

Smith, K. L. & Hessler, R. R. (1974). Respiration of benthopelagic fishes: *in situ* measurements at 1230 meters. *Science, Washington*, **184**, 72–3.

Smith, K. L. & Hinga, K. R. (1983). Sediment community respiration in the deep-sea. In *The Sea*, Vol. 8, ed. G. T. Rowe, pp. 331–70. New York: Wiley-Interscience.

Smith, K. L. & Howard, J. D. (1972). Comparison of a grab sampler and large volume corer. *Limnology and Oceanography*, **17**, 142–5.

Smith K. L., Laver, M. B. & Brown, N. O. (1983). Sediment community oxygen consumption and nutrient exchange in the central and eastern North Pacific. *Limnology and Oceanography*, **28**, 882–98.

Smith, K. L. & Teal, J. M. (1973). Deep-sea benthic community respiration: An *in situ* study at 1850 m. *Science, Washington*, **179**, 282–3.

Smith, K. L. & White, G. A. (1982). Ecological energetic studies in the deep-sea benthic boundary layer: *in situ* respiration studies. In *The Environment of the Deep Sea*, eds W. G. Ernst & J. G. Morin, pp. 279–300. Englewood Cliffs, New Jersey: Prentice-Hall.

Smith, K. L., White, G. A., Laver, M. B. & Haugsness, J. A. (1978). Nutrient exchange and oxygen consumption by deep-sea benthic communities: Preliminary *in situ* measurements. *Limnology and Oceanography*, **23**, 997–1005.

Smith, K. L., Williams, P. M. & Druffel, E. R. M. (1989). Upward flux of particulate organic matter in the deep North Pacific. *Nature, London*, **337**, 724–6.

Smith, W. & Grassle, J. F. (1977). Sampling properties of a family of diversity measures, *Biometrics*, **33**, 283–92.

Smith, W., Grassle, J. F. & Kravitz, D. (1979*a*). Measures of diversity with unbiased estimates. In *Ecological Diversity in Theory and Practice*, eds J. F. Grassle, G. P. Patil, W. Smith & C. Taillie, pp. 177–91. Fairland, Maryland: International Co-operative Publishing House.

Smith, W., Kravitz, D. & Grassle, J. F. (1979*b*). Confidence intervals for similarity measures using the two sample jackknife. In *Multivariate Methods in Ecological Work*, ed. L. Orloci, C. R. Rao, & W. M. Stiteler, pp. 253–62. Fairland, Maryland: International Publishing House.

Snelgrove P. V. R. & Haedrich, R. L. (1987). Structure of the deep demersal fish fauna off Newfoundland. *Marine Ecology – Progress Series*, **27**, 99–107.

Snider, L. J., Burnett, B. B. & Hessler, R. R. (1984). The composition and distribution of meiofauna and nanobiota in a central North Pacific deep-sea area. *Deep-Sea Research*, **31A**, 1225–49.

Soetaert, K. & Heip, C. (1989). The size of nematode assemblages along a Mediterranean deep-sea transect. *Deep-Sea Research*, **36A**, 93–102.

Sokal, R. R. & Ogden, N. L. (1978*a*). Spatial autocorrelation in biology. 1. Methodology. *Biological Journal of the Linnaean Society*, **10**, 199–228.

(1978*b*). Spatial autocorrelation in biology. 2. Some biological applications of evolutionary and ecological interest. *Biological Journal of the Linnaean Society*, **10**, 229–49.

Sokolova, M. N. & Pasternak, F. A. (1964). Quantitative distribution of bottom fauna in the northern parts of Arabian Sea and Andaman Sea. *Trudy̆ Instituta Okeanologii*, **64**, 271–96 (in Russian).

Somayajulu, B. L. K., Sharma, P. & Berger, W. H. (1983). ^{10}Be, ^{14}C and U-Th decay series nuclides and ^{18}O in a box core from the central north Atlantic. *Marine Geology*, **54**, 169–80.

Somero, G. N., Anderson, A. E. & Childress, J. J. Transport, metabolism and detoxification of hydrogen sulfide in animals from sulfide-rich marine environments. *Reviews in Aquatic Sciences* (in press).

Somero, G. N., Siebenaller, J. F. & Hochachka, P. W. (1983). Biochemical and Physiological Adaptations of Deep-Sea Animals. In *The Sea*, Vol. 8, ed. G. T. Rowe, pp. 331–70, New York: Wiley-Interscience.

Sorem, R. K., Reinhart, W. R., Fewkes, R. H. & McFarland, W. D. (1979). Occurrence and character of manganese nodules in DOMES sites A, B, and C, east equatorial Pacific Ocean. In *Marine Geology and Oceanography of the Pacific Manganese Nodule Province*, eds J. L. Bischoff & D. Z. Piper, pp. 475–527. New York: Plenum Press.

Sorokin, Y. I. (1978). Decomposition of organic matter and nutrient regeneration. In *Marine Ecology*, Vol. IV, ed. O. Kinne, pp. 501–616. London: John Wiley.

Southward, A. J. (1989). Animal communities fuelled by chemosynthesis: Life at hydrothermal vents, cold seeps and in reducing sediments. *Journal of the Zoological Society of London*, **217**, 705–9.

Southward, A. J. & Dando, P. R. (1988). Distribution of Pogonophora in canyons of the Bay of Biscay: factors controlling abundance and depth range. *Journal of the Marine Biological Association of the United Kingdom*, **68**, 627–38.

Southward, A. J., Southward, E. C., Dando, P. R., Barrett, R. L. & Ling, R. (1986). Chemoautotrophic function of bacterial symbionts in small Pogonophora. *Journal of the Marine Biological Association of the United Kingdom*, **66**, 415–37.

Southward, A. J., Southward, E. C., Dando, P. R., Rau, G. H., Felbeck, H. & Flugel, H. (1981). Bacterial symbionts and low $^{13}C/^{12}C$ ratios in tissues of Pogonophora indicate unusual nutrition and metabolism. *Nature, London*, **293**, 616–20.

Southward, A. J. & Southward, E. C. (1982). The role of dissolved organic matter in the nutrition of deep-sea benthos. *American Zoologist*, **22**, 647–59.

Southward, E. C. (1979). Horizontal and vertical distribution of Pogonophora in the Atlantic Ocean. *Sarsia*, **64**, 51–5.

(1986). Gill symbionts in thyasirids and other bivalve molluscs. *Journal of the Marine Biological Association of the United Kingdom*, **66**, 889–914.

(1987). Contribution of symbiotic chemoautotrophs to the nutrition of benthic invertebrates. In *Microbes in the Sea*, ed. M. Sleigh, pp. 83–118. Chichester: Ellis Horwood.

(1980). Development of the gut and segmentation of newly settled stages of *Ridgeia* (Vestimentifera): implications for relationships between Vestimentifera and Pogonophora. *Journal of the Marine Biological Association of the United Kingdom*, **68**, 465–87.

Spärck, R. (1951). Density of bottom animals on the ocean floor. *Nature, London*, **168**, 112–13.

(1956a). Background and origin of the expedition. In *The Galathea Deep-Sea Expedition*, pp. 11–17. London: Allen & Unwin.

(1956b). The density of animals on the ocean floor. In *The Galathea Deep-Sea Expedition*, pp. 196–201. London: Allen & Unwin.

Stahl, D. A., Lane, D. J., Olsen, G. J. & Pace, N. R. (1984). Analysis of hydrothermal vent-associated symbionts by ribosomal RNA sequences. *Science, Washington*, **224**, 409–11.

Stanley, D. J. (1971). Bioturbation and sediment failure in some submarine canyons. *Vie et Milieu*, **22**, 541–55.

Starikova, N. D. (1970). Vertical distribution patterns of dissolved organic carbon in sea water and in interstitial solutions. *Okeanologiya*, **10**, 988–1000 (in Russian, English summary).

Stehli, F. G., Douglas, R. & Kafescegliou, I. (1972). Models for the evolution of planktonic foraminifera. In *Models in Paleobiology*, ed. T. J. M. Schopf, pp. 116–28. San Francisco: Freeman.

Steimle, F. W. & Terranova, R. J. (1988). Energy contents of northwest Atlantic continental slope organisms. *Deep-Sea Research*, **35A**, 415–23.

Stein, D. L. (1980). Description and occurrence of macrourid larvae and juveniles in the northeast Pacific Ocean off Oregon, U.S.A. *Deep-Sea Research*, **27A**, 889–900.

Stein, D. L. & Pearcy, W. G. (1982). Aspects of the reproduction, early life history, and biology of macrourid fishes off Oregon, U.S.A. *Deep-Sea Research*, **29A**, 1313–29.

Stein, J. L., Cary, S. C., Hessler, R. R., Ohta, S., Vetter, R. D., Childress, J. J. & Felbeck, H. (1988). Chemoautotrophic symbiosis in a hydrothermal vent gastropod. *Biological Bulletin. Marine Biological Laboratory, Woods Hole Mass.*, **174**, 373–8.

Stock, J. H. (1978). Abyssal Pycnogonida from the North-eastern Atlantic Basin, part 1. *Cahiers de Biologie Marin*, **19**, 189–219.

Stockton, W. L. & DeLaca, T. E. (1982). Food falls in the deep-sea: occurrence, quality, and significance. *Deep-Sea Research*, **29A**, 157–69.

Stordal, M. C., Johnson, J. W., Guinasso, N. L. & Schink, D. R. (1985). Quantitative evaluation of bioturbation rates in deep ocean sediments. II. Comparison of rates determined by ^{210}Pb and ^{239,240}Pu. *Marine Chemistry*, **17**, 99–114.

Strathmann, R. R. (1978). The evolution and loss of feeding larval stages of marine invertebrates. *Evolution*, **32**, 894–906.

Streeter, S. S. (1973). Bottom water and benthonic foraminifera in the North Atlantic: glacial-interglacial contrasts. *Quaternary Research*, **3 (1)**, 131–41.

Streeter, S. S. & Shackleton, N. J. (1979). Paleocirculation of the deep North Atlantic: 150,000 year record of benthic foraminifera and oxygen 8. *Science, Washington*, **203**, 168–70.

Suchanek, T. H., Williams, S. L., Ogden, J. C., Hubbard, D. K. & Gill, I. P. (1968). Utilization of shallow-water seagrass detritus by Caribbean deep-sea macrofauna: ^{13}C evidence. *Deep-Sea Research*, **32A**, 201–14.

Suess, E. (1988). Effects of microbial activity. *Nature, London*, **333**, 17–18.

Suess, E., Carson, B., Ritger, S. D., Moore, J. C., Jones, M. L., Kulm, L. D. & Cochrane, G. R. (1985). Biological communities at vent sites along the subduction zone off Oregon. *Bulletin of the Biological Society of Washington*, **6**, 475–84.

Sulak, K. J. (1977). The systematics and biology of *Bathypterois* (Pisces, Chlorophthalmidae) with a revised classification of benthic myctophiform fishes. *Galathea Report*, **14**, 49–108.

   (1982). A comparative taxonomic and ecological analysis of temperate and tropical demersal deep-sea fish faunas in the western North Atlantic. Unpublished Ph.D. dissertation. University of Miami, Florida.

Sulkin, S. D. & van Heukelem, W. F. (1980). Ecological and evolutionary significance of nutritional flexibility in planktonic larvae of the deep-sea red crab *Geryon quinquedens* and the stone crab *Menippe mercenaria*. *Marine Ecology – Progress Series*, **2**, 91–5.

Svavarsson, J. (1984). Ischnomesidae (Isopoda: Asellota) from bathyal and abyssal depths in the Norwegian and North Polar Seas. *Sarsia*, **69**, 29–36.

Svedrup, H. U., Johnson M. W. & Fleming R. H. (1942). *The Oceans*. New Jersey: Prentice-Hall.

Swift, S. A., Hollister, C. D. & Chandler, R. S. (1985). Close-up stereo photographs of abyssal bedforms on the Nova Scotian Rise. *Marine Geology*, **66**, 303–22.

Swinbanks, D. (1985*a*). Japan finds clams and trouble. *Nature, London*, **315**, 624.

(1985*b*). New find near Japan's coast. *Nature, London*, **316**, 475.

Swinbanks, D. D. & Shirayama, Y. (1984). Burrow stratigraphy in relation to manganese diagenesis in modern deep-sea carbonates. *Deep-Sea Research*, **31A**, 1197–223.

(1986*a*). High levels of natural radionuclides in a deep-sea infaunal xenophyophore. *Nature, London*, **320**, 354–7.

(1986*b*). A model of the effects of an infaunal xenophyophone on ^{210}Pb distribution in deep-sea sediment. *La Mer*, **24**, 69–74.

Swinghamer, P. (1983). Generating ecological hypotheses from biomass spectra using causal analysis: a benthic example. *Marine Ecology – Progress Series*, **13**, 151–66.

(1985). Observations on size-structure and pelagic coupling of some shelf and abyssal benthic communities. In *Proceedings of the Nineteenth European Marine Biology Symposium*, ed. P. E. Gibbs, pp. 347–59. Cambridge: University Press.

Tabor, P. S., Deming, J. W., Ohwada, K. & Colwell, R. R. (1982). Activity and growth of microbial populations in pressurized deep-sea sediment and animal gut samples. *Applied and Environmental Microbiology*, **44**, 413–22.

Taghorn, G. L. (1982). Optional foraging by deposit-feeding invertebrates: Roles of particle size and organic coating. *Oecologia, Berlin*, **52**, 295–304.

Taghorn, G. L., Nowell, A. R. M. & Jumars, P. A. (1980). Induction of suspension feeding in spionid polychaetes by high particulate fluxes. *Science, Washington*, **210**, 562–4.

Takahashi, K. (1986). Seasonal fluxes of pelagic diatoms in the subarctic Pacific 1982–1983. *Deep-Sea Research*, **33A**, 1225–51.

(1987). Seasonal fluxes of silicoflagellates and *Actiniscus* in the subarctic Pacific during 1982–1984. *Journal of Marine Research*, **45**, 397–425.

Tanone, E. & Handa, N. (1980). Some characteristic features of the Avertical profile of organic matter in recent sediments from the Bering Sea. *Journal of the Oceanographical Society of Japan*, **36**, 1–14.

Taylor, L. R. (1961). Aggregation, variance and the mean. *Nature, London*, **189**, 732–5.

Tendal, O. S. (1972). A monograph of the Xenophyophoria (Rhizopodea, Protozoa). *Galathea Report*, **12**, 7–103.

(1979). Aspects of the biology of Komokiacea and Xenophyophoria. *Sarsia*, **64**, 13–17.

(1985*a*). A preliminary account of the Komokiacea and the Xenophyophorea. In *Peuplements Profonds du Golfe de Gascogne*, eds L. Laubier & C. Monniot, pp. 263–6. Brest: Institut Français de Recherche pour l'Exploitation de la Mer.

(1985*b*). Xenophyphores (Protozoa, Sarcodina) in the diet of *Neopilina galatheae* (Mollusca, Monoplacophora). *Galathea Reports*, **16**, 95–8.

Tendal, O. S. & Gooday, A. J. (1981). Xenophyophoria (Rhizopoda, Protozoa) in bottom photographs from the bathyal and abyssal NE Atlantic. *Oceanologica Acta*, **4**, 414–22.

Tendal, O. S. & Hessler, R. R. (1977). An introduction to the biology and systematics of Komokiacea (Textlariina, Foraminiferida). *Galathea Report*, **14**, 165–94.

Tendal, O. S., Swinbanks, D. D. & Shirayama, Y. (1982). A new infaunal xenophyophore (Xenophyophorea, Protozoa) with notes on its ecology and possible trace fossil analogues. *Oceanologica Acta*, **5**, 325–9.

Tendal, O. S. & Thomsen, E. (1988). Observations on the life position and size of the large foraminifer *Astrorhiza arenaria* Norman, 1876, from the shelf off Norway. *Sarsia*, **73**, 39–42.

Terborgh, J. (1971). Distribution on environmental gradients: theory and a preliminary interpretation of distributional patterns in the avifauna of the Cordillera Vilcabamba, Peru. *Ecology*, **52**, 23–40.

Thiel, H. (1972*a*). Die Bedeutung der Meiofauna in küstenfernen benthischen Lebensgemeinschaften verschiedener geographischer Regionen. *Verhandlungen der Deutschen Zoologischen Gesellschaft, Helgoland*, **65**, 37–42.

(1972*b*). Meiofauna und Struktur der benthischen Lebensgemeinschaft des Iberischen Tiefseebeckens. *'Meteor' Forschungsergebnisse* D, **12**, 36–51.

(1975). The size structure of the deep-sea benthos. *Internationale Revue des Gesamten Hydrobiologie*, **60**, 575–606.

(1979*a*). Structural aspects of the deep-sea benthos. *Ambio Special Report*, **6**, 25–31.

(1979*b*). First quantitative data on the deep Red Sea benthos. *Marine Ecology – Progress Series*, **1**, 347–50.

(1982). Zoobenthos of the CINECA area and other upwelling regions. *Rapport et procès-verbaux des réunions. Conseil permanent internationale pour l'exploration de la mer*, **180**, 323–34.

(1983). Meiobenthos and nanobenthos of the deep sea. In *The Sea*, vol. 8, ed. G. T. Rowe, pp. 167–230. New York: Wiley-Interscience.

Thiel, H. & Hessler, R. R. (1974). Ferngesteuertes Unterwasserfahrzeug erforscht Tiefseeboden. *U M S C H A U in Wissenschaft und Technik*, **74**, 451–3.

Thiel, H., Pfannkuche, O., Schriever, G. Lochte, K., Gooday, A. J., Hemleben, C., Mantoura, R. F. G., Patching, O., Turley, C. M. & Riemann, F. & Phytodetritus on the deep-sea floor in a central oceanic region of the northeast Atlantic. *Biological Oceanography*, **6** (1988/1989), 203–39.

Thiel, H., Pfannkuche, O., Theeg, R. & Schriever, G. (1987). Benthic metabolism and standing stock in the central and northern deep Red Sea. *Marine Ecology: Pubblicazione, della Stazione Zoologica di Napoli* **I**, 8, 1–20.

Thistle, D. (1978). Harpacticoid dispersion patterns: Implications for deep-sea diversity maintenance. *Journal of Marine Research*, **36**, 377–97.

(1979*a*). Deep-sea harpacticoid copepod diversity maintenance: The role of polychaetes. *Marine Biology*, **52**, 371–6.

(1979*b*). Harpacticoid copepods and biogenic structures: Implications for deep-sea diversity maintenance. In *Ecological Processes in Coastal and Marine Systems*, ed. R. J. Livingstone, pp. 217–31. New York: Plenum Press.

(1980). A revision of Ilyarachna (Crustacea, Isopoda) in the Atlantic with four new species. *Journal of Natural History*, **14**, 111–43.

(1981). Natural physical disturbances and communities of marine soft bottoms. *Marine Ecology – Progress Series*, **6**, 223–8.

(1982). Aspects of the natural history of the harpacticoid copepods of San Diego Trough. *Biological Oceanography*, **1**, 225–38.

(1983*a*). The stability-time hypothesis as a predictor of diversity in deep-sea soft-bottom communities: A test. *Deep-Sea Research*, **30A**, 267–77.

(1983*b*). The role of habitat heterogeneity in deep-sea diversity maintenance. *Deep-Sea Research*, **30A**, 1235–45.

(1988). A temporal difference in harpacticoid-copepod abundance at a deep-sea site: caused by benthic storms? *Deep-Sea Research*, **32A**, 1015–20.

Thistle, D. & Eckman, J. (1988). Response of harpacticoid copepods to habitat structure at a deep-sea site. *Hydrobiologia* **167/168**, 143–9.

Thistle, D. & Sherman, K. M. (1985). The nematode fauna of a deep-sea site exposed to strong near-bottom currents. *Deep-Sea Research*, **32A**, 1077–88.

Thistle, D. & Wilson, G. D. F. (1987). A hydrodynamically modified, abyssal isopod fauna. *Deep-Sea Research*, **34A**, 73–87.

Thistle, D., Yingst, J. Y. & Fauchald, K. (1985). A deep-sea benthic community exposed to strong bottom currents on the Scotian Rise (Western Atlantic). *Marine Geology*, **66**, 91–112.

Thomson, J. W. (1874). *The Depths of the Sea*. London: Macmillan.

Thompson, B. E. (1980). A new sipunculan from southern California, with ecological notes. *Deep-Sea Research*, **27A**, 951–7.

Thompson, I., Jones, D. S. & Dreibelbis, D. (1980). Annual internal growth banding and life history of the ocean quahog *Arctica islandica* (Mollusca: Bivalvia). *Marine Biology*, **57**, 25–34.

Thompson, J. & Wilson, T. R. S. (1980). Burrow-like structures at depth in a Cape Basin red clay core. *Deep-Sea Research*, **27A**, 197–202.

Thorndike, E. M., Gerard, R. D., Sullivan, L. G. & Paul, A. Z. (1982).

Long-term, time-lapse photography of the deep ocean floor. In *The Ocean Floor*, eds R. A. Scrutton & M. Talwani, pp. 255–75. New York: John Wiley.

Thorson, G. (1946). Reproduction and larval development of Danish marine bottom invertebrates. *Meddelelser fra Kommissionen for Danmarks Fiskeri- og Havundersogelser*. Kjobenhavn, Serie: Plankton. Bind 4, 523 pp.

(1950). Reproduction and larval ecology of marine bottom invertebrates. *Biological Reviews*, **25**, 1–45.

(1955). Modern aspects of marine level-bottom animal communities. *Journal of Marine Research*, **14**, 387–97.

Thunnell, R. C. & Reynolds L. A. (1984). Sedimentation of planktonic foraminifera: seasonal changes in species flux in the Panama Basin. *Micropaleontology*, **30**, 243–62.

Thurston, M. H. (1979). Scavenging abyssal amphipods from the North-East Atlantic Ocean. *Marine Biology*, **51**, 55–68.

Tietjen, J. H. (1971). Ecology and distribution of deep-sea meiobenthos off North Carolina. *Deep-Sea Research*, **18**, 941–57.

(1976). Distribution and species diversity of deep-sea nematodes off North Carolina. *Deep-Sea Research*, **23**, 755–68.

(1984). Distribution and species diversity of deep-sea nematodes in the Venezuela Basin. *Deep-Sea Research*, **31A**, 119–32.

Tietjen, J. H., Deming, J. W., Rowe, G. T., Macko, S. & Wilke, R. J. (1989). Meiobenthos of the Hatteras Abyssal Plain and Puerto Rico Trench: abundance, biomass and associations with bacteria and particulate fluxes. *Deep-Sea Research*, **36A**, 1567–77.

Tipper, J. C. (1979). Rarefaction and rarefiction — the use and abuse of a method in paleoecology, *Paleobiology*, **5**, 423–34.

Tirmizi, N. M. (1966). Crustacea Galatheidae. *John Murray Expeditions, Scientific Reports*, **11**, 169–234.

Toggweiler, J. R. (1988). Deep-sea carbon, a burning issue. *Nature, London*, **334**, 468–9.

Tokiska, T. (1953). *Ascidians of Saganmi Bay collected by His Majesty the Emperor of Japan*, Tokyo: Iwanami Shoten.

Trutschler, K. & Samtleben, C. (1988). Shell growth of *Astarte elliptica* (Bivalvia) from Kiel Bay (Western Baltic Sea). *Marine Ecology – Progress Series*, **42**, 155–62.

Tucholke, B. E., Hollister, C. D., Biscaye, P. E. & Gardner, W. D. (1985). Abyssal current character determined from sediment bedforms on the Nova Scotian continental rise. *Marine Geology*, **66**, 43–57.

Tufail, A. (1987). Microbial communities colonising nutrient-enriched marine sediment. *Hydrobiologia*, **148**, 245–55.

Tunnicliffe, V. (1988). Biogeography and evolution of hydrothermal-vent fauna in the eastern Pacific Ocean. *Proceedings of the Royal Society of London*, Series B, **233**, 347–66.

Tunnicliffe, V., Garrett, J. F. & Johnson, H. P. (1990). Physical and biological factors affecting the behaviour and mortality of hydrothermal vent tubeworms (vestimentiferans). *Deep-Sea Research*, **37A**, 103–25.

Tunnicliffe, V., Juniper, S. K. & de Burgh, M. E. (1985). The hydrothermal vent community on Axial Seamount, Juan de Fuca Ridge. *Bulletin of the Biological Society of Washington*, **6**, 453–64.

Turekian, K. K. (1976). *Oceans*. Englewood Cliffs, New Jersey: Prentice-Hall.

Turekian, K. K., Cochran, D. P., Kharkar D. P., Cerrato, R. M., Vaisnys, J. R., Sanders, H. L., Grassle, J. F. & Allen, J. A. (1975). Slow growth rate of deep-sea clam determined by ^{228}Ra chronology. *Proceedings of the National Academy of Science of the United States of America*, **180**, 2829–32.

Turekian, K. K., Cochrane, J. K. & Nozaki, Y. (1979). Growth rate of a clam from the Galapagos hot spring field using natural radionuclide ratios. *Nature, London*, **280**, 385–7.

Turley, C. M., Lochte, K. & Patterson, D. J. (1988). A barophilic flagellate isolated from 4500 m in the mid-North Atlantic. *Deep-Sea Research*, **35**, 1079–92.

Turner, R. D. (1973). Wood-boring bivalves, opportunistic species in the deep sea. *Science, Washington*, **180**, 1377–9.

(1977). Wood, molluscs, and deep-sea food chains. *Bulletin of the American Malacological Union, Inc.*, **1977**, 13–19.

(1985). Notes on molluscs of deep-sea vents and reducing sediments. *American Malacological Bulletin*, Special Edition No. 1, 23–34.

Turner, R. D. & Lutz, R. A. (1984). Growth and distribution of molluscs at deep-sea vents and seeps. *Oceanus*, **27**, 54–62.

Turner, R. D., Lutz, R. A. & Jablonski, D. (1985). Modes of molluscan larval development at deep-sea hydrothermal vents. *Bulletin of the Biological Society of Washington*, **6**, 167–84.

Tyler, P. A. (1980). Deep-sea ophiuroids. *Oceanography and Marine Biology: an Annual Review*, **18**, 125–53.

(1986). Studies of a benthic time-series: reproductive biology of benthic invertebrates in the Rockall Trough. *Proceedings of the Royal Society of Edinburgh*, **88B**, 175–90.

(1988). Seasonality in the deep-sea. *Oceanography and Marine Biology: an Annual Review*, **26**, 227–258.

Tyler, P. A. & Billett, D. S. M. (1988). The reproductive ecology of elasipodid holothurians from the NE Atlantic. *Biological Oceanography*, **5**, 273–96.

Tyler, P. A. & Gage, J. D. (1980). Reproduction and growth of the deep-sea brittlestar *Ophiura ljungmani* (Lyman). *Oceanologica Acta*, **3**, 177–85.

(1982a). The reproductive biology of *Ophiacantha bidentata* (Echinodermata: Ophiuroidea) from the Rockall Trough. *Journal of the Marine Biological Association of the United Kingdom*, **62**, 45–55.

(1982b). *Ophiopluteus ramosus*, the larval form of *Ophiocten gracilis* (Echinodermata: Ophiuroidea) from the Rockall Trough. *Journal of the Marine Biological Association of the United Kingdom*, **62**, 485–6.

(1984*a*). The reproductive biology of echinothurid and cidarid sea urchins from the deep-sea (Rockall Trough, northeast Atlantic Ocean). *Marine Biology*, **80**, 63–74.

(1984*b*). Seasonal reproduction of *Echinus affinis* (Echinodermata: Echinoidea) in the Rockall Trough, northeast Atlantic Ocean. *Deep-Sea Research*, **31A**, 387–402.

Tyler, P. A., Grant, A., Pain, S. L. & Gage, J. D. (1982). Is annual reproduction in deep-sea echinoderms a response to variability in their environment? *Nature, London*, **300**, 747–9.

Vaccaro, R. F., Capuzzo, J. M. & Marcus, N. H. (1981). The oceans and U.S. sewage sludge disposal policy. *Oceanus*, **24**, 55–59.

Vale, F. K. & Rex, M. A. (1988). Repaired shell damage in deep-sea prosobranch gastropods from the western North Atlantic. *Malacologia*, **28**, 65–79.

Valentine, J. W. (1973). *Evolutionary Paleoecology of the Marine Biosphere*, New Jersey: Prentice-Hall.

Valentine, J. W., Hedgecock, D. & Barr, L. G. (1975). Deep-sea asteroids: high genetic variability in a stable environment. *Evolution*, **29**, 203–12.

Van Dover, C. L., Berg, C. J. & Turner, R. D. (1988*a*). Recruitment of marine invertebrates to hard substrates at deep-sea hydrothermal vents on the east Pacific Rise and Galapagos spreading center. *Deep-Sea Research*, **35A**, 1833–49.

Van Dover, C. L., Franks P. J. S. & Ballard, R. D. (1987). Prediction of hydrothermal vent locations from distributions of brachyuran crabs. *Limnology and Oceanography*, **32**, 1006–10.

Van Dover, C. L., Fry, B., Grassle, J. F., Humphris, S. & Rona, P. A. (1988*b*). Feeding biology of the shrimp *Rimicaris exoculata* at hydrothermal vents on the Mid-Atlantic Ridge. *Marine Biology*, **98**, 209–16.

Van Dover, C. L., Szuts, E. Z., Chamberlain, B. C. & Cann, J. R. (1989). A novel eye in 'eyeless' shrimp from hydrothermal vents of the Mid-Atlantic Ridge. *Nature, London*, **337**, 458–60.

Van Praet, M. & Duchateau, G. (1984). Mise en évidence chez une Actinie abyssale (*Paracalliactis stephensoni*) d'un cycle saisonnier de reproduction. *Compte rendu hebdomadaire des séances de l'Académie des Sciences, Paris*, **299**, 687–90.

Vangenechten, J. H. D., Aston, S. R. & Fowler (1983). Uptake of americium-241 from two experimentally labelled deep-sea sediments by three benthic species : a bivalve, a polychaete and an isopod. *Marine Ecology – Progress Series*, **13**, 219–228.

Vaugelas, J. de (1989). Deep-sea lebensspuren: remarks on some echiuran traces in the Porcupine Seabight, northeast Atlantic. *Deep-Sea Research*, **36**, 975–82.

Verwoort, W. (1985). Deep-water hydroids. In *Peuplements Profonds du Golfe de Gascogne*, ed. L. Laubier & C. Monniot, pp. 267–97. Brest: Institut Français de Recherche pour l'Exploitation de la Mer.

Vinogradova, M. E. & Tseitlin, V. B. (1983). Deep-sea pelagic domain (Aspects of bioenergetics). In *The Sea*, Vol. 8, ed. G. T. Rowe, pp. 123–65. New York: Wiley-Interscience.

Vinogradova, N. G. (1959). The zoogeographical distribution of the deep-water bottom fauna in the abyssal zone of the ocean. *Deep-Sea Research*, **5**, 205–8.

(1962*a*). Vertical zonation in the distribution of the deep-sea benthic fauna in the ocean. *Deep-Sea Research*, **8**, 245–50.

(1962*b*). Some problems of the study of deep-sea bottom fauna. *Journal of the Oceanographical Society of Japan*, 20th Anniversary Volume, 724–41.

(1969*a*). The vertical distribution of the deep-sea bottom fauna. In *The Pacific Ocean. Biology of the Ocean*, Book 2. *The Deep-Sea Bottom Fauna, Pleuston*, ed. V. G. Kort, pp. 125–53. Moscow: Izd-vo 'Nauka' (in Russian).

(1969*b*). The geographical distribution of the deep-sea bottom hauls. In *The Pacific Ocean Biology of the Ocean*, Book 2. *The Deep-Sea Bottom Fauna, Pleuston*, ed. V. G. Kort, pp. 154–81. Moscow: Izd-vo 'Nauka' (in Russian).

(1970). Deep-sea ascidians of the genus *Culeolus* of the Kurile-Kamchatka Trench. *Trudy Instituta Okeanologii*, **86**, 489–512.

(1979). The geographical distribution of the abyssal and hadal (ultra-abyssal) fauna in relation to the vertical zonation of the ocean. *Sarsia*, **64**, 41–50.

Vinogradova, N. G., Kudinova-Pasternak, R. K., Moskalev, L. I., Muromtseva, T. L. & Fedikov, N. F. (1974). Some regularities of the quantitative distribution of the bottom fauna of the Scotia Sea and the deep-sea trenches of the Atlantic sector of the Antarctic. *Trudy Instituta Okeanologii*, **98**, 157–82 (in Russian, English summary).

Vinogradova, N. G., Levenstein, R. Y. & Turpaeva, E. P. (1978*a*). Quantitative distribution of bottom fauna in research field of 16th voyage of sci. res. vessel 'Dimitry Mendeleev'. *Trudy Instituta Okeanologii*, **113**, 7–21 (in Russian, English summary).

Vinogradova, N. G., Zezina, O. N. & Levenstein, R. J. (1978*b*). Bottom fauna of the deep-sea trenches of the Macquarie complex. *Trudy Instituta Okeanologii*, **112**, 174–92 (in Russian, English summary).

Vivier, M.-H. (1978). Influence d'un déversement industriel profond sur la nématofaune (canyon de Cassidaigne, Mediterranée). *Tethys*, **8**, 307–21.

Volckaert, F. (1987). Spatial pattern of soft-bottom Polychaeta off Nova Scotia, Canada. *Marine Biology*, **93**, 627–39.

Wakefield, W. W. & Genin, A. (1987). The use of a Canadian (perspective) grid in deep-sea photography. *Deep-Sea Research*, **34A**, 469–78.

Walker, H. A. & Paul, J. F. (1989). Ocean dumping of sewage sludge. *Maritimes*, **33(2)**, 15–17.

Walker, M., Tyler, P. A. & Billett, D. S. M. (1987*a*). Biochemical and calorific contents of deep-sea aspidochirotid holothurians from the northeast Atlantic Ocean. *Comparative Biochemistry and Physiology*, **88A**, 549–51.

(1987*b*). Organic and calorific content of the body tissues of the deep-sea elasipodid holothurians in the northeast Atlantic Ocean. *Marine Biology*, **96**, 277–82.

Warén, A. (1984). A generic revision of the family Eulimidae. *Journal of Molluscan Studies, Supplement 13*, 1–96.

(1988). *Neopilina goesi*, a new Caribbean monoplecophoran dredged in 1869. *Proceedings of the Biologial Society of Washington*, **101**, 676–81.

(1989). New and little known molluses from Iceland. *Sarsia*, **74**, 1–28.

Warén, A. & Bouchet, P. (1989). New gastropods from East Pacific hydrothermal vents. *Zoologica Scripta*, **18**, 67–102.

Warén, A. & Sibuet, M. (1981). *Ophieulima* (Mollusca, Prosobranchia), a new genus of ophiuroid parasites. *Sarsia*, **66**, 103–7.

Warner, G. F. (1977). On the shapes of passive suspension feeders. In *Biology of Benthic Organisms*, ed. B. F. Keegan, P. O. Ceidigh & P. J. S. Boaden, pp. 567–76. Oxford: Pergamon.

Warren, B. A. (1981). Deep circulation of the World Ocean. In *Evolution of Physical Oceanography*, eds B. A. Warren & C. Wunsch, pp. 6–41. MIT Press.

(1983). Why is no deep water formed in the North Pacific? *Journal of Marine Research*, **41**, 327–47.

Warwick, R. M. (1984). Species size distributions in marine benthic communities. *Oecologia, Berlin*, **61**, 32–41.

Weatherly, G. L. & Kelley, E. A. (1985). Storms and flow reversals at the HEBBLE site. *Marine Geology*, **66**, 205–18.

Weaver, P. P. E. & Schultheiss, P. J. (1983). Vertical open burrows in deep-sea sediments 2 m in length. *Nature, London*, **301**, 329–31.

Weibe, P. H., Madin, L. R., Haury, L. R., Harbison, G. R. & Philbin, L. M. (1979). Diel vertical migration by *Salpa aspersa* and its potential for large-scale particulate organic matter transport to the deep-sea. *Marine Biology*, **53**, 249–55.

Wenner, C. A. (1979). Notes on fishes of the genus *Paraliparis* (Cylopteridae) on the middle Atlantic continental slope. *Copeia*, **1979(1)**, 145–6.

Wenner, C. A. & Musick, J. A. (1977). Biology of the morid fish *Antimora rostrata* in the western North Atlantic. *Journal of the Fisheries Research Board of Canada*, **34**, 2362–8.

Wenner, E. L. (1978). Some aspects of the biology of deep-sea lobsters of the family Polychelidae (Crustacea, Decapoda) from the western North Atlantic. *Fishery Bulletin*, **77**, 435–44.

(1980). Notes on the biology of a deep-sea penaeid, *Benthesicymus bartletti* Smith. *Crustaceana*, **38**, 290–4.

Wenner, E. L. & Boesch, D. F. (1979). Distribution patterns of epibenthic decapod Crustacea along the shelf-slope coenocline, Middle Atlantic Bight, USA. *Bulletin of the Biological Society of Washington*, **3**, 106–33.

Wetzel, A. (1981). Ecological and stratigraphic significance of biogenic structure in Quaternary deep-sea sediments off NW Africa. *Meteor Forschungsergebnisse*, Reihe C, No. 34, 1–47 (in German, English summary).

Wheatcroft, R. A., Smith, C. R. & Jumars. P. A. (1988). Dynamics of surficial trace assemblages in the deep-sea. *Deep-Sea Research*, **36A**, 71–91.

Whittaker, R. H. & Fairbanks, C. W. (1958). A study of plankton copepod communities in the Columbia Basin, southeastern Washington. *Ecology*, **54**, 46–65.

Wiebe, P. H., Copley, N., Van Dover, C., Tamse, A. & Manrique, F. (1988). Deep-water zooplankton of the Guayamas Basin hydrothermal vent field. *Deep-Sea Research*, **35A**, 985–1013.

Wiebe, P. H., Madin L. P., Harbison G. R. & Philbin L. M. (1979). Diel vertical migration by *Salpa aspera* and its potential for large scale POM transport to the deep-sea. *Marine Biology*, **53**, 249–55.

Wieser, W. (1953). Die Bezeihung zwischen Mundhohlengestalt, Ernahrungsweise und Verkommen bei freilebenden marinen Nemotoden. Eine okologisch-morphologische Studie. *Arkiv for Zoologi (Ser. II)*, **4**, 439–84.

(1960). Benthic studies in Buzzards Bay II. The meiofauna. *Limnology and Oceanography*, **5**, 121–37.

Wigley, R. L. & Emery, K. O. (1967). Benthic animals, particularly *Hyalinoecia* (Annelida) and *Ophiomusium* (Echinodermata), in sea-bottom photographs from the continental slope. In *Deep-Sea Photography*, ed. J. B. Hersey, pp. 235–49. Baltimore: Johns Hopkins Press.

Wigley, R. L. & Theroux, R. B. (1975). Deep-sea red crab, *Geryon quinquedens*, survey off northeastern United States. *Marine Fisheries Review*, **37**, 1–28.

Wikander, P. B. (1980). Biometry and behaviour in *Abra nitida* (Muller) and *A. longicallus* (Scacchi) (Bivalvia: Tellinacea). *Sarsia*, **65**, 255–68.

Williams, A. B. & Chace, F. A. (1982). A new caridean shrimp of the family Bresiliidae from thermal vents of the Galapagos Rift. *Journal of Crustacean Biology*, **2**, 136–47.

Williams, A. B. & Rona, P. A. (1986). Two new caridean shrimps (Bresiliidae) from a hydrothermal field on the Mid-Atlantic Ridge. *Journal of Crustacean Biology*, **6**, 446–62.

Williams, P. J. le B. (1975). Biological and chemical aspects of dissolved organic matter in sea water. In *Chemical Oceanography*, 2nd Edn., eds J. P. Riley & G. Skirrow, pp. 301–63. London: Academic Press.

Williams, P. M., Druffel, E. R. & Smith, K. L. (1987). Dietary carbon sources for deep-sea organisms as inferred from their organic radiocarbon activities. *Deep-Sea Research*, **34A**, 253–66.

Williams, R. & Moyse, J. (1988). Occurrence, distribution and orientation of *Poecilasma kaempferi* Darwin (Cirripedia: Pedunculata) epizoic on *Neolithodes grimaldi* Milne-Edwards and Bouvier

(Decapoda: Anomura) in the Northeast Atlantic. *Journal of Crustacean Biology*, **8**, 177–86.

Williamson, D. I. (1982). The larval characters of *Dorhynchus thomsoni* Thomson (Crustacea, Brachyura, Majoidea) and their evolution. *Journal of Natural History*, **16**, 727–44.

Wilson, G. D. (1983*a*). Variation in the deep-sea sopod, *Eurycope iphthima* (Assellota, Eurycopidae): depth-related clines in rostral morphology and in population structure. *Journal of Crustacean Biology*, **3**, 127–40.

(1983*b*). Systematics of a species complex in the deep-sea genus *Eurycope*, with a revision of six previously described species (Crustacea, Isopoda, Eurycopidae). *Bulletin of the Scripps Institution of Oceanography*, **25**, 1–64.

Wilson, G. D. F. & Hessler, R. R. (1987*a*). Speciation in the deep sea. *Annual Review of Ecology and Systematics*, **18**, 185–207.

(1987*b*). The effects of manganese nodule test mining on the benthic fauna in the North Equatorial Pacific. In *Environmental Effects of Deep-Sea Dredging*, eds F. N. Speiss, R. R. Hessler, G. Wilson & M. Weydert. Final report to the National Oceanic and Atmospheric Administration on contract NA83–SAC–00659. 24–86. Scripps Institution of Oceanography reference 87–5, La Jolla, California, 86 pp.

Wilson, J. B. S. (1979*a*). The distribution of the coral *Lophelia pertusa* (L.) [*L. prolifera* (Pallas)] in the north-east Atlantic. *Journal of the Marine Biological Association of the United Kingdom*, **59**, 149–62.

(1979*b*). 'Patch' development of the deep-water coral *Lophelia pertusa* (L.) on Rockall Bank. *Journal of the Marine Biological Association of the United Kingdom*, **59**, 165–77.

Wilson, M. (1982). *Challenger* reveals potentially important roughy resource off Tasmania. *Australian Fisheries*, **41**, 2–3.

Wilson, R. R. (1988). Analysis of growth zones and microstructure in otoliths of two macrourids from the North Pacific abyss. *Environmental Biology of Fishes*, **21**, 251–61.

Wilson, R. R. & Kaufman, R. S. *et al.* (1987). Seamount biota and biogeography. In *Seamounts, Islands and Atolls*, eds B. Keating, P. Fryer, R. Batiza & G. Boehlert, pp. 355–77. Geophysical Monograph No. 43. Washington: American Geophysical Union.

Wilson, R. R. & Smith, K. L. (1984). Effect of near-bottom currents on detection of bait by the abyssal grenadier fishes *Coryphaenoides* spp., recorded *in situ* with a video camera on a free vehicle. *Marine Biology*, **84**, 83–91.

Wilson, R. R. & Waples, R. S. (1983). Distribution, morphology, and biochemical genetics of *Coryphaenoides armatus* and *C. yaquinae* (Pisces: Macrouridae) in the central and eastern North Pacific. *Deep-Sea Research*, **30A**, 1127–45.

(1984). Electrophoretic and biometric variability in the abyssal grenadier *Coryphaenoides armatus* of the western North Atlantic, eastern South Pacific and eastern North Pacific Oceans. *Marine Biology*, **80**, 227–37.

Wimbush, M. (1976). The physics of the benthic boundary layer. In *The Benthic Boundary Layer*, ed. I. N. McCave, pp. 3–10. New York: Plenum Press.

Wimbush, M. & Munk, W. (1970). The benthic boundary layer. In *The Sea*, Vol. 4, ed. A. E. Maxwell, pp. 731–758. New York: Wiley-Interscience.

Wingstrand, K. G. (1985). On the anatomy and relationships of recent Monoplacophora (Mollusca). *Galathea Report*, **16**, 7–94.

Wirsen, C. O. & Jannasch, H. W. (1983). *In situ* studies on deep-sea amphipods and their intestinal microflora. *Marine Biology*, **78**, 69–73.

(1986). Microbial transformations in deep-sea sediments: free-vehicle studies. *Marine Biology*, **91**, 277–84.

Wishner, K. F. (1980*a*) Aspects of the community ecology of deep-sea benthopelagic plankton, with special reference to the gymnopleid copepods. *Marine Biology*, **60**, 179–187.

(1980*b*) The biomass of deep-sea benthopelagic plankton. *Deep-Sea Research*, **27A**, 203–216.

Wolff, T. (1956*a*). Isopoda from depths exceeding 6000 meters. *Galathea Report*, **2**, 85–157.

(1956*b*). Crustacea Tanaidacea from depths exceeding 6000 meters. *Galathea Report*, **2**, 187–241.

(1960). The hadal community, an introduction. *Deep-Sea Research*, **6**, 95–124.

(1961). Animal life from a single abyssal trawling. *Galathea Report*, **5**, 129–62.

(1962). The systematics and biology of bathyal and abyssal Isopoda Asellota. *Galathea Report*, **6**, 1–320.

(1970). The concept of the hadal or ultra abyssal fauna. *Deep-Sea Research*, **17**, 983–1003.

(1971). Archimède dive 7 to 4160 metres at Madeira: observations and collecting results. *Videnskabelige Meddelelser fra Dansk naturhistorisk Forening*, **134**, 127–47.

(1976). Utilization of seagrass in the deep sea. *Aquatic Botany*, **2**, 161–74.

(1979). Macrofaunal utilization of plant remains in the deep sea. *Sarsia*, **64**, 117–36.

(1980). Animals associated with seagrass in the deep sea. In *Handbook of Seagrass Biology: an Ecosystem Perspective*, ed. R. C. Phillips & C. P. McRoy, pp. 119–224. New York: Garland Press.

Woodhead, D. S. & Pentreath, R. J. (1983). A provisional assessment of radiation regimes in deep-sea ocean environments. In *Wastes in the Ocean*, Vol. 3, eds P. K. Park, D. R. Kester, I. W. Duedall & B. H. Ketchum, pp. 133–52. J. Wiley & Sons.

Woodin, S. A. (1983). Biotic interactions in recent marine sedimentary environments. In *Biotic Interactions in Recent and Fossil Benthic*

Communities, eds M. J. S. Tevesz & P. L. McCall, pp. 3–38. New York: Plenum Press.

Woodin, S. A. & Jackson, J. B. C. (1979). Interphyletic competition among marine benthos. *American Zoologist*, **19**, 1029–43.

Woods, D. R. & Tietjen, J. H. (1985). Horizontal and vertical distribution of meiofauna in the Venezuela Basin. *Marine Geology*, **68**, 233–41.

Worthington, L. V. (1970). The Norwegian Sea as a Mediterranean basin. *Deep-Sea Research*, **17**, 77–84.

Wright, J. E. (ed.) (1977). *Introduction to the Oceans*. Milton Keynes, U.K.: The Open University.

Wüst, G. (1961). On the vertical circulation of the Mediterranean Sea. *Journal of Geophysical Research*, **66**, 3261–71.

Wyrtki, K., Magaard, L. & Hager, J. (1976). Eddy energy in the oceans. *Journal of Geophysical Research*, **81**, 2641–6.

Yayanos, A. A. & Dietz, A. S. (1983). Death of a hadal deep-sea bacterium after decompression. *Science, Washington*, **220**, 497–8.

Yayanos, A. A., Dietz, A. S. & Van Boxtel, R. (1979). Isolation of a deep-sea barophilic bacterium and some of its growth characteristics. *Science, Washington*, **205**, 808–9.

(1981). Obligately barophilic bacterium from the Mariana Trench. *Proceedings of the National Academy of Science of the United States of America*, **78**, 5212–15.

Yingst, J. Y. & Aller, R. C. (1982). Biological activity and associated sedimentary structures in Hebble-area deposits, western North Atlantic. *Marine Geology*, **48**, 7–15.

Yingst, J. Y. & Rhoads, D. C. (1980). The role of bioturbation in the enhancement of microbial turnover rates in marine sediments. In *Marine Benthic Dynamics*, eds K. R. Tenore & B. C. Coull, pp. 407–21. Columbia: University of South Carolina Press.

Young, C. M. & Cameron, J. L. (1987). Laboratory and *in situ* flotation rates of lecithotrophic eggs from the bathyal echinoid *Phormosoma placenta*. *Deep-Sea Research*, **34A**, 1629–39.

(1989). Development as a function of depth in the bathyal echinoid *Linopneustes longspinus*. In *Reproduction, Genetics and Distribution of Marine Organisms*, eds J. S. Ryland & P. A. Tyler, pp. 225–31. Copenhagen: Olsen & Olsen.

Young, D. K., Jahn, W. H., Richardson, M. D. & Lohanick, A. W. (1985). Photographs of deep-sea lebensspuren: a comparison of sedimentary provinces in the Venezuela Basin, Caribbean Sea. *Marine Geology*, **68**, 269–301.

Zarenkov, N. A. (1969). Decapoda. In *Biology of the Pacific Ocean*. Part II. *The Deep-Sea Bottom Fauna*, ed. L. A. Zenkevitch, pp. 79–82 (in Russian, translated by U.S. Naval Oceanographic Office, Washington, D.C.).

Zenkevitch, L. A. (1966). The systematics and distribution of abyssal and hadal (ultra-abyssal) Echiuroidea. *Galathea Report*, **8**, 175–83.

Zenkevitch, L. A. & Birstein, Y. A. (1956). Studies of the deep-water fauna and related problems. *Deep-Sea Research*, **4**, 54–64.

(1960). On the problem of the antiquity of the deep-sea fauna. *Deep-Sea Research*, **7**, 10–23.

Zenkevitch, L. A. & Murina, V. V. (1976). Deep-sea Echiurida of the Pacific Ocean. *Trudў Instituta Okeanologii*, **99**, 102–14 (in Russian, English summary).

Zezina, O. N. (1975). On some deep-sea brachiopods from the Gay Head–Bermuda transect. *Deep-Sea Research*, **22**, 903–12.

(1976). On the determination of growth rate and production of brachiopod species *Pelagodiscus atlanticus* (King) from bathyal and abyss. *Trudў Instituta Okeanologii*, **99**, 85–90 (in Russian, English summary).

(1981). New and rare cancellothyroid brachiopods. *Trudў Instituta Okeanologiya*, **115**, 155–64 (in Russian, English summary).

Zibrowius, H. (1980). Les scleractinaires de la Méditerranée et de l'Atlantique nord-oriental. *Memoires de la Institut Océanographique, Monaco*, **11**, 284 pp.

Zibrowius, H., Southward, E. C. & Day, J. H. (1979). New observations on a little known species of *Lumbrinereis* (Polychaeta) living on various cnidarians, with notes on its recent and fossil scleractinian hosts. *Journal of the Marine Biological Association of the United Kingdom*, **55**, 83–108.

Zobell, C. E. & Johnson, F. H. (1949). The influence of hydrostatic pressure on the growth and viability of terrestrial and marine bacteria. *Journal of Bacteriology*, **57**, 179–89.

Zobell, C. E. & Morita, R. A. (1957). Barophilic bacteria in some deep-sea sediments. *Journal of Bacteriology*, **73**, 563–8.

Zonenshayn, L. P., Murdmaa, I. O., Baranov, B. V., Kuznetsov, A. P., Kuzin, V. S., Kuz'min, M. I., Avdeyko, G. P., Stunzzhas, P. A., Lukashin, V. N., Barash, M. S., Valyashko, G. M. & Demina, L. L. (1987). An underwater gas source in the Sea of Okhotsk West of Paramushir Island. *Oceanology*, **27**, 598–602 (English translation of *Okeanologiya*).

Species index

Page numbers in italics refer to figures.

Subject index

Page numbers in italics refer to figures.